Discipline
In Our
Schools

Discipline In Our Schools

An Annotated Bibliography

Compiled by
Elizabeth Lueder Karnes,
Donald D. Black,
and
John Downs

GREENWOOD PRESS
Westport, Connecticut • London, England

Copyright Acknowledgment

The dissertation titles and abstracts contained here are published with permission of University Microfilms International, publishers of *Dissertation Abstracts International* (copyright © by University Microfilms International), and may not be reproduced without their prior permission.

Library of Congress Cataloging in Publication Data

Karnes, Elizabeth Lueder.
  Discipline in our schools.

  Includes indexes.
  1. School discipline—United States—Bibliography.
I. Black, Donald D. II. Downs, John III. Title.
Z5814.D49K37 1983   [LB3012]   016.3715   83-12847
ISBN 0-313-23521-X

Library of Congress Catalog Card Number: 83-12847
ISBN: 0-313-23521-X

First published in 1983

Greenwood Press
A division of Congressional Information Service, Inc.
88 Post Road West, Westport, Connecticut 06881

Printed in the United States of America

10 9 8 7 6 5 4 3 2 1

CONTENTS

PREFACE

This book is designed to provide educators with the most comprehensive source of information available regarding social behavior problems and discipline in American schools.

Since the conception of this project and the eventual publication of this bibliography, we have literally had thousands of opportunities to work with and to hear about hundreds of students displaying behavior problems in school settings. Without a doubt, the problem is tremendous and the need for more and better answers continues to grow. School administrators and teachers throughout the country are utilizing a vast array of methods, programs, and procedures for working with the social problems presented by students. This book's volume and breadth of coverage is a credit to American educators and their interest in helping our youth become productive members of our society.

This book not only brings together a listing of effective published procedures, but is also designed to encourage readers to generate and disseminate information regarding effective tools useful in assisting and teaching those students displaying inappropriate classroom behaviors. The authors, in an attempt to meet those needs, followed the lead provided by Father Edward Flanagan, the founder of Boys Town, who said, "There are no bad boys. Only bad environments, bad training, bad thinking and bad examples."

In addition to providing a "Home" for over 400 children and youth, Boys Town also provides a comprehensive educational program, including instruction and training in the area of social behavior—that same area addressed by this text on discipline. The youth who reside and attend school at Boys Town have had, for the most part, a history of unsuccessful school experiences. Many had below average or failing grades, others did not get along with teachers, administrators, or their peers, while others had dropped out of school completely. It is the intent of the Boys Town Schools to "turn on" these "turned off" students and to give them the skills they need to succeed academically, vocationally, socially, and spiritually, not only at Boys Town, but also in their community school, in higher education, or on the job.

Because of its unique student population, we have implemented programs designed to be used by both teachers and administrators for improving students' adult and peer interactions as well as classroom behavior. Implementation of these techniques has involved intensive teacher and administrative training in classroom/school management and social skill instruction.

Training programs, developed at Boys Town and now being implemented in both public and private schools throughout the country, include the following:

The Motivation System
A comprehensive behaviorally oriented program that provides teachers with specific skills necessary for managing and motivating student behavior. Included in the training are:

1) procedures for implementing and utilizing a token economy;

2) a structured process, referred to as the Teaching Interaction, designed to be used by teachers for assisting students in learning appropriate social skills; and

3) a problem-solving procedure used by teachers to help students learn how they can solve some of the day-to-day problems they face both in and out of school.

Social Skills in the Secondary School (S⁴)
Specifically designed for teachers of high school age youth and incorporating many of the same components found in the Motivation System. Also included in the S^4 Program are the steps necessary for effectively initiating and writing behavioral contracts with students.

Crisis Intervention
Complementing both the Motivation System and S^4 Programs are the administrative procedures for assisting disruptive youth. This set of procedures is composed of a sequential set of instructional components including procedures for:

1) de-escalating disruptive behavior;

2) obtaining and maintaining instructional control;

3) teaching alternative behaviors; and

4) preparing students for classroom reentry.

This set of procedures is designed for school administrators who realize the need to teach social skills to those students who have not learned to appropriately interact with peers and/or adults in the school setting.

We would like to thank the following Boys Town employees for their assistance in the completion of this book: Donna Richardson, search service manager, who completed the data base search; Carolyn Seybold and Linda Brunz, who typed the manuscript; and Jayne Larson, manager of special communications, and Karen Thomas, senior word processing technician, for adapting the manuscript to magnetic media text editing format. Without these persons' efforts, this book would not have reached fruition.

E. Karnes

D. Black

J. Downs

Discipline
In Our
Schools

1.

BOOKS

1001.   Ackerly, R. L. and Gluckman, I. P. <u>The Reasonable Exercise of Authority, II</u>. Reston, Virginia: National Association of Secondary School Principals, 1976.

This document was prepared in order to provide principals and other administrators with information and guidance on their duties and powers as determined by constitutional and statutory interpretation in the hopes that such information will help them stay out of the courts. More specifically, the document considers the basic and general legal principles of due process and suggests acceptable approaches to the necessary and reasonable exercise of authority by school officials. After a lengthy discussion of due process, a number of related topics are discussed individually. The topics are freedom of expression, student publications, personal appearance, religion and patriotism, civil rights, codes of behavior, student property, weapons and drugs, extracurricular activities, discipline, corporal punishment, student participation in student governments, the right to petition, and student records. See ERIC Abstract ED 117845.

1002.   Andersen, C. M. and Barbe, W. B., Editor. <u>Classroom Activities For Modifying Misbehavior In Children</u>. New York, New York: The Center For Applied Research In Education, Incorporated, 1974.

This handbook gives the teacher a collection of ready activities for dealing effectively with a broad range of misbehavior within the classroom. The activities presented offer ways in which the teacher can deal with such problems in a manner that will produce the desired results. The activities included are those which have proven to work best in modifying misbehavior in the classroom, such as making contract, establishing a time out booth, setting up a token economy, and using indirect behavior control. There are intended to provide models for dealing appropriately with each area of concern, and are not meant to be all inclusive in describing all cases of misbehavior. Each activity gives the teacher a workable plan for carrying out behavior control -- objectives, necessary procedures, specific procedures and supplementary discussion. The teacher is shown how to administer effective punishment, how to respond most effectively to misbehavior and how to use the many methods that are available for modifying misbehavior. Sections include: 1) Who is the chronic misbehaver?, 2) Don't say anything -- Do something!, 3) Using punishment, 4) Bribes versus rewards, 5) The time out technique, 6) Setting up a token economy, 7) Manipulating disrupting behavior cues, 8) Using indirect behavior control, 9) Truancy.

1003.   Archer, D. K. Humane Atmosphere Within The School. Dubuque, Iowa: Kendall/Hunt Publishing Company, 1976.

Respect and cooperation among all people should be a goal of this age. It can hardly be expected that individuals will respond to this vital need of the twentieth century unless their children are taught to respect one another. To foster the type of learning environment which will encourage people to recognize the dignity and worth of all mankind; trust, confidence, cooperation, concern, tolerance, civility, and sharing must be considered necessary. Such an environment is described in this book as a humane atmosphere. The prerequisites for establishing such an atmosphere are discussed in detail. Included are guidelines for maintaining a humane atmosphere within the classroom. To allow the reader a greater opportunity to be exposed to some of the problems and possible solutions to these problems within the classroom, each chapter contains case studies. These case studies can be used by the individual reader as thought provoking; they may be used for classroom discussions or may be given by the instructor as a class assignment of a problem solving nature. Included are the following chapters: 1) Establishing a humane climate, 2) Dignity and mutual respect, 3) Accountability, 4) Unreasonable demands, 5) Decision making, 6) Leadership.

1004.   Axelrod, S. Behavior Modification For The Classroom Teacher. New York: McGraw Hill Book Company, 1977.

The author has provided a detailed description of how teachers and other educators may apply behavior modification techniques in classroom settings. In chapter one he describes basic behavioral principles and means of applying principles in the classroom. In the second chapter less basic but important useful procedures are discussed. Chapter three presents means by which teachers can accurately and convieniently measure student behavior. The author describes research designs which educators can employ to determine with great certainity which factors cause an improvement in pupil performance. In the fourth chapter the author provides many examples of how teachers and other school personnel have used behavior modification procedures to solve a variety of classroom problems. In the final chapter, he presents some of the most commonly asked questions about behavior modification and offers some interesting answers to these important questions.

1005.   Baker, B. Steps to Independence. Champaign, Illinois: Research Press, 1976.

This series of four resource guides and a twenty-one page guide for their use, is designed to help parents of special children use behavioral modification techniques to teach self-care skills and to develop behavior control. The guides are entitled "Early Self-Help Skills," "Intermediate Self-Help Skills," "Advanced Self-Help Skills" and "Behavior Problems." Suggestions are provided for step-by-step development of skills. Numerous examples, illustrations, and diagrams are included for clarification of concepts and procedures. The guide provides a description of the series, guidelines of establishing a parent training program, a performance inventory of self-help skills, and sample checklists and charts for recording level of skill and progress. See ERIC Abstract IN028556.

1006.   Baker, B. L. et al. Behavior Problems. Champaign, Illinois: Research Press, 1976.

This research guide is designed to help parents develop a program for changing behavior problems in their children. The guide begins with chapters dealing with identifying and examining problem behavior. This is followed by suggestions for initiating a behavior modification program, including changing the antecedents and consequences of the behavior. The final chapter deals with handling self-stimulating behaviors such as rocking, flapping arms, or banging objects together, self-abusive behaviors, and fear. See ERIC Abstract IN028559.

1007.   Bailey, R. E. and Kackley, J. C. Positive Alternatives to Student Suspensions: An Overview. Washington, D.C. Bureau of Elementary and Secondary Education, 1977.

The prevention and resolution of student behavior problems with the goals of the Positive Alternatives to Student Suspension Program involving schools in Pinellas County, Florida. Workshops for staff and administrators aimed toward creating a humanized caring school. Classroom activities attempted to create situations in which students and teachers to get to know and appreciate each other. Programs for students run by a psychologist and social worker aimed at self exploration and personal growth. Encounter groups for interactions through values clarification, transactional analysis, and other applied behavioral science techniques. Parent training groups fostered open communication, sharing of concerns, problem solving, and values clarification using techniques from parent effectiveness training, behavior modification, and transactional analysis. A time out room provided a place where students could talk out personal problems before the problems became discipline problems. A "student's school survival course" allowed students to receive positive feedback from teachers and other students. A "student's home survival course" used Reality Therapy, transactional analysis, and rational behavior therapy to help students explore positive alternatives for resolving problems at home. During the two years in which the program operated, it had significantly fewer student suspensions than did control schools. See ERIC Abstract ED 165347.

1008.   Bailey, W. J. Managing Self-Renewal In Secondary Education. Englewood Cliffs, New Jersey: Educational Technology Publication, 1975.

Authors seeks to answer the question, "How does a secondary school make improvements without resorting to radical approaches which simply will not be acceptable in most communities?" In order to make maximum changes that are constructive and effective over long periods of time, the administrator must adopt an organization for change and growth for his miniature society known as the school. This book explains how a system of operations can be adopted that will enable his schools to be viable. A viable school is one that is capable of constant growth and change, in fact, is constantly effective and dynamic. The primary emphasis is placed on organizing a secondary school that can negotiate changes as seen from the inside by the educators on the firing line. The book contains practical and simple procedures, which, if followed with the proper dedication, can help to develop a modern, progressive, and viable secondary school. Chapters include: 1) Philosophical Input For Self-Renewal, 2) How To Plan For The Charge Of Change, 3) Ways To Maximize The Change, 4) Organize For Viability, 5) Design Instructional Strategies For Individuality, 6) Planning For The Future, 7) Develop A Performance System Of Student Evaluation, 8) Controlling Interventions, 9) Schedule And Group For Flexibility.

1009.   Baruth, L. G. and Eckstein, D. G. The A.B.C.'s of Classroom Discipline. Dubuque, Iowa: Kendall/Hunt Publishing Company, 1976.

The philosophy underlying this book is based upon alternative methods of achieving power and authority, methods which paradoxically give teachers more influence in their classrooms, not less. Such a system is built on a democratic concept which views people as being worthwhile. The result of such innovative teaching approaches is that neither students nor teachers lose and that the educational process is en-hanced for everyone. The emphasis is on practical classroom applications which have been supported by relevant theory, practice and research. A programmed text approach is implemented in this book. Typical chapters have an introductory pro section, followed by various programmed materials. The theoretical orientation of the book originated with Alfred Adler and Rudolf Dreikurs. Based upon the belief that the child is a social being who is motivated to find a place at home, school, and in the world-at-large. All behavior is purposeful or goal-directed, indicating various ways and means each person has discovered to gain status and significance. Chapter Two examines basic mistaken goals of children with Chapter Three describing ways for teachers to recognize and deal with ineffective behaviors. Chapter Four discusses the use of encouragement and consequences as a means of improving classroom atmosphere, while classroom meetings are the topic of Chapter Five. Chapter Six demonstrates ways to increase positive pupil behavior. Representative examples of elementary, middle and high school conflicts are presented in Chapter Seven. Additional readings, charts and a crossword puzzle are included in the appendix and bibliography.

1010.   Beatty, J. B. The Onion Sandwich Principle And Other Essays On Classroom Management. Columbus, Ohio: Charles E. Merrill Publishing Company, 1973.

The purpose of the book is to help teachers and perspective teachers meet some of their needs in the area of maintaining discipline in the most productive ways, in order to free them to teach more creatively and examine the process of learning and education with new perspective. Essays include: 1) The Onion Sandwich Principle And Other Observations On Rewards, 2) The Answer Is Probably Awareness -- But What Was The Question? 3) The Essay That Isn't There, 4) Some Thoughts On Individualized Instruction, 5) On Individual Differences: E. Pluribus Unum Or Then Again, Maybe Not, 6) On Resolving A Paradox: Learning Takes Place In An Individual, Education Takes Place In A Group, 7) Divide And Conquer -- Or Teach As The Case May Be, 8) The Group As A Resource For Affective Learning, 9) How To Maintain Discipline In Your Classroom, 10) Kingwood: A Complex Token Economy System For The Educable Mentally Retarded, 11) You Could Have A Great Future In Modeling, My Dear, 12) The Teacher: Hidden Resource In The Classroom, 13) Creative Teaching: Personal Style In Action, 14) Self-evaluation: A Gift That Keeps On Giving, 15) So, How Come It Does Not Work? A series of observation, 16) Conclusion, More Or Less, 17) Post Script And Other Assorted Responses To Fatigue.

1011.   Benton, F., Jr. Studies in Campus Law--The Legal Issues of Pratz vs. Louisiana State Board of Education. Baton Rouge, Louisiana: Franklin Press, Inc., 1971.

"The issue raised in this court case is whether a state supported institution of higher education may, through the establishment of reasonable parietal regulations, requires students to live and eat their meals in facilities provided by the institution." Included are the following sections: part 1) the legal issues of the Pratz case, part 2) studies in campus law.

1012.   Bessell, H.   Methods in Human Development: Theory Manual.   LeMesa,   California: Human Development Training Institute, 1972.

This manual, developed by psychologists at the Human Development Training Institute, describes techniques for understanding and dealing with the behavior and development of young children. The major objective of the book is to help elementary school teachrs improve communication their pupils. The manual offers conceptual tools for fostering healthy child development and for re-orienting children who exhibit signs of emotional disturbance. The manual is presented in two parts. Part 1 examines major concerns and procedures of the human development program and describes how these key elements inter-relate. This section covers the child and his development, the magic circle arrangement in which students and teachers sit and talk, activities by grade level, the role of the teacher and rating scales. Part 2 considers the three main themes of the curriculum: 1) awareness, 2) mastery, and 3) social interaction. Background information from psychological literature is presented for each theme and methods are indicated for reinforcing positive behavior in situations such as lying, stealing, repression, withdrawl, and overcompensation. See ERIC Abstract ED 148695.

1013.   Blaker, K. E. 'Behavior Modification. Morristown, New Jersey: General Learning Press, February, 1976.

The goal of this book is to have all teachers and counselors thoroughly trained in the theory and techniques of applied behaviorism. Upon completion of this book, the author hopes that the reader will be able to 1) conceptualize how behavior is acquired, altered, maintained, and eliminated according to the consequences that are associated with the behavior, 2) to clarify and detail basic strategies that can be employed by educators who are teaching new and adaptive behaviors, 3) to recognize the conceptual differences between behaviorism and other, more traditional explanations of human behavior, 4) to identify the variables that are necessary to explain, plan, and analyze the applications of reinforcement theory, and 5) to present an illustration of how behavioral strategies can be generally implemented in a classroom. The book will be most beneficial to students if it can become a springboard and guide for activity, experimentation and discussion.

1014.   Block, E. E., Covill-Servo, J. & Rosen, N. F.   Failing Students--Failing   Schools--A   Study   of   Dropouts   and Discipline in New York State. Rochester, New York: A Statewide Youth Advocacy Project, April 1978.

The problem out-of-school youth is one of major significance to the economic and social well-being of the State of New York. Each year in New York State, new dropouts join those from the preceding year and form a state pool of about a quarter of a million 16 to 20 year olds seeking employment. The combination of under-schooling and under-employment has bred a young people who have few aspirations and great alienation from the traditional societal values. This report focuses on under-schooling. The authors have sought to determine: 1) How many students leave, 2) Why they leave, 3) How school systems respond to students who: fail to keep up in class, fail to attend, and fail to follow the customary and accepted pattern of classroom in-school behavior, (4 What local schools in state government can do to reduce the number of youths out of school. Included are the following chapters: 1) The Dropouts, 2) Achievement, 3) Discipline, 4) Suspension, 5) Truancy, 6) Over Sixteen, 7) Need for Appropriate Education, 8) Findings and Recommendations.

1015.   Bluming, M. and Dembo, M. H. Solving Teaching -- A Guide For The Elementary School Teacher. Pacific Palisades, California: Good Year Publishing Company Incorporated, 1973.

To find the most obvious and recurring problems that plague teachers, the authors conducted a survey of teachers from schools with varying demographic factors, asking them to complete this statement, "My biggest problem in teaching is ..." The completed statements plus a review of recent research studies on teaching problems help determine which problems would be included in the book. The authors feels that the most successful teachers are the most flexible teachers but to be flexible they most know the proven techniques, innovative ideas and varied approaches that might be effective in any given situation. The beginning teacher may use this book to provide him or her with a backlog of ideas to begin with, the experienced teacher may use the book to replinish his ideas. The book is divided into four chapters. Chapter One describes a systematic approach to classroom problems by presenting a model for decision making. Chapter Two describes symptoms that reveal possible causes of disruptive behavior, analyses each cause and develop several plans for dealing with the cause. Chapter Three considers various plans for effective use of time -- including ways of alleviating clerical fatigue, of saving student work from the wastebasket, and of dealing with ones personal adversion to parts of the curriculum he is required to teach. Chapter Four discusses learning problems of the individual child and plans to enhance pupil learning -- for example, how to keep precocious readers from being bored, what to do about children good in math but lagging in reading; this chapter also investigates individualized learning on a limited scale and pupil-team learning.

1016.   Bolmeier, E. C. <u>Legality of Student Disciplinary Practices</u>. Charlottsville, Virginia: The Michie Company, 1976.

The main purpose of this book is to draw attention to court cases which determine the legal principles to serve as guidelines for adopting practices most conducive to better student discipline. Included are the following chapters: 1) Introduction; 2) The In-Loco Parenthis Doctrine; 3) Due Process and School Discipline; 4) Administration of Corporal Punishment; 5) Exclusionary Practices: Suspension-Expulsion; 6) Unorthodox Practices of Disciplining; 7) Conclusions and Implications.

1017.   Bommarito, J. W. <u>Preventive And Clinical Management Of Troubled Children: Contributions From Field, Dynamic And Psycoeducational Theorist (A Learning Theory Appraisal)</u>. Washington, D.C.: University Press Of America, 1977.

Included in this book are the contributions of Jacob Kounin, his findings, discussions and conclusions. Part Two discusses the contributions of Rudolph Dreikurs -- Adlerian Psychology As Applied To The Classroom. In Section Two the author discusses basic principles, general methods and treatment, and the distinctive Dreikurian trademark -- natural and logical consequences. Part Three presents influence techniques, background data, categories of influence techniques, task assistance -- the removal of frustration, reality and value appraisal, envoking the pleasure-pain principle, classroom control, and a discussion. Part Four presents life spaced interviewing with background information, psychological factors, operational prothesis, discussion, and inconsistencies and additional criticism.

1018.   Bossert, S. T. <u>Tasks and Social Relationships in Classrooms--A Study of Instructional Organization and Its Consequences</u>. New York: Cambridge University Press, 1979.

The research reported in this book rests on the simple observation that it is within the context of daily activities that teachers and students made judgments about themselves and others, interact and form social ties, and experience social sanctions. The study was designed to examine how the structure of activities, particularly the nature of common, recurrent instructional tasks, shape both teacher and pupil behavior. Extensive observations of several elementary school classrooms and interviews with teachers and pupils provide an in-depth look at how variations in certain forms of instruction affect a teacher's use of individualized versus formalized control, the allocation of instructional assistance among pupils, the formation of children's friendship ties and peer groups, and the development of norms of group competition and cooperation. Chapter One, presents the perspective guiding the research. It differs from traditional treatments of classroom structure and draws on concepts from small group and industrial work studies to characterize the social organization of instruction and its consequences for interpersonal interaction. Chapter Two, describes the study design and its rationale. Of particular note, is the longitudinal and comparative nature of the research in which a sub group of children was observed for two school years. This enables concrete comparisons to be made among teachers and among children who experienced similar and differenct classroom organization, effectively controlling for personal characteristics to alluminate structural effects. Chapter Three, provides a descriptive ethnography of four of the classroom studies. It gives a natural history of events without attempting to categorize or analyze the nature of classroom structure. Chapter Four, examines the teacher-pupil relationship in detail. The effects of different instructional organizations on group management, the exercise of control, and the allocation of special instructional assistance are analyzed in the light of competing personality and organizational explanations of teacher behavior. Chapter Five, describes the consequences of classroom structure for peer relations. How pupil/peer groupings formed and changed throughout the school year, and how academic performance played a different role in shaping friendship ties in the different classrooms demonstrate the way in which the structure of activities shapes peer competition and cooperation. Chapter Six is an over-view of the relationship between a classroom's instructional organization and patterns of teacher and pupil interaction. The final chapter, Chapter Seven, presents some implications of this research for studying the effects of classroom structure on pupil achievement and on normative socialization.

1019.   Brigham T. A., Hawkins, R., Scott, J. W., McLaughlin, T. F. <u>Behavior Analysis In Education--Self-Control And Reading</u>. Dubuque, Iowa: Kendall/Hunt Publishing Company, 1976.

This book is divided into three major sections but united by a single approach, behavior analysis. What behavior analysis and how does it differ from such things as behavior modification, behavior therapy, operant learning theory, etc.? Behavior analysis is simply a general approach to the study of human activity. The two major features of the approach are its concern with the behavior of the individual and the experimental analysis of that behavior. In contrast to behavior modification and/or behavior therapy which have been concerned mainly with changing deviant behavior, behavior analysis focuses on analyzing and teaching effective behavior. Included are the following sections: 1) Self-control in the classroom, 2) Behavior analysis research in reading, 3) Current topics in behavior analysis: a potpourri.

1020.   Brophy, J. E. and Evertson, C. M. <u>Texas Teacher</u>
<u>Effectiveness: Classroom Coding Manual</u>. Washington, D.C.:
National Institute of Education, 1978.

This coding manual was developed for the Texas Teacher
Effectiveness Study and is intended to be self-contained.
The coding system provides for extensive coding of student
initiated questions and comments, opinion questions, and
expanded private work contracts, both teacher initiated and
student initiated, including extensive coding of quality and
type of behavioral context. The focus for this sytem was on
teacher behavior, since the larger research questions
involved the relative effectiveness of teacher process
behaviors in producing student learning. However, the
system can be readily adapted to account for individual
student interaction with teachers by including a space for
coding a student number.

1021.   Brophy, J. E. and Putnam, J. G. <u>Classroom Management in</u>
<u>the Elementary Grades</u>. <u>Research Series No. 32</u>. Washington,
D.C.: National Institute of Education, July, 1979.

The literature on elementary classroom management is
reviewed. Topics include student characteristics and
individual differences, preparing the classroom as a
learning environment, organizing instruction and support
activities to maximize student engagement and productive
tasks, developing workable housekeeping procedures and
conduct rules, managing groups during instruction, motivating and shaping desired behavior, resolving conflict and
dealing with students' personal adjustment problems, and
orchestration of these elements into an internally consistent and effective system. Promising teacher education
approaches are discussed in the closing section. See ERIC
Abstract ED 167537.

1022.   Brown, A. R. and Avery, C. <u>Modifying Children's Behavior</u>
<u>-- A Book Of Readings</u>. Springfield, Illinois: Charles C.
Thomas, Publisher, 1974.

This book represents a book of readings on behavior modifica-
tion with children. It was compiled to disseminate informa-
tion to special education and regular teachers. Included
are the following chapters: 1) The Origin Of Behavior
Modification With Exceptional Children, 2) Behavior Modifica-
tion: The Current Scene, 3) Modification And Maintenance Of
Behavior Through Systematic Application Of Consequences, 4)
Learning Theory Approaches To Classroom Managment: Rationale
And Intervention Techniques, 5) Precision Techniques In The
Management Of Teacher And Child Behaviors, 6) Freedom To
Fail: The Morality Of Behaviorism In Education Or Why The
Big Fuss Over Behavior Mod? 7) Behavior Modification:
Limitations And Liabilities, 8) How To Make A Token System
Fail, 9) The Reinforcement Of Cooperation Between Children,
10) The Alteration Of Behavior In A Special Classroom, 11)
The Use Of "Emotive Imagery" In The Treatment Of Childrens'

Phobias, 12) Classical And Operant Factors In The Treatment Of A School Phobia, 13) Token Reinforcement Programs In Special Classes, 14) Behavior Modification Of An Adjustment Class: A Token Reinforcement Program, 15) The Effects Of Loud And Soft Reprimands On The Behavior Of Disruptive Students, 16) The Santa Monica Project: Evaluation Of An Engineered Classroom Design With Emotionally Disturbed Children, 17) Behavior Modification Of Children With Learning Disabilities Using Grades As Tokens And Allowances As Backup Reinforcers, 18) A Behavior Modification Classroom For Head Start Children With Problem Behaviors, 19) Effects Of Teacher Attention And A Token Reinforcement System In The Junior High School Special Education Class, 20) The Timer-Game: A Variable Interval Contingency For The Managment Of Out-Of-Seat Behavior, 21) Behavior Modification: Where Do We Go From Here?

1023.   Brown, D. Changing Student Behavior: A New Approach To Discipline. Dubuque, Iowa: William C. Brown Company, 1971.

There are three major purposes of this book. First, an attempt is made to provide the classroom teacher with a means by which she can maintain adequate classroom control while maintaining an atmosphere which will maximize academic and personal development. Emphasis is placed on developing patterns of behavior which allow self-control as opposed to the imposition of external restraints. A second objective is to provide the teacher with a rationale for developing his or her own procedures. What is attempted is to provide a rationale for developing positive behavior patterns and then taking a random sample of the problems which a teacher faces, illustrate how the rationale can be implemented. A topic of the book is an attempt to place the teacher's role in the behavioral change process in a proper perspective. Included are the following chapters: 1) Rationale for developing positive behavior patterns, 2) Classroom discipline 3) Developing specific skills, 4) The pupil personnel team and behavioral development, 5) Identification of behavioral problems.

1024.   Brown, D. G. Behavior Modification in Child and School Health--An Annotated Bibliography on Applications with Parents and Teachers. Rockville, Maryland: National Institute of Mental Health, 1973.

The establishment of behavior modification as a treatment approach in mental health is a development of far-reaching significance. The use of behavior modification by parents and teachers as therapists is a very recent development. Considerable evidence has now accumulated that suggests behavior modification therapy, compared to traditional therapies, has several important advantages in work with children, including 1) greater effectiveness, 2) greater efficiency, 3) greater specificity of results in therapy, 4) greater applicability to a wider segment of population of children, and 5) greater utilization of a treatment method.

Groups other than professional personnel in mental health, including parents and teachers can carry out the behavior therepudic process. Most of the references in this bibliography are concerned with therapeudic process. Most of the references in this bibliography are concerned with reports on parents and teachers who were trained to carry out the therapeudic process involving children with a wide range of emotional and behavioral problems. Included are children who were hyperactive, distractible, negativistic, oppositional, aggressive, rebellious, destructive, delin-quent, over-dependent, withdrawn, socially isolated, unable to relate to peers, autistic, psychotic, self-injurious, eneuretic, disturbed in sleep or eating, stutters, school adjustment or classroom behavior problems, educational failures or low achievers, truancy or dropouts, culturally disadvantaged, and mentally retarded. While the focus is on consultations by mental health in related personnel to parents and teachers, many oᶠ the references are equally relevant to other care-giving ɣɼoups concerned with children and youth, such as physicians, public health nurses, case-workers, pastoral counselors, occupational and recreational therapists, and juvenile officers.

1025.   Buckley, N. K. & Walker, H. M. Modifying Classroom Behavior--A Manual Of Procedure For Classroom Teachers. Champaign, Illinois: Research Press, 1974.

The program lessons in this book are designed to explain the theory and technique of classroom behavior modification. It has been written for use for teacher trainees and practicing teachers. The attempt has been made to keep the book as brief and non-technical in its terminology and concepts as possible. In developing the format of the text, the authors chose to incorporate both pros and programmed items to form a semi-programmed content. This design was selected to enhance reader interest and at the same time make use of the advantages of programmed instruction. Programmed instruc-tion has been shown effective in learning materials because it incorporates 1) immediate feedback, 2) small steps, 3) active responding, 4) self-pacing. The chapters are divided into sets. Each set represents a different concept impor-tant to the chapter focus. Each set begins with a pro section designed to present all the materials. Included are the following sections Part I Basic Principles a) how behaviors are learned, b) why behaviors continue to be performed (maintained), c) how behaviors can be eliminated, d) measuring behavior Part 2 Application includes section E Modifying Classroom Behavior. The authors stress that 1) behavior change is an observable alteration in over-behavior, 2) behavior technology has been found to be superior to traditional psychotherapy in producing behavior change, 3) the primary goal of therapeutic applications of learning theory is to weaken or stamp out deviant behavior, 4) in prosthetic applications, the primary goal is to build in or condition behaviors whose operant levels are low, 5) behavior modification techniques are usually programmed to increase or decrease behavior rates, 6) shaping is used to establish totally new responses in the individual's behavior repertoire.

1026.   Buckley, N. K. and Walker, H. M. Modifying Classroom Behavior -- Revised. A Manual of Procedure for Classroom Teachers. Champaign, Illinois: Research Press Company, 1978.

This book is written for teacher trainees and practicing teachers. The attempt has been made to keep the book as non-technical and brief in its terminology and concepts as possible without omitting relevant information. The authors chose to incorporate both pros and programmed items to form a semi-programmed content. This design was selected to enhance reader interest and at the same time make use of the advantages of programmed instruction. Programmed instruction has been shown effective in learning material because it incorporates a) immediate feedback, b) small steps, c) active responding and de-self-pacing. Programmed items are selected to give feedback to the reader regarding understanding of the pros material. It is important that the reader respond actively to each of the items and these items or frames incorporate classroom application of the concepts. Included in this book are the following chapters: 1) How behaviors are learned, 2) Why behaviors continue to be performed (maintained), 3) How behaviors can be eliminated, 4) Measuring behavior, 5) Modifying classroom behavior.

1027.   Buford, W. B. Managing Classroom Behavior: Six Alternatives. Durham, North Carolina: Child Advocacy Center. 1973.

The purpose of this book is to present a passage that introduces through readings, discussions, writing and role playings, six different alternatives for managing surface classroom behavior. It was not designed to force a point of view other than the belief that children are better off with teachers who accept responsibility for their behavior toward children. By becoming more aware of alternative techniques, it is expected that the teacher will be able to make choices and thereby accept more readily responsibility for his actions. To facilitate the effective use of the book there is included what is called an "objectives and learning activity task checklist." The package is organized around 15 performance objectives which the participant is expected to achieve. Under each of these objectives the check sheet provides a list of learning activity tasks necessary for the completion of the specific performance objective.

1028.   Bushell, D. Classroom Behavior--A Little Book for Teachers. Englewood Cliffs, New Jersey: Prentice-Hall, Inc., 1973.

It is the thesis of this book that important changes in education can occur only in the classroom. Nothing will alter the basic fact that the real change in education can occur only inside the classroom. It is the individual teacher who commands the power to change the system. Administrative authority, laws, and vast sums of money can make things easier or more difficult but they cannot do the job. The job that must be done can be done only by those who teach children. Included are the following sections: 1) Teaching, 2) Some Principles of Learning/Teaching, 3) Objective Progress Records, 4) Learning is a Participant Sport, 5) Eliminating Problem Behavior, 6) Teacher Motivation, 7) Getting it All Together.

1029.   Cantor, L. and Cantor, M. "Assertive Discipline -- A Take Charge Approach For Today's Educator." Seal Beach, California: Cantor and Associates, 1976.

This book is an outgrowth of professional efforts in working directly with children with behavior problems and consulting with classroom teachers on how to deal effectively with such children. It resulted primarily from an exposure to the theoretical and practical aspects of Assertion Training. This training is a systematic approach designed to help individuals learn more effectively to express their wants and feelings, a means for increasing their ability to get their needs met in both personal and professional relationships. These skills will enable individuals to stand up more effectively for their wants and feelings, while at the same time not abusing the rights of others. The focus is on three general response styles of individuals: non-assertive, assertive and hostile. Chapters in this book include: 1) Power To The Teacher, 2) Discriminating Response Styles, 3) Road Blocks To Assertive Discipline, 4) Your Wants And Needs: What Are They? How Do You Get Them Met?, 5) Verbal Limit Setting, 6) Limit Setting Follow-through: A Promise Not A Threat, 7) Positive Assertion: Verbal And Follow-through, 8) But What If They All Do It? -- Assertive Classroom Management Skills, 9) The Assertive Discipline Plan And Other Persistency Building Procedures, 10) Asking For Help: The Use Of Assertive Skills With Parents And Principals, 11) In Conclusion: Assertive Discipline Comes Down To The Issue Of Choice.

1030.   Carbonari, S. A. "Discussion: The Role Of Teachers And Paraprofessionals In The Classroom." In Behavior Modification: Issues And Extensions. New York: Academic Press, 1972.

This is a critical examination of O'Leary's contention that paraprofessionals should be utilized as behavior modifiers in the classroom. Data are presented to illustrate that there is a greater need for training teachers than paraprofessionals in behavior modification techniques. See ERIC Abstract 0766650-4.

1031.   Carew, J. V. and Lightfoot, S. L. Beyond Bias --
Perspectives on Classrooms. Cambridge, Massachusetts:
Harvard University Press, 1979.

The research reported in this book was conducted with four
teachers and eighty children. Studied with the teacher as
the central figure, difference and deviance, the social
context of school and community, and an observation of
teachers and children in the classroom. After explaining
the research study, each of the teachers is looked at
individually in Part Two. Appendices include a Teacher-
Child Interaction Coding Manual, A Child Focused Observation
Coding System and Supplementary Statistical Information.

1032.   Cartan, K. W. The Communicatively Disordered Child.
Austin, Texas: Learning Concepts, Inc., 1977.

With the emphasis on mainstreaming in the 1970's, the
regular class teacher is now expected to meet the needs of
exceptional children in his or her classroom, along with the
other children in the class. The problem is that most
regular class teachers have little or no preparation in the
area of educating exceptional children. Regular class
teachers need basic information regarding the various
exceptionalities, and more specifically, practical suggestions which they can emply to enhance the mainstreamed
exceptional child's personal and educational development.
This book was written to fill this need. The author hopes
that providing definitions, theories about causes, characteristics of various disorders, guidelines for referrals, and
practical suggestions for classroom activities, that the
task of educating the communicatively disordered child will
be much easier. The following questions are answered in
this book: What is an articulation disorder? What causes
articulation disorders? To whom do I refer? What can
teachers do? What is a voice disorder? What causes these
disorders? What are the common voice problems? What can
teachers do? What is stuttering, what causes it? How does
it develop and what can teachers do? What is a communication and language disorder? What causes communication and
language disorders and what can teachers do?

1033.   Carter, R. D. Help! These Kids Are Driving Me Crazy.
Champaign, Illinois: Research Crafts Company, 1972.

This book gives teachers knowledge of workable techniques
for humane classroom control, many of which have been known
and used for years. It includes the following chapters: 1)
Living, behaving, and changing, 2) Strengthening desirable
behaviors, 3) Weakening undesirable behaviors, 4) Hints,
tricks of the trade and details, 5) An experiement, 6) Doing
your own thing, 7) An outlined summary. Appendices include
a) survey quiz, b) a classroom point system, and c) some
payoffs for school aged kids.

1034.   Chamberlin, L. J. and Carnot, J. B. (Eds.) Improving School Discipline. Springfield, Illinois Charles C. Thomas, Publisher, 1974.

Authors state that developing effective instruction while maintaining positive student behavior is one of the most urgent and recurring problems found in the teacher profession. Management of student behavior is a definite aspect of effective teaching. This book provides concrete references to achieve results in instruction developed by teachers with advice in administrating the daily educational program. The book gives the reader a frame of reference which increases his ability to understand problem behavior and deal effectively with it. It offers a positive action approach to teaching. The material is designed for use by teachers and college students preparing to enter the teaching profession, parents, school administrators, and experinced teachers as well. Chapters include: 1) Concepts of discipline and instruction, 2) Discipline in the public schools, 3) Common causes of disciplinary problems, 4) The teacher's role, 5) The administrator-supervisor-parent rolls, 6) Preventive discipline, 7) Corrective discipline, 8) Therapeutic discipline, 9) Psychological approaches, 10) Legal approaches.

1035.   Chase, J. A. "Differential behavioral characteristics of non-promoted children." Genetic Psychology Monographs, 86, (November, 1972): 219-277.

Author investigated the non-promotion of first time first graders in relation to the factors of intelligence, perceptual ability, physical and developmental status, achievement, classroom behavior and teacher judgement. Three hundred and nine first graders were given a battery of tests. The sixty-five subjects who were not promoted were best discriminated by teacher judgement variables and scores on the Metropolitan Readiness Test. See ERIC Abstract 0-71350-2.

1036.   Chernow, F. B. and Chernow, C. Teaching The Culturally Disadvantaged Child. West Nyack, New York: Parker Publishing Company Incorporated, 1973.

Included in the book are activities that raise children self-image, techniques that make disruptive children actually want to gain positive peer approval, materials using low reading levels but high interest levels, approaches to learning that utilize the senses, appeals to instruction that are multi-ethnic, involvement of parents and community in the learning process, approaches to the three R's that are practical, subjects that are relevant to the needs of pupils, materials for pupils that are free and inexpensive, activities that help build confidence and respect, and steps to ensure good classroom management. This book is designed for the teacher who wants to refine and develop his or her expertise in reaching the disadvantaged

children who people today's schools. Included are the
following chapters: 1) Establishing a positive favorable
relationship with your class, 2) How you can develop good
discipline from the very beginning, 3) How you can get and
maintain parental support and cooperation, 4) How to use
school resource people effectively, 5) Tested guidance
techniques in teaching the disadvantaged, 6) How to teach
reading to the disadvantaged -- after others have failed, 7)
Teaching basic math skills to the disadvantaged, 8) How to
teach language arts successfully to the disadvantaged, 9)
Techniques that get the disadvantaged interested in social
studies, 10) Teaching science to the disadvantaged student,
11) Fresh approaches to teaching other subjects to the
disadvantaged, 12) How you can build a bridge from your
classroom to your community, 13) Learning materials that can
help in teaching the disadvantaged, 14) How to evaluate the
progress of your disadvantaged students.

1037.   Child Behavior Equals You.   Briarcliff Manor, New York,
Benchmark Films, 1973.

This fifteen minute film is designed to show both adolescent
students and adults how children learn behavior. The film
stresses the influences of the community, the school, and
the family in the process of development. Animation is used
to present stiuations in which the adult child interaction
is contributing to learned behavior. For example, an infant
is shown crying; the mother picks up the infant; and the
infant learns to cry in order to receive attention. The
film suggests that the adults should ignore the crying baby
and give attention when the infant is happy. There is an
emphasis in the film on behavior modification concepts,
including negative and positive reinforcement. This film is
appropriate for junior and senior high classes as well as
adult basic education. See ERIC Abstract IN025579.

1038.   Clarizio, H. F.   Toward Positive Classroom Discipline.
New York: John Wiley and Sons, Inc., 1971.

Classroom discipline is one of the most difficult problems
confronting teachers. The adequate preparation of teachers
in this regard has been impeded by the lack of a science of
discipline in any strict sense. The purpose of this book is
to inform both perspective and experienced teachers about
new techniques developed from the practical application of
learning theory principles. It is intended for use by
professionals such as counselors, psychologists and social
workers who consult with teachers concerning problem children, as well as the teachers themselves. The techniques
discussed are offered as a starting point in the development
of a how to do it book. Included are the following
chapters: 1) A Learning Theory Approach to Classroom
Discipline, 2) The Use of Reward, 3) Modeling and Observational Learning, 4) Extinction Procedures, 5) Punishment: A
New Look, 6) Overcoming Anxieties Through Desensitization,
and 7) Implementing Positive Disciplinary Procedures.

1039.   Clarizio, H. F.   <u>Toward Positive Classroom Discipline</u>.
(Second Edition).   New York: John Wiley & Sons, Inc., 1976.

Classroom discipline continues to be one of the most
difficult problems confronting teachers. The adequate
preparation of teachers in this regard has been impeded by
the lack of a science of discipline in any strict sense.
Today we are witnessing rapid advances in scientific know-
how with respect to classroom discipline. These advances
have come from the practical applications of learning theory
principles. The purpose of this book is to inform both
prospective and experienced teachers about these techniques.
It also should prove valuable to those professionals who
consult with teachers concerning problem children such as
counselors, psychologists, and social workers. The techniques discussed here are offered as a starting point in the
development of a "how to do it" book. They are not presented as the final word on disciplinary strategies but are
given as first approximations that undoubtedly will be
improved on in the light of further research and experience.
Included are the following chapters: 1) A Learning Theory
Approach to Classroom Discipline, 2) The Use of Reward, 3)
Modeling and Observational Learning, 4) Extinction Procedures, 5) Punishment: A New Look, 6) Overcoming Anxieties
Through Desensitization, 7) Implementing Positive Disciplinary Procedures.

1040.   Collins, M. T. and Collins, D. R.   <u>Survival Kit For
Teachers (And Parents)</u>.   Pacific Palisades, California:
Good Year Publishing Company Incorporated, 1975.

Discipline-classroom behavior-classroom management is a
major and universal concern of teachers, administrators,
parents and students. The kit contains the most
comprehensive combined listing and treatment of behaviors
ever published. In-service and pre-service teachers,
counselors, administrators, and parents can use the list of
324 behaviors as a ready referrence for coping with student
behavior. The behaviors were gleaned from live surveys of
classroom teachers, a systematic review of professional
periodicals and books and a recall of many years of school
experience as students, teachers, counselors and administrators. The capsules written for the behaviors are
vignettes dealing with the psychology of the behavior. The
options immediately following each capsule provide specific
alternatives for coping with the behaviors. This book can
provide solid discussion material for faculty meetings and
workshops. Its use as a communication medium during parent-
teacher conferences is also suggested. Author also suggests
that the capsules and options be discussed with the child
whose behavior is upsetting and let him chose an option as a
resolution to his difficulty. The appendix includes concise
descriptions of 26 procedures frequently referred to in the
capsule and options.

1041.   Connecticut Education Association. <u>Bridge Over Troubled Waters--Report Of Connecticut Education Association Bridge- port Discipline Study Panel, January, 1973.</u> Hartford, Connecticut: Connecticut Education Association, 1973.

Discipline results from the general state of health of the total system. If everyone--teachers, administrators, school board, students, parents,--are all working together to achieve the same ends, school discipline can be excellent. If school discipline is considered to be a problem, that problem is really only a symptom resulting from the more fundamental problems of people in conflict over aims and the ways to achieve them. Sections include: 1) Climate, 2) Communications, 3) Programs, 4) Personnel, 5) Discipline.

1042.   Connors, E. T. <u>Student Discipline And The Law.</u> Bloomington, Indiana: Phi Delta Kappa Educational Foundation, 1979.

This publication establishes some general guidelines for teachers and administrators to follow when disciplining students. While the law is frequently complex, some fairly simple rules to thumb can be gleaned from an examination of State and Federal court cases concerning the legality of student discipline procedures. Controlling student disci- pline is an integral element of the educational process. The use of disciplinary techniques should be encouraged as a means of helping students gain the most from their educa- tional opportunity. Educators do have broad powers when dealing with student conduct through disciplinary means. As long as there is no blatant violation of the students' constitutional rights, the courts are reluctant to substi- tute their judgement for those of educators. Educators must be aware of their legal limitations in administering discipline. The purpose of this publication is to help to enlighten those concerned with student discipline as to the legal status of various discipline techniques. Included are the following sections: 1) Corporal punishment, 2) Suspen- sion and expulsion, 3) Searches and seizures, 4) Regulations governing married and/or pregnant students, 5) Discipline and students' first amendment rights, 6) Regulating students' dress and hair styles, 7) Regulating students grades, diplomas, graduation, 8) Making reasonable rules and developing a student handbook.

1043.   Cultice, W. W. <u>Positive Discipline For A More Productive Educational Climate.</u> Englewood Cliffs, New Jersey: Successful School Administration Series, Prentice-Hall, Incorporate, 1969.

This booklet is designed to provide guidance in the impor- tant area of discipline. Discipline theory must be modified and adjusted to remain compatable with current concepts of education. This material, for purposes of effective analysis and emphasis, is organized around the major areas of discipline problems and each problem is treated separately. The author feels that the right to learn and the responsbility to perform should be the foremost consideration in handling transgressors whose infractions constitute an imposition upon their peers, teachers, and school program in general. This booklet is an attempt to help the administrator to use positive discipline to create a productive educational climate. Chapters include: 1) The Concept And Function Of Discipline -- Evolution Of Discipline, Forming The Disciplinary Policies Of The School, The Need For A Written Discipline Policy, Some Tips On Good Classroom Discipline, Universal Tips On Positive School Discipline, 2) Implementing The Program -- Basic Guidelines In Building A Program, Setting A Positive Pace, The Role Of The Counselor, 3) The Need To Create A Positive Basic Curriculum -- The Need For A Creative Lesson, Encouraging Students To Set Their Own Standards, 4) Identifying Physical Problems -- Managing Large Groups, 5) Student Attendance -- Absence Procedure, Understanding Minority Student Problems, Understanding Minority Parent Problems.

1044.   Daniels, L. K. (Ed.) The Management of Childhood Behavior Problems in School and at Home. Springfield, Illinois: Charles C. Thomas, Publisher, 1974.

This book is problem centered and describes detailed procedures for the management of the most common behavior problems encountered in elementary and secondary school classrooms. There are three major sections. The first deals with avoidance problems or behavior that should be increased. The second introduces approach problems which consist of behaviors that should be decreased. The basis for such a division rests on the assumption that all human behavior can be delegated to one of these categories and can be modified by increasing response probability in relation to particular persons, situations, or tasks. The third and last part presents the child's parents as therapists and describes ways in which they can collaborate with teachers in changing behavior. Part one introduces six major areas that concern the classroom teacher and describes behavior that must be increased with instructional objectives are to be attained. These areas include achievement to various academic subjects, promptness in preparing for classes, speaking out and participating in class discussion, tendencies to withdraw and become isolated, unrealistic fears or anxieties, and a completion of such tasks as picking up toys, tying shoes, and personal grooming. These are activities in which the teacher needs to increase pupil participation and deficiencies in them have been of traditional concern to members of the profession. Part two presents five major areas that affect classroom management and include activities that must be decreased to attain goals of instruction. These include physical aggression, inappropriate talking, lack of attention, generally disruptive behavior, and self-indulgence. Part three is devoted to the role of parents in the problem-solving process, an area of practical precedence that has received

very little attention in texts prepared for professionals.
The article selected for this section emphasized the
techniques that may be successfully used by parents and
parallel material presented in part one and two for the
classroom teacher.

1045.   Davis, J. E. Coping With Disruptive Behavior -- What
Research Says To The Teacher. Washington, D.C.: National
Education Association, 1974.

Author states that most students try to adapt their behavior
to that of other students in the classroom. When a student's behavior forms a consistent pattern, he or she has
established a status in the classroom and therefore has a
definite role. Although individual students may try to
fulfill certain needs through their classroom roles, in
general their behavior is complimentary to that of their
peers. Research indicates that disruptive behavior tends to
develop in the classroom when individual roles tend to
conflict with one another. The conflicts occur more in
student-student relationship than in teacher-student relationships, because the roles of students are more subject to
change than are the relatively fixed roles of teachers in
relation to students. This report reviews recent findings
of research on various methods that teachers may use to
modify, redirect, or otherwise influence disruptive
behavior. In order to maintain a classroom climate in which
learning can take place. Chapters include: 1) Methods of
handling disruptive behavior -- the teacher-dominant
approach, the analytic approach, the behavioristic approach,
the student-centered approach, the teacher-student interaction approach, 2) Application of methods, 3) Reward and
punishments, 4) Group strategies -- group counseling,
sociodrama, establishing group codes, 5) Classroom environment, 6) Curriculum, 7) Teaching style.

1046.   Deitz, S. M. and Hummel, J. H. Discipline in the Schools
-- A Guide to Reducing Misbehavior. Englewood Cliffs, New
Jersey: Educational Technology Publications, 1978.

The main purpose of this book is to teach alternatives by
presenting and explaining a large variety of procedures from
which a teacher may choose when faced with problems of misbehavior. This book can be useful to a variety of practitioners, including prospective or practicing teachers,
individuals working in day-care centers, parents and others.
The book is divided into three sections. Before each section is a brief discussion introducing the various contents
of the section. Section One, deals with issues and identifying, defining and measuring misbehaviors and also with
evaluating programs for their reduction. Chapter Two, discusses ten procedures which have been found effective for
reducing or eliminating misbehavior. The first four either
use adversive events and/or produce some form of aversive
behavioral side effects. The last six procedures reduce
misbehavior through more positive or productive teacher-

student interactions. In Section Three, are summaries, and discussion of some implications and conclusions derived from the other sections. Through studying these issues, the reader should gain practical expertise in the following areas: 1) analyzing and defining misbehavior, 2) measuring misbehavior, 3) implementing a misbehavior reduction program following one of the ten suggested procedures, and 4) evaluating the effects of a misbehavior reduction program.

1047.   Dembo, M. H. Teaching for Learning: Applying Educational Psychology in the Classroom. Santa Monica, California: Goodyear Publishing Company, Inc., 1977.

The author states that the book was written because teachers need more detailed information about specific aspects of the teaching-learning process, rather than encyclopedic knowledge of all content in education psychology and teachers need to know how to use educational psychology to make better teaching decisions. The following components of the book are the author's attempts to translate these assumptions into a textbook that is an alternative to the many textbooks already in the field. He based the book on an instructional model identifying the major variables of the teaching-learning process: individual differences, teacher behavior, instructional objectives, theories and principles of learning, methods of teaching, and evaluation of student behavior and achievement. After presenting the model in chapter one he discusses individual differences in chapters two and three. Chapter four demonstrates how teachers interact with and affect the behavior of different students. Chapter five covers the issues and procedures involving the use of instructional objectives, while chapters six, seven and eight consider the conceptual and practical aspects of theories of learning and the resulted methods of teaching for attaining classroom objectives. Chapters nine and ten outline ways to measure and evaluate student progress. The author has tried to focus on the most relevant theories, principles and research findings for each of the variables. Developmental concepts are discussed primarily under individual differences, and Piagetian theory is covered under cognitive learning theory. Learning theories and methods of teaching are organized by their theoretical orientations -- behaviorism, coginitivism, and humanism, to help the reader understand the theory behind the practice. The author begins each chapter with a brief orientation to acquaint the reader with the issues and concerns of the chapter. Finally, he has interspersed questions throughout the text that ask the reader to take a stand on various issues or require them to think about personal experiences in school. These questions encourage the reader to examine personal beliefs about the teaching-learning process. Follow-up activities at the end of each chapter maintain this self inquiring process.

1048.   Dettre, J. R.   <u>Decision Making In The Secondary School</u>
<u>Classroom--Toward   Preparing   The   Diagnostic   Teacher</u>.
Scranton: Intext Education Publishers, 1970.

This book is an attempt to focus through the secondary
school setting to relevant matters in teaching in the
secondary school. The book attempts to create a secondary
school setting with attendant problems as a basis for both
introducing and incorporating relevant material about
teaching in the secondary school and developing a process
related to problem solving and decision making in the
classroom. The overall aim of the materials and the process
is to provide students at both an in-service or pre-service
level with an opportunity to broaden their notions of what
teaching is, to increase their level of transfer of learning
to their own classroom and to develop for them a way of
analyzing problems that will permit the students to operate
at a level in their own classroom that is beyond that of a
simple classroom technician. In Part 2 of the materials the
process used to deal with the problems is developed. The
approach is to develop a situation in detail and then
step-by-step to use the process to treat the situation.
Included is a detailed consideration of the nature of the
information available both in terms of substance and form.
The next step is to organize the information by means of
classifying and sequencing the data. The analysis of the
sample situation proceeds on through seven steps. In Part 3
a detailed description of the school attendance district is
provided along with a curriculum guide, teacher handbook,
faculty roster and administrative profiles, state supervisory reports and two sample class rosters. This material
is designed to: 1) provide useful information needed in
analyzing and treating the problems provided and 2) delimit
the involvement with the problem, particularly in terms of
helping control the degree of manipulation the teacher might
be prone to make of variables related to outcomes and
strategies. Part 4 includes a list of 43 problems concen-
trated in the areas of professional welfare, personal
welfare, pupil welfare, institutional welfare, and community
welfare. The problems are arranged in terms of the degree
of complexity perceived in the problem situation.

1049.   Dollar, B.   <u>Humanizing Classroom Discipline--A Behavioral</u>
<u>Approach</u>. New York: Harper and Rowe Publishers, 1972.

The concepts and techniques that are explored and analyzed
in this book represent suggested activities that the author
felt will accomplish certain objectives. First, the teacher
learns to effectively reinforce students' correct responses.
Conversly, the teacher learns methods and techniques to
discourage students' misbehavior. Finally, the teacher
learns to verbally communicate fundamental principles of
behavior: that learning does not occur without reinforcement; that aggression teaches aggression; that punishment
alone merely teachers the student how to avoid future punishment; that punishment is the withdrawl of reinforcement;

that punishment combined with reinforcement is the only effective way of changing behavior. That text provides a three step modeling procedure for effecting optimum classroom discipline.

1050.   Doob, H. Codes of Student Discipline and Student Rights. Arlington, Virginia: Educational Research Service, Inc., 1975.

Student discipline continues to be one of the major concerns of educators and laymen. The development and administration of discipline codes that are both educationally and legally sound have gained importance in recent decades. In part, the emergence of administrator concern about student discipline and student rights has been attributed to the increased social awareness of students and the public at large. As students and their parents have come to challenge certain restrictions, and as local, state, and federal courts have begun to stress the rights of students within the school, administrators have addressed themselves to the substantive and procedural aspects of student discipline. The purpose of this report is to 1) present findings of a recent educational research service inquiry regarding written codes of student discipline and 2) to replicate examples of selected codes. This publication is intended to serve school administrators by providing basic information, positive suggestions, and examples pertaining to student codes.

1051.   Dreikurs, R. Maintaining Sanity in the Classroom: Illustrated Teaching Techniques. New York: Parker & Rowe, Publishers, 1971.

The purpose of this book is to encourage teachers, who in these troubled times, are beginning to doubt their own ability to motivate children in school, and who are either accepting defeat and are leaving the teaching profession, or who are resigned to a fate of failure and misery until such time when they can retire. The aim is not to tell teachers how to teach any particular subject, but rather how to create an atmosphere conducive to learning and enjoyment. This can be achieved if they share their responsibility with the students, understands what makes them tick, recognize their aspiration and help them to realize their hopes. The child can function fully in the classroom only if he feels accepted by the group as a worthwhile member. His ability and willingness to function depends on what is called his "social interests" disturbances and deficiencies indicate a lack of social interest, of concern with the welfare of others. The restriction of social interest is usually due to inferiority feelings, to the doubts of the child to find a place through useful means. It is the task of the teacher to help the child to overcome his mistaken self-evaluation and, thereby, increase his social interests. For this reason, the art of encouragement is one of the most crucial tools that can be used to correct and improve the adjustment

each child is making. Included are the following chapters:
1) Theoretical Premises, 2) Diagnostic Techniques, 3)
Effective Democratic Methods, 4) Coping with Specific
Problems, 5) Parental Involvement.

1052.   Dreikurs, R. & Cassel, P. Discipline Without Tears.
(Second Edition) New York: Hawthorn Books, 1974.

Presently our school system is in a dilemma regarding
discipline. The controversy over punishment cannot be
resolved unless we give teachers alternative effective
techniques for dealing with children who misbehave and
refuse to learn. In a well organized primary classroom,
where the teacher is skilled and stimulating the students to
learn what they need to learn, there are few discipline
problems. If the teacher believes in educating the whole
child, there is ample opportunity for the development and
expression of creativity through art, music, dance and the
language arts. When a problem arises, the teacher immediately asks some questions. Was the assigned work too
difficult for some, or was it too easy and consequently
boring? Was the lesson preparation adequate? Was the
presentation stimulating and exciting? Was it too long or
too short? Have the pupils been given sufficient time to
finish, and are there opportunities for fast workers to do
challenging enrichment? The way in which the teacher
answers these questions indicates what action she can take
to improve the situation. If she is satisified that her
teaching methods are suitable, she may next go to the hidden
curriculum for some answers. In that hidden curriculum may
live a child with a health problem, either physical or
mental; a recent disappointment such as a death of a pet; or
an exciting anticipation of a happy event. The teacher
should be aware of the difference between a temporary upset
and a deeper more permanent problem. When a teacher really
knows his or her class she or he is sensitive to the pupils'
reactions, and if a personal problem is the cause of the
disturbance she is able to offer effective guidance. However
if disturbing behavior or resistance to learning is repeti-
tive, she or he can learn to diagnose the purpose of the
childs mistaken goals, to understand the private logic of
the child, and to redirect his behavior. Included are the
following chapters: 1) What kind of teacher are you? 2) A
rewarding alternative: teaching the democratic way. 3) How
does a child grow? 4) Understanding the modern child. 5)
Competition. 6) Encouragement. 7) Logical consequences,
not punishment. 8) Conflict solving and how to deal with
tyrants. 9) Is your class a group? 10) The class discussion period. 11) Typical problems and their solutions. 12)
Examples that stopped the tears. Included in this publication is also a workbook entitled "Discipline Without Tears."

1053.   Drucker, P. F. People And Performance: The Best Of
Peter Drucker On Management. New York: Harper's College
Press, 1977.

This selection on management deals with the major dimensions of management: as a persons craft and as a tool for achievement; as an intellectual discipline in its own right; as people working alone and working together; as society's organ for the performance of vital social tasks; and as an integrating, synthesizing function in a complex and changing world. It aims at giving students an idea of management, the feel of an experience that otherwise is still ahead of them. All the chapters in the book have been developed out of many years of practice as advisor to, and diagnostician for, management and organizations. There are six sections in this book. Section One discusses what management is. Why do we have management and managers? How did management emerge and develop? And what is management concerned with? Section Two deals with what a manager is. What does he or she do? Section Three turns to what is being managed and asks what an institution is. What are its realities? What are its tasks? And what has to be done to enable it to perform and to contribute? Section Four is concerned with organization and structure -- with identifying the work needed and placing it in relation to the entire organization and to all its individual parts. Section Five focusus on people and their work. What do we know about work and working? What do we know about people in jobs, their needs, their aspirations and their problems? What does todays student have to know to be effective and satisfied as as employee tomorrow? Finally, in Section Six, management and organization are looked at from the outside, from society and culture. The emphasis throughout the book is on people and performance.

1054.   ERIC Clearinghouse on Early Childhod Education. Behavior Modification in the Classroom: An Abstract Bibliography. Catalog #139. Washington, D.C.: National Institute of Education, 1975.

This selected bibliography contains references to 75 ERIC documents and journal articles on the subject of behavior modification in the pre-school and elementary school classroom. Included are samples of programs in which behavior modification has been used, descriptions of how to use behavior modification techniques, research on the effectiveness of behavior modification techniques, and discussion of critical issues related to behavior modification. See ERIC Abstract ED 118245.

1055.   Fagen, S. A., Long, N. J. & Stevens, D. J. Teaching Children Self-Control--Preventing Emotional and Learning Problems in the Elememtary School. Columbus, Ohio: Charles E. Merrill Publishing Company, 1975.

This book discusses freedom and responsibility. The authors believe that the increasing incidence of disruptive behavior in the classroom reflects an educational neglect of skills needed for prevention of serious learning and emotional problems. The authors have moved to a position that disruptive behavior signifies a limitation in skills--on the part of either the child or the educational system. Their thinking has changed as a result of careful analysis of children's disruptive behavior. Through a process of class-room observation, literature review, and shared reflection they have identified a core set of eight skills that seem to determine an idividiual's capacity to maintain free control over his or her own behavior. The book is organized into three parts. Part one presents the theoretical and concep-tual structure upon which the self-control curriculum is based. Part two describes the eight curriculum areas and their subsidary units and tasks. Part three describes important issues pertaining to the self-control curriculum and provides closing remarks. The eight curriculum areas include: selection, storage, sequencing and ordering, anticipating consequences, appreciating feelings, managing frustration, inhibition and delay, and relaxation.

1056.   Fagen, S. A. and Hill, J. M. Behavior Management -- A Competency Based Manual For In-Service Training. Montgomery County Public Schools, Rockville, Maryland: In-Service Teacher Training For Main Streaming Series, Psyco Educa-tional Resources, Incorporated, 1977.

This manual is intended for personnel responsible for in-service programming in local education agencies. The manual can be flexibly used to conduct 1) A one semester in-service course, 2) Individual workshops at the local school or area level. Authors feel that the one area of greatest concern to classroom teachers is the management of student behavior. Teachers over-estimate the frequency and intensity of acted out behavior and often worry about their own reactions to such behavior. With exposure to sound principles and techniques for handling and preventing behavior problems, these same teachers develop confidence in their ability to maintain classroom order and discipline. This training manual is intended to help teachers prevent and survive difficult encounters with student behavior. Included are prevention modules 1) Establishing behavior values, standards, and limits, 2) The operant strategy of one of three educational approaches, 3) Strategies for reinforcing behavior values, Coping module 4) Discusses teaching acceptance of and coping with frustration, Interven-tion module 5) Presents surface management techniques for intervening and disruptive school behavior and module 6) Present life space interviewing. There are six components of each module. The first is an overview of the module. Next the objectives give a brief run down of what the instructor is expected to provide participants. The third component is the instruction unit guide. The fourth component is the basic instructional material section and the fifth component is the assessment tasks/criteria. The final component includes supplemental resources.

1057.   Faust, N. F. Discipline And The Classroom Teacher. Port
Washington, New York: Kennikat Press, 1977.

A number one concern of teachers throughout the nation is
"Disciplinary Problems." The purpose of this book is to
assist teachers in acquiring the secure feeling of being
able to establish well disciplined classes in which adequate
learning may take place. A central goal of the author is to
help the teacher meet such needs of youngsters as will
encourage these young people to be self-controlled individuals who are willing to take advantage of their opportunities. The authors intent is to assist many teachers in
gaining the background knowledge needed to work with young
people that will assure teachers of healthy survival in the
classroom. There is further hope of the author that through
the book many teachers may be lead to the conviction that
the teacher's existence in the classroom can be rewardingly
productive. Several chapters are devoted to handling disadvantaged youth in discipline and learning. Much of the
book is concerned with the discipline of all types of
youngsters. Included are the following chapters: 1) Disadvantaged Youth And The Problem Of Discipline, 2) Disciplining Disadvantaged Youth Through Effective Teaching, 3)
Special Handling Of The Disadvantaged Child, 4) Managerial
Antidotes For Disciplinary Problems, 5) Affective Antidotes
For Problems In Discipline, 6) Cognitive Antidotes For
Behavior Problems 7) Lesson Planning And Presentation As
They Relate To Discipline, 8) Handling Youth Through
Questioning, 9) Ways Of Dealing With Disciplinary Problems,
10) Specific Problems And How To Handle Them, 11) Case
Studies In Discipline.

1058.   Fine, M. J. & Walkenshaw, M. R. The Teacher's Role Into
Classroom   Management.   Dubuque,   Iowa: Kendall/Hunt
Publishing Company, 1973.

Authors stress some of the following principles of a
humunastic orientation toward classroom management 1)
management procedures are part of the total curriculum, 2) a
humanistic curriculum emphasizes both the cognitive and
effective development of the child, 3) the nucleus of a
humanistic curriculum is a facilitative teacher-child
relationship, 4) the nucleus of humanistic management
procedures is a facilitative teacher-child relationship, 5)
a facilitative teacher-child relationship is characterized
by teacher respect and caring for the child, 6) respect and
caring for the child requires that the child participate in
deciding what happens to him, 7) the child may need to be
educated as to his capability of participation, 8) it is
through such participation that the child learns to assume
more responsibility for his own behavior. Included in the
book are the following chapters: 1) What's happening in the
classroom, 2) A viewpoint on human development, 3) A framework on intervention, 4) Intervention: minimal investment
strategy, 5) Intervention: formal strategy, 6) Brief case
studies, 7) Where do we go from here?

1059.   Fishteim, R. <u>Classroom Psychology</u>. Brooklyn, New York: Book-Lab Incorporated, 1973.

The technique of anticipating needs is particularly useful when dealing with children who manifest behavior problems. The anticipatory approach is based upon the understanding the motivations of each child with such problems, and preparing, in advance, to forestall the undesirable behavior. Successful application of the principle of anticipating needs requires knowledge and understanding of the children as they will appear before the teacher in the classroom. In Part I the author considers the needs of very specific types of students who can be readily classified into definite categories. In Part II she considers more general teaching problems and discusses techniques for solutions applicable to children in the class as a whole. In Part III she considers some of the teacher's problems not as a professional but as a person who is groping with as much uncertainty and need for understanding as anyone else. The book classifies children as 1) The hyperactive child, 2) The aggressively unresponsive child, 3) The fearful one, 4) The outsider, 5) The exceptionally bright child, 6) The day dreamer, 7) The chronic absentee, 8) The foul mouth kid.

1060.   Foster, H. L. <u>Ribbin', Jivin', and Playin' The Dozens -- The Unrecognized Dilemma of Inner-City Schools</u>. Cambridge, Massachusetts: Ballinger Publishing Company, 1974.

The author states that there are three underlying reasons why we have not been able to educate more urban black children. The first is institutionalized white racism. The second, is the fear people have of those exhibiting unfamiliar and different life styles. The third, related to and to some extent a consequence of the first two, is that urban educators are playing the game of teaching and learning in inner-city schools by the wrong rules. This book provides most inner-city teachers and administrators with whole new insights about what they have been experiencing without understanding. His chapter on discipline is unique in its dealing with the gut issues teachers in inner-city schools face all the time. His discussion of the conflict between the teachers and the inner-city students lifestyle reflects an intimate knowledge of the situation. Chapters include: 1) Introduction 2) The Unrecognized Dilemma of Inner-City Schools 3) A Historical Perspective Concerning Inner-City Conditioning Experiences 4) Jive, Lexicon and Verbal Communication 5) Ribbing, Jiving and Playing the Dozen 6) Discipline 7) Summing Up.

1061.   Galloway, D. <u>Case Studies In Classroom Management</u>. New York, New York: Longman, Incorporated, January, 1977.

These case histories are about the daily challange of class- room teaching. They show how problems can develop in fundamentally normal children, and in many cases they illustrate how imaginative teachers have found ways to help

children with intransigent learning and behavior problems
without labeling them maladjusted and without removing them
to a special school. Each case history is preceded by two
or three main points, intended to focus the readers attention on the crucial issues. The questions deliberately
cover a ride range, some are suitable for students in their
first year or two of training, others could be used in
sensitivity training for teachers specializing in conseling.
Cooperation between schools and other agencies is a
reacurring theme.

1062.   Glavin, J. P. <u>Behavioral Strategies For Classroom
Management</u>. Columbus, Ohio: Charles E. Merrill Publishing
Company, 1974.

This text focuses on modifying disruptive behavior in the
regular classroom. It deals with the current issues which
accompany the use of behavior modification techniques in
schools. The reader is also informed about the various
aspects of behavioral approaches: what each is, how it is
applied, when it should be used, and how it should be
evaluated. The following chapters are: 1) The mergence of
special and regular education, 2) managing classroom
behavior, 3) behavior modification as applied today, 4) some
reflections on behavior modification in the classroom, 5)
modeling and vicarious reinforcement, 6) social reinforcement, 7) contingency contracting: from teacher to self-
control, 8) peer tutoring, 9) self management in learning,
10) individualization and structure in the classroom. The
goal is to find a satisfcatory way to facilitate behavior
modification not only in a special classroom, but also in a
regular classroom, for the current lack of manpower and
funds makes the initiation of this kind of program infea-
sible. This book is an attempt to describe a realistic
concept which will enable the regular classroom teacher to
more clearly see his place in the management of childrens
problems.

1063.   Glavin, J. P. (Ed.) <u>Ferment In Special Education</u>. New
York: M. S. S. Information Corporation, 1974.

This book is motivated by the author's experiences in
teaching the introductory course on the exceptional child to
graduate and advanced undergraduate students. Students
should gain firsthand familarity with significant articles
in the field of special education. Most of the articles
selected for inclusion in the book have been used over
several semesters and have continued to attract the interest
of students and to emphasize some of the major theoretical
and practical issues in special education. Included are the
following sections: 1) Introduction, 2) Application in the
classroom, 3) Evaluation, 4) Curriculum: cognitive, effective, creative, 5) Early education of disadvantaged children, 6) Types of programs, 7) Trends and controversies, 8)
Research and service needs.

1064.   Gnagey, T. How to Put Up with Parents -- A Guide for Teenagers. Ottawa, Illinois: Facilitation House, 1975.

These materials are designed to assist students in grades junior high through adult in understanding the basic principles of human behavior and how the family environment may be modified by using behavioral techniques. The book describes the characteristics of good parents, character- istics of human behavior, and some common problem parent personality traits and how to deal with them. See NIMI 035-357.

1065.   Gnagey, W. J. Maintaining Discipline in Classroom Instruction. New York: MacMillan Publishing Co., Inc., 1975.

The material in this book is meant to bridge the research- implementation gap so that classroom teachers can begin immediately to improve the learning atmosphere for their students. A positive, humanistic, reward-centered approach pervades most of the techniques described in this book. Also included is recent material on effective punishment. Included are the following chapters: 1) Defining Classroom Discipline; 2) Preventing Classroom Misbehavior; 3) Controlling Deviance Directly; 4) Controlling Deviance by Proxy; 5) Reconditioning Student Behavior; 6) Using Punish- ment Constructively; 7) Increasing Self-Control; 8) Applying Glasser's Reality Therapy: An Eclectic Approach.

1066.   Gnagey, W. J. The Psychology of Discipline in the Classroom. London: The MacMillan Co., 1968.

This book is an attempt to bring together the adventure of classroom teaching and the precise statistical operation of the research scientist. Its goal is to illustrate the latest findings in discipline research with authentic incidents from living classrooms. The purpose is to provide the classroom teacher with a versatile tool for helping deviant students become more efficient learners. In Chapter 1, the five components of deviancy episode appear in a classroom disaster that highlights their dynamic inter- action. Chapters 2 through 6 focus on these essential aspects, bringing the results of clinical and experimental research to bear on each one in turn. In Chapter 7, a psychological model of deviancy control is employed to organize and facilitate the application of the material in the other chapters. The final chapter describes and analyzes five case studies in which the psychological model is systematically applied.

1067.   Goldstine, A. P. and Krasner, L. Classroom Management: The Successful Use of Behavior Modification. New York: Pergamon Press, Inc., 1972.

The purpose of this book is to: 1) supply the reader with a set of principles about changing behavior, and to place those principles within the historical context of the development of treatment with children, 2) present research evidence documenting the efficacy of such procedures in the classroom, 3) discuss how teachers can implement such procedures for both preventing problems and for dealing with existing problems, and 4) influence the direction of research in the area of classroom management by making both educators and psychologists aware of a rapidly developing field, by describing both the advantages and the disadvantages of some of the research in this book, and by pointing out directions which future research might take. The articles in the book were selected because the research was conducted in the classroom or because they have direct relevance for classroom management. Twenty-seven of the articles include data from the classroom itself. Another criterion for selection of articles was the adequacy of design of the study; case studies were generally avoided. Included in the book are the following chapters: 1) Behavior Modification with Children, 2) Psychotherapy with Children: Evaluations, 3) Praise and Positive Forms of Teacher Attention, 4) Classroom Punsihment, 5) Modeling, 6) Token Reinforcement Programs: Extrinsic Reinforcers, 7) Token Reinforcement Programs: Intrinsic Reinforcers, 8) The Effect of Peers as Therapeutic Agents in the Classroom, 9) Programmed Instruction in Teaching Machines, 10) The Effective Use of Para Professionals, and 11) Self-Management.

1068.   Good, T. L. & Brophy, J. E. <u>Looking In Classrooms</u>. (Second Edition) New York: Harper & Row, Publishers, 1978.

The authors have included content in this book that will increase the reader's ability to conceptualize, measure and improve classroom behavior. Case study techniques are included in order to help readers to actually use the case study as a tool. The management chapters, which are strongly oriented toward preventing this behavior, include behavior modification concepts and the group techniques recommended by Glasser. Included are the following chapters: 1) Classroom life, 2) Teacher awareness, 3) Scene in classrooms, 4) Teacher expectations, 5) Modeling, 6) Management 1: preventing problems, 7) Management 2: coping with problems effectively, 8) Individualization and open education, 9) Classroom grouping, 10) Instruction, 11) Inproving classroom teaching.

1069.   Goodwin, D. L. and Coates, T. J. <u>Helping Students Help Themselves--How You Can Put Behavior Anaylsis Into Action In Your Classroom</u>. Englewood Cliffs, New Jersey: Prentice Hall, Incorporated, 1976.

This book is divided into three sections: Chapters one and two introduce basic concepts and assumptions in behavior analysis; Chapters three through nine describe behavior analysis in detail, and are designed to facilitate its application rather than merely discuss theory; and Chapters ten through thirteen discuss some novel applications of

behavior analysis. This book is designed as a practical
handbook to be used in the classroom to provide a day-to-day
program for truly helping students help themselves.
Included are the following chapters: 1) New tools for
teaching: an introduction to behavior anaylsis, 2) Setting
the stage for effective learning, 3) The four steps in
behavior anaylsis, 4) Selecting parts, 5) Assessment:
seeing the forest and the trees, 6) Reinforcement and punishment, 7) Strategy planning, 8) Planning your approach, 9)
Implementing your strategy: all systems are go, 10) Establishing token economies in the classroom, 11) Learning new
skills, 12) Teaching students self-control, 13) Teaching
behavior anaylsis, 14) Invitation to the future: doing it
your way.

1070.   Gordon, T. T.E.T. Teacher Effectiveness Training. New
York, New York: Peter H. Wyden publishers, 1974.

This book demonstrates teacher effectiveness training
step-by-step, with dozens of case histories and dialogues
and it should be used by teachers and parents. It is
designed for young people of all ages, for all types of
learning and discipline problems. It has been successful
for public and private schools, preschools, and for parents
dealing with learning difficulties in the home. Its institutional acceptance is nationwide with 45 universities given
college credit for T.E.T. The book contains two chapters on
the following areas: 1) teacher-learner relationships: the
missing link, 2) a model for effective teacher-student relationships, 3) what teachers can do when students problems,
and two types of verbal communication and their effects on
students: a catalogue, 4) the many uses of active
listening, 5) what teachers can do when students give them
problems, 6) how to modify the classroom environment to
prevent problems, 7) conflict in the classroom, 8) the no
lose method of resolving conflicts, 9) putting the no lose
method to work: other uses of method three in schools, 10)
when values collide in school, 11) making the school a
better place for teaching and a special section on how to
handle learning problems in the home: the parent-teacher-
student relationship.

1071.   Grey, L. Discipline Without Fear--Child Training During
The Early School Years. New York: Hawthorn Books, Inc.,
1974. Sequel to Discipline Without Tyranny: Child Training
During The First Five Years.

The author shows parents how to deal with negative behavior
in both normal and handicapped children from the ages of
five to twelve. These are difficult years for both the
child and the parents. As the child learns to adjust to
dramatically new physical and social environments, the
parent-child relationship changes: the teacher becomes a
substitute parent, and if substantial conflicts exist
between the parents' disciplinary methods and those of the
teacher, the results may be traumatic. During this period

of readjustment the child is also discovering his parents' limitations. They are no longer the God-like beings they previously seemed to be. In order to help parents cope with the problems that arise during these critical years, the author illustrates theoretical principles of behavior with examples of both successful and unsuccessful disciplinary methods. And because much behavior exhibited by the school age child is a direct result of the school experiences, the author discusses what is wrong with schools, how they can be changed, and how to work directly with teachers, principals, and Boards of Education to improve the system and benefit the child. Included are the following chapters: 1) The critical years, 2) The young child's personality, 3) Effective ways to deal with school age children at home, 4) Children with handicaps, 5) The family counsel, 6) School problems and parental responses, 7) What is wrong with our schools?

1072.   Gudmundsen, A., Williams, E. & Lybbert, R. B. You Can Control Your Class. Salt Lake City, Utah: Class Control Associates, 1978.

The thesis of this book is that discipline must be taught and mastered thoroughly. Mere exposure is not sufficient. Discipline is the very foundation upon which all success rests, including academic success. The ultimate goal is to teach the student the ability to know how to act appropriately in diverse settings where there may not be set rules. This book emphasizes the more elementary phases of discipline and is prepared with the realization that teachers can control their students in class. Teachers can plan, initiate and implement desirable changes which will put the teacher in command rather than continuing to tolerate deteriorating situations that will eventually make the job intolerable. Included are the following chapters: 1) time and effort to gain control, 2) letting the students know, 3) three cardinal rules, 4) the miracle of self-starting, 5) four important considerations, 6) the voice, 7) punishment, 8) random ideas on control, 9) a principal's perspective.

1073.   Halsted, D. L. and Streit, F. Analysis in Depth -- Discipline -- Causes and Remedies of Problem Behaviors in School. Highland Park, N. J.: Essence Publications, 1977.

Successful behavior change appears to have been accomplished by training school administrators and teachers in the use of behavior modification techniques in the classroom. Adaptations using group process and competition also have shown promise. These techniques are described within this publication in the following chapters: 1) Introduction; 2) Factors Associated With Problem Behaviors In Children; 3) Controlling Classroom Behavior.

1074.   Hamerlynck, L. A., Handy, L. C., Mash, E. J. (Eds.) Behavior change--methodology, concepts and practice. Champaign, Illinois: research press, 1974.

The topics discussed in this book derive from the complex interaction in terms of data forms, data section and analysis, ethical concerns, and the need to explore concepts of stimulus control, multiple schedule, heterogeneous chains, and adaptive behavior typology to account for complex social interactions and develop procedures for analyzing them. Included are the following sections, 1) methodological problems in development, 2) conceptual issues, 3) new applications and developments.

1075.   Hargreaves, D. H., Hester, S. K., and Mellor, S. J. Deviance in Classrooms. Boston, Massachusetts: Routledge & Kegan, Paul, 1975.

This book has been written for two audiences, social scientists and teachers. The authors have sought to make a contribution to the theory of deviance and to give insight into their research procedures and the way in which they generated theory. The object was to attempt to understand classroom deviance and to generate a more adequate conceptual framework and contribute to the theory of deviance. The authors also attempted to lay some foundations to the development of practical insights into everyday problems of teachers. Included are the following chapters: 1) A Critical Introduction to Labelling Theory, 2) Deviance and Education, 3) Rules in School, 4) Rules in Context, 5) The Imputation of Deviance, 6) A Theory of Typing, 7) The Typing of Deviant Pupils, 8) Reactions to Deviants, 9) Implications.

1076.   Haring, N. G. and Phillips, E. L. Analysis and Modification of Classroom Behavior. Englewood Cliffs, N.J.: Prentice-Hall, Inc., 1972.

This book deals with two basic procedures: analysis, pinpoints relationship between the child's observable behavior and the factors in the environment that evoke it; the other, behavior modification, is the process of altering conditions or events which are related to the behavior of concern so that it will change in the desired direction. It is a strategy that demands a structured environment in which the teacher change according to both the child's responses and those that a teacher wishes to evoke in order to accomplish an educational or behavioral objective. Included are the following chapters: 1) Vocabulary and Methodological Concepts; 2) Review of Research; 3) Behavior Analysis and Design of Programs; 4) Behavior Modification in the Classroom; 5) Programmed Instruction and Behavioral Control; 6) Roles of School Personnel; 7) Working with Parents; 8) Case Studies of Behavior Modification.

1077.   Harmin, M. & Sax, S. A Peaceable Classroom -- Activities To Calm And Free Student Energies. Minneapolis, Minnesota: Winston Press, 1977.

This book includes five sets of activities for teachers to try 1) discharging tensions and freeing energies, 2)

clearing the mind, 3) relaxing consciousness, 4) centering
the self, 5) giving the self messages. The activities in
the book are based on the assumption that persons can make
decisions to influence the tone and colors of the feelings
and flow and depth of their intellegence. They can learn to
influence their inner prostheses much like they learn to
influence the prostheses of things around them. This
results in people learning how to use themselves and use
themselves in a world more fully, more effectively, and more
joyfully. Included in the book are the following chapters:
1) What is this book all about, 2) Activities for discharging tensions and freeing energies, 3) Activities for
clearing the mind, 4) Activities for relaxing consciousness,
5) Activities for centering the self, 6) Activities for
giving the self messages, 7) Some questions we have heard
and answers we have given, 8) An occasion to reassess one's
teaching, 9) Applications to counseling, 10) About
resources.

1078.   Harris, M. B. Classroom Uses Of Behavior Modification.
Columbus, Ohio: Charles E. Merrill Publishing Company,
1972.

This book is written for students of psychology and education as well as for practicing teachers. The first two
sections give an introduction to the methods and principles
embodied in the articles which are included in order to
provide a foundation for those who do not possess a background in educational psychology and experienced in reading
journal articles. Comments are also given for each article
to assist the reader in seeing some of the implications of
the paper for the practicing teacher. The focus of the book
throughout is on applicability to the classroom situation.
Included are the following sections: 1) Basic principles of
learning and behavior modification, 2) Conducting and
evaluating behavior modification projects, 3) Studies
attempting to increase certain behaviors, 4) Studies
attempting to decrease certain behaviors, 5) More complex
studies, 6) Practical and theoretical issues.

1079.   Heitzmann, W. R. & Staropoli, C. Student Teaching,
Classroom Management, And Professionalism. New York: N. S.
S. Information Corporation, 1974.

The articles included in this book related to student
teaching, classroom management, and professionalism are
designed to increase the reader's positive and affective
knowledge and consequently result in a successful program.
The readings have been chosen to aid a student teacher in
obtaining the finest teaching experience possible. This is
a period of exploration and experimentation -- the student
teacher with the encouragement and support of the cooperating teacher and the university supervisor should utilize
several successful instructional strategies in the classroom. Included are the following general areas: student
teaching, with articles on humanizing teacher education, the

teaching center, the prospective teacher as observer, intent, action, and feedback and the use of video tape. The second section on classroom management includes articles on teachers' expectancies, the self-fulfilling prophesy, the textbook, open verses closed classrooms, report cards, testing, discipline, the use of behavior modification, disciplined and the disadvantaged child. The third section on professionalism includes articles on quality research, interpersonal relations, unionism, and the superintendent.

1080.   Hemphill, J. K. & Rosenau, F. S. Educational Development -- A New Discipline For Self-Renewal. Eugene, Oregon: University of Oregon Printing Department, 1970.

This book was written on the assumption that American public schools and teacher training institutions can and will renew themselves and adapt to the needs of a changing society. A further assumption is that an emerging new discipline -- educational development -- can play a catalytic role in the change process while at the same time, acting as a force for conservation in public education. This group of articles focuses solely on development in the research, development and evaluation domain. The research phase in the late 1960's and early 1970's was in large measure the respon- sibility of university based professors and research institutes. The vocus of evaluation in education at this time is diffused. Included are the following sections: 1) Background and Theory 2) Planning and Developing 3) Evaluating and Revising 4) Disseminating and Installing 5) Funding 6) Managing.

1081.   Hilde, R. The Rod Versus The M & M's.--Plain Talk On The Principles Of Discipline In Home And Classroom. Mountain View, California: Pacific Press Publishing Association, 1976.

This book presents the reader with ideas concerning the most important task ever entrusted to men and women--the educa- tion and character development of children. Author states that the right admixture of strictness and toleration, justice and mercy must be found in the home and in the school. This book organizes and rationalizes what parents and educators have know and need to know about discipline. Chapters include: I Enlisted, The Great Objective, A Terrible Mistake, The Thread Of Requests Verses The Chain Of Command, The Better Method, Don't Be A Trust Buster, As A General Rule, Rules Are Too General, Too Hard Heads Are Better Than None, The Rod Versus The M & M's, I See What You Mean, The Eloquence Of Silence, The Best Instruments For Discipline, The Golden Rule, The Era In Airing Errors, Mercy, From Playground To Battlefield, From Pain To Joy, A Step In The Right Direction, A Good Look At The Unseen, Reproof Positive, Something Better, They All Belong.

1082.   House, E. R. and Lapan, S. D. <u>Survival In The Classroom</u>
<u>-- Negotiating With Kids, Colleagues, And Bosses</u>. Boston,
Massachusetts: Allen & Baken, Incorporated, 1978.

This book is intended as a message to teachers. It
describes some of the most pressing concerns of the teachers
professional life--concerns such as discipline, testing,
principals, parents, and teacher organizations. The theme
of the book is that teachers face an overwhelming set of
demands from a wide range of groups: kids, colleagues,
administrators, parents, school boards, and interest groups.
Included in the book is a chapter on discipline and control
in the classroom with sections on 1) recalling the not-so-
good old days, 2) greener pastures school district--the
teachers committee on discipline: a three act play, 3)
teacher responses to misbehavior, 4) methods of managing
classroom problems, 5) classroom problems games, 6) selected
recommendations for classroom control and management.

1083.   Howard, E. R. <u>School Discipline Desk Book</u>. West Nyack,
New York, Parker Publishing Company, 1978.

This book begins by explaining to teachers and adminis-
trators how to improve discipline in the elementary or
secondary school. It then goes on to divide the information
into the following sections: (1) Getting It Together In An
Urban High School--A Snapshot of Cleveland High School in
Seattle (2) Shaping Up the School I--Conducting A Campaign
Against Crime and Violence (3) Shaping Up A School
II--Handling Discipline Problems Effectively (4) Shaping
Up The School III--Helping Teachers Reduce Discipline
Problems (5) Turning Losers into Winners--Unrigging the
School (6) Increasing Student Involvement In The Schools
Activity Programs (7) Improving Student Morale By
Modifying the Curriculum (8) Achieving More Effective
Discipline By Improving Self-Esteem--A Snapshot Of What's
Happening in Cottage Lane, New York. References and a
bibliography are included.

1084.   Howie, P. A. and Winkleman, G. <u>Behavior Modification: A</u>
<u>Practical Guide for the Classroom Teacher</u>. West Nyack, New
York: Parker Publishing Company, Inc., 1977.

The author states that the dynamic principles of behavior
modification can make every teacher's job more stimulating
and rewarding. The major purpose of this book is to provide
practical guidelines and specific know-how to translate
tested approaches into action quickly an easily. Although
the concepts and practices of behavior modification can be
applied in many settings with individuals of many different
ages, the effective programs and techniques described in
this book will have special significance for the classroom
elementary school teacher. The book enables teachers to
begin analyzing and changing procedures almost immediately.
The first part of the book will acquaint the teacher with
some basic terminology. How old is behavior modification?

What did Pavlov and Skinner contribute? What is behavior
modification? The second section of the book deals with key
aspects of the teacher role. What is the structure of
behavior patterns that the teacher has setup in the classroom? Is the teacher encouraging behaviors that he would
really like to eliminate? What specific changes could be
made in a way the teacher arranges her room or his room the
furniture and the use of materials? What inexpensive commerical materials will help the teacher strengthen this
approach? How can the teacher recognize the materials he or
she has to fit in with the new goals? The next portion of
the book provides practical techniques for coping with a
number of common behavior patterns. Which approach is best
for a disruptive child? What can the teacher do to help a
withdrawn child? How can the teacher use a existing
resources most effectively? How can the teacher analyze and
overcome such problems when there is no school psychologist
or counselor available? The final section of this book
provides answers to important questions currently being
asked about the use of behavior modification in todays
schools. How can an educator use such methods in situations
other than the self contained classroom? How can specialists be used without depending upon them too much? How can
your administrator help? How can parents change from being
part of the problem to becoming part of the solution?
Chapters include: 1) getting a realistic view of behavior,
2) clarifying key factors that affect behavior, 3) analyzing
your present reward systems, 4) structuring a program of
behavior modification in self contained classrooms, 5)
arranging your room to produce behavioral change, 6)
assigning tasks to produce behavioral change, 7) meeting
individual needs in a group setting, 8) helping the disruptive child, 9) helping the quiet child, 10) helping the
defeated child, 11) developing a program of behavior modification beyond the self contained classroom, 12) using school
and home resources to a better advantage, 13) changes that
last.

1085.   Hunter, C. P. "Classroom Observation Instruments And
Teacher In-Service Training By School Psychologist." School
Psychology Monograph, 3, 2 (Fall, 1977): 45-88.

Author provides information about instruments that are
available for use in observing classroom behavior and
illustrates the use of observation instruments as part of
in-service training activities for teachers by school
psychologists. The first section is a review of different
types of instruments that are available for use by school
psychologists. Methodological concerns are discussed which
relate to each type of instrument. The second section of
the paper describes an approach that is used in teach
in-service training, using the data obtained from particular
instruments as a basis for teacher conferences with school
psychologists. See ERIC Abstract 0704962-3.

1086.   Hurt, H. T., Scott, M. D., McCroskey, J. C. Communication In The Classroom. Reading, Massachusetts: Addison-Wesley Publishing Company, 1978.

The purpose of this book is to explain basic communication concepts and it intergrated those concepts into learning environments. Included are the following chapters: 1) Introduction, 2) The process of human communication, 3) Communication and learning, 4) Information acquisition in the classroom, 5) Communication and information processing in the classroom, 6) Non-verbal communication in the class-room, 7) Perception of teachers as communication sources in the classroom, 8) Motivations to communicate in the class-room, 9) Communication apprehension, 10) Expectencies in the classroom, 11) Communication, interpersonal solidarity, and student needs, 12) Conflict in the classroom.

1087.   Johnson, D. W. and Johnson, R. T. Learning Together and Alone -- Cooperation, Competition, and Individualization. Englewood Cliffs, New Jersey: Prentice-Hall, Inc., 1975.

This book examines the learning process to determine the most favorable conditions for fulfilling instructional goals in the classroom. It shows how the usual guiding force -- inappropriate competition -- handicaps achievement in a survival of the fittest structure. In contrast, coopera-tion, which requires sharing, helping, communication and concern, creates more favorable growth. The strategies suggested are based on sound research that show clear results from cooperative methods within which competition and individualization take a natural place. The authors showed that when goal structures concentrate on interaction patterns and interdependencies, achievement will go up, attitudes will become more positive and missing skills will be mastered. The book tells how to establish cooperating procedures that build relationship and trust within the group. The teacher then implements appropriate goal structures in the instructional program, based on the ideas suggested in the book and the skills promote a more produc-tive, cooperative attitude that increases the accomplish-ments within the classroom. Included in the book are the following chapters: 1) increasing teachers' effectiveness and fun, 2) goal structures, learning processes, and instructional outcomes, 3) re-examination of the use of cooperative, competitive and individualistic goal struc-tures, 4) selecting the appropriate goal structure: no need to flip a coin, 5) implementing goal structures: building a bridge from theory to practice, 6) student acquisition of appropriate skills, 7) Are you ready? putting it all together, 8) monitoring the classroom: listening, watching and reflecting, 9) evaluating outcomes and communicating results, 10) teacher concerns and classroom management: last minute advice.

1088.   Johnson, L. B. & Bany, M. A. Classroom Management --
         Theory And Skill Training. New York, New York: The
         MacMillan Company, 1970.

This book concentrates upon improving teachers' effectiveness in the management dimension of teaching. To understand
only the behavior of individuals is not enough. It is
necessary to understand the collective behavior of children
in the classroom group, as well as the factors that
influence this behavior. This book advances a theoretical
understanding and focuses on the development of teacher
skills and patterns of classroom activities. The instructional aspects are discussed only in relation to the management of classrooms or problem situations. One purpose of
this book is to present an action packed training program
which will enable teachers to cope effectively with classroom management problems. Included are the following
chapters: 1) New ways of perceiving and thinking, 2) An
operational concept of classroom management, 3) Dynamics of
organizational behavior in the classroom setting, 4)
Achieving unity and cooperation, 5) Establishing standards
and coordinating work procedures, 6) Using problem solving
to improve conditions, 7) Changing established patterns of
group behavior, 8) Maintaining and restoring morale, 9)
Handling conflict, 10) Minimizing management problems.

1089.   Jones, V. F. Adolescents with Behavior Problems:
         Strategies for Teaching, Counseling, and Parent Involvement.
         Boston, Massachusetts: Allyn & Dacon, Inc., 1980.

Professionals working with adolescents frequently state that
they become frustrated in their attempts to serve as useful
resources to adolescents. The purpose of this book is to
assist professionals in understanding the factors that
elicit adolescents' unproductive behaviors and to offer a
variety of strategies for preventing behavior problems as
well as for assisting adolescents in modifying their
behavior. A strong emphasis is placed on providing concrete
teaching and counseling strategies. The book does not focus
on one particular theoretical approach or one counseling
paradigm, but rather offers a broad socio behavioral
approach to examining causes, preventions, and mofidication
and behavior. The book is based upon the belief that
unproductive behavior is caused by the interaction of an
environment that fails to meet adolescents' legitimate needs
and the adolescents' skilled emphasis that prevent them from
responding in productive ways to their environment. A basic
concept presented throughout the book states that professionals should examine both their style of interacting with
adolescents and the extent to which their demands and
expectations respond productively to adolescents' developmental needs. The book's organization requests a small kind
of dimensional to examining and modifying unproductive
behavior. Part one provides an overview of adolescents'
psychological and developmental needs and examines the
relationships between these needs and unproductive

adolescent behavior. Part two explores the impact various patterns of interpersonal communication have on adolescent behavior. The initial chapter focuses on important decisions adults must make in determinging how they will interact with adolescents. This is followed by a presentation of communicatiion skills which facilitate positive therapeutic interactions. The final chapter focuses on methods for assisting adolescents in developing productive communication skills. Part three examines the ways in which school environments can be altered so as to more effectively meet legitimate adolescent needs, and thereby significantly reduce acting-out and avoidance behavior. An emphasis is placed on practical teaching strategies that can be employed by regular classroom teachers. Part four presents a wide range of practical strategies for assisting adolescents in altering their behavior. The strategies discussed in part four are organizaed under the general headings of self-observation, behavioral counseling and behavior contracting. Part five acknowledges the important roll that the family plays in influencing adolescents' behavior. The section begins by examining the feelings and needs experienced by parents whose adolescents are having difficulty adjusting to society and its institutions. This is followed by a discussion of strategies professionals can employ in responding to these parents and involving them in working cooperatively with school personnel. Finally, several models are presented for providing parents with individual and group instruction in skills which will enable them to interact more effectively with their adolescent children.

1090.   Kaplan, P. It's Positively Fun. Denver, Colorado: Love Publishing Company, 1974.

This book contains the collection of positive reinforcement techniques in order to provide students with rewarding experiences. The 56-page book includes awards, free-time passes, right to rent and bonus point systems, contracts, accomplishment sheets, and school-time communications. The reinforcers are made by utilizing cartoon type characters. The sheets are perforated and may be duplicated. The materials are appropriate for students in kindergarden through grade four. See NIMI 031-047.

1091.   Karlin, N. S. & Berger, R. Discipline And The Disruptive Child--A Practical Guide For Elementary Teachers. West Nyack, New York: Parker Publishing Company, Incorporated, 1972.

This book is designed to help elementary teachers handle their discipline problems, problems that are encountered in every grade. It is a book of methods and techniques. It will aid the teacher by placing in his or her hands the ways and means of working with disruptive children. In the book are procedures with which to experiment and consequently to teach students. It will also help the teacher to comprehend childrens needs, and to make the teacher aware of the problems. Chapters have been devoted to the major tasks of troublesome children--to understanding them and to coping with them in your classroom. The book begins with material to help the teacher see himself as the leader of the class. Next he is given insights into the problems children may be faced with in their daily lives. Then he will find suggestions that will help him to work on solutions to these problems or to live with them when solutions are impossible. Chapters follow on working with a child who has learning problems and with those who are quarrelsome or openly aggresive in their behavior. The problems arising with a hyperactive child, with the underachiever and with the non motivated child are discussed. Other chapters are devoted to the child with difficulties at home, the child who has a phobia and does not come to school, and the child who isolates himself from other youngsters. There is a chapter also on students who are seriously disturbed and those who are mentally ill. At the end of the book is a questionnaire which will help a teacher look at himself objectively. Chapters include: 1) Establishing yourself as the teacher, 2) Recognizing the children with problems, who cause the problems in your classroom, 3) Basic methods for working with children with problems--the troubled child, 4) Getting the parents to cooperate with you, 5) The child with learning problems, 6) Working with the fighter or quarreler, 7) Fulfilling the needs of the attention seeker and the hyperactive child, 8) The underachiever and the non motivated child, 9) The child with problems at home, 10) The school phobic, the truant and the loner, 11) The physically handicapped child and the child of poverty, 12) The drug abuser and the child who drinks, 13) The seriously disturbed child, 14) A self-analysis questionnaire for every teacher.

1092.   Keller, F. S. and Ribes-Inesta, E. Behavior Modification -- Applications to Education. New York: Academic Press, 1974.

The studies appearing in this book were reported at the second symposium on Behavior Modification held at the National Autonomus University of Mexico, in Mexico City, January, 1972. The purpose of the symposium was to set forth and examine a series of problems related to the use of behavior analysis and education. The significance of radical change in education as a fundamental feature of social development was a matter of constant concern in each of the contributions in this book. The studies ranged from those in which specific variables were employed in experimentation at the pre-school level to a consideration of behavior analysis in relation to revolutionary change in societal control. Contributors to this book include: B. F. Skinner, Robert Wahler, Jore Peralta, Sidney W. Bijou, Florente Lopez, Montrose Wolf, Elery Phillips, Dean Fixsen, Harold Cohen, Emilio Ribes-Inesta, Daniel O'Leary, Rodolpho Sant' Anna, Teodoro Ayllon, and Patricia Wright, Benjamin Dominguez, Felipe Acosta, Dementrio Carmona and C. B. Ferster.

1093.   Klein, R. D., Hapkiewicz, W. G. and Roden, A. H.
Editors. Behavior Modification in Education Settings.
Springfield, Illinois: Charles C. Thomas publisher, 1973.

The major portion of this book of readings is devoted to a
sampling of articles which illustrate the rationale behind
and the utilization of operant principles in classroom
behavior modification. The operant section has been
specifically divided into four chapters. The introduction
provides a brief summary of basic operant conditioning
principles and the methodological procedures used to implement these principles in the classroom. The next three
chapters contain studies which are direct applications by
teachers of preschool children, school age children and
children in special education classes. An attempt has been
made to classify the studies according to the broad area of
behavior which is being modified, such as academic behavior,
or social behavior. Although the categories are not always
mutually exclusive, it is believed that a more organized
presentation is made by using such a classification. The
operant section is followed by a section on respondent
principles in education. An introductory paper is presented
which briefly explains basic respondent techniques and
suggests various ways in which they apply to the classroom.
Also included are several studies which deal with the treatment of emotional behavior, such as test anxiety and stage
fright in school settings. The final two sections, are
concerned with the training of educators in the application
of learning principles and a discussion of problems and
ethical issues related to the use of those principles.

1094.   Kluball, C. Will Everyone Please Stand Still For The
Picture? Philadelphia, Pennsylvania: Dorrance & Company,
1973.

This book is a collection of individual incidences when
students were behaving inappropriately. It is a series of
individuals and some of their reactions to the classroom and
related subjects. Included are the following sections: 1)
Will everyone please stand still for the picture?, 2) Lesson
plans, 3) The town, 4) The school, 5) The principal, 6) The
kids, 7) The ranch, 8) The attitudes, 9) The reading lab,
10) Introduction to diary. The diary then included individual events that happen in this particular classroom and how
the teacher responded to inappropriate behaviors exhibited
by the students.

1095.   Knight, R. S.; et al. "Students' rights: issues and
constitutional freedoms." The Analysis of Public Issues
Program. Boston, Massachusetts: Houghton Mifflin, 1974.
122p.

This monograph examines the broad topic of student rights
and focuses in turn on the number of related constitutional
issues. Chapter I presents some of the social changes
affecting American education and briefly touches on many of

the sources of school-based conflict. Chapter 2 deals
specifically with the issue of school dress codes and
efforts by school officials to control students' appearance.
Chapter 3 examines student rights to freedom of expression
and the limits on those rights in the school setting.
Chapter 4 presents the right to privacy as it applies to
students in school. Chapter 5 deals with the issues of
student freedom, school discipline, and students' constitutional right to due process. Chapter 6 reviews the social
problems facing American schools and examines the philosophical issue of how much freedom is too much. The book is
intended for possible use is secondary social studies
classes. See ERIC Abstract #ED 147925.

1096.   Know-Net Dissemination Project. Bibliography of
Washington State Materials on School Discipline. Tumwater,
Washington, July, 1981.

Included in this bibliography are various materials on
school discipline. Included are sections on books, professional articles, other articles, research, Eric Microfiche
collections, films, speakers, and other resources.

1097.   Kohut, S. & Range, D. G. Classroom Discipline: Case
Studies and Viewpoints. Washington, D. C.: National
Education Association, 1979.

This book is designed for the pre-service and in-service
teacher concerned about classroom management and discipline
as an aspect of learning. It is an attempt to bridge the
gap between the theoretical and practical dimensions of
learning with important implications for daily interaction
and communication between teachers and pupils in kindergarten through high school. The text is designed for undergraduate and graduate courses and practicums or as a workshop or in-service program reference for teachers and other
educators. The case studies and illustrations included in
the book are actual, real life situations observed,
recorded, documented and contributed by teachers, administrators and para professionals throughout the country. The
case studies represent problems and issues common to urban,
suburban and rural school districts and school personnel.
The basic purpose of the text is to provide concerned classroom practitioneers with a practical guide for understanding
and improving classroom communication with the expressed and
ultimate goal of enhancing that aspect of learning which is
so important to teacher and learner alike -- discipline.
Chapters include: 1) Perspective on Discipline, 2)
Discipline: Theory, Research and Practice, 3) Case Studies:
Early Childhood and Elementary Education, 4) Case Studies:
Middle School, Junior and Senior High School.

1098.   Kolesnik, W. B. Humanism and/or behaviorism in
education. Boston: Allyn & Bacon, Inc., 1975.

This book presents a comparison of humanism and behaviorism

as they pertain to education. The first chapter draws
attention to some of the major problems and issues in
education and examines a dozen criticisms of our schools;
the rest of the book relates behaviorism and humanism to
these issues and criticisms. The second chapter summarizes
the basic principles and assumptions of humanism. The third
deals with the educational implications of humanistic
psychology and the kinds of practices that humanistic educators recommend. Chapter four presents an overview of the
principles and assumptions of behavioral psychology.
Chapter five is concerned with the implications of, and
recommendations based on, that system. Chapter six attempts
to help the readers synthesize the two apparently conflicting positions and to integrate what they might perceive
as the more attractive features of each. The book is
primarily intended for prospective teachers in educational
psychology, foundations of education, and philosophy of
education courses.

1099.   Kolesnik, W. B. Motivation -- Understanding and
Influencing Human Behavior. Boston, Massachusetts: Allyn
and Bacon, Incorporated, 1978.

The purpose of this book is to help the reader to understand
and influence human behavior, particularly in the area of
education. The book addresses itself to two main questions:
1) why do people behave as they do? 2) how can teachers
effectively motivate students to study, learn, develop their
potentialities, observe necessary classroom regulations, and
otherwise do what they should like them to do. Included in
this book are the following chapters: 1) An Introduction to
Motivation, 2) Unconscious Motivation, 3) Individual and
Social Dimensions, 4) The Pay-Off of Human Behavior, 5)
Interpretations and Expectations, 6) Toward Self-Fulfill-
ment, 7) Intrinsic Motivation, 8) Extrinsic Motivation, 9)
Motivation in Classroom Management, 10) Motivation Toward
Scholastic Achievement.

1100.   Koren, E. T. Flexible Guidance In The Elementary School:
Tested Techniques For A Stress-Free Classroom. New York:
The center for applied research in education, 1974.

This handbook is designed to help the classroom teacher
develop and maintain a sound emotional climate for children
to learn. Its aim is to provide him or her with guidance
tools for smoother classroom functioning; it also seeks to
give the teacher an insight into the guidance roles of the
supervisor in counsel, while providing him or her with
guidelines for working with them. The handbook is designed
to meet the needs of teachers in terms of ongoing guidance
programs. It is written with an eye toward the workable
everyday interrelationships between the teacher, supervisor,
guidance personnel, and the children. Included are the
following chapters: 1) Teaching in a guidance-oriented
school, 2) Ways to recognize each child's importance, 3)
Working with a counselor, 4) Working with the administrator,

5) Working with the parent, 6) Using creative dramatics and role playing in the guidance of children, 7) Guiding children through art experiences, 8) Developing a guidance related tutorial program, 9) Using the sociogram and other guidance techniques, 10) Working with classroom groups, 11) Dealing with children with special behavioral problems, 12) Guidance in the ghetto, 13) Guidance through creativity, 14) Dealing with records and confidentiality, 15) A humanistic approach, appendix--films and film strips.

.101.   Kostiuk, N., Barkan, E., & Rocco, J. Improving Behavior -- One Hundred Applications For The Elementary Classroom. Morristown, New Jersey: Silver Berdette Company, 1979.

This book is written for a teacher who asks for practical ideas and suggestions for improving behavior in his or her classroom. The book contains one hundred practical applications in behavior modification. The book has been organized with each application as a self contained unit. Each of the one hundred five practical applications is divided into three parts: situation describing a typical classroom problem that a teacher might face, strategy, a step-by-step, easily followed procedure for coping effectively with a situation or preventing future ones from arising; rationale, the reasons for using a particular strategy. The strategies involve theses that are practical, positive in scope, educationally sound, and fun for children. They are equally applicable to urban, surburban and rural areas. The strategies have multiple uses and are not restricted to the particular situation mentioned. They can be expanded to other situations and used with children of different personalities, ages and grade levels, as well as in the teaching of different subjects or discipline.

102.   Kujoth, J. S. The Teacher And School Discipline. Metuchen, New Jersey: The Scarecrow Press, Incorporated, 1970.

This anthology is intended for elementary and secondary school teachers and principals, faculty and students of education, and others who work with groups of children or who are preparing to do so. Effective discipline is a prerequisite to effective education and the authors suggest that the problem of discipline cannot be bypassed in the school classroom. This book is an attempt to assemble help from a number of sources in the form of principals, guidelines, comparisons, psychologies, lessons from experience, test cases, research findings, and practical experiments relating to school discipline. The book contains 46 articles and is divided to six parts according to the general approach taken or types of subject matter treated. Part 1 discusses theoretical concepts, principles and background factors such as comparison of school discipline in different countries. Part 2 focuses upon psychological elements such as fear, setting limits, creativity in discipline, discipline by contract. Part 3 deals specifically with the control element. Part 4 sets forth a variety of practical guidelines for maintaining effective discipline. Part 5 offers first aid to those who are having problems with discipline. Part 6 discusses last resorts for handling particularly severe discipline problems.

1103.   Langstaff, A. L. and Volkmor, C. B. Contingency Management. Columbus, Ohio: Charles E. Merrill Publishing Company, 1975.

This book illustrates and describes a very effective technique for motivating students. This method, based on the work of Lloyd Homme, is called Contingency Management and it is a contracting system in which the students' successful task completion is consistently rewarded by free time activity. The students and the teacher actually enter into an agreement. The teacher promises to provide free time for students to engage in self chosen activities which they enjoy; the students agree to complete a specific amount of academic work in order to earn their free time. Chapters include: 1) Contingency Management Basic Principles, 2) Contingency Management in the Classroom, 3) Planning a Contingency Management Program--I, 4) Planning a Contingency Management Program--II, 5) Implementing a Contingency Management Program, 6) Maintaining and Adapting the System.

1104.   Larson, K. "School Discipline in an Age of Rebellion." West Nyack, New York: Parker Publishing Company, Inc., 1972.

Attempts to answer these questions: How can we work with militant groups to improve our schools? How can we help the youth "rebellion" to build a better nature? The author examines the politics of confrontation, the how to of working effectively with militant groups, and the process of channeling the energies of anger into positive directions. He examines the new problems of the classroom teacher and offers specific guidelines for effective teaching and learning today. Special consideration is given to the handling of severely alienated youth. Attention is also given to the improvement of curriculum and arrangements for learning. Included are the following sections: 1) an anatomy of a revolution, 2) living with militancy in schools, 3) coping with the narcotics problems, 4) the teacher works with militant youth, 5) a contemporary rationale for school discipline, 6) maintaining justice law and order in the school, 7) working with alienated youth, 8) human relations education, 9) policies and regulations affecting discipline, 10) improving the climate for learning, 11) action review.

1105.   Lavin, P. Anecdotes to Develop Social and Self-Awareness with Elementary School Children. Midland, Michigan: Pendell Publishing Company, 1973.

The author presents a series of anecdotes that describe the
most common behavioral problems encountered in elementary
school children. Each is then subject to an analysis which
can aid and guide the educator. The purpose of the stories
is to provide teachers and guidance counselors with
materials which might be used as a catalyst for helping
children to understand their own behavior and how it affects
other persons. In each of the anecdotes, an attempt is made
to present a situation in which school children might find
themselves. The main characters are youngsters who exhibit
a particular type of maladaptive behavior and their failure
to respond in a socially appropriate manner results in
creating difficulties for themselves and for the people with
whom they interact.

1106.   Lemlech, J. K. Classroom Management. New York, Harper &
Row, Publishers, 1979.

The purpose of this book is to assist teachers with their
classroom preparation by describing classroom management
procedures and by suggesting ways to work with students and
other adults to create learning environments and to develop
effective classroom and instructional practices. Included
are the following chapters: 1) Teacher behavior, 2)
Managing group behavior, 3) Evaluating progress, 4) The
missing link: parent-teacher relations, 5) Management and
leadership in the classroom, 6) Development, management, and
evaluation of learning centers, 7) Ideas for learning
centers, 8) Instructional tactics, I, 9) Instructional
tactics, II, 10) Improving teaching performance.

1107.   Long, J. D. & Frye, V. H. Making It Till Friday: A
Guide To Successful Classroom Management. Princeton, New
Jersey: Pinceton Book Company, 1977.

The purpose of this book is to provide teachers and
perspective teachers at all grade levels with practical
suggestions for managing their classes more effectively.
Many of the problems that provade the lives of teachers and
students are amenable to solutions: seemingly unmotivated
students can be helped to become interested in school, agressive students can learn to cooperate, shy students can learn
to interact appropriately. Included in this book are the
following chapters: 1) An introduction to classroom management, 2) The eye of the beholder, 3) Setting the stage for
desirable behavior, 4) Accenting the positive, 5) Managing
disruptive behavior, 6) Working with others, 7) Guiding
students towards self-management, 8) Right and wrong:
ethical and legal problems of classroom management, 9)
Putting it all together.

1108.   Long, J. D. and Williams, R. L. Classroom Management
With Adolescents. New York, New York: M. S. S. Information
Corporation, 1973.

The first major section of this book deals with the
possiblity of self management by adolescents. Critics of
behavior modification have been quite concerned about the
extent to which the source of behavioral control is external
to the student. Ideally the student should learn to control
his own contingencies, supply his own setting events, and
produce his own rewards and punishments. The studies
included in section one describe the logistics for achieving
these possibilities. Section two indicates the comparative
effectiveness of contracts with different types of high
school population. Section three investigates the possiblity of modifying adolescents' behavior via teacher
attention. The last two sections of the book attempt to
appraise the impact of operant procedures on academic performance and social problems. Section I is self-management
of behavior, 2) Contingency contracting, 3) The role of
teacher attention, 4) Applications to academic performance,
5) Applications to social problems.

1109.   Louisiana State Department of Education. Crime and
disruptive behavior--a module of instruction for colleges of
education in the state of Louisiana. Baton Rouge,
Louisiana, January, 1980.

This module is a mini-unit of instruction developed by a
writing committee composed of college of education deans,
teachers throughout the state of Louisiana and the state
department of educational personnel. A basic premise around
which this module is built is that the aims of education and
classroom discipline must be compatable--to help youth to
self directing and to assume responsibility for their
actions. Basically, the approaches by noted specialists in
the area of discipline have induced the creation of an
educational environment wherein: 1) overall school and
individual classroom roles are lucid, concise and enforceable, 2) teachers and administrators use a variety of techniques to deal with misbehavior, in short, a) the behavior
determines the technique, b) students are provided with
options, c) no one method is used to deal with all forms of
misbehavior, 3) teachers are well acquainted professionally
and socially and feel comfortable helping one another with
educational problems, 4) parents in the community work with
the school personnel in helping to build responsible
behavior in students, 5) the school administration provides
effective leadership in formulating some basic definitions
of the words discipline, punishment, and responsible
behavior; and inducing the agreement and adherence to these
definitions by the school community; and 6) teachers and
students enjoy sharing experiences on the school campus and
away from school. This brief synthesis presents a solid
foundation upon which to build a discipline module. The
suggested modular topics which are included in the manual
correspond closely to the six point which constitute an
educational environment conducive to the development of
self-directing behavior.

1110.   Lovitt, T. C. <u>Managing Inappropriate Behavior In The Classroom</u>. Reston, Virginia, The Council For Exceptional Children, 1978.

The intent of this monograph is to help teachers to manage disruptive behaviors. An effort is made to provide a number of strategies that may be useful in establishing peaceful situations. In the first section several approaches are discussed that pertain to the general, comprehensive management of classes. Included in the second section are several strategies that may be used with individuals who display inappropriate behaviors. Included are the following chapters: 1) Preliminary strategies, 2) Individually orientated management systems, 3) Group oriented management systems, 4) Using the techniques--a final word.

1111.   Lynn, E. M. <u>Improving Classroom Communication: Speech Communication Instruction For Teachers</u>. Urbana, Illinois: Clearing House On Reading And Communication Skills, 1976.

This publication is intended primarily for use by departmental administrators and instructional developers from both the speech communication and education field. The rationale and course descriptions are offered to assist readers in convincing their colleagues: 1) That perspective and practicing classroom teachers have special needs for instruction in the skills in classroom communication, 2) That such skills and awareness are not innate, but must and can be learned through appropriate instruction and practice, 3) That the scope and diversity of a teachers communication needs cannot be met solely through traditional education courses, 4) That courses need to be tailored to address teachers' special communication needs, 5) That the study of speech communication protheses has a necessary relationship to understanding and improving teacher-student and student-student interaction in the class. The problem of discipline in conjuction with speech communication is discussed.

1112.   MacDonald, W. S. and Tanabe, G. <u>Focus on Classroom Behavior -- Readings and Research</u>. Springfield, Illinois: Charles C. Thomas, Publisher, 1973.

This collection of papers is intended to suggest directions for the application of behavioristic principles, and to suggest to teachers the range of problems which yield to behavioral analysis. Section One, "Understanding pupil behavior through behavioral analysis," consists of five papers dealing with theoretical issues in which student activities can be better understood through behavioral modification studies. Section Three, "Behaviorism and the Teacher," presents to the readers some approaches to preparing teachers to work with difficult students, and some issues relevant to the roll of the teacher made pertinent by behavioral analysis.

1113.   Mante, D. R., Mathisen, B. W. <u>How To Develop A Model
School And Model Classrooms For Young Children--A Guide For
Administrators And Teachers</u>. Redwood City, California:
Educational Publications, 1977.

This book presents a list of ideas to help administrators
and teachers develop a model school for young children.
Included are the following chapters: 1) Introduction, 2)
How to develop a school philosophy, 3) How to unify and
train a staff, 4) How to develop an effective environment,
5) How to prepare an individualized setting with what you
have, 6) How to teach in a individualized setting, 7)
Components of the school day, 8) Discipline, 9) How to build
a partnership with parents, 10) Positive approaches to
discipline. Included in the appendices are sample letters
to parents, selected suppliers of materials, selected
reference books, and a sample questionnaire.

1114.   Marshall, M. Kimbrough. <u>Law And Order In Grade Six: A
Study Of Chaos And Innovation In A Ghetto School</u>. Little,
Brown and Company. Boston, Massachusetts. 1972. 241P.

This book deals with the development and details of a
variant of the open classroom technique, based upon the
author's experiences as a sixth grade teacher at the Martin
Luther King, Jr. Roxbury, Massachusetts, Middle School.
There were four major differences in this system as opposed
to conventional classrooms: 1) Kids sit in groups spread
around the room rather than in rows; 2) Worksheets in seven
subject areas--Mathematics, English, Social Studies,
Spelling, Creative Writing, General, and Reading--are put in
pockets scattered around the outside of the room every
morning Monday through Thursday, 3) On these station days,
the students are free to move around the room and do the
worksheets in any order they like, as long as they finish
all seven by the end of the day, and 4) The teacher's
responsibilities are: a) Writing worksheets for seven
subjects the night before and running off copies first thing
in the morning, b) Moving around the room during the station
time helping people with the work and any other problems, c)
Planning other activities for the remaining part of the day
after the stations are finished, d) Correcting the stations
with the whole class in the last hour of the day, and e)
Evaluating progress in the traditional subjects weekly. See
ERIC Abstract ED 066528.

1115.   Martin, R. <u>Legal Challenges to Behavior Modification --
Trends in Schools, Corrections and Mental Health</u>. Champaign,
Illinois: Research Press, 1975.

Modifying behavior is the business of many of our public
institutions, most notably schools, corrections, and mental
health programs. The clients of these institutions and the
general public want such benefits of behavior modification
as education, rehabilitation, and training for success in
society. But, the techniques used and the procedures

through which they are offered, are the source of increasing legal problems. Because of rapid changes, and many chases still unappealed, this book focuses on trends in the law. It is aimed as an audience of practioners of behavior-change and administrations of such programs and public institutions. The organization of the book reflects the planning and implementation of a behavior change program rather than being grouped around legal doctrines. Any potential client, or a friend or an attorney counseling that client, should be challenged to raise many questions about a proposed program -- not to defeat efforts at treatment, but rather to make it the very best possible. Included are the following factors: 1) growing legal challenge, 2) the decision to intervene, 3) consent, 4) selecting a strategy, 5) establishing goals, 6) motivating behavior change, 7) contractual problems, 8) accountability: compliance and effectiveness, 9) supervision and control, 10) records, 11) remedies, and 12) conclusions.

1116.   Martin, R. & Lauridsen, D. Developing Student Discipline And Motivation--A Series For Teacher In-Service Training. Champaign, Illinois: Research Press, 1974.

Authors stress that providing a humane and responsive environment for our children is the most important responsibility of our schools. Most teachers need to know alternatives to threats, physical punishment, medication and excluding children from school. Recent research in educational psychology and sociology have made alternatives available and a widely used method for structuring learning in a responsive environment is detailed in the book. The material is presented in a workshop format. The application of the techniques should raise questions of professional issues and ethics. Chapters include: 1) Do you have a behavior problem?, 2) Observing your own behavior, 3) Analyzing the classroom environment, 4) Basic principles of human behavior, 5) Planning for change, 6) Using social reinforcers, 7) Using non-social reinforcers, 8) How did it work?

1117.   Maryland State Department Of Education. Approaches To School Discipline--A Selective Review Of The Literature. Number Two. Baltimore, Maryland: Maryland State Department Of Education, October, 1973.

Approaches to school discipline are a concern of experienced as well as inexperienced teachers and school administrators. This publication is intended to bring together in convenient form a selective review of the literature on several approaches to school discipline. Sections include: 1) Definitions of discipline, 2) A psychoanalytic model, 3) A behavior modification model. A bibliography is included.

1118.   McCarthy, J. A. and Reigel, R. H. Beyond Coping: Managing Problematic Behavior. Plymouth, Michigan: Model Resourece Room Project, 1981.

In attempting to deal with the many individual problems which occur at the secondary level, classroom teachers often voice frustration with the behavior some students show. Frequent requests for suggestions and support have been heard, particularly regarding assistance in managing behaviors which have become problematic. Beyond Coping is intended to provide a parallel reference to maladies and remedies, with special emphasis given to frequently recurring behavior problems at the secondary level. Each suggestion listed may or may not be appropriate for a given situation; teacher judgement and careful review of progress is essential. There are several principles of behavior management which must be kept in mind in order for the suggestions in this book to be of value. These include: 1) Clarify your expectations 2) Be consistent 3) Use a positive approach 4) Consider the theme of the behavior 5) Consider the frequency and type of behavior. The book is divided into the following sections: 1) Getting there 2) Being there 3) Staying there 4) Elaboration.

1119.   Mehan, H. Learning Lessons--Social Organization in the Classroom. Cambridge, Massachusetts: Harvard University Press, 1979.

Included in this book are chapters on 1) Looking Inside School, 2) The Structure of Classroom Lessons, 3) The Structuring of Classroom Lessons, 4) Competent Membership In The Classroom Community. The author covers such topics as comparing differences between schools and examining the internal life of schools, research strategies in the study of the classroom, the conduct of the inquiry, organization of classroom lessons, interactional sequences in classroom lessons, achieving order under normal classroom circumstances, revealing the basic turn-allocation apparatus of classroom lessons, achieving order under unusual classroom circumstances, approaches to competence, interactional competence in the classroom, the production of academically correct and interactionally appropriate responses, students' initiation rights, the interpretation of normative demands in the classroom, learning classroom lessons, the nature of findings from constitutive ethnography, a comparison of approaches to classroom interaction, conversation in the classroom and in everyday life, directions for classroom interaction research.

1120.   Menges, R. J. The Intentional Teacher: Controller, Manager, Helper. Monterey, California: Brooks/Cole Publishing Company, 1977.

This book is to be used to introduce the study of teaching and learning to undergraduates preparing for human service professions. Professional school students and those who work with learners as youth leaders, religious educators, counselors, school administrators, professors, and social workers may also find this point of view pertinent. One way to consider the variety of teaching/learning activities is to conceptualize three teacher roles. Depending on objectives and other circumstances, a teacher sometimes assumes the role of controller, sometimes the role of manager, and sometimes the role of helper. These roles are illustrated in chapter one, and each is described further in subsequent chapters. Intentionality is the dimension underlined the conception of teaching by the author. The intentional teacher is the one whose actions and intentions are congruent. Such teachers know what they intend and are able to select appropriate means for themselves and for their students to actualize those intentions. The final chapter of the book discusses intentions in some detail and suggests ways teachers might clarify intentions and come closer to achieving more in practice.

1121.   Metz, M. H. <u>Classrooms and Corridors--The Crisis of Authority in Desegregated Secondary Schools.</u> Berkeley, California: University of California Press, 1978.

The guiding questions throughout this book concern the ways staff members and students and the schools as whole organizations, address the twin task of pursuing education and maintaining civility, safety and order. The two schools described are far from typical, but they provide an unusually informative context for understanding the relationship between the pursuit of education and the pursuit of order, because both ends were especially difficult to achieve. The schools were recently desegregated and still adjusting to changes in the student population. They contained children of an age particularly unlikely to be readily cooperative and civil with their teachers or with one another. And, they were dominated by working class black children at a time of rising black consciousness and by upper middle class white children at a time when restlessness among this group was close to its height. Included are the following chapters: 1) The Schools of Canton, 2) Organizational Tensions and Authority in Public Schools, 3) Teachers' Definitions of Classroom Relationships, 4) Students; Definition of Classroom Relationships, 5) Classroom Interaction: The Teachers Adjust to the Students, 6) Classroom Interaction: Principled Conflict, 7) The Problem Order in the School At Large, 8) Faculty Culture and Student Order, 9) The Principals' Impact on the School, 10) Differences in Student Culture at Chauncey & Hamilton, 11) Beyond Campus.

1122.   Millman, H. L., Schaefer, C. E. and Cohen, J. L. <u>Therapies for School Behavior Problems</u>. San Francisco: Jossey--Bass publishers, 1980.

Among the major tasks of childhood are learning and socializing in school, and problems faced by children arise very quickly in the educational process. Weaknesses within the educational system can cause problems in the child or exaggerate already existing ones. This book attempts to provide a variety of methods to reduce these problems and to enhance the psychological, social, and cognitive development of children in schools. The book is directed to those who have the responsibility of dealing with problems that arise in the educational process from preschool through high school. Included are the following sections: 1) classroom management problems, 2) immature behaviors, 3) insecure behaviors, 4) habit disorders, 5) distrubed peer relations, 6) disturbed relationships with teachers.

1123.   Morreau, L. E. and Daley, M. F. Behavioral Management in the Classroom. New York: Appleton-Century-Crofts, 1972.

This text, a programmed text in behavioral management, is intended for school administrators, curriculum specialists, in-service teachers and students in university courses in education, programmed instruction or behavior modification. Included in the book are sections on behavior, identifying a behavior, behavioral sequencing, measuring a behavior, the behavior recording sheet, recording a paragraph, preparing a graph, recording, high and low probability behavior, tasks, arranging a contract, micro-task size, increasing the micro-size, reinforcing events, setting a criterion level, sequence of contract events, termination of the RE, RE and task areas, the RE menu, program evaluation, re-evaluation, post-test on contingency management principles, model answers and a bibliography.

1124.   Morse, W. C. Classroom Disturbance: The Principal's Dilemma. Arlington, Virginia: The Council for Exceptional Children, 1971.

This monograph discusses what principals have talked about, as well as how they have examined the situation with classroom disturbances. The premise is, there is no one who will back or help bring about the new design in special education more effectively than that special educator, the principal, whether he be elementary, middle school, junior high school or high school. In the exploration of this problem there are several topics covered in the book: The School's Role in Prevention and Rehabilitation; The Types of Pathology One Can Expect to Find; and What the Principal Himself Can Do About Particular Children in His School in His Role as a Special Educator. Included are the following chapters: 1) The New Role for Schools: Prevention and Rehabilitation; 2) The Current Crisis; 3) Planning; 4) Patterns of Pupil Maladjustment; 5) The Special Role of the Principal: Dealing with Disturbed Pupils.

1125.   Myers, H. S. Fundamentally Speaking. San Francisco, California: Strawberry Hills Crest, 1977.

Included in this book is a chapter entitled "The Departure from Discipline." It discusses the permissive attitudes of schools today. The author stresses that the child must be taught how to behave and how to follow rules. He must be made to understand that rules are designed to benefit the majority, and that if he violates the rules that he will be punished. In addition to behavioral discipline, the child must also be taught to discipline his mind. He must be taught to develop good work and study habits and how to set priorities and be responsible. The author feels that schools are not teaching discipline. He divides his book into the following sections: 1) The Problem -- The Illiteracy Invasion, The Slob Syndrome, The Departure From Discipline, The Absence of Attractiveness, The Paucity of Patriotism, The Condemnation of Competition; 2) The Causes -- The Boards of Education, The Teachers' Unions, Tenure, Failure, Ability Grouping, Learning Stations, Phonics, New Math, New Grammar, Federal Funds, Textbooks; 3) The Solution -- Involvement, A Bit of History, Alternatives, The Rebirth of Fundamental Education, The Results, The Opposition, and the Challenge. The final chapter deals with a guide to starting a fundamental school -- helpful organizations and suggested readings.

1126.   National Association of Secondary School Principals. Disruptive Youth--Causes and Solutions. Reston, Virginia: The National Association of Secondary School Principals, 1977.

Aggressive behavior by youth is causing a serious situation both in the schools and on the streets. In fact, problem youths in some schools are of sufficient numbers to threatened the morale of the general student body and the quality of the educational program. A principal forced to spend a majority of time with misbehaving students has few hours to devote to program improvement and staff development. The formation of a state-wide task force in Maryland on programs for disruptive youth was first proposed in 1973 by the Maryland Association of Secondary School Principals. The primary purpose of the task force was to identify programs for youths who could not function in a contemporary school setting. This book discusses the results of the task force.

1127.   National Association of Secondary School Principals. Report on Educational Programs for Disruptive Youth. Rifton, Virginia, 1977.

Aggressive behavior by youth is causing a serious situation both in the schools and on the street. Problem youth in some schools are of sufficient numbers to threaten the morale of the general student body and the quality of the educational program. A principal forced to spend a majority of time with misbehaving students has precious few hours to devote to program improvement and staff development. This monograph profiles the causes of disruption and proposes some practical, concrete solutions. Six objectives were set forth for the Task Force working in this study 1) Define disruptive youth; 2) Identify the scope of the disruptive youth problem; 3) Identify and review existing alternative programs for disruptive youth through a. visitations, b.

review of literature and research, c. use of consultants; 4) Recommend specific educational programs needed for disruptive youth; 5) Assist local education systems in establishing pilot projects; 6) Recommend legislation needed for implementation of needed programs.

1128.   National Education Association. Discipline and Learning: An Inquiry Into Student-Teacher Relationship. Washington, D.C.: National Education Association, 1975.

Discipline and learning are integrally related. Discipline is necessary for learning, and defective learning is a form of discipline. Today, discipline is acknowledged as one of the most pressing concerns of the community at-large. This book offers the classroom teacher some approaches to the general topic of discipline from a historical perspective as well as the contemporary point of view. It discusses punishment and order and justice, and it shows teachers way to approach the more serious problems attached to maintaining discipline in the classroom, as well as ways of helping students arrive as some discipline. Included are articles dealing with the following topics: 1) Discipline, 2) Historical Perspective, 3) Punishment, 4) Behaviorism, 5) Student Response to Control, 6) Special Issues Today, 7) Order and Justice.

1129.   National Education Association. Discipline and Learning: An Inquiry into Student-Teacher Relationships. Revised Edition. Washington, D.C.: National Education Association, 1977.

The question of discipline permeates all aspects of learning. Discipline gives form to the content of learning; consequently, a study of one involves the other. The chapters in this book present the challenge of learning as seen by differing professionals--teacher and administrator, counselor and psychologist, school board member and lawyer. The purpose is to stimulate discussion in the general area of discipline, in the hopes of helping teachers consider the possibilities for learning that lie uniquely in each classroom situation. Included are the following chapters: 1) Discipline; 2) Historal Perspective; 3) Punishment; 4) Behaviorism; 5) Student Response to Control; 6) Special Issues Today; 7) Order and Justice.

1130.   National Education Association. Discipline in the Classroom. Revised Edition. West Haven, Connecticut: National Education Association Publications, 1974.

The articles in this booklet reflect a broad spectrum in their approach to discipline in the teaching process. Even though discipline is now called classroom control, these articles indicate that some educators questions the desirability of precise prescription in the classroom. Running through the articles is a common thread: discipline is less a problem when the instructional content and process are interesting and relevant, constitutes stimulating activities, and arouse natural curiosity. Since, as many of the articles point out, what constitutes meaningful curriculum or stimulating activities for one student may be irrelevant for another, the matter of motivating individual students appears to be the critical problem. However, since some students become discipline problems despite meaningful curriculum, other approaches are suggested. These approaches range from an attempt to match a teacher's teaching style to a student's learning style, to a straight to behavior modification where the forms of behavior -- and not the attitudes behind behavior -- are the primary concern. See ERIC Abstract ED 095629.

1131.   Naurer, A. Corporal Punishment Handbook. Berkeley, California: Generation Books, 1977.

Corporal punishment is the infliction of pain upon the body of the child because of an act of disobedience, omission of an assigned task or the commission of an error. It does not include temporary restraint of a child nor the removal of a weapon from a child bent on destruction. Included in this book are sections on the following areas: 1) definition, 2) examples, 3) history, 4) defenders, 5) areas of agreement, 6) questional defenses, 7) agruments for abolition, 8) scientific evidence, 9) opinions of the respected, 10) medical opinion, 11) how to reassess a discipline policy, 12) trouble spots, 13) disruptive students, 14) school caused disruption, 15) alternatives, and 16) list of reading.

1132.   O'Leary, K. D. and O'Leary, S. G. Classroom Management: The Successful Use of Behavior Modification. New York: Pergamon Press, Inc., 1972.

The purposes of this book are to 1) Supply the reader with a set of principles about changing behavior and to place those principles within the historical context of the development of treatment with children, 2) Present research evidence documenting the efficacy of such procedures in the classroom, 3) Discuss how teachers can implement such procedures for both preventing problems and dealing with existing problems, 4) Influence the direction of research in the area of classroom managemnt by making both educators and psychologist aware of a rapid redevelopment field, by describing both the advantages and disadvantages of some of the research in this book, and by pointing out directions which future research might take. The articles in this book were selected because the research was conducted in the classroom or because they have direct relevance for classroom management. Greatest emphasis was placed on the former and twenty-seven of the thirty-seven articles include data from the classroom itself. Another criteria for selection of articles was the adequacy of design of the study; case studies were generally avoided. Included are the following chapters: 1) Behavior Modification with Children, 2)

Psychotherapy with Children: Evaluations, 3) Praise and Positive Forms of Teacher Attention, 4) Classroom Punishment, 5) Modeling, 6) Token Reinforcement Programs: Extrinsic Reinforcers, 7) Token Reinforcement Programs: Intrinsic Reinforcers, 8) The Effects of Peers As Therapeutic Agents in the Classroom, 9) Programmed Instruction in Teaching Machine, 10) The Effective Use of Paraprofessionals, 11) Self-Management, 12) The Implementation of Behavioral Principles in the Classroom.

1133.   O'Leary, K. D. & O'Leary, S. J. Eds. Classroom Management--The Successful Use of Behavior Modification. Second Edition. New York: Pergamon Press, Inc., 1977.

The purposes of this book are to 1) Supply the reader with a set of principles about changing behavior and to place these principles within the historical context of the development of treatment of children. 2) Present research evidence documenting the efficacy of such procedures in the clasroom. 3) Discuss how teachers can implement such procedures for both preventing problems and dealing the existing problems. The book is intended for under-graduate students in education and psychology, for teachers who are currently working in the field, and for clinical, education, and school psychologists who consult with teachers about educational problems. The books contains explanations of basic terminology, it introduces the reader to the field of behavior modification with children in some detail; comments are made about each article in the book, and the concluding chapter discusses the implementation of the procedures illustrated throughout the book. Included are the following chapters: 1) Behavior Modification With Children, 2) Teacher-Editors' Comments, 3) Classroom Punishment-Editors' Comments, 4) Modeling, 5) Children As Change Agents, 6) Token Reinforcement Programs, 7) Self-Management, 8) Environmental Assessment and Change, 9) Implementation.

1134.   Osborn, D. K. and Osborn, J. D. Discipline is Classroom Management. The University of Georgia: Education Associates, 1977.

As beginning teachers this book is written for them. Because the most difficult task is not the mastery of subject matter content but rather the task is learning how to deal effectively with children. Effective discipline in classroom management techniques are learned. A teacher can master the necessary skills. This book attempts to help the teacher do this. The following chapters are included: 1) will the real problem child please stand up, 2) a double continuum: a new look at discipline, 3) how children learn, 4) two research designs that really help teachers, and 5) techniques of classroom management.

1135.   Paley, V. G. White Teacher. Cambridge, Massachusetts: Harvard University Press, 1979.

The author presents a personal account of her experiences teaching kindergarten in an integrated school within a predominantly white, middle class neighborhood. In a series of episodes and carefully observed moments, she provides an unsparingly honest self examination of her own growth toward a new understanding of children, whatever their differences. She begins by recognizing and learning to deal with her own subtle forms of prejudice. The book records a strong applicacy of integrated education. She firmly believes that diversity of experience, if approached sensibly, enriches the learning process.

1136.   Pattavina, P. and Gotts, E. A.   The Outer Dimensions of Classroom Conflict Training Package.   Trainer's Manual. CONSERT Project.   Washington, D.C.:   Bureau of Education for the Handicapped, July, 1981.

The materials described in this manual are based on a series of anecdotes of conflict situations in secondary classrooms. The situations focus on emotional and behavioral problems of adolescents. The manual is intended to be used with a video tape cassette that depicts 15 vignettes of classroom events in which student behavior problems are portrayed. A series of teacher's response forms is provided for each episode, offering choices between five clusters of teacher behaviors. The clusters are: 1) Authoritative--Appealing to Outside Authority, 2) Neutral Facilitation, 3) Incentive Manipulation, 4) Interview and Supportive Intervention, and 5) Deliberate Ignoring.   The Vignettes are presented in narrative form along with the work sheets and may be used with or without the accompany video tape. See ERIC Abstract ED 199216.

1137.   Payne, J. S., Polloway, E. A., Kauffman, J. M. and Scranton, T. R. Living in the classroom: the Currency based token economy. New York: Human Sciences Press, 1975.

Various types of token economies and contingency contract systems are emerging throughout private and public educational programs. These behavior modification programs were originally designed to assist the teacher in classroom management and motivate children to learn. Although these programs have purportedly been moderately to highly successful, they have been criticized on the grounds that they are irrelevant to basic and humanistic education. The author seeks to answer these questions: 1) what do token systems have to do with basic education?, 2) can they contribute to the achievement of humanistic goals?   The purpose of this book is to explain how to develop an educationally relevant and humanistic system through the use of the currency based economy.   The goal is to help the teacher establish a currency based token economy that will make education in the classroom more relevant to the lives of children in today's society.   The book is intended to be a resource for methods courses for elementary, secondary, and special education teachers as well as supplementary reading for introductory courses in education and behavior modification. Included are the following chapters: 1) justification of the currency based token economy, 2) how the currency based token economy works, 3) identification and acquisition of reinforcers, 4) classroom management in the traditional sense, 5) how to begin living in the classroom, 6) store keeping, 7) banking, 8) thoughts on psychological existence.

1138.   Pearson, C. Resolving Classroom Conflict. Palo Alto, California: Learning Handbooks, 1974.

Cooperation, communication, and awareness can grow in a classroom. The purpose of this book is to offer suggestions, insights and experiences, which will help the teacher build a responsible, equitable classroom. Included are the following chapters: 1) What's The Problem? 2) Child -vs-Child -vs- Child -vs- Child... 3) Child -vs- Teacher -vs-Child -vs- Teacher... 4) Child -vs- System -vs- Child -vs-System... 5) Child/Teacher -vs- System -vs- Child/Teacher -vs- System... 6) Formulas.

1139.   Phay, R. E. "Suspension and Expulsion of Public School Students." Eric/Cem State of the Knowledge Series, No. 10." Washington, D.C.: National Center for Educational Research and Development, 1971. 49p.

This mongraph reviews and analyzes decisions dealing with suspension or expulsion of students by public school authorities. It focuses on court cases that reaffirmed, amplified or extend entrenched in constitutional and common law principles undergirding the public educational system in the U.S. The authors considers the traditional elements of procedural due process and concludes that to comply with minimum requirements of procedural due process administrators must 1) give the student adequate notice of the grounds of the charges and the nature of evidence against him, 2) conduct a hearing unless the student waives it, and 3) take action only if it is warranted by the evidence. See ERIC Abstract ED 048672.

1140.   Phillips, E. L. Analysis and Modification of Classroom Behavior. Englewood Cliffs, New Jersey: Prentiss-Hall, Inc. 1972.

This book deals with two basic procedures: 1) Analysis, pinpoints the relationship child's observable behavior and the factors in the environment that evoke it; the other, behavior modification, is the process of altering those conditions or events which are related to the behavior of concern so that it would change in the desired direction. It is a strategy that demands a structured environment which the teacher can change according to both the child's responses and those the teacher wishes to evoke in order to accomplish an educational or behavioral objective. Included are the following chapters: 1) Vocabulary and Methodological Concepts, 2) Review of Research, 3) Behavior Analysis and Design of Programs, 4) Behavior Modification In the Classroom, 5) Programmed Instruction and Behavioral Control, 6) Rolls of School Personnel, 7) Working With Parents, 8) Case Studies of Behavior Modification.

1141.   Phillips, G. M., Butt, D. E. and Metzger, N. J. Communication in Education--A Rhetoric of Schooling and Learning. New York: Holt, Reinhard and Winston, Inc., 1974.

The focus of this book is on communication, and the rhetorical view that is adopted proposes that the teacher reach his own educational goals by helping his students achieve their goals. Implicit is the question, "What is the Point of Bringing People Together in a Classroom if They are not Able to Communicate Fully and Freely with Another?" The author focuses on the classroom conditions that would make such communication possible. Included are the following chapters: 1) Examining our Assumptions About Speech, 2) Interpreting Communication Behavior, 3) Child Language Development, 4) Understanding What Happens When Humans Communicate with One Another, 5) Human Needs and the Responsibility of the School, 6) Winning and Losing: The Rhetoric of Goal Seeking, 7) The Clinical Responsibility of the Speech Teacher, 8) Building the Communication Atmosphere in the Classroom, 9) A Taxonomy of Possible Contents for Instructional Program in Oral Communication.

1142.   Presbie, R. J. and Brown, P. L. Behavior Modification. Washington, D.C.: National Education Association, 1976.

This report reviews some of the most relevant findings from the extensive research which has been done thus far in the area of behavior modification. It summarizes the more important, practical, concrete, and classroom tested procedures which research shows to be effective in improving students' academic and social behaviors. Included are the following chapters: 1) Behavior Modification Equals Behavior Improvement, 2) Methodology of Using Behavior Modification Procedures, 3) Behavior Modification Change Procedures, 4) Learning More About Behavior Modification.

1143.   Prutzman, P., Burger, N. L., Bodenhamer, G. and Stern, L. The Friendly Classroom for a Small Planet -- A Handbook on Creative Approaches to Living and Problem Solving for Children. Wayne, New Jersey: Avery Publishing Group, Inc., 1978.

There is an urgent need for effective educational responses to the growing concern among educators, administrators and parents over violence, vandalism and the interpersonal hostilities and conflicts that too often get in the way of effective learning in the classroom. It is also widely recognized that the educational needs of those children who fail to learn, although they may be docile rather than troublesome, may require special effort. There has been a growth of program efforts to help teachers and students deal constructively with conflict situations and to build the kind of classroom community in which mutual respect forms a basis for acting responsible. These programs aim at common goals: to help teachers and students create a classroom climate in which people respect themselves and each other, cooperation is the rule rather than the exception, learning can go forward unimpeded by squabbles and hostilities, all children are equally valued and get an equal chance to shine, and students and teachers learn specific skills of communication, cooperation and conflict resolution that can be applied within and beyond the classroom period. This book has three main goals to help in the classroom, 1) to develop toward a community in which children are capable and desirous of open communication, 2) to help children gain insight into the nature of human feelings, capabilities, strength, to share their own feelings and become aware of their own strengths, and 3) to help each child to develop self-confidence about his or her ability to think creatively about problems and begin to prevent or solve conflicts. Included are the following chapters: 1) Creative Response--Meeting the Challenge of Violence, 2) An Idea Grow--The Roots of Violence, 3) Preparing and Planning--Some Preliminary Considerations, 4) Getting Started--Your Role as Facilitator, 5) The Challenge of Integration--Moving Beyond the Workshop Approach, 6) Let's Get Acquainted--Exercises that Help Remember Names, 7) Freeing Ourselves Up--Loosening Up Activities, 8) Let's Build Community--Learning to Cooperate, 9) Do You Hear Me? -- Learning to Communicate, 10) We are All Special--Acclamation of Ourselves and Others, 11) A Notebook About Me--Creating a Treasured Possession, 12) Let's Make an Instrument--An Affirming Activity for Everyone, 13) Sometimes We Can All Win--Creative Conflict Resolution, 14) How About That Bully? -- Some Conflict Scenarios, 15) Doesn't Anyone Understand? -- The Needs to Share Feelings, 16) How Did it Work? -- Let's Evaluate, and 17) Why Just in Classrooms? -- Expanding Our Skills to Meet Wider Needs.

1144.   Rice, D. L. Classroom Behavior From A to Z. Belmont, California: Lear Siegler, Inc., 1974.

This book was written as a tool for the elementary teacher to use in the management of classroom behavior. In order to manage classroom behavior effectively, it is necessary to understand a child and to establish a working relationship with the child. The teacher must react to the child as an individual and also as a group member. Included in this book is a behavior index and bibliography.

1145.   Richardson, E. The Environment of Learning -- Conflict and Understanding in the Secondary School. London, England: Heinemann Educational Books, Ltd., 1973.

This book is about personal relationships in the secondary schools and about the way emotional undercurrents affect the work that any teacher is doing with his classes. These themes are discussed in the concrete terms of school organization--the methods of leadership, the layout of rooms, the patterning of a time-table, staff leadership and organization. Chapters include: 1) Human Relations in the School; 2) The Teacher and the Form or Tutorial Group; 3) Patterns of Leadership and Control; 4) Loneliness, Isolation and the Fear of Rejection; 5) The Physical Setting and its Influence; 6) Teachers, Pupils and Time Schedules; 7) Freedom, Discipline, and Creative Invention; 8) Learning, Performance and Evaluation; 9) The Teacher and His Colleagues; 10) The Social Organization of the School; 11) Teaching and Living.

1146.   Rogers, D. M. Classroom Discipline--An Idea Handbook for Elementary School Teachers. New York: Center for Applied Research in Education, Inc., 1972.

This book addreses itself to the normal classroom situation with typical classroom discipline problems. It presents normal inhabitants, their problems, and how some of them have been solved. It includes several chapters on morale building and concrete, proven ideas for promoting individual self-confidence and esprit de corps. It also provides several chapters on mundane behavior problems, together with specific techniques which humane, excellent teachers are using with success in today's classrooms. The primary purpose of the book is to help the teacher stimulate thinking and imagination. Confronted with youngsters' impulsive antics and problems, the classroom encounters teachable moments. Atmosphere is the essence of a natural classroom control and the right blend of components for an outstanding atmosphere is difficult to convey. The book can be used as a six-week campaign. The ideas presented are guidelines and not arbitrary rules.

1147.   Rothman, E. Troubled Teachers. New York, David McKay Company, Inc., 1977.

The author who is a principal of one of America's most problem riddled schools paints a portrait of classroom education in America today: how it destroys the very minds and spirits it is supposed to build according to Rothman. She demonstrates how teachers can turn the system around to make it work for today's youth. She provides practical advice that can help teachers teach rather than rule and she shows how to turn aggression into a positive force, how to understand how violence is an expression of undisclosed needs, and how to transform apathy into the curiosity that is a natural part of childhood. Chapters include: 1) teachers need children more than children need teachers, or the art of self deception, 2) the methology of teaching, 3) the power of the system and self-entrampment, 4) power games teachers play with students, 5) violent teachers, 6) the prison syndrome, 7) to be loved, young, and immortal, 8) the romantics, 9) the rebels: the true and the pseudo, 10) black is to black as white is to white, 11) the incestuous supervisor, 12) teacher training and the fortress mentality, 13) sugar coated unionism, 14) teaching is the pursuit of aggression.

1148.   Rovetta, C. H. & Rovetta, L. Teacher Spanks Johnny--A Handbook For Teachers. Stockton, California, The Willow House Publishers, 1968.

This handbook has been written to inform teachers, administrators and school board members of the rights, responsibilities and risks involved in corporal punishment situations, to present authoritative material in this area, to remove teacher confusion, and hence to lessen many classroom problems and tensions. Ignorance of the law is no excuse, and teachers without knowledge of rules and regulations in reference to corporal punishment may wrongfully punish a pupil and find themselves involved in a lawsuit because of acts performed with the best of intentions. Chapters include: 1) Teacher Right To Punish, 2) Extent of Teacher Right To Punish, 3) Offenses Committed By Pupils, 4) Forced Used On Pupil By Teacher, 5) Instruments Used To Punish Pupils, 6) Motive Of Teacher, 7) Teacher Liability Problems, 8) Trends, 9) Defenses Favoring Teacher, 10) Types of State Statutes Dealing With Corporal Punishment, 11) Selected Cases, 12) Discipline: Understanding the Pupil Lessens Need To Punish, 13) Epilogue: Dear Teacher and a Bibliography.

1149.   Rubel, R. J. "Assumptions Underlining Programs Used To Prevent Or Reduce Student Violence In Secondary Schools." Washington, D.C.: National Institute For Juvenile Justice And Delinquency Prevention, Department Of Justice, 1978. 28P.

This is one of 52 theoretical papers on school crime and its relation to poverty. This paper explores programs designed to prevent or to reduce student crime or violence in secondary schools that are based on the assumption that pupils are competent to make rational decisions and take rational actions, and programs that assume that pupils are not competent. Program areas explored are organizational modification, curricular/instructional programs, security systems, and conseling services. The paper concludes that programs of many different kinds are needed to deal effectively with problems of crime and violence in schools. See ERIC Abstract ED 157201.

1150.   Ruben, A. G. Our Teachers are Crying: A Positive Approach to Solving Classroom Problems. New York: MSS Information Corporation, 1975.

This book describes how to organize and lead teacher consultation groups so that teachers can learn to improve their attitudes toward themselves and their students. Explicit guidelines to leaders of consultation groups have been detailed so that any person interested in leading such a group should be able to do so from reading the book. The following chapters in the book are: 1) Teachers in Trouble; 2) The Group is the Thing; 3) You as the Leader; 4) What to Do When Things Go Wrong; 5) Sitting in on a Consultation Group for Teachers; 6) Solving Classroom Problems; 7) Evaluating the Consultation Group Experience; 8) Future Directions for Teacher, Education, Institutions and School Systems.

1151.   Rubin, R. A. and Balow, B. "A Longitudional Survey Of School Behavior Problems." "Interim Report Number 25." Washington, D.C.: National Institute Of Education, 1977. 24P.

This report desceibes an investigation to determine the frequency and consistency with which elementary school children are identified with their teachers over a period of years, as presenting behavior problems within the school setting. A large sample of urban white children, measured on the number of school related variables were followed through the course of their elementary school years. A teacher rating of behavior was obtained for 1570 children over 70 year period. Subjects with a least three ratings were divided into groups: no problem, behavior problem, and inconsistent classifications. Resulting data include: 1) An analysis of behavior problems by sex and grade level, 2) Cumulative reading totals, 3) A comparison of the three subject groups on the school related variables. See ERIC Abstract ED 147012.

1152.   Ruble, D. N. and Nakamura, C. Y. "Young Children's Task Versus Social Orientations." Washington, D.C.: Office Of Education, Department Of Health Education And Welfare, 1971. 23P.

The purpose of this study was to examine small children's tendencies to be task or socially oriented in a experimental situation. Two independent variables were chosen: Field dependents-independents and sex. It was expected that field-dependents subjects and girls would tend to be more socially oriented, while field-independents subjects and boys would tend to be more task oriented. The results from the two experiemental tasks used generally failed to confirm the hypotheses. The possibility that social orientation may sometimes serve as a task-avoidant strategy is discussed. See ERIC Abstract ED 063037.

1153.   Schofield, D. and Dunn, P. Student Rights and Discipline. Burlingame, Calif.: Association of California School Administrators, 1977.

Flexibility on the part of school administrators is of prime importance to the success of a discipline program. Principals set the tone of their schools and are responsible for seeing that disciplinary techniques evolve with the school's and the students' changing needs. The administrator must treat each case as unique and seek to determine with the student the reasons for his behavior and possible methods for improving it. Such procedure will help to make sure that discipline is effectively addressed to causes rather than symptoms and can also encourage the student to see the educator as a positive rather than a negative force in his life. Included are the following chapters: 1) Introduction: The Philosophical Roots; 2) The Basis for Authority: In Loco Parentis; 3) The Verdict of the Courts: Students Have Rights; 4) Interpreting Rights and Freedoms; 5) Practical Aspects of Rights and Discipline; 6) Conclusions.

1154.   Schreiber, D. (Ed.), "The School Dropout." Washington, D.C.: National Education Association, 1964.

This volume is a collection of papers presented at a symposium on school dropouts. Participants represented the disciplines of both education and the social sciences. It was hoped that the multi-disciplinary contributions might crystalize a contextual statement about the nature of the dropout problem as well as indications for effective educational intervention. See ERIC Abstract ED 029914.

1155.   Shipman, H. and Foley, E. Any Teacher Can ... A Systematic Approach to Behavior Management and Positive Teaching. Chicago, Illinois: Loyola University Press, 1973.

This book is a discussion of Shipman's study of operant conditioning and behavior modification research. Sister Helen Shipman discusses her experiences in dealing with behavior management and positive teaching. She includes the following sections: 1) Positive Teaching; 2) Grandma's Law; 3) How to Begin; 4) Ground Rules; 5) A Token Economy; 6) Helps for Learning; 7) Problems and Discipline; 8) Shaping New Behavior.

1156.   Silberman, M. L., Allender, J. S. & Yanoff, J. M. (ED S). Real Learning--A Source Book for Teachers. Boston, Massachusetts, Little, Brown & Company, 1976.

This book is adaptable to the needs of various education courses, in-service programs, and individual teachers at all levels of schooling who are interested in improving the learning climate in the classroom. It is suitable for a wide range of purposes, from independent study to a program for large groups. It contains extensive activity suggestions and guidelines for inquiring into its contents. The reading cover a broad range of issues and views then do other books on humanistic approaches in education. It is the hope of the authors that this teacher source book will facilitate the constructive changes needed in education today. Included are the following chapters: 1) involving learners, 2) guiding, thinking and learning, 3) educating for emotional growth, 4) learning to work in groups, 5) creating freedom and limits, 6) building active teacher roles. The activity section includes the following chapters: 1) involving learners, 2) guiding, thinking and learning, 3) educating for emotional growth, 4) learning to work in groups, 5) creating freedom and limits, 6) building active teaching roles.

1157.   Silver, R. A. Developing Cognitive And Creative Skills Through Art--Programs For Children With Communication Disorders For Learning Disabilities. Baltimore, Maryland: University Park Crest, 1978.

The main purpose of this book is to call attention to art procedures found useful in developing concepts of space, of sequential order, and of class or group of objects. The procedures were developed in studies of children with hearing impairments, language impairments, or learning disabilities. The second purpose of this book is to provide art techniques for evaluating cognitive and creative skills of children and adults who cannot communicate well verbally. Part I is concerned with the roles art can play in cognition, adjustment, and assessment. It is also concerned with the needs to reexamine low expectations of intellectual and artistic ability, and to demonstrate that the handicapped can be truly gifted. Part II is concerned with art procedures found useful in remediating cognitive deficits and in identifying cognitive skills. These include the ability to associate and requisite concepts through drawing from imagination, the ability to perceive and represent concepts of space through drawing from observation, and the ability to order sequentially through painting, modeling clay, and predictive drawing.

1158.   Singh, S. P. Guidelines for Developing Contextual Conceptualization in the Training of Education Personnel for Young Children: An Approach for the Prevention of Learning and Behavior Problems. Washington, D.C.: Bureau of Educational Personnel Development, 1973.

Guidelines are presented for a program to prepare educational personnel to work with young children to explain learning and behavior disabilities despite adequate intelligence, hearing, vision, motor capacity and emotional adjustment. The program provides the following skills and competencies: 1) skills and identification of perceptual abilities, communication skills, self-concepts, principles of learning, the understanding of self, 2) competencies and utilizing types of responses, questioning, and stimuli for effective teaching, 3) knowledge of subject content, 4) ability to utilize skills and competencies in designing educational programs and performance in the classroom. See ERIC Abstract ED 080150.

1159.   Singh, S. P. <u>Inter-disciplinary Seminar for the</u>
<u>Prevention of Learning and Behavior Problems Among Young</u>
<u>Children</u>. Washington, D.C.: Bureau of Educational
Personnel Development, 1975.

A graduate inter-disciplinary seminar is described which was
held at the University of South Florida during the 1972-73
school year, on the prevention of learning and behavior
problems in young children. Faculty members from the areas
of Anthroapology, Guidance, Special Education, Early Childhood and Linguistics led presentations and discussions on
topics relating to the behavior of young children. See ERIC
Abstract ED 097790.

1160.   Slavin, R. E. <u>Teams-Games-Tournament: A Student Team</u>
<u>Approach to Teaching Adolescents With Special and Emotional</u>
<u>and Behavioral Needs</u>. Baltimore, Maryland: Center for
Social Organization of Schools Report, Johns Hopkins
University, November, 1975.

The use of teams-games-tournament is described, an instructional technique involving student teams and learning games,
as an alternative classroom structure for children with
special needs. A study was conducted in which the TGT and
individualized instruction were compared, using 39 7th-9th
graders in a school for adolescents of normal intelligence
who have problems with human relationships and academic
tasks. Results confirm hypotheses that TGT would exceed
individualized instruction on social connectiveness, pro-
academic peer norms, frequency of peer tutoring and percent
of time on task. A five month follow up showed that former
TGT students distributed among 6 new classes were still
interacting with their peers both on and off task more than
control students. However, the TGT students were off task
more than control students at the time of the follow up
observation. See ERIC Abstract 1081355-5.

1161.   Sloane, H. N. <u>Classroom Management Remediation And</u>
<u>Prevention</u>. New York: John Wiley & Sons, Incorporated,
1976.

This book is organized around the practical difficulties of
the experienced elementary and junior high school teacher.
A problem approach is used. Each chapter defines a set of
problems, which are followed by discussions of the factors
that account for the behavior. Specific procedures both
preventative and remedial, are then presented. Classroom
management perse is not a useful objective. Although status
may accrue to the teacher who has a class that looks
orderly, or at least is not overly chaotic, the ultimate
goal is the production of beneficial changes to the
students. All learning progresses better with a systematic
program, and this program requires some limits and some
management. Included are the following chapters: 1)
Solving behavior problems before they solve you, 2)
Out-of-seat, talking out, and overactive behaviors, 3)

Agressive behaviors, 4) Crying and tantrums, 5) Over-quiet, isolate behavior, 6) Creating an attentive class, 7) Work completion, 8) Work routines, 9) Reducing cheating, 10) Management systems and general disruption.

1162.   Smith, D. H. (ED.) Disruptive Students. Albany, New York: Bureau Of School Social Services, New York State Education Department, April, 1974.

A committee explored ways of helping school districts develop more effective programs for disruptive students. Findings revealed the need for the developement of local guidelines to satisfy each school district's needs and for reliable feedback. The report presents efforts to sample various local approaches to the problem and represents feedback from a two day workship that utilized some of the best imformed persons who work with disruptive students in New York. Discussion topics range from discriptions of the scope, identification, prevention, and legal aspects of this behavior. 2) The security measures needed to prevent such behavior. Pertinent illustrations are provided that include descriptions of approaches by one suburban school district, some city schools, some special classes and schools, several large urban school, and some positive alternatives to student suspension. See ERIC Abstract #ED 084632.

1163.   Smith, G. "Guidance Packet." Washington, D. C.: Office Of Education, Department Of Health, Education and Welfare, January, 1980.

Functions of guidance groups, the guidance counselor, the advocacy program, and the guidance committee of the High School in the Community, New Haven, Connecticut, are described. HSC, High School in the Community, was designed to provide a choice of learning environments within the public school system. It serves students dissatisfied with their previous school experience. Guidance groups consists of a staff member who doubles as a guidance teacher and approximately 20 students. Guidance teachers keep track of students' attendance and academic records. Advise students regarding personal or school related problems, acts as advocates and as liaison between the guidance counselor and the student, and meet with parents. The guidance counselor works individually with students planning to graduate, with students who need more counseling than the guidance teacher can give, and with the student membership coordinator. This advocacy program is designed to deal with behavior problems. Procedures include first and second offense meetings with a guidance teacher, counsel, member of the administrative unit, parents, and a student advocate to assist the student in preparing his or her case. Recommendations deriving from the second offense hearing entails either assigning the student a work project, involving outside professional help for the student, or referring the student for placement in another educational program. The guidance committee consists of four members including one student, one parent and acts as a form for all guidance-related ideas and problems. See ERIC Abstract #ED 175787.

1164.   Smith, W. F. (Comp.). Ways to Understanding: A Teacher In-Service Conference Funded Through the Emergency Assistance Program, United State Office of Education, for Priority I Teachers. Washington, D.C.: Office of Education, Department of Health, Education and Welfare, May, 1973.

The in-service workshop reported in this document was part of a staff development program for teachers in thirty-nine elementary and middle schools. It was funded under a Grant from the United States Office of Education under provisions of Emergency School Assistance Program. Each workshop consisted of a one-day group presentation followed by small group discussions. Included in this workshop was a section on "Discipline in Desegregated School" by J.J. Salamone. See ERIC Abstract ED 072170.

1165.   Smith, W. I. Guidelines to Classroom Behavior. Brooklyn, New York: Book-Lab, Inc.

The author presents some general thoughts on classroom behavior and presents interesting chapters on the following: 1) Some General Thoughts; 2) Two Negatives Don't Make a Positive; 3) Something to Fight For; 4) Keep the Main Goals in Mind; 5) Improving the Sense of Responsibility; 6) Doing the Unexpected; 7) Know Thyself; 8) The Quest for Attention; 9) The Jujitsu Method; 10) Getting the Gangs Together; 11) Here Comes the Judge; 12) Making Life Easier; 13) Flexible Routines; 14) Parent Cooperation; 15) One More Time Now--A Quick Review.

1166.   Solomon, D. and Kendall, A. J. Children in classrooms -- an investigation of person-environment interaction. Chicago, Illinois: Spencer Foundation, 1980.

This book describes a research project which was supported by a grant from the Spencer Foundation, Chicago, Illinois, and was conducted under the auspices of the Montgomery County Public Schools, Rockville, Maryland. Included are the following chapters, 1) persons and environments, 2) students in classrooms, 3) the pilot study, 4) the main study: general plan and data collection procedures, 5) deriving dimensions of classroom environment, 6) deriving dimensions of child characteristics and educational outcomes, 7) identifying classroom types and child types, 8) effects of classroom types and child types on outcomes, 9) effects of classroom dimensions and child dimensions on outcomes, 10) summary, conclusion, and implications.

1167.   Stainback, S. B. Classroom Discipline--A Positive Approach. Second printing. Springfield, Illinois: Charles C. Thomas, publisher, 1977.

This book is written to provide specific guidelines for the prospective and beginning teacher concerning techniques of classroom control, as well as to provide a helpful reference for the experienced teacher. The major focus is toward a concise compilation of discipline techniques that have been found to be effective through practical application. These techniques can be used to humanize classroom management because they offer a viable alternative to out moded techniques of classroom control such as physical punishment. The text is divided into four sections. Section one presents three distinct strategies for educating children who exhibit disruptive behavior. The purpose is to provide a brief comparison of the operate conditioning strategy adopted by the authors, with two other popular strategies. Section two includes preventive techniques for maintaining classroom discipline. It also suggests measures to employ after the disruptive behavior has occurred. These are practical techniques that can and should be implemented in almost any classroom. Section three provides two specific plans, based on operant conditioning principles for modifying the behaviors of extremely disruptive students. Also included in this section are a discussion of various items that can be used as reinforcers in a school setting and the presentation of ethical issues involved in the use of an operate conditioning approach. Section four consists of supplementary selected articles that outline ways of preventing and/or handling discipline problems. Only articles written specifically for classroom teachers are presented.

1168.   State Department of Education of South Carolina. <u>Alternatives to School Disciplinary and Suspension Problems</u>. Columbia, S. C., State Department of Education, 1976.

This book provides information as to various alternatives that can be used in seeking solutions to disciplinary problems. Included are the following chapters: 1) Discipline Problems; 2) Alternative Program; 3) Legal Rights of Students; 4) Laws on Discipline; 5) Conclusions.

1169.   Stebbins, R. A. <u>Teachers and meaning--definitions of classroom situations</u>. Leiden, the Netherlands: E. J. Brill, 1975.

Both of the hypotheses are presented in this monograph, 1) teachers tend to avoid provoking their most troublesome students when confronting them or when considering a confrontation with them for disorderly behavior, 2) teachers have a disorderly behavior set, or a readiness to act to avert or arrest misconduct, which is part of the definition of disorderly behavior situations, but which is activated only under certain conditions, 3) teachers who instruct large groups of low ability pupils have a complex custodial orientation toward their work, 4) teachers view the chronically tardy as an insoluble problem, which must be indured despite its continued threat to their aim of

intellectual training. Included are the following sections:
1) the definition of the situation, 2) further theory and
conceptual relatives, 3) studying the definition of the
situation, 4) the meaning of disorderly behavior I, 5) the
meaning of disorderly behavior II, 6) the meaning of
academic performance I, 7) the meaning of academic performance II, 8) the meaning of tardiness, 9) toward relevance.
This is publication 10 in the series of monographs and
theoretical studies in sociology and anthropology in honor
of Nels Anderson.

1170.   Stenhouse, L. Discipline in Schools: A Symposium. New
York: Pergamon Press, 1967.

In the first paper in this collection the author has placed
the idea of discipline in a broad, educational setting,
relating it to some central strands of educational theory,
to problems of curriculum, and to different stages of
schooling. He has attempted to set the teachers' responsibility for discipline and for the general pattern of his
relations with his pupil in the context of the nature and
purposes of the education. In the second paper, the editor
has attempted an analysis of the dynamics and mechanisms of
discipline in the classroom, building a model from concepts
developed in social psychology and the sociology of small
groups. The third paper analyzes, on a sociological base,
the factors in the environment of the pupils outside the
school which bear on the problem of discipline in the classroom. The fourth paper is psychological in its approach.
It considers discipline in the context of child development
and alerts teachers to those abnormal patterns of behavior
which suggests the need for clinical treatment. The final
paper concentrates on two areas which seem to present
recurrent difficulties to students: namely, the relation of
freedom to discipline and the justification of punishment.
These problems are clafied by philosophical techniques,
which exemplifies the modern conception of the role of
philosophy in educational thinking.

1171.   Stephens, T. M. (Ed.) The Charles E. Merrill Series On
Behavioral Techniques In The Classroom. Columbus, Ohio:
Charles E. Merrill Publishing Company, 1974.

This book is one in a series devoted to a particular aspect
of schooling and/or behavioral methodology. This text
focuses on modifying disruptive behavior in the regular
classroom. It deals with the current issues which accompany
the behavior modification techniques in schools. Various
aspects of behavioral approaches are discussed as well as
how each is applied, when it should be used, and how it
shall be evaluated. Behavioral analysis utilizes the
following basic procedures for changing behavior in children: 1) Selecting a target of behavior, 2) Changing the
behavior's consequences, 3) Keeping records, 4) Shaping the
behavior, 5) Continuously evaluating the data. The first
section of the book critically evaluates the present

position of applying behavior modification in various classroom settings. Chapter one introduces the readers to current trends in education for handling behavior problem children. The interaction between the child and his classroom environment in creating deviant behavior is stressed in Chapter two. Behavior modification procedures as they are most commonly applied today, and a critical evaluation of these procedures are presented in Chapters three and four. Section two of this book discusses different types of reinforcement procedures and teaching strategies which could help make behavior modification more practical for the regular classroom teacher. The critical question asked of each procedure is whether it is feasible to apply in a regular classroom setting. The topics in section two present hierarchy of procedures and strategies leading ultimately to self-managed and intrinsic reinforcement. The remainder of the volume is devoted to concomitant topics often felt to be useful or necessary to applying behavior modification in the classroom, but which are seldom emphasized, or even mentioned, in textbooks on the subject. The importance of individualizing instruction, in the various facets of classroom structure are discussed in Chapter ten. The final chapters stresses the vital role of the regular class teacher in the successful implementation of the behavioral approach to teaching.

1172.   Stephens, T. M. <u>Social Skills in the Classroom</u>. Columbus, Ohio: The Ohio State University, 1979.

Materials in this handbook were developed to be used within a directive teaching approach. Directive teaching is skill training oriented within a diagnostic-prescriptive model of teaching. First, the behavior is defined and stated in observable terms, specifying both the movements which make up the behavior and the conditions under which the behavior is to occur. Second, the behavior is assessed, and the student's level of performance on a particular skill ids determined. Third, teaching strategy are prescribed to fit the student's needs as determined by assessment. Step one. Defined behaviors to be taught. Step two. Assess target behaviors. Step three. Develop instructional strategy. Step four. Evaluate the effectiveness of the strategy. Included in the book are the following chapters: 1) Introduction to Teaching Classroom Social Skills, 2) Indexing and Coding System, 3) Social Skills List, 4) Care for Environment, 5) Dealing with Emergencies, 6) Lunchroom Behavior, 7) Movement Around Environment, 8) Accepting Authority, 9) Coping With Conflict, 10) Gaining Attention, 11) Greeting Others, 12) Helping Others, 13) Making Conversation, 14) Organized Play, 15) Positive Attitude Toward Others, 16) Playing Informally, 17) Property-Own and Others, 18) Accepting Consequences, 19) Ethical Behavior, 20) Expressing Feeling, 21) Positive Attitude Toward Self, 22) Responsible Behavior, 23) Self Care, 24) Asking and Answering Questions, 25) Attending Behavior, 26) Classroom Discussion, 27) Completing Tasks, 28) Following Directions,

29) Group Activities, 30) Independent Work, 31) On Task Behavior, 32) Performing Before Others, and 33) Quality of Work.

1173.   Stevens, D. M. & Benson, W. W. Strategies for Instructional Management. Boston, Massachusetts, Allyn & Bacon, Inc., 1979.

Professional efforts and instructional outcomes constitute the major targets of the strategies of management in developing a strong instructional program with its chosen acceptable goals. This means that the concept of account- ability becomes one of testing not whether a person should be continued in or dismissed from position but rather whether the professional effort has been appropriately supported and applied so that the outcome selected for the total program are being achieved. The chapters in this book present many aspects of this concern. The examples of strategies following many sections in the book are intended to bring the general discussion into sharp focus so that action has an acceptable payoff both for those instituting the action and for the recipients of the action. Included are the following chapters: 1) management acceptability, 2) instructional impact--response areas, 3) synthesis of purpose and effort, 4) reciprocities as building blocks, 5) loyalties and influences, 6) talent and decisions, 7) categories of work process, 8) relationships of goals and processes, 9) delegation of instructional tasks, 10) coordination of instructional tasks, 11) the antecedents to action, 12) auditing as continuous evaluation, 13) multi- faceted accountability, 14) direction through indirection, 15) directed self management, 16) strategies and the strategist.

1174.   Stoops, E. and King-Stoops, J. Discipline or Disaster? Bloomington, Indiana: The Phi Delta Kappa Educational Foundation, Fastback Series, 1972.

Included in this book are sections on the following areas concerning discipline: 1) Discipline as a way of life -- basis for discipline, kinds of discipline, sources of discipline, current need for discipline, parents and discipline, students and discipline, criteria for school discipline, 2) Discipline policies for the district, the building and the classroom -- discipline policies for the district, discipline policies for the building, discipline problems for the classroom, 3) Classroom discipline -- or disaster for the teacher -- general tips on classroom control, problem types and problem situations, 4) How to avert disaster -- criteria for establishing classroom standards, sample questions standards, sample standards for the playground.

1175.   Stoppleworth, L. J. Everything is Fine Now that Leonard isn't Here. New York: MSS Information Corporation, 1973.

This book takes the point of view that the most disturbing behavior in a classroom is learned behavior; that is, that it is maintained in existence by the consequences that it receives from its immediate environment. In the first part of this book, representative articles have been included to illustrate divergent ways of looking at distrubed behavior in general, including the effects of labels and stigma and the sociological influences on the identification of deviant behavior. The second part of the book is devoted exclusively to the consideration of various environmental consequences for disturbing behavior in educational settings. The authors feel that teachers posses the technology with which to manage much of the disturbing behavior they are presented with each day. The problem of teachers becomes how to use childrens energy to manage the disturbing behavior in an efficient and satisfying and educationally productive way.

1176.   Storen, H. F. The Disadvantaged Early Adolescent: More Effective Teaching. New York: McGraw Hill Book Company, 1968.

This book is addressed to future teachers and the treatment of the junior high school years contains records of teachers presently in the field. Chapter I, summarizes the characteristics of disadvantaged youth. Chapter II, deals with the problems of establishing rapport, motivation, and discipline. Chapter III, focuses on diagnosing the students' needs and readiness. Chapter IV, examines the selection and organization of the content of the academic experience. Chapter V, deals with the methods used for presenting the content, the importance of structure, flexible planning, and discussion techniques. See ERIC Abstract ED 033994.

1177.   Stradley, W. E. & Aspinall, R. D. Discipline In The Junior High/Middle School: A Handbook For Teachers, Counselors And Administrators. New York: The Center For Applied Research In Education, Incorporated, 1975.

Teachers and other educators working with middle/junior high students usually feel this age group is the most difficult group with which to work as far as classroom discipline is concerned. Often children of this age are labeled unruly, uncooperative, misunderstood, unpredictable, lacking self discipline and hard headed. This age level also reveals such traits as sensitiveness, feelings of insecurity, desire to be recognized, and a need for direct understanding and guidance. This book has been written for middle level teachers who are looking for ideas, methods and techniques that will help them work more effectively with the paradoxical entities known as pre and early adolescence. It places special emphasis on the specific areas about which middle school and junior high teachers have expressed most concern--respect for authority, peer relationships, student teacher conflicts, attendance, group and individual behavior and vandelism. Chapters include: 1) Using preventive discipline approaches, 2) Helping students improve their self images, 3) Methods for developing respect for authority, 4) Improving student peer relationship, 5) Resolving student teacher conflicts, 6) Techniques for reducing attendance problems, 7) Reducing acts of vandalism, 8) Solving behavior problems outside the classroom, 9) Dealing with student group problems, 10) Utilizing a discipline ladder of referral.

1178.   Striefel, S. Teaching a Child to Imitate--A Manual for Developing Motor Skills in Retarded Children. Lawrence, Kansas: H and H Enterprizes, Inc., 1974.

This book is a significant work in the area of behavior management for handicapped children. The techniques presented here will find a wide application in various studies where both professional and paraprofessionals, as well as parents are engaged in efforts to train retarded children in basic motor imitation. This publication is designed to be used by parents, teachers, institutional workers and therapists who may or may not be familiar with behavior management principles. The program is intended to help such workers establish or improve the imitative skills of handicapped children so they can learn more complex skills such as speech and self-help. The ability to imitate is basic to the social and speech development of any child. This work is intended to help handicapped learners acquire the imitation skills they must have to travel the road toward normalization. Included are the following chapters: 1) Introduction, 2) Reinforcement, 3) Entry Behaviors, 4) Preliminary Phases of Motor Imitation Program, 5) Motor Imitation Program, 6) Training, and 7) Miscellaneous.

1179.   Sulzer-Azaroff, B., & Mayer, G. R. Applying Behavior-Analysis Procedures with Children and Youth. New York: Holt, Rinehart and Winston, 1977.

Applied behavior analysis is the applied branch of the field known alternatively as operant conditioning or as the experimental analysis of behavior, which is a laboratory based area of knowledge. To fully understand the procedures for educating children by means of the principles of applied behavior analysis, an understanding of the laboratory derived principles is necessary. This book provides this background information. It describes schedules of reinforcement, stimulus control, DRO, DRL, multiple schedules, successive approximation, extinction and many other concepts and procedures established in laboratory studies. The authors have described laboratory based findings so that readers can easily understand the basic principles of operant conditioning. A set of general goals is provided in the book at the beginning of each unit. The study-guide is included to be used with the traditional course foremat to guide learning or as a discussion, recessitation, or laboratory manual. Included are the following chapters: 1) Introduction to Applied Behavior Analysis with Children and

Youth, 2) Goal Selection: Initial Considerations, 3) Goal
Selection: Ethical Considerations, 4) From Goals to Objec-
tives, 5) Selecting Observational Systems, 6) Interval
Recording and Implementing Observational Systems, 7) Con-
siderations in Selecting and Implementing Procedural
Strategies, 8) Increasing Behavior: Reinforcement, 9)
Selecting Effective Positive Reinforcers, 10) Implementing
Effective Reinforcement Procedures, 11) Reducing Behavior:
Extinction, 12) Stimulus Control: What is it?, 13) Stimulus
Control: Arranging Behavioral Antecedents, 1., 14) Stimulus
Control: Arranging Behavioral Antecedents, 2., 15) Stimulus
Control: Failing, 16) Teacher Behavior.

1180.   Sulzer, B. & Mayer, G. R. Behavior Modification
Procedures--For School Personnel. Hinsdale, Illinois: The
Dryden Press, Inc., 1972.

This book applies many of the operant learning principles
that govern human behavior to the modification of behavior
in the school setting. It is a pragmatic text that has been
written primarily for elementary and secondary school
educators, such as teachers, administrators, school
psychologists, counselors, social workers and others concerned with the development of children. The book is
divided into six main sections. The first chapter is an
introductory chapter. It provides the reader with a basic
overview and a model for a behavior modification program.
Part One, discusses the use of various procedures designed
to increase the occurrence of existing behaviors; Part Two,
the application of procedures designed to teach new
behaviors; Part Three, methods for maintaining behavior;
Part Four, methods for reducing behaviors; Part Five, on
carrying out and evaluating the program has been written
primarily for those who will be engaged in educational
consulting research activities. Preceding each chapter,
specific student learning objectives are listed. The completion of these objectives is used by the student as his
criterian for mastery of the chapter. Each chapter also
contains a number of practical exercises that have been
field-tested by over one hundred students.

1181.   Sylvester, R. The Elementary Teacher And Pupil Behavior.
West Nyack, New York: Parker Publishing Company, 1971.

The proper study of the elementary school is the school
itself. The rapid changes now occuring in our society
demand that the schools educate citizens who can function
responsibly with a mimimum of imposed control. This is a
book on classroom behavior written for the 1970's. It is
addressed to the teacher in the elementary classroom, but it
assumes that the ideas will be carried out jointly by
teacher and pupil--not by the teacher on the pupil as was
traditional in books in earlier years but by teachers and
pupils exploring and experimenting together on how best to
live with each other in a classroom society that mirrors
greater society in many significant ways. The book suggests

many explorations that teachers and pupils can make as they
try to define the essential nature of the school, discover
the conflicts that exist in societal values, create a school
environment that all can live and work in, examine the
present role of traditional behavior categories and
controls, and seek ways to developing self-discipline.
Included are the following chapters: 1) Turning the child's
needs to learning challenges, 2) The conflicting values that
affect pupil behavior, 3) Projecting responsible adult
society in your classroom, 4) Observing your students as a
group and as individuals, 5) Creating a wholesome and
attractive school environment, 6) Using imaginative teaching
methods to increase positive behavior, 7) Understanding the
hidden causes for misbehavior, 8) Responding respectively to
misbehavior, 9) Helping children to develop self-discipline.

1182.   Tanaka, J. Classroom Management--A Guide for the School
Consultant. Springfield, Illinois: Charles C. Thomas,
Publisher, 1979.

School consultation may include a broad range of activities
and involve numerous school personnel addressing a variety
of problem areas. Within this broad context, it is difficult for the consultant to function effectively. He must
define his role as a consultant, identify the areas of
agreement that should be negotiated with the teacher and
principal, and acquire an understanding of the behavior
principles upon which the development of classroom management procedures are based. This book is intended for use by
the school consultant and includes the following parts: 1)
Preparation for Consultation; 2) Problem Solving; 3)
Consultation Experiences.

1183.   Tanner, L. N. Classroom Discipline for Effective
Teaching and Learning. New York: Holt, Reinhart and
Winston, 1978.

This book is designed for anyone who is interested in
orderly classrooms, places where learning can take place.
Classroom teachers, college instructors, school administrators and parents may find answers for their concern about
school discipline in the body of knowledge and the set of
guiding principles for classroom management. It is a
practical guide for those who will be or are practicing
education. It is designed for use in courses which deal
with methods of teaching and for the classroom teacher who
may be experiencing disciplinary problems. Included are the
following chapters: 1) The Nature of Discipline, 2) Discipline and Development, 3) Discipline and the Curriculum, 4)
Discipline and Teaching, 5) Lack of Attention and Teacher
Expectation, 6) Discipline in Special Settings, 7) The
Ecology of Classroom Discipline, 8) Socializing the
Unsocialized, 9) Dealing with Discipline Problems, 10)
Discipline and the Needs and Rights of Children.

1184.   Thoresen,   Carl   E.   (Ed)   Behavior   Modification   in
Education--the   Seventy   Second   Year   Book   of   the   National
Society   for   the   Study   of   Education,   Part   1.   Chicago,
Illinois: the university of Chicago press, 1973.

The purpose of this yearbook is to A) provide a perspective
on the historical and contemporary development of behavior
modification, B) analyze and synthesize the work on the
subject as it relates to education theory, C) stimulate
inquiry by professional educators as to the applicability of
behavior modification in educational practice, D) identify
and deal with the issues of behavior modification as it
relates to education, E) broaden professional perspectives
of educational decision makers concerning behavior modification. Included are the following sections: 1) teaching in
the classroom, 2) specific problem areas, 3) behavioral
systems, 4) problems and prospects.

1185.   Todd, K. R. Promoting Mental Health in the Classroom. A
Handbook for Teachers. Washington, D.C.: U.S. Government
Printing Office, 1973.

This handbook is a course of study to teach teachers at all
grade levels to understand, implement, and teach to their
students the causal approach to human behavior. Provided
are thirteen guide units designed to help the teachers: 1)
Recognize the need for promoting mental health in the classroom, 2) Understand the causes and effects of behavior, 3)
Change behavior in the classroom, 4) Teach students the
causal approach to behavior in different curriculum areas,
5) Develop curriculum materials for the classroom that will
promote mental health, 6) Promote individualization and
self-directed learning, 7) Understand group dynamics and
inter-group relationships. See ERIC Abstract ED 084209.

1186.   Turney, C. and Cairns, L. G. Classroom Management and
Discipline--Series 3 Handbook. Sidney, Australia: Sidney
University Press, Sidney Micro Skills Unit, 1976.

The Sidney Micro Skills are being used in a variety of
settings and in a variety of ways. They have been employed
in pre- and in-service education of primary and secondary
school teachers, in military education, in training practice
teacher supervisors, in the educating of teachers, in
research projects and in parent education. The book
presents an introduction to the skilled courses, this introduction dealing specifically with classroom management and
discipline. Chapter One, includes an introduction to the
skills courses. Chapter Two, deals with writings on classroom management and discipline and Chapter Three, deals with
skill of the classroom management and discipline. A
selected bibliography is included.

1187.   The University of the State of New York. Disruptive
students. The state education department bureau of school
social services, Albany, New York, 1972.

Included in this publication is a practice which describes the disruptive student who is usually defined as one who interferes with the learning process. Sections include: 1) introduction and scope, 2) legal aspects in security in secondary schools, 3) identification and prevention, 4) special schools, classes and alternative programs, 5) elementary school programs, 6) school policy, and 7) illustrations. These illustrations include sections on suburban school districts, city schools, schools for boys, special classes in schools, security in large urban schools, and positive alternatives to student suspension.

1188.   Upstein, C. Classroom Management In Teaching: Persistant Problems And Rational Solutions. Reston, Virginia: Reston Publishing Company Incorporated, 1979.

This book is a reasoned approach to living with children for a large part of the day and helping them become everything they are capable of. Included are the following chapters: 1) Solutions Based On Physical Management, 2) Solutions Based On Management Of Time, 3) Solutions Based On Pupil-Teacher Communication, 4) Solutions Based On Pupil-Pupil Communication, 5) Solutions Based On Curriculum, 6) Long-term Solutions, 7) The Philosophical Basis For The Solutions, 8) Fate Control For The Teacher. Author attempts to identify those human problems that arise in a specific setting -- the classroom. They are problems faced by teachers of children whoever and wherever they are. Given certain contingencies, certain consequences, certain common behaviors appear. The author has attempted to draw together what is known in the educational profession about changing behavior, synthesizing it, and applying it to specific classroom behaviors.

1189.   Vest, L. S. and Summers, V. M. Procedures on Classroom Organization for the Primary Teacher. New York: Exposition Press, 1971.

This handbook for the elementary teacher provides a practical approach to classroom organization and pupil control. It is the belief of the authors that teachers enter the classroom with a sincere desire for success as well as enthusiasm for their roles as teachers. However, they soon lose their feeling of effectiveness and security because they become bogged down from lack of a structured system of organization. Teachers have expressed a need for meaningful learning activities which can be given to children as they engage in work at their seats. These activities should present a progression of readiness skills in eye, hand and motor coordination. They should help build a good attitude toward learning. The following chapters are included in this book: 1) Classroom Organization; 2) Suggested Instructional Procedures; 3) Experience Charts; 4) Beginning Grouping for Use of Materials; 5) Beginning Independent Seat Work.

1190.   Vogelsberg, T. & Porcella, A. <u>When Your Child</u>
<u>Misbehaves</u>. Logan, Utah: Utah State University, 1975.

This sixty page paper back book is designed to assist
parents in dealing with their children's less desirable
behavior patterns. It utilizes rules and brief examples to
help parents deal with behaviors such as teasing, sulking,
whining, tantrums, and hitting. It also uses behavior
modification approaches with charts, reinforcers, and
complete instructions. See ERIC Abstract IN028554.

1191.   Volkman, C. S. <u>The Last Straw--A Handbook of Solutions</u>
<u>to School Behavior Problems</u>. San Francisco, California: R
and E Research Associates, Inc., 1978.

This reference book is conceived as an experiental resource
aid for elementary teachers, designed to investigate many
typical classroom problems and their possible solutions.
Some of the behavior areas or problem categories are
generalized in order to allow for convenient problem identi-
fication. Included are an Introduction, Sorting the
Haystack: Philosophy of Investigating Behavioral Problems,
Setting the Foundation to Behavior Patterns, First
Clenchers, Heart Breakers and Night Tossers, Debriefing and
Desensitization.

1192.   Volkmore, C., Langstaff, A., and Higgins, M. <u>Structuring</u>
<u>the Classroom for Success</u>. Columbus, Ohio: Charles E.
Merrill Publishing Co., 1974.

Authors discuss the use of behaviorist techniques in the
classroom with fundamental humanistic learnings as well.
They stress that the affective environment is every bit as
important as the teaching methods of techniques used by the
teacher. Their philosophy stressed an open activity based
environment, allowing for the individual development of each
student within it. Included are the following chapters: 1)
Overview of Open Education; 2) Room Environment; 3) Creating
Activity Centers; 4) Behavior Management Principles; 5)
Behavior Management in the Classroom; 6) Individualized
Instruction; 7) The Open Classroom-Some Ideas on How to
Start.

1193.   Vredevoe, L. E. <u>Discipline</u>. Dubuque, Iowa: Kendall/Hunt
Publishing Company, 1971.

The purpose of this book is to bring together the
theoretical and practical aspects of the problems relating
to behavior in the school and community. Although the
greatest emphasis is upon the school, the practices and
solutions are also applicable to the home and community.
The principals's recommendations and suggestions are the
result of twenty years of study and travel by the author.
The selective law cases present principle summariein
Behavior Control, 4) Responsibility and Accountability, 5)
School Discipline in Europe, Middle East, Canada and Mexico,

6) Corporal Punishment and Behavior, 7) Embarrassment and Ridicule As a Means of Discipline, 8) Dealing With Tantrums on Both Sides of the Desk, 9) Group vs Individual Punishment, 10) Good Lesson Planning Develops Good Discipline, 11) Reading Ability and Behavior, 12) Changing Patterns of Behavior in Socioeconomic and Ethnic Groups, 13) Vandalism, Strikes and Riots, 14) Desegregation and School Discipline, 15) The Courts and School Discipline, 16) Innovative Practices in Behavior Control, 17) New Breed, New Challenge, New Hope.

1194.   Walker, J. E. and Shea, T. M. Behavior Modification -- A Practical Approach for Educators. New York: C.V. Mosvy Company, 1976.

This text was written to provide experienced teachers, teachers in training and paraprofessionals with a guide for the application of behavior modification techniques in special and general educational settings. It is designed to aid teachers working in self-contained classes in resource centers, teachers engaged in itinerant and consultative services, and regular and secondary regular classroom teachers having responsibility for normal and handicapped children. It may be used as a basic text for pre-service and in-service courses or as a self-study guide. The discipline of behavior modification is introduced in Chapter I. The basic principle of behavior modification is presented in Chapter II. The exposition of each principle is supplemented by practical examples from classroom teaching experiences. Chapter II also includes a list of reinforcers for application in the classroom. In Chapter III the reader is given step-by-step instructions for modifying behavior in the classroom. Each step is discussed and exemplified. Several specific methods for increasing acceptable behaviors and decreasing unacceptable behaviors are reviewed in Chapters IV and V. In the final chapter the ethics of behavior management are discussed, and the alternatives to the techniques recommended in the text are explored. This chapter concludes with a presentation of guidelines for the use of suggested intervention. The text is written in non-technical language for maximum readibility by a broad audience of professionals, paraprofessionals, and college students. The primary goal of the work is the ethical, effective, and efficient management of the behavior problems of children as they learn to explore, manipulate, and ultimately controls their world.

1195.   Wallen, D. and Wallen, L. L. Effective Classroom Management -- Abridged Edition. Boston: Allyn and Beacon, Inc., 1978.

The authors have been concerned with the tunnel vision evidenced in much of the literature dealing with classroom management. Simple, uni-dimensional solutions are offered to what are, in actuality, complex, multi-dimensional problems. The concerned teacher is offered a choice between such widely divergent and contradictory panaceas as open education and behavior modification. The intent of the authors is to make this study of classroom management multi-dimensional. They have accomplished this by focusing on three major roles of the teacher; instructional manager, group leader, and counselor.

1196.   Webster, S. W. Discipline in the Classroom--Basic Principles and Problems. San Francisco, California: Chandler Publishing Company, 1968.

This book has two major aims. First, it seeks to help the reader develop a frame of reference that will enhance his ability to understand problem behaviors and to deal effectively with them. In striving to realize this objective, the book emphasizes that persistent acts of pupil malbehavior must never be viewed as isolated incidents. Such acts should be seen as products of possible inter-actions among several factors which include the personality of the student, the personality of teacher, and the human and physical environments of the classroom. The second part of the book aims to reinforce what the reader might have learned from the first part by providing him with opportu-nities to consider case reports of specific student behavior problems. The book has two major divisions. Part one contains six chapters. The initial chapter discusses the multi-faceted nature of discipline and presents the frame of reference which is stressed throughout the book. The next two chapters deal with those factors influencing the attitudes and behaviors of children and adolescents, with special attention to disadvantaged and certain ethnic minority students. Chapter four focuses upon the teacher as a possible contributing factor to the behavior problems which arise in his class. Ideas and considerations are suggested for dealing with incidental, as well as persistent and more serious forms of student malbehavior in chapter five, along with behavior modification principles that appear to have important implications for teachers. Chapter six contains a brief discussion of the roles of a teacher in his relation with the students. Part two of the book con-tains four sections. The first section presents ten cases of student malbehavior, section B contains the first diagnostic analysis of each case problems. Section C presents information that supplements each case problem. Section D presents the reviewers' final analysis of the problems in their suggested strategies for dealing with them successfully.

1197.   Welch, I. D. & Schutte, W. Discipline: A Shared Experience. Fort Collins, Colorado: Shields Publishing Company, Inc. 1973.

Discipline, in its most effective form, is a shared expe-rience. Too often, it can become a sort of psychological tug-of-war between teachers and students. The classroom becomes a battleground on which teachers seek to subdue and coerce students into doing things that teachers think are important and the students do not. As a consequence of the battleground approach to discipline, many schools have become grim and sometimes inhumane places. The authors maintain that children learn discipline when it is person- ally meaningful to them and shared with concerned and significant others. Children do not learn to make decisions by having decisions made for them; nor do they learn responsibility by being denied responsibility. Responsi- bility and self-control are learned best when the opportu- nity to assume responsibility is readily available and when the opportunity is a shared and an experienced with others. Various situations that teachers and parents will encounter with discipline concerns are presented in this book. Sections include: 1) Introduction,   2) Responding to the Negative,   3) Pay Attention to the Good Things,   4) The Do's and Dont's of Discipline.

1198.   Welsh, R. S.   Delinquency, Corporal Punishment, in the Schools.   Washington, D.C.:   Department of Health, Education and Welfare, 1979.

One of the fifty-two theoretical papers on school crime and its relation to poverty. This book reports that there is a growing trend in this country to blame youth crime on parental over-permissiveness. Available data failed to support this and show that all types of crime, including school crime, develop within families and school systems emphasizing obversive and authoritarain discipline tech- niques. Also, racism and personal injustice are more common in an authoritarian atmosphere. Of all types of obversive behaviors, corporal punishment appears most apt to induce aggression. A theory relating delinquent aggression to the severity of parental discipline is sketched out, and it is suggested that a National effort be made to discourage the use of corporal punishment as a socially acceptable child- rearing technique. Since corporal punishment tends to produce both fear and anger, it's continued use in the school can only be counter productive to the learning process. A joint effort should be made to train teachers in non-obversive but effective techniques of pupil control. In addition, individual teachers need the support of well trained guidance personnel who are willing to enter homes and work with the behavioral problems at their source. See ERIC Abstract ED 158369.

1199.   Wenk, E. and Harlow, N.   School, Crime and Disruption. Davis, California: Responsible Action, 1978.

This anthology which was sponsored by the National Institute of Education is part of a national effort to respond to the school crime problem by gathering and disseminating informa- tion on its volume were solicited for a collection of papers sponsored by the office of the secretary of the Department of Health, Education and Welfare and compiled by the Research Center of the National Counsel of Crime and

Delinquency. This earlier work was based on a nationwide solicitation effort to obtain and interdiscipliinary collection of theoretical papers on the causes of crime in the nation's schools. With an emphasis on its relationship to poverty. The remainder of the papers were developed specifically for this anthology. The collection begins with two papers describing approaches to the study of crime in schools -- a prerequisite to the implementation of effective prevention program. These papers are followed by a group of seven articles which are primarily explanitory, suggesting coherent theories of causation, but which also offer concrete suggestions for altering conditions in school or society which contribute to school crime. The third category of papers differ from the second primarily in emphasis. While drawing on various theories of crime causation these eight papers concentrate specific programs of actions which can be taken to reduce school crime. Included in the book are the following articles: 1) studing school crime, 2) the social organization of the high school, 3) scholastic experiences, self-esteem and delinquent behavior, 4) aesthetic factors in school vandalism, 5) the obsolescence of adolescence, 6) school crime, power and the student sub-culture, 7) delinquent behavior in the public schools, 8) school community linkages, 9) value orientations and delinquency, 10) human relations training in school settings, 11) decentralization reconsidered, 12) the human ecology of school crime, 13) negotiating school conflict to prevent student delinquency, 14) training specialists to work with disruptive students, 15) the child care apprenticeship program, 16) tomorrow's education, 17) democratic education and the prevention and the prevention of delinquency.

1200.   Wheeler, A. H. & Fox W. L. A Teacher's Guide to Writing Instructional Objectives. Lord, Kansas: H & H Enterprizes Inc., 1972.

The goals of American education are based on the needs of individuals living in a modern technological society. Our educational goals are derived from a philosophy which springs from the realities of living in a contemporary society, from the values inherent in the democratic way of life, and from the characteristics and needs of the individual. In order to help the individual realize these goals, American education has experienced a significant increase in the scope and depth of educational programs. The rising costs of expanded educational programs, and the desperate need to ensure that every individual has mastered the basic functional language and arithmetic skills, has resulted in a definite trend toward making the teacher accountable for his or her practices. Teachers have found that the evaluation of instruction requires a clear specification of the expected changes in student performance. If students can demonstrate expected changes in their performance as a result of the instructional program, the teacher has powerful evidence for suggesting that the instructional

program is the specification of the outcome of instruction.
Clearly specified instructional objectives are required if
we are to objectively evaluate the effectiveness of our
educational program. This book is a programmed guide for
educators who wish to learn to write instructional objectives which clearly specify desired educational outcomes in
terms of observable behavior. This booklet presents a
system for writing instructional objectives in terms which
clearly describe the desired final outcome of the instruction, which state the conditions under which the final
behavior will occur, and which specify that criteria by
which the final performance is judged. Included are the
following chapters: 1) Introduction, 2) Specifying Educational Outcomes--Educational Goals, Educational Objectives,
Instructional Objectives, 3) A System for Writing Instructional Objectives, 4) Exercises in Writing Instructional
Objectives, 5) Three Categories of Action Verbs -- 1. Action
verbs that are directly observable, 2. Ambiguous action
verbs, 3. Action verbs that are not directly observable, 6)
Translating Educational Goals into Instructional Objectives,
7) Exercises in Translating Educational Goals into Instructional Objectives, 8) References.

1201.   Wiener, D. N.   Classroom Management of Discipline.
Itasca, Ill.:   F. E. Peacock Publishers, Inc., 1972.

This book presents the views of a psychologist as an objective observer and changer of human behavior, to add to the
views of the classroom teacher, and a systematic approach to
the maintenance of classroom discipline and to training in
self-discipline, to add to the first aid and improvisation
approaches to the handling of classroom problems. Included
are the following chapters: 1) A Theory of Discipline and
Achievement; 2) Purposes and Problems of Classroom Discipline; 3) Structuring the Classroom for Discipline Achievement; 4) Setting Goals and Tasks; 5) Implementing Tasks; 6)
Follow-Up; 7) Learning Problems of Students; 8) Emotional
Problems of Students; 9) Teachers' Personal Problems and
Classroom Discipline.

1202.   Wise, J. H. (Ed.)   Proceedings--Conference on Corporal
Punishment in the Schools: A National Debate.   Washington,
D.C.:   National Institute of Education, U.S. Department of
Health, Education and Welfare, February 18, 1977.

The Child Protection Center of Children's Hospital National
Medical Center, Washington, D.C., hosted a national invita-
tional conference on child abuse. One section of that
conference, supported in part by funds from the National
Institute of Education, devoted an intensive two and one-
half days to a singular topic: Corporal Punishment in the
Schools. The examination of corporal punishment in the
schools proved both unprecedented and timely; unprecedented,
in the fact that for the first time the question of corporal
punishment was seriously considered and intensively discussed within the overall framework of a national conference

on child abuse; timely because just three months prior to
the conference the Supreme Court had heard oral arguments
for the first time on corporal punishment in the schools.
This conference was specifically designed to present a
balanced cross section of opinions on this ontroversial and
understudied issue. The conference was also designed to
examine corporal punsihment from a variety of perspectives.
The eight formal papers presented examines historical and
constitutional considerations; debated inherent philosophical, moral, ethical and practical issues; analyzed and
reported on corporal punishment practices and excesses in
our Nation's classrooms today; surveyed the current status
of state statutes regarding corporal punishment; provided a
scientific over view and appraisal of the effect of physical
punishment on children's behavior and emotions; and finally,
presented an initial examination of corporal punishment from
a cross cultural perspective. In addition, an open forum
dialogue was held which included representatives of three
national associations: The American Federation of Teachers,
The American Psychological Association, and the National
Parent-Teacher Association.

1203.   Yong, D. P. **The Legal Aspects of Student Dissent and
Discipline in Higher Education**. Athens, Georgia: Institute
of High Education, University of Georgia, 1970.

The purpose of this publication is to aid all those concerned with higher education to better understand the legal
parameters within which higher education operates and the
limits to which students may carry dissent in seeking to
force change. Included are the following chapters: 1)
Introduction; 2) Nature of Discipline in Higher Education;
3) Relationship Between the Student and the School; 4)
Relationship Between Courts and Education; 5) Due Process
and Student Dissent in Discipline in Higher Education; 6)
Equal Protection in Student Dissent and Discipline in Higher
Education; 7) Judicial Intervention in Scholastic Affairs;
8) Private Colleges and Universities; 9) Guidelines for
Disciplinary Proceedings in Public Institutions for Higher
Education.

1204.   Ziegler, C. L. "Struggle in the Schools: Constitutional
Protection for Public High School Students." Princeton
University, Woodrow Wilson Association Monograph Series,
School of Public and International Affairs, 1970.

Included in this monograph are cases dealing with the
constitutional rights of students in secondary schools.
Case studies are presented.

2.

DISSERTATIONS AND PAPERS

2001.   Alcorn, R. D.   "An Analysis of the Relationship of Discipline Practices of Teachers and the School Climate." Ph.D. Dissertation, United State International University. Dissertation Abstracts International, 38 (3-A), 1219. Order no. 77-16,395, 1977.

The problem of the study was to determine if positive practices regarding discipline are related to a positive school climate. One objective of the study was to test the following hypotheses: 1) There is a relationship between teachers' self-perceptions of discipline practices and school climate in low-income schools, and 2) There is a relationship between teachers' self-perceptions of discipline practices and school climate in middle-income schools. Subject groups consisted on one hundred ninety-six teachers in ten low-income and six middle-income schools. The three main conclusions resulting from this study were: 1) there is a strong relationship between the self-perceptions of teachers in low-income schools regarding the use of positive discipline practices and the school climate; 2) male teachers, in both low- and middle-income schools, use positive discipline practices slightly more frequently than female teachers; and 3) teachers with over four years experience use positive discipline practices slightly more frequently than teachers with less than four years experience.

2002.   Adams, C. L.   "An Exploration of First, Third, and Sixth Grade Students' Observable Behaviors and Verbal Responses elicited by a Specific Listening Task." Ph.D. Dissertation, Southern Illinois University at Carbondale. Dissertation Abstracts International, 38 (10-A), 5904. Order no. 7804241, 1978.

The major purpose of this study was to observe elementary school students; overt behaviors during a listening task, to investigate the relationship of these factors to the child's comprehension of the content of the task shown by free retelling and responses to questioning, and to investigate how these observable behaviors and comprehension related to the child's classroom listening performance and academic ability and performance as assessed by classroom teachers. Twenty first grade, twenty third grade, and twenty sixth grade students were randomly selected from elementary attendance centers of a school district in southern Illinois. Multiple regression analyses revealed that observed behaviors of maintaining eye contact most of the time during listening, of appropriate facial expressions, and twisting and shifting body position were comprehension-enhancing the behavior of excessive hand movements was comprehension detracting.

003.   Alfonso, R. "The School Behavior of Children With Good and Poor Self-Concepts: A Case Study." Ed.D. Dissertation, University of Pennsylvania. Dissertation Abstracts International, 38 (5-A), 2542-2543. Order no. 77-24,173, 1977.

The purpose of this study was to determine the patterns of behavior of children with good and poor self-concepts. From this, insight was gained as to the relationships, inter-actions, and elements which enhance or deter self-concept development. Eleven fourth and fifth grade children in a suburban, middle class elementary school served as the subjects of the study. The participants were divided into two groups: children with good self-concepts and children with poor self-concepts as defined by the Piers-Harris Children's Self-Concept Scale. The school experiences of the children were monitored throughout one school year by means of pupil, teacher, and parent interviews, observations with accompanying anecdotal records, and sociometrics. The data disclosed distinct patterns of behavior for the two groups. socially, the good self-concept group had more extensive interaction with their peers as work group and play group members. In contrast, the poor self-concept group not only had far fewer positive interactions with their classmates, but also had developed behavior patterns which caused their peers to reject them. Academically, the children with good self-concepts displayed consistent achievement. They considered their roles as students important, as did their parents who provided supportive home environments. Accordingly, they displayed positive attitudes towards the tasks required of them in school. Conversely, the children with poor self-concepts wanted to be successful in school, but, for the most part, were not. They often displayed negative and some sometimes hostile attitudes in school. Likewise, anxiety resulting from family problems often inhibited their ability to function well in school.

2004.   Allen, L. S. "An Examination of Academic and Behavioral Characteristics of Boys and Girls Who Have Been Identified as Learning Disabled." Ed.D. Dissertation. University of Northern Colorado, 1975.

The purpose of this study was to examine the academic and behavioral characteristics of the learning disabled boy and the learning disabled girl and to compare an contrast their characteristics with those of the normal boy and the normal girl. The subjects included in this study were 30 children who were identified as learning disabled including 15 boys and 15 girls. In addition, 30 children who were identified as normal were used including 15 boys and 15 girls. The children were taken from 18 different elementary schools in Jefferson County, Colorado. The children included were first and second gradres who ranged in age from six years seven months to eight years four months. Data concerning the subjects were obtained in the following way: 1. Behavioral characteristics of the subjects were obtained by having each child's teacher fill out the Devereux Elementary School Behavior Rating Scale (DESB). 2. Academic characteristics of the subjects were obtained by using the total score on the Comprehensive Test of Basic Skills (CTBS). The scores were obtained through the Testing Office of Jefferson County Public Schools. 1. Learning disabled children of both sexes score significantly lower than normal children on standardized achievement tests. 2. Teachers are referring children to equal academic achievement for placement into classrooms for the learning disabled regardless of sex. 3. Teachers perceive learning disabled children of both sexes as exhibiting more problem behaviors than normal children. 4. Learning disabled boys exhibit more overtly aggressive behavior than learning disabled girls. 5. Sex differences do exist in several behavioral areas, including Disrespect-Defiance, Inattentive-Withdrawn, Irrelevant-Responsiveness, and Need Closeness to the Teacher. 6. Learning disabled girls exhibit a need for closeness to their teacher to a significantly higher degree than learning disabled boys or normal girls. 7. Learning disabled girls display higher achievement anxiety than normal girls. 8. Normal children of both sexes are seen by their teachers as displaying better understanding of material presented in class than learning disabled children. 9. Normal children of both sexes are seen by their teachers as displaying more self-motivation than learning disabled children. Order No. 76-10, 822, DAI.

2005.   Allen, S. A. "A Study to Determine the Effectiveness of a Positive Approach to Discipline System for Classroom Management." Ed.D. Dissertation, North Texas State University. Dissertation Abstracts International, 39 (11). DAI no. 7911061, 1978.

This study reports on an investigation of the effectiveness of the "Positive Approach to Discipline" (PAD) system for classroom management. The subjects for this study were teachers and students located in a Middle School in a large, urban school district. Data were collected on the number of students referred to administration during ten weeks of the first quarter: the same teachers participated in a four day workshop on the concepts and techniques of the PAD system. The teachers agreed to participate in ten follow-up sessions. Data were collected on the number of students referred to administration during ten weeks of the second quarter. The findings of the study indicate that: 1) teachers utilizing the PAD system significantly reduced the number of students referred to administration, and 2) teachers utilizing the PAD system significantly reduced the number of Black students referred to administration, and 3) the PAD system was effective in reducing the number of students suspended from school. On the basis of the findings and conclusions of this study, the following recommendations are made. 1) It is recommended that the PAD system be utilized by teachers who are sending students to administration for unacceptable classroom behavior. 2) It is recommended that the PAD system be implemented in school districts interested in reducing the high incidence of suspensions from school.

2006.   Allwhite, A. G.   "A Comparison of Fourth Grade Students Who Have Participated in a Modified DUSO D-2 Classroom Guidance Program and Those Who Have Not."   Ed.D. Dissertation, The University of Tulsa.   Dissertation Abstracts International, 36 (3-A), 1297-1298.   Order no. 75-20,678, 1975.

The purpose of this study was to determine if measurable differences existed in certain personal and social dimensions between a group of fourth grade students having classroom guidance, utilizing the DUSO D-2 materials, and a group of fourth grade students not included in these guidance activities. The variables selected for investigation were academic achievement, school behavior, peer relations, self-esteem, and social self-esteem. Data were gathered from forty-one, low achieving Ss which had been randomly-assigned to either the experimental or control class. The criterion instruments utilized in this assessment included: 1) the Science Research Associates Achievement Series, multilevel edition, language usage subtest, 2) a Teacher Behavior Ratings of Pupils, 3) a Sociometric Election, 4) the Social Self-Esteem Scale, and 5) the Piers-Harris Self-Concept Scale. In addition, the experimental teacher's observations concerning the treatment were reported. The results, based on the t-value data, revealed there was no statistical difference (p .05) between participants and non-participants in the classroom guidance program when comparing their respective levels of self-esteem, social self-esteem, language usage achievement, peer relations, and school behavior as measured by the criterion instruments. The experimental teacher observed basically three benefits of the treatment process: 1) increased sharing of ideas by nonverbal students, 2) increased sharing of personal concerns, and 3) initiation of closer teacher-pupil relationships.

2007.   Arce, A. H. "Classroom Management Approach Preferences of Teacher as Related to the Reading Achievement of Their Respective Students." Ed.D. Dissertation, University of Houston. Dissertation Abstracts International, 39 (11). DAI no. 7910527, 1978.

This study examined the nature and extent of the relationship between teachers' expressed classroom management approach preferences and the academic achievement of their respective students. There is no statistically significant relationship between elementary teachers' authoritarian, behavior modification, "cookbook," group process, instructional, permissive, and socioemotional climate classroom management approach preferences and the mean grade equivalent reading achievement change scores of their students. This study was a correlational study in which a measure of classroom management approach preferences of a teacher was correlated with the mean reading achievement gain of his or her students. For purposes of this study the teachers' expressed preference for a classroom management approach was considered the independent variable. Change in reading achievement score was considered as the dependent variable. As an operational measure of classroom management approach preferences, the Management Approach Preference Inventory (Weber and Cunningham, 1977) was administered to each of the teachers who constituted the sample of the study. Student achievement was assessed through use of the Iowa Tests of Basic Skills, Form 5. There were no statistically significant relationships between elementary teachers' expressed classroom management approach preferences and the academic achievement of their respective students.

2008.   Anderson, R. F. "Using Guided Fantasy and Modeling to Modify the Acting-Out Behavior of Fifth Grade Boys." Ph.D. Dissertation, The University of Florida. Dissertation Abstracts International, 36 (12-A), 7859. Order no. 76-12, 042, 1976.

This study sought to identify the impact of three different group treatments (modeling, fantasy and modeling plus fantasy) on the acting-out behavior of fifth grade boys. Questions posed related specifically to the differences between pretest to post-test mean gain scores of the three treatment groups plus a control group. The study employed 48 fifth grade males from three Alachua County Schools. After initially screening all fifth grade males from the three schools on the Acting Out Scale, 48 were randomly selected and assigned to the four groups. All subjects were pre- and posttested during two-week periods with a teacher rating scale, ratings to taped responses by subjects to anger producing situations, a peer perception device and frequency counts on times disciplined. The taped responses were made by the counselor in each school and rated by trained judges for level of aggressiveness. The acting-out scales and discipline reports were recorded by the subject's teacher, while the classroom play was administered by the school counselor. Each group was conducted by the school counselor and consisted of ten sessions. The modeling group listened and reacted to a tape of a boy handling a hierarchy of anger producing situations by using self-control. The fantasy group listened and reacted to a tape in which they were instructed to imagine themselves involved in the same situations that the model faced. The combined modeling plus fantasy group listened and reacted to both tapes. The control group was given unstructured time to talk with each other, draw pictures or play games. Each hypothesis was stated in reference to each measure utilized in the study and each was tested as a null hypothesis. Each was rejected if the probability of the obtained result was less than the predetermined level of significance (.05). An overall trend toward decreasing acting-out behavior in the three treatment groups is apparent in the raw data. Generalizing effects of the experimental condition may be in evidence.

2009.   Andros, G. C. "Modifying the Effectiveness of Secondary Reinforcement Through Its Pairing With Tangible Rewards." Ed.D. Dissertation, The University of Tennessee. Dissertation Abstracts International, 33 (11-A), 6167-6168. Order no. 73-12,380, 1973.

The main objective of this study was to increase the effectiveness of teacher praise through its pairing with tangible rewards in the natural classroom setting. A secondary purpose was to determine the relative effectiveness of three classroom management conditions: (1) contingently applied teacher praise and ignoring behavior; (2) contingently applied teacher praise and ignoring behavior with the administration of unexchangeable points for appropriate student behavior; and (3) contingently applied teacher praise and ignoring behavior with the administration of exchangeable points for tangible rewards as related to appropriate student behavior. The study was conducted in four seventh grade classrooms. The results of this study indicate that (1) contingent teacher praise is an effective means of increasing appropriate student behavior; (2) contingent teacher praise increases in its effectiveness over time; (3) the pairing of tangible rewards with contingent teacher praise enhances the rate of increase, rather than the final outcome, in the effectiveness of contingent teacher praise; and (4) the awarding of unexchangeable points with contingent praise increases the effectiveness of contingent teacher praise only during the point administration period.

2010.   Baldwin, M. A. "Activity Level, Attention Span, and Deviance: Hyperactive Boys in the Classroom." Ph.D. Dissertation, University of Waterloo. Dissertation Abstracts International, 37 (10-B), 5341. 1977.

Using an observational methodology, activity level, attention span, and deviant behavior were studied in 15 hyperactive boys (mean age 100.60 months), 15 control boys (mean age 99.40 months), and 15 control girls (mean age 97.27 months) in elementary school classrooms. Each subject was observed for 40 min. spread over a four day period and a stylized behavior commentary describing his actions was recorded on audio tape. Measures of activity level obtained were the frequency, total duration, and mean bout length of a large number of objectively defined behaviors. The various stimuli which the subjects attended to and the amounts of time spent attending to them served as measures of attention. Deviancy was examined by coding the subject's actions as being either appropriate or inappropriate in the classroom, by noting the frequency of occurrence of certain behaviors such as hitting and by recording the nature of teacher and peer interactions directed towards the subjects. A series of stepwise discriminant analyses indicated that the hyperactive boys, as compared to the control children, engaged in significantly more locomotion and standing, in more gross bodily movements while seated, such as turning, leaning, and shifting, in longer bouts of leg movements, and in more purposeless or extraneous hand movements. The hyperactives also talked for a significantly greater amount of time, and displayed more extraneous head movements. Analysis of the attentional data indicated that there were no significant differences between the hyperactive and control groups in the length of attention span for all stimuli or in the number of different stimuli attended to. The hyperactive boys were found to have significantly longer attention spans for nonacademic stimuli, such as parts of their bodies, while the control children had longer attention spans for academic materials and the teacher. The behavior of the hyperactive boys was found to be more socially inappropriate than that of the controls and the hyperactives received significantly more negative interactions from both their teachers and their peers than did the controls. Relatively few differences were found between the control boys and girls on any of the measures of activity level, attention or appropriateness.

2011.   Baris, Mitchell A. "Social Ecological Correlates of the Impact of Elementary Schools Upon Behavior of Students." Ph.D. Dissertation, University of Colorado, 1976. Dissertation Abstracts International, 36 (11-B), 5856-5857. Order no. 76-11,545.

Mental health consultation to the elementary school is defined from a social-ecological standpoint where the school is viewed as an environmental sub-system functional within the context of the larger ecological system, the community, with which it is interactive. Hypotheses of the relationship between organizational affect and individual student behavior are derived from the ecological principles of 1) inter-relatedness, 2) recycling of resources, 3) individual styles of adaptation to environment, and 4) evolutionary succession. Data on systems and individuals were collected from the principals and faculties of twenty-four north-eastern Colorado elementary schools. Follwing scale valida-tion operations, data was analyzed by means of serial step-wise regressions. The technique provided for the identifica-tion of the most potent of the system affect and demographic variables as predictors of the parameters of individual student behavior measured in the study. Results indicate that organizational affect predicts to the mean of student need achievement 59%, aggression 56%, anxiety 76%, academic disability 97%, extroversion 27%, and total disability 65%. All are significant at p .01. School and community demo-graphic variables predict 43% to the mean of student need achievement, 47% to aggression, 60% to anxiety, 77% to academic disability, 77% to extroversion, and 52% to total disability. However, only anxiety, academic disability, extroversion, and total disability are significant at p .01. The results lend supporting evidence to the contention that affective dimensions of organizational environment con-tribute powerfully to the personalities manifested by individuals functional within that system. More specifi-cally, the results support system consultation as a viable mental health intervention strategy in the elementary school and imply its widescale practical application in effecting behavior change in students.

2012.   Bar-Lev, Yechiel. "The Effectiveness of Parent Training Programs of Their Children's Motivation, Calssroom Behavior, and Achievement." Ph.D. Dissertation, Arizona State University. Dissertation Abstracts International, 37 (5-A), 2521-2522. Order no. 76-24,870, 1976.

The purpose of this study was to determine whether 1) as a result of parent's participation in a parent training pro-gram, it is possible for them to increase motivation, desirable classroom behavior, and achievement in their elementary school age children? 2) the parent training program will be effective for non-helping parents or only for helping parents? A list of all students from third to eighth grade who lived with both parents was compiled. Based on the teacher's evaluation, the list of the parents was divided into two groups 1) helping parents and 2) non-helping parents. From each group a sample of 24 parents was randomly selected. Sixteen parents from each group were assigned to the experimental group. The other 16 parents (8 helping and 8 non-helping) were assigned to the control group. A model for parental training was developed. The activities and the techniques employed in the model were derived from a number of motivational theories and from other models. The findings showed that it was possible for the parents to increase motivation and desirable classroom behavior in their children. Also, it was concluded that the parent training program was effective for both helping and for non-helping parents.

2013.   Barnett, J. B. "Effects of Self-Management Instruction and Contingency Management to Increase Completion of Work." Ph.D. Dissertation. The Ohio State University, 1973.

The purpose of this study was to examine the effects of self-management instruction and contingency management to increase amount of work for non-productive students. Thirty students who were selected from 113 students had the lowest percent of completed contracted tasks on a five-day language arts contract during pre-treatment period. The thirty students were randomly divided into Experimental 1 and Experimental 2 groups. Experimental 1 students received self-management instruction during first-treatment period but were not required to implement the instructional procedures taught. Self-management instruction involved describing and demonstrating how a five-day language arts contract can be divided into daily schedules with least preferred tasks scheduled at the beginning of the language arts period and the most preferred tasks at the end. Experimental 1 students were required to develop daily schedules during the third treatment period. Experimental 2 students never received self-management instruction. Statistical analysis revealed unclear effects of self-management instruction. Contingency management treatment was given to both experimental groups. Since both experimental groups received contingency management at the same time, the effects of contingency management could not be made by comparing data from two independent samples. The effects of contingency management treatment was significant when comparing both experimental groups before and during contingency management treatment (t test of two correlated means). When comparing the data from the first four weeks of the study (before contingency management treatment) with the data from the last four weeks of the study (during contingency management treatment) significant differences for both experimental groups occurred at the .01 significance level. Order No. 73-26, 768, DAI.

2014.   Baugh, E. H. "The Relationship Between Performance on Observational and Laboratory Measures of Attention in Previously Identified High- and Low-Risk Grade One Pupils." Ph.D. Dissertation, York University. Dissertation Abstracts International, 39 (11-B), 5535.

From a preschool screening program involving 4,034 pupils, norms were developed for the Caldwell Preschool Inventory. Children identified as high or low risk by their Inventory scores were also administered the Bender Gestalt test in Kindergarten, and teacher ratings were obtained in grades one, two and three. No relationship was found between Bender Gestalt predictions of risk and those from the Inventory suggesting that the Inventory does not include a measure of visual-motor integration. Teacher ratings yielded inconclusive results. In a further study, 32 first grade children in four schools, matched for age, sex, and risk level (by Inventory score) were observed for five days in the classroom under a four category coding system of attending behavior. A visual attention task requiring response to a colored light and an auditory attention task requiring response to a particular digit in a series were also administered to each subject individually. No relationship was found between risk level and attending behavior on any measure.

2015.   Becklund, J. D. "An Experimental Analysis of a Self-Monitored Treatment Package and Its Specific Components in Reducing the Disruptive Social Behaviors of Mildly Handicapped Male Adolescents." Ph.D. Dissertation, University of Oregon. Dissertation Abstracts International, 40 (9-A), 4996. Order no. 8005751, 1980.

The major purpose of the present study was twofold: (a) to determine the effects of a self-monitored treatment package (SMP) on reducing a specified disruptive behavior for each subject, and (b) to determine if either of the specific components of the package facilitates a behavior change in a differential manner, e.g., was one component more powerful than the other in producing a change in the target behavior. The SMP was comprised of four variables. These were combined to form two package components: (a) subject's self-recording and self-charting the frequency of the disruptive behavior, and (b) an externally imposed performance goal and contingent reinforcement. Three mildly handicapped male adolescents at the seventh grade level served as subjects. The self-monitored treatment package was effective in reducing the frequency of the target behavior for Subject 1 and somewhat equivocally for Subject 2. No discernible effects were observed for the third subject. A lower level of intellectual functioning and environmental classroom variables were viewed as possible reasons for the lack of effects for the third subject. The components analysis revealed that for Subject 1 and Subject 2 there were no differences between the two pull-out conditions in facilitating a change in the target behavior. There were differences, however, in the rate observed of the target behavior for each subject during the pull-out conditions relative to full package implementation. During each pull-out condition, the rate observed for Subject 1 was higher than the rate condition was equivalent to the rate observed during SMP. No conclusions could be drawn for the third subject.

2016.   Beecher, Ronnie. "Teacher Approval and Disapproval of Classroom Behavior in Pre-Kindergarten, Kindergarten and First Grade." Ph.D. Dissertation, Columbia University. Dissertation Abstracts International, 35 (2-B), 1015. Order no. 74-17,837, 1974.

The study was conducted to compare teacher verbal approval and disapproval patterns in pre-kindergarten, kindergarten and first grade. Classes included in the study were four first grades, four kindergartens and four pre-kindergartens (two private and two public), or twelve classes in total. The study was an observational study using the Teacher Approval and Disapproval Observation Record. A wide variety of classroom activities at each grade level were systematically sampled. Observation time per grade was 1200 minutes. Total observation time was 3600 minutes. The analyses performed on the observed pupil behaviors included: 1) Examination of descriptive data including frequencies of teacher approval and disapproval for pupil behaviors. 2) The degree of relationship between teacher verbal approval patterns, and between teacher verbal disapproval patterns for the grades. 3) The prediction of the first grade teacher verbal approval pattern from teacher verbal approval patterns in previous grades. Results suggested the following conclusions about teacher verbal approval and disapproval behavior in the classroom: 1) Teacher verbal approval patterns for pupil behavior in pre-kindergarten, kindergarten and first grade were unrelated. A major difference was that academic behavior such as reading and arithmetic behaviors received more teacher approval in first grade than in other grades. 2) The first grade teacher approval pattern could not be predicted from teacher approval patterns in previous grades. 3) Teacher verbal disapproval patterns for pupil behaviors in the three grades were unrelated. In general, teachers disapproved of inappropriate classroom behavior and incorrect academic responses.

2017.   Behre, Alice C. "Behavior Rehearsal Techniques Used With Groups of Elementary Students Identified as Disruptive." Ph.D. Dissertation, University of Maryland. Dissertation Abstracts International, 37 (2-A), 798. Order no. 76-17,775, 1976.

The purpose of this study was to determine whether a behavior rehearsal technique would modify the disruptive behavior of children identified as disruptive in the classroom. The influence of the technique was determined by a measure of the criterion behavior, disruptive classroom behavior, before and after treatment. The following questions were posed: 1) Does participation in a behavior rehearsal program affect disruptive behavior of students in the classroom? 2) Is there a difference between behavior rehearsal and behavior rehearsal combined with behavior assignments, in affecting disruptive behaviors? 3) Is there a difference in the effect of disruptive behavior between groups who have non-disruptive students as models during the program, and groups of students who are all identified as disruptive? Sixty students from the four, fifth, and sixth grades in two elementary schools participated. Analysis of the data revealed that behavior rehearsal was an effective technique in reducing disruptive classroom behavior. The independent variables, assignment and modeling, combined with behavior rehearsal, did not affect the influence of the treatment at the .05 level of significance.

2018.   Beisner, L. R. "Self-Analysis procedures as related to teacher perception of verbal and non-verbal behaviors." Dissertation Abstracts International. <u>38</u> (10a), April, 1978.

Study deals with teachers' perception of verbal and non-verbal behaviors of children as compared to self-analysis procedures.

2019.   Bell, S. H. "The Effects of Sociodrama on the Adaptive and Maladaptive Behaviors of Elementary School Boys." Ph.D. Dissertation, University of Georgia, 1976.

The effects of sociodrama on the adaptive and maladaptive behaviors of elementary school boys were examined in three groups of six boys each. ONe group was used as a control for the Hawthorne Effect; the second, as a control for teacher expectation effects and for changes as a function of involvement with a male counselor. In the experimental group, children listened to one of Aesop's Fables and then played out the social conflicts described. The forty-five minute sessions were conducted twice a week for eight weeks. In-school behaviors of the children were recorded by neutral observers on a checklist of adaptive and maladaptive behaviors. Case reports for each child in the experimental group were also prepared. Analysis of results indicated no statistically significant differences between groups, although a comparison between the control and experimental groups was in the expected direction. Methodological suggestions are presented for further research of this type. See ERIC Abstract ED 139006.

2020.   Belsky, M. B. "The Relationship of Mother-Child Interaction to Dependency Behavior in First Graders." Ph.D. Dissertation, Fordham University. Dissertation Abstracts International, 34 (1-A), 165-166. Order no. 73-16,045, 1973.

This study sought to investigate whether systematic relationships could be identified between different patterns of mother-child interactions as observed in a problem solving situation and dependency behaviors of the child in school. The study examined the relationships within the interaction process using an expanded model in which the effects of the child on the mother as well as the effects of the mother on the child were considered, and the possible outcomes defined in terms of reinforcement contingencies consonant with social learning theories. Major Issues included: 1. What is the effect of dependency initiation in the mother-child interaction situation on the child's school behavior? 2. Is there a relationship between the type of response by mother to an initiation of a dependency interaction and dependency behavior of the child in school? 3. Is there a relationship between the type of response by the child to an initiation of dependency interaction by the mother and the extent of initiation of dependency behavior by the mother? Results included: 1. Initiation of dependency in the mother-child interaction situation had no relationship to school dependency behavior. The amount of initiation was thus not predictive of dependency behavior with teacher. Only the response contingencies within the interaction situation (accept, ignore, or reject) related to school behavior. 2. Boys with mothers who accepted the dependency by helping them, showed more dependency in school, while mothers ignoring or rejecting scores were not related to dependency behavior in school. Girls with mothers who ignored dependency initiations showed less dependency in school, while mothers' high accepting or rejecting scores were not related to school dependency behavior. The child had a definite effect on mother's behavior within the interaction process. Children who accepted rather than rejected or ignored their mothers' dependency overtures had mothers who initiated more. 4. When a task was introduced and the mothers were busy, they were more likely to perform the task for sons and to ignore daughters.

2021.   Benlifer, Ginger E. "Hand-Raisers and Non-Hand-Raisers: Academic and Personality Profiles." Ph.D. Dissertation, Yeshiva University. Dissertation Abstracts International, 38 (4-B), 1856. Order no. 77-20,283, 1977.

This study examined the academic and personality profiles of groups of sixth grade children who were classified according to the frequency of their hand-raising behavior in a normal classroom setting, and their level of competence on an academic task. The children were identified first as hand-raisers, moderate-hand-raisers and non-hand-raisers, and second, within these groups, as informed or uninformed. The study investigated primarily whether hand-raisers and non-hand-raisers differed in their achievement test scores, I.Q., need for approval, test anxiety, global and school-related self-concept and extraversion, and whether teachers evaluated the academic competence of these groups as different. The results of the study suggested that the specific overt classroom behavior of hand-raising is strongly and positively related to I.Q. and to varied areas of achievement test scores, even outside the context in which hand-raising is measured. Hand-raisers were found to receive more positive evaluations, be less in need of approval, less test anxious, and higher in global and school-related self-concept, all of which follow from there being such a strong positive relationship between hand-raising and I.Q. and achievement.

2022.   Berenberg, M. B. "Achievement, Attendance, Discipline and Self-Concept of Ninth-Grade Students in Traditional and Alternative Programs." Ph.D. Dissertation, Fordham University. Dissertation Abstracts International, 38 (1-A), 193. Order no. 77-14,860, 1977.

This study sought to determine whether exposing ninth-grade students to alternative or traditional programs would have any differential effects upon their academic and nonacademic educational outcomes. The study grew out of the great need, expecially on the junior high school level, for empirical research into the effectiveness of a contemporary educational phenomenon known as the "free school movement." This movement is based upon the principles and practices of humanistic psychology and is characterized by greater student involvement and participation in individual and group decision making processes in school. The subjects in this study were 170 ninth-grade students from a middle- to upper- class suburban community. The experimental group spent ninth grade in the alternative half-day school-within-a-school program, and the two control groups spent ninth grade in the traditional program in the same school. Results indicated that exposure to the experimental or control treatments produced no significant differences between the groups on the hypothesized variables. Supplementary analyses revealed that boys scored significantly higher than girls in each group on most cognitive variables, and that girls in the experimental group tended to have more latenesses than any other group of boys or girls. It was concluded that these findings occurred as a result of insufficient separation of the alternative program from the traditional one to allow for maximization of experimental variance. It was also concluded that half-day programs such as the one under investigation, in which students are exposed to both alternative and traditional school environments and practices each day, produce conflicts and confusion which may interfere with the intended effects of the program.

2023.   Bien, N. Z. "An Evaluation of a Broad-Scale, School-Based Psychotherapeutic Intervention With Adolescents Who Have Adjustment Problems." Ph.D. Dissertation, Rutgers University The State University of New Jersey. Dissertation Abstracts International, 36 (5-B), 2458-2459. Order no. 75-24,660, 1975.

An objective and thorough evaluation of a psychotherapeutic intervention was conducted in a school system. Forty seventh-grade students were chosen for the intervention on the basis of low academic motivation, family problems, or referrals to the vice principal for discipline. Four groups were designed: one group received behavioral group therapy, teacher conferences, and parent conferences; a second group received only behavioral group therapy and teacher conferences; a third group received teacher conferences, and a fourth group received no treatment. The groups were measured on grades, attendance, disciplinary referrals, teacher comments, and classroom behavior. While not statistically significant, certain trends suggested that the full treatment package was superior to partial intervention and that the addition of program elements to the treatment package promoted a positive treatment outcome. The article considered the problems inherent in evaluation and the conditions necessary for the solution of these problems.

2024.   Bjorklund, Lorimer R. "The Identification of Student Disruptive Behavior in Industrial Arts and the Application of Simulation to These Problems." Ph.D. Dissertation, The Ohio State University. Dissertation Abstracts International, 40 (7-A), 3834-3835U. Order no. 8001696.

The purposes of this study were to identify student disruptive behavior problems which occur in industrial arts laboratories and classrooms and to develop and field test simulation materials to depict several selected problems. Five videotaped incidents were created to provide decision-making experiences in industrial arts teacher education for pre-service and in-service teachers. A check list type instrument titled the Student Disruptive Behavior Check List (SDBCL) was developed to identify frequent and bothersome disruptive behavior problems. The target population for the SDBCL inventory was composed of 1728 Minnesota industrial arts teachers. Five of the fifteen most "significant" disruptive behavior problems were selected to be developed into simulated incidents and were videotaped. Conclusions based on the findings indicated that: 1) bothersome and frequent disruptive behavior problems can be identified by industrial arts teachers, 2) teacher education students are able to identify specific simulated incidents and suggest decisions and actions for the treatment and control of disruptive behavior, and 3) future teachers will project positive attitudes toward IALPS materials.

2025.   Blust, R. S. "Perceived Organizational Press, Personal Ideology and Teacher Pupil Control Behavior." D.Ed. Dissertation, The Pennsylvania State University. Dissertation Abstracts International, 38 (5-A), 2436. Order no. 77-23, 213, 1977.

The relationship of teacher pupil control ideology and perceived organizational press with teacher pupil control behavior was investigated. Teacher pupil control ideology referred to the personal beliefs that teachers have in regard to pupil control, not necessarily actual teacher behavior. Organizational press was defined by teacher perceptions of the pupil control ideology of their teacher colleagues and the building principal. Pupil control behavior, the dependent variable, referred to the actions of teachers in the school environment while interacting with or directing students. The instruments were Willower, Eidell, and Hoy's Pupil Control Ideology (PCI) Form; Packard and Willower's modification of the PCI Form to tap teacher perceptions of the colleague and principal PCI; and Helsel and Willower's Pupil Control Behavior (PCB) Form. Two school districts consented to participate in the investigation, each district provided two secondary schools. A sample of ninety-five classroom teachers and 2,170 students was surveyed. The analyses utilizing multiple regression indicated tht teacher PCI and organizational press were significantly related to teacher PCB. Clearly, teacher PCI was the best predictor of teacher PCB for the total sample of ninety-five teachers.

2026.   Bolstad, O. D. "The Relationship Between Teachers' Assessment of Students and the Students' Actual Behavior in the Classroom." Ph.D. Dissertation, University of Oregon. Dissertation Abstracts International, 35 (8-B), 4160-4161. Order no. 75-3863, 1975.

The present study examined the relationship between the labels and ratings that teachers provided of students in their classrooms and the actual behavior that these students exhibited. Assessment data were collected from five class-rooms in an initial sample and six classrooms in a replica-tion sample. Third and fourth grade public school teachers were asked to select boy and girl pairs whom they would label as: (1) "Best behaved" in terms of classroom behavior, (2) the most typical or "average behaved," and (3) the "least well behaved" in classroom conduct. Teachers were then asked to rate each of these six students on three retrospective rating scales relevant to the classroom con-duct dimension. After the ratings were completed, direct behavioral observations of the selected students were con-ducted over an extensive time sample of 200' minutes per child. Both high and low base rate behaviors were sampled in the observations. The results of this investigation indicated that teachers were quite accurate in their assess-ment of students' behavior.

2027.   Bond, R. B. "The Effects of Three Short-Term Interven-tions on Disruptive Sixth-Graders in Transition." Ph.D. Dissertations, Texas Woman's University. Dissertation Abstracts International, 40 (1-B), 440. Order no. 7915865, 1979.

The effects of three short-term intervention programs on chronically disruptive sixth-graders (n = 24) were measured during their transition from elementary to middle school. Treatment programs included Multi-faceted Psychological Consultation (n = 6), Limited Psychological Consultation (n = 6) and Time-Out Class Placement (n = 6). A fourth group, Traditional Intervention, was served by existing school staff and was designated as a control group (n = 6). Fifth-grade teachers rated subjects' school behavior (Devereux Elementary School Behavior Rating Scale and Portland Problem Rating Scale) in late spring. Sixth-grade teachers provided both a second prerating early in the fall term and posttest ratings after six weeks of intervention. Parents rated their children's behavior at home (Walker Problem Behavior Identification Checklist) prior to initiation of interven-tion programs and again at their conclusion. Subjects also rated themselves on self-concept (Piers-Harris Children's Self-Concept Scale) immediately before and after the treat-ment period. Results revealed that the most intensive intervention program, Multi-faceted Psychological Consultation, was significantly superior to both other treatment groups and the control group in increasing self-concept of subjects. No significant differences between groups were found on home behavior, nor on either of the two measures of behavior in the classroom. Results are discussed with regard to their comparison to previous research findings and possible causative factors.

2028.   Boone, S. L. "Language, Cognition and Social Factors in the Regulation of Aggressive Behavior: A Study of Black, Puerto Rican, and White Children." Ed.D. Dissertation, Rutgers University The State University of New Jersey. Dissertation Abstracts International, 36 (7-A), 4338. Order no. 76-1102, 1976.

The purpose of this study was to investigate the "Language-Aggression Hypothesis." This hypothesis suggests that measurable high language proficiency is associated with low observable aggression and low language proficiency is associated with high observable aggression. The language-aggression hypothesis was derived from Pavlov's excitation-inhibition model which suggests that language serves as a "second-signalling system," and, as such, directs and controls behavioral activities. While the main focus to this study was to investigate the language-aggression hypothesis, consideration was given to qualitative differences in aggressive behaviors as a function of family-income, race, age, number of parents in household and school membership. Further data on differences in free speech and its relationship to the former variable were treated. The subjects were 55 Black, 25 Puerto Ricans and 52 White male fourth, fifth, and sixth graders selected from schools within the Newark public school system. Aggression was measured using an adaptation of the physical and verbal categories employed by Walter Pearce and Dahms. The vocabulary subtest of the WISC, Metropolitan Reading Test (Elementary Form), and measures of free speech were used to measure language proficiency of subjects. The language-aggression hypothesis appears to hold for comparisons among Black subjects and Puerto Rican subjects tested and observed within the study, but it does not appear to hold for White subjects tested and observed within the study. While the language proficiency scores for children from middle-income families were higher than the scores of children from low-income families, the aggression results were not significantly different. There was a tendency, however, for children from low-income families to display more verbal, physical and total aggression than children from middle-income families.

2029.   Borko, H. "Factors Contributing to Teachers' Preinstructional Decisions About Classroom Management and Long-Term Objectives." Ph.D. Dissertation, University of California, Los Angeles. Dissertation Abstracts International, 39 (09). DAI no. 7906162, 1978.

The purpose of this study was to examine the effects of
several factors -- educational beliefs, information (cues)
about students, and estimates of student attitudes -- on
teachers' preinstructional decisions. Two major sets of
analyses were conducted. The first set used a general
linear model to examine teachers' estimates of student
aptitudes. Models were constructed to predict teachers'
judgments from information about students and educational
beliefs. The second set of analyses used a general linear
model to investigate factors contributing to teachers'
preinstructional decisions. Two alternative models were
constructed to predict each decision. One model used
information about students and educational beliefs; the
other used educational beliefs and estimates of student
aptitudes. Teachers' estimates of student aptitudes could
be fit with simple additive models which included information about only a small number of student cues. Teachers'
preinstructional decisions could be fit with simple one- or
two-factor models which included information about the one
most relevant cue and either one or no measure of educational beliefs. The models that predicted teachers' decisions from educational beliefs and estimates of student
aptitudes were also main effects models which included at
most four factors. When all decisions were considered
together, general academic competence was the most salient
student aptitude.

2030.   Boudin, Henry M. "The Ripple Effect in Classroom
Management." Ph.D. Dissertation, The University of
Michigan. Dissertation Abstracts International, 31 (12-A),
6395. Order no. 71-15,104, 1971.

This study was designed to measure the effects of the
application of behavior modification techniques to a class
member in increasing his frequency of task relevant behavior. It was also hypothesized that the ripple effect,
defined as the degree to which the frequency of task
relevant behavior of another class member is dependent upon
the frequency of task relevant behavior of the target child,
will effect an increase in the frequency of task relevant
behavior for other class members as well. The study was
carried out in 5 classrooms. In each classroom, 2 or 3
behavior modification techniques were compared to test which
was more effective in increasing the adaptive behavior of
the target child and the other class members. The treatment
variables compared were: public versus private contingencies, groups versus individual reinforcements, feedback
versus reinforcement, acceleration versus deceleration, and
a behavior chose for modification by the teacher on the
basis of its negative qualities versus a maladaptive
behavior chosen for modification by the investigator on the
basis of its high frequency. A return to baseline design
was used in each classroom. The conclusions of this investigation were that: 1) There is strong evidence to support
the conclusion that behavior modification techniques will
increase the frequency of adaptive behavior and decrease the

frequency of maladaptive behavior of children to whom the behavior modification techniques are applied. 2) There is strong evidence to support the conclusion that through the ripple effect, class members who are witness to the application of behavior modification techniques to a target child will increase their frequency of adaptive behavior, and decrease their frequency of maladaptive behavior as well. 3) There is some evidence to support the conclusion that through the ripple effect, those class members who are nearer to a target child to whom a behavior modification technique is applied, will increase their frequency of adaptive behavior and decrease the frequency of maladaptive behavior to a greater extent than those class members who are positioned further away from the target child.

2031.   Boyd, W. D. "Inservice Training in Behavior Management for Special Education Teachers." Ed.D. Dissertation, The University of Alabama. Dissertation Abstracts International, 34 (10-A), 6479. Order no. 74-9335, 1974.

The purpose of the study was to determine which of three approaches to inservice behavior management training allowed teachers the most time to use for teaching behavior instead of controlling behavior. This determination was evaluated through observation of teacher classroom behavior by observers. Three approaches to inservice behavior management training with Special Education teachers were implemented and compared. Participating teachers received training in appropriate behavior management techniques either through development of specific behavior modification skills, individual management by appropriate decision making or teacher consultation on specific problem behaviors. A Lindquist Type I experimental design was used for evaluation purposes. This design permitted evaluation of both differences in inservice behavior management training approaches and differences in preinservice and postinservice teacher behaviors. The results of the two way analysis of variance showed no significant difference between inservice approaches or between pre- and postinservice teacher behaviors.

2032.   Bradley, R. H. "Sex, race, socioeconomic status, locus of control and classroom behavior among junior high school student." Ph.D. Dissertation, the University of North Carolina at Chapel Hill, 1974.

The study was designed to investigate the following five sets of relationships: 1) the relationship between sex, race, and socioeconomic status variables and generalized perceptions of internal external control of reinforcement, 2) the relationship between sex, race, and socioeconomic status variables and perceptions of internal external control of reinforcements in intellectual, social and physical situations, 3) the relationship between sex, race, socioeconomic status variables and the stability and locus of control dimentions of causality, 4) the relationship between generalized perceptions of control over reinforcements and specific achievement oriented behaviors, 5) the relationship between perceptions of control over reinforcements in intellectual situations and specific achievement oriented behaviors. Results of the study were as follows, 1) it was determined that whites were more internal than blacks and middle class individuals were more internal than lower middle and lower class individuals; males and females do not differ. Whites were more internal than blacks regarding unsuccessful outcomes. Females were more internal than males regarding success for outcomes.

2033.   Branch, C. V. "An Investigation of Inferred and Professed Self Concept-As-Learner of Disruptive and Nondisruptive Middle School Students." Ed.D. Dissertation, The University of Florida. Dissertation Abstracts International, 36 (2-A), 771-772. Order no. 75-16,360, 1975.

The purpose of this study was to examine the self concept-as-learner of a group of middle school students identified as disruptive. Two secondary purposes were to determine if a relationship exists between self concept-as-learner and amount of disruptiveness, and to compare the Florida Key, an inferred measure of self concept-as-learner, with the school-academic subscales of the Self-Esteem Inventory, a measure of professed self concept-as-learner. Five hypotheses were tested: There will be a significant difference between disruptive and nondisruptive students on inferred self concept-as-learner. There will be a significant difference between disruptive and nondisruptive students on professed self concept-as-learner. There will be a relationship between the number of disruptions and inferred self concept-as-learner. There will be a relationship between the number of disruptions and professed self concept-as-learner. There will be a significant correlation between students' scores on the Florida Key and the school-academic sub-scale of the Self-Esteem Inventory. The sample consisted of 208 disruptive and 208 nondisruptive students drawn from a population of 3,254 students in four rural and urban Florida middle schools. In testing the first two hypotheses, multivariage analysis of variance was used to determine the differences between disruptive and nondisruptive students' scores on the two instruments. A four-way analysis of variance indicated significant differences between the disruptive and nondisruptive students' scores on both the Florida Key and the SEI school-academic subscale. In testing the third hypothesis, a multiple regression analysis and a Pearson product moment coefficient of correlation were used to show linear and quadratic curvilinear relationships between the number of disruptions and inferred self concept-as-learner. No significant relationships were found. In testing the fourth hypothesis, a Pearson product moment coefficient or correlation was used to determine the relationship between the number of disruptions and professed self concept-as-learner. No significant relationship was found. In testing the fifth hypothesis to determine the significance of the correlation between the Florida Key and the school-academic subscale of the SEI, a matrix of the correlations and a correlation coefficient were used. A statistically significant relationship was found.

2034.   Brand, M. "A Study of the Effectiveness of Simulation Techniques in Teaching Behavior Management Skills to Undergraduate Music Education Majors." Ph.D. Dissertation, University of Miami. Dissertation Abstracts International, 37 (5-A), 2706. Order no. 76-24,890, 1976.

The purpose of this study was to compare the relative effectiveness of simulated encounters with behavior management problems and the traditional lecture-discussion method in teaching behavior management skills to undergraduate music education majors prior to their student teaching experiences. To test the hypothesis that simulated encounters with behavior problems significantly affect the behavior management skills and attitudes of music education majors as measured by the: 1) Behavior Management Skills Inventory (MTAI), and 2) ability to handle actual behavior problems in a school setting as appraised by qualified observers; an experiment involving fifty-two music education majors at the University of Miami was conducted. While the experimental simulation treatment utilized in this study did not appear to be superior to the control treatment when measured in relation to the development of attitudes and responses to hypothetical situations; both treatments appear to be equally effective. However, when subjects from both groups were placed into an actual classroom teaching situation, the members of the experimental treatment group proved to be superior to those drawn from the control group.

2035.   Brannon, J. M. "The Impact of Teacher Stage of Concern and Level of Use of a Modified Reality Therapy Discipline Program on Selected Student Behaviors: A Discriminant Analysis Approach." Ed.D. Dissertation, The University of Mississippi. Dissertation Abstracts International, 38 (7-A), 4037. Order no 77-28,952, 1978.

The purpose of this study was to investigate the effects of a Teacher Corps inservice education program designed to train teachers in the implementation of an innovative discipline program. The problem was to determine if the level to which satellite teaching teams implemented the training would produce significant differences in student self concept, locus of control, teacher/student relationships, and behavioral ratings. In addition a semantic differential was used to obtain a measurement of satellite teaching team attitudes toward the discipline program. The degree to which the modified Reality Therapy discipline program was implemented was determined through two assessments: 1) the State of Concern (SoC) aroused by the discipline program; and 2) the Level of Use (LoU) of the discipline program. Since all teaching teams received the same training these

two assessments were used to identify those satellite
teaching teams who were maximizing and minimizing the use of
the discipline training. A representative random sample of
students was drawn from the classrooms of each teaching
team. These students were assessed to obtain a measurement
of their self concept, acceptance of achievement responsibility, teacher/student relationships, and classroom
behavior. The following conclusions were reached: 1) A
well planned inservice program can be an effective means to
implement an innovative discipline program to improve classroom behavior. 2) Both teacher state of concern and level
of use of an innovative program are related to how that
program is used and its outcomes. 3) The teacher stage of
concern is an accurate predictor of teacher attitudes toward
an innovative program. 4) The teacher level of use is a
measure of teacher behavior and is relatively independent of
teacher attitudes toward the innovative program.

2036.   Bray, M. C. "A Comparison of Counselor Attention,
Counselor Attention Plus Modeling, and Supervised Study
Control Treatments in Changing Study Habits, Attitudes,
Behaviors, and Grades." Ed.D. Dissertation, The University
of North Carolina at Greensboro. Dissertation Abstracts
International, 39 (6-A), 3362-3363C. Order no. 7824295,
1978.

The purpose of this study was to compare counselor attention, counselor attention plus modeling, and supervised
study control treatments in changing students' study habits
and attitudes, grades, and class behaviors. Several hypotheses were investigated. Among them were: 1) counselor
attention will produce significantly greater change in
appropriate study habits, behaviors, and attitudes, and in
grade point averages than will the control condition; 2)
modeling plus counselor attention procedures will produce
significantly greater change in appropriate study habits,
behaviors, and attitudes, and in grade point averages than
will the control condition; 3) IQ levels and treatment
levels will interact. Other relevant contrasts were
examined as they appeared. Twenty-seven high school sophomore volunteers were stratified by IQ level, then randomly
assigned to either a counselor attention, a counselor attention plus modeling, or a supervised study control group.
Treatment for the attention group consisted of nine meetings
which involved initial rules and instructions and later
discussions of grades, study behaviors and attitudes toward
school. The investigator reinforced subjects with praise,
smiles, nods, and physical contact for expressing positive
attitudes toward school and for working efficiently at the
correct time. No significant treatment effect differences
existed for study habits, study attitudes, or grade point
averages. For the study habits variable, the counselor
attention treatment mean was significantly higher than means
for the modeling or control condition at the low IQ level.
Significant treatment main effects were found for teacher
rating 3 ("speaks positively of school and own work"), but

these were qualified by an interaction of treatment method and these were qualified by an interaction of treatment method and IQ. Within the average IQ level the ratings for the counselor attention condition and for the modeling condition subjects were significantly more favorable than those for students in the control condition. Within the low IQ level, counselor attention treatment subjects received significantly more favorable teacher ratings than those of the modeling or control groups.

2037.   Bricker, Audrey J. "A Program to Increase the Effectiveness of Regular Education Teachers in the Behavioral Management of Mainstreamed Children." Psy.D. Dissertation, Rutgers University The State University of New Jersey, 1980. Dissertation Abstracts International, 40 (12-A, Pt. 1), 6196. Order no. 8011321.

Mainstreaming, a system of progressive inclusion of handicapped students into regular education settings has been adopted by many public school systems as the major procedure for providing education for the handicapped in compliance with interpretations of the mandates of Public Law 94-142, the Education For All Handicapped Children Act. A review of the literature reveals that integration of handicapped children has been occurring in the United States with minimal or no advance preparation for the regular education teacher involved in the mainstreaming process. The primary goal of the program is to aid and assist in the effective delivery of educational services to mildly handicapped students by increasing regular education teachers skills and knowledge pertaining to: 1) federal, state and local laws which affect the education of handicapped children; 2) special characteristics and needs of handicapped students; 3) special education resources available to regular educators; 4) behavioral techniques for classroom management of maladaptive behaviors; 5) the use of communications skills to improve interpersonal functioning with students and other faculty. A program evaluation design was developed in order to obtain technically adequate information to aid the evaluation client(s) to make informed decisions about the design, performance, and impact of the program. The evaluation design includes the following strategies: a) evaluability assessment; b) process evaluation; c) outcome evaluation; and d) consumer evaluation. Specific methods of information collection, data analysis and information dessemination are explicated. Methods of analyzing the contribution of the program components in order to determine which are essential to achieving the desired outcomes are outlined in a four year evaluation time line which includes construction, program dismantling and reconstruction of the program periods. Methods of dissemination of a final evaluation report have been recommended.

2038.   Bridge, E. A.   "The Effect of Behavioral Techniques
Within an Intensive Design Upon Elementary School Children's
Attending Behavior."   Ph.D. Dissertation, Michigan State
University. Dissertation Abstracts International, 34 (9-A),
PT 1), 5616. Order no. 74-6010, 1974.

The purpose of this study was to measure the change in
attending behavior exhibited by elementary age students
through the application of a token economy and behavioral
contracts through the use of an intensive design. The study
was conducted over a 4-month, 73 school-day period of time.
Initially 4 teachers were selected who in turn submitted the
names of youngsters demonstrating nonattending behavior in
the classroom. From this list of referrals 11 children were
randomly selected to participate in the study. Prior to the
study 4 teachers were trained in the use of token economies
and behavioral contracts. Concurrently, a trained observer
began 1 20-minute daily observation of each child's attending and nonattending behavior, during phase one. This
daily observation was continued for the duration of the
study. In the second phase each teacher initiated a treatment program with each individual child. Five of the 11
students received contracts, while the remaining 6 received
tokens. In the third phase of the study the teachers withdrew the treatments while the observer continued to record
the classroom behavior. The teachers again utilized a
treatment technique in the fourth phase of the study. The 5
children who had received contracts now used tokens, while
those children who had received tokens initially now used
contracts. In the fifth phase of the study the treatments
were again withdrawn, while the children's behavior was
still continuously observed. The teachers used whichever of
the two treatments they felt most effective in increasing
attending behavior in the sixth phase of the study. Due to
the nature of the intensive design procedure, the hypotheses
were stated for both individual and group analysis. A
number of criterion measures was used to evaluate change in
attending behavior. These were: (1) the Behavior Analysis
Form, (b) the Achievement Motivation Scale, (c) the Academic
Achievement Scale, (d) the Assignment Completion Scale, and
(3) the Individual Student Evaluation Scale. The results of
the analyzed data indicate that the two treatments techniques were able to produce significant changes in each
child's attending behavior on both a meaninful and a
statistical level (p.05). From a statistical standpoint
there was no order effect in the presentation of treatments,
nor was there a superior treatment across subjects. The
Achievement (academic and motivation), Assignment Completion, and Individual Student Evaluation Scales data revealed
some mean changes between phases, but these were unique to
both teacher and student. The Teacher Research Evaluation
analysis data revealed that teachers consistently rated the
study on the positive end of the continuum with little
fluctuation between phases.

2039.   Brighouse, V. L. "Teacher-Controlling Behavior as Related to Selected Pupil and Classroom Variables." Ed.D. Dissertation, University of Southern California. Dissertation Abstracts International, 38 (8-A), 4540-4541P. 1978.

The study investigated the relationship between teacher-controlling behaviors (TCB) in grades one through three and the following selected pupil and classroom variables: 1) participation in the California Early Childhood Education (ECE) program, 2) teaching experience, 3) teacher person-ality factors, 4) pupil achievement, 5) pupil independent behavior, and 6) pupil self-concept. The problem was chosen because of the following theoretical concerns: 1) the teacher has significant impact on the classroom both in the development of classroom climate and on student cognitive and affective outcomes: 2) the classroom behavior of the teacher is largely one of a controlling or directive nature; and 3) research is sparse in the area of teacher-controlling behaviors, especially research which uses classroom observa-tion as a means of investigating links between TCB and pupil classroom variables. It was concluded that 1) Controlling functions are the most predominant of teacher behaviors. 2) Few cognitive and affective pupil and classroom variables in both ECE and non-ECE classes relate to TCB. 3) Relation-ships between selected pupil classroom variables exclusive of TCB may be significant.

2040.   Brinker, R. P. "Predicting Children's Classroom Behavior From Teachers' Classroom Behavior and Psychometric Descriptions of Children." Ph.D. Dissertation, George Peabody College for Teachers. Dissertation Abstracts International, 37 (5-B), 2539-2540. Order no. 76-21,618, 1976.

The purpose of the present study was to isolate the input and process variables which are associated with children's classroom behavior. Three categories of children's class-room behavior were used as dependent measures: a) the rate of children's academic involvement (the combined rate of hand-raising and academic verbalizations); b) the rate of attentive behavior; c) the rate of off-task behavior. The five sets of predictor variables were: a) demographic descriptions of children (IQ and achievement test scores); b) identification of children's problems (academic, behavioral, combination) for which teachers requested special assistance; c) nominal identification of teachers; d) a general sample of the teachers' verbalizations to the class; e) a sample of the teachers' and peers' behavior towards the target child. Second grade children (N = 117) from the classes of 44 teachers were observed. The class-room observation schedule was a time sampling procedure in which three pieces of information were recorded every 10 sec. Teachers' verbalizations to the class were classified into one of ten mutually exclusive and exhaustive categories during the first 3 sec. of each 10-sec. interval. The behavior of the target child (the same child for an entire 30-min. observational period) was classified into one of ten mutually exclusive and exhaustive categories during the second 3 sec. of each 10-sec. interval. The remainder of each 10-sec. interval was used to classify the behavior of teacher or peers directed toward the target child. The analyses revealed that the rates of both children's academic involvement and attentive behavior were associated with the rates of various categories of teachers' antecedent verbalizations and post-response events. The antecedent verbalization categories associated with academic involvement and attentive posture were a) responsive verbalizations (verbalizations in response to children's verbalizations) and b) questions to individuals. The rate of teachers' responsive verbalizations was positively correlated with the rate of academic involvement and negatively correlated with the rate of attentive behavior. The rate of questions to individuals was positively correlated with the rates of both academic involvement and attentive posture.

2041.   Brooks, R. C. "A Study to Establish Behavioral and Other Correlates of the Pupil Control Ideology Form at the Junior and Senior High School Level." Ph.D. Dissertation, The University of Iowa. Dissertation Abstracts International, 38 (4-A), 1762-1763. Order no. 77-21,120, 1977.

The primary purpose of this study was to examine the relationship between a teacher's pupil control ideology and the number and type of pupil/teacher conflicts that are sent to the administration as "discipline referrals". More specifically, this study obtained Pupil Control Ideology (PCI) scores from the teaching staffs of three junior high schools and one senior high school. After their PCI scores were obtained, the teachers were classified into a custodial-humanistic dichotomy at the median of the distribution of scores. These data were then analyzed to determine if a teacher's classification of the basis of their pupil control ideology was related to the frequency and type of pupil/teacher conflicts referred to the administration for adjudication. Significant differences were found between mean scores and showed that: 1) Custodial teachers not only had more total pupil/teacher conflicts than did humanistic teachers, they had more of all types of conflict reported at all levels investigated. 2) Junior high teachers (grades 7, 8, 9) were more custodial in PCI orientation and also had more pupil/teacher conflicts than senior high teachers. 3) Male teachers were more custodial and reported more pupil/teacher conflicts than female teachers. As a result of the significant findings, it is projected that Pupil Control Ideology and subsequent teacher behavior are related and that a teachers' responses on the PCI form could allow one to predict the way in which a teacher can be expected to behave in the area of reporting pupil/teacher conflict.

2042.   Broughton, S. F., Jr.   "Direct and Collateral Effects of Positive   Reinforcement,   Response-Cost,   and   Mixed Contingencies   for   Academic   Performance."   Ph.D. Dissertation, University of Georgia.   Dissertation Abstracts International, 37 (8-B), 4131.   Order no. 77-4102, 1977.

The purpose of this study was to examine the relative effects of three academic contingency systems on the dependent measures of academic performance and classroom behavior.   The three contingency systems were positive reinforcement, response-cost, and a mixed positive rein- forcement and response-cost system.   It was predicted from the available literature that all three contingency systems would cause persistent increases in the accuracy of academic performance and improvements in classroom behavior.   Thirty- three fourth- and fifth-grade pupils served as subjects. Four remedial math classes were randomly assigned to one of the three contingency systems or to an untreated control condition.   The findings of the study supported the results of earlier studies which had indicated that modification of academic performance produced significant and persistent changes in both academic performance and classroom behavior. The implementation on contingencies produced signficant improvements in all three contingency groups in academic performance and classroom behavior when compared to pretreat- ment baseline levels and untreated control subjects.   When contingencies were discontinued, treatment levels of academic performance were maintained for all three contin- gency groups.   The positive reinforcement and response-cost groups remained above control group performance levels while the mixed contingency group did not.   On-task behavior remained at treatment levels and above control group levels for all three contingency groups when contingencies were withdrawn.

2043.   Brown, Carolyn.   "The Effects of Self-Observation on Oral Classroom Participation and Locus of Control."   Ph.D. Dissertation, Arizona State University.   Dissertation Abstracts International, 37 (3-A), 1396-1397.   Order no. 76-19,814, 1976.

The purpose of this study was to determine whether or not self-observation would both improve the oral classroom participation of ninth-grade students as well as help those students move toward a more internal locus of control. Forty-seven male and 38 female ninth-grade students were assigned to three experimental groups defined as self- observation (S-O), observation plus reinforcement (S-O + R), and no-treatment control group (C).   Five observers assigned to ten classrooms recorded the same behavior as the students.   The results indicated that 1) self-observation did not have a significant effect on the classroom participa- tion of students whether or not they were reinforced and regardless of their classification as internal or external; 2) externals who were not reinforced for self-observation became significantly more internal, whereas neither

internals or externals changed in LOC when they were reinforced; and 3) overall treatment produced significant
improvement of the locus of control on scores of externals.

2044.   Brown, D. M. "Teacher Training in the Use of Operant
Principles to Reinforce Assertive Behavior in Elementary
School Children." Ed.D. Dissertation, Memphis State
University. Dissertation Abstracts International, 37 (8-A),
4975-4976. Order no. 77-4199, 1977.

The purpose of this study was to determine whether assertiveness in children could be increased through the training of
teachers in the use of operant principles to reinforce
assertive behavior. Effects of this training on other
student personality traits were also studied. The teacher
training program was conducted with four fourth-grade
teachers over a period of ten weeks. The program emphasized
positive reinforcement of five assertive behaviors: 1)
assertive talk, 2) expression of feelings, 3) disagreement,
4) asking why, and 5) talking about self. The effects of
the teacher training program were examined by assessing two
areas: the students' perceptions of various personality
traits as measured by the Children's Personality Questionnaire (CPQ), and the actual frequency of observed assertive
behaviors in the classroom. Equivalent forms of the CPQ
were administered to the students (N=82) before and after
teacher training. Classroom observations of the five
assertive behaviors by at least two raters were also made
before and after implementation. A multivariate analysis of
variance test, computed on the pretest and posttest data of
the CPQ, indicated that there was a significant difference
(p .001) in the pretest and posttest personality profile of
the children. The two factors of major interest in this
study were Factor E, assertiveness, and Factor C, ego-
strength. Results for Factor E suggested that there was a
significant increase (p .001) in the assertiveness of the
students after the teacher training program. Students saw
themselves as being more assertive, independent and dominant
in the four classes individually. Results for Factor C
indicated that there was a significant increase (p .001) in
the ego-strength of the students after implementation of the
teacher training program. Upon completion of the program,
students in all four classes appeared to be relatively calm,
stable, and socially mature and were also better prepared to
cope effectively with others.

2045.   Brown, Lorraine H. "Student Socioeconomic Status and
Teacher Pupil Control Behavior." Ph.D. Dissertation, The
Pennsylvania State University. Dissertation Abstracts
International, 35 (3-A), 1369. Order no. 74-20,908, 1974.

The purpose of this study was to examine the relationship
between school socioeconomic status (SES) and the pupil
control behavior of teachers. It was hypothesized that
teachers in low SES schools would exhibit more custodial
pupil control behavior than teachers in middle socioeconomic

status schools. The influence of school racial composition was also examined. The instrument designed to measure pupil control behavior was the Pupil Control Behavior Form (PCB Form) developed by Helsel and Willower. Prototypic custodial and humanistic behavior are described, and teachers are assigned scores by students completing this form. School SES was established by ranking occupations of heads of households for 20 percent of the student population. The population from which the sample was drawn was public secondary students of the Philadelphia Standard Metropolitan Statistical Area. The sample consisted of 16 secondary schools -- 4 predominantly black, low SES schools, 4 predominantly black, middle SES schools, 4 predominantly white, low SES schools, and 4 predominantly white, middle SES schools. The findings indicate that for the schools examined, the hypothesis that teachers in low SES schools will exhibit more custodial pupil control than teachers in middle SES schools is rejected. This suggested that socio-economic status does not influence teachers' pupil control behavior in the same manner as previous research shows it influences teachers' pupil control ideology.

2046.   Brown, P. O. "A Comparison of Self-Esteem, Anxiety, and Behavior of Black and Non-Black Underachieving Elementary School Students in Open and Stratified Classrooms." Ed.D. Dissertation. Columbia University, 1973.

The purposes of this study were: 1. to determine whether students in selected fourth, fifth, and sixth grade open and traditional (stratified) classes differed in terms of self-esteem or level of anxiety; 2. to determine whether selected black and non-black students reading two grades below norm in the open classes differed in terms of self-esteem, anxiety, and behavior from selected black and non-black students in the stratified classes. One open and one stratified class on the fourth, fifth and sixth grades were selected for this research. There were sixty-nine students in the open classes and sixty-five in the stratified class. The two fourth grade classes were located on the upper west side of Manhattan. The two fifth and sixth grade classes were located in a suburb of White Plains, New York. A total of six classes was involved in this study. Castaneda's Children's Manifest Anxiety Scale and Coopersmith's Self-Esteem Inventory were administered to all students in the six classes to measure anxiety and self-esteem. The results indicated no significant difference in level of anxiety or self-esteem between the total groups of students in the open and stratified classes. But there was a significant difference in self-esteem between the students in the open and stratified fourth grade classes, with the students in the open class demonstrating a significantly higher level of self-esteem. The findings indicated no significant difference in the self-esteem of the selected underachievers in the open and stratified classes. The data did show a significant difference in the level of anxiety between the selected black underachievers in the open and stratified settings. Order No. 73-31, 264, DAI.

2047.   Browning, B. D.   "Effects of Reality Therapy on Teacher Attitudes, Student Attitudes, Student Achievement, and Student Behavior." Ed.D. Dissertation. North Texas State University, 1978.

This study investigated whether Reality Therapy classroom management techniques could be used effectively to improve teacher attitudes, student attitudes, student achievement, and student classroom behavior. The data for this study were obtained by the use of a Semantic Differential, Pupil Achievement record, student tardy report, and student discipline report. The Semantic Differential consisted of seven key concepts related to the research problem. Bipolar adjectives were used to rate each concept. Concepts used in the study were rules, school, teacher, assistant principal, grades, discipline, and self. Teachers and students were administered the Semantic Differential prior to and following the treatment. Student grade point average was tabulated prior to and following Reality Therapy treatment, as was incidence of student discipline as measured by tardies, referrals to office, and suspensions. Experimental and control group subjects were comprised of eighth grade teachers and students from two junior high schools. Experimental group teachers were exposed to twenty hours of Reality Therapy prior to the treatment period. Both the experimental and control teachers and student groups were administered a pre- and post-assessment with the instruments used to secure data for the study. Fourteen eighth grade teachers comprised the experimental group. The experimental student group consisted of 345 students and the control group was comprised of 323 students. The study was conducted over a six-week period. The findings of the study support the following conclusions. 1. Reality Therapy inservice education and implementation of Reality Therapy Teaching techniques in classroom produce significant changes in the way teachers regard student discipline. 2. Implementation of Reality Therapy practices in junior high classrooms produces positive changes in attitude toward school environment. 3. Implementation of Reality Therapy techniques in junior high classrooms does not seem to be effective in producing changes in student attitude toward self. 4. Implementation of Reality Therapy techniques in junior high classrooms can be effective in producing higher student grade point averages. 5. Reality Therapy techniques in junior high classrooms are not effective in producing lower rates of student misbehavior. Order No. 7824637, DAI.

2048.   Browning, M. E. "The Relationships Among Secondary
School Teacher Role Orientation, Pupil Control Ideology, and
Pupil Control Behavior." Ed.D. Dissertation, Northern
Illinois University. Dissertation Abstracts International,
40 (11-A), 5658. Order no. 8011156, 1980.

This investigation arose from a concern about the relationships between teachers' pupil control ideology and behavior
and the often conflicting expectations held for them as
professionals and as employees of highly bureaucratized
organizations. The study generated information relative to
the following questions: (1) What relationships exist among
teachers' professional role orientation, their employee role
orientation, and their pupil control ideology (the study's
three independent or predictor variables)? (2) How well do
teachers' professional role orientation, their employee role
orientation, and their pupil control ideology predict their
pupil control behavior (the study's dependent or criterion
variable)? Two questionnaires were used to gather data. A
questionnaire for teachers collected demographic information
(age, sex, parental status, years of education, and years of
teaching experience) and teachers' responses items from
Corwin's Professional Orientation Scale, Corwin's Employee
Orientation Scale, and the Pupil Control Ideology Form
developed by Willower et al. A questionnaire for students
was the Pupil Control Behavior Form developed by Helsel and
Willower. A sample of 140 teachers in a large suburban high
school district was randomly selected for the study. In
addition, two classes of students were randomly selected for
each teacher for purposes of collecting data on the
teacher's pupil control behavior. The data suggest three
primary conclusions: (1) Whereas there is a significant
relationship between teachers' views of themselves as
employees of an organization and their pupil control
ideology, neither of these variables is significantly
related to teachers' views of themselves as professionals.
(2) Teachers' pupil control ideology and professional role
orientation are significantly related to their pupil control
behavior. Moreover, whether examined singly or in combination, teachers' pupil control ideology is consistently the
best predictor of their pupil control behavior. (3) With
respect to the demographic characteristics taken singly and
in combination the strength of the study's significant
relationships consistently greater for parents, for respondents age 30 to 39, and for respondents with Master's
Degrees plus credits.

2049.   Brownlee, E. M. "Verbal Approval and Disapproval of
Urban Black Pupils' Classroom Behaviors Relative to the Race
and Sex of the Teacher." Ph.D. Dissertation, Columbia
University. Dissertation Abstracts International, 37 (6-B),
3043-3044. 1976.

The major purpose of this study was to determine whether
black and white teachers, male and female teachers emitted
different rates of verbal approval and disapproval in

response to the classroom behaviors of black pupils. Accordingly, the following research questions were posed: 1) Do black teachers differ from white teachers in their distribution of verbal approval and disapproval to black pupils? 2) Do male teachers differ from female teachers in their distribution of verbal approval and disapproval to black pupils? 3) Do black and white teachers, male and female teachers differ in their rates of a) instructional or managerial approval and b) instructional or managerial disapproval? The subjects, 40 elementary school teachers, included 10 black males, 10 black females, 10 white males, and 10 white females. The teachers were drawn from eight elementary schools located in predominantly black, low-income areas of the inner-city. Each teacher was observed on three separate occasions for 25-minutes each time. The Teacher Approval-Disapproval Observational Record (TAD) was used to record approval-disapproval interactions. Male and female teachers were not found to emit significantly different rates of verbal aproval or disapproval. No differences were found between their rates of a) instructional or managerial approval nor b) instructional or managerial disapproval. The observed similarity between male and female teachers in their rates of verbal approval and disapproval was discussed in terms of the social role influence interpretation of teacher behavior.

2050.   Brownsmith, C. L. "The Skill Acquisition Model: Behavior Rehearsal as a Method for Developing Pro-Social Adaptive Behaviors in Elementary School Children." Ph.D. Dissertation, Indiana University. Dissertation Abstracts International, 37 (11-B), 5825. Order no. 77-10,956, 1977.

This study has investigated the application of the response acquisition model in teaching pro-social classroom behavior to elementary students. Six students were nominated by teachers to participate in the behavior rehearsal intervention program because of inappropriate or inadequate social behaviors in the regular classroom. Classroom conflict situations were written and tape recorded based upon informal observation and teacher interviews and related pro-social behaviors were stipulated for use in behavior rehearsal of these classroom stiuations. The students attended 20 minute individual intervention sessions twice weekly for four weeks in which they listened to two tape recorded classroom conflict situations and enacted behavior rehearsals for each situation. The Socio-Behavioral Interaction System was employed to record observational data in the regular classroom for the target students. Results indicated that the percent-time of cooperative behavior increased significantly for two students, though these results were not replicated for the remaining four students. Discussion of difficulties encountered in systematic observation in a naturalistic setting is provided. The experimenter suggests the need for careful definition of behavioral categories to be used in observation. Finally, the individual student's behaviors are examined informally to determine those characteristics which differentiated the two students with increases in cooperative behavior from the others. The possibility that variability in classroom performance may be a primary reason for teacher's identification of these students as behavior problems is presented for the purposes of future research.

2051.   Bruyere, D. H. "The Effects of Client-Centered and Behavioral Group Counseling on Classroom Behavior and Self Concept of Junior High School Students Who Exhibited Disruptive Classroom Behavior." Ph.D. Dissertation, University of Oregon. Dissertation Abstracts International, 36 (3-A), 1299. Order no. 75-18,723, 1975.

The purpose of this study is to compare the effects of client-centered and behavioral group counseling on the classroom behavior and self-concept of junior high school students who exhibited disruptive classroom behavior and to reexamine the theoretical premises of each counseling methodology. The 96 students participating in the study were enrolled in three public junior high schools in an industrial community of 35,000. These students had exhibited disruptive classroom behavior as reported by observers, and self-concept as measured by the Tennessee Self Concept Scale. The null hypothesis that there would be no significant differences among the four groups in conduct grade point average was retained. Significant difference at or exceeding the .05 level permitted rejection of the null hypothesis that there would be no significant difference among the four groups in teachers' behavior ratings, frequency of disruptive classroom behavior, and self-concept. Analysis of the data revealed that the client-centered group demonstrated a significantly greater reduction in frequency of disruptive classroom behavior as reported by observers, and that the behavioral group showed significant improvement in general classroom behavior as assessed by teachers, on the Modified Haggerty-Olson-Wickman Behavior Rating Scale. The four groups differed significantly on ten of the 44 Tennessee Self Concept Scale variables. The client-centered, behavioral and placebo groups demonstrated stability of self concept and constructive personality change while the control group demonstrated lowered self concept and personality deterioration. Evaluation of the group experience by students participating in client-centered and behavioral groups indicated that perceived changes in the self and in behavior varied between the two groups. These self-evaluations of change were compared by those made by teachers and classroom observers. It appeared that a positive change in observable behavior was not dependent upon a change in self perception, and that a change in self perception did not necessarily result in observed positive changes in behavior.

052.   Bryant, D. M. "Attention Training Procedures for
Distractible Children: Is EMG Biofeedback Effective."
Ph.D. Dissertation, The University of North Carolina at
Chapel Hill. Dissertation Abstracts International, 40
(5-B), 2402. Order no 7925891, 1979.

Electromyogram (EMG) biofeedback has been suggested as a
training procedure to help distractible children learn to
become more attentive in class. The purpose of this study
was to compare such a procedure with a behavioral attention
training method and two types of control groups: Pseudofeedback and no-treatment groups. Subjects were 32
elementary school children (7 girls and 25 boys), aged 6-11,
who were referred by their teachers because of their
problems in paying attention in class. Subjects were
randomly assigned to one of four groups, 8 subjects per
group. 1) Biofeedback subjects received 7 sessions of
frontalis EMG biofeedback training. Feedback was a tone
that varied in frequency as EMG level changed. 2) Pseudofeedback subjects received 7 sessions of similar training,
except, for them, the tone was not contingent upon EMG
Level. However, they were led to believe that it was. 3)
Attention Training subjects received 7 sessions of a
behavioral procedure that involved goal-setting and self-
monitoring. 4) Control group subjects were tested on the
same schedule as other subjects. Biofeedback subject rapidy
learned to lower frontalis EMG levels, while the EMG Levels
of Pseudofeedback subjects remained constant. This study of
EMG biofeedback in distractible children ployed more experimental controls that any other study to date. The results
do not support the hypothesis that it is an effective way to
teach distractible children to "pay attention." Some hyperactive children are reported to have very high muscle
tension levels, but these distractible children did not.
Excessive muscle tension appears not to be the cause of the
distractibility. Within a biofeedback session, subjects
concentrate well and were attentive to the feedback stimuli.

053.   Burck, E. L. "An Evaluative Study of the School Outreach
Services Project: A School Community Effort to Help
Selected Junior High School Students." Ed.D. Dissertation,
East Texas State University. Dissertation Abstracts
International, 37 (5-A), 2597-2598. Order no. 76-24,912,
1976.

The purpose of this study was to determine if students,
subjected to a special treatment of social work intervention
over a period of four months, will show greater improvement
in reading, arithmetic computation, school attitude, and
classroom behavior than will students who received only
regular school services including the Center for Special
Instruction program. The study spanned a period of four
months. The experimental group consisted of twenty-six
Miami Springs Junior High School students, and the control
group consisted of twenty-six Madison Junior High School
students. Three hypotheses were formulated to determine if

differences did exist in the areas of reading, arithmetic, and school attitude. Each hypothesis was accepted denoting no difference in acievement. The descriptive analysis of the classroom behavior data indicated that the control group had slightly more positive responses than did the experimental group. Students who have been subjected to intensive social work intervention for a four-month period may not show greater improvement in reading, arithmetic computation, school attitude, and classroom behavior, than do students who have only received the regular school services including the Center for Special Instruction program.

2054.   Burka, Aden A.   "Procedures for Increasing Appropriate Verbal Participation in Special Elementary Classrooms." Ph.D. Dissertation, The University of Rochester. Dissertation Abstracts International, 38 (6-B), 2848-2849T. Order no. 77-25,433, 1977.

The present study represents a continuation of efforts by the Classroom Management Training Project (CMTP) to develop social skills-oriented methods of classroom management and performance-oriented methods of teacher training. In this study the teachers of three special elementary classrooms were first trained in basic skills of limit-setting and the shaping of on-task behavior during a seat work lesson format, and subsequently they were trained in a newly developed set of discussion leader skills. The goals of the intervention were to reduce the amount of disruptive student behavior and to increase the amount of the students' appropriate verbal participation during group discussions. Each classroom had approximately 10 children. The age range in one class was 10-11 years, and in the other two, 12-13 years. Data were collected during a daily 20-30 minute academically-oriented discussion period by three members of the school's staff. Disruptive student behavior was measured using an event recording system and included both inappropriate talk and out of seat. Appropriate verbal participation, generally defined as pupil verbalizations where were "on topic" and addressed to the class as a whole, were measured using a duration recording system. The results indicated that during baseline all three classrooms were characterized by relatively high rates of pupil disruption and relatively little appropriate verbal participation. Instructing the three teachers had inconsistent effects. Skill Training I was successful in eliminating pupil disruption, and this low rate of disruption was stable throughout the remainder of the study. As predicted, all three classrooms showed increases in appropriate verbal participation following these two training sessions.

2055.   Burns, Harriet M.   "The Effect of the Use of Systematic Behavior Observation Procedures on the Perception of Severe Behavior Problem Children by Teachers." Ph.D. Dissertation, University of Minnesota. Dissertation Abstracts International, 35 (12-A, Pt. 1), 7753-7754. Order no. 75-12,047, 1975.

This study reports the effects of training in the use of a systematic observation procedure, The Pupil Observation Schedule (Wood, 1973), on teacher descriptions of the behavior of "problem" students viewed on videotapes. The population of 115 teachers (elementary/secondary, regular education/special education) were divided into experimental and control groups. The experimental group was trained in the use of the POS. The control group was given written directions for the use of the POS but no instruction. Three fifteen minute video tapes of three teenage boys in a residential treatment center were shown to the entire group of teachers. Teachers were asked: 1) to make a decision to refer/not refer each of the three boys shown on the tapes to a special setting for children with severe behavior problems, 2) to list all of the behaviors observed, 3) to indicate the two behaviors most influential in making the refer/not refer decision. No differences were noted between elementary and secondary school teachers on any of the variables. There was no difference between the Special Learning and Behavior Problem (Special Education) teachers and the regular teachers in the percent recommending referral. However, the S.L.B.P. teachers noted a larger mean number of behaviors than did the regular teachers.

2056.   Butler, K. O. "Attribution and intervention: a comparison of teachers' and pupils' perceptions of disruptive behavior." Ph.D. Dissertation, United States International University, 1975.

The problem of this study was to investigate whether teachers and pupils differ in their perception of the causes of disruptive behavior that occurs in the schools. The two main objectives of the study were 1) to determine if teachers and pupils perceive the same of different factors as causing disruptive behaviors, and 2) to determine if there is a relationship between the perception of causes and the conception of intervention strategies appropriate to remediate it. From the study it was concluded that teachers and pupils differ in their perceptions of the causes of disruptive behavior, teachers tend to attribute the causes to characteristics and traits of the active pupil, pupils tend to attribute the causes to entities and circumstances within the situational context and there is a negative association between the perception of cause and the conception of intervention strategy appropriate to remediate disruptive behavior from many teachers.

2057.   Byrd, G. W. "The Degree of Attraction Toward a Model and the Subsequent Learning of Classroom Contingency Management." Ph.D. Dissertation, The University of Oklahoma. Dissertation Abstracts International, 36 (8-A), 5141. Order no. 76-3088, 1976.

The primary purpose of this study was to attempt to determine whether positive and negative attraction toward a teacher affects the student's ability to learn from that teacher. An additional goal was the investigation of the effects of learning classroom contingency management on pre-service teachers' attitudes towards students in grades K-12. The third and final goal of this study was to investigate the effects of a simulated presentation versus a printed presentation on the learning of classroom contingency management. A significant difference at the .05 level was obtained between the positive and negative attraction toward a teacher in subsequent learning. No significant difference was found for the last two variables.

2058.   Candelario, G. "The Relationship of Biorhythms and Student Behavior: Critical Days, Physical, Emotional, and Intellectual Biocurves and Their Influence on High School Students' Behavior at the Time of Suspension From School." Ph.D. Dissertation, Michigan State University, 1979.

The general problem was to investigate the relationship between the behavior of students at the time they were suspended from school and the twenty-three day physical, twenty-eight day emotional, and thirty-three day intellectual cycles plus the critical day propositions of the popular theory of biorhythms. The investigation took place in three high schools in the southwestern part of Michigan. 141 students who were suspeded during October, 1977, and February, 1978, comprised the sample. The selection of the subjects was restricted to those students who were suspended because of self-initiated behavior. Because the theory is applicable to all humans from the moment of birth to the time of death, no differentiation was made for sex, age, grade levels, socio-economic status or condition of mental or physical health. The subjects' birth dates were used to draw individual biocharts. The critical days, non-critical days, and the high and low cycles of each student's biorhythms were obtained using the "birth charts" found in Bernard Gittelson's Biorhythm: a Personal Science. Biocharts were also computed with simple pencil and paper operations and the Kosmos I "bio-calculator." Chi-square analysis was used and the selected level of significance was .05. It was hypothesized that there would be no difference between the number of students suspended during their critical days and the number of students suspended during their non-critical. Chi-square analysis of all possible combinations of critical and non-critical days and the discrete categories of critical and non-critical days did not prove statistically significant and the null hypothesis was not rejected. A second hypothesis stated that there would be no difference between the number of students suspended during the low cycles of their physical, emotional, and intellectual biorhythms and the number os students suspended during the high scycles. The application of chi-square procedures did not demonstrate any significance when all possible combinations of high and low biorhythmic phases and the discrete categories of high and low biorhythmic cycles were scrutinized. Again, the null hypothesis was not rejected. 1) The results did not provide any evidence that biorhythms exerted any significant impact during the times when students' behavior caused them to be suspended from school. The basic assumption of the study that suspension-behavior was directly influenced by bio-rhythms was found to be false. 2) Biorhythms do not exist as an influence on human behavior, and the popular theory promulgated by George Thommen and Bernard Gittelson is without merit. Order no. 7921136, DAI.

2059.   Carducci, Ronald J.   "A Comparison of I-Messages with Commands in the Control of Disruptive Classroom Behavior." Ph.D. Dissertation, University of Nevada, Reno, 1976. Dissertation Abstracts International, 36 (11-B), 5783. Order no. 76-11,352.

Sixty-four students in two 5th grade public school classes served as experimental subjects in a study designed to test the relative effectiveness of two modes of teacher responses -- I-Messages and commands -- to reduce the frequency of disruptive classroom behavior. Each classroom teacher was trained to deliver commands and I-Messages in response to disruptive student behavior. I-Messages consisted of a description by the teacher of the student or students' disruptive behavior, the teacher's feelings in reaction to such behavior, and an explanation of how the disruption interfered with the teacher's ability to meet her needs. Commands consisted of explicit orders to the student or students to either stop a disruptive behavior, start an appropriate behavior, or stop a disruptive behavior and start an appropriate behavior. Classroom #1 experienced an ABAC reversal design sequence (A=Baseline$_1$, B=Command condition, A=return to Baseline$_2$) followed by a comparison of the I-Message condition (C=I-Message condition) with baseline. Classroom #2 experienced an ACABC reversal sequence (A=Baseline$_1$, C=I-Message$_1$ condition, A=Baseline$_2$, B=Command condition) followed by a return experimental I-Message$_2$ condition (C). Per minute frequency of speaking-out and out-of-seat behavior was recorded in both classrooms during all baseline and experimental conditions. It was concluded that: 1) The teachers' exclusive use of I-Messages (i.e., without the additional use of consequences such as reinforcement or loss of privileges) was effective in reducing the frequency of disruptive behavior. 2) The teachers' use of I-Messages was more effective than commands in reducing the frequency of disruptive behavior. 3) The teahcers' use of I-Messages during the I-Message$_1$ period in Classroom #2 appeared to cause an across-condition decrease in the frequency of speaking-out and out-of-seat behavior. 4) I-Messages appeared to be effective in reducing the rate of disruptive behavior even though delivered by the teachers at a relatively low frequency rate. 5) The use of I-Messages was taught to both classroom teachers during a four hour training period.

2060.   Carella, S. D. "Discipline Judgments of Disruptive Behaviors by Individuals and Dyads Differing in Moral Reasoning." Ph.D. Dissertation, The University of Oklahoma. Dissertation Abstracts International, 38 (4-A), 1990. Order no. 77-21, 368, 1977.

One hundred and ten (110) male and female teacher education students completed a objective test of moral development (Defining Issues Test) and were ranked according to their scores of higher principled moral reasoning. Forty-eight (48) students were chosen as subjects from this population by randomly selecting sixteen (16) students from the upper, middle, and lower twentieth percentiles. Each participant viewed two vignettes depicting classroom disturbances with a dyad partner. The participants were asked to write their individual recommendations regarding how the disturbances should be handled and the reasons for the recommendations. In addition, each participant was asked to rate how severe he/she perceived the disturbances. The first vignette was perceived as more severe than the second vignette by the five judges. In regard to disciplinary judgments those of higher principled subjects tended to be less severe and more appropriate than those judgments of lower principled subjects. In addition, higher principled subjects perceived the classroom disturbances as less severe than lower principled subjects. There was no evidence to support the hypothesis that change would occur as a result of combining subjects of different levels or moral reasoning. However, significant interactions indicated that mixed moral dyads tended to evoke different judgments than matched moral dyads and that mixed dyads did not perceive the disturbances in the same way as matched dyads.

2061.   Carlson, R. E. "Training Teachers in Reinforcement: A Teacher-Student Interaction Analysis." Ph.D. Dissertation, University of Houston. Dissertation Abstracts International, 35 (7-B), 3549-3550. Order no. 75-1027, 1975.

Fifty-eight subjects were sampled randomly from a population of 510 teachers participating in the Teacher Development Centers; reinforcement training program located in three elementary schools. Fifty-eight classrooms were involved in the study. Approximately 1,800 students were observed in their classrooms during the study. Observations were made by 15 trained observers for twenty (20) minutes on each of three (3) successive days before and after treatment. Baseline or pre-treatment data were collected three (3) weeks prior to the first 40 hours training, cycle one. Post-treatment data were collected three (3) weeks after the second cycle of 40 additional hours of training. A time lapse of 15 weeks occurred between the first cycle of training and the second training cycle. Total training was 80 hours. A more positive learning environment was established. Theoretically, a positive environment will facilitate an individual's proacting with his environment.

Since the teachers manifested significantly more positive (approving) behaviors and significantly fewer negative (disapproving) behaviors toward students, the students should have been more expressive toward or solicitous of this source of approval: the teachers or the significant others. The students were not more solicitous of the teachers. There were no significant differences between pre-treatment and post-treatment observations of solicitation behaviors by students toward teachers.

2062.   Carson, W. M. "A Study of the Effects of Training Teachers Through Group Consultation to Decrease Pupils' Attention-Getting Behaviors." Ph.D. Dissertation, State University of New York at Buffalo. Dissertation Abstracts International, 34 (9-A, PT 1), 5618-5619. Order no. 74-4387, 1974.

This study determined the usefulness of training teachers through a group consultation process to decrease attention-getting behaviors on the part of their pupils. A major concern of this study was to investigate the applicability of a model of group consultation that focused on the behavior and/or problems external to the teacher that could prove to be a useful and productive one for counselors and other in the mental health profession who work at the elementary school level. A second concern of this study was to add to the limited body of knowledge concerning consultation. This study attempted to define the theory model, concretize the roles and functions of the consultant, and relate the results of the consultation process to the outcome for the client. It was hypothesized in this study that those teachers involved in the consultation process and who used video tape for feedback during the follow-up period would produce effective decreases in certain maladaptive pupil behavior. Three treatment conditions were established to carry out the study. The control condition was comprised of those teachers who received "no treatment." The experimental I condition received the training through group consultation plus the use of video tape for observing their pupils during the follow-up period. The experimental II condition received the training through group consultation plus in-classroom observation of their pupils during the follow-up period. The teachers who received the training plus the use of video tape during the follow-up period showed significant (p.05) decreases in their pupils' attention-getting behaviors when compared with the control and experimental II groups.

2063.   Carter, Lonnie T. "A Strctured Human Relations Program for Teachers: An Experiment in Classroom Management." Ph.D. Dissertation, Marquette University, 1973. Dissertation Abstracts International, 34 (5-A), 2380. Order no. 73-27,498.

This study was undertaken to determine the effects of a structured in-service human relations program on certain attitudes and behaviors of teachers. Changes in teacher's behaviors were assessed by nonreactive measures, 1) discipline cards, 2) psychological referrals, and 3) counseling referrals. The major objective of the program was the development of more positive coping techniques for certain specified problem behaviors. The theoretical framework for this human relations program was Dreikurs' model for understanding maladaptive behaviors in children and adolescents. The problems focused upon were presented in six structured sessions as follows: 1) <u>Session One</u> - Students who are rebellious. 2) <u>Session Two</u> - Students who have asocial values. 3) <u>Session Three</u> - Students and others who use alienating language. 4) <u>Session Four</u> - Students who hurt others (physically) for no apparent reason. 5) <u>Session Five</u> - Students who seek attention. 6) <u>Session Six</u> - Students who misbehave when left unsupervised for a short time. Experimental and control groups of ten each were established from three Title One public schools; one elementary, one junior high school, and one high school. The experimental groups viewed films, role played, and dealt with written materials which presented specific and concrete examples of the above-mentioned behaviors. The subjects then attempted to determine ways of handling these situations in the most positive fashion. The study proposed that in this manner the experimental subjects would develop more positive coping techniques and that the development of these techniques would be reflected in certain attitudinal and behavioral changes. An evaluation of the accumulated data revealed that there were no significant differences in MTAI scores for experimental and control subjects. In regards to discipline cards, the experimental group submitted significantly fewer cards than the control group at the elementary school level. However, there was no significant differences in the number of discipline cards submitted for the junior high and high school samples. The number of psychological and counseling referrals were significantly less for the experimental groups at the elementary and junior high school levels. Once again no significant differences appeared among the high school sample in regard to the submission rate of these two variables.

2064.   Cartledge, G. "A Preliminary Investigation into the Effects of Social Skill Teaching Strategies on Attending Behavior." Ph.D. Dissertation, The Ohio State University. Dissertation Abstracts International, 36 (8-A), 5194. Order no. 76-3398, 1976.

This investigation was designed to study the effects of social modeling and praise on observable attending and on-task behaviors. As part of a larger social skills curriculum project, it was theorized that certain observable social behaviors could be taught using teaching strategies which incorporated behavioral approaches. Fifteen public school third, fourth and fifth grade subjects, identified as poor attenders, were used in this study. The fifteen subjects were assigned to one of three study groups (N=5), according to grade level and baseline attending scores. A multiple baseline-reversal design across conditions and groups was employed. Intervention consisted of 1) teacher praise in the classroom for attending behaviors and 2) small group instruction outside the classroom for attending, using social modeling strategies. Classroom observations by trained observers were conducted throughout the study. These procedures resulted in no significant observable changes in attending behaviors in the classroom. Although it appeared that the teaching strategies may have been effective in increasing attending in the modeling sessions, generalization did not occur to the classroom. It was concluded that, to be effective, behaviors should be taught in the settings where they are desired and for generalization to occur highly developed mechanisms are required.

2065.   Chernick, E. "An Exploratory Study of the Effect of the Feingold Diet on Reading Achievement and Classroom Behavior." Ed.D. Dissertation, Hofstra University. Dissertation Abstracts International, 40 (11-A), 5722. Order no. 8008437, 1980.

The primary purpose of study was to evaluate effectiveness of dietary change for children with learning/emotional problems. Nutritional program based upon Feingold's theory that synthetic flavors, colors, and salicylates acted as central nevous system irritants for children demonstrating "pharmacological individuality." Controlled study of 15 hyperactive children placed on Feingold's elimination diet resulted in reduced hyperactivity noted by teachers. In another study parents reported improved behavior for 93 percent of hyperactive children placed on diet. In double-blind crossover study no changes noted by parents or teachers but improved behavior noted in preschool group, supporting Feingold's hypothesis that younger children demonstrated faster, more positive, reaction to diet. Subsequent study revealed 70 percent hyperactive children presented positive allergic reactions as compared to 15 to 20 percent for population at large.

2066.   Cherry, James H. "A Study of Reality Therapy as an Approach to Discipline in the Classroom." Ed.D. Dissertation, Illinois State University, 1975. Dissertation Abstracts International, 36 (11-A), 7369. Order no. 76-9906.

The problem of this study was to assess the effects of a Reality Therapy program on irresponsible students in a secondary school setting during a three-week experimental treatment period. In particular, it was hypothesized that a three-week Reality Therapy program would increase the rate of appropriate classroom behavior and decrease the rate of inappropriate classroom behavior. The sample of students was drawn from the secondary school population at University High School, Normal, Illinois. Data for the study were collected by observers on a Student Rating Sheet designed by

Thomas, Becker, and Armstrong. The observers recorded both
the students' appropriate and inappropriate behavior on a
dialy basis during the study. 1) Neither the appropriate
nor inappropriate student behavior exhibited statistically
significant changes as a result of the three-week experimental treatment. 2) While the Reality Therapy approach did
not produce a statistically significant outcome, investigation of the total treatment period revealed no negative
effect because of the use of Reality Therapy in the classrooms under treatment. 3) Assessment of the extended treatment period resulted in the general conclusion that specific
student behaviors exhibited stronger positive trends than
general behavior categories.

2067.   Cheuvront, Herbert L. "Use of Behavior Modification
Concepts with Adolescent Underachievers to Improve School
Achievement Through Attitude Change." Ph.D. Dissertation,
United States International University, 1975. Dissertation
Abstracts International, 36 (4-b), 1940. Order no.
75-22,653.

The purpose of the study was to test the effectiveness of a
brief summer training program, using behavior modification
principles, in bringing about improvement in academic performance through changes in attitudes found to be most
closely associated with underachievement. The specific
objectives of the research were: 1) To determine if a
combination of programmed fantasy experiences for improving
self-image, relaxation training, assertiveness training,
desensitization to aversive stimuli, and training of parents
in the use of behavior modification principles in dealing
with their children would produce greater attitude changes
than no training in any of these techniques. 2) To determine if specific combinations of techniques may be more
effective in producing attitude change than no training in
techniques. 3) To determine if specific combinations of
techniques may be more effective in producing attitude
change than no training in techniques. 4) To determine the
interrelationships among changes in achievement and changes
in the various attitudes, shown to be related to achievement. Eighty subjects were chosen from public schools by
the following criteria: age range of thirteen to sixteen
years; IQ range of ninety or above; letter grades of "D" or
"F" on more than half their report card marks for preceding
school year or scores of more than two years. Eight groups
were formed on the basis of personal convenience. Six
groups were trained two hours a day for three weeks in a
variety of self-controlled behavior modification techniques.
One "placebo" group met but received no particular training.
One control group received testing only and attended no
meetings. Analysis of the data indicated that combined
group scores showed a significant increase in grade points
and in self-esteem. Definite positive trends were recorded
in each of the other categories. The fact that the control
group was one of the groups showing a significant improvement in grades and the lack of significant interaction among

groups on all measurements resulted in failure to reject any of the null hypotheses. It was concluded that the program had a positive influence, but that it was overshadowed by strong uncontrolled environmental stimuli, particularly relating to family relationships.

2068.   Chiesa, Daneta D. "The Effects of Teacher Training in Behavior Analysis and Human Relations on Student Classroom Behavior." Ed.D. Dissertation, George Peabody College for Teachers. Dissertation Abstracts International. Order no. 75-12,429, 1975.

One goal of teacher training is to instruct teachers in how to effect change in student classroom behavior. Empirical studies indicate that by training teachers in behavior analysis and human relations skills teachers can effect change in student academic behaviors. Studies also indicate that teachers trained in behavior analysis can effect change in off-task student classroom behavior. However, no studies are available which indicate teachers trained in human relations skills or a combination of behavior analysis and human relations skills can effect change in off-task student classroom behavior. This study was designed to examine if teachers systematically trained in behavior analysis and human relations skills could effect change in off-task student classroom behavior. The results of this investigation indicated significant differences were found among the five treatment groups. No significant differences were found among the three rating conditions. No significant interaction was found among groups and subjects within groups. It was concluded from these findings that teachers systematically trained in behavior analysis and human relations skills can demonstrate knowledge of the principles conveyed by their performance on paper-and-pencil tests, verbal contributions, and role-playing during training sessions and still not be able to effect a significant change in off-task student classroom behavior.

2069.   Choy, Steven J. "A Comparative Analogue Study of Techniques Used to Teach Classroom Management Skills." Ph.D. Dissertation, University of Utah. Dissertation Abstracts International, 38 (7-A), 4105. Order no. 77-27,710, 1977.

University students were trained in behavior modification using one of three techniques: Lecture; Lecture with Video-taped Modeling; Lecture with Role-playing. The comparative effects of the training procedures were measured by the subjects' acquired knowledge of behavior modification principles and their actual application of these principles in a simulated classroom. There were no differences among the training groups in the acquisition of behavior principles as measured by a paper-and-pencil test. The groups did, however, differ in their actual use of these skills. The subjects in both the modeling and role-playing groups generally attended more to the children's appropriate behaviors and less to their inappropriate behaviors than the lecture group. The modeling and the role-playing groups, however, did not differ significantly from each other. Implications for teacher training are that the less expensive lecture with videotaped modeling procedure is preferable to lecture with role-playing.

2070.   Christiansen, Gary A. "Minicourse 23: Classroom Management Through Positive Reinforcement -- A Preliminary Field Study." Ed.D. Dissertation, University of Pittsburgh. Dissertation Abstracts International, 37 (7-A), 4295. Order no. 77-687, 1977.

The purpose of the study was to conduct a preliminary field study of Minicourse 23: Class Management through Positive Reinforcement developed by the Far West Laboratory for Educational Research and Development. The study population consisted of twelve elementary grade level teachers enrolled in the graduate school of Education at Edinboro State College. The teachers received three hours graduate credit for their participation in the study. Each teacher participated in the series of studies and exercises in the graduate classroom and teacher classroom that together comprise the elements of the Minicourse experience. The Minicourse developes the use of positive reinforcements in the classroom by means of a general introduction followed by the lesson or chapter each on Teacher Verbal and Nonverbal Reinforcement, Activities and Privileges, and Classroom Environment types of reinforcement. Reinforcement concepts and activities are presented in the form of print and videotape materials prepared by Far West. The Minicourse was a success in terms of the data produced by the Questionnaires which showed that the teachers as a group increased the amount of teacher-student interaction and individualization, increased freedom to choose materials, and improved rates of study in the classroom. This success is further implied by the identified decrease in the teacher use of negative reinforcements and the overall improvement in the classroom environment and behavior of individual students and the class as a whole as perceived by the teacher. The Minicourse was a success in terms of the data produced by the Observation Event Recording Instrument which shows the teachers as a group increasing the amount and use of the three forms of reinforcement (Teacher Verbal and Nonverbal, Activities and Privileges, and Use of the Environment) based on observation of Precourse and Postcourse videotapes of teaching behavior.

2071.   Church, J. S. "Effect of Individual and Group Cue-Reinforcement Counseling as Interventional Techniques for Modifying Elementary Classroom Behaviors." Ph.D. Dissertation, University of Kentucky. Dissertation Abstracts International, 33 (8-A), 4083. Order no. 72-29,262, 1973.

This research investigated the effectiveness of structured individual personal-vocational cue-reinforcement feedback counseling and structured group vocational cue-reinforcement feedback counseling, each treatment being administered on a three-week time interval and on a two-week time span, as interventional procedures to modify the patterns of behavior of elementary school children. Overall, the results from using explicitly described counseling strategies and a powerful assessment instrument revealed that the females' behavioral patterns were effected in that they increased their own estimations concerning their realistic, outdoor, manual skills and were judged in like manner by their peers. In addition, the females became less shy and reticent, asserting themselves and became more positive in their leadership skills, personal adjustment and effort and motivation. The males were viewed as being less disruptive and impulsive and as being more controlled. The males' vocational interest behaviors were also enlarged. In conclusion, this study indicated that it is possible to answer the question of what kind of treatment is best for what kind of person with what kind of behavior.

2072.   Clark, R. P. "Comparative Effects of Instruction, Self-Monitoring, and Self-Reinforcement on Teacher Attending Behavior." Ed.D. Dissertation, The University of Tennessee. Dissertation Abstracts International, 36 (3-A), 1385. Order no. 75-18,948, 1975.

A major purpose of the present study was to assess the relative merits of instruction in contingent teacher attention, self-monitoring, and self-reinforcement on teacher approval and disapproval to disruptive classroom students. Other objectives were to assess the reliability of teacher self-recorded data and to determine whether a relationship between the frequency of approval and disapproval occurred as a function of the experimental conditions. Five junior high school teachers in an urban school system served as subjects. Each teacher identified two students in their classes regarded as disruptive or nonparticipating. Teachers and students were observed for 55 days. Data on teacher rates of approval and disapproval to target students and student rates of appropriate and inappropriate behaviors were collected to ascertain the effectiveness of experimental conditions. The results showed that instruction had little effect upon either positive teacher or student behavior. Self-monitoring approval had no clear effects on teacher approval or disapproval, although students under this condition reduced their inappropriate behavior. Teachers under the self-monitoring disapproval phase reduced their disapproval, but a decrease in approval rates and appropriate student behavior also occurred. Self-reinforcement increased teacher approval but had ambiguous effects on disapproval and student behaviors. Agreement between teacher self-recorded data was low for both approval and disapproval. Teacher rates of approval and disapproval failed to show systematic variation with respect to each other as a function of the experimental treatments.

2073.   Clarkson, P. J.   "Effects of Parent Training and Group Counseling on Children's Functioning in Elementary School." Ed.D.   Dissertation,   University   of   Massachusetts. Dissertation Abstracts International, 39 (8-A), 4726-4727P. Order no. 7901980, 1979.

The purpose of this study was to determine if changes could be demonstrated in the classroom performance of sixty-seven public school elementary school students after their parents had received a nine-week Systematic Training for Effective Parenting (STEP) program and the children themselves had received group counseling using the Developing Understanding of Self and Others (DUSO) program. It was hypothesized that parent training and group counseling would produce measurable change in the classroom performance of students from the regular population of the school. It was further hypothesized that parent training would bring about change in the children's behavior at home as perceived by their parents. Classroom performance was measured in the areas of classroom behavior, academic achievement, self-concept, and attendance. At-home behavior was evaluated by the parents using a behavior rating scale and parent questionnaires. Students, from Grades 1 through 6, in an elementary school in western Massachusetts and their parents volunteered for participation in the study in response to a letter sent to the whole population of the school. The children were assigned to three experimental groups and a control group. Group 1 (N=14) was composed of children who received group counseling and whose parents received parent training; Group 2 (N=17) was composed of children who did not receive group counseling, but whose parents did not receive parent training; and Group 4 (N=20) was the control who neither received group counseling nor did their parents receive parent training. Analysis of the data showed that there were no significant differences in the classroom performance of the subjects between the treatment groups. Nor were their significant results between any of the treatment groups and the control groups. Three possible explanations for these results were offered: 1) the techniques used to measure classroom behavior did not have the capability of measuring the changes expected, 2) the expected changes may take longer to develop in the regular school population than the time intervals used in this study, and the treatment had no effect on the subjects.

2074.   Clay, C. M.   "The Utility of Behavioral Descriptions for Predicting Self Concepts in Children."   Ed.D. Dissertation, The   University   of   Tennessee.   Dissertation   Abstracts International, 39 (6-A), 3463. Order no. 7823316, 1978.

The purpose of this study was to determine what classroom behaviors (Task Relevant, Verbalization, Aggressive, Noise Making, and Social Conduct) are predictive of self-concept in fourth grade students. Subjects for the study were 30 students, 15 boys and 15 girls, ranging in age from nine to ten years. Two undergraduate college students trained in behavioral observation techniques observed the classroom behavior daily for 30 minutes. During this time students worked on scheduled English assignments. A time sampling technique was utilized to collect data on task related (on-off), disruptive behavior (verbalization, aggressive, noise making) and social conduct. A frequency count was used in tabulating teachers' negative and positive comments. The study demonstrated that several classroom behaviors are predictive of self-concept in an educational setting. Specifically, the following behaviors were significantly related to self concept: on task behavior, inappropriate social conduct, and aggressive behavior. In contrast the following additional behaviors were not significantly related to self-concept: off task behavior, appropriate social conduct, verbalization, and noise making. The combination of variables which are the best predictors of self concept include the following: on task behavior and inappropriate social conduct: and on task behavior and aggressive behavior.

2075.   Cocreham, E. A. "A Study of the Effect on Attitude, Knowledge and Evaluation of Teachers Working with Elementary School Children After Participation in a Behavioral Modification Inservice Program." Ed.D. Dissertation, Brigham Young University. Dissertation Abstracts International, 36 (3-A), 1386. Order no. 75-19,722, 1975.

The purpose of this study was to determine the effects of an inservice program emphasizing implementation of behavior modification techniques in the classroom on a) teacher attitude regarding behavior modification, b) teacher evaluation of behavior modification, and c) teacher knowledge of basic principles of behavior modification. The participating 80 teachers, 40 in the experimental group and 40 in the control group, were volunteers from four experimental schools in the Burbank and the Los Angeles Unified School Districts. Based on the results of this study, it was concluded that 1) there was no significant change in attitude on the part of teachers participating in the inservice, 2) there was a significant difference in behavior modification content knowledge gained on the part of participating teachers, 3) teachers placed significantly greater evaluation on behavior modification after participating in the inservice, and 4) there was no significant positive relationship between evaluation of and increased knowledge of behavior modification on the part of teachers in the inservice program.

2076.   Cohen, E. N. "Pupil Behaviors as Indicators of Teacher Success." Ph.D. Dissertation, Columbia University. Dissertation Abstracts International, 39 (4-A), 2138. Order no. 7819316, 1978.

This study examined the influence of naturally occurring pupil behaviors on teachers' self judgment of success. It pinpointed observable pupil behaviors that were identified by teachers as indicators of teacher success, and examine how these behaviors naturally occurred in classrooms, and how teachers verbally approved of these behaviors. A two-phase methodology was used. In Phase 1, elementary and secondary teachers (N=100) viewed video-tapes of social studies classes and then wrote descriptions of pupil behaviors which would indicate success. In Phase 2, observations were conducted in junior high school classes using the Teacher Pupil Behavior Inventory, an instrument which allows two observers in a classroom to simultaneously record verbal and nonverbal pupil behaviors and teacher verbal approval feedback. In Phase 1 teachers identified both verbal and nonverbal pupil behaviors as indicators of teacher success. Verbal behaviors included answers to teacher questions, both correct and incorrect and on-task initiated responses including comments, questions, and expressions of enjoyment or interest. The nonverbal pupil behaviors included on-task attention and facial expressions of enjoyment. Classroom observations in Phase 2 indicated that while some indicators of teacher success occurred frequently during a class session, others were infrequently exhibited. Pupils rarely demonstrated either verbal or non-verbal questions occurred on the average of once per minute of instructional time. The major finding in this study was that there was no significant difference between the frequency of either verbal or nonverbal pupil indicators of teacher success in the "most successful" or "least successful" class sessions. One interpretation of this finding was that teachers' self-rating of effectiveness in teaching a class session may only be influenced by pupil behavior which differs considerably from that behavior they would expect to observe. The behavior of pupils in the average tract classrooms observed in this study did not vary greatly from day to day, and, therefore, no meaningful discrepancy may have been created between the pupil behavior a teacher may have expected and what actually occurred. In the absence of such sharp variations in pupil behavior, teachers' judgement of success may have been based upon self-monitoring of their own behavior and their goals of subject-matter competence in a lesson.

2077.   Coleman, L. M.   "Behavioral Contrast Between Classrooms." Ph.D. Dissertation, University of Georgia. Dissertation Abstracts International, 36 (8-A), 5141-5142. Order no. 76-2217, 1976.

This study was concerned with the occurrence of behavioral contrast between classrooms. The significance and the need to study behavioral contrast and its ramifications were discussed. Four teachers and two elementary grade student sections served as subjects in this study. Two teachers with consecutive classes with a third grade student section served in the positive behavioral contrast paradigm. Two teachers with consecutive classes with a fourth grade section served in the negative behavioral contrast paradigm. Conceptually, when one section of students was shared by two teachers in consecutive class periods, these class periods were viewed as components of a cycle in a multiple schedule, where the teachers function as discriminative stimuli. By applying appropriate schedules of reinforcement within these components, behavioral contrast effects were demonstrated. Manipulating the reinforcement schedules for teacher attention (praise or ignore) in the first, changed component, the contrast effects were observable in the second, unchanged component. These behavioral contrast effects were positive when there was an increase in the rate of target behavior and negative when there was a decrease in the rate of target behavior in the second, unchanged component. Two pardigms, specific to generating either positive or negative contrast were performed. Contingent teacher attention schedules (praise or ignore) served as independent variables. Appropriate academic behavior among 10 target students in a student section served as the dependent variable, the target behavior. Target students were not identified to teachers during the study. All four experimental hypotheses were supported by the data. When the first teacher was changed from praise to ignore schedules, the rate of target behavior increased in the second class where the teacher remained on a praise schedule throughout the study. Further, there was a decrease in rate of target behavior in the second class when the first teacher was returned to a praise schedule. These results were consistent with the definition of positive behavioral contrast.

2078.   Coman, P. N.   "An Examination of the Relationship Between Preferred and Observed Classroom Management Behaviors of Elementary   School   Teachers."   Ed.D.   Dissertation. University of Houston, 1978.

The purpose of this study was to explore the relationship between the classroom management approach preferences of teachers and their classroom managerial behavior. Seven hypotheses were formulated for the study; each one tested the relationship posited to exist between a specific teacher classroom management approach preference and the teacher managerial behaviors characteristic of that approach. The seven classroom management approaches which were examined were those identified by Weber (1977). They were the: 1. authoritarian; 2. behavior modification; 3. common sense; 4. group process; 5. instructional; 6. permissive; and 7. socio-emotional climate approaches. The independent variables were teacher preferences regarding seven classroom management approaches as measured by the Management Approach Preference Inventory (MAPI) (Weber and Cunningham, 1978); the dependent variables were teacher classroom managerial behaviors as measured on the Management Approach Behavior Observational System (MABOS) (Coman, Goldstein, Peacock, and Weber, 1978). The sample consisted of thirty-five volunteer elementary school teachers. They were the subjects for observational study and the respondents to the MAPI. The results of this study suggested the following conclusions: 1. that a statistically significant relationship exists between the expressed preferences that teachers have for authoritarian, behavior modification and instructional classroom management approaches and their use of the behaviors descriptive of these approaches; 2. that a statistically significant relationship exists between clusters of management approach preferences and clusters of corresponding management approach behaviors, specifically those including the behavior modification, common sense, group process, instructional and permissive approaches; and 3. as a result, limited support is given to the MAPI as a reliable and valid predictor of classroom managerial behavior. Order No. 7901212, DAI.

2079.   Conard, R. J.   "Long and Short Term Effects of a Teacher Training "Package" on Teacher and Student Behavior."   Ph.D. Dissertation, University of Kansas.   Dissertation Abstracts International, 39 (7-A), 4188-4189L.   Order no. 7824783, 1979.

The effects of a teacher training "package" upon selected teacher and student behaviors, student daily academic performance, and student achievement test performance were investigated.   The package, including videotaped lessons, objective performance criteria, classroom performance feedback and mastery learning requirements, increased teachers' use of selected teaching techniques and increased student on-task behavior.   Daily student academic performance did not change as a result of the training package.   However, student achievement test scaled scores increased more for trained teachers' classes than for untrained teachers' classes.   A possible trend toward teachers' decreasing use of trained teaching techniques was noted after training was completed, despite weekly maintenance feedback, suggesting that more powerful maintenance procedures may be necessary. However, student on-task rates remained at training levels, and teachers' instances of attending to off-task student behaviors continued to decrease.

2080.   Cook, C. H.   "An Investigation of the Post Treatment Effects of Teacher Tracking on Teacher Praise and the Behavior of Low Achieving, Inattentive Students."   Ph.D. Dissertation, University of Oregon.   Dissertation Abstracts International, 40 (9-A), 4998.   Order no. 8005757, 1980.

The investigation was an attempt to evaluate the effects of teacher tracking during a maintenance period on rates of teacher praise and levels of appropriate behavior of target students.   These variables were studied under two conditions: teacher tracking of target student behavior, and no teacher tracking of target student behavior.   (Teacher tracking was defined as observation and recording of target student behavior at 10 minute intervals.   At the end of each interval, teachers were required to record whether each target student was working or not working).   The study was conducted during a six week period that followed successful completion of a behavioral treatment program in three primary grade classrooms. The target students were 10 low achieving, inattentive students. The program included training teachers to track target student behavior, and to pair praise with backup reinforcers for appropriate behavior. The 10 target students in the treatment program served as subjects for the study, along with their teachers. Rates of praise in the tracking and no tracking conditions were compared. No significant differences were found between the continuous tracking and no tracking teachers. The within classroom analyses yielded similar nonsignificant results. Comparisions between students' appropriate behavior levels under tracking and no tracking conditions indicated that tracking was also ineffective as a procedure for maintaining improvements in student behavior. Visual inspection of the data indicated a moderate degree of relationship among rates of teacher praise to individual target students on a given day. It was concluded that teacher praising and student behavior were under the control of variables other than teacher tracking for the period of this study.

2081.   Cook, J. H. "The Effects of Small Group Counseling on the Classroom Behavior of Sociometrically underchosen Adolescents." Ed.D. Dissertation, University of Georgia. Dissertation Abstracts International, 33 (9-A), 4827. Order no. 73-5670, 1973.

The purpose of this study was to examine the effects of small group counseling on the classroom behavior and level of social acceptance of sociometrically underchosen and withdrawn students. The treatment consisted of 20 group counseling sessions of 55 minutes each over a period of eleven weeks. The two treatment groups consisted of eight eighth grade boys from an Atlanta, Georgia, high school. Four of the boys in each group were sociometrically under-chosen students and four were highly chosen students who served as models. The counseling approach used consisted of an involvement phase and a structured relearning phase. The procedures of Reality Therapy developed by William Glasser were followed in the involvement phase. The relearning phase was a behavioral approach which placed emphasis upon social interaction and the evaluation of behavior in the group setting. An empirical case study design permitted the presentation of data on an individual basis. Daily observa-tions of classroom behavior were made on each individual. Observations occurred 10 minutes daily for 16 weeks. Obser-vations began three weeks before counseling and continued three weeks following counseling. Spauldings' Coping Analysis Schedule for Educational Settings (CASES), an instrument designed to translate all overt behavior into a particular category or style of response, was used to make the observations. Two hypotheses were tested on a group basis. These hypotheses concerned changes in the frequen-cies of negative behaviors and mean change in positive choices by peers from pretest to posttest. Wilcoxon's matched pairs signed-ranks test was used pretest changes in negative behaviors and a t-test was computed to compare positive choices by peers. Data were examined on an individual basis: therefore generalized conclusions were difficult to formulate. Sociometric data and CASES data, to a lesser extent, clearly indicated that there was movement for some of the students, although not for all. The implications of these findings were discussed in the study. Only those conclusions which represented summary statements for all students are presented here. They include the following: 1) Differences in the frequency of negative behaviors or pre-counseling and post-counseling observations were not significant. 2) Differences in mean change in positive choices by peers were significant on a comparison of pretest and posttest measures. The null hypothesis concerning gains in positive choices was rejected. An empirical examination of the data collected to evaluate the hypothesis concerning the relationship between positive choices on the sociometric and changes in negative behaviors showed no correlation between these variables. The null hypothesis concerning positive choices and negative behaviors was not rejected.

2082.   Copeland, R. E. "The Effects of Principal Implemented Techniques on the Behavior of Pupils." Ph.D. Dissertation, University of Kansas. Dissertation Abstracts International, 34 (7-A), 3983-3984. Order no. 73-30,797, 1974.

Four investigations were carried out regarding the effects of various principal initiated procedures on the behavior of elementary school children. Eighty children including kindergarten, first, third and fifth graders served as subjects. In Experiment I when three chronically absent children attended school, the principal entered their classrooms and praised them for being present. In Experiment II three low achieving subjects were sent to the principal's office to receive praise contingent on meeting predetermined criteria in word recognition and addition tutoring sessions. In Experiment III a principal assigned cafeteria job was made contingent on a low achieving child meeting criteria in word recognition and arithmetic tutoring sessions. Experiment IV assessed the effects a principal implemented procedure had on the academic functioning of 74 third graders. Twice weekly in two classrooms the principal recognized both improving students and the highest performing students regarding their work on addition study sheets. In all four experiments the target behaviors increased when the principal applied the treatment contingencies. The application of multiple baseline and reversal designs revealed that there was a functional relationship between the children's behavior and the principal implemented procedures.

2083.   Courtney, C. L. "A Study of the Effects of Adlerian Behavioral Consultation With Teachers on the On-Task Behavior and Achievement of Fourth-Grade Children." Ph.D. Dissertation, University of Southern Mississippi. Dissertation Abstracts International, 39 (4-A), 2061. Order no. 7818960, 1978.

The purpose of this study was to investigate the effects of an Adlerian behavioral consultation program with teachers on the on-task (attentive and non-disruptive) behavior and achievement of elementary school children who had been identified by their teachers as students least involved in classroom instruction. The research questions which guided the study were as follows: 1. What are the effects, if any, of an Adlerian behavioral consultation model used with fourth-grade teachers on the on-task (attentive and non-disruptive behavior of fourth-grade students identified as least involved in instruction? 2. What are the effects, if any, of an Adlerian behavioral consultation model used with fourth-grade teachers on the achievement of fourth-grade students identified as least involved in instruction? The population of this study consisted of 48 student subjects who were randomly selected from a total population of students who met criteria for student selection and were in self-contained fourth-grade classrooms in the St. Vrain Valley School District, State of Colorado. The experimental group and the control group each consisted of 24 students (eight students from three different classrooms). Teachers of students in the experimental group participated in treatment, an Adlerian behavioral consultation program. Teachers of students in the control group did not participate in any known form of treatment or consultation regarding management of classroom behavior. The research hypothesis that the student subjects in the experimental group, students whose teachers participated in Adlerian behavioral consultation, would be significantly more on-task (attentive and non-disruptive than the student subjects in the control group was not supported. The research hypothesis that academic achievement scores of the student subjects in the experimental group, students whose teachers participated in Adlerian behavioral consultation, would be significantly higher than academic achievement scores of the student subjects in the control group was not supported. The group means for grade level equivalent scores in reading subtest achievement did differ significantly, with the experimental group scoring higher than the control group. Thus, this hypothesis was partially supported.

2084.   Covington, A. M. "A Study of Principal Behavior in Management of Student Discipline." Ed.D. Dissertation, Columbia University Teachers College, 1979.

The purposes of this study were to describe and analyze a self-report by principals of their behavior in the management of certain discipline problems; to determine the degree of difference of reported behavior between and among principals in three different school populations; and to identify the relationship between principal behavior regarding discipline and reading level of students in school, age of principal, sex of principal, years in present school as principal, experience as principal, and racial composition of schools. To discover the approaches used in the management of discipline problems, 53 elementary school principals were selected from the New York City public school system and asked to respond to a questionnaire. Four approaches were investigated: the diagnostic (D), the authoritarian (A), the permissive (P), and the behavioristic (B). The results showed that most principals were diagnostic in their approach to student discipline. There was no significant relationship found between the D, A, P, and B scores and the reading level of students, years in present school as principal, experience as principal, and racial composition of schools. Significant relationships were found for the D scores and the age of principal (p .02), the P scores and the age of principal (P .01), and the A scores and the sex of principal (p .002). There was no significant difference in the management of the most serious behaviors and the least serious behaviors. Order no. 7923579, DAI.

2085.   Cowart, Joseph B. "Establishing a Behavior Analysis Program in an Elementary School." Ph.D. Dissertation, University of Utah. Dissertation Abstracts International, 35 (1-A), 253. Order no. 74-15,108, 1974.

The objective of this project was to establish a behavior analysis program in an elementary school. A central reinforcement system was established as the core of the program. This system enabled the faculty/staff to reinforce the students' appropriate behaviors by giving them points on slips of paper. The children could trade the points for some tangible reinforcer such as candy, toys, etc. Four other tasks were accomplished as a part of establishing the program. These tasks were: 1) in-service training for the faculty/staff, 2) implementation of the training, 3) establishment of a behavior modification demonstration classroom, and 4) in-service training for the non-classroom faculty/staff. The outcomes are indicated by the overall reduction in the number of children being referred for discipline.

2086.   Cowen, R. J. "Grandma's Rule With Group Contingencies: A Cost-Efficient Means of Classroom Management During Reading Circle." Ph.D. Dissertation, University of Pittsburgh. Dissertation Abstracts International, 39 (03). DAI no. 7816828, 1977.

The present study made use of two different incentive procedures designed to reduce disruptive behavior during reading circle. Both were based on Grandma's Rule; however one was relatively inexpensive, while the other was significantly more expensive. The less expensive procedure had the teacher keeping track of "good work" via a stop watch, giving the class feedback only when disruption was occurring. With the more expensive procedure, the class not only got a reminder from the teacher when disruption was occurring, but also received continuous feedback about the amount of "good work" it had done from a stop clock (visible to everyone). The contingent reinforcement for both techniques was free time for preferred activities. Students of five elementary school classrooms (grades one through three) served as subjects. Dependent variables were "out of seat," "talking to neighbors," and "off-task." An ABCB multiple baseline design was employed where the stop watch procedure was introduced after baseline, then the stop clock, and finally the stop watch again. The design addressed the following theoretical and practical questions: 1) Would the procedures be effective on an absolute basis in reducing class disruption during reading circle? 2) Would the stop clock be incrementally more effective than the stop watch in this setting? 3) If so, would the additional decrement be worth the cost of the stop clock, at $125 per classroom? Results indicated that both techniques were effective on an absolute basis in reducing the level of occurrence of all three dependent variables. Moreover, the stop clock offered no incremental advantage over the less expensive stop watch. Several teachers became more adept at handling disruptions over time, and this seemed to represent a simple practice effect rather than a systematic difference between the effects of the procedures.

2087.   Crowder, Nettie J. "Training Elementary School Children in the Application of Principles and Techniques of Behavior Modification." Ph.D. Dissertation, University of Kansas, 1974. Dissertation Abstracts International, 36 (6-B), 3029.

The purpose of this study was to demonstrate a procedure for teaching behavioral principles and techniques to children, enabling them to select and modify behaviors of concern to them. Six children, ages 10 through 13, met twice weekly for approximately five weeks to receive instruction, using a semi-programmed text "Secrets for Children: An Elementary Guidance Course in Behavior Change," written by this author. Each child selected a behavior he/she wished to change, measured that behavior, and using an applied behavior analysis research design, implemented appropriate baseline and experimental conditions, with reliability measures. Each child was able to complete his/her behavior change project with at least modest or, in some cases, significant success. Consumer satisfaction questionnaires and other data from parents suggested that they saw their children as profiting from their experience in the behavioral program and showing fewer problem behaviors following the program.

2088.   Cummings, L. O., III. "Social Intelligence and Classroom Adaptive Behavior." Ph.D. Dissertation, The University of North Carolina at Chapel Hill, 1979.

The purpose of this study was to investigate the relationships between social intelligence and classroom behavior
patterns. Predictive measures employed were four tests of
social intelligence, sex, race, CAT IQ scores, and socioeconomic status. The criterion measure used was the
Devereux Elementary School Behavior Rating Scale. The four
social intelligence tests, Expression Grouping, Missing
Cartoons, Social Translations, and Cartoon Prediction, were
designed to measure cognition of behavior areas in M.P.
Guilford's SOI model of intelligence, SES was determined
from job information provided by the students' parents.
Jobs were rated using the Duncan SES scale. The subjects
were 146 sixth grade students from two middle schools. The
sample was composed of 36 black males, 37 while males, 36
black females, and 37 while females. Students were administered the four tests by the author in classroom groups.
They were rated on the DESBRS by their teachers. The
research supported both of the research hypotheses in that
statistically significant canonical correlations were found
between the predictor variables and the DESBRS ratings. The
four social intelligence tests had a canonical R of .63 with
a pattern of DESBRS ratings. All eight predictor variables
had a canonical R of .71 with a pattern of DESBRS ratings.
One social intelligence test, Social Translation, added
significantly to sex, race, IQ, and SES in predicting the
DESBRS factor identified by canonical correlation. The
pattern of DESBRS ratings identified on both of the
canonical correlations was labeled "understanding classroom
requirements." Students of above average IQ were found to
score average or above average on all the social intelligence tests except Social Translations where they had a
wide range of scores. Students of average or below average
IQ were found to score both above and below average on all
the social intelligence tests. Order no. 8005028, DAI.

2089.   Dadey, William J. "An Investigation of the Relationship
Between Perceived Classroom Verbal Behavior of Teachers and
Frequency of Discipline Problems." Ph.D. Dissertation,
Syracuse University, 1971. Dissertation Abstracts
International, 32 (8-A), 4274. Order no. 72-6565, 1972.

The purpose of the study was to investigate the relationship
between perceived classroom verbal behavior of teachers and
frequency of discipline problems. The design of the study
was based on a correlational analysis of a number of independent variables and one dependent variable. The two main
independent variables considered were: students' perceptions and teachers' perceptions of the verbal behavior of
teachers. Four other independent variables that were
studied included: sex of the teacher, experience of the
teacher, subject area taught by the teacher and quality of
teaching. The only dependent variable considered in the
study was frequency of discipline problems. Sixteen
hypotheses involving these variables were studied by
organizing the data for each of the variables in the form of
ranks. An analysis of the relationships of these ranks was

then made utilizing Spearman's rank-difference correlation coefficient. The study itself was conducted in a suburban secondary school in Central New York. It utilized a random sample of 30 teachers and 600 students. A portion of the data was collected by administering the Verbal Behavior Q-Sort to teachers and the Student Perceptions of Teacher Influence Questionnaire to students. Other data was obtained from rankings performed by various staff personnel and an analysis of the actual number of discipline referrals made by each teacher in the sample to the administrator in charge of discipline. Some of the statistically significant findings of the study are as follows: 1) Teachers who used more direct influence, as perceived by their students, had a higher frequency of discipline problems. 2) Experience of the teacher and subject area taught by the teacher were significant factors in the relationship between perceived verbal behavior of teachers and frequency of discipline problems. Sex of the teacher was not a significant factor in this relationship. 3) Teachers who perceived the ideal teacher to use more praise and encouragement had a higher frequency of discipline problems. Teachers' perceptions involving the other Flanders' teacher-talk categories showed no relationship to the frequency of discipline problems. 4) Teachers who wre perceived to be the least effective had the highest frequency of discipline problems. 5) Rankings of teachers performed by department chairmen on the basis of quality of teaching produced ranks which were statistically concordant.

2090.   Daniels, K. R. "Adults as Compound Discriminitive Stimuli in a Token Economy Classroom." Ph.D. Dissertation, University of Louisville, 1972.

Studies in the basic animal research area have indicated that the strength which two individuals discriminative stimuli show singly is summated arithmetically when the two stimuli are presented in a simultaneous compound. An attempt was made in this study to show that this basic principle held also in the applied human operate situtation; specifically a behavior analysis based token economy system for first grade children. Two classrooms containing four groups of students and an outside control group were employed in this experiment. All groups in each classroom received two different teachers successively in single stimulus training. Two groups received a segment in which the amount of reinforcement given by the teacher assistant was four tokens for each red line reached with a red line specifying that two to three pages of material were to be completed for token reinforcement. The other two groups received a segment in which the teacher assistant delivered eight tokens to each child for each red line reached. The overall suggested that an analysis of the natural environment in terms of the sources of compound discriminitive stimulus control are useful.

2091.   Daniels, Robert W. "A Comparison of Student-Managed and Teacher-Managed Reward Techniques with Primary Age Children." Ph.D. Dissertation, Kent State University. Dissertation Abstracts International, 35 (10-A), 6509. Order no. 75-7449, 1975.

Behavior modification interventions have proven to be effective and precise. Consequently, there is concern about the control of human behavior. The schools specifically have been attacked for their rigidity and preoccupation with control. The goals of behavior modification within the school situation have been criticized as preserving order and quiet, while stifling independence and creativity. If students can be taught behavioral self-control methods, they might then be able to shape their own environments and be less at the mercy of some outside agent of control. One part of the moral dilemma of behavior control might also be avoided. The burden of control would then be on the student rather than the teacher, parent, or therapist. If a person is able to utilize self-control techniques in one situation, the use of the method can generalize to other problem areas. Feelings of self control and competence should then ensue. This study investigated the effectiveness of two methods of self reward compared to a method of teacher-managed reward and to a method employing no systematic rewards. The study was done in four heterogeneously grouped first-grade classrooms, which are considered a representative sample. Classes were randomly assigned to treatment groups. Three days of baseline data were gathered prior to the ten-day treatment period. Conclusions were drawn that self-reinforcement methods can be as effective as traditional teacher-reinforcement methods in changing classroom behavior. It was further concluded that young children can be taught self-management techniques without having experienced a systematic external control procedure. The results also pointed out that students can be taught specific verbal-mediation skills to promote self-reinforcement. Another important conclusion was that a parent, teacher, or therapist might be able to avoid the issue of behavioral control by presenting self-management techniques to be used at the discretion of the client.

2092.   Davis, R. A. "The Impact of Self-Modeling on Problem Behaviors of School-Age Children." Ph.D. Dissertation, The University of Arizona. Dissertation Abstracts International, 36 (7-A), 4342-4343. Order no. 76-1397, 1976.

The effects of self-modeling were observed on problem behaviors of three elementary-school-age children. A single subject design with a multiple-baseline technique was utilized. Subjects were observed for a total of 45 school days. Baseline was recorded by the actual teachers of the subjects in two cases and by the teacher's aide in the other. Treatment was done in the natural environment. Problem behaviors were targeted, and, after a baseline

phase, the subjects were video-taped role-playing a script
of the appropriate behavior. The video-tape recording was
done in the natural environment. Following another baseline, the subjects viewed themselves on video-tape once each
day throughout the treatment phase. Dramatic increase in
the frequency of appropriate behavior was observed on all
target behaviors. The effects were maintained over a post-
treatment phase.

2093.   DeEsch, J. B.   "The Use of the Ohlsen Model of Group
Counseling with Secondary School Students Identified as
Being Disruptive to the Educational Process." Ph.D.
Dissertation, Indiana State University. Dissertation
Abstracts International, 36 (7-A), 4253-4254. Order no.
75-29,876, 1976

The purpose of this research was to examine the effects of
group counseling with secondary students identified as being
disruptive to the educational process among the following
variables: 1) changes in specific school behaviors; 2)
changes on a self concept measure; 3) achievement of idiosyncratic goals; and 4) changes in academic achievement.
The study was conducted in three secondary schools of the
Pennsbury School District, a suburban district northeast of
Philadelphia, Pennsylvania. The schools involved in the
study included grades seven through ten and has a cross-
section of socio-economic levels. The subjects were
selected from the 10 percent of the total student body most
frequently referred to the discipline office during the
first ten weeks of school. Each subject met the criteria
for being a client and was committed to the group counseling
experience following a presentation and intake interview.
All research subjects were randomly assigned to one of the
two major groups: the Treatment Group or the Delayed Treatment Control Group. Within each of these two major groups,
the research subjects were placed in counseling groups at
the counselors' discretion and within the guidelines
prescribed by Ohlsen (1970). Five criterion measures were
used to determine outcomes of the counseling experience: a
Pupil Behavior Inventory, and Idiosyncratic Goal Rating
Form, the Tennessee Self Concept Scale, a grade-point-
average index, and the frequency of referrals to the discipline office. All research subjects had a pre-measure prior
to any group counseling contact. Following a ten week
treatment for the Treatment Group all subjects had a post-
measure. At this point the Delayed Treatment Control Group
was terminated from the study although they did have an
opportunity to participate in a group counseling experience
not associated with the results of this study. Ten weeks
after the post-measure a follow-up measure was taken for
Treatment Group subjects. Ten null hypotheses, five related
to change within the Treatment Group and five related to
comparing the Treatment Group to the Delayed Treatment
Control Group, were investigated. The five null hypotheses
testing for differences between the measurement periods
within the Treatment Group resulted in four producing

statistically significant levels of change (p .05). The treated subjects improved their self concept as measured by the Tennessee Self Concept Scale, Idiosyncratic Self Rating Form scores, grade-point-average index, and reduced the number of referrals to the discipline office. No change occurred in the teachers' rated Pupil Behavior Inventory score. The five null hypotheses testing for differences of scores observed between the Treatment Group and Delayed Treatment Control Group resulted in one producing a statistically significant level of difference (p .05). The referrals to the discipline office decreased for the treated group while there was an increase in frequency for the control group; this difference was statistically significant.

2094.   Denning, E. N. "An Analysis of the Effects of Differing Socio-Emotional Classroom Climates on Students Who Have Been Identified as "High Risk" in Terms of Emotional Handicaps." Ph.D. Dissertation, University of Oregon, 1976.

This study investigated the effects of different socio-emotional classroom climates on students identified as suseptible to or already evidencing emotional handicaps. From the total primary school population in Kitimat, British Columbia, 115 students were screened out as "High Risk." The criterian for such status was a negative two or a negative three position on the continuum of Relatability-alienation as determined by a procedure combining perceptions of teacher, peers, and self. Three types of socio-emotional classroom climate were identified from the teachers' verbal behavior: 1) indirect, 2) average, and 3) direct. It was concluded that type of social-emotional classroom climate, as determined by the predominant style of teacher influence, exerts considerable influence with regard to other students who are already experiencing limitations in range of behavioral freedom exhibit either a resolution, a maintenance, or a compounding of these handicaps over the period of one year. The conditions for such resolution, maintenance, or compounding tend to show a dependence on indirect, average, or direct climates respectively.

2095.   Desselle, Richard E. "Experiential Learning Program Effects on Classroom Behaviors. Ph.D. Dissertation, University of Georgia. Dissertation Abstracts International, 35 (10-A), 6452. Order no. 75-8126, 1975.

The study was conducted to determine if fourth graders who had received human relations training would be observed as more cooperative in their behavior in class. Self-report, peer perceptions and teacher ratings were also measured to test for other change that may have occurred through training. This was a pilot study to consider the feasibility of using human relations training to influence student behavior. The findings indicate that changes can be fostered if enough time is devoted to an area by competent trainers.

2096.   Diamond, Ivan L. "A Study of the Use of Corporal
Punishment in Selected Middle Schools and Junior High
Schools in the State of Michigan." Ph.D. Dissertation, The
University of Michigan.   Dissertation Abstracts
International, 37 (3-A), 1322. Order no. 76-19,118, 1976.

The problem of this investigation was to determine the
perceived use of corporal punishment in selected Middle
Schools and Junior High Schools in the State of Michigan.
The following research questions were investigated: 1) The
extent the principal administers or allows others to administer corporal punishment to students. 2) The extent the
principal believes corporal punishment should be administered by himself or others. 3) The extent teachers believe
the principal administers or allows others to administer
corporal punishment. 4) The extent teachers believe the
principal should administer or allow others to administer
corporal punishment. 5) The extent the principal believes
corporal punishment is more effective than keeping a student
after school, assigning essays, withholding privileges, or
calling a student's parents as a punishment. 6) The extent
teachers believe corporal punishment is more effective than
keeping a student after school, assigning essays, withholding of privileges, or calling a student's parents as a
punishment. These data were obtained from a questionnaire
mailed to a random sample of 100 Middle School and 100
Junior High School Principals in the State of Michigan. 1)
Corporal punishment was being administered, to varying
degrees, to students in the Middle Schools and the Junior
High Schools involved in the study. 2) No statistically
significant difference at the .05 level of confidence was
found in the perceived use of corporal punishment in Middle
Schools and Junior High Schools for any of the six research
questions. 3) A corollary finding of statistically significant difference at the .01 level of confidence existed in
the use of corporal punishment with males as opposed to
females. Males were found to be subjected to a statistically greater level of corporal punishment than females. 4)
Teachers in a majority of the Middle Schools (66%) and
Junior High Schools (64.2%) surveyed are allowed to administer corporal punishment. Counselors in a majority of the
Middle Schools (84.2%) and Junior High Schools (87.3%)
surveyed are not allowed to administer corporal punishment.
5) A large majority of the Middle School and Junior High
School Principals (85.2%) indicated that they believe
corporal punishment is effective.

2097.   Dicker, Saul S. "The Theory and Practice of Corporal
Punishment in the Public and Private Secondary Schools of
Boston: 1821-1890. Ph.D. Dissertation, The Catholic
University of America.   Dissertation Abstracts
International, 31 (3-A), 1047. Order no. 70-16,456, 1970.

The purpose of the study was threefold: first, to document
the history of the theory and practice of corporal punishment in the public and private secondary schools of Boston

between 1821 and 1890; second, to discover whether or not the psychological insights of such European educators as Johann Pestalozzi were being taught in and implemented by the Normal Schools of Boston; third, to find the role of the private secular secondary schools of Boston in the replacement of corporal punishment with more efficacious disciplinary techniques. The major findings of the study revealed that corporal punishments were the primary, and often the only, method of school discipline in the public secondary schools until written legislation in 1890 declared them illegal. Normal School graduates, although instructed in European methodology, often sought positions outside the city of Boston. The English High School, established at Boston in 1821, attempted to interest the student in a more varied curriculum than the Latin Grammar School, and stood as a singular success and paradigm for imitation. Finally, the private secular secondary schools, able to attract better educated personnel than the public schools, abandoned corporal punishment twenty-five years before Public School Superintendent Edwin P. Seaver mandated against it.

2098.   Dobbins, J. B. "The Relationships Between School Climate and Teacher Attitudes and Behavior in Managing Their Classrooms." University of Texas: Austin. 1977.

Discussed are the social atmosphere among faculty members as a measure of school climate and school size and socioeconomic status of students and teaching experience, teacher attitudes and student on-task behavior among elementary school teachers. See ERIC Abstract 0384060-2.

2099.   Douglas, A. C. "An Assessment of the Effect of a School-Wide Positive Approach to Discipline and Classroom Management in a Suburban Junior High School." Ed.D. Dissertation, North Texas State University. Dissertation Abstracts International, 40 (07), Sec A, P3931. Order no. 8000783, 1979.

The purposes of this study were 1) to determine if a specific set of classroom management-discipline procedures have a positive effect on student attitude and involvement and 2) to determine if a specific set of classroom management discipline procedures will have a positive effect on teachers and students as shown by results on teacher and student opinion inventories, reduction in discipline cases, and increased student involvement in clubs, mini-courses, student government and intramurals. There were two junior high schools that participated in this study. Both schools were located in a suburban setting in the same school district. The experimental school used the positive approach to discipline and the control school did not. The population of the experimental school was composed of 850 students and fifty teachers. The population of the control school was 750 students and forty-four teachers. Students in both schools were randomly selected and given the Student Opinion Inventory. All teachers in both schools were given the

Teacher   Opinion   Inventory.   The   findings   of   this
investigation support the following conclusions concerning
junior high schools.   1) A positive approach to discipline
can be expected to have a significant positive impact on
students' opinions of school.   2) A positive approach to
discipline can be expected to have a significant positive
impact on teachers' opinions of school.   3) A positive
approach to discipline can be expected to have a significant
positive effect on school atmosphere as evidenced by fewer
discipline cases and increased student involvement.   4) A
positive approach to discipline will result in increased
teacher participation in areas such as sponsorship of
student   clubs,   mini-courses   and   other   extra   curricular
activities.

2100.   Dovey, R. L.   "A Program of Constructive Reaction to
Negative Student Behavior Problems in a High School in a
Small City."   Ed.D. Dissertation, University of Pittsburgh.
Dissertation Abstracts International, 33 (8-A), 3995.   Order
no. 73-4149, 1973.

It was the purpose of this study to devise, implement, and
evaluate a program of constructive reaction to negative
student behavior problems in a high school located in a
small city.   The applied theory or action research was the
method used in the study.   Its function was to provide a
directional   discipline   by   which   theory,   experimentally
derived, was translated into practice.   The study was
divided into three phases.   The first phase included: (1)
the   identification   of   the   negative   student   behavior
problems: (2) the data showing the number of suspensions and
detentions for the 1970-1971 school year; and (3) the
results of the first opinion survey distributed to 500
parents, 500 students, and 50 teachers.   The second phase of
the study included the attempted improvements implemented
for and during the 1971-1972 school year, which included
the: (1) formation of a Discipline Advisory Committee, (2)
review and revision of student discipline policies, (3)
orientation of policies to all students, (4) discussion
meetings with first and second year teachers, and (5)
working with students having many or serious negative
behavior problems.   The third phase of the study included:
(1) the data showing the number of suspensions and detentions for the 1971-1972 school year and comparing it with
the 1970-1971 school year; (2) the results of the second
opinion survey distributed to the same 500 parents, 500
students, and 50 teachers as in the first phase; and (3) the
relating of attitude changes of parents, students, and
teachers toward negative student behavior problems over the
two year period of the study.   It was concluded that suspensions increased considerably over the two year period.   The
orientation program for first and second year teachers
showed a favorable response.   The referrals to the probation
office showed a favorable response.   During both school
years, the majority of parents and teachers indicated

agreement or better with most of the student control policies of the school. The majority of students indicated disagreement with the policies.

2101.   Drummond, D. J. "Self-Instructional Training: An Approach to Disruptive Classroom Behavior." Ph.D. Dissertation, University of Oregon. Dissertation Abstracts International, 35 (8-B), 4167-4168. Order no. 75-3869, 1975.

This study examines the feasibility and effectiveness of a self-instructional (SI) training procedure for reducing disruptive behavior of 3rd- and 4th-grade children. The SI training paradigm was adaped from Meichenbaum and Goodman (1971), who combined modeling, verbal reinforcement, and self-reinforcement with a conceptualization of the develop- ment of the behavior-controlling functions performed by language. In terms of the primary goal of reducing class- room disruptiveness, the superiority of self-instructional training over a procedure which controls for demand characteristics was not demonstrated by observational data. However, the finding that teachers rated children in the self-instructional condition as significantly less disrup- tive than children in the control condition, suggests the need for further research in which observational data from a wider range of school activities are collected.

2102.   Duray, M. M. "Characteristics of Children Perceived by Teachers as Displaying Positive and Negative Attention- Getting Behaviors." Ph.D. Dissertation, Indiana State University. Dissertation Abstracts International, 38 (8-A), 4580. 1978.

This study was designed to investigate if fourth grade children, grouped by sex and by positive or negative atten- tion-getting behavior, could be differentially described on a set of nine characteristics including positive or negative early recollections, birth order, family size, locus of control socioeconomic status, classroom acceptance, need achievement, need for approval, and cognitive ability. The sample was composed of thirty-seven boys and forty-eight girls from twenty fourth grade classrooms in thirteen elementary parochial and public schools in southern and west central Indiana. The boys' criterion groups were signifi- cantly differentiated by the nine variables. Those variables contributing the most to the separation of the boys' groups were family size, socioeconomic status, need for approval, classroom acceptance, need achievement, birth order, and locus of control. Positive attention-getting boys were higher than negative attention-getting boys in socioeconomic status, need for approval, classroom acceptance, and locus of control They came from smaller families, were later-born, and were lower in need achieve- ment. The girls' criterion groups were significantly discriminated by eight of the nine variables. Need achieve- ment was not a differentiating characteristic for the girls.

Those variables contributing the most to the separation of the girls; groups were family size, cognitive ability, and locus of control. Implications for teacher consultation and parent education in dealing with positive and negative attention-getting boys were drawn particularly from the contributions of the variables of need for approval, peer acceptance, and need achievement.

2103.   Duricko, Allen J. "The Free-Choice Free-Time Approach to Management of Classroom Behavior: A Replication and Introduction of Self-Control Features." Ph.D. Dissertation, Arizona State University, 1974. Dissertation Abstracts International, 35 (5-B), 2425. Order no. 74-25,800.

A contingent free-time approach was employed in a fourth-grade low-level math class to reduce the frequency of disruptive talking-out and out-of-seat behaviors among 18 students. A five-minute free time, which provided a choice of appealing activities, was available to students on an individual basis, contingent upon no talking-out nor out-of-seat behavior during a preceding segment of class time. Measures of concomitant changes in academic performance, and of behavior generalization to another classroom setting, were also made over the seven-week duration of the study. There were seven experimental conditions: baseline 1 (clearly-stated class rules based upon the teacher's expectations for student behavior); free-choice free-time 1 (introduction of contingent free time involving teacher control of access to reinforcers); baseline 2 (removal of the contingent free time and maintenance of class rules); free-choice free-time 2 (reinstatement of contingent free time); self-control 1 (continued use of contingent free time, with student responsibility for self-assessment, self-recording, and self-administration of reinforcement, with teacher feedback); self-control 2 (continuation of self-control procedures without teacher involvement); and, baseline 3 (removal of contingent free time and maintenance of class rules). Analysis of the data showed that the free-choice free-time approach significantly decreased the frequency of both disruptive behaviors and that the introduction of self-control procedures produced a further reduction in the rates of disruptive behaviors. Additionally, the academic performance of the students displayed significant improvement, both quantitatively and qualitatively, during phases in which target behaviors were brought under contingency control. Finally, it was shown that the improved behaviors effected by contingent free-time procedures generalized to a second classroom setting.

2104.   Dye, J. C. "Values Clarification as a Discipline Alternative for the Middle School." Ph.D. Dissertation, The University of Florida, 1979.

The problem of this study was to use the Gordon Personal Profile in indentifying students who might become disciplinary problems and to assess the use of values

clarification and self-study exercies of the type first
introduced by Sidney Simon in the treatment and possible
prevention of disciplinary problems. Subjects for the study
were 2,105 male and female students in grades eight and nine
of two double-session junior hight schools in Hillsborough
County, Florida. All subjects were given the Gordon
Personal Profile during the first full week of school in the
1977-78 school year and their scores on that test were
correlated with their frequency of referral to an administrator for disciplinary action the same year. The use of
the scores on the Gordon Personal Profile with sex added as
a variable permitted the correct classification of 88% of
the cases in the study. This effect was significant. The
45 students in each of the two selected schools with the
greatest number of referrals to an administrator for disciplinary action for the 1976-77 school year were randomly
assigned to one of the three treatment groups. One group
received treatment with the values/self-study packet, "A
Guide to the Study of Me," in an individually guided manner
during the second through the eleventh week of the school
year. Another group received treatment with the same
values/self-study packet in a small group setting. The
small group met for a period of forty minutes one day a week
during the second through the eleventh week of school. The
third group received no treatment and served as a control.
Sixty of the original ninety subjects were in attendance at
the close of the study. There was no significant difference
in the frequency of referral for those students who received
the treatment individually, those who received the treatment
as a group, and those who received no treatment. It was
concluded that exposure to values clarification and self-
study did not reduce the frequency of referral to an administrator for disciplinary action. It was also concluded that
the Gordon Personal Profile can be used to identify
violators of school policy prior to their referral for
disciplinary action as a result of violating that policy.
Order no. 7921924, DAI.

2105.   Eastman, Brenda G. "Cognitive Self-Instruction for the
Control of Impulsive Classroom Behavior: A Generalization
Training Model." Ph.D. Dissertation, The University of
Florida, 1980. Dissertation Abstracts International, 41
(1-B), 349. Order no. 8016526.

The effectiveness of cognitive self-instruction training as
a remedial intervention for school children exhibiting
behavior problems such as impulsivity or distractibility has
been demonstrated in experimental settings. The results of
those studies which have included a measure of generalization to the classroom have been more equivocal. The aim of
the present study was to evaluate the viability of a training program in cognitive self-instruction as a practical
means of achieving desired changes in task-related behavior
and performance which were generalizable to the classroom.
The training paradigm was modified to facilitate generalization, and environmental conditions were arranged to foster

the use of the cognitive self-instruction strategy. Specifically, these conditions included the provision of verbal cues and social reinforcement by the regular classroom teacher. The criterion measures of generalization were on-task behavior, measured by a behavior observation technique of interval sampling, and performance on academic work. Eleven first grade children attending a public elementary school participated. Children were nominated by their teachers on the basis of disruptiveness in the context of academic work periods and selected on the basis of Conners' Abbreviated Teacher Rating Scale. Two groups were formed, equated on Metropolitan Achievement Test Total Reading scores, and baseline levels of on-task behavior and academic performance on reading seatwork. The treatment group initially received three daily one half hour sessions in cognitive self-instruction training. The second group served as an attention-practice control group. Following this initial training period, no significant improvements in levels of on-task behavior and academic performance occurred within the context of a group design. Despite the provision of an additional training period, no group increases occurred on either measure. However, individual subject trends toward substantial improvement in on-task behavior occurred for a majority of the treatment group. The attenuated outcome of cognitive self-instruction training is discussed from the standpoint of a need for a critical two-pronged shift in research emphasis. First, a metacognitive approach which emphasizes the transsituational nature of cognitive strategies as well as the pervasiveness and breadth of the training experience may facilitate generalization and the acquisition of broad, general strategies. The second crucial research direction must be toward analyses of the cognitive processes necessary to task approach and solution. The isolationist position of cognitive self-instruction research to date is highlighted, with the suggestion that researchers in the area must become conversant with related research in the areas of cognitive and developmental psychology if the goal of altering behavior is to be achieved.

2106.   Eberle, J. "A Descriptive Study of Teacher-Pupil Verbal Interaction in Informal Classrooms." Ed.D. Dissertation. State University of New York at Buffalo, 1978.

The study was designed to describe and analyze the quantity and quality of teacher-pupil verbal dyadic interaction in the informal classroom. Data were obtained in four elementary self-contained, informal classrooms, selected on the basis of criteria established by the researcher. The study focused on four types of interaction (substantive, procedural, self-reference, behavioral) in six classroom settings: large group with reading or recitation, large group without reading or recitation, small group with reading or recitation, small group without reading or recitation, individualized with reading or recitation, individualized without reading or recitation. With the help of a wireless microphone, twenty half-hour periods of teacher-pupil verbal dyadic interaction were recorded in each classroom (two first-grade classrooms, one second-grade, one fifth-grade). The eighty recordings were analyzed to determine the differences in quantity and quality of teacher-pupil interaction on the basis of <u>sex</u>, <u>achievement</u> <u>levels</u>, behavior characteristics, <u>need</u> <u>for</u> <u>attention</u>, and <u>degree</u> <u>of</u> <u>motivation</u>. The nature of interaction was examined with reference to the four types of interaction, the six classroom settings, the initiator of the interaction (teacher or pupil), length of interaction (brief or extended), levels of teacher questions (process, product, choice, opinion), patterns of teacher feedback to student responses following teacher questions. The M.A.P.S. Program (A Multiple Analysis Program System for Behavioral Science Research, Version 2.0) and the Monroe Calculator, Model 1930 were used to analyze the data. The following are among the findings obtained through the analysis: 1. Some children initiated and received little or no attention, others initiated and received a large share. 2. The flow of communication was much more under the control of the teachers than of the students. 3. There was an inordinate amount of time given to procedural matters. 4. Little time was spent on praising or criticizing children. 5. There were relatively few significant differences among the five comparison groups: males - females, high achievers - low achievers, well behaved children - poorly behaved children, children in need of little attention - children in need of much attention, highly motivated children - poorly motivated children. Order No. 7906758.

2107.   "The Effects of Democratic Classroom Procedures on the Behavior of 9- to 11-Yr-Old Children." Ed.D. Dissertation, University of Northern Colorado. Dissertation Abstracts International, 38 (8-A), 4751. Order no. 7730860, 1978.

The objective of this research was to determine whether the behavior of children taught by teachers enrolled in a course in democratic classroom management techniques becomes less detrimental and more responsible as measured by the Pupil Behavior Rating Scale. The subjects of this study were children, grades three through five, attending Middle Island School District No. 12, Middle Island, New York, randomly selected from in-tack classes of teacher volunteers. Three experimental classes, whose volunteer teachers were enrolled in a behavior management inservice course, and three control classes, whose volunteer teachers were not enrolled in a behavior management inservice course, yielded 138 subjects, with one each of Grades 3, 4, and 5 in both experimental and control groups. The twelve-week inservice course was designed on the Adlerian-Dreikurs model wherein democratic methods of classroom management were taught, including a theoretical psychological base, effective intervention techniques, improved communications skills, and continuing teacher-parent involvement. It was recommended that: 1) This research be replicated. 2) The inservice course design be broadened to include greater participant involvement in its planning and execution, that it cover a full school year, and that abundant opportunities for feedback and evaluation be provided the participants. 3) The PBRS be redesigned to attach more accurate Adlerian-Dreikurs values to the items.

2108.   Ellison, E. J. "Classroom Behavior and Psychosocial Adjustment of Children from Single- and Two-Parent Families." Ed.D. Dissertation. University of California, Los Angeles, 1979.

This study compared the classroom behavior and psychosocial adjustment of children from divorced or separated, mother-headed, single-parent families with that of children from two-parent families. Two questions were addressed. First, are there differences in the classroom behavior of single- and two-parent children? Second, do single-parent children differ from the two-parent children in their overall psychosocial adjustment within the school setting? In this study, attachment theory was utilized as the conceptual framework after similarities were noted in the responses of children to parental separation (as reported in the clinical literature) and the responses of young children to an unwilling separation from an attachment figure. In keeping with the life-span perspective, attachment was concep-tualized as a system of behaviors which enable the individual to achieve a balance between exploring the environment and maintaining close contact with another person. Consequently, an observational schedule was devised to record the children's gaze direction, proxemic, tactile and verbal behavior toward teachers and peers in the class-room. The sample consisted of 19 single-parent and 19 two-parent children between the ages of eight and eleven years. The children were from upper-middle class families and were matched on the basis of age, sex and classroom. For single-parent children, the mean number of months since parental separation was 36. The gaze direction, proxemic, tactile and verbal behavior of each child was observed an average of 46 minutes, in on-minute time segments, by four trained observers who were unaware of the child's family status. Data on the children's psychosocial adjustment were obtained from teacher ratings on the Louisville School Behavioral Checklist. Analysis on the data revealed many similarities in the classroom behavior of both single- and two-parent children with both groups exhibiting strong same sex peer preferences. Teachers rated single-parent children as being significantly more maladjusted on the Academic Disability subscale of the Louisville School Behavior Check-list (p .01). Differences were also noted in the patterns of correlations between teacher ratings of Academic Dis-ability and the children's behavior. For two-parent chil-dren, significant positive correlations were found between Academic Disability ratings and their proxemic, tactile and verbal behavior involving teachers. For single-parent chil-dren, significant negative correlations were found between

Academic Disability ratings and their proxemic, tactile and verbal behavior involving male peers. These findings suggest that maintaining successful relationships with male peers may play an important role in the socialization of single-parent children. The results also suggest that attention must be paid to a number of intro-classroom variables such as teacher-child and child-child interactions, in addition to the extra-classroom variables that have traditionally been used to explain the possible differences in the academic performance of single- and two-parent children. Order no. 7921391, DAI.

2109.   Ens, J. "The Ideology Behavior Interface: A Comparison of High School Teachers' Pupil Control Ideology and Behavior as Perceived by Themselves and Their Students." D.Ed. Dissertation, University of Oregon. Dissertation Abstracts International, 36 (9-A), 5973-5974. Order no. 76-5162, 1976.

The purpose of this study was to examine and compare three elements related to the problem of pupil control: the beliefs or ideology of teachers regarding pupil control processes, the perceptions of teachers in regard to their own pupil control behavior and finally, students' perceptions of teachers' pupil control behavior. The study was focussed on two areas. First, the three major variables - teacher ideology, teacher perception of behavior and student perception of behavior regarding pupil control - were examined for all teachers, for male and female teachers, and for experienced and inexperienced teachers. The second aspect of the study examined the effects that the degree of consonance between teacher ideology and self-perception of practice had on students' perceptions of teacher behavior. The sample of teachers and students for the study was drawn from the high schools of the Public Education System in Saskatoon, Saskatchewan, Canada. Data was collected through questionnaires distributed to the selected teachers and students. Teacher ideology was measured by the Pupil Control Ideology Form. Teacher perception of behavior was measured by a revised form of the Pupil Control Behavior Form. The relationships between pupil control ideology and teacher and student perceptions of teacher behavior were examined by computing correlation coefficients for the two pairs of variables. The effects on students of the degree of consonance between teacher ideology and self-perception of behavior were examined by constructing a two by two crossbreak based on dichotomizations of teacher PCI Form scores and teacher PCB Form scores. This crossbreak created four sub-groups of teachers: those teachers whose self-perception of behavior and ideology were consonant in the humanistic section of the dichotomy; those teachers who were consonant in the custodial section; those who were dissonant with a humanistic self-perception of practice and a custodial ideology; and those who were dissonant with a custodial self-perception of behavior and a humanistic ideology. The results showed a positive but not significant relationship between teacher ideology and teacher perception of behavior. The correlation coefficient between teacher ideology and student perception of behavior was positive and significant but the variance accounted for was less than ten percent. No significant differences between male and female teachers, or experienced and inexperienced teachers were shown by the results.

2110.   Etchegoinberry, Paul L. "The Effects of Group Centered Counseling on the Attitudes, Feelings, and Behavior of Chicano Inner City EMRT Students." Ph.D. Dissertation, University of Southern California. Dissertation Abstracts International, 35 (9-A), 5811. Order no. 75-6411, 1975.

The purpose of this study was to examine the effects of group centered counseling on the three variables on 1) school alienation, 2) study anxiety, and 3) school behavior among Chicano EMRT high school students attending a large inner city school. The basic conclusion is that group centered counseling, which emphasizes the conditions of empathy and respect, had a significant effect on the attitudes, feelings, and school behavior of Chicano EMRT students attending a large inner city high school.

2111.   Evans, D. F. "Effects of Behavior Management Training on Teachers' Attention and the Behavior of Their Retarded Pupils." Ph.D. Dissertation, The University of Arizona. Dissertation Abstracts International, 36 (8-B), 4152. Order no. 76-3793, 1976.

Teachers of mentally retarded elementary school children were given eight weeks of training in classroom behavior management. The first half of training was purely didactic; the second half of training included in-class practice of behavior modification skills by the teachers. Topics covered during the weekly, 90-minute sessions included: reinforcement, extinction, timeout, shaping, fading, prompting, punishment, and problem solving. Each week teachers received handouts summarizing material presented during the session. Pre- and posttraining measures of teachers' knowledge of behavior modification principles and techniques were taken. Weekly observations were made of teacher-pupil interaction in the classrooms. Teacher attention was coded as Verbal Praise, Verbal Reprimand, Verbal-neutral, Physical Praise, Physical Punishment, and Physical-neutral. Antecedent pupil behavior was coded as Appropriate Verbal, Inappropriate Verbal, Appropriate Physical, and Inappropriate Physical. Interactions between teachers and targeted behavior-problem pupils were coded separately from interactions between teachers and non-targeted pupils. Of the 20 observational measures, only Appropriate Verbal behavior of targeted children showed a significant effect for didactic training versus diadactic training plus in-class practice of behavior modification skills.

2112.   Faison, Ruth A. "A Study of Specified Behavioral Changes in Four Groups of Sixth Grade Boys Using: 1) Group Counseling, 2) Group Counseling and Multi-Media presentation, 3) Multi-Media Presentation, and 4) No Treatment." Ph.D. Dissertation, St. Louis University. Dissertation Abstracts International, 33 (3-A), 969. Order no. 72-23,926, 1972.

Using three counseling treatments: 1) a multi-media presentation alone; 2) multi-media presentation and three group counseling sessions; 3) four group counseling ses- sions, and a control group (no treatment), this investiga- tion was designed to study changes in behavior in five dimensions of classroom behavior: classroom conduct, academic motivation and performance, socio-emotional state, teacher dependence, and personal behavior. 1) It appears that behavior can be changed by exposing the pupil to a social model of the desired behavior. 2) A social model presented through a multi-media mode can contribute to change in behavior in pupils. 3) A series of group counseling sessions can contribute to change in behavior in pupils.

2113.   Fanning, F. W. "The Effects of Classroom Instruction in Behavioral Principles Upon Student Tardiness Behavior." Ph.D. Dissertation, The Ohio State University. Dissertation Abstracts International, 33 (4-B), 1761, 1972.

The focus of this study was to investigate the probability of behavioral changes occurring in high school students as a result of classroom instruction in behavioral principles and their application. The general hypothesis tested in this study was that a student's tardiness behavior will decrease as a result of classroom instruction in behavioral principles and the student's self-application of these principles on his own tardiness behavior. All results of this study indicated that behavioral instruction always had a decelerating effect upon tardiness, when any effect was noted. It never increased tardiness. None of the results indicated that either the sole condition of observation of tardiness, or the control instruction, had any effect on the tardiness behavior of any group or individual. The results of all group data and the majority of the individual behavior change results supported the tested hypothesis, that a student's tardiness behavior will decrease as a result of classroom instruction in behavioral principles and the student's self-application of these principles on his own tardiness behavior.

2114.   Farmer, Willie S. "Legal Provisions Concerning the use of Corporal Punishment in Pupil Discipline of the Public School Districts in the State of Mississippi." Ed.D. Dissertation, University of Colorado at Boulder, 1977. Dissertation Abstracts International, 38 (5-A), 2447. Order no. 77-24,206.

The purposes of this study were fourfold: 1) to document corporal punishment policies and procedures in the public school districts of Mississippi; 2) to review and analyze school district policy statements on rules and regulations concerning corporal punishment; 3) to review court decisions on corporal punishment nationally and in the Mississippi public schools; and 4) to develop a prototype policy that is in accordance with policies and legal principles. This study was undertaken to ascertain the status of corporal punishment as a means of pupil control in the public schools of Mississippi. In addition, it was the intent to develop a statewide perspective and a legal position on the use of corporal punishment. The population of the study consisted of 150 public school districts in the State of Mississippi. The following conclusions were drawn from the study: 1) The study concludes that corporal punishment is a major means of controlling pupil discipline in the Mississippi schools, and much discretion cncerning its use is left to the building level personnel. The administrators and teachers have a definite right and duty to maintain discipline in the school. 2) From the data it can be concluded that the type and degree of corporal punishment administered by the administrator/teacher gives consideration to the age, sex, weight, size and physical condition of the pupil. 3) The administrators and teachers have essentially the same right as a parent in disciplining children under their super-vision, except that a teacher or an administrator may be held liable both in a civil court as well as on criminal charges, while the parent is liable only criminally. 4) The responsibility for establishing policies and procedures concerning corporal punishment administration is vested in the school board of each district in Mississippi. 5) The study seems to indicate that superintendents support corporal punishment as an effective means of dealing with pupils. It is concluded that corporal punishment is frequently administered to pupils in grades five through nine.

2115.   Fennema, John E. "The Process and Product of Classroom Discipline: A Description of Behavioristic and Humanistic Approaches and the Development of a Biblical Alternative." Ed.D. Dissertation, University of Georgia, 1975. Dissertation Abstracts International, 36 (8-A), 5209. Order no. 76-2226.

Maintaining discipline is anticipated by the pre-service teacher as being the number one problem of the classroom. It is imperative for consistency within disciplinary proce-dures to view discipline within the gestalt of the total educational scene. This means that effective discipline must be consistent with one's philosophical, psychological, and curricular beleifs and practices. Because one's beliefs most likely fall partially outside of the framework presented by the behaviorist and humanist, it is necessary that pre-service and in-service teahcers be encouraged to develop alternative approaches to classroom discipline which

reflect their personal philosophical positions. This
dissertation presents three views of discipline -- the
behavioristic, the humanistic, and the biblical. First, the
philosophical and psychological frameworks of each of these
viewpoints are developed; then the implications for preventive discipline (curriculum and classroom management) and
corrective discipline are stated. The philosophic position
presents the various perspectives on the origin of man, the
nature of man, and the purpose of man's existence. This is
followed by the psychological perspectives on the motivation
of behavior and the learning process. The behavioristic
approaches to preventive and corrective discipline include
the following techniques: priming, prompting, programming,
sequencing, satiation, extinction, incompatible alternatives, and negative reinforcement. The humanistic
approaches to preventive discipline include the development
of a facilitative atmosphere, a student-centered emphasis, a
dynamic curriculum, and the use of discovery approaches.
The humanistic approaches to corrective discipline first
offer insight into factors which may influence misbehavior
and then present a description of approaches taken by Haim
Ginott, William Glasser, and Rudolf Driekurs. The biblical
approaches to classroom management reflect a balance between
a teacher/curriculum dominance and a student/needs dominance. All have their proper place within a balanced,
unified classroom. Both teachers and students have unique
responsibilities within the positions they fill. The
teacher is to give responsible guidance and leadership. He
is placed in authority by God; but that authority can never
usurp the student's freedom and dignity. The biblical
approach to discipline seems to be more in harmony with that
of the humanist than with that of the behaviorist. The
philosophical framework differs to a great extent, but the
approaches to preventive and corrective discipline have many
similarities. That is noteworthy since Christian discipline
has often been perceived as being authoritarian in nature
rather than humane or humanitarian.

2116.   Fereday, L. P. "Investigation of Teacher Behaviors and
Characteristics Related to Frequency of Student Disciplinary
Referrals." Ed.D. Dissertation, The University of Oklahoma,
1979.

This investigation examined teacher behaviors and characteristics as they relate to frequency of student disciplinary
referrals. A middle school in an integrated urban school
district was the investigation site. Student Disciplinary
Referral Forms were collected for the first semester of the
1978-79 school year. Referral Forms were tabulated individually for each basic subject teacher. A frequency distribution was constructed using the number of Student Disciplinary Referral Forms per teacher as the criteria. The
three teachers at the upper end of the frequency distribution comprised the sample for the exploratory study. Data
for the investigation was gathered by the following methods:
1) Teacher Interviews; 2) Projective Instruments; 3)

Analysis of Records; 4) Analysis of Discipline Referrals; 5) Student Interviews; 6) Classroom Observations. In addition to the value of describing a phenomenon as it existed, profiles of both the teacher who initiated a low number of student disciplinary referrals and the teacher who initiated a high number of student disciplinary referrals were developed. The investigation also led to insights that prompted recommendations and possible hypotheses for further research. Order no. 8003801, DAI.

2117.   Fine, Richard M. "The Application of Social Reinforcement Procedures to Improve the School Attendance of Truant Chicano Junior High School Students." Ph.D. Dissertation, Arizona   State   University.   Dissertation   Abstracts International, 35 (3-A), 1442-1443. Order no. 74-19,284, 1974.

The purpose of this study was to investigate the utility of a paraprofessional and indigenous high school student administering social reinforcement procedures to improve the school attendance of truant junior high bilingual disadvantaged students. This research attempted to demonstrate the practical and useful application of behavior modification principles as well as the role of paraprofessional and youth resources to modify problem behaviors in a public school setting. The population included in this study were truant lower socio-economic Chicano junior high school students who attended a local junior high in Tempe, Arizona during the school year 1972-73. From the results of this study, the following conclusions were drawn: 1) The systematic application of social reinforcement procedures was an effective method to modify truant behavior. 2) The utilization of paraprofessional and indigenous high school youth as effective treatment administrators of these learning procedures is justified. 3) The presence of group social rewards helped to improve school attendance. 4) The strength of the treatment program was most effective in reducing absenteeism during the continuous (first) phase of reinforcement and subsequently dimished over time. 5) The treatment group significantly differed from the control group in improving school attending behavior during treatment, following treatment (extinction), and also in follow-up the subsequent school year.

2118.   Finkelstein, M. "Perceived Parental Acceptance and Control and Classroom Behavior: A Test of the Predictive Validity of Schaefer's Configurational Model." Ph.D. Dissertation, University of Maine. Dissertation Abstracts International, 36 (10-B), 5254. Order no. 76-7428, 1976.

The primary purpose of this study was to determine whether or not the utilization of Schaefer's configurational model can predict children's classroom behavior. This model treats the child-perceived variables of parental acceptance and control interactionally. The Children's Reports of Parental Behavior Inventory was administered to 67 girls and

74 boys enrolled in the fifth and sixth grades of two rural elementary schools in Maine. Hostile-Aggressive, Neurotic, and Withdrawn-Dependent behavior were defined for each child by factor scores derived from their teachers' ratings on the Burks Behavior Rating Scales. The interaction between the perceived parental acceptance and control variables did not reach an acceptable level of significance for any of the three behaviors under study. However, nine out of a possible 24 correlations between the perceived parent variables and the children's behavior variables reached a significance level of .05 or better. Maternal and paternal acceptance were found to be negatively related to boys' Hostile-Aggressive behavior. Maternal control was found to be positively related to boys' and girls' Hostile-Aggressive and Neurotic behaviors. Paternal control was found to be positively related to boys' Hostile-Aggressive behavior and girls' Neurotic and Withdrawn-Dependent behavior.

2119.   Finney, Frank. "The Design, Development, and Evaluation of a Minicourse in Positive Classroom Management." Ph.D. Dissertation, Washington State University. Dissertation Abstracts International, 35 (1-A), 298. Order no. 74-16,363, 1974.

The purpose of this study was to design and develop a minicourse in positive classroom management for a competency-based curriculum and to determine the effectiveness of a minicourse, compared with a group lecture presentation. The minicourse incorporated a variety of principles of curriculum development in a systems approach to instructional design. The component materials that were developed included a programmed booklet, a videotape, and a package of printed materials. Forty-eight pre-service teachers enrolled in a Language Arts methods course for elementary teachers at Washington State University during the Fall Semester, 1972, participated in the study. The study was incorporated into the regular instructional program for the course. The two sections of students were identified as minicourse and lecture treatment groups. One group of students studied the self-contained, individualized minicourse and the other group attended a group lecture presentation. Both groups received approximately the same amount of instructional time. Prior to and immediately following the different instructional methods, students viewed a simulated classroom incident which showed student behavior that was interfering to learning. Students described in writing how they would plan a program to manage the inappropriate behavior in the classroom. These management paradigms were later typewritten and judged by five graduate teaching assistants who had participated in a training program in classroom management. Paradigms were judged according to the number of positive management principles and the degree of completion of each principle. Analysis of the data indicated that students in the minicourse and lecture groups experienced increased levels of learning which, though different in magnitude, were statistically significant.

Students utilizing the minicourse demonstrated significantly higher performance in writing positive management principles, both number and degree of completion, than students in the group lecture presentation. A student questionnaire, utilized to appraise the system, clearly indicated student approval for the minicourse and endorsement of an instructional strategy comprised of independent and small group study.

2120.   Fleming, E. E. "The Effects of Facilitative Communications Training of Mothers on Behavior of Elementary School Children." Ph.D. Dissertation, The University of Mississippi. Dissertation Abstracts International, 36 (7-A), 4346-4347. Order no. 76-452, 1976.

The purpose of this study was to determine the relative effects of Carkhuff's (1969) model of facilitative communications training of mothers on behavior of their elementary school children. The sample consisted of volunteers (45 mothers and 69 children in the second and third grades) in Tupelo, Mississippi. The mother-child dyads were randomly assigned to two experimental and a control group (N=46 because one mother had two children). Twenty-three children, whose mothers were not in the groups, were used as a fase control group. The groups were randomly assigned to trainers so that the trainers had one subgroup within each major group. The two trainers were doctoral students. Mothers assigned to Experimental Group I (E_1) were trained using the Carkhuff (1971) paradigm. Carkhuff's model provides for systematic training of therapeutic core dimensions of empathy, respect, concreteness, genuineness, confrontation, and immediacy. Mothers assigned to Experimental Group II (E_2) participated in a general discussion group, and no training was provided on the core dimensions. Mothers assigned to the Control group (C) only met for testing. The experimental groups met for ten hours, five two-hour sessions, including testing time. All mothers assigned to the groups were administered the Carkhuff Communication Discrimination Index to assess their communication and discrimination skills and the IPAT: Anxiety Scale Questionnaire to assess their general anxiety level. The findings indicated that the mothers' interpersonal functioning significantly improved. The children's behavior ratings were significantly changed at home but not at school. Also, the children's learner self-concepts were not significantly affected by the training of the mothers.

2121.   Fontana, D. B. "The Effects of Behavior Modification on Locus of Control, Self-Concept, Reading Achievement, Math Achievement, and Behavior in Second Grade Children." Ph.D. Dissertation, St. John's University. Dissertation Abstracts International, 36 (8-B), 4197-4198. Order no. 76-2984, 1976.

This study investigated the effect of behavior modification classroom techniques including a token economy system on locus of control, self-concept, reading achievement, math achievement, and behavior in second graders. There were 85 children in four classes. Two were experimental classes and two were controls. Pre- and posttesting was done with the Nowicki-Strickland Locus of Control Scale for Children, the Piers-Harris Children's Self Concept Scale, and the Wide Range Achievement Test, Reading and Math sections. Weekly observations were made of each child's behavior to obtain the mean number of disruptive intervals (those in which a disruptive behavior occurred) for the base period which was two weeks and the experimental period, fifteen weeks. Subjects were categorized by treatment group, the experience level of the teacher (more experienced vs less experienced), and the sex of the subjects. It was concluded that the treatment, behavior modification, only had a significant effect on the experimental children's behavior which improved. Neither locus of control nor self-concept changed significantly in either their treatment or control group. The math achievement score of the control group was significantly higher than that of the control classes. The experience level of the teacher did not significantly affect any variable under study.

2122.   Fontius, J. A. S. "Relationships of School Climate and Congruence of Administrator, Teacher, and Student Perceptions Regarding Discipline to the Degree of Severity of Discipline Techniques Used in Schools." Ph.D. Dissertation, The University of Wisconsin-Madison, 1979.

The purpose of this study was to determine the degree of the relationships between school climate and the congruence of administrator, teacher, and student perceptions regarding discipline to the degree of severity of discipline techniques used in schools. The framework for the study was that of general system stheory and social systems theory. The first 12 null hypotheses were tested by the following general hypothesis: There is no significant relationship between school climate, as measured by the OCDQ Climate Profile and Similarity Scores, and the degree of severity of discipline techniques used in schools, as measured by the Index of Degree of Severity of School Discipline Techniques. The last three hypotheses were tested by the following general hypothesis: There is no significant difference between the congruence of administrator, teacher, and student perceptions regarding discipline and the degree of severity of discipline techniques used in schools. Data were collected from 29 elementary schools of a large urban district. The sample included 29 principals, 192 intermediate level teachers and 1,118 fourth, fifth, and sixth graders. The instrumentation used in this study included the Organizational Climate Description Questionnaire, Form IV; the Modified Lufler School Discipline Survey; the Modified Lufler Student Discipline Survey; and the Index of Degree of Severity of School Discipline Techniques. The Organizational Climate Description Questionnaire provided data for determing the school climate. The Modified Lufler

Surveys provided data pertaining to the discipline techniques used in schools as perceived by administrators, teachers, and students. The degree of severity of discipline techniques used in schools was measured by the Index of Degree of Severity of School Discipline Techniques developed by the writer. Order no. 7927170, DAI.

2123.   Fortune, L. A. "The Effects of Multidimensional Elementary School Counseling on the Self-Concepts and Classroom Behavior of Alienated Elementary School Children." Ed.D. Dissertation. Washington State Univeristy, 1975.

The purpose of this study was to identify alienated elementary school children and implement a structured multidimensional elementary counseling program. The study sought to determine the effect of change in alienated children's feelings about themselves, classroom behavior, and school attendance resulting from this intervention process. Children were selected by their teachers from the fourth, fifth, and sixth grades in three elementary schools, in Tacoma, Washington. They participated in a counseling process which consisted of five major elements: An individual "plan of attack," individual and group Counseling, parent involvement, and teacher involvement. The instruments used in this research project were The Piers-Harris Self Concept Scale and the Devereux Elementary School Behavior Rating Scale. Data were also collected on tardies and absences. No statistically significant differences were found between the treatment and control groups on the Piers-Harris Self Concept Scale. However, despite a lack of statistical significance, according to the manual a gain of 5 points for a group mean has been shown to indicate more positive self-concepts. On the basis of this rationale, the treatment group did make positive gains in self-concept. Significant differences were found between the total treatment and control groups on the Devereux scale. The control total group decreased and differed from the treatment group on the classroom distrubance, disrespect-defiance, external blame, and achievement anxiety. The treatment group increased and differed from the control group on creative initiative. The treatment group also showed a trend toward increased comprehension. No significant differences were noted on impatience, external reliance, inattentive-withdrawn, irrelevant responsiveness, or need closeness to teacher. It was concluded that multidimensional elementary school counseling did have a positive effect on the self-concepts and classroom behavior of alienated elementary school children. The nature of the change for the control group on the Devereux scale revolved around a response to the controlling efforts in a school: Reduced classroom disturbance, disrespect-defiance, and external blame. The changes for the treatment group indicated increased involvement both academically and with people. Increased comprehension, creative initiative, and need closeness to teacher while reduced external reliance and inattentive-withdrawn behavior. The latter types of behavior are interpreted to be incongruent with alienation. Order No. 75-16, 169, DAI.

2124.   Fotsch, L. P. "Relationship of Student Perceptions to Selected Dimensions of Interpersonal Behavior of the Professional Staff in Schools." Ph.D. Dissertation, The University of Wisconsin. Dissertation Abstracts International, 33 (9-A), 4723. Order no. 72-31,676, 1973.

The general objective of the study was to examine the relationships between perceptions of students and perceptions of their teachers and certain selected classroom and human relations practices of the teachers. Factor analysis of the data pertaining to elementary and high school class characteristics using the IMAGE-factoring procedure revealed twenty-eight factors and four of them were rotated to simple structure by the varimax procedure. The four factors accounted for almost half of the total item variance. The four factors, as interpreted by the investigator were: Pupil Acceptance of Teacher, Classroom Order, Cohesiveness and Participation. Three hypotheses and four ancillary questions focused on the relationships that might exist between students' attitudes and perceptions of the four major factors and their teachers' perceptions of school climate and of their principal's executive professional leadership, and managerial and social support. The relationship between teachers' classroom perceptions of their principal's executive professional leadership, managerial tions of their principals's executive professional leadership, managerial and social support were also investigated. The population for this investigation is based on the students and professional adults in eight Wisconsin school systems. The sample includes all students present in random sample of the eleventh grade English classes, the teachers of these students, all school principals and additional professional adults randomly selected until thirty percent of all professionals were represented. The findings of the study found few significant relationships between students' perceptions of items related to "Acceptance of Teacher," "Classroom Order," "Student Cohesiveness," and "Student Participation" and teachers human relation practices in the classroom. However, there were some indications that favorable perceptions of students were positively correlated with classroom practices which encourage greater student participation, even though many of the correlations were not large enough to be significantly greater than zero. In general, there were no relationships between students' perceptions and their teachers' perceptions of school climate and their teachers' perceptions of their principal's executive professional leadership, managerial and social support. Some significant relationships were found between teachers' perceptions of school climate and their perceptions of the executive professional leadership, managerial and social support of their principal.

2125.   Franklin, Wallace J.   "The Effect of T-Groups on Pupil Control Ideology and Pupil Control Behavior of Student Teachers in Secondary Schools." Ed.D. Dissertation, University of Kansas. Dissertation Abstracts International, 37 (8-A), 4739-4740. Order no. 77-2216, 1977.

Researchers have pointed out that pupil control is a problem in the public schools. Since the socialization press in the school leans toward a custodial orientation and since there is support for the assertion that controlling behavior should lean toward the humanistic end of the continuum, a strategy was designed to counteract the current direction of the socialization press. This investigation was guided by the following questions: Will a T-group intervention strategy based on humanism result in student teachers' acquiring a more humanistic pupil control attitude than they would normally acquire? Will their performance reflect this humanistic attitude as perceived by their students? This study revealed that change initiated through T-group intervention strategy made no significant differences in PCI among groups. The results also indicate that the amount of treatment made no significant difference in student teachers' PCI.

2126.   Fredman, Marvin E.   "Two Self-Concept Variables, Pupil Classroom Behavior, and Academic Achievement Among Upper Elementary School Males." Ph.D. Dissertation, Temple University. Dissertation Abstracts International, 37 (4-A), 2073. Order no. 76-22,094, 1976.

This study had two distinct purposes. The first was to investigate whether the school self-concept has a stronger relationship to academic achievement than does the global or generalized self-concept and whether pupil classroom behavior is related significantly to academic achievement. The second purpose was to investigate the notion that human functioning can best be explained as a result of the interaction of both personality theory and reinforcement theory principles. The student population consisted of 190 fifth and sicth grade males enrolled within a white, middle to upper-middle class school district in Pennsylvania. All of the males were students in regular public school classes. Language Arts teachers rated the boys' classroom behavior on the Quay-Peterson Behavior Problem Checklist. 1) There was significant differences in intelligence test scores among the three research groups: the Appropriate group had the highest mean I.Q. score, the Withdrawn group had the next highest, and the Aggressive group had the lowest. 2) There was a significant and positive relationship between I.Q. and the school self-concept and between I.Q. and academic achievement. The relationship between I.Q. and generalized self-concept was not significant. 3) Neither of the two self-concept vairables had significant relationships with achievement when I.Q. was statistically controlled. Only the school self-concept had a significant and positive relationship with achievement when I.Q. was not statistically

controlled.   4) When I.Q. was statistically controlled,
there were no significant differences in achievement scores
among the resarch groups when achievement was defined as a
combination of both "Word Meaning" and "Paragraph Meaning"
scores.

2127.   Freebery, J. W.   "Reading achievement down, discipline
problems   up: reserving   this   middle   school   trend."
Individual Practicum for EDD Nova University.   123p, 1978.

Discipline records and reading test scores revealed that
students in the Redding Middle School, Middletown, Delaware,
were achieving low reading scores, while the number of
discipline referrals remained high.   This report discusses
how the school's teachers and administrators succeeded in
changing the direction of this trend, increasing reading
achievement, while reducing discipline referrals.   A master
check-list was developed, with objectives, activities, and
strategies to implement major changes in school organization, staff training, reading programs, and discipline
programs.   Bloom's Theory of Mastery and Learning to improve
student competency in reading through sequential instruction, assessment, and achievement feedback was used.
Glasser's Theory of Reality Therapy provided students and
teachers with practical problem solving strategies for
dealing with potential discipline problems before administrative intervention.   A 20% reduction in referrals and a
substantial increase in reading achievement scores resulted
from this study.   See ERIC Abstract #ED 154371.

2128.   French, M. D.   "A Study of Kohlbergian Moral Development
and Selected Behaviors Among High School Students in Classes
Using Values Clarification and Other Teaching Methods."
Ed.D.   Dissertation,   Auburn   University.   Dissertation
Abstracts International, 38 (5-A), 2521.   Order no. 77-24,
495, 1977.

The moral development and selected behaviors of 182 students
in two urban Southern public high schools were assessed
under two experimental teaching methods.   Two teachers, one
at each school, taught three similar classes in terms of
subject and grade for one semester using a lecture approach
in one, a humanistic values clarification approach in
another, and their regular teaching methods in the third.
Rest's Defining Issues Test of moral judgment development
was administered to all the students in these classes at the
beginning and end of the semester.   Direct classroom
behavior observation was used to assess behavior differences
in terms of attentiveness, opinions, expressed, interactions, and control required to maintain order.   Analysis
of observational data indicated that some behaviors, i.e.,
interactions and opinions offered, were significantly higher
in the values clarification classrooms, which would be
expected because of the nature of that pedagogical approach.
There were no statistically significant differences in

attendance, attentiveness or degree of teacher control required among the three groups.

2129.   Freudman, J. D.   "Reflection-Impulsivity and Pupil Attentive Behavior in the Classroom." Ph.D. Dissertation, Columbia University. Dissertation Abstracts International, 34 (10-B), 5166. Order no. 74-8175, 1974.

The purpose of this study was to investigate: 1) the relationship between pupil conceptual tempo, as defined by the reflection-impulsivity dimension (R-I) and pupil attentive behavior in the classroom; and 2) the relationship between teacher conceptual tempo and the attentive behavior of their pupils. Pupil subjects consisted of 246 Caucasian boys drawn randomly within classes of 41 third, fourth and fifth grade classes in six schools, two of which were public and four of which were parochial schools. Of the 246 pupils, 90 were from public schools and 156 from parochial schools. Hypothesis 1 was concerned with the expectation that five "decision time" scores on measures of the RI dimension would be positively correlated with the frequency of observed pupil attention scores. Hypothesis 2 was concerned with the expectation that two "quality of response: scores on measures of the RI dimension would be negatively correlated with the frequency of observed attention scores. The results indicated that neither the "decision time" nor the "quality of response: scores on pupil RI tests were related to observed pupil attention scores. An additional measure of pupil attention, obtained from teacher ratings of pupils, was also shown not be be related to pupil RI scores.

2130.   Frye, V. H. "The Comparative Effects of Two Types of Teacher Consequences on Student Verbalizations." Ed.D. Dissertation, The University of Tennessee. Dissertation Abstracts International, 33 (8-A), 4172. Order no. 73-2447, 1973.

The major purpose of the study was to assess the efficacy of specific approval and nondirective teacher attention in increasing higher order student verbalizations, i.e., verbalizations which involve expressing opinions, speculating, comparing, giving reasons, examples or illustrations, and evaluating given information. Disruptive behavior was also monitored to determine whether changes occurred in frequencies of this behavior when treatment conditions were in effect. Three groups of junior high school students participated in the study. Each group was observed for one hour four days a week and a record was made of the time large group discussions began or terminated during the observation period. Teacher attention appeared to have a facilitative effect in increasing higher order student verbalizations. However, neither specific approval nor nondirective attention appeared consistently superior to the other across the three groups. The introduction of a higher percentage of higher order teacher questions without a concomitant increase in teacher attention appeared insufficient to stimulate much increase in higher order student responding. The findings suggest that teacher attention may be a component in reaching the commonly stated educational goal of promoting higher levels of thinking, inquiry and criticism.

2131.   Fuchs, Douglas H. "The Relationship Between Reading Gain and School Behavior Among Fourth, Fifth and Sixth Grade Disabled Readers." Ph.D. Dissertation, University of Minnesota, 1978. Dissertation Abstracts International, 39 (2-A), 774. Order no. 7813396.

Many children who have reading problems also manifest disturbing behavior in their classrooms, a relationship which has been substantiated by much clinical and empirical evidence. The effects of various remedial programs on reading skill has been well established, but the bulk of the research has ignored the behavioral facet of the relationship. Specifically, there have been few attempts to find out if improving a child's ability to read also improves his behavior in the classroom. Instead, the effort in these studies has been to assess the child's performance in reading achievement only. Related, non-reading clasroom behavior goes largely unexamined. The first and primary objective of the present study was to investigate the amount and nature of changes in classroom behavior concomitant with change in reading performance among seriously disabled fourth, fifth and sixth grade children enrolled in a remedial reading program. Assuming that improvements in class conduct were observed together with gains in reading in the classroom in which reading remediation took place, a second purpose of the present study was to assess the extent of transfer of such changes in conduct from the remediation room to the regular classroom. A control group was employed to assess the importance of improved reading skill as a causal factor in this presumed relationship. The behavior of children assigned to the experiemntal group was observed in both the room in which remedial activities occur and in the regular classroom. Observing in the regular classroom in addition to the remedial room seemed important since previous research found improvement in behavior to be specific to the situation in which academic improvement took place. In order to explore the possibility of transferring presumed improved behavior in the remedial setting to the regular classroom, teachers and parents of a randomly selected subgroup of experimental subjects received periodic, formal feedback on the children's progress in the remedial reading program. Both the experimental and control groups showed a statistically significant and important improvement in reading from pre- and post-treatment testing. Experimentals showed higher mean raw scores than the controls on the three reading measures employed, but none of these differences in raw scores were found to be statistically significant. Experimentals manifested statistically significant and dramatic reductions in frequency of disturbing behavior in the remedial reading room. A comparison of the treatment groups' raw score frequencies revealed that the experimentals behaved somewhat more appropriately than controls in the regular classroom, although this difference was not statistically significant.

2132.   Fugate, J. E., II. "The Use of a Picture Preference Scale to Predict Antisocial Behavior." Ph.D. Dissertation, The Ohio State University. Dissertation Abstracts International, 40 (10-A), 5411. Order no. 8009277, 1980.

Delinquent behavior in the schools is a concern of society. Need for an accurate instrument to predict delinquency was established. The purpose of this study was to determine the appropriateness and usefulness of the Ohio State Picture Preference Scale (OSPPS) for predicting antisocial behavior in junior high male students. A three step research plan to ascertain the usefulness of the OSPPS in discriminating between antisocial behavior and socially acceptable behavior was outlined. Briefly, the steps were as follows: Step One: An OSPPS Antisocial Behavior Key was developed by analyzing the responses of known criminals and noncriminals to the OSPPS. Step Two: Sample group data were obtained from the files of Wedgewood Junior High School. These data consisted of three test scores (The Ohio State Picture Preference Scale, Internality-Externality Scale, and Kvaraceus Delinquency Proneness Scale), teacher predictions, and copies of Corrective Measurement Communications usually called discipline slips. Step Three: These sample group data were interpreted through the use of correlational analysis and by comparing mean scores. When data from the sample group were analyzed, it was found that no statistically significant relationships existed between the Ohio State Picture Preference Scale and any of the four instruments that measured delinquency proneness. Also, a comparison of mean scores between high group scores on the OSPPS and low group scores on the OSPPS showed no significant level of difference. All eight hypotheses were rejected. The OSPPS Antisocial Behavior key does not measure the same thing that the Kvaraceus Delinquency Proneness Scale, Internality-Externality Scale, Teacher Predictions, or Discipline Slips measure. It was found that The Ohio State Picture Preference Scale, at this stage of development, is not useful in predicting antisocial behavior.

2133.   Fuller, Deena S. "Instructional Strategies for Changing Expressed Opinions Toward Classroom Behavior Management." Ed.D. Dissertation, The University of Tennessee. Dissertation Abstracts International, 34 (11-A), 7042. Order no. 74-11,244, 1974.

Behavior modification is a controversial subject which elicits acclaim from some and disdain or even outright hostility from others. Proponents of behaviorism often assume that empirically establishing effectiveness and then teaching the specific technology will insure dissemination of behavior modification throughout educational realms. Obviously, this has not been the case. An increasing body of literature indicates the need to deal with people's ethical and philosophical objections to behavioral technology. The present study demonstrates that a teaching approach dealing with such objections enhances the students' affinity for behavior modification as well as teaching the technology. The effects of three treatment conditions (A, B, and Control) on expressed opinions regarding classroom behavior modification were examined in six graduate level courses. Each A and B treatment was administered in two educational psychology classes; two control classes (nonbehavioral, curriculum and instruction courses) were included primarily as a point of comparison. Treatments A and B involved separate content approaches for teaching a course in classroom behavior management. The experimental treatment classes were equivalent in overall format; however, Treatment A emphasized ethical dimensions of behavior modification while Treatment B emphasized procedures for objectively analyzing classroom behavior. A behavior modification opinionnaire was administered three times (pre, midterm, and posttreatment) in all A, B, and Control classes. A high score on the opinionnaire indicates positive affect toward behavior modification. In A and B classes a course examination was administered pre, midterm, and posttreatment. Subjects had the option of taking it at any or all of the administrations with the highest score being counted toward their grade. Midterm examination scores and each student's total accumulated points were the indices of academic achievement in A and B classes. Analysis of the opinionnaire data indicated that Treatments A and B produced significantly greater endorsement of behavior modification than did the control condition. Also, Treatment A proved to be more facilitative of positive affect toward classroom amangement than did Treatment B. This conclusion was supported by opinionnaire responses and verbal behavior in class.

2134.   Fuller, Joye M. "An Evaluation of the Home-School Behavioral Management Program Implemented in an Intermediate Classroom for the Emotionally Disturbed." Ed.D. Dissertation, University of Kansas, 1971. Dissertation Abstracts International, 32 (4-A), 1941. Order no. 71-27,221, 1971.

The Home-School Behavioral Management Program (HSBMP) developed by the Institute for Behavioral Improvement, has been utilized as a procedure for involving parents in affecting change in daily classroom behavior, both academic and social, of children in special education classrooms. This program has previously been used with over 200 children placed in special education classrooms in a suburban school district. The present study was designed to study the effects of the HSBMP on specific academic performance of children who were placed in a classroom for the emotionally disturbed in a public school setting. The HSBMP provides a formal and active involvement of the parent in affecting change within the classroom setting. The daily procedures implemented in the classroom in which the present study took place were based on the Structured Approach. These procedures were in effect prior to, and continued throughout the present investigation. This study represents the first reported investigation to determine effects of the HSBMP on specific academic tasks in any setting. Daily measurement of five aspects of Spelling and Reading was used in order to assess the effects of initiating the HSBMP with four children in a classroom for the emotionally disturbed who were of intermediate age range. One pupil served as a control subject. The HSBMP was implemented with Spelling and two aspects of Reading. Data were recorded in two additional aspects of Reading although no contingencies were placed on the performance. The HSBMP was found to be successful in affecting change in the academic performance of children who are considered emotionally disturbed when measured in terms of percent and number correct. The HSBMP was successful in affecting change in the academic performance of children who were enrolled in a classroom operating under the Structured Approach which involved procedures of individualized planning for academic tasks, immediate verbal feedback, and a weekly reporting system. Changes in the performance in specific academic tasks of Spelling and Reading were demonstrated when the HSBMP was implemented with four children. The use of the HSBMP resulted in differential change in various academic tasks. The most marked change in performance was observed in the area of Spelling. Little generalization was seen in the two aspects of Reading which were measured although no HSBMP was implemented at any time.

2135.   Gaasholt, Marie G. P. "Teacher and Pupil Behaviors Related to Classroom Organization and Management." Ed.D. Dissertation, University of Oregon, 1972. Dissertation Abstracts International, 33 (9-A), 4980. Order no. 73-7893.

The purpose of this study was to investigate classroom organization and management. Three components: 1) teacher planning; 2) classroom behavior of teacher, and; 3) classroom behavior of pupils, were examined. Fifteen fourth, fifth and sixth grade classes were randomly selected for this study. Observers obtained nine daily measure of: a) physical events related to teacher planning; b) rates of specific teacher and pupil behavior; c) teacher evaluations of organization; and d) additional notes regarding organization or management. After all 135 classroom observations wre completed the investigator interviewed each teacher. The data were analyzed three ways: 1) A Pearson Product Moment correlation matrix based on the rates of teacher and pupil behavior was input for factor analysis; 2) medians and best fit slopes were calculated for the rates of teacher and pupil behaviors; and, 3) checklist data and interview responses were tallied and numerically tabluated. Nine factors showing a relationship among tacher and pupil behaviors were identified. Twenty-six significant correlations between specific teacher and pupil behaviors were revealed. Physical events related to teacher planning were not significantly related to pupil behavior. Teacher planning of classroom procedures was not significantly related to classroom behavior of teacher and pupils. Teacher evaluations of organization were not significantly related to pupil behavior.

2136.   Gang, M. J. "Empirical Validation of a Reality Therapy Intervention Program in an Elementary School Classroom." Ph.D. Dissertation, The University of Tennessee. Dissertation Abstracts International, 35 (8-B), 4216. Order no. 75-3592, 1975.

The present study investigated the effect of a Reality Therapy Intervention Process (RTIP) on selected behaviors of six students in the elementary school classroom. Three major questions were investigated: 1) Does the RTIP result in changes in student behavior in the classroom? 2) If so, will differential effects associated with the class of behavior (i.e., desirable, undesirable, or both) to which the teacher responds have any effect? More specifically, will there be a greater or lesser impact on the student if the teacher implements the RTIP responding to: the student's desirable behavior only; the student's undesirable behavior only; or both the student's desirable and undesirable behavior. 3) How durable are any observed changes in student or teacher behavior when E withholds feedback from the teacher? The data collected strongly suggested that the RTIP was effective in modifying behavior. Problem behaviors decreased and desirable behaviors increased for each of the target students. In addition, it appeared that the teachers felt that the establishment of an ongoing, genuine relationship between the student and the teacher was an essential condition for the successful outcomes achieved.

2137.   Gardner, W. E. "The Effects of Intergrade Tutoring With Group Guidance Activities on the Reading Achievement, Self-Concept, Attitudes Toward School and Behavior of Third and Fourth Grade Tutors and on the Reading Achievement and Behavior of First and Second Grade Tutees." Ed.D. Dissertation. Wayne State University, 1973.

The major prupose of this study was to investigate the effects of intergrade directed tutoring with group guidance activities on the reading achievement, self-concept, attitudes toward school, and behavior of third and fourth grade low-achievers in a Detroit inner-city public elementary school. A secondary purpose of the study was to measure the effects of directed tutoring and group guidance activities on the reading achievement and behavior of first and second graders (tutees) involved in the project. Research instruments used were: 1. The California Reading Tests, Upper Primary and Lower Primary, Forms W and X, 2. Bills' Elementary School Index of Adjustment and Values, 3. A semantic differential scale, 4. A teacher evaluation

form, and 5. A parent's informal questionnaire. The study
was undertaken in the Detroit City Schools. Letters were
sent to the parents of 104 pupils requesting written
permission for them to participate in the project. The
subjects were entered into the program only after the
written consent of the parents were returned to the school.
All written permissions were granted before the program
began. Staff orientation was conducted by the investigator,
who was also the school principal, in an effort to apprise
the staff of the project. Orientation was also provided for
104 pupils who had been selected to participate in the
project. 1. No significant difference was found between
the experimental subjects, by groups, and the control
subjects, by groups on pre-test reading achievement mean
scores. 2. Not all experimental tutee groups showed gains
in reading achievement greater than did all the control
tutee groups, as was predicted. 3. All experimental tutor
groups showed gains in reading achievement greater than
those of the control tutor groups, as was predicted. 4.
The experimental tutors, as a group, showed gains in reading
achievement greater than those of the experimental tutees,
as a group. Order No. 73-31, 723, DAI.

2138.   Garza, G. "A Study of Teacher-Student Interaction in
Sixth Grades of Ethnically Imbalanced Schools." Ph.D.
Dissertation, The University of Texas at Austin.
Dissertation Abstracts International, 37 (8-A), 4819. Order
no. 77-3902, 1977.

A study of teacher-student interaction data as they related
to attitudes and classroom climates in 63 sixth-grade classrooms in 15 ethnically imbalanced schools in the Houston
Independent School District was made during the 1972-73
school year. Specifically, the investigation focused on
selected characteristics of teachers in ethnically
imbalanced school environments and on the perceived and
observed social behavior of students in these same schools.
Four instruments (the Teacher Information Questionnaire,
Minnesota Teacher Attitude Inventory, Student Behavior
Scale, and Classroom Interaction Schedule) were used to
collect data from the following areas: 1) teacher characteristics; 2) teacher perception of classroom behavior; 3)
observed teacher behavior; and 4) observed student behavior.
The stepwise discriminant analysis and the stepwise multiple
regression analysis procedures were used to analyze the data
in response to two questions: 1) Were selected characteristics of teachers in ethnically imbalanced schools related
to the positive or negative social behavior of students as
perceived by their teachers? 2) In ethnically imbalanced
schools, was observed student social behavior related to 1)
selected characteristics of teachers and 2) observed teacher
behavior? Student social behavior was described as 1)
cooperative behavior, 2) uncooperative behavior, 3) affiliative behavior (group allegiance, belonging), and 4) bored
behavior. In answer to the first question, the findings
clearly indicated the existence of high correlations between

teacher perceptions of the positive or negative social behavior of students in ethnically imbalanced schools and the teachers' attitudes, number of years in the present school, age, sex, and ethnicity. In answer to the second question, the findings significantly supported the hypothesis that teachers' attitudes, number of years of teaching expierience, number of years in the present school, age, sex, ethnicity, dominance, permissiveness, encouragement, and the perception of students' social behaviors had a direct relationship to the observed social behaviors of students in ethnically imbalanced schools.

2139.   Gilberg, B. M. "The Development of Children's Cognitive and Affective Role-Taking Abilities in Relation to Aggressive Behavior in the Classroom." Ph.D. Dissertation, Iowa State University. Dissertation Abstracts International, 38 (7-A), 4012. Order no. 77-29,835, 1978.

The relationship between cognitive and/or affective role-taking and aggressive behavior in the classroom was the central interest in the study. In addition, the relationship between role-taking ability and grade level, and the relationship between role-taking ability and general intelligence were investigated. There were 39 first-grade and 45 third-grade boys interviewed individually to obtain measures of role-taking ability and a peer rating of aggression. Teachers' ratings of aggression and estimates of the children's general intelligence also were obtained. There were no significant relationships between role-taking ability and ratings of aggression in the first or third grade. There also were no developmental differences in role-taking ability. Ancillary results suggested a significant inverse relationship between affective role-taking and teachers' ratings of aggression when test scores from both grades were considered together. In addition, teacher and peer ratings of aggression and third grade children's scores on the Stanford Achievement Test.

2140.   Glenn, Myra C. "Changing Attitudes Towards Corporal Punishment in the Age of Jackson." Ph.D. Dissertation, State University of New York at Buffalo, 1979. Dissertation Abstracts International, 40 (9-A), 5156. Order no. 8005662.

This dissertation explores changing cultural attitudes towards discipline in the northern United States by focusing on the anti-corporal punishment efforts of nineteenth-century common school, naval, and family reformers. These reformers' numerous writings on discipline, as well as their participation in well publicized corporal punishment controversies reveal a crucial shift in values away from external coercion and towards internalized self-control. Central Questions in my study are: Why did these reformers view corporal punishment, as a "relic of barbarism"? Why did they repeatedly stress the importance of internalized moral restraints in their discussions of punishment and discipline? Were their views shared by other citizens and legitimized into law? The dissertation contends that growing condemnation of corporal punishment reflected both humane concerns and interest in effective social control. Widespread denunciation of corporal punishment as "barbaric" and "degrading," for example, attested to concern for the huyman rights of abused victims. Opponents of the lash and rod stressed, at the same time, that internalized moral restraint was the most effective basis for social control in a mobile, rapidly changing republic. These arguments reflected a profound desire to develop a new basis of social discipline, satisfying the traditional need for order and yet responsvie to the complex demands and opportunities of an industrializing society. A final section of this study explores the lack of public interest in wifebeating. Thus the dissertation concludes by considering the boundaries and limits of the anti-corporal punishment movement in antebellum America.

2141.   Glenwick. D. S. "Training Impulsive Children in Verbal Self-Regulation by Use of Natural Change Agents." Ph.D. Dissertation, The University of Rochester. Dissertation Abstracts International, 37 (1-B), 459. Order no. 76-14,758, 1976.

Forty impulsive fifth- and sixth-graders participated in a project intended to help them become more reflective problem-solvers. The study hypothesized that training the youngsters' parents and teachers would be more effective than training only the children. The target children were divided into five groups: (1) a parents and teachers combined group, where both teachers and parents were trained, but not the youngsters; (2) a teachers alone group; (3) a parents alone group; (4) a children alone group, where the experimenter worked directly with the pupils; and (5) an untrained control group. Training consisted of eight 45-minute sessions over a four-week span and involved verbal self-instructional procedures which entailed modeling, self-guiding speech, and self-reinforcement. Sessions involving parents tended to emphasize behavioral and interpersonal situations and nonacademic skills, while those involving teachers focused primarily on educational tasks. The children's group was exposed to a combination of all of these problems. Cognitive and intellectual performance, academic achievement, classroom behavior, and home behavior were the dependent variables. The most consistent gains for the experimental groups were produced on the Wide Range Achievement Test, especially on the reading subtest. Only slight improvement occurred in cognitive and intellectual abilities, except for the Matching Familiar Figures Test of impulsivity. No classroom behavior changes were reported, but parents who participated perceived gains in home behavior.

2142.   Golden, B. R. "An Evaluation of the Effectiveness of Two Guidance Programs on the Academic Achievement, Attendance, Citizenship, Self-Concept, and Behavior of Junior High School Students." Ph.D. Dissertation, University of Utah. Dissertation Abstracts International, 38 (4-A), 1889-1890. Order no. 77-21,952, 1977.

The purpose of the study was to determine the relative effectiveness of two types of guidance experiences on groups of junior high school students with respect to grade-point average, attendance, citizenship ratings, self-concept ratings, and behavior ratings. One experience described as open-traditional represented a minimally structured approach and was based on interventions associated with a non-directive counseling model. The other approach was structured and based on activities which have been described as enhancing self-concept, i.e., self-disclosure, intra and interpersonal exercises to increase self-awareness, role playing, using the first person in communication, etc. Forty-eight junior high school students were selected from a larger group of 80 students identified as having a poor self-concept. The students were randomly assigned to one of three treatment groups. The findings from the analyses indicated that there were no significant differences in the means of the post-scores between the three treatment groups. The analysis to determine interaction effects of counselor and treatment indicated that interaction with one counselor was related to a significant difference in attendance.

2143.   Golden, F. "The Modification of Attending Behavior in Elementary School Children by Imitation and Direct Reinforcement Under the Mediation of Delayed Video Tape Playback." Ph.D. Dissertation, West Virginia University, 1973.

The current investigation was primarily designed to assess the relative efficacy of programs incorporating different vicarious and direct reinforcement techniques as means of producing appropriate attention to school work in normal elementary school children. Previous research findings had supported the utility of both vicarious and direct reinforcement techniques in the elicitation of behavior change in children. This study attempted to utilize these techniques to remedy a universal problem of the educational system; that is, to assist children in attending to academic stimuli. A further aim was to examine the feasibility of using vicarious and direct reinforcement procedures with entire classrooms, rather than with single children or small groups of children. The practicality of using automated video tape recording equipment in facilitating behavioral change was also examined within the context of the treatment intervention program. The Paradigm was designed to produce behavioral change working with whole classes of children, and the results were generally supportive of such paradigm. Children identified as both good and poor attenders benefitted from the experimental manipulations. The poor attenders appeared to exhibit the most substantial improvement. The utility of automated video tape procedures as a facilitator of behavioral change in behavior modification programs was further substantiated.

2144.   Goldstein, J. M. "Managerial Behaviors of Elementary School Teachers and Student On-Task Behavior." Ed.D. Dissertation, University of Houston. Dissertation Abstracts International, 39 (7-A), 4018-4019T. Order no. 7901203, 1978.

The purpose of the study was to examine the relationship between seven specific clusters of teacher managerial behaviors and student on-task behavior in the elementary school. Seven directional hypotheses were formulated to examine the relationship between seven specific clusters of teacher managerial behaviors and student on-task behavior. Teacher behavior modification, group process, and socioemotional climate managerial behaviors were posited to have a positive relationship with student on-task behavior. Teacher authoritarian, common sense, and instructional managerial behaviors were posited to have a negative relationship with student on-task behavior. Given the hypotheses the study was designed to test, the independent variables were the seven clusters of teacher managerial behaviors: authoritarian, behavior modification, common sense, group process, instructional, permissive, and socioemotional climate. The dependent variable was student on-task behavior. The subjects were thirty-five volunteer elementary school teachers from school districts in the Houston metropolitan area. Teachers in the study represented nine elementary schools. Teachers in grades one through five participated in the study. Teacher managerial behaviors were recorded and coded using the Managerial Approach Behavior Observation System (Coman, Goldstein, Peacock, and Weber, 1978). Student on-task behavior was recorded and calculated using the Student Engagement Rating System (Evertson and Anderson, 1978). The results of the study suggested the following conclusions: a) teacher authoritarian managerial behaviors had a significant negative relationship to student on-task behavior, b) teacher group process managerial behaviors had a significant positive relationship to student on-task behavior, c) teacher permissive managerial behaviors had a significant negative relationship to student on-task behavior, and d) teacher socioemotional climate managerial behaviors had a significant positive relationship to student on-task behavior.

2145.   Goldstein, Marci-Ann F. "Classroom Management: Assertion Training for Teachers. A Six Month Follow Up." Ed.D. Dissertation, Temple University, 1979. Dissertation Abstracts International, 41 (8-A), 3379. Order no. 8025084.

The problem was to ascertain the perceptions of teachers relative to the impact of the program "Classroom Management: Assertion Training for Teachers" at pretest, posttest, and six month followup. The specific areas studied were: 1) teachers' perceptions of their abilities to feel and act assertive, 2) teachers' perceptions of their feelings of self-esteem, 3) the effective use of Assertion Training in classroom management, and 4) the value of this particular program model. The general research hypotheses for this study were that: 1) there is a significant difference in teachers' perceptions of their ability to act and feel assertive, prior to training in the program entitled "Classroom Management: Assertion Training for Teachers" immediately following training and at a six month followup; 2) there is a significant difference in teachers' perceptions of their own feeling about self, prior to training in the program entitled "Classroom Management: Assertion Training for Teachers" immediately following training and a six month followup; and 3) there is a significant difference in the perceptions of teachers' value of the program entitled "Classroom Management: Assertion Training for Teachers" six months after training. The results of data analysis, utilizing analysis of variance revealed a signifi-cant F probability of .008 between subjects, and a signifi-cant F probability of .017 within subjects on the RAS. Analysis indicated significant differences between group means for the total TSCS and yielded a significant F proba-bility within subjects of .029. No significant differences were obtained on the Identity subscale. Significant differences did not exist on the Self-Satisfaction subscale. Analysis of the Behavior subscale yielded a significant F probability of .027 within subjects. Mean scores on the Moral-Ethical Self subscale did not differ significantly. Significant differences within subjects did exist on the Personal Self subscale, a significant F probability of .024 was revealed. Analysis indicated a significant F proba-bility of .001 within subjects on the final TSCS subscale, Social Self. A significant difference between groups was detected in one of six areas of the RPEQ that of Abilities to Assert, although mean scores were higher in every area for the treatment group than for the control group.

2146.   Golladay, W. M. "Maintaining Student Behavior by Increasing and Maintaining Teacher Contingent Reinforcement Rate." Ed.D. Dissertation, University of Virginia. Dissertation Abstracts International, 33 (7-A), 3380-3381. Order no. 72-33,361, 1973.

This study was an attempt to evaluate (1) the teacher train-ing technique most effective in increasing and generalizing the contingent use of praise, and (2) the consequent effects of each training method on the child's "on task" behavior. The three training methods consisted of: (a) reading a behavior modification text, (b) weekly training sessions based on the behavior modification text and feedback in use of praise, and (c) weekly training sessions, feedback, and the use of a cueing device. Generally, it was found that the cueing device was the only effective means of signifi-cantly increasing and maintaining contingent praise but that the other training methods were somewhat effective reducing the use of punishment and increasing the use of more contingent praise. Student "on task" behavior responded to and maintained with the significant increase in the use of praise.

2147.   Graham, K. M. "Effects of a Companion Counseling Program on Elementary School Children." Ed.D. Dissertation. Lehigh University, 1976.

Companion Counseling is a theapeutic procedure developed from new manpower resources in a variety of mental health settings. Companion programs involve volunteers who spend regular weekly time in a one-to-one relationship with a troubled person. This study investigated whether male or female school children with same sex college companions would show positive differences when compared to a con-trolled group on various criterian measures. The measures included a personality evaluation, a self-esteem inventory, behavior rating scale, school attitudes scale and school grades. Comparisons were also made of trained companions, untrained companions, and a control group on the measures. Self-descriptions of the college students who participated as companions were analyzed from pre-test and post-test results. Results indicated no significant difference between children with companions and a controlled group on a personality measure, self-esteem inventory, behavior rating scale, and school attitudes scale. In addition, there were not significant differences among children with trained companions, children with untrained companions, and a controlled group on four criterian measures. On a fifth measure, school grades, children with trained companions received significantly higher grades, when compared to children with untrained companions and a controlled group. There were no significant effects due to sex of the children.

2148.   Greene, D. "Immediate and Subsequent Effects of Differential Reward Systems on Intrinsic Motivation in Public School Classrooms." Ph.D. Dissertation, Stanford University. Dissertation Abstracts International, 35 (9-B), 4626. Order no. 75-6854, 1975.

Achieving generalization of treatment effects from contin-gent reinforcement systems has proved far more difficult than producing the effects themselves. Some insight into this difficulty may be provided by the social psychology literature on overjustification, wherein it has been demon-strated that if a subject who regards an activity as an end in itself can be induced to regard this activity as a means to some ulterior end, the subject's interest in the activity, in the absence of the expectation that it will lead to the ulterior end, will be decreased. The present study was designed to explore the possible utility of an overjustification analysis in understanding generalization findings in "token economy" studies, as as a step toward conceptual and empirical convergence of operant and non-operant psychology. The pattern of results suggested that reinforcing engagement with an intrinsically interesting activity will not produce overjustification unless some cue is provided to make the instrumentality of such engagement salient to the subject. "Cognitive" and "operant" strategies for producing generalization from token economies were contrasted, and it was argued that the former promote attributions of intrinsic motivation as well as extrinsic motivation, while the latter are likely to prove counter-productive in the long run.

2149.   Greene, Ruth L. "The Effects of Group Counseling and Consultation on the Classroom Behaviors and Attitudes of Selected Elementary School Children." Ed.D. Dissertation, University of Massachusetts. Dissertation Abstracts International, 37 (1-A), 132. Order no. 76-14,688, 1976.

The purpose of this study was to measure the effects of a particular group counseling teacher consultation treatment on the classroom attending behaviors and attitudes of selected urban elementary school children. Group counseling and consultation involved the use of behavioral contracts and a token economy. An additional purpose of the study was to evaluate whether an increase in classroom attending behavior would also increase the percentage of assignments that each child completed. Five third grade children were selected from a group of fourteen students who were recommended for counseling because of non-attending behavior. A three phase intensive design procedure was used to measure individual attending behavior over successive observations and to compare the group counseling teacher consultation treatment phase behavior with the before and after baseline phase behavior. The results of the study indicated an increase in the children's attending behavior during the treatment phase and a decrease in attending behavior during the second baseline phase. Thus, it can be concluded that the observed changes in the children's behavior were a result of the group counseling teacher consultation intervention.

2150.   Greenstein, S. "Comparison of the Effectiveness of Three Different Categories of Reinforcement With Three Different Age Groups." Ph.D. Dissertation, The University of North Carolina at Chapel Hill. Dissertation Abstracts International, 36 (6-B), 3042. Order no. 75-29,031, 1975.

The aim of this study was to provide elementary school teachers with guidelines for choosing which reinforcer would be most effective with different pupils. Following a suggestion in the literature it was hypothesized that children move developmentally from responding to concrete externalized reinforcers toward an increased responsiveness to abstract reinforcement. Three categories of reinforcers which are employable within the classroom and which differ on the hypothesized developmental continuum, were chosen.

The categoreis chosen from comparison were Material, Socal and Symbolic Reinforcement. In order to obtain a criteria by which the experimental conditions could be considered representative of the diversity within each category, an effort was made to maximize the effectiveness of each reinforcer. To test the developmental hypothesis 100 male students at each of three age levels (first, third and fifth graders) were assigned to one of four experimental conditions (Control, Material Reinforcement, Social Reinforcement, Symbolic Reinforcement). Each of these subjects was administered a variation of the W.I.S.C. Coding task under conditions of reinforcement and again in extinction. The primary finding was that the predicted interaction effectiveness did not occur, which casts serious doubt upon the developmental hypothesis. A secondary finding of considerable importance was that the material reinforcement group was not significantly different from control on extinction measures.

2151.   Greer, J. B. "Adlerian Psychology Applied to Secondary Teacher Inservice." Ph.D. Dissertation. The University of Arizona, 1978.

The deterioration of the traditinal roles between adults-youth, parent-child, labor-management, male-female, student-teacher has led to the development of many approaches to deal with these conflicts. In the student-teacher relationship, many teachers still maintain an autocratic approach in dealing with students. As a results of this relationship, communication between these two groups has disintegrated, resulting in frustration and defeat on the part of teachers. Three instruments were used for both pre and post treatment data. The instruments were the Behavior Concepts Inventory Education Model, and Inventory of Selected Student Behavior, and the revised Winnetka Scale for Rating School Behavior and Attitudes. Both teacher groups rated between five and seven "problem" students in their classrooms at the pre and post treatment phase. A third group of non-involved teachers rated these same students to test the possibility of generalized perceived behavior change. The treatment program consisted of seven bi-weekly sessions, one-and-a-half hours in length. Counselor-consultants from The University of Arizona and a resident consultant gave presentations on Adlerian-based principles and techniques for use in the classrooms. Analysis of pre-post tests indicated comparable scores between experimental and comparison groups at the pre-test phase. Post-test score analysis indicated the experimental group made significant score gains in the theory and application of the Education Model, as well as greater positive change in their perception of student behavior than did teachers in the comparison group. In comparing ratings of students by involved comparison teachers and non-involved group teachers, the scores showed similar ratings. Significant differences were found by the experimental group teachers' student ratings as compared to non-involved teacher ratings of the same students, with experimental teachers rating their students higher. This indicated that either behavior changed only in the experimental classrooms and did not generalize to other classrooms, or that no behavior change occurred, only a change in preception of behavior. It was concluded that the Education Model was an effective method for providing secondary school teachers with a conceptual and theoretical base for the understanding of student behavior and provided teachers with skills needed to apply this knowledge in practical classroom situations. The program also provided directional support in the Education Model's effectiveness in altering teacher perception of student behavior. Order No. 7909444, DAI.

2152.   Griffin, James T., Jr.   "A Study to Develop Procedural Guidelines for the use of Corporal Punishment in the Elementary, Intermediate, and High Schools in the Birmingham, Alabama, City School System."   Ed.D. Dissertation, The University of Alabama, 1977. Dissertation Abstracts International, 39 (4-A), 1952. Order no. 7818869.

The purpose of this study was to develop procedural guidelines which the personnel of the Birmingham City School System could follow in the administration of corporal punishment. Specific legal guidelines based on the actual needs of the principals in the Birmingham City System did not exist at the onset of this study. A legal base was established upon which data gathered from Birmingham principals could be analyzed. The procedure utilized a questionnaire to survey elementary, intermediate, and high school principals and advisors. A panel of experts and an item analysis were employed as the validation procedure. The questionnaire was mailed to thirty-four principals. The analysis was used to determine deficiencies in legal knowledge related to corporal punishment within the group of principals surveyed. The effect of having a recent school law course was compared to the amount of legal knowledge possessed by the principals, the choice of implements used to administer the punishment, and the principals' attitude toward corporal punishment. An assessment of the favorability of the sample group as a whole toward corporal punishment was undertaken. The following findings were presented: 1) Birmingham City School principals presently possess adequate legal knowledge on corporal punishment. 2) The analysis of legal guideline questions from the questionnaire showed a high level of understanding of the law relating to corporal punishment. 3) There was no significant relationship between having a recent school law course and the amount of legal knowledge possessed. 4) There was no significant relationship between having a recent school law course and the type of implement used to administer corporal punishment. 5) There was no significant relationship between having a recent school law course and the principals' attitude toward corporal punishment. 6) There was a significant relationship between the principals with regard to their favorable attitudes toward corporal punishment.   7) Seven specific legal guidelines related to the administration of corporal punishment were developed.

2153.   Grogan, Jimmy H.   "Precise Personal Management as it Relates to Changes in Adolescent Behavior."   Ph.D. Dissertation, Saint Louis University.   Dissertation Abstracts International, 37 (4-A), 1986-1987.   Order no. 76-22,543, 1976.

The purpose of this study was to examine Precise Personal Management as it relates to changes in adolescent behavior. This is a technique for helping individuals understand, control, and change their own behavior.   It appears suited to adolescents in three ways: a) It provides daily data that is helpful since adolescents often change markedly from day to day.   b) It encourages self-counting, charting, and management.   c) It allows examination of those behaviors which are observable only to the person experiencing the thought or feeling and those behaviors which an outsider could observe.   This study suggests that adolescents can identify, chart, and change their own behaviors.   The study further suggests that adolescents can gain control of themselves and their environments without the use of formal modification change procedures.

2154.   Grosman, J. F.   "A Systematic Codification of Sources, Methods, and Target Populations in Behavior Modification for Exceptional Children and Youth (1949-1976) (Volumes I-IV)." Ed.D. Dissertation, Columbia University Teachers College. Dissertation Abstracts International, 40 (9-A), 5000.   Order no. 8006814, 1980.

This review analyzes a sample of 500 research studies using behavior modification with exceptional children and youth in educational settings.   The purpose of the review is twofold. First, it fulfills the need for a single reference which reviews and statistically analyzes the methods and results published research in the field.   Second, this review identifies the trends in research methodology and teaching strategies by the analysis of the data obtained from the research studies reveiwed.   A data base was established extracting specific information from the 500 studies.   The data collected fell into four distinct areas: (1) information on the author and reference in which the study was published: (2) information on the subjects and settings of the study: (3) information on the observational recording and design, and (4) information on the teaching (behavioral) strategies and their results.   A data collection form was created for the purpose of providing a means which all information from each study could be presented in a concise yet complete manner.   The data from the 500 studies reviewed were subsequently compiled and analyzed using descriptive statistical measures.   Data collection forms on which were recorded pertinent information extrapolated from each of the studies used in this review comprise Volumes II, III, and IV of the dissertation.

2155.   Groves, John T. "A Description of Student-Cueing
Behavior, Teacher-Management Responses, and Self-Reported
Teacher-Management Conceptions in an Elementary Classroom.
Ph.D. Dissertation, Michigan State University. Dissertation
Abstracts International, 40 (12-A), 6130. Order no.
8013743.

In this study, three factors that contribute to management
exchanges are examined: student behaviors that may function
as management cues for teachers, teacher-management
responses, and teacher-management conceptions. One elementary school teacher and ten students were identified for
observation purposes. The teacher was selected on the basis
of education and teaching experience. Classroom observations were conducted for the purpose of numerically
identifying those students who were most frequently involved
in management exhanges with their teachers. The students
who were most frequently involved were chosen. The descriptive analysis indicated a narrow range of recorded student
behaviors. Three of the listed twenty-four student
behaviors represented a majority of the total recorded
behaviors. The most frequently recorded student behaviors,
in order, were 1) working on task, 2) talking with
neighbors, and 3) aimlessly walking. Maintaining teacher
actions were the most frequently recorded management
responses. Two maintaining actions, redirection to ask and
reduction of frustration, represented the majority of
recorded teacher-management responses. The frequency of
self-reported general teacher-management conceptions
emphasized student- and teacher-related responsibilities.
The specific teacher attitudes stressed student social-
emotional learning. The initial explanatory analysis
indicated that teacher-management responses were not equally
distributed among recorded student behaviors. The majority
of management responses that were applied to recorded
student behaviors were maintaining actions. These were
directed toward potentially disruptive student behaviors.

2156.   Guarnaccia, V. J. "The Effectiveness of Rule Codes in
Reducing Misbehavior in Elementary School Classes." Ph.D.
Dissertation, Hofstra University. Dissertation Abstracts
International, 33 (6-B), 2810. Order no. 72-31,955, 1972.

The applicability of using formal rule codes to reduce
misbehavior in regular elementary school classes and the
viability of directly involving pupils in deciding on rule
code contingencies were investigated in this study. A
comparison was made between rule codes which contain pupil
suggestions for handling misconduct and rule codes which
contain teacher suggestions. Variables such as pupil
achievement motivation, pupil liking for the teacher,
teacher consistency in applying the rule code contingencies
and teachers' perceptions of how closely the rule codes
resemble their regular classroom procedures were also
investigated to determine their effect on rule breaking
behavior. Five fifth grade and five sixth grade classes in

one elementary school were used in this study. The results
of this study indicated that all classes showed a significant reduction in rule violations regardless of which rule
code was being used. Classes using Pupil Codes which were
represented to them as Teacher Codes and classes which
participated in developing rule code contingencies had
significantly fewer rule violations during the experimental
phase than classes under any other experimental conditions.
The variables of achievement motivation, pupil liking for
the teacher, teacher consistency and teachers' perceptions
did not show significant effects in this study.

2157.   Gutkin, T. B. "The Modification of Locus of Control
Among Lower Class, Minority, Elementary School Students: An
Operant Approach." Ph.D. Dissertation, The University of
Texas at Austin. Dissertation Abstracts International, 36
(10-A), 6551-6552. Order no. 76-8038, 1976.

This study investigated the efficacy of operant techniques
for the modification of children's locus of control. The
subjects were 125 lower class, black, fourth and fifth grade
students. The experimental treatment consisted primarily of
individual social and token reinforcement which was made
contingent upon "appropriate" student behavior. All reinforcements were accompanied by an explicit verbal statement
which linked each reward to the specific student behavior
which had earned it. It was expected that the treatment
would underscore and make maximally explicit for each
student the relationship between his own personal behavior
and the manner in which the environment responded to him.
It was hypothesized that an understanding of the contingent
nature of this relationship would result in a more internal
locus of control. The studnets in the placebo classes
received noncontingent reinforcement and non-contingent,
individualized attention. This treatment was designed to
control for the rewards and increased attention which the
experimental students received. The students in the control
classes received no treatment per se. Despite the fact that
prior to the treatment period there were no significant
differences between the participating classes, the experimental classes were significantly more internal than either
the placebo or control classes following the treatment
period. The magnitude of these differences, although highly
significant from a statistical perspective, were rather
small (1-2 points) and of questionable educational and
clinical importance. It was hypothesized that time spent by
students in non-experimental classrooms, inconsistent use of
social reinforcement, and the short length of the treatment
period all combined to dilute the impact of the treatment
and reduce the size of the locus of control shifts. It was
concluded that the results were sufficient to warrant the
further investigation of operant techniques as a tool with
which to modify student locus of control.

2158.   Haesloop, M. D.   "An Analysis of Off-Task Classroom
Behavior."   Ph.D.   Dissertation,   Columbia   University.
Dissertation Abstracts International, 34 (8-B), 4018.   Order
no. 74-1487, 1974.

This study was designed to provide normative information
about the nature and occurrence of off-task behavior in a
sample of normal elementary school classrooms.   In addition,
selected correlates of off-task behavior were examined.
Teacher activities which immediately preceded, or coincided
with, a pupil's return-to-task were also noted.   The study
was conducted in seven fourth-grade classrooms in three
schools in a suburban, white upper-middle-class public
school district.   Each classroom was observed 11 times
during various instructional periods.   A total of 124 pupils
were selected as off-task subjects.   A two-phase observation
procedure was employed in the study.   An adaptation of the
Jackson-Hudgins Observation Schedule was used to determine
the percentage of pupils off-task at the beginning of each
classroom visit (Phase I).   Those students who were observed
to be off-task during the first phase comprised the pool of
off-task subjects for the subsequent 20 minute observation
period (Phase II).   During Phase II of each classroom observation, pupils were randomly selected from the pool of
off-task subjects and were observed in turn.   The activities
in which pupils engaged when they were off-task were
categorized and observed in sequence.   The duration of each
activity was recorded in seconds.   In order to determine a
standard measure of off-task behavior for each off-task
subjects, the mean number of five-second-units off-task per
observation was calculated.   During Phase II, teacher
activities were noted when off-task pupils returned-to-task.
Results of the study indicated that significant differences
in the frequency of off-task behavior occurred among the
three schools but not between classrooms within each school.
Pupils were found to vary considerably in the amount of
off-task behavior they exhibited.   A small percentage of
pupils in each classroom contributed more than the other
students of observed off-task behavior.   When the extreme
group of off-task subjects were examined across schools,
boys and girls were represented in almost equal numbers.

2159.   Hammond, J. M.   "Children of Divorce: A Study of Self-
Concept,   School   Behaviors,   Attitudes,   and   Situational
Variables."   Ph.D.   Dissertation.   The   University   of
Michigan, 1979.

The two-fold purpose of this study was, first, to investigate the differences in self-concept, school behavior, and
attitudes between children of intact and divorced families
and, second, to obtain specific data from children of
divorce on the positive and negative effects of divorce on
themselves.   The 165 participating students were third
through sixth graders at two selected public elementary
schools.   Eighty-two of the children were from families

where parents were separated or divorced and were selected
by identifying all of these children in grades three through
six. The remaining 83 children were from intact families
and were chosen by stratified systematic sampling with a
random start. Children who had lost a parent through death
were not included in this study. Classroom teachers
provided information on reading and mathematics achievement
and completed the Walker Problem Behavior Identification
Checklist (WPBIC) for each child in their class participating in the study. All of the students were administered
the Piers-Harris Self-Concept Scale, and the Attitude Toward
Family Questionnaire. Children whose parents were separated
or divorced also completed the Hammond Children of Divorce
Questionnaire. Data from teachers indicated there were no
significant differences in reading the mathematic achievement between children of intact and divorced families. The
teachers, on the WPBIC, rated the boys of divorced families
significantly higher than boys from intact families in the
school problem behaviors of "acting out," and "distractibility," while there were no significant differences
between females on these measures. As measured by the
Piers-Harris scale there were no significant differences in
self-concept between children of intact and divorced
families. Data from the Attitude Toward Family Questionnaire revealed that males of divorced families rated their
family significantly less happy than did males of intact
families; there were no significant differences between
females. Males of divorced families were also significantly
less satisfied with the time and attention they received
from parents than were males of intact families. Children
of divorce reported significantly more often than children
of intact families that divorce could have a positive effect
on their lives, and that they have no control over reuniting
their parents. Both children in divorced and intact groups
agreed that children do not cause parental divorce. Data
from the Hammond Children of Divorce Questionnaire disclosed
the negative and positive effects of divorce for the children and their recommendations for school counselors.
Children of divorce reported that the most negative effect
of divorce was "not seeing one parent as often" and the most
positive effect was "parents not fighting as much anymore."
Order no. 7916719, DAI.

2160.   Hardage, Nell C. "A Comparison of the Efficacy of
Treatments of Classroom Behavior Management and Group
Counseling for Use with Potential Dropouts." Ph.D.
Dissertation, University of Southern Mississippi, 1972.
Dissertation Abstracts International, 33 (4-A), 1436. Order
no. 72-26,551.

This study was conducted to evaluate and compare the
efficacy of treatment between classroom behavior management
and group counseling employed to increase on-task behavior,
social interactions, grade-point average and school attendance of potential dropouts. The sample population was
chosen from five elementary schools of Forrest County and

Hattiesburg, Mississippi, which had a combined enrollment of 563 pupils in the fifth and sixth grades. A total number of fifteen fifth and sixth grade teachers were randomly assigned in groups of five to each of the following groups for a period of twelve weeks: 1) Classroom Behavior Management, 2) Group Counseling, and 3) Control Group. Thirty potential dropouts identified by the Demos D Scale and the Dropout Rating Scale were assigned to each of the three groups, making a combined total of ninety subjects. The five teachers who were randomly assigned to Group I had a consultant in classroom behavior management. Five doctoral students in guidance trained by the Madsen Method served as the consultants. These five teachers received feedback from the consultant based on observations of the potential dropouts. The five teachers who were randomly assigned to Group II permitted the potential dropouts to be removed from the classroom one hour per week to receive group counseling. Five doctoral students trained in attitudinal group counseling served as the counselors for each of the five counseling groups. The five teachers who were randomly assigned to Group III received no treatment. The thirty potential dropouts identified in the classroom of the five teachers in Group III served as the control for the experiment. Data were collected for the four variables: 1) observation of on-task behavior, 2) sociometric status, 3) grade-point average, and 4) school attendance, pre-treatment, mid-treatment and post-treatment. A two-way analysis of variance was performed on the obtained data. The 5 percent level was accepted as statistically significant. The following findings are indicated from this study: 1) Classroom Behavior Management procedures and Group Counseling have differential effects on on-task behavior, social status and grade-point average of potential dropouts. 2) When teachers utilize a Classroom Behavior Management approach, on-task behavior and grade-point averages of potential dropouts increase.

2161.   Hardy, Robert E. "The Effects of Praise on Selected Variables in Secondary School Classrooms: A Behavior Modification Approach. Ed.D. Dissertation, Western Michigan University, 1971. Dissertation Abstracts International, 32 (10-A), 5546. Order no. 72-12,708.

Thirty-six high school students were assigned by the process of computer class scheduling to one of three psychology courses taught by three different teachers. The study consisted of the three teachers establishing ten days of no verbal praise, ten days of verbal praise, and ten days of no verbal praise. During the ten day periods, trained raters kept count of the number of student hand raising responses and verbal responses. Following each ten day period, the students were tested for their study habits and their image of the teacher. Multiple factor analysis of variance was used to analyze the data. Verbal praise was not statistically significant as a generalized reinforcer. A concomitant finding was the individual teacher differences had a statistically significant effect on verbal and hand raising responses, and on teacher image. In addition, verbal and hand raising responses were correlated with study habits and teacher image; the results were mixed with a range from -.34 to .72.

2162.   Hartje, Jack C.   "Premackian Reinforcement of Classroom Behavior Through Topic Sequencing." Ph.D. Dissertation, Arizona   State   University.   Dissertation   Abstracts International, 33 (3-A), 1020. Order no 72-23,165, 1972.

In a test of Premack's model of reinforcement, 108 fifth-grade students at Cactus Wren Elementary School were randomly assigned to three groups. All subjects partici-pated in 15 daily 90-minute experimental sessions. Prior to initiating the treatment, all of the subject's preferences for reading, social studies, and science were measured by means of a ten-point rating scale. Ratings for each of the three topics ranged from zero ("I don't like it") to ten ("I like it very much"). On the basis of the pretest ratings, it was possible to determine for each subject his least preferred (L), intermediate or middle (M), and highes rated (H) topic. Control group subjects were allowed to freely choose which of the three topics they would study. This constituted the only distinction between the two treatment groups and the Control group. It was predicted that since Control subjects did not undergo either a reinforcing or punishing Premackian contingency, posttest preference measures would not differ from pretest values. Unfortu-nately, Control scores changed in the same manner as the two treatment groups.

2163.   Hartwell, M. R.   "An Evaluation of an In-Service Program Concerning the Disciplinary Approach of Dr. Rudolf Dreikurs." Ed.D. Dissertation, University of Massachusetts. Dissertation Abstracts International, 36 (2-A), 704-705. Order no. 75-16,559, 1975.

A number of approaches for dealing with classroom management and discipline have evolved during the past decade. Among them is an approach developed by Dr. Rudolf Dreikurs. The approach is the focus of this study. Dreikurs's method is currently being taught to teachers and counselors at several major American universities as well as by private consul-tants conducting in-service training within school systems. Little formal research has been conducted to determine the impact of such training on the primary recipients of the technique: the students in those teachers' classrooms. The problem addressed by this study was the need to gather data which justifies and supports the notion that Dreikurs's method is an effective way to deal with discipline problems in the public schools within the classroom. Teachers were recruited to take part in an in-service training program in Dreikurs's method. The course lasted eight weeks during which teachers attended weekly 2 1/2 - 3 hour sessions plus a full day Saturday workshop. Teachers were instructed in

Dreikurs's method and encouraged to implement what they had learned in their classrooms between sessions. Teachers were asked to identify two disturbing and one model child from each of their classrooms. The teachers were asked to complete a behavior checklist for each of these children both before the course began and three weeks following termination of the course. They were also asked to complete an inventory regarding their own attitudes and behaviors on the same schedule and to develop a project that would reflect their understanding of the content of the course. A checklist was developed to evaluate these projects. Feedback questionnaires were completed after each session of the course and at its conclusion. Three levels of change were examined and/or tested by the instruments listed above in the course of the study: knowledge of teachers regarding behavior problems and Dreikurs's methods for dealing with them, attitudes of teachers on several dimensions commensurate with Dreikurs's theories and behavioral change in the participating teachers and in the students as perceived by their teachers. The checklist developed for use in evaluating the teachers' projects indicated a high degree of cognitive competence in Dreikurs's method. From 73 to 10 percent of the teachers demonstrated successful learning in items that dealt with diagnosis and immediate redirection of misbehavior as well as in classroom discussion skills. Scores on the teachers' inventories of their own attitudes and behaviors tended to cluster about the mid-points of the continuum scales used in interpretation. Change scores on this formal instrument were negligible. Teachers did report notable attitudinal changes on the final feedback questionnaires and in their projects, however. Comparison of the pre-and post-treatment behavior checklists that were completed by the teachers for each of their students showed considerable positive change in the disturbing children. The model children retained their initial scores for the most part. Apparently, the Dreikurs program either affected the teachers' perceptions of their disturbing children or indeed was instrumental in helping the teachers work with some of the children to mitigate disturbing behaviors. In interviews, feedback questionnaires and individual projects the teachers reaffirmed the findings of the behavior checklists with 79 percent making specific statements that indicated positive significant change in at least one of their disturbing children.

2164.   Hauger, B. E. "Arena of Conflict: A Study of Perceptions Regarding Selected Student Discipline Policies." Ed.D. Dissertation, University of Southern California. Dissertation Abstracts International, 34 (7-A), 3757-3758. 1974.

The purpose of this study was to analyze and compare perceptions of students, parents, and educators toward selected discipline policies existing in high schools in Southern Califonia. A random sampling technique was used to select eight public high schools of grades 9-12 or 10-12, with a minimum average daily attendance of 500 or more, in Los Angeles, Orange, or Riverside Counties. Three populations in each school were sampled-students, parents, and educator. Respondents were interviewed and responded to thirty-one questions on an agree-disagree basis. Also, they were asked to provide solutions to four questions. (1) Parents, students, and educators had a tendency to hold similar perceptions regarding tardy policies. (2) Parents and students had a tendency to hold similar perceptions regarding smoking policies. (3) Students and educators had a tendency to hold different perceptions regarding smoking policies. (4) Parents and educators had a tendency to hold similar perceptions regarding smoking policies. (5) Parents and students had a tendency to hold different perceptions regarding dress code policies. (6) Students and educators had a tendency to hold similar perceptions regarding dress code policies. (7) There was a definite difference of perception between parents and students regarding closed campus policies. (8) Parents and educators had a tendency to hold similar perceptions regarding closed campus policies. (9) Parents listed parent conference as their top alternative to suspension for enforcement of tardy policies. Students and educators listed detention. (10) Parents and educators listed work crews as their top alternative to suspension for violation of smoking policies. (11) Students listed formation of a smoking area as their top alternative. (12) Students felt attendance problems were the main reasons for a closed campus. (13) Parents stated control of non-students on campus was the main reason for a closed campus.

2165.   Hawkins, J. L. "A Comparison of the Effects of Two Types of Reinforcement Techniques on Academic and Nonacademic Classroom Behaviors of Underachieving Elementary Students." Ph.D. Dissertation, University of California, Los Angeles. Dissertation Abstracts International, 35 (5-B), 2404. Order no. 74-24,591, 1974.

An important question in reinforcement application to educa- tion is whether Positive Reinforcement is more effective than Response Cost in reducing inappropriate classroom behavior and increasing academic output of behavior problem children, or those with learning disabilities. This study examines the issue of the relative effects of these two types of reinforcement techniques and the effect on relevant behaviors. Nine male subjects, ages 10.7 to 11.3 were selected from three different schools; one classroom from each. All children in each of the classrooms were rated by the teacher using a Quay Behavior Checklist, and the nine subjects selected were all from the category 'conduct dis- order.' A token system was devised around a specific rein- forcement schedule wherein each subject was exposed to a Baseline (no token involved), a Positive Reinforcement dispensing tokens contingent upon appropriate behavior and a Response Cost withdrawing tokens contingent upon inappro- priate behavior condition. Academic output was found to have significantly increased during Positive Reinforcement

and Response Cost conditions as compared to Baseline condition. A significantly larger increase was found during the
Response Cost condition. An analysis of deviant behaviors
showed very similar effects. It was concluded that, within
limitations set forth in the study, Response Cost was significantly better than Positive Reinforcement in increasing
academic output and reducing inappropriate classroom
behavior.

2166.   Hazzard, J. C. "Effects of Behavioral Consultation on
Teacher Application and Transfer of Behavior Management
Principles." Ph.D. Dissertation, The University of Arizona.
Dissertation Abstracts International, 38 (5-A), 2557. Order
no. 77-24, 934, 1977.

The effects of a behavioral consultation model which
utilized brief interviews to impart learning principles and
implement application of these principles by three public
school classroom teachers was studied. Intervention interviews were interspaced and success was measured by daily
observation of teachers' application of verbal and nonverbal reinforcement for attending behaviors of referred
children. In each classroom one child was the subject of
teacher consultation while behaviors of other problem children were measured in an effort to establish if transfer of
the intervention plan had occurred. It was found that a
treatment plan which involved behavior change on the part of
a cooperative teacher could be established without extensive
time and training, that verbal and non-verbal reinforcement
for attending behavior could increase that behavior among
studied children, and that some transfer of learned principles toward students other than the targeted child may be
possible but that direct cueing was necessary to initiate
transfer of learned principles in most studied cases.

2167.   Heath, B. L. "Application of Verbal Self-Instructional
Procedures to Classroom Behavior Management." Ph.D.
Dissertation. University of Minnesota, 1978.

The purpose of this study was to evaluate the feasibility
and effectiveness of using a verbal self-instructional (VSI)
training procedure for producing generalization of reduced
disruptive and increased appropraite classroom behaviors.
The study examined whether VSI training provided a "better"
behavior modification procedure. By "better" it was meant
that it would satisfy one of the major concerns expressed
about behavior modification, i.e. lack of generalization of
behavior change to new (previously not treated) situations
or over time. Subjects were second and third graders from a
rural school district in York County, Maine. Subjects were
recruited through an explanatory letter/consent form sent to
parents of all second and third graders in the two participating schools. From the pool of children given parental
permission, sample population was selected on the basis of
two criteria: 1. referral to the school psychologist for
"classroom behavior problems" and 2. significantly high

scores on the Low Need Achievement and Aggression subscales
of the School Behavior Checklist. The eighteen subjects
were randomly assigned to one of three conditions.
Cognitive-VSI subjects learned a specific self-instructional
strategy for bringing their classroom behaviors under their
own cognitive control. Cognitive-control subjects met with
the tutor for equivalent amounts of time and sessions as the
Cognitive-VSI subjects. They were exposed to identical
materials and engaged in the same general activities, but
they did not receive the VSI portion of the training.
In-class control subjects received only the same assessment
battery as did the two treatment groups. The study was
unable to demonstrate that the VSI training was effective in
producing the desired changes in classroom behaviors.
Consequently, generalization of behavior change could not
occur. Order No. 7906326, DAI.

2168.   Hedberg, J. D. "Pupil Control Ideology of Middle School
Teachers and Its Relationship to Student Alienation and to
Selected Organizational and Teacher Variables." Ph.D.
Dissertation, Michigan State University. Dissertation
Abstracts International, 34 (3-A), 1024-1025. Order no.
73-20,348, 1973.

The ideology of teachers with regard to pupil control was
studied in randomly selected Michigan schools which were
organized in 6-8 and 7-9 grade structures. The study
attempted to determine if a relationship existed between a
teacher's pupil control ideology and such teacher characteristics as sex, teaching experience, educational attainment,
area of first teaching assignment, type of certification,
and age. In addition, school pupil control ideology (mean
scores of teachers) was considered in relation to depart-
mentalization within the school, size of school, organizational structure, and student alienation. Questionnaires
provided the major source of data for both the pupil control
ideology of teachers and the degree of alienation of
students. The Tutor Tutee (TT) Form, a scale for alienation
developed by Frank P. Besag, was administered to 1,866
sixth-, seventh-, eighth-, and ninth-grade students in the
twenty-three schools. A principal components analysis was
used to identify possible sub-dimensions of alienation.
Schools ranged in size from 400 to 1,000 pupils and were of
moderate to moderately-high socioeconomic status. Schools
were predominantly white and involved all classifications of
population density--rural, urban fringe, town, city, and
metropolitan core. A "custodial" pupil control orientation
is one which stresses maintenance of order and teacher-pupil
status differences, is distrustful of students, utilizes a
punishment-centered approach to pupil control, views
behavior in moralistic terms, and tends to treat pupils
impersonally. An "humanistic" orientation stresses two-way
communication between pupils and teachers is optimistic
about the ability of students to be self-disciplined and
responsible, views pupil behavior in psychological and
sociological terms, encourages close teacher-pupil relations

and de-emphasizes teacher-pupil status differences. Through analysis of the data the following conclusions were drawn: 1) Secondary-certified teachers were more custodial than elementary-certified teachers. 2) Male teachers were more custodial than female teachers. 3) There was no interaction between certification and sex of teachers--sex and certification had no differential effect in relation to pupil control ideology. 4) Teachers with 7 or more years of teaching experience were more custodial than teachers with 1-3 years and 4-6 years of experience.

2169.   Henderson, Carlesta E. "The Effect of In-Service Training of Music Teachers in Contingent Verbal and Nonverbal Behavior." Ed.D. Dissertation, Columbia University. Dissertation Abstracts International, 33 (8-A), 4218-4219. Order no. 73-2601, 1973.

This study was designed to investigate the effectiveness of in-service teacher training in increasing contingent use of academic and social approval and decreasing contingent disapproval by music teachers. The study was limited to observations of twenty-seven music teachers in classroom situations in public schools of District IV, East Harlem, of New York City. The results of the research show that ten days of in-service training, one and one-half hours each day, did not change the groups teaching behaviors except for disapproval behavior which did, indeed, change. Disruptiveness was decreased and greater classroom control was noted. The findings of this research project suggest that a combination of after-school in-service training utilizing video taped observations combined with more classroom visitation during the training may increase the effectiveness of consultant teacher-training techniques.

2170.   Herndon, Angie D. "A Comparison of Cognitive and Affective Classroom Management Procedures." Ed.D. Dissertation, Auburn University, 1980. Dissertation Abstracts International, 41 (6-A), 2562. Order no. 8028572.

The purpose of this study was to investigate differential effects of pre-service instruction in cognitive and affective classroom management procedures on 1) the knowledge of classroom mangement techniques, 2) pupil control orientation, and 3) reponses to simulated situations of field-dependent and field-independent teacher trainees. Thirty-five pre-service teachers were randomly assigned by cognitive style to one of two treatment conditions, respectively, instruction in affective or cognitive classroom management procedures. Knowledge of classroom management approach taught, attitudes toward pupil control, and responses to simulated student-teacher situations were collected. Analyses of resulting data indicated that training in a particular classroom management approach brings about different knowledge of classroom management techniques $F(1,31) = 70.72,p$ .001, dissimilar orientations toward student control $F(1,31) = 8.12,p$ .01, and distinct skills in responding to student initiated statements and questions, $F(1,31) = 605.03,p$ .001. The cognitive style of the pre-service teachers also had higher cognitive achievement scores than the field-dependent subjects while field-dependent subjects had higher affective achievement scores than the field-independent subjects, $F(1.31) = 7.03,p$ .05. However, the field-independent subjects in both treatment conditions were more responsive to the treatments than the field-dependent subjects in both conditions $F(1,31) = 11.74,p$ .01. Field-dependent subjects were also signifi-cantly more authoritarian or less humanistic than field-independent subjects while field-independent subjects were more humanistic than field-independent subjects were more humanistic than field-dependent subjects $F(1,31) = 7.04,p$ .01.

2171.   Hett, G. G. "The Modification and Maintenance of Attending Behavior for Second-, Third-, and Fourth-Grade Children." Ph.D. Dissertation, University of Oregon. Dissertation Abstracts International, 34 (3-A), 1128-1129. Order no. 73-20,211, 1973.

The primary purpose of this study was to evaluate behavior modification procedures for improving the attentional behavior of elementary school children who engage in high rates of nonattending behavior. The intent of this study was to demonstrate, using a control group design, that the attending of treatment subjects could be increased during a school term and would maintain, at a level significantly higher than control subjects, throughout the remainder of the school year. The secondary purpose of this study was to demonstrate that increases in attending would result in concurrent increases in academic performance. Subjects were enrolled in second-, third-, and fourth-grade public school classrooms. A total of 27 subjects, who emitted low rates of attending, were selected for this study, each from a separate classroom. Once identified, each subject was randomly assigned to either the direct intervention, teacher training, or control group. Treatment for subjects assigned to direct intervention involved undergraduate students developing the intervention procedures in each of the nine classrooms involved. Following treatment, weekly post-treatment visitations were made to each school to provide teachers with further consultation, feedback from the obser-vation data being collected, and praise for program mainte-nance. Treatment for subjects assigned to the teacher training condition involved nine teachers meeting for three seminar sessions, at which time treatment procedures were discussed. These sessions were followed by the writer making five weekly school visitations, then four bi-monthly visits or telephone calls to each teacher to provide further consultation, feedback, and praise for program maintenance as was done with teachers in Group 1. Control subjects were seen weekly by the writer during the within-treatment phase and bi-monthly during the post-treatment phase of this study. Topics of interest to each subject were discussed.

Although there were significant gains in both attending and academic performance for all groups across time and a significant interaction effect among groups in attending, the interaction among groups on achievement scores was not found to be significant.

2172.   Heverling, J. M. "Using Superordinate Goals to Reduce Negative Behavior Among Elementary Pupils." Ph.D. Dissertation, Saint Louis University. Dissertation Abstracts International, 39 (3-A), 1292. Order no. 7814574, 1978.

This study was undertaken to determine the effectiveness of superordinate goals in reducing negative behavior among normal elemenatry pupils as reflected in teacher ratings of student social growth. Forty-nine racially mixed fourth grade students constituted the experimental group. The control group consisted of 48 students selected for their equivalence to the experimental subjects. A "Self-Control Trophy" served as the superordinate goal object. The experimental students were engaged in a superordinate goal program over a 16-week period. An examination of the data showed significant growth for the experimental group in three of the four indices studied, i.e., cooperates with others, obeys classroom rules, and obeys playground rules. Examination of the discipline referral count revealed a 60% drop in the experimental group during the treatment period, whereas the reverse of this trend occurred within the control period. The findings suggest that peer group influence when allied with appropriate superordinate goals can be a very powerful and persuasive tool in promoting school discipline.

2173.   Hewins, Charles F., Jr. "An Overview of the Positive Alternatives that Behavior Modification Techniques offer to Discipline in Secondary Schools and Guidelines for Implementation." Ed.D. Dissertation, University of Wyoming, 1978. Dissertation Abstracts International, 40 (10-A), 5268. Order no. 8008016.

The purpose of this study was to collect and organize guidelines which could be used by educators who wish to implement a positive discipline program in their schools. Additionally, this study identified and provided a written review of seventeen existing positive discipline programs found in the United States' secondary schools. The approach used to develop the suggested implementation guidelines was 1) to conduct a computer search using the Bibliographic Data Base Search Services (BDS), and a review of literature concerning positive discipline programs presently in operation within secondary schools in the United States, 2) to identify as many such programs as possible, 3) to request information about the philosophies and methods employed from the twenty-three identified programs, 4) to review the information provided by the seventeen programs which responded to the request for information, and 5) to use questionnaires to collect any necessary information not previously obtained by the above procedure. The following findings were found to be warranted: 1) Based on the materials supplied the writer, all programs were successful. 2) Certified classroom teachers comprised the majority of program personnel in thirteen of the seventeen programs. 3) Support from all publics for the individual programs was in direct relation to the amount of personal involvement put forth. Support for the programs generally followed this descending order: teachers, the rest of the school staff, students, parents and community members. 4) The more people directly involved with the program, the greater the requirement and need for in-service training. 5) All detention programs required a facility, while a specific facility was not required by intervention and prevention programs.

2174.   Hickey, Dolores F. "The Attitudes of Colorado High School Counselors Toward Behavior Modification as They Understand It." Ed.D. Dissertation, University of Denver, 1975. Dissertation Abstracts International, 36 (3-A0, 1307. Order no. 75-16,806.

The purpose of this investigation was to ascertain the attitudes of high school counselors toward the use of behavior modification as they understand it. This information was compared to the knowledge the counselors had of behavior modification techniques. Attitudes were also compared to the variables of the counselors' age, sex, amount of education, recency of training, and the socioeconomic status of the school (as perceived by the counselors). The investigation focused on a sample of eighty (out of six hundred and thirty-two) public high school counselors in the State of Colorado. The subjects responded to the instruments (Information Schedule, Attitudes Scale, and Quiz) and were interviewed by the investigator in their own schools. It was determined that the age of counselors, the count of education they had, and the recency of their training were not correlated to the attitudes they held regarding the use of behavior modification. The amount of knowledge a counselor had about behavior modification did have a significant correlation with attitudes. In addtion, it was clear that as knowledge increased, the attitudes toward the use of behavior modification tended to be more positive. Female counselors in this study tended to have more positive attitudes toward the use of behavior modification. And counselors who perceived their schools as serving students of higher socioeconomic status held attitudes that were more positive toward the use of behavior modification. One of the primary conclusions drawn from this investigation was that most counselors have had very little exposure to a behavioral approach.

2175.   Hickman, Michael S. "The Correlation of Measures of Adaptive Behavior and Intelligence in Educable Mentally Retarded Elementary School Students." Ed.D. Dissertation, Texas Woman's University. Dissertation Abstracts International, 37 (7-A), 4281. Order no. 77-746, 1977.

Thirty-five educable mentally retarded public elementary school subjects chosen randomly from two public school systems were administered a measure of intelligence and their teachers completed a measure of adaptive behavior. A Pearson product-moment coefficient of correlation was calculated to determine the degree of association between the various measures of intelligence and adaptive behavior. These correlations were tested for significance. Few significant correlations were calculated. Those which were significant indicated a positive association between performance measures of intelligence and measures of adaptive behavior.

2176.   Higgins, Andy J.   "Social Consequences Associated with the Application of Operant Conditioning Interventions in Classroom Settings." Ph.D. Dissertation, Kent State University. Dissertation Abstracts International, 35 (1-A), 259. Order no. 74-15,063, 1974.

The present study examined the social consequences which accompanied the application of operant conditioning interventions which were directed at modifying the inappropriate and unacceptable classroom behaviors of an aggressive kindergarten boy and a withdrawn first grade girl. Video-tape recordings were made of the target children, the selected nontarget children and the teachers throughout the duration of the present study. Target children's and nontarget children's classroom behaviors were scored as desirable, inappropriate or unacceptable. Teachers' reinforcement interactions with children were scored as either positive or negative. Peer interactions were scored as either positive or negative. Children's perceptions of the target children were obtained through the administration of pre- and post-picture sociometric tests. The results of the present study indicated that both operant conditioning interventions were successful in modifying the classroom behaviors of the aggressive and withdrawn target children.

2177.   Hillhouse, E. D.   "A Survey of Selected Missouri Principals and Assistant Principals' Attitudes Pertaining to Classroom Discipline." Ed.D. Dissertation, Saint Louis University. Dissertation Abstracts International, 40 (05). Order no. 7923824, 1979.

The problem was to analyze the attitudes or perceptions of selected Missouri school principals concerning pertinent aspects relating to classroom discipline and/or teacher effectiveness. The project involved a collection and presentation of administrative responses in an attempt to relate such toward a meaningful discourse that might be employed by educators in the disposition of their duties. The study population resulted in 247 elementary and secondary principals and assistant principals, randomly selected from The Missouri School Directory - 1976-77. The study population was presented an opinionnaire which consisted of twenty-five statements and two priority listings that dealt with such

problems as teacher preparation, school discipline, classroom management, corporal punishment, school curriculums,
teacher dismissals and functions of a strong teacher. The
responses ot the statement were placed on a rating scale of
4 points. The two listings enabled administrators to rank
in order of priority their responses to items related to
teacher dismissals and functions of a strong teacher. The
findings gave support to a number of conclusions. Discipline was perceived as being a serious problem in the public
schools today. The evidence gathered indicated that
colleges are graduating teachers better equipped in their
subject area but lacking in the areas of public relations
and classroom management (discipline). The need for
colleges to devote more effort in training teachers in classroom control and discipline was recognized. Corporal punishment was supported. Guiding and directing was viewed as the
major function of a strong teacher and students were
believed to learn better in the controlled self-contained
classroom.

2178.   Hinojosa, D. "A Study of the Relationships Between the
Organizational Climate, the Pupil Control Ideology and the
Self-Esteem and Power Dimensions of the Students' Self-
Concept in Selected Elementary Schools in the Corpus Christi
Independent School District." Ph.D. Dissertation,
University of Houston. Dissertation Abstracts Inter-
national, 34 (11-A), 6901-6902. Order no. 74-11, 854, 1974.

The problem of the study was to determine the relationships
between the organizational climate and pupil control
ideology as perceived by teachers, and the self-esteem and
power dimensions of the students' self concept as perceived
by the students. More specifically the study examined and
tested the following hypotheses: 1) Teachers who perceived
their schools to have open climates will be more humanistic
in their pupil control ideology. 2) The more open the
organizational climate the higher the pupil self-esteem. 3)
The more open the organizational climate the greater the
students' sense of power. 4) The more humanistic the pupil
control ideology the higher the pupil self-esteem. 5) The
more humanistic the pupil control ideology the greater the
students' sense of power. The study involved a smaple of 29
teachers and 779 students. In the Spring of 1973 the
teachers were asked to respond to the Organizational Climate
Description Questionnaire and the Pupil Control Ideology
Questionnaire. These two sets of data were then correlated
with the self-esteem and power scores obtained from the
Children's Self-Social Constructs Test. The analysis of the
data revealed several important results. First, the results
of the data indicated that Analysis of Variance was more
appropriate than the Pearson R technique. The results
yielded no correlations that were statistically significant.
On the other hand, Analysis of Variance of the organizational climate, self-esteem and power data sets yielded
F-ratios that were significant at the .01 level. Specifically, what this finding indicated was that the teachers

with more open climate scores had students that socred
higher on the self-esteem and power dimensions of the
Children's Self-Social Constructs Test. One other important
result was the correlation obtained from the OCDQ and FVIAS
relationship. In this set of data the correlation was
.3075; though not statistically significant the correlation
coefficient was positive and in the right direction in the
OCDQ and FVIAS relationship.

2179.   Hochschild, R. M. "Teacher Rated Student Maladjustment
in   Open,   Transitional,   and   Traditional   Classroom
Environments." Ph.D. Dissertation, State University of New
York at Buffalo. Dissertation Abstracts International, 37
(5-B), 2508-2509. Order no. 76-26,531, 1976.

This study investigated whether open, transitional, and
traditional classroom environments influenced teacher
reported rates and types of student maladjustment and
techniques used to work with problem behavior. A classroom
was classified as open, transitional, or traditional
depending on its score on the Preliminary Screening
Procedure, a classroom observation and teacher interview
instrument that measured student choice, materials,
activities, social groupings, and teacher activity. Twenty-
two classrooms containing 583 children were included in the
study. There were seven open classrooms, ten transitional
classrooms, and five traditional classrooms. Student maladjustment was measured using teacher ratings of overall
adjustment. Types of student maladjustment were measured
using the Student Behavior Rating Scale, which included the
AML Behavior Rating Scale, and the Devereaux Elementary
School Behavior Rating Scale. Behavior Management techniques were measured using the Teacher Technique Questionnaire devised for this study. The results indicate that the
three classroom environments differ significantly in terms
of teacher reported rates of student maladjustment (p =
.0017). Open and traditional classrooms also differ significantly (p = .0033). Open classrooms have the lowest rate
(13.9%), followed by transitional classrooms (27.8%) and
traditional classrooms (32.9%). Teachers provide no
evidence that the distribution of problem behavior types or
the amount of any particular problem behavior among maladjusted students is different in open, transitional, and
traditional classrooms (p .10). Open, transitional, and
traditional classroom teachers report they use different
types of techniques in working with the dependent child but
not with the aggressive child (p .10). Open classroom
teachers rely more on student choice and peer involvement,
and traditional classroom teachers rely more on teacher
activity and punishment. The results indicate that
measurable aspects of the classroom environment like student
choice, activities, materials, social groupings, and teacher
activity may have a major effect on rates of student
maladjustment. If the results are related to classroom
environment, then a primary prevention model aimed at

promoting "optimal" classroom environments is a logical and promising strategy for promoting mental health in the schools.

2180.   Hoffman, R. A. "Relationships Between Primary Process Functioning and Aspects of Adjustment in Elementary School Boys." Ph.D. Dissertation, New York University. Dissertation Abstracts International, 37 (9-B), 4684. Order no. 77-5413, 1977.

This was a study of relationships between primary process functioning and aspects of adjustment. The basic assumption was that the interplay and relative dominance between the primary and secondary processes have a bearing upon adaptive functioning. The sample consisted of a group of elementary school boys, twenty each from grades two, four and six. All the boys were Spanish surnamed, fluent in English, and attended an inner-city public school. Ages ranged from 7.5 to 13.3 years. Primary process functioning was measured through Rorschach protocols scored with Holt's manual. Adjustment was considered within the context of classroom behavior through the use of teacher checklists. (Conners' Behavior Rating Scale), peer-group sociograms and IQ scores. The basic thrust of the investigation was that defense effectiveness--adaptive control and modulation of primary process thinking which emerges during Rorschach testing -- would predict adjustment measured along a variety of dimensions. A major aspect of the study was essentially an examination of the DE score's construct validity; four of the six main hypotheses dealt with this concept. Supplementary analyses, which were conducted in post hoc examination of data, followed the propositions of the main hypotheses, but used different scores to represent subjects' attempts to control primary process thinking. The bulk of the significant findings came from supplementary analysis and the need for cross validation is particularly great. DE scores correlated significantly with a behavioral measure of adjustment that considered withdrawing reactions--this cross-validates a finding from an earlier primary process study of adjustment in an adult sample. There was agreement between judgments about adjustment made from children's figure drawings scored for indications of emotional disturbance (Koppitz' system) and the mean DE ratings of the children. Cumulatively, four findings support the proposition that examining controls of aggressive imagery in terms of how directly, and by inference how freely, subjects communicate responses, should predict unsocialized, aggressive behavior--none of the supplementary predictions using scores that measure only amount or blatancy of aggressive ideas was sustained. The number of popular and near popular responses was negatively related to defiant and aggressive behavior; but this held only for the oldest group of children.

2181.   Horowitz, L. T. "The Academic and Behavioral Effects of
a Behavior Problem Child in the Public School Classroom."
Ph.D.   Dissertation,   University   of   South   Carolina.
Dissertation Abstracts International, 36 (4-A), 2101-2102.
Order no. 75-16,484, 1975.

The purpose of this study was to determine whether the
presence of a behavior problem child or children in a normal
classroom negatively affects the behavior and academic output of the other members of the class. Problem children in
third-grade classes in a large rural school were identified
by means of the WPBIC. Those classes meeting specific
criteria -- no more than two children above the minimal
score for problem behavior and the rest of the class below
the cutoff for normal behavior -- served as experimental
classes. Twelve of the normal students from each of three
classes which qualified were chosen at random to serve as
experimental subjects were transferred during the experiment
leaving a total of 34 experimental subjects. Behavior of
the subjects during a structured seatwork assignment during
math period was recorded by observers. Percentage of
attending, nonattending, and disruptive behaviors was
recorded as well as the percentage of problems correct and
attempted on the specifically designed seatwork exercises.
The study consisted of three phases -baseline, experimental,
and baseline. During both baseline phases observations were
taken several times a week over a period of weeks. During
this time the behavior problem child or children were
present in class as usual. The experimental phase consisted
of a four-week period during which the problem child or
children were present in class as usual. The experimental
phase consisted of a four-week period during which the
problem child or children were removed from math class and
tutored elsewhere every day. Observation periods during
this time occurred without the presence of the problem
child. All five measures were compared for each treatment
phase and by classes via analysis of variance. Three
measures varied significantly across treatments -- attending
behavior, problems correct, and problems attempted. By
means of a Duncan's multiple range test it was determined
that for attending behavior the significant difference was
accounted for solely by the difference between baselines.
Because of the expected increase in the two academic
measures across the three months of the study a t test was
employed which compared the means for the experimental
phases with the averaged means for the two baselines for
both academic measures. An overall positive effect was
found for the experimental phase for both measures. Specifically it was noted that in terms of classes a significant
effect for the experimental phase occurred only for classes
1 and 2. For problems attempted, only class 2 varied
significantly.

2182.   Houser, M. E.   "An Examination of Student Compliance and
Attitude as a Function of Gender and Classroom Control
Technique."   Ph.D.   Dissertation,   University   of   Toronto.
Dissertation Abstracts International, 38 (10-A), 6013-6014.
Order no. 7802756, 1978.

This study was designed to identify the results of a
teacher's classroom utilization of certain means of social
influence, e.g., bases of social power by examining differences in 1) the level of student compliance as a function of
the social influence strategy employed by the teacher, 2)
the effectiveness of each social influence strategy to
produce compliance as a function of the sex of the subject
and 3) the attitude of the student toward the teacher as a
function of the social influence strategy employed by the
teacher.   A total of 588 subjects participated in the study,
297 female and 289 male, from 24 separate fourth, fifth and
sixth grade elementary classrooms.   Significant differences
in both student compliance and attitude toward the teacher
were observed as a function of the power base strategy
employed by the teacher.   Student compliance was highest in
the coercive power condition, followed by the informational,
legitimate, reward, referent and control conditions in order
of decreasing student compliance.   Significant sex differences in student compliance as a function of the power base
strategy employed by the teacher were not observed.
Attitude toward the teacher significantly varied as a function of power base, with subjects in the coercive power
group holding the most favorable attitudes followed by the
legitimate, reward, informational, control and referent
power conditions.   The findings of this study are potentially valuable for those in the classroom setting.   The
results suggest both in terms of the effect of the power
base strategy upon compliance and resultant attitude toward
the teacher that coercive power is the most desirable power
base for a teacher to use in the classroom and informational
and legitimate power are the second and third most desirable
influence strategies.

2183.   Huddleston, R. J.   "The Effects of a Reinforcement-
Counseling Procedure on the Social Behavior and Sociometric
Status of Elementary School Students."   Ph.D. Dissertation,
University of Oregon.   Dissertation Abstracts International,
33 (9-A), 4836. Order no. 73-7906, 1973.

This study was designed to assess the effectiveness of a
Behavioral Counseling procedure which was designed to
improve the sociometric status of elementary students by
assisting them to increase the frequency of their rewarding
and cooperative behavior while in the presence of their
peers.   A sociometric instrument was administered to the
third, fourth and fifth grade students attending Lincoln
School in Eugene, Oregon.   Forty of these students who were
sociometrically-ranked in the lower half of their respective
classrooms and who indicated a desire to get along better
with their classmates were randomly assigned to one of two

treatment conditions, Reinforcement-Counseling or Inactive Control. Twenty students assigned to the Reinforcement-Counseling condition were again randomly assigned to one of four counseling group. A counseling curriculum was administered to the students in the four counseling groups. Each group met twice weekly for five weeks. Students in the Inactive Control condition received no treatment. Following the completion of the curriculum, the sociometric instrument was readministered to the students. Then the forty students originally chosen for study were randomly reassigned into groups of four. Each group of students then participated on a series of work tasks and observations of the counseled and uncounseled students' rewarding and cooperative behavior were taken while they participated on the tasks. Analysis of the results revealed no significant differences between students in the Reinforcement-Counseling and those in the Inactive Control condition on gain in sociometric choices or in their behavior while participating on the series of work tasks. It was concluded that the Reinforcement-Counseling procedure was ineffective in increasing the rate of low status students' cooperative and rewarding behavior.

2184.   Hummel, J. H. "Training and Generalization of Elementary School Teachers in the Use of Eight Behavior Reducing Procedures." Ph.D. Dissertation, Georgia State University. Dissertation Abstracts International, 37 (8-A), 4986-4987. Order no. 77-1547, 1977.

The purpose of this study was to evaluate the training of elementary school teachers in the use of eight different procedures for reducing inappropriate classroom behaviors, and to assess whether there was generalization of this training by the teachers to application within their classrooms. All subjects were pre- and posttested with three instruments: an achievement test, an attitude survey and a behavior rating scale. Subjects in one experimental group also were observed in their classrooms periodically through the study. The observers coded inappropriate student behaviors and ascertained which behavior reducing procedure the teacher(s) used and how often they used a specific procedure during a session. Experimental group 1 (n=19) received written materials only. Experimental group 2 (n=12) received the written materials plus a class on the procedures that met bi-weekly at Mimosa Elementary School. Experimental group 3 (n=12) also received the written materials and the class, plus the teachers in this group were observed 1 or 2 times per week for 10 weeks. The control group (n=23) received no treatment, but were pre- and posttested. The posttest means of the written assessments for the four groups were analyzed using a one-way analysis of covariance with the appropriate pretest mean as the covariate in each analysis. When significance was discovered with the analysis of covariance, Scheffe's S-method was used to determine where the significance lay. Three of the six subscales of the behavior rating scale and both the achievement test and the attitude survey were significant at the .05 level. Visual inspection of the graphed results of the observational data for both student behavior and teacher procedures failed to indicate actual changes in either inappropriate student behaviors or teacher procedures.

2185.   Ide, K. N. Concurrent Validation of the Self Observation Scales, Intermediate Level, Using as Criteria Teacher Rated Classroom Behavior of White Students in Grades 4 Thru 6." Ed.D. Dissertation, Duke University. Dissertation Abstracts International, 38 (12-A), 7230-7231. Order no. 7807606, 1978.

The purpose of the research was to determine whether the Self Observation Scales (SOS), Intermediate Level, is an effective instrument for Classifying 450 white males and 405 white females in grades 4 thru 6 into the same discrete behavioral categories as those assigned by their respective teachers. Since the purpose of the research was concerned with the extent to which inventory item responses may be used to estimate an individual's present standing on a criterion, a concurrent validity study of the SOS was conducted. From the stated purpose of the research, the following hypotheses were derived and subjected to statistical analysis: 1) The proportion of white male subjects who are correctly classified into each behavioral criterion category on the basis of the subjects' responses to the items on the intermediate level Self Observation Scales does not differ significantly from the proportion of correct classifications expected by chance alone. 2) The proportion of white female subjets who are correctly classified into each behavioral criterion categroy on the basis of the subjects' responses to the items on the Intermediate Level Self Observation Scales does not differ significantly from the proportion of correct classifications expected by chance alone. The subjects of the research consisted of 450 white males and 405 white females in grades 4 thru 6 who had completed the SOS and were classified by their teacher into one or more of seven discrete behavioral categories described on the SOS Student Information Form: Socially Insecure, Behaviorally Disruptive, Low Self-Esteem, Emotionally Over-Reactive, Aggressive, Verbally Disruptive, and Exceptionally Healthy.

2186.   Jacobs, Paul C. "Modifying Impulsive Behavior of Second Grade Boys Through Cognitive Self-Instruction: Intensity of Training Related to Generality and Long Range Effects." Ph.D. Dissertation, Wayne State University. Dissertation Abstracts International, 35 (7-A), 4252-4253. Order no. 74-29,816, 1975.

This research was designed to assess the efficacy of modeling plus cognitive self-instruction as a viable training procedure for the modification of impulsivity. Different intensities of training were looked at in order to determine maximum effectiveness of the training procedures. In addition, transfer effects and durability of changes in conceptual tempo were investigated. It was hypothesized that the boys receiving modeling plus cognitive self-instruction would significantly decrease impulsive responding immediately after training, demonstrate the greatest amount of transfer effects and maintain these changes on a one-month delayed posttest in comparison to those not receiving training. In addition, it was hypothesized that those receiving the greatest intensity of training would perform significantly better on all dependent measures. Predictions concerning the comparison of the subjects in each condition on the immediate posttest were not confirmed. The subjects who received modeling plus cognitive self-instruction for a three-week period did not significantly decrease impulsive responding or evidence superior performance on any of the generalization measures in comparison to subjects in any of the other treatment conditions or control group.

2187.   Jalovick, J. M. "Pupil Control Ideology and Openness of Teachers' Beliefs and Practices." Ed.D. Dissertation, Rutgers University The State University of New Jersey. Dissertation Abstracts International, 38 (7-A), 3910-39110. Order no. 77-27,968, 1978.

The investigation dealt both with the development of a measure of teachers' beliefs about children's learning and knowledge and with the relationship between these attitudes and their attendant classroom practices and control orientations. The following hypotheses guided the inquiry: The more open the classroom practices of the teacher, the less custodial the pupil control ideology. The more open the teacher's beliefs about children's learning and knowledge, the less custodial the pupil control ideology. The more open the teacher's beliefs about children's learning and knowledge, the more open the classroom practices. In addition, all three major constructs were further examined in terms of selected demographic variables.

2188.   Jenkins, A. E., III. "Reducing Classroom Discipline Problems Among 20 Selected Classroom Teachers at Hamilton Junior High School." Practicum submitted in partial fulfillment of the requirements for the degree of Ed.D., Nova University, 1976.

The author had the task of creating discipline in a junior high school where he was made principal. He isolated the students and faculty who were involved in the most discipline referrals. He created a program that grouped the students with the most referrals with the teachers who made the most referrals in an inter-disciplinary cluster. The performance objectives for students and teachers are presented along with the teacher development program and the student curriculum. The teaching development program focused on self evaluation and teaching methods that take into consideration student attitudes and abilities. See ERIC Abstract ED 136413.

2189.   Johnson, A. O., Jr. "Missouri In-School Suspension Programs: A Descriptive Study of the Rationale, Structure, Common Usage and Success in Reducing the Number of Suspension." Ph.D. Dissertation, Walden University, Florida, 1979. 151p.

A study of the in-school suspension programs of 25 junior and senior high schools in Missouri with enrollments of 1,000 or more revealed that the programs have similar rationales and structures, have no total shared responsibility for the program between the central office and school administration, need to clarify the reasons for and type of suspensions assigned, were not in common usage, in successfully reduced the number of suspensions. Pertinent literature is discussed in the documentation of the study, several programs are described, and the questionnaire used to gather the data is included. See ERIC Abstract ED 173907.

2190.   Jones, T. R. "A Study of Citizen, Teacher, and Administrator Attitudes Regarding Preferred Student Disciplinary Alternatives in Public High Schools." Ed.D. Dissertation, East Texas State University. Dissertation Abstracts International, 38 (11-A), 6435-6436. Order no. 7805468, 1978.

The purpose of the study was to determine if selected citizens, teachers, and administrators had similar attitudes regarding the techniques utilized to achieve good student discipline in public high schools. The population sample represented randomly selected citizens, teachers, and administrators from two chosen school districts. The participants responded to a questionnaire which identified preferences as to which one disciplinary alternative from among six was considered most appropriate for each of eighteen specified discipline problem situations. 1) Among the three groups investigated, a trend existed for citizens to be the most lenient in their preferences, with teachers being more severe, and for administrators being the most severe. 2) As citizens expressed concern for school discipline, it seemed that this did not necessarily infer a desire for more severe discipline, but possibly more attention to the disciplining process itself for the benefit of the individual student and society. 3) In-school suspension was considered appropriate for students using alcohol, smoking where prohibited, and stealing school property. 4) Citizens preferred counseling with students more frequently than did teachers and administrators. 5) Citizens with no children tended to be the most lenient when expressing preferences for discipline.

2191.   Joy,   A.   D.   "Classroom   Organization   and   Classroom
Behavior: A Study of Children's Behavior in Differentially
Organized   Classroom   Types."   Ph.D.   Dissertation,   State
University of New York at Buffalo.   Dissertation Abstracts
International, 38 (9-A), 5325.   Order no. 7732670, 1978.

Differences   in   the   behavior   of   pupils   in   classrooms
organized   according   to   open   and   traditional   educational
philosophy   were   investigated.   A   consideration   of   the
existing   literature   pointed   toward   the   documentation   of
differences   in   children's   actual   classroom   behavior   as   an
important   element   in   the   evaluation   of   both   short-term   and
long-term   effects   of   differing   education   practices.   On   the
basis   of   scores   derived   from   the   Preliminary   Screening
Procedure,   a   quickly   administered   multidimensional   screening
instrument   assessing   aspects   of   classroom   organization
structure,   32   third   and   fourth   grade   classrooms   were
assigned   to   three   experimental   groups,   Open,   Low   Transitional and High Transitional.   Trained observers carried out
procedures   specified   in   the   Observation   Schedule   for   Pupil
Activity   in   Classrooms   during   four   forty-five   minute   observation   periods   in   each   classroom,   coding   the   behavior   of   each
of   four   children   among   seven   specified   dimensions: Task
Learning   Character,   Task   Behavior   Mode,   Involvement,   Task
Social   Grouping,   Task   Social   Character,   Social   Interacton
and   Choice.   Differences   among   classroom   groups   were   predicted   and   found   in   the   number   of   task   options   available   in
different   classrooms   types,   and   in   the   percentage   of   time
children   schedule   their   own   activities.   Differences   among
classroom   types   were   predicted   and   not   found   in   the   amount
of   student-structured   activity   in   different   classroom   types
and   in   the   number   of   social-group   options   in   different
classroom   types.   No   differences   among   classroom   types   were
predicted,   and   none   were   found   in   the   area   of   time   spent   in
productive   learning   and   student   involvement   in   work
activity.   The   results   extend   understanding   of   classroom
processes,   document   practical   differences   that   result   from
differing   educational   philosophies,   and   add   to   the   growing
body   of   literature   evaluating   open   education   programs.
Results   suggest   that   differences   among   classroom   types   are
not   as   great   as   the   public   debate   over   educational   philosophy   might   suggest,   but   large   enough   to   warrant   further
attention for the research community.

2192.   Kaeck,   D.   J.   "The   Modification   of   Emotionally   Disturbed
Behavior   Through   Teacher   and   Peer   Taining."   Ph.D.
Dissertation, Utah State University.   Dissertation Abstracts
International, 40 (2-B), 921.   Order no. 7917963, 1979.

The   purpose   of   the   investigation   was   to   develop   and   field
test   a   practical   program   for   the   mainstreaming   of   behaviorally   disturbed   children   into   regular   fifth-grade   classrooms.
The   10   day   training   program   emphasized   the   training   of   both
teachers   and   peers   as   therapeutic   agents.   It   focused   upon
the   teachers'   behaviors   in   terms   of   establishing   classroom
rules,   praising   and   ignoring,   minimizing   reprimands,

individualizing instruction, and providing naturally-occuring reinforcers to the children. The program enlisted the aid of the peers in terms of utilizing them as tutors, models, and as reinforcing agents or therapists. The children were taught to self-monitor their attention to appropriate and inappropriate behaviors and role playing techniques were used. Multiple baseline designs were used to assess the effects of intervention in five classrooms and on the target behaviors of ten children identified as emotionally disturbed. Treatment effects were replicated across students and teachers in three experiments. Substantial reductions in inappropriate behaviors were obtained while significant academic gains in reading and math were fostered. The results indicated that this approach was effective, efficient, and suitable for a variety of elementary classrooms.

2193.   Kahn, Wallace J. "Self-Management: A Study of the Differential Effects of Self-Observation, Self-Observation with External Feedback, and External Feedback on the Duration of On-Task Behavior of Children." Ph.D. Dissertation, University of Maryland. Dissertation Abstracts International, 35 (7-A), 4159-4160. Order no. 75-1806, 1975.

This experiment was designed to study the differential effects of self-observation, self-observation paired with external feedback, and external feedback on childrens' positively valued on-task behavior. In order to test the different effects that any one or a combination of these feedback modes had on the duration of on-task behavior, a factorial design with 2 dimensions (self-initiated feedback and external feedback) was utilized. Thirty-two sixth-grade students within one school were selected for this study. These students were judged by their arithmetic teachers to be on-task less than 50% of each class period. The 32 children participating in this study were randomly assigned to 1 of the 3 treatment conditions or to a control group. Although these findings substantiate the effectiveness of self-observation when upplemented by an external monitoring system, they do not support previous research indicating that self-initiated or externally provided feedback on a positively valued behavior is intrinsically reinforcing if the information indicates an increase in the desired behavior. A discrimination explanation derived from a learning pardigm was offered to clarify the present findings.

2194.   Kalus, J. M. "Analysis of Hawaii Secondary School Discipline Variables." Ph.D. Dissertation, Waldon University, Hawaii. 1978. 288p.

The purpose of this study was to examine student discipline problems in 21 high schools in Hawaii. Literature was reviewed concerning the youth revolution as it affects students in the public school and concerning discipline problems unique to the Hawaiian public schools. Data were collected through a questionnaire administered to selected students, teachers and school administrators. Principals reported truancy as the most frequently occurring problem. Principals reported that burglary, vandalism, smoking and drug use were reported frequently. Fighting and disorderly conduct occurred with moderate frequency. It was established that a school's enrollment size is positively correlated with crime rate. No association was found between school-community relations and crime rate. Twelve recommendations were suggested. See ERIC Abstract ED 170868.

2195.   Kane, G. M. "Effects of Contingency System Upon Academic and Inappropriate Behaviors in a Laboratory and a Third Grade Classroom Setting." Ph.D. Dissertation, University of Kansas. Dissertation Abstracts International, 33 (7-B), 3346-3347. 1973.

The present experiments were an attempt to analyze the relationship between inappropriate (study) behaviors and academic performance, and the effect of contingencies upon both behaviors. The first laboratory study compared the academic performance of three sisters (aged 5, 7, and 9 years) under baseline condition, a condition in which assignment completion within a fixed time was reinforced, and a condition in which assignment completion within a fixed time with a specific accuracy was reinforced. In addition the rates of inappropriate behaviors were recorded throughout the comparisons. The rate of academic performance of all three subjects was increased when assignment completion within a fixed time was reinforced. However, the accuracy of the performance deteriorated. When the accuracy requirement was added, the accuracies increased to a level above the criterion set by the experimenter. The inappropriate behavior was higher during baseline conditions than when consequences for academic performance were in effect. In the second laboratory study, baseline performance was compared to performance in a condition in which reinforcement was contingent upon the nonoccurrence of inappropriate behaviors.

2196.   Kane, J. F. "A Comparison of Learning Disabled Children With Learning Disabled Adolescents Relative to Non-Learning Disabled Peers in Terms of Selected Achievement, Affective and Behavioral Variables." Ed.D. Dissertation, The Johns Hopkins University, 1979.

Based on the lack of previous research and potential applications within the field, the present study was designed to investigate the questions -- 1) what effect does being learning disabled have on achievement, attitudes toward self and school, and classroom behavior? and 2) how do learning disabled (LD) adolescents differ from LD children with respect to the aforementioned variables? Four groups of subjects participated in the study: 1) Learning Disabled Children (LDC), 2) Learning Disabled Adolescents (LDA), 3)

Non-learning Disabled Children (NLDC), and 4) Non-learning Disabled Adolescents (NLDA). From these four groups, two additional groups were created: 1) Learning disabled students (LDS) which was LDC and LDA combined, and 2) Non-learning disabled students (NLDS) which was NLDC and NLDA combined. The following research hypotheses were tested: Hypothesis 1 - LDS will score significantly lower than NLDS on measures of academic ahcievement. Hypothesis 2 - LDS will demonstrate significantly poorer attitudes toward self and school than NLDS. Hypothesis 3 - LDS will demonstate significantly less favorable classroom behavior than NLDS. Hypothesis 4 - LDA will demonstate significantly greater retardation on measures of academic achievement than LDC relative to non-disabled peers. Hypothesis 5 - LDA will demonstrate significantly poorer attitudes toward self and school than LDC relative to non-disabled peers. Hypothesis 6 - LDA will demonstate significantly less favorable class-room behavior than LDC relative to non-disabled peers. On the basis of the data analyses, hypotheses 1 and 3 were supported (p .05). Hypotheses 2 and 6 were not supported. LDA demonstrated greater retardation on measures of reading vocabulary and arithmetic (but not on reading comprehension) than LDA relative to non-disabled peers. LDA demonstrated significantly poorer (p .05) attitudes toward school, (but not toward self) than LDC relative to non-disabled peers. There were both heuristic and practical implications of the aforementioned conclusions. Theoretical contributions included support of previous research indicating that LD students perform lower than NLD in academic achievement and that academic deficits among LD children continue into adolescence. In addition, new insights were provided into the nature of the LD adolescent including the observations that 1) academic deficits might be cumulative over time, 2) learning disability does not appear to impact upon self-concept (contrary to previous research), and 3) attitude toward school declines as LD students become older. Order no. 7914305, DAI.

2197.   Kaplan, M. A. "A Packaged Operant Conditioning Program and Pupil Behavior." Ph.D. Dissertation, Arizona State University, 1979.

The purpose of this study was to investigate the effects of a packaged operant conditioning program upon the behavior of elementary pupils in regular classroom settings. More specifically, the study was directed at assigning disposi-tions to hypotheses structured around three research ques-tions: 1) To what extent will the number of targeted class misbehaviors change as a result of the operant conditioning program? 2) To what extent will the number of pupil refer-rals to the principal's office change as a result of the operant conditioning program? 3) To what extent will teacher assessment of pupil behavior change as a result of the operant conditioning program? The sample was composed of all individuals in the fourth and sixth grades of a public school in a large city district. Prior to the

experiment, pupils were ranked by IQ and assigned in rota-
tion to one of our classes at each level. Class groups were
further adjusted in order to obtain a balance according to
size, age, and sex. Of the eight total classes, four were
team taught; and four were self-contained. All contained
approximately 30 pupils. The data analysis revealed a
significant reduction in class misbehaviors and a significant improvement in pupil behavior ratings with no differences attributed to grade level, team, or self-contained
settings. While the investigation found that the packaged
operant conditioning program did not reduce the number of
discipline referrals to the principal's office, it was noted
that the referral rate remained low during all observation
periods. Order no. 8003298, DAI.

2198.   Karafin, G. R. "An Observational Study Assessing the
Behavioral Goals of an Affective Curriculum." Ed.D.
Dissertation, Temple University. Dissertation Abstracts
International, 38 (4-A), 2001. Order no. 77-21, 769, 1977.

This report proposed that affective curricula which proport
complex behavioral goals need to include systematic, objective, behavioral assessments outside the course structure
within the evaluation program in order to validate the
degree of the curriculum's success. It was the purpose of
this investigation to demonstrate the use of a systematic,
objective behavioral assessment technique to evaluate the
impact of an affective curriculum on its participants. The
Achievement Competence Training (ACT) program was assessed
using the Spaulding pupil observation system: Coping
Analysis Schedule for Educational Settings (CASES). After
comparing the matching ACT behavioral goals and CASES
behavior categories, the hypotheses generated were that the
fifth-grade children participating in the ACT curriculum
would score a significantly higher frequency than would the
uninstructed fifth-grade control children in the CASES
categories: 1) Self Directed Activity; 2) Paying Close
Attention; 3) Integrative Sharing and Helping; 4) Integrative Social Interaction; and 5) Integrative Seeking and
Receiving Support. A total of 72 students randomly selected
from twelve field test classrooms participated in the study.
The results indicated that overall the ACT students did not
behave significantly differently in the routine classroom
setting than did Non-ACT students; however, a striking
finding revealed that the ACT program effected more similar
behavior patterns among classrooms for the hypotheses
behaviors which reflected ACT skills. These results
suggested that the ACT program consolidated participating
classroom styles to reflect more similar behavior patterns
in situations which occurred after the course hours. More
affective programs need to include behavioral observation as
a confirming assessment technique in their evaluation programs, and statements made by curricula developers regarding
the impact of their programs should be viewed in light of
this recommendation. Program statements regarding

behavioral changes among participants need to be reviewed with caution unless direct behavior assessments were made.

2199.   Kavanagh, Thomas E.   "Early Intervention and Prevention of Classroom Management Problems: A Planning Study for Teacher   Training."   Psy.D.   Dissertation,   Rutgers University, The State University of New Jersey, 1978. Dissertation Abstracts International, 39 (1-A), 240. Order no. 7800198.

The purpose of this study was to research the area of prevention of emotional and educational disorders in the public schools and, based on a knowledge of the practice and theory in this area, to design and plan a program which would meet the needs of one particular school system given its present resources and existing constraints. Based on a review of expert opinion on approaches to the definition of normality, an operational definition of a healthy personality was suggested for use in the school system. This definition was one which stressed efficient function and took into account such factors as individuality, culture, and situation specificity, and did not imply that either conformity or deviation was inherently desirable. After a review of the nature and scope of school maladjustment, the concept of and need for preventive strategies was presented. An analysis and examination of prevention programs in the public schools revealed a need to demonstrate the value of prevention through controlled research.   In addition, there were a number of major deterrents to the successful implementation of preventive strategies that needed to be anticipated. The basic hypothesis of this planning study became one which implicitly stated that a logical way to further immunize vulnerable children against the deleterious effects of prolonged school failure was to equip their teachers with an armamentarium of specific skills and techniques which would maximize their effectiveness in the classroom and prevent more serious problems from occurring in their students.   A behavioral education program which emphasized those procedures teachers needed to increase their effectiveness in the classroom was described and proposed with a plan for its evaluation.   After the relevant literature pertaining to objectives and procedures of the behavioral education training program was reviewed, there followed a discussion of the limitations and liabilities of this philosophy and method of school practice. It was concluded that, while the selection of any prevention program clearly involves constraining factors, a properly planned and administered behavioral education teacher training program could offer a systematic, concrete, and effective way not only to prevent psychological harm created by prolonged school failure, but also to promote personal competencies in young school children.

2200.   Kayden, Michele G.   "Teachers' Pupil Control Ideology and Classroom Management Behavior."   Ph.D. Dissertation, The Pennsylvania State University.   Dissertation Abstracts International, 37 (6-A), 3497. Order no. 76-26,841, 1976.

This study was designed to examine the relationship between teachers' pupil control ideology and their classroom management behavior. Teacher pupil control ideology was defined as teacher attitudes and beliefs regarding pupil control or student discipline, and was measured on a humanistic-custodial continuum. Teacher classroom management behavior was defined as observable techniques employed by teachers to manage student deviancy and promote work involvement in academic settings. The teacher sample was drawn from four inner city elementary schools in a large northeastern urban school district. The Pupil Control Ideology (PCI) Form which measured teacher orientations toward pupil control and an Information Sheet which provided emographic information were completed by forty-nine teachers who volunteered to participate in the study. Five null hypotheses were formulated to explore the relationship between teacher pupil control ideology and teacher classroom management behavior. These state that there would be no significant association between teacher pupil control ideology and withitness, overlapping, momentum, smoothness, or total teacher classroom management behavior, which included teacher behavior across the four KMOT categories. Pearson product-moment correlation coefficients were computed to test these hypotheses. The same statistical treatment was employed to explore the relationship between teacher pupil control ideology and the CSM and LMM factors of the KMOT. No statistically significant relationship was found between teacher pupil control ideology and observed classroom management behavior.

2201.   Keadle, M. E. "A Study of the Relationships Between the Perceptions of Teachers of the Organizational Climate and Selected Cognitive and Noncognitive Variables Associated with Elementary Students." Ph.D. Dissertation, University of Maryland. Dissertation Abstracts International, 37 (6-A), 3307. Order no. 76-27,400, 1976.

The problem of this study was to investigate possible relationships between organizational climate in schools and selected student variables. The questions raised were: 1) Do students in schools characterized by open climates achieve more cognitive learning than do students in schools characterized by closed climates? 2) Do students in schools characterized by open climates exhibit higher self-concepts than do students in schools characterized by closed climates? 3) Do students in schools characterized by open climates exhibit more desirable classroom behavior than do students in schools characterized by closed climates? 4) Do students in schools characterized by open climates hold higher perceptions of their teachers' feelings toward them than do students in schools characterized by closed climates? A random selection of twenty-four public elementary schools from Baltimore County, Maryland, constituted the sample of this study. The organizational climate of these schools was measured by having the teachers of the schools complete the Organizational Climate Description

Questionnaire (OCDQ). 1) The hypothesis that schools whose
organizational climates are characterized as "open" will
tend to result in higher student achievement, higher student
self-perceptions, more favorable classroom behavior, and
higher students perceptions of their teachers' feelings
toward them, than in schools whose organizational climates
are characterized as "closed" was not supported. 2) The
hypothesis that in open climate schools, as compared to
closed climate schools, as stronger positive relationship
exists between students' perceptions of their teachers'
feelings toward them and student achievement, student self-
perceptions, and classroom behavior was not supported.

2202.   Keesee, J. T.   "The Effects of a Behavioral Management
Class on Students Exhibiting a High Rate of Unsatisfactory
Conduct." Ed.D. Dissertation, University of Illinois at
Urbana-Champaign.   Dissertation Abstracts International, 36
(05). DAI no. 75-24,337, 1975.

The purposes of this participant observation investigation
were 1) to summarize the research following an applied
behavioral analysis which has relevance for public school
classrooms, e.g., as administrative alternatives to discipline; and 2) to discuss the selected important considerations involved in an applied behavioral analysis of deviant
behaviors.   The following reinforcers were utilized in the
behavioral management classroom to manage unacceptable
subject behaviors: 1) the Premack principle and token
economy procedure, 2) student self-evaluation, 3) the self-
contained classroom, 4) punishment procedure (non-corporal
in nature to include time out and systematic exclusion), 5)
teacher attention, and 6) vicarious reinforcement.   The
behaviors to be managed were 1) aggression, 2) gross motor
activities, 3) noise making, 4) orienting, and 5) verbalizations.   Finally, the writer delineated the implications of
the study for classroom behavior management as well as for
future research.

2203.   Kerney, Jean C.   "The Efficacy of an Adlerian Child
Guidance Study Group on Changing Teachers' Attitudes Toward
Children's Behavior."   Ph.D. Dissertation, Ohio University.
Dissertation Abstracts International, 41 (2-B), 673.   Order
no. 8016644.

The purpose of this study is to evaluate the effect an
Adlerian child guidance study program, "Coping with Kids,"
has on teacher attitudes toward discipline.   These attitudes
are measured by the Minnesota Teacher Attitude Inventory
(MTAI).   The author of the instrument defines these
attitudes as the ability to win affection of pupils, fond-
ness for pupils, understanding of pupils' behavior and
ability to maintain a desired form of discipline (Borich,
1977).   The Adlerian concept on which this study group is
based tends to emphasize those attitudes that are being
measured by the Minnesota Teacher Attitude Inventory (MTAI).
In addition, the study is to determine if an attitude change

is experienced by the teacher groups during a six week period following the termination of the treatment. "Coping with Kids" is a telecourse which was developed at Ohio University in an attempt to teach Adlerian child guidance principles. This program gives teachers skill training in specific methods of preventing conflicts between teacher and child - such as understanding the mistaken goals and private logic of misbeahvior, natural and logical consequences, and methods of verbal and nonverbal encouragement. Random sampling procedures were used in the process of assigning subjects to the treatment group and control group. The elementary teacher subject pool consisted of thirty-two (n = 32) subjects and the secondary teacher subject pool consisted of thirty (n = 30) subjects. Fifteen elementary (n = 15) school teachers were randomly assigned to the elementary study group and fifteen secondary school teaches were assigned to the secondary study group. The other teachers in the subject pool became the control group. The number of teachers assigned to the treatment and to the control group was determined in part on the basis of the number of teachers volunteering to participate in the study group. Each study group met twice a week. Each session was scheduled for one and one-half hours. The study groups were led by the same leaders (the author and a trained school counselor) for the entire treatment. When the groups were divided into smaller groups (n = 7 or 8) for activities, discussions and shared experiences, the facilitators alternated (i.e. every other session) among the subgroups to maximize consistency of treatment across the study groups. The "Coping with Kids" teacher study group has shown that not only can teacher attitudes toward children be changed toward a positive direction, but that the change can be maintained over time. It appears that the study group, when combined with the videotaped lecture, is an effective teacher training instrument. The small study gorup gave the participants the opportunity to interact with people who were experiencing similar situations. In a general sense, the Adlerian model seems to provide a valuable framework upon which to build teachers' understanding of students and potentially to improve the quality of classroom management. The current findings add further evidence to the importance of providing teachers with practical management skills and support for teacher trianing workshops and teacher study groups within the school system.

2204.   Kindall, L. M. "To Praise and Ignore Classroom Behaviors or to Praise and Punish Classroom Behaviors: That is the Question." Ed.D. Dissertation, The University of Tennessee. Dissertation Abstracts International, 34 (11-A), 7048. Order no. 74-11, 264, 1974.

The effects of two combinations of teacher supplied social consequences on disruptive and appropriate classroom behaviors were investigated. Six white male adolescents (three in each class) served as subjects. They were selected on the basis of their frequent disruptive behaviors. Observer reliability was computed. Each observer was required to attain a minimum reliability score of 85%. Samples of both teacher and student behaviors were recorded. The study involved a multiple baseline design with reversals. Four basic experimental conditions were introduced and replicated: 1) baseline; 2) praise for appropriate behaviors in combination with ignoring disruptive behaviors; 3) reversals; and 4) praise for appropraite behaviors plus soft reprimands for disruptive behaviors. In one class the order of conditions was reversed. The results showed that though both approaches were effective in producing desirable behaviors, the praise soft-reprimand strategy was slightly more effective than the praise-ignore strategy in producing such behaviors. Further analysis indicated that the behavior also changed more rapidly in the desired direction during the praise soft-reprimand sessions, which partically accounted for the overall difference. The teacher's reactions to the two approaches indicated a preference for both. That is, she concluded that she would use a combination of both approaches with emphasis on the use of praise.

2205.   Kitay, Gerald L. "A Study of the Relationship of Classroom Openness to Student Behavior and Self-Concept as a Learner." Ph.D. Dissertation, University of Maryland. Dissertation Abstracts International, 36 (2-A), 885-886. Order no. 76-17,812, 1976.

This study investigated the relationship of open education in the classroom to student behavior and self-concept as a learner. The classroom was the unit of investigation. "Openness" was assessed by averaging teacher ratings of their classroom obtained early and late in the school year on the Walbert-Thomas Questionnaire. A total of 53 fifth grade teachers and 1,346 fifth grade students provided the data analyzed in the study. Classroom measures obtained included mean student a) SCAL scores, b) "Positive Behavior" scores, and c) "Negative Behavior" scores. The results indicated that the correlations between classroom openness and both self-concept as a learner and "Positive Behavior" were positive but statistically nonsignificant; the relationship between classroom openness and "Negative Behavior" was inverse and statistically significant at the .01 level.

2206.   Klein, A. R. "Hyperactive and Active Boys in the Classroom: A Naturalistic Assessment of Teacher Ratings, Classroom Behaviors, Peer Interactions and Perceptions, and Subtypes of Hyperactives." Ph.D. Dissertation. Indiana University, 1978.

Teacher ratings, peer perceptions, peer interactions, and classroom behaviors of 17 hyperactive and 17 active elementary school age boys, nominated by their teachers, were compared using multivariate analyses of variance and planned comparisons in order to better describe and assess hyperactivity in its most problematic setting -- the classroom. Hyperactive boys and their active comparisons were 1. rated by their teachers on Conners Teacher Rating Scale, a behavior checklist for hyperactivity, 2. rated by their peers via a sociometric measure, "The Class Play" and 3. observed and rated on 17 behavioral variables using time-sampling procedures for one morning and one afternoon spaced a week apart. Hyperactive boys were significantly more anxious, inattentive, hyperactive, and had worse conduct problems and peer relations than did active boys as described by their teachers on the Conners Teacher Rating Scale. Additionally, they were chosen by peers for more negative roles on the sociometric measure than were actives. They were also chosen less often as "a true friend" and were less frequently reciprocally chosen for positive roles by their own chocies for these roles among their classmates than were active boys. Overall observed group differences between hyperactives and actives were found to be highly significant (p=.005) in the morning analyses and approached significance (p=.075) for the afternoons. In all three classroom situations (teacher-led, seatwork and unstructured activities), hyperactives were more off-task than were actives being involved either in activities other than those designated by the teacher or in disruptive, high activity level actions. There were no interactions between groups (hyperactive and active) and various classroom activities. Order No. 7906715, DAI.

2207.   Kleinbord, Kolman M. "Teaching Social Reinforcement Classroom Management Skill to Elementary School Student Teachers: A Selected Programmed Textbook Approach." Ph.D. Dissertation, University of Miami, 1972. Dissertation Abstracts International, 33 (6-A), 2714. Order no. 72-31,898.

The investigation was conducted to determine if student teachers who have read a selected programmed textbook on classroom management which follows the social reinforcement paradigm would: 1) learn defined effective classroom management techniques; 2) know these techniques on a paper and pencil assessment and consistently apply them to actual pupil classroom behavior; and 3) not change their reported attitudes about pupils or the teaching profession from positive to negative, as a result of the student teaching experience. A sample of convenience of 15 student teachers was drawn, and subjects are randomly assigned to one of three treatment gorups: 1) control group (C); 2) a group (E_1) in which each subject received a copy of the selected programmed textbok, Modifying Classroom Behavior: A Manual of Procedures for Classroom Teachers (Walker and Buckley, 1970), and 3) a group (E_2), which received collaboration from the investigator, in addition to receiving the selected programmed textbook, The Minnesota Teacher Attitude Inventory (MTAI) and a cognitive assessment instrument developed by the investigator were administered to each subject prior to and immediately after the five-week treatment period. There were no statistically significant differences among the groups in either type of student teacher attention.

There was a measurable difference in favor of E_2 (p 0.068) in reduced attention to inappropriate pupil classroom behavior. There were no statistically significant differences among the scores of the three groups on the five factors of the MTAI or in their knowledge of the techniques of classroom management. There was a measureable but non-significant increase in scores obtained on the cognitive assessment instrument in favor of C. There was no consistent classroom application of the techniques of classroom maangement in the groups. The attitudes of the student teacher neither changed nor improved significantly during the experience.

2208.   Knauss, J. W. "The Effects of Group Assertiveness Training on the Aggressive Behaviors and Self-Concepts of Fourth Grade Boys." Ed.D. Dissertation, The University of Tennessee. Dissertation Abstracts International, 38 (9-A), 5356. Order no. 7802014, 1978.

The literature suggests that direct behavior observation is the preferred methodology for assessing changes in the aggressive behaviors of children. Furthermore, it has been suggested that teachers can be reliable observers of aggressive behavior. However, many questions remain to be answered. The present study presented an opportunity to explore the question of whether a teacher checklist can be used as a reliability check on more precise observations. Subjects for the study were twelve fourth grade boys. The subjects were divided into two groups of six boys each. The study followed a multiple baseline design with staggered and continuous treatment. It was hypothesized that: 1) The frequency of aggressive behaviors would decrease as a result of assertiveness training. 2) The self-concepts of the boys in the program would increase an alpha level of 0.05 was selected as the level of statistical significance. The data for the teacher checklist and the behavioral observations was analyzed using the Pearson product-moment coefficient of correlation. The correlations were significant for only two of the subjects. Therefore, it was concluded that the data does not support the viability of using a teacher checklist as a reliability check rather than a second observer.

2209.   Knight, R. F. "The Relationship Among Selected Teacher Attributes and Frequency of Student Disruptive Behavior Referrals." Ed.D. Dissertation, Temple University. Dissertation Abstracts International, 39 (4-A), 1960. Order no. 7817389, 1978.

This study investigated the relationship between the number of disruptive behavior referrals made by teachers and the teacher attributes of (1) sex, (2) race, (3) age, (4) years of teaching experience, (5) kind of baccalaureate degree (education or noneducation), (6) major subject area taught, (7) number of days absent, (8) sponsorship of activity or club, and (9) parenthood. The study sought to identify those attributes which appeared to be associated with the larger number of reported classroom disruptions with the hope that this identification may be helpful for those who employ, assign, and develop inservice activities for teachers. The investigation was conducted in a large junior high school in Baltimore, Maryland. All of the eighth grade teachers in the school were included in the teacher population (n=37). The student sample included all the eighth grade students of the school for whom a student disruptive behavior referral was made by one of the teachers in the teacher population (student sample n=287). The nine (9) identified teacher attributes variables were compared with four (4) referral variables: (1) number of referrals, (2) sex of students referred, (3) types of referrals, and (4) general academic ability of class assignments of students referred. A panel of three judges (a teacher, an administrator, and a supervisor) read the 2,833 disruptive behavior referral reports made and agreed upon fourteen categories of referrals. These were then codified into three types of referrals: Type A: (1) class cutting and (2) classroom disruptions. Type B: offenses directed toward the teacher personally; (3) disobedience, (4) insubordination/disrespect, (5) and verbal abuse. Type C: offenses not directed toward the teacher; (6) fighting, (7) hallwalking without a pass, (8) use of lavatory without a pass, (9) leaving building or campus without permission, (10) use of profanity, (11) smoking, (12) tardiness to classroom or to school, (13) theft, and (14) vandalism. 1. Sex. Female teachers made more referrals than did male teachers. 2. Race. White teachers made more referrals than did black teachers. 3. Age. Teachers thirty years of age or under made more referrals than did teachers over thirty years of age. 4. Years of Teaching Experience. Teachers with five or less years of experience made more referrals than did teachers with more years of experience. 5. Kind of Baccalaureate Degree. Teachers with noneducation baccalaureate degrees made more referrals than did teachers with education baccalaureate degrees. 6. Major Subject Area Taught. Teachers of major subjects (English, foreign languages, mathematics, science, and social sutdies) made more referrals than did teachers of minor subjects (art, home economics, industrial arts, music, physical education, and reading). 7. Number of Days Absent. Teachers with the fewer days of absence made the greater number of referrals. 8. Sponsorship of Activity or Club. Teachers who sponsored clubs or activities made the greater number of referrals. 9. Parenthood. Teachers with children of their own made fewer referrals than did teachers with no children.

2210.   Krell, S. K. "Improving Student Lunchroom Behavior Through the Utilization of Behavioral Techniques." Ph.D. Dissertation, Case Western Reserve University. Dissertation Abstracts International, 39 (6-A), 3473. Order no. 7823812, 1978.

Inappropriate behaviors of students in the school lunchroom is the concern of principals, parents and lunchroom staff

members.   This study attempted to show that positive reinforcement in a school cafeteria setting constituted an
effective method of changing specific target behaviors of
the students.   The target behaviors included staying in
seat, placing litter in the proper receptacle, sponging the
table and removal of litter from around the table.   During
in-service workshops, the lunchroom staff members received
training in the application of behavioral techniques.   They
then applied these techniques in a behavior modification
lunchroom program.   The participants in this study were
students in grades four through six at an elementary school.
The number of students involved in the lunchroom program
fluctuated daily with a range from 55 to 112.   There were
four teacher aides, one teacher and the researcher implementing this program.   Each table of students had to earn a
specified number of checkmarks during the 30 minute lunchroom period in order to be dismissed from the lunchroom for
free play.   Checkmarks were awarded by the lunchroom staff
to students performing the target behaviors.   The results
indicated that during the periods when staff used positive
reinforcement for target behaviors and ignored inappropriate
behaviors there was an increase in: 1) students staying in
their seats; 2) placing the litter in the proper receptacle;
3) sponging their tables; and 4) a decrease in the amount of
litter around and under the tables.   The program also showed
a reduction of negative statements by the lunchroom staff
coinciding with an increase in target behaviors of the
students.   The changes in the behaviors of the staff members
seemed due to the implementation of the behavioral lunchroom
program and appeared to bring about a change in the target
behaviors of the students involved in the study.

2211.   Kroungold, M. H.   "The Effects of Type of Praise and Type
of Reward on Response Maintenance and Intrinsic Motivation."
Ph.D. Dissertation, Syracuse University.   Dissertation
Abstracts International, 40 (12-B, PT 1), 5817.   Order no.
8013387, 1980.

The effects of different types of praise and reinforcement
were examined in a setting that closely approximated classroom token economies.   Subjects were 65 third graders, and
the target activity involved solving math problems.   Intrinsic motivation was defined by performance levels which
occurred in the absence of extrinsic rewards and by enjoyment ratings.   The design included baseline, reinforcement,
and follow-up phases.   No reinforcement was delivered during
baseline or follow-up, and the nature of reinforcement and
praise differed for the five conditions.   Reward groups
either earned tangible incentives or free time to spend with
specific activities.   Praise was either administered by the
teacher or self-administered.   Training in self-praise was
done by self-instructional procedures whereby praise was
faded from overt to covert levels.   A control group received
neither token nor social rewards.   The results indicated
that follow-up enjoyment ratings and performance levels were
significantly lower than baseline for reinforcement and

control groups with no differences between the reinforcement
and control groups. Greater intrinsic motivation was found
for the tangible groups relative to the free time groups.
No significant differences were found for the praise manipulations.

2212.   Kutch, Lloyd L.   "The Effects of Contingency Management
Techniques   by   Teachrs   on   Classroom   Behaviors   of
Institutionalized   Delinquent   Adolescent   Boys."   Ed.D.
Dissertation, Oklahoma State University, 1971.   Dissertation
Abstracts   International,   33   (2-B),   936.   Order   no.
72-21,918.

This study was conceived and designed to explore the effects
of contingency management techniques by teachers upon the
behavioral responses in the classroom of institutionalized
delinquent boys.   The design emphasized the training of
teachers in contingency management technqiues including the
determining of desirable behaviors of contingencies, the
effective application of tangible reinforcers, and the use
of a partial reinforcement schedule.   The independent variables were the reinforcement principles, the physical setting, curriculum, and the teacher's ability in applying
reinforcement techniques for modification of behavioral
responses.   Thus, the focus was upon the teacher as a manipu-
lator   of   reinforcing   agents   in   controlling   classroom
behavior.   The dependent variables were the behaviors to be
modified.   The subjects for the study were the seventh grade
class, randomly selected from the Helena State School for
Boys at Helena, Oklahoma.   The results of the investigation
generally upheld the hypotheses.   The systematic application
of tangible reinforcers led to modification of student
behavior into relatively stable patterns.   It had been
hypothesized that the reinforcement techniques would cause
an increase in total time-on-task, an increase in the
frequencies of educationally relevant behaviors such as:
questions, answers, comments, pupil-pupil interaction, and
hand-raising, and a decrease in the frequencies of digres-
sive verbal and motor behaviors.   These hypotheses were
tenable and were not rejected.   It was also hypothesized
that the frequency of aggressive verbal and motor behaviors
would   decrease   from   Control   to   Experiment,   and   that
increases in desired behaviors in the experimental group
would result in an increase of the responses under the
control group.   The changes in frequency were not significant at the level of confidence established and both
hypotheses were rejected.

2213.   Lantz, H. J.   "The Alteration of Behavior in the Classroom   Setting."   Ph.D.   Dissertation,   West   Virginia
University.   Dissertation Abstracts International, 33 (7-B),
3311-3312. Order no. 73-841, 1973.

An intervention procedure directed at changing teacher and
pupil behavior in the classroom setting was developed to
meet the criteria of minimal disruption of routine classroom

activities, modest cost of professional time, follow-up data showing that intervention effects persist, and low response cost to the teacher. The investigation centered on an attempt to modify children's rates of appropriate and inappropriate behaviors by attempting to change the teachers' rate of approving and disapproving responses. Results showed experimental teachers differed significantly from control. Set, and feedback plus set, brought about significant increases in teacher approval and children's appropriate behavior, with concomitant decreases in teacher disapproval and children inappropriate behavior.

2214.   Lasley, Thomas J. "Perceived Student Misbehavior Within the Context of Classroom Interactions: A Participant Observation Study."   Ph.D. Dissertation, The Ohio State University, 1978.   Dissertation Abstracts International, 39 (2-A), 547-548. Order no. 7812357.

Extensive research has shown that the setting in which a phenomenon is observed affects the nature of the findings. The present research on perceived misbehavior was undertaken, therefore, in a setting where behavioral phenomena occur naturally, in the classroom. The data were inductively analyzed to determine how teachers and students defined, perceived and reacted to misbehavior. The study is exploratory and designed to generate data about behavior treated by classroom participants as misbehavior. The data were collected from April 22 to June 6, 1977. The classes observed were in two junior high schools -- one was an innver-city school and the other suburban. The teacher in the inner-city school was a female with five years of teaching experience while the suburban school teacher was a male with six years of teaching experience. Teachers were asked to assess how troublesome student behavior was during each class period. A moderately troublesome class for each teacher was then selected and observed every day it was in session. The themes are organized around three categories: coping, challenging and interactions affecting authority. The first category of coping consists of two themes: maintaining cool and relieving boredom. The themes in this category focus on how students cope with the teacher's exercise of power in the classroom. The second category of challenging is organized into three themes: aggressing smarting-off and ignoring. This category of classroom behaviors deals with how students directly or indirectly challenge or eroed the teacher's use of power and ability to exercise authority in the classroom. The final category examines classroom interactions affecting teacher authority and include the themes of transitioning, nonresponding and faceworking. These themes focus on classroom interactions which directly affect the teacher's ability to exercise or maintain authority.

2215.   Laspina, Anthony V. "The Effect of Applied Reality
Therapy Methods Upon Creative Thinking and Behavior." Ph.D.
Dissertation, University of Southern Mississippi.
Dissertation Abstracts International, 37 (4-A), 1991. Order
no. 76-23,016, 1976.

The study was conducted to determine if Applied Reality
Therapy methods as advocated by William Glasser have any
effect upon creative thinking and behavior. Increases in
creative thinking were measured by alternate Verbal Forms of
the Torrance Tests of Creative Thinking. Increases in on-
task behavior were measured by trained observers in the
classroom using an unpublished behavior rating form by
Charles Madsen. Hypotheses were that significant differences would occur between experimental and control-placebo
composite groups and subgroups from pretests to posttests.
Statistical analysis revealed that significant differences
occurred for the Fluency scale and for the Verbal Forms as a
whole. Further analysis revealed that no increases occurred
for experimental groups in regard to these two variables.
Therefore, none of the hypotheses were supported by the
data.

2216.   Lauback, A. R. "School-Controlled Conformity of Dress
for Teenagers and Its Relation to Selected Behaviors and
Security-Insecurity." Ph.D. Dissertation, The Pennsylvania
State University. Dissertation Abstracts International, 34
(3-A), 1033-1034. Order no. 73-20,100, 1973.

This study was designed to explore aspects of issues raised
by educational administrators concerning their beliefs that
students exhibit more socially desirable behavior when they
are dressed more carefully or in more conventional dress. A
stratified random sample of 640 students was chosen from
four secondary schools in the same county in eastern
Pennsylvania. Two schools with well defined dress codes
(referred to as code schools) and two schools with no
specific dress codes (referred to as no code schools) were
included in the sample. Equal numbers of girls and boys
from eighth and eleventh grades from each school were
tested. Hypotheses were designed to test exploratory concepts which might be used in furthering studies of teenage
behavior and dress. The instrument used to test the
hypotheses included an 80-item list of girls' dress and an
80-item list of boys' dress from which students chose dress
items for their own sex which they would like to wear to
school often, sometimes, or never. The instrument also
included a Behavior Test designed to determine the level of
behavior which respondents though they had attained, and a
social security-insecurity inventory to determine the level
of students' security. Multiple choice and open end questions secured students' feelings about types of dress or
grooming practices. Findings confirmed four hypotheses and
partially confirmed a fifth. Significant correlations were
found between behavior scores for girls and boys and their
selection of certain items of dress which they would like to

wear to school if there were no restrictions. Girls and boys with positive behavior more often chose frequently worn items considered by school authorities as acceptable for school wear. Girls and boys with negative behavior more often chose items which were less frequently worn and usually banned by dress codes.

2217.   Lawrence, A. N. "An investigation of some side effects of the use of individual tangible reinforcement contingencies in the elementary school classroom." Ph.D. Dissertation, the University of Connecticut, 1975.

The purpose of this study was to investigate the effects of a behavior modification program carried out on a single elementary school student on the behavior of non reinforced students in the class and of the teacher. Student behaviors of concern included on task behavior, interactions with a target, and effective responses toward both the target and other students. Teacher behaviors study included physical proximity and positive and negative feedback to students. The behavior of all the students in two classrooms was observed by means of the Behavioral Observation Schedule for Pupil and Teachers. Teacher behaviors were recorded using a modified version of the same schedule. The results showed that non-reinforced students significantly increased the frequency of on task behavior from baseline to treatment conditions as a function of the successful modification of the targets' off task behavior. Sociometric ratings received by the target and non reinforced students improved over the course of the experiment, but only in the fourth grade class.

2218.   Lawrence, J. D. "Teacher Perception of Student Threat to Teacher Status and Teacher/Pupil Control Ideology." Ed.D. Dissertation, The Pennsylvania State University. Dissertation Abstracts International, 38 (10-A), 5826-5827. Order no. 7803340, 1978.

This study sought to determine whether differences in teachers' perceptions of student threat to teacher status were related to teachers' pupil control ideology. Three major, and two related minor hypotheses were developed for testing: H.1. Teacher custodialism will be directly related to secondary teachers' perceptions of student threat to teacher status. H.1.B. Elementary teachers' custodialism will be directly related to elementary teachers' perceptions of student threat to teacher status. H.2. Secondary teachers will perceive greater student threat to teacher status than elementary teachers. H.3. Secondary teachers will be more custodial than elementary teachers. The first major hypothesis and the first minor hypothesis related to it were not able to be rejected at the .01 level. The second related minor hypothesis was not able to be rejected at the .05 level. Hypotheses two and three were not able to be rejected at the .001 level. Based on the results, it appears that there is a relationship between teachers' perceptions of student treat to teacher status and teachers' pupil control ideology; and that secondary teachers both perceive a greater student threat to teacher status and are more custodial than elementary teachers. Limited additional analysis was also done focusing on the relationship of the demographic data to teachers' pupil control ideology and to their perception of student threat to teacher status.

2219.   Lawther, J. W. "The Differential Influence of Peer Behavior Modification and Class Discussions on Selective Child Characteristics of Middle School Students." Ph.D. Dissertation, University of South Carolina. Dissertation Abstracts International, 37 (10-A), 6278. Order no. 77-6770, 1977.

The study investigated the influence of two types of group sessions on disruptive classroom behavior. Teachers were trained by the counselor to hold group discussions which focused on the encouragement of acceptable classroom behavior. The teachers then held six group discussions of the peer behavior modification type or the class discussion type. The study asked questions regarding disruptive student behavior, the counselor as consultant training teachers, the use of group discussions at three levels. Specifically, they were these: 1) What is the influence of teacher training in behavior modification on teacher know-ledge of behavior modification concepts? 2) What is the influence of teacher training in class discussion? 3) Does peer behavior modification differ from class discussions in its influence on the following: a) disruptive behavior of sixth, seventh, and eighth grade students?, b) the scores of sixth, seventh, and eighth grade students on the Self Percep-tions Index (SPI)?, c) the scores of sixth, seventh, and eighth grade students on the Peer Acceptance Index (PAI)? Three measures of changes in the students' behavior were ascertained from pre-posttest scores on 1) the Self Percep-tions and Peer Acceptance Indices of the Mac B Personal Competence Inventory, 2) detention hall assignments, and 3) observers recording classroom behaviors on the Pupil Enthusiasm Inventory. The detention hall assignment and the observer data dependent variables revealed no significant behavior change although decreases in the number of disrup-tive behaviors were noted. Satisfactory reliability measures were obtained for the SPI and the teacher training tests. The SPI of the Mac B revealed a significant differ-ence in treatment for seventh graders who were in the behavior modification treatment. Their self perception scores were significantly better than the control group at the seventh grade level. The PAI revealed that the sixth grade students in the Class Discussion group scored signifi-cantly better than the control group indicating improved peer acceptance as a result of treatment at the sixth grade level. The study supports the hypothesis that a middle school counselor can make a difference on what some students think of themselves and others by consulting with teachers on leading class discussions.

2220.   Lessard, B. L. E. "Charting Positive and Negative Behavior in an Elementary School and Classroom." Ed.D. Dissertation, University of Kansas, 1979.

Much effort in educational research has focused on both student behavior and student learning. The effects of behavior on learning have long been a major concern among the public and educators. No evaluation of the effects of school behavior on classroom behavior and classroom behavior on learning has been reported. Therefore, this study used the Standard Celeration Chart and related statistics to compare these behaviors. The effects of attempts to improve the school climate and classroom climate were recorded on both positive and negative behavior. This permitted recording effects of changing the school climate on classroom behavior. At the same time, the quality of learning was measured in three separate curriculum within the classroom which permitted the measurement of effects of changes in school climate and classroom climate on student learning. The independence of school positive behavior from school negative behavior is seen from January to May when the negative behavior decelerated by +2.3 per month without any corresponding acceleration in school positive behavior. The independence of classroom positive behavior from classroom negative behavior is seen when in September and October they both accelerate. November and December negatives accelerate and positives decelerate, and then in Marcy, April and May they both decelerate. Conclusions included: 1) Changes in positive behavior are independent of changes in negative behavior in both school and classroom. 2) Changes in school positive and negative behavior are independent of changes in the positive and negative behavior of a classroom in a school. 3) Changes in school behavior were related to changes in the school environment and changes in classroom behavior were related to changes in the classroom environment. 4) Classroom learning quality was related to curriculum changes and was independent of both classroom behavior and school behavior. Order no. 7925869, DAI.

2221.   LeVan, Richard R. "Development and Assessment of a Teacher-Implemented Self-Instructional Program for Management of Hyperactivity and Associated Behavior in the Classroom." D.Ed. Dissertation, The Pennsylvania State University. Dissertation Abstracts International, 41 (10-B), 3896. Order no. 8107602.

The school psychologist's role as consultant to teachers in the management of hyperactive children in the classroom is discussed. Current literature focusing on etiology and management of hyperactivity is reviewed. Attention is given to the development and applications of self-instructional training programs directed at improving self-regulation. This study was designed to evaluate a self-instructional training program implemented by teachers in their classrooms with consultive support of the school psychologist. The primary measures of program effects were observed levels of inappropriate task and conduct behaviors. Ratings, a measure of reflection-impulsivity, and a measure of visual-motor skill were also employed. Fidelity to program, use of self-instructional techniques in general teaching, and teachers' opinions of the program were also assessed. Relationships among dependent measures were analyzed. Twenty students enrolled in a school program for learning disabled children were selected according to criteria that specified hyperactivity, disruptive classroom behavior, and absence of retardation or significant physical handicap. Students from the affiliated regular school program selected on similar criteria served as controls for three of the dependent measures. Four groups of five students from the learning disabilities program received self-instructional training provided by teachers in the classroom. Results suggest that the program was moderately effective in reducing the inappropriate general conduct behaviors. Older subjects responded more favorably. The efficacy of self-instructional training directed at improving on-task behavior was not demonstrated. However, task behavior of some subjects did improve during the conduct phase. Analyses of other dependent measures indicate a significant reduction in errors on a matching task and a significant pretest and posttest reduction in teachers' ratings of inappropriate behavior. There were no gains in response latency, visual-motor work, teacher ratings of positive behavior, or parent ratings of behavior at home. Teachers were successful in carrying out the program lessons but they did not show techniques consistent with the program in their regular classroom teaching. Teachers' evaluations of the program were generally positive. Correlational study failed to demonstrate any significant relationships among direct observation of behavior, teacher ratings, and parent ratings. There was also an inverse relationship between competence in selecting a correct response on the matching task and direct observations of inappropraite conduct.

2222.   Lever, E. B. "Reactions of Teachers to Photographs of Boys Differing in Facial Attractiveness, Behavior, and IQ Label." Ph.D. Dissertation. University of Southern California, 1979.

The purpose of this study was to investigate the relationship of retarded children's attractiveness, IQ, and adaptive behavior to teachers' reactions toward them. The following questions were posited: 1. Do teachers' expectations for a retarded child's academic and social performance in the regular class vary as a function of attractiveness, IQ label, and behavior? 2. Do teachers' attitudes toward a retarded child vary as a function of attractiveness, IQ label, and behavior? 3. Do teachers respond more negatively to unattractive than to attractive children? 4. Do teachers respond more negatively to EMR-labeled than to average IQ-labeled children? 5. Do teachers respond more negatively to EMR descriptions than to behavioral descriptions of regular-class children? The independent variables

were facial attractiveness (attractive vs. unattractive), IQ
label (EMR vs. average IQ), and behavioral description
(typical EMR behavior vs. typical regular-class behavior).
Eight combinations of these variables were possible. The
stimulus for each combination was a picutre of a fifth-grade
boy. The variables were randomly combined (one photograph,
one lable, one description) within the confines of the eight
possible combinations to form the stimulus child for each
condition. A picture of each stimulus child was attached to
a 23-item questionnaire designed to measure teachers' expectations for the attitudes toward the child's performance in
a regular fifth-grade class. The dependent variables were
teachers' total questionnaire scores, teachers' expectation
scores, and teachers' attitude scores. A random sample of
109 teachers from middle-class schools was selected.
Findings were that teachers' expectations for and attitudes
toward the children depicted in the questionnaire varied
significantly with IQ labels and behavioral description.
Teachers' responses did not vary significantly with the
attractiveness of the children. Conclusions reached were:
1. Label and description of a child's behavior and IQ can
significantly influence teachers' expectations for and
attitudes toward that child. 2. Regular-class teachers can
develop different expectations for and attitudes toward a
retarded child, based on behavior and IQ label. Teachers
had lower expectations for and more negative attitudes
toward children labeled EMR than they did children labeled
as being of average intelligence; they had lower expectations for and attitudes toward EMR than they did regular-
class behavior. 3. The effect of attractiveness on
teachers' predictions for children's academic performance
was not significant.

2223.   Levine, Mary A. "Teachers' Attitudes Toward Corporal
Punishment and its Alternatives in the School Environment."
Ph.D. Dissertation, Indiana University, 1977. Dissertation
Abstracts International, 38 (5-A), 2523. Order no.
77-22,663.

The purpose of the study was to ascertain teachers' attitudes toward alternatives to corporal punishment in the
school environment and to determine, by contrast with
various alternative methods of discipline, teachers' attitudes toward corporal punishment itself. The study was
motivated by five elements which were as follows: 1) Educa-
tionists, as well as the general American public, regard the
maintenance of systems of discipline in schools as
essential. 2) The history of corporal punishment as a
vehicle of discipline in American schools parallels the
development of public education in America. 3) From
earliest times, severity characterized the implementation of
corporal punishment in U.S. schools. 4) Criticism and
rejection of corporal punishment of pupils as inhumane,
cruel, and unethical dates to the time of Quintillian in the
first century A.D. 5) Despite criticism of corporal punishment since the Renaissance, such punishment is currently

permitted legally and with social sanction in all but three
states of the fifty states of the U.S. 1) A substantial
minority of public school teachers sampled opposed the use
of corporal punishment in all instances specified on the
opinionnaire. 2) Teachers generally opposed the use of
corporal punishment and accorded it a rank of thirteen among
fourteen tactics of discipline suggested in the opinionnaire. 3) Teachers generally opposed corporal punishment
along with other tactics of a severe, punitive nature.
Suspension, dismissal from class, detention after school,
and expulsion were among the punishments most widely
rejected by the teachers sampled. 4) Participants in the
inquiry, for the most part, regarded the tactic of the
individual pupil conference as the most efficacious tactic
of school discipline. It also was the most widely employed
alternative to corporal punishment.

2224.   Levy, B. B. "Teachers' Judgments of Achievement-Related
and Pupil Role Behaviors of Elementary School Girls and
Boys."   Ph.D.   Dissertation,   Columbia   University.
Dissertation Abstracts International, 35 (10-B), 5085.
Order no. 75-7518, 1975.

Many investigators have speculated that teachers evaluate
pupils according to a variety of dimension simultaneously,
with "pupil role" concerns (character development and
institutional adjustment) overriding "achievement-related"
concerns (sustained achievement and intellectual development). Some educators have argued that boys are "emascu-
lated" in the elementary school; other claimed that both
sexes are "sex-typed" along traditional lines. A Classroom
Anecdotes task was developed to gather data on these two
issues, i.e., the relative influence of achievement-related
and pupil role behavior on teachers' judgments of a child's
behavior and the influence of pupil sex on these judgments.
The instrument consisted of five anecdotes describing the
behavior of an individual pupil in a classroom situation.
Each anecdote included an achievement-related (AR) behavior
and a pupil role (PR) behavior. AR behaviors sampled were
task independence, social/emotional independence, initiation, achievement striving, and expectation of success. PR
behaviors sampled were: sociability, considerateness, care-
fulness, obedience and diligence. Eight versions of the
instrument representing all possible combinations of AR
(positive or negative), PR (positive or negative), and pupil
sex (girl or boy) were administered to 259 female upper
elementary teachers from urban and suburban area with an
average of four years teaching experience. The major
findings were: 1) As hypothesized, teachers valued "achievement-related behaviors over "pupil role" behaviors. On both
the one word choice and teacher reaction choice measures,
teachers clearly indicated more concern for AR than for PR
behaviors; 2) Contrary to expectation, teachers differed
little in their responses to the behaviors of boys and
girls. Neither the desirability ratings, one word choices,
reaction choices, or open-ended responses indicated any sex

differences. However, PR positive boys were rated as less typical than PR negative ones, and more PR labels were added to describe the behavior of AP+PR- girls than girls in the other conditions or AR negative boys.

2225.   Lieber, E. K. "The Effects of Teacher Leadership on Pupil Morale and Compliance in Primary Classrooms." Ph.D. Dissertation, University of California. Dissertation Abstracts International, 37 (5÷A), 2775-2776. Order no. 76-25,218, 1976.

This study had two major objectives: 1) to investigate the relationship between teacher leadership behavior and pupil morale and compliance in primary classrooms and 2) to determine the feasibility of applying large-scale survey research methods to a very young respondent population. Teacher leadership was conceptualized as composed of three inter-related dimensions: Task, Authority, and Expressiveness. The interaction effect of these dimensions was termed a mode of teacher behavior, or teaching style. A mode was any combination of varied levels of performance on the three dimensions at the same time. Pupils in 33 first-grade classes in 12 schools of varying socioeconomic levels, and located in seven difference districts in Southern California were included in the sample. Data were analyzed through the use of multiple regression analysis, graphic presentations of plotted scores, and correlational analysis. The findings of the study appeared to indicate the following: 1) The higher the teacher task dimension, the lower the authority dimension of the teacher. 2) The higher the expressive dimension of the teacher, the higher the teacher task dimension. 3) The lower the authority dimension of the teacher, the higher the expressive dimension.

2226.   Liebroder, B. T. "Evaluation of an Elementary Guidance Program." Ph.D. Dissertation, University of Utah. Dissertation Abstracts International, 37 (6-A), 3422. Order no. 76-27,410, 1976.

In 1973, the Granite School District began an elementary guidance program which included the addition of full-time counselors in three elementary schools. This program was intended to be developmental in nature and was supported by funds appropriated by the Utah State Legislature specifically for guidance services to elementary school students. The problem of this study was to determine whether students' participation in the elementary guidance program resulted in any measurable changes in their attitudes, differences in their classroom behaviors, or differences in parents' perceptions of student attitudes and behaviors. Additionally, the study attempted to determine whether there was a relationship between the attitudes of the teachers and changes in student attitudes. A District supported evaluation program was carried out during the 1973-1974 school year. Two hundred twenty third and fourth grade students, ten teachers, and three counselors from three schools within the

Granite School District participated in the study. The students were randomly divided into five experimental and five control groups. Counselors worked with the experimental students for a five month period. Significant differences were obtained in one of the three schools on 1) the Interpersonal Effectiveness Diagnosis, 2) non-disruptive off-task classroom behaviors; and 3) disruptive off-task classroom behaviors, favoring the experimental students. Further, significant differences in the amount of classroom disruptive off-task behavior were obtained between experimental and control groups in a second school.

2227.   Lightel, D. G. "The Effectiveness of the Adlerian Model in Elementary School Counseling." Ph.D. Dissertation, Kent State University, 1974.

The purpose of this study was to investigate the application of the Adlerian group counseling model to three significant groups within the life space of selected second and third grade students, and to attempt to determine which of the three group applications would result in the most significant positive change in the child's behavior. A total of thirty-six second and third grade boys and girls participated in the study. The Adlerian group counseling approach was used as the counseling model in the three experimental groups. In Approach A, the students met for group counseling with the counselor one-half hour twice weekly for a ten-week period. In Approach B, the students met for group counseling one-half hour twice weekly with the counselor, and their mothers also met with the counselor once a week for 1½ hours for a ten-week period. In Approach C, the students met for group counseling one-half hour twice weekly with the counselor, and their teachers also met with the counselor once a week for one hour for the ten-week period. In Approach D, the students served as a control group, meeting only for testing sessions. It was hypothesized (H_1) that the children in the three experimental groups would show greater constructive behavior change than the children in the control group. Results of the analysis of covariance design indicated support for this hypothesis in only one of the three stated expectations included in the definition of constructive behavior. Results of the Newman-Keuls Test indicated that the three experimental groups did significantly better than the control group on the California Text of Personality. It was hypothesized (H_2) that all children in the double treatment approaches would show greater constructive behavior change than children in the single treatment approach. Results of the analysis of covariance design as applied to the California Test of Personality, Gronlund's Sociometric Questionnaire, and the Stilwell-Santoro Behavior Checklist necessitated rejection of this hypothesis. It was hypothesized (H_3) that the children in the double treatment approach, featuring parent group counseling and child group counseling, would show greater constructive behavior change than those children in the double treatment approach featuring teacher group counseling and child group counseling.

Results of the analysis of covariance design as applied to the California Test of Personality, Gronlund's Sociometric Questionnaire, and the Stilwell-Santoro Behavior Checklist, necessitated rejection of this hypothesis. It was hypothesized (H_4) that the children in the three experimental groups would show greater increase of acceptance by peers than the children in the control group. Results of the analysis of covariance design as applied to the California Test of Personality, Gronlund's Sociometric Questionnaire, and the Stilwell-Santoro Behavior Checklist, necessitated rejection of this hypothesis. It was hypothesized (H_5) that the children in the double treatment approach, featuring teacher group counseling and child group counseling, would show greater increase of acceptance by peers than children in the single treatment approach or children in the double treatment approach featuring parent group counseling and child group counseling. Results of the analysis of covariance design as applied to the California Test of Personality, Gronlund's Sociometric Questionnaire, and the Stilwell-Santoro Behavior Checklist, necessitated rejection of this hypothesis. It was hypothesized (H_6) that the children in the double treatment approach, featuring parent group counseling and child group counseling, would show greater increase of acceptance by peers than the children in the single treatment approach. Results of the analysis of covariance design as applied to the California Test of Personality, Gronlund's Sociometric Questionnaire, and the Stilwell-Santoro Behavior Checklist, necessitated rejection of this hypothesis. Order no. 75-14, 223, DAI.

2228.   Likins, T. R. "An Exploratory Study of the Cooperation on Low Achieving Junior High School Students." Ed.D. Dissertation, Stanford University. Dissertation Abstracts International, 34 (1-A), 93-94. Order no. 73-15,008, 1973.

This study is addressed to the question of what can be done for the low achieving student in our public schools. At the outset of this study we contended that low achieving students are victims of their own expectations or failure. These students have been conditioned by years of experience with the school and their parents to accept this expectation. Twenty 8th grade students were selected on the basis of their record of poor achievement to participate in the Cooperative Class. The class met four hours a day for the Spring semester of 1972. Credit was given for Social Studies, Math, English and Physical Education. It was hypothesized that the Cooperative Class would result in a number of measurable changes in the students involved. 1) Class participation level would increase. 2) Class activity level would increase. 3) Academic self-concept would improve. 4) Achievement level would increase. 5) Consensus concerning academic "goodness" would decrease. To establish comparative judgement criteria for academic self-concept and achievement level, two control groups were established. A Non-Treatment Equivalent Group of similar students in the traditional class and an Alternative Treatment Group of low achievers in a contained classroom. Participation and activity levels were measured periodically as process variables in the Cooperative Class only. Consensus of academic "goodness" was measured by questionnaire in the last week of the semester. Results indicated that: 1) Class participation level did not increase. It did however maintain an unusually high level of involvement for the entire semester. 2) Class activity level did not increase. Rather, it kept a consistent very high level for the semester, peaking in the last few weeks. 3) Academic Self-Concept as a class improved significantly when compared to either control group. 4) Achievement level increased significantly in each area tested. 5) Consensus concerning academic "goodness" was nearly identical to the data collected by Hoffman in traditional classes.

2229.   Lillenfield, B. M. "Teacher Identification of Children with School-Related Problems: Predictive Validity Six Years Later." Ed.D. Dissertation, Rutgers University The State University of New Jersey. Dissertation Abstracts International, 36 (10-A), 6557. Order no. 76-8698, 1976.

In February 1967, as part of a state of New Jersey early identification procedure, teachers of grades K-6 of the public schools of "Fairview" (a pseudonym for a racially and socially diverse industrial suburb, population 30,000) filled out an idenficiation card (referred to as IDF-NF) on each child in their classroom, described any persistent problem(s) then experienced by the student and coded such problems into the area(s) of functioning affected, i.e., academic, behavioral, physical, or their multiples, defined in the study as an academic problem combined with a behavioral and/or physical problem. Teachers wrote "no problem" on the cards of children believed not to be then experiencing persistent difficulties. IDF-NJ cards were collected, briefly perused by child study team members, and placed in storage where they remained until the present researcher, at the time a doctoral student in school psychology, received in July 1972, permission from school authorities to follow up the later school outcomes of children coded differentially by their teachers in 1966-67. Major null hypotheses were as follows: a) no difference in academic outcomes in June 1967 among children coded differentially in February 1967, b) no difference in academic outcomes in June 1973 among children coded differentially in February 1967, and c) no difference in behavioral outcomes in June 1973 among children coded differentially in February 1967. After a year long data search, 396 (65%) of the original 611 February 1967 problem group students and 411 (64%) of the original 638 control group (equated by race and sex to the February 1967 problem group) were found either to be still enrolled or to have dropped out of the Fairview schools. Ratios of boys to girls and white students to black students were approximately 2:1 in the problem and control groups separately in February 1967 and in June 1973. With the exception of kindergarten codings, all null hypotheses were rejected at p .001 for various grade level groupings and race and sex subgroups. Children with behavioral problems of a nonaggressive nature not combined with academic problems, and children with physical problems not combined with academic problems had academic outcomes 6½ years later similar to control group children.

2230.   Lillenstein, H. P. "Modality: Its Relationship to Behavior and Self-Concept. Ph.D. Dissertation, State University of New York at Buffalo. Dissertation Abstracts International, 39 (3-A), 1343. Order no. 7817058, 1978.

The primary purposes of this research investigation were to study the factors of self-concept and overt behavior and to correlate these factors with children's modes of perceptualization (modalities) and the modality stimulation provided by the classroom teachers. The sample of children used in the study was drawn from the population of first and third grade students in a large centralized school district's elementary school. First and third grade students who had greater proficiency in visual tests were designated as Visual Learners, those who had greater proficiency on auditory tests were designated as Auditory Learners, and those who showed no preference or greater proficiency on either visual or auditory tests were designated as Multimodal Learners. It was hypothesized that there would be correlations between self-concept and modality preference, between overt behavior and modality preference, between first and third graders of like modality preference, and linear relationships between overt behavior and self-concept for children of like modality preference and between children's modality preferences and the modality of the classroom. The major hypotheses proposing the effect of modality preference upon the criterion variables of self-concept and overt behavior were not supported. The results of the analyses of the data on the major hypotheses demonstrated that there were no significant differences across modality groups or grade levels on either of the two variables under investigation. The major hypotheses proposing relationships between the two criterion variables and the relationship between the criterion variables and the modality of the classroom were supported. The results of the analyses of the data demonstrated that there was a significant relationship between overt behavior and self-concept for children showing a preference for auditory modality, but not for visual modality preference children, and a significant relationship between the variables when the children's modalities matched the modality to the classroom.

2231.   Ling, M. S. "A Study of Classroom Behaviors Constrasting the Behavior of Children With Auditory and Visual Screening Ability With the Behavior of Children With Poor Screening Ability in Grades One Through Six." Ed.D. Dissertation, Oregon State University, 1976.

The purpose of this study was to compare classroom behaviors of students whose tests indicate high average or better figure-ground discrimination skills with those learners whose figure-ground discrimination skills were rated as low average or less. Auditory and/or visual problem and nonproblem groups were formed on the basis of scores on the Goldman, Fristoe, Woodcock Test of Auditory Discrimination and the Children's Embedded Figures Test. Behaviors were rated on the Devereux Elementary School Behavior Rating Scale. One hundred and ninety-six students were tested in this study. Ten teachers rated the classroom learning behaviors of each student in their respective classrooms. It was concluded, that the ability to screen visually greatly enhanced the acquisition of comprehension learning behaviors at grade levels three, four, five and six. Students who had visual screening problems relied on external factors for assistance significantly more often than did the non-problem group. Intermediate level students who had auditory screening problems were significantly more often than did the non-problem group. Intermediate level students who had aduitory screening problems were significantly more often a part of classroom distrubance and of disrespect and defiance than the non-problem group.

2232.   Loeber, M. S. "The Relationship Between Classification and Consequences of Student Behavior in Three Primary Classrooms." Ph.D. Dissertation, Queen's University at Kingston. Dissertation Abstracts International, 40 (5-B), 2373-2374U. 1979.

The present study was designed to explore the effect of the use of students' and teachers' own classification of behavior for the analysis of observational data. In each of three primary grade classrooms the behavior of three target students and their teachers were coded sequentially. Every 6 seconds the behavior of a target student and teacher were noted. A total of 72 hours of observational data was collected. The classifications by the students and teachers were compared in order to arrive at an index of agreement on the classification of behaviors both among the teachers and also between student and teacher. The observational data were used for two purposes. First, the data gave information about rates of behaviors in classrooms. The broad spectrum, ecological approach afforded comparisons between the rates of different student and teacher behaviors. Second, the observational data were analyzed using both the student's and the teacher's classification. Probabilities and conditional probabilities were derived from these analyses. The conditional probabilities of teacher behavior given student behavior were examined for the purpose of establishing whether the teacher responded differentially to various classes of student behavior. It was also determined to what extent the student's classification of his own behaviors was related to the teacher's classification of those behaviors and to what extent it was related to the teacher behaviors that followed the student behaviors. The

results of the study support the use of individual, as
opposed to single, uniform classification systems. The
agreement on the classification of behaviors among teachers
and between teacher and student was low. Rates of behavior
found to be of interest were the following: on average, the
teacher was not involved with the target student 71% of the
time. The teacher's noninvolvement tended to serve as a
discriminative stimulus for the student's undesirable
behavior. Teacher approval rates and rates of teacher
behavior directed exclusively to the target student were
also related to the rates of undesirable student behavior.

2233.   Loehfelm, Elizabeth E. "Rates of Classroom Behaviors by
Sex Compared to Teacher Approval/Disapproval Rates." Ph.D.
Dissertation, Columbia University, 1975. Dissertation
Abstracts International, 35 (10-B), 5085-5086.

Teacher comments and pupil behaviors were observed and
recorded to answer the following questions: 1) When teacher
comments are recorded and analyzed, do teachers respond
differently with approval and disapproval to boys' behavior
than to girls' behavior, as was found by Waters? 2) When
pupil behaviors are recorded and analyzed, a. what types of
pupil behaviors occur in the calssroom? b. what is the
frequency of these pupil behaviors? 3) What are the actual
schedules of presumed reinforcement used by the teachers for
each behavior? 4) How do these reinforcement rates relate
to the frequency of the behavior? 5) Do the frequency of
these behaviors and the schedules of reinforcement vary with
the sex of the child? Fifteen teachers, five in each of the
first, third, and fifth grades, were observed using the
Teacher Approval/Disapproval Observation Record (TAD). Each
teacher was observed for three 20 minute periods, and
teacher approvals and disapprovals were recorded, as was the
sex of the pupil(s) to whom the comment was directed. When
computing rates of approval and disapproval per observed
minute it was found that over grade boys received more
disapproval than did girls (p. .05). There were no significant differences in rates of approval. Rates of approval
decreased as grade level increased whereas rates of disapproval showed very little variation with grade level.
Ninety pupils were observed; three boys and three girls
randomly chosen from each of the fifteen classrooms used
during the first part of the study. Each pupil was observed
for nine five-minute intervals extending over four days, and
all overt pupil behaviors that were observed were recorded
on the Timeline Pupil Behavior Observation Instrument.
Teacher approvals and disapprovals given to the pupils
observed during an observation interval were also recorded.
When pupil behaviors were compared across grade levels, it
was found that on-task learning behaviors and instruction-
oriented on/off task behaviors increased with grade level,
and pupil behaviors conflicting with learning, as well as
all other categories of behavior, decreased with grade
level. Boys and girls were found to have the same frequencies of behavior across all categories of behavior. Teacher

rates of approval and disapproval expressed in terms of a ratio to number of pupil behaviors showed the rates of presumed reinforcement to be very low. It was concluded that teacher approval and disapproval were not being used differentially for boys and girls. It was also concluded that teacher approvals and disapprovals are being used in response to pupil behaviors rather than as an effective means of classroom management.

2234.   Long, James D. "The Comparative Utility of Structured Lessons, Group and Individually Contingent Events, and Conditioned Reinforcers in Modifying Classroom Behaviors." Ed.D.   Dissertation,   The   University   of   Tennessee. Dissertation Abstracts International, 33 (5-A), 2173-2174. Order no. 72-27,482, 1972.

A major purpose of the study was to assess the relative merits of group versus individually contingent consequences in modifying the classroom behavior of adolescents. Other major purposes were to determine whether student conduct would improve with the implementation of structured lessons and to ascertain whether improvements would occur with the awarding of points as a consequence for appropriate behavior without the use of backup reinforcers. Eight students in an inner-city seventh grade classroom of 32 blacks served as the subjects. They were selected by the teacher as the most disruptive students who were in regular attendance. The eight subjects and the teacher were observed daily for 60 days in math and for 67 days in geography. Treatments were applied successively in math and geography, and, except for the final phase in geography, a session in one class always corresponded to a session in the other class period. Every treatment condition in math yielded statistically higher levels of appropriate student behavior than the baseline. Both the structured lessons and points phases resulted in increased percentages of appropriate classroom behaviors, but their power to modify student behaviors enough to estab- lish a semblance of effective classroom control was not demonstrated.

2235.   Lowman, B. C. "The Identification and Modification of Classroom Behavior Associated with Internal and External Loci of Control Among Fourth Grade Students." Ph.D. Dissertation, The University of North Carolina at Chapel Hill.   Dissertation Abstracts International, 36 (6-A), 3517-3518. Order no. 75-29,048, 1975.

This study was designed to investigate two questions: 1) what student classroom behaviors are associated with having an internal or external locus of control orientation and 2) can the classroom behaviors of external children be changed by means of weekly goal-setting conferences with their teacher. Each of these questions was investigated in separate studies. Differences in classroom behavior between internals and externals, blacks and whites, and males and females were examined in the first study. Behavioral differences between a group of external black females who participated in goal-setting conferences and a group who did not were investigated in the second study. In the first study, fourth graders were identified as very internal or external by the Intellectual Achievement Responsibility scale. A behavioral rating system for making classroom observations was then developed for use in this study. First, ten internal and ten external children were observed for thirty minutes each while engaged in structured learning activities. Analyses of these observations resulted in a nineteen-category behavioral rating system divided into three major areas, autonomous, teacher-related and peer-related behavior. Results of the first study are as follows: 1) With respect to the ratings of the nineteen behavioral categories: a) externals and internals differ significantly in terms of their classroom behavior, b) the sexes do not differ, c) the races do not differ, d) there is a significant locus of control-sex interaction in terms of the classroom behavior. 2) With respect to percentages of total time spent in autonomous, teacher-peer-related activities, there are no significant differences between internals and externals, the sexes, or the races. 3) Internals exhibit significantly (p .001) more continuous, task-oriented behavior than externals. The effect holds across sex and race groups. In the second study the goal-setting procedures involved one teacher with one student in a half-hour weekly conference in which they discussed and selected behavior and achievement goals for the student to concentrate on for the coming week. The student's progress during the week past was also reviewed. The effects of this goal-setting on these children was compared to the effects of no treatment on an equal number of children by means of a multivariate analysis of variance carried out on each of the following dependent variables: 1) the percentage of total classroom time spent in the four behavioral categories which differentiated internals and externals, 2) the percentages of total time spent in the other fifteen categories of behavior, and 3) the percentage of total time spent in autonomous, teacher-and peer-related activity. Results of the second study are as follows: 1) With respect to the four categories of behavior which best differentiate internals and externals, the goal-setting group changed significantly more than the control group in three of the four categories. 2) With respect to the other fifteen behavioral categories, there are no differences between the treatment and control group. 3) With respect to the percentages of total time spent in autonomous, teacher- and peer-related activity, the treatment and control groups do not differ.

2236.   Luster, June T.   "The Effect of Classroom Management Training on the Interactive Process of Student Teachers and Pupils." Ph.D. Dissertation, University of Pittsburgh, 1980. Dissertation Abstracts International, 41 (8-A), 3537. Order no. 8028114.

The purpose of this study was to investigate the relationships among process variables occurring in the classrooms of student teachers who participated in a training program in classroom management. The process variables specified aspects of the student teacher-pupil classroom relationships concerning: a) student teachers' Pupil Control Ideology (PCI); b) frequency of pupil off-task behavior; and c) frequency of classroom management strategies utilized by student teachers during the practicum experience. Classroom Management Training sessions emphasized theory and application of management techniques through: a) observing classroom behaviors; b) simulating classroom interaction, and c) implementing management strategies when in the unique setting of the classroom. Twelve student teacher participants were involved in this study. Six pairs of student teachers from an eastern, urban university who chose inner city practicum schools were equally divided into experimental and control groups. Student teachers from both groups experienced two practicums in different grade placements during a 15 week semester. Subjects were placed in experimental and control groups on the basis of classroom assignment of the practicum experience. There was one student teacher from the experimental and one from the control group in the same classroom at different time intervals. Through this design the variables of cooperating teacher and pupils were held constant. A pre-post test with treatment and control design was used with student teachers from three elementary schools in one inner city school district. The Pupil Control Ideology (PCI) From was selected to measure attitudes of student teachers toward pupils on a custodial-humanism continuum. Higher scores indicated individuals with a more custodial pupil control orientation while lower scores inferred a more humanistic control orientation. The second type of instrument used to analyze the effect of treatment was direct observation of both student teachers and pupils in student teacher directed classrooms. The third type of data collected was from interviews with both groups of student teachers involved in this study. The experimental group began Classroom Management Training during their first two weeks as student teachers. Participants met one afternoon each week at a central location for two hours. The results of this study support the need for direct training in classroom management for pre-service teachers. Heretofore, ways of dealing with pupil misbehavior has been left up to "trial and error" learning for student teachers. The rationale behind this approach seems to be that management of pupil behaviors is an "individual's personal decision." Consequently, student teachers in their first classroom experience may practice ineffective management strategies. Since the purpose of student teaching is for students to simulate the role of the teacher, those behaviors practiced during that time are likely to be repeated in the future. Therefore, this study highlights the need for teacher education programs to offer a systematic approach to classroom management in the development of professional educators.

2237.   McDermott, Raymond P.   "Kids Make Sense: An Ethnographic
Account   of   the   Interactional   Management   of   Success   and
Failure   in   one   First-Grade   Classroom."   Ph.D.   Dissertation,
Stanford   University.   Dissertation   Abstracts   International,
38 (3-A), 1505.   Order no. 77-18,265, 1977.

The bulk of the dissertation consists of a detailed description of the moment-to-moment interactional behavior of two
groups of children sitting around a table with a teacher in
a first-grade classroom.   Their behavior was recorded on
videotape on one day in May, 1974 and was transferred later
onto 16mm film for more precise viewing.   Both groups are
involved in what they call reading lessons.   One group is
considered the top group; it is made up of children who are
successfully learning how to read and who are behaving in
ways the teacher regards as proper.   The other group is the
bottom group; it is made up of children who are having
difficulties learning to read and who are constantly in
trouble with the teacher.   In everyday terms, the children
in the top group are orderly and bright and the children in
the bottom group are disorderly and not so bright.   The
detailed description of the participants' activities successfully demonstrates 1) that there is equivalent order and
regularity in the behavior of both groups, 2) that this
order represents an active accomplishment on the parts of
all involved, and 3) that this accomplishment of order, no
matter how institutionally regressive, can be understood in
terms of an effort on everyone's part to make sense in
common with others around them.   Thus, the dissertation
attempts to document how both failing and successful children and their teacher make sense.   Accordingly, it should
raise doubts about the institutional assumptions which force
us to sort young children into such categories as successful
and failing.

2238.   McEwen, J. H.   "An Examination of the Effects of
Manipulating Instructional Objectives and Choice of Study
Methods in the Behavior of Secondary School Students."
Ed.D.   Dissertation,   The   University   of   Tennessee.
Dissertation Abstracts International, 33 (8-A), 4181-4182.
Order no. 73-2473, 1973.

The present research was designed to examine the effects of
communicated instructional objectives and of choice of study
methods in reaching those objectives as a means of changing
the behavior of disruptive students.   Primary questions to
be answered were: (1) would students study more in class,
complete more work and make better grades when explicit
objectives were given to them; and (2) would appropriate
behavior and academic achievement increase if students were
permitted to choose the method of study they wanted to use
in reaching instructional objectives.   This design permitted
the analysis of the effects of instructional objectives and
of choice of study methods on the target students' classroom
behaviors, test scores, and number of pages completed in the
textbook.

2239.   McKeown, D. O., Jr.   "Generalization to the Classroom of Principles of Behavior Modification Taught to Groups of Teachers."   Ph.D.   Dissertation, University of Georgia. Dissertation Abstracts International, 34 (6-B), 2943-2944. Order no. 73-31, 925, 1973.

The present study investigated the effectiveness of several methods of instructing teachers in principles of behavior modification.   Twenty teachers were matched and assigned to four conditions: 1) teachers who participated in a labora- tory group, as well as receiving a written manual; 2) teachers who participated only in the laboratory group; 3) teachers who received only written manual and; 4) teachers who did not receive either source of information.   The groups were evaluated on their increase in knowledge and on the decrease of disruptive behaviors in the classroom.   With regard to an increase in knowledge, subjects who partici- pated in a laboratory group increased knowledge compared to subjects who did not participate in a laboratory group.   A significant interaction suggested that group participation plus a written manual was superior to group participation or a manual alone, both of which were superior to the control group.   The analysis of disruption in theacher's classrooms indicated a significant decrease in disruptive behavior. However, a significant interaction indicated that this change was due largely to a decrease in disruptive behavior in the classrooms of teachers who had participated in a laboratory group on behavior modification principles. Further, there were moderate to high correlations between increase in knowledge and decrease in disruptions.

2240.   McKinley, Wayne E.   "Attitudes and Perceptions of Attitudes Toward the Disciplinary Behaviors of Teachers and Administrators   Within   a   Selected   School."   Ph.D. Dissertation,   Northwestern   University.   Dissertation Abstracts International, 35 (10-A), 6401-6402.   Order no. 75-7955, 1975.

The primary research questions addressed during this study were: Do intergroup differences exist within a selected school in attitudes toward the disciplinary behaviors of teachers and administrators?   Are there varying perceptions by groups of the attitudes of other groups toward the disci- plinary behaviors of teachers?   Significant differences were predicted on the basis of role-set and attribution theory. Further purposes of the study were: 1) To analyze and explain significant intergroup differences, or the lack of them, in attitudes and perceptions of attitudes; 2) To describe and analyze group beliefs within the school about specific disciplinary practices; 3) To predict the theoret- ical impact of the findings of the study upon the school organization as a social system.   As predicted, discrepan- cies were found between groups in attitudes and perceptions of attitudes toward disciplinary behaviors.   Somewhat unexpectedly, attitudinal discrepancies were more numerous than incongruities in perceptions of attitudes.   One notable

attitudinal difference was that the typical teacher supported his own disciplinary behaviors significantly more
than he supported the disciplinary behaviors of other
teachers. The attitudes of groups were in general perceived
quite accurately; this is especially true in relation to
perceptions of the attitude of students. The major exception to the genral case of keen perception was that pupil
personnel services staff members were perceived to be more
closely aligned with teachers and administrators than with
students in their attitude toward the disciplinary behaviors
of teachers; this perception is false.

2241.   McLaughlin, R. E. "Behaviorally Oriented Techniques for
the Remediation of Academic Underachievement in High
Potential Intermediate School Students." Ed.D.
Dissertation, The Pennsylvania State University.
Dissertation Abstracts International, 37 (11-A), 7046.
Order no. 77-9773, 1977.

The study was designed to investigate if high potential,
underachieving boys in a private, residential school could
be helped by either or both of two remediation programs
utilizing behavior modification techniques. More specifically, the problem was to determine if these brief, uncomplicated, and inexpensive procedures could induce significant
improvements in the subjects' 1) achievement related
behaviors in the classroom and student home, 2) self-
concepts, 3) attitudes toward achievement, 4) personality
traits' scores, 5) achievement test scores, and 6) grade
point averages (GPA's). Eighty high potential (IQ 110 or
greater) underachieving (GPA 2.4 or worse) sixth through
ninth grade students were randomly assigned to one of four
groups. These four groups were then randomly assigned to
one of four experimental conditions. Group One was a no
treatment control. Group Two was an attention placebo
control. Group Three was a treatment condition in which the
subjects' teachers and houseparents were taught, in four
one-hour sessions, how to 1) analyze the students' achievement patterns, 2) strengthen and increase achievement
promoting behaviors, and 3) weaken and decrease achievement
interfering behaviors. Group Four was a treatment condition
in which the subjects' teachers and houseparents were
exposed to the same program as in Group Three. The criteria
measures were: 1) GPA's, 2) achievement test scores
(Stanford), 3) self-concept scores (Piers-Harris), 4)
achievement attitude scores (experimenter designed), 5)
personality traits; evaluations (experimenter designed), and
6) behavior ratings in the classroom and student home
(experimenter designed). The results of this study suggest
that, in the private school, during the course of one school
year, behavior modification techniques can be employed to
significantly improve (.05 level) high potential under-
achievers' 1) self-concepts and attitudes toward achievement, 2) achievement related behaviors in the classroom and
student home, 3) grade point averages. The data indicate
that the students' self-concepts and attitudes toward

achievement can be changed significantly by the psychologist working exclusively with the teachers and houseparents (Group Three); however, to bring about statistically significant improvements in the subjects' GPA's requires the added dimension of the psychologist working directly with the students in small groups (Group Four). It was also found that while significant improvement in specific target behaviors associated with underachievement can be induced by the psychologist teaching behavior modification techniques to the subjects' teachers and houseparents, even greater improvements are accrued when, in addition, behavioral counseling is provided to the students. The results suggest that working directly with underachieveing students, as well as their teachers and houseparents, is justifiable even though this dual approach requires over double the psychologist's time.

2242.   McMillan, Richard K. "The Effects of a Personality Improvement Program Upon the Self-Concepts, Attitudes Toward Others, and Personality Characteristics of School Incorrigibles." Ph.D. Dissertation, The University of Michigan. Dissertation Abstracts International, 33 (9-A), 4845. Order no. 73-6874, 1973.

The purpose of this study was to explore the effectiveness of a recently inaugurated educational program for school incorrigibles that had been developed and implemented in Flint, Michigan, in terms of changes in self-concept, attitudes toward others, and personality characteristics. The program which was selected was the Personality Improvement Program (PIP) which was a joint effort of the Flint Community Schools and the Genesee County Probate Court. PIP was designed as a behavioral modification program that tried to alleviate the chronic behavioral and/or truancy problems of school incorrigibles by placing them in a day-care treatment center for six weeks and then providing support services for six additional weeks after the students were returned to their regular schools. PIP was seen as producing positive results upon the subjects for a short period of time.

2243.   Margeson, Carol I. "A Comparison of Aggression and Perception of Aggression in Self and Others: A Study of Negro and White Third Grade Students in Integrated and Segregated Schools Settings in the Rural South." Ph.D. Dissertation, University of North Carolina at Chapel Hill. Dissertation Abstracts International, 35 (1-B), 484. Order no. 74-15,365, 1974.

This study compared the classroom aggression of Negro and white third-graders in integrated and segregated classrooms in a southern rural community. Since southern Negroes have been described as passive and self-abnegating, it was anticipated that Negroes would be less aggressive than whites. This pattern holds in segregated classrooms, but in newly integrated settings, it is breaking down: integrated

Negroes were reported to be more aggressive than integrated
whites. Traditional sex-role patterns did not break down:
Negro and white boys were reported to be more aggressive
than their female counterparts. Negroes and whites reacted
differentially to classroom settings. Negroes appeared to
interpret segregation as punishing, and reacted with low
levels of aggression and little freedom of expression.
Conversely, whites appeared to interpret segregation as a
sign of their superiority, and felt comfortable enough to
react with freedom of expression, including expression of
aggression. Negroes interpreted integration as a sign of
improved status, and responded with high levels of aggression and a good deal of individual variability in behavior,
whereas whites interpreted being placed in classrooms with
low caste, low class Negroes as punishing and reacted with
strikingly low levels of aggression and very little
individual variability in behavior. In integrated classrooms, the highly aggrressive, low class Negroes provided
their middle class white classmates with examples of how not
to behave. Integrated Negroes appear to enjoy a sense of
freedom of expression in a social situation that is
historically new for them in the south.

2244.   Marholin, D. "The Development of Independent Social and
Academic Behaviors in an Elementary Classroom." Ph.D.
Dissertation, University of Illinois at Urbana-Champaign.
Dissertation Abstracts International, 36 (9-B), 4735. Order
no. 76-6855, 1976.

Eight 5th and 6th grade behavior-problem children in one
public elementary school classroom performed various
academic tasks during baseline and two reinforcement conditions: 1) reinforcement for being on task and nondisruptive, and 2) reinforcement for the accuracy and rate of
their academic work itself. The design of the experiment
constituted an ABCBC individual-subject analysis in which
each child was sequentially exposed to a baseline period (A)
followed by a series of ontask (b) and academic reinforcement (c) conditions. Following each of these conditions,
the teacher was absent for a portion of each session (probe
conditions) for 3 successive days. In the teacher's
absence, on-task behavior was markedly reduced and disruptive and neutral behaviors were markedly increased, regardless of the reinforcement condition in operation. In addition, the teacher's absence resulted in a marked reduction
in academic accuracy and rate during baseline and both
reinforcement conditions. The observed difference between
the two reinforcement conditions was especially prevalent
between the second presentations of both reinforcement
conditions. In a similar manner, a greater number of
problems were attempted in the teacher's absence during both
conditions in which accuracy and rate of academic performance were being reinforced than the two conditions in which
on-task behavior alone was being reinforced. In contrast,
the two different reinforcement contingencies had no differential effect on academic accuracy in the teacher's absence.

2245.   Marino, M. F. "The Effectiveness of Teacher-Centered
Versus Case-Centered Consultation in the Reduction of
Classroom Management Errors and Negative Classroom Behavior
of Students." Ph.D. Dissertation, Temple University.
Dissertation Abstracts International, 36 (12-A), 7956.
Order no 76-12,016, 1976.

This study compared teachers, who received consultation in
classroom management, and teachers, who received consultation in the diagnosis and remediation of a referred student.
The first purpose was to determine whether providing
teachers with consultation in classroom management resulted
in a significant mean decrease in management errors. The
second purpose was to determine whether a change in the
managing behavior of the teachers resulted in a significant
mean decrease in the negative classroom behavior of the
students. Fifty first- through sixth-grade teachers were
randomly selected (N = 137), 25 being randomly assigned to
the teacher-centered consultation group and performed a
psychodiagnostic evaluation of a referred student from the
class of each teacher assigned to the case-centered consultation group. The teachers received "consulting or evaluation" time for 5-weeks, 1-1/2 hours per week. (1) There was
no significant pre-treatment difference between the teacher-
centered and case-centered consultation group. (2-3) The
differences between both the pre- and post- and pre- and
follow-up-observation results indicated that the group and
observation main effects were not significant and that the
interaction effects were significant. Analyses of both
significant interaction effects, using the Morrison Post-Hoc
Test (1967), indicated that the mean decreased in withitness, overlapping, and total number of classroom management
errors were significant. (4) The differences between the
post- and follow-up-observation results indicated that the
group and observation main effects were not significant and
that the interaction effect was significant. However,
analysis of the significant interaction effect, using the
Morrison Post-Hoc Test (1967), indicated that there were no
significant mean decreases for any of the dependent measures
considered separately. Teacher-centered consultation was an
effective technique for significantly reducing the mean
frequency of withitness, overlapping, and total number of
classroom management errors. Therefore, the teachers'
improved their ability to (a) select correct deviancy
targets and do something about the deviancy before it became
more serious or began to spread to other children; and (b)
recognize and deal with two issues simultaneously when two
different issues were concurrently present.

2246.   Marotto, R. A. "Posin' To Be Chosen: An Ethographic
Study of Ten Lower Class Black Male Adolescents in an Urban
High School." Ed.D. Dissertation, State University of New
York at Buffalo. Dissertation Abstracts International, 39
(3-A), 1234-1235E. Order no. 7814236, 1978.

The investigation described the way a group of ten lower class black male adolescents, the "Boulevard Brothers," behaved in an urban public high school, "Verland," explained the way their behavior affected themselves, the teachers and administrators, and the entire school organization, and then developed an understanding of why these black males behaved the way that they did. Data was collected primarily through participant observation, extensive interviews, and supplemented with written documentation. The descriptions were gathered during a seven month period in which the researcher attended Verland High School daily, associated himself with the Boulevard Brothers, attended some classes, ate in the cafeteria, "hung out" in the halls, and took part in their informal corridor activity. The Brothers accepted him on the basis of his actions, and it made little difference to them that he was a white former teacher. In the lexicon of a Brother, most of his school day was spent "cuttin' classes, stayin' in the cafeteria, and hangin' in the hall 'posin' to be chosen' to show 'what he is about,' 'n it's all 'bout bein' a 'real live nigger'". Academically phrased, while in school the Boulevard Brothers developed a perspective of non involvement with the general academic structure of the organization. They seemed to prefer peer-involvement to academic activities and deliberately <u>chose</u> to <u>flout</u> the school's rules in order to establish and participate in a <u>class cutting routine</u>. This indigenous routine afforded the Brothers the time to act out a streetcorner behavior repertoire or life style that brought them recognition and enhanced their reputation in the eyes of their peers. It was suggested that the tendency of the Boulevard Brothers to maintain a close-knit, in school group that exhibited a street corner life style within an established class cutting routine was a natural consequence of the school's basic organizational structure and the streetcorner frame of reference utilized by the Brothers to deal with that structure. Specifically, the school denies students freedom, masses and fails to differentiate them, and keeps them powerless; whereas the group's streetcorner frame of reference motivates the Brothers to develop a style that will bring them recognition, differentiation, and emulation. This style is conveyed through dress, demeanor, and the effective use of words (i.e., "gamin'"). The Brother's effective use of words shows him to be in verbal control, and by extension, in control of the social setting -- the school. Thus, the Brothers; streetcorner perspective allows the school to become a proving grounds for ghetto talents. In sum, the Brothers' anomalous class cutting routine preserves the group's informal structure and gains for them and their ghetto streetcorner-oriented peers the recognition or status denied by Verland's formal organization. As a result, the Brothers "lose by winning." They win the status conferred by their peers, but lose out on the formal instruction articulated by their teachers.

2247.   Martin, L. S. "An Investigation of Pupil Control Ideology and Personality Characteristics of High and Low Achieving Pupils." Ph.D. Dissertation, The University of Connecticut. Dissertation Abstracts International, 33 (9-A), 5571-5572. Order no. 77-4285, 1977.

The purpose of this study was to determine if an interaction between teacher style and certain noncognitive dimensions of students is related to pupil achievement outcomes. Briefly, the variables under examination were the following: 1) Pupil Control Ideology (PCI): The degree to which the teacher believes that control must be exercised over the behavior and learning of the students (Willower, 1967). 2) Dependence-Proneness: The degree to which students rely on teacher direction, supervision and support in their work (Flanders, 1960). 3) Intellectual Achievement Responsibility (IAR): The degree to which a student believes that he is responsible for his own successes and failures in intellectual-academic achievement situations (Crandall et al., 1965). 4) Teacher Perceived Competency: A teacher judgment measure in which students are assessed as either working at capability or below capability (Martin, 1976). The problem, generally stated, is: What is the relationship of the teacher's pupil control ideology to the achievement outcomes of pupils with differing intellectual achievement responsibility orientations and dependence-proneness? Questions were addressed to the data concerning the relationships among variables, interactions between variables, and differences related to teacher and pupil characteristics. The results of this investigation did not confirm the hypothesized relationship and interaction effects of teacher control ideology and pupil personality characteristics. Conclusive findings were that: 1) Across the board, high dependent-prone pupils were high achievers based on the TPC measure (p .01). 2) Across the board, findings support other research in the area that highly internal pupils were higher achievers (IAR and TPC measures) at the .05 level of probability. 3) As measured by the IAR and dependence-proneness questionnaires, there was a high correlation between internality and dependence-proneness (p .001). 4) Analysis of teacher control ideology and demographic data revealed that age, length of time teaching, and sex were significantly related to teacher control ideology, older teachers, more experienced teachers, and males being higher scorers on the PCI (high teacher control).

2248.   Martin, Oneida L. "An Analysis of Classroom Management Behaviors Used by Selected Secondary English Teachers." Ed.D. Dissertation, The University of Tennessee. Dissertation Abstracts International, 41 (10-A), 4270. Order no. 8108160.

The purpose of this study was to determine how selected effective secondary English teachers managed classroom time, students, and materials to achieve instructional goals and objectives. The study was conducted in the Chattanooga,

Tennessee Public School District during the Spring quarter 1980. Data were collected from interviews and classroom observatinos. Two interviews were conducted with the participants, and seventy-five classes were observed. Prior to observing classes, the participants were asked five open-ended questions about classroom plans. After all classes had been observed, the participants were asked five open-ended questions about how instructional decisions are made and how management skills were acquired. Log forms were used to record verbal and physical teaching behaviors. The time of the behaviors was also recorded. Content analyses were used to analyze the data. Two instruments were designed for the purposes of identifying, coding, and analyzing instructional and managerial behaviors; identifying, coding, and analyzing how the teachers manage classroom time, students, and materials. Effective instructional and managerial behaviors obtained from the literature review were the criteria used. Two people were trained to identify and code the behaviors from the narrative logs. The researcher analyzed the data. Some of the major findings of the research were: 1) planning, organizing, decisionmaking, mantaining, and disciplining were the management skills most often used by the teachers; 2) the management skills were used to present instructional tasks and activities and create and maintain an academic learning environment; 3) the management skills were also used to manage classroom time, students, and materials; 4) the teachers were not aware that behaviors were managerial; 5) students also used management skills, and 6) basic skills such as planning, organizing, and decision-making can be acquired through preservice and inservice education programs.

2249.   Marwell, B. E. "Responsiveness to Social Reinforcement and Learning Under Two Reinforcement Conditions." Ph.D. Dissertation, The University of Wisconsin-Madison. Dissertation Abstracts International, 36 (8-A), 5153-5154. Order no. 75-19,082, 1976.

The efficacy of using token-tangible reinforcers to improve the performance of children who are both low performers and low in responsiveness to social reinforcement was tested on 80 second-grade children in a small-town Wisconsin school. It was hypothesized that for some children who are performing poorly in school, lack of appropriate reinforcers, rather than lack of ability is a major problem. Identification of children who are not responsive to social reinforcement and introduction of other (tangible) reinforcers, was predicted to improve performance. The experiment testing these assumptions involved: 1) classification of subjects as high, medium or low in responsiveness to social reinforcement (RSR); 2) baseline measure of task performance under social reinforcement (Paired Associates I); and 3) measure of task performance under token-tangible reinforcement (Paired Associates II). Sixty subjects comprised the experimental group. Responsiveness to social reinforcement was measured using the two-hole marble dropping task, where the experimenter attempted to change the subject's preference for one of two holes through the use of social reinforcement. Subjects were classified as high, medium or low RSR. The paired associates tasks were two experimenter designed eight-pair lists, with numerals as stimulus items and pictures of common objects as response items. PA tasks were used because of evidence indicating their relationship with school achievement. The major findings were: 1) no generality of social reinforcer effects across the two experimental tasks, RSR and PA I; 2) no relationship between RSR and school achievement, as had been suggested in the literature; 3) correlations between PA tasks and school achievement were uniformly low, in contrast to Stevenson's early findings of moderate, significant relationships and corroborating other recent evidence on the lack of relationship between these variables; 4) a correlation of .26 (p .05) was found between IQ and the second PA task.

2250.   Matthews, D. B. "The Effects of Reality Therapy on Reported Self-Concept, Social Adjustment, Reading Achievement, and Discipline of Fourth and Fifth Graders in Two Elementary Schools." Ph.D. Dissertation, University of South Carolina. Dissertation Abstracts International, 33 (9-A), 4842-4843. Order no. 73-3606, 1973.

The purpose of this investigation was to explore a method in the affective domain, Reality Therapy or classroom meetings, and to study its effects on reported self-concept, social adjustment, reading achievement, and discipline. Only a relatively small amount of research is available on techniques for teachers to use in the affective domain. The following research hypotheses were tested: 1) Classes of students who participate in Reality Therapy for four months will score significantly higher (p .05) on Personal Adjustment (self-concept) of the California Test of Personality than similar classes of students who participate in the open language arts program. 2) Classes of students who participate in Reality Therapy for four months will score significantly higher (p .05) on Social Adjustment of the California Test of Personality than similar classes of students who participate in the open language arts program. 3) Classes of students who participate in Reality Therapy for four months will score significantly higher (p .05) on the Metropolitan Reading Test than similar classes of students who participate in the open language arts program. 4) Classes of students who participate in Reality Therapy for four months will score significantly lower (p .05) on the Walker Problem Behavior Identification Checklist than similar classes of students who participate in the open language arts program. The sample for the study was composed of two hundred twenty-one fourth and fifth graders. The results of the study may be summarized as follows: 1) Self-concept scores from the subtest Personal Adjustment of the California Test of Personality increased from pretest to posttest with both treatments, Reality Therapy and an open language arts period, but neither method was significantly

superior to the other, therefore, hypothesis one was not
accepted. 2) Social adjustment scores from the subtest
Social Adjustment of the California Test of Personality
decreased for both groups from pretest to posttest with
neither group showing a significant difference from the
other group; therefore, hypothesis two was not accepted. 3)
Reading achievement scores from the Metropolitan Reading
Achievement Test increased for experimental and control
groups with neither group being significantly different from
the other; therefore, hypothesis three was not accepted. 4)
The scores from the Walker Problem Behavior Checklist of the
experimental group differed from the control group for discipline at the .01 level of confidence. Reality Therapy
appeared to be a better technique for decreasing discipline
problems than the open language arts period for the experiment; therefore, hypothesis four was accepted.

2251.   Mattice, E. L. "Dreikurs' Goals of Misbehavior Theory:
Child and Teacher Generation of a Neo-Adlerian Construct."
Ed.D.   Dissertation,   The   University   of   Tennessee.
Dissertation Abstracts International, 37 (8-A), 4994. Order
no. 77-3662, 1977.

Adler's theory of personality was forwarded by Dreikurs who,
in attempting to develop specific Adlerian techniques,
modified some of Adler's concepts. Dreikurs' four goals of
misbehavior theory were discussed in this context. Child
and teacher ability to generate goals of misbehavior (via
nominal group technique), teacher methods of classifying the
statements teachers generated, and teacher and school
psychologist ability to classify goals in a Dreikurs format
plus an Other category were assessed. The intrarater
consistency and interater agreement of classification judgements was tested. In addition, three psychologists knowledgeable in the area of Individual Psychology classified
child and teacher generated statements as to their interpersonal quality and goal orientation. In all, 36 children
(6 each from grades 3,5,6,7,8, and 12), 24 elementary school
teachers, 6 school psychologists, and 3 psychologists
familiar with Adler and Dreikurs took part in this study.
Children generated 52 different statements and teachers 62.
Results indicated that although children and teachers are
able to formulate interpersonal goal statements, the task is
a difficult one, particularly for teachers. Teachers seemed
to feel that setting events and instincts were major factors
controlling children's misbehavior. Teacher agreement as to
classification of teacher generated statements within
Dreikurs' categories varied widely. The majority of school
psychologists placed the majority of statements into
categories with intrarater consistency and interrater agreement. The three psychologists familiar with Adler and
Dreikurs were in perfect agreement on approximately half of
the statements--slightly higher agreement was found on goal
status judgments than on judgments of interpersonal quality.

2252.   Mazzei, J.   "The Use of Feedback and Reinforcement in
          Controlling   Maladaptive   Classroom."   Ph.D.   Dissertation,
          West Virginia University, 1972.

          The study was designed to compare the relative efficiency of
          feedback and reinforcement techniques in dealing with overt
          motor responses which are incompatible with classroom study
          behavior. Subjects with 12 elementary school children who
          worked on arithmetic problems at their desk while their
          teacher worked in small reading groups. Behavioral observa-
          tions were reported for baseline, experimental and follow-up
          trials. The results support the major predictions based on
          Greenwald's 1970 analysis of feedback mechanisms. Negative
          feedback combined with reinforcement from maladaptive
          responses yielded significantly greater decreases in maladap-
          tive classroom behavior than did positive feedback or rein-
          forcement alone.   The difference between the divergent
          feedback and reinforcement groups during the experimental
          trials was significant as was the difference between the
          divergent feedback and positive feedback groups.

2253.   Meanor, G. C. "A Study of the Effects of a Short, Daily
          Relaxation Period on Some Important Behaviors of Secondary
          School   Students."   Ed.D.   Dissertation.   University   of
          Houston, 1978.

          The primary purpose of this study was to ascertain the
          effect of a daily, short relaxation period on the general
          anxiety level of a group of secondary school students. Also
          to be examined were the effects of this session on the
          frequency of discipline problems and the rate of absenteeism
          among the participants. Finally, the positive or negative
          reactions of the students to the process itself, indicating
          their abilities to perform the process, were observed. The
          following hypotheses were posed. A short, daily relaxation
          period incorporated into the regularly-scheduled education
          program of secondary school students will significantly
          reduce: A. the index of general anxiety, B. the number of
          disciplinary offenses serious enough for students to be sent
          to the office by the teachers, C. the number of incidences
          of days of absences of the participants, and D. the posi-
          tive or negative reactions of the participants to the relaxa-
          tion period indicating their ability to carry out the
          process will bhe significantly related to the extent of
          reduction in general anxiety, disicplinary problems, and the
          number of absences. The population consisted of a regularly-
          scheduled, high school psychology class of thirty-one
          members. The comparison group was comprised of a senior
          English class from within the same institution. Objective
          data for this study was gained by means of 1. the IPAT
          Anxiety Scale Questionnaire (ASQ), 2. the discipline cards
          on file in the assistant principals' offices, 3. the atten-
          dance records on file in the attendance office, and 4. the
          administration of The Adapted Osis Relaxation Session
          Questionniare. The investigation found no significant
          differences between treatments or groups in those areas of

concern i.e. anxiety, discipline offenses, and absentee
rates.   The   relationship   between   positive   or   negative
reactions to the process and the anxiety levels among the
participants, was statistically significant.   Although the
ANCOVA'S showed no significant difference between treatments
and groups, the means for anxiety levels of the experimental
group did decrease from a pre-test to a post-test at the end
of the treatment period, but then rose again as evidenced by
a post-post-test given six weeks after the end of the class.
Neither discipline offenses nor absentee rates abated
appreciably, but individual cases were encouraging.   Order
No. 7910529, DAI.

2254.   Miller, J. J.   "Specifying Cross-Temporal Stability and
Cross-Dimensional Causal Models for Children's Classroom
Behavior,   Interpeer   Social   Competence,   and   Level   of
Cognitive Functioning Using Longitudinal Data Obtained in
Two Replication Samples."   Ph.D. Dissertation, University of
California,   Los   Angeles.   Dissertation   Abstracts
International, 38 (6-A), 3387-3388C.   Order no. 77-25, 342,
1977.

This study examined the stability over the early elementary
school years of three latent variable dimensions, and the
cross-dimensional causal effects resulting from each latent
dimension on the other dimensions.   Using data obtained from
a large-scale longitudinal investigation which had sought
means for the early identification of young elementary-age
children with school learning problems, the study explored a
wide range of alternative causal model structures; finally
selecting and subjecting to empirical test a set of "Best-
Fitting" causal models.   There was, in general, no basis
from these analyses for the hypotheses that a child's in-
class behavior is largely a function of the child's level of
cognitive functioning.   Classroom behavior, in all four
years of these longitudinal data, was causally distinct from
a child's level of cognitive functioning.   A child's same-
year role-appropriate classroom behavior consistently had
significant causal effect on the child's school performance,
and such effects were in addition to the effects of a
child's level of cognitive functioning onto the child's
later school performance.   Thus, a child's level of cognitive functioning and the child's current class behavior were
the principal determinants of the child's later school
performance.   This study argued for a conception of
stability as the stability of causal structure over time.

2255.   Milstein, I. T.   "Socially Incompetent Behavior of
Students as Described by Their Junior and Senior High School
Teachers."   Ph.D. Dissertation, University of Oregon.
Dissertation Abstracts International, 36 (7-A), 4403-4404.
Order no. 76-957, 1976.

In 1970 a study entitled "Measures of Social Incompetency in
Adolescence: was undertaken by deJung and Edmonson (1972).
The purpose of the study was to determine how teachers

identify and describe their junior high school students as
Socially Incompetent or Socially Competent. The study
attempted to follow-up the same students into two semi-rural
senior high schools geographically near the junior high
schools of 1970. The sample consisted essentially of those
students remaining in the school system after three years.
Ninety-five students names were given in class rosters to
fifty-eight teachers in two semi-rural schools. The procedures were essentailly the same as followed by the deJung
and Edmonson Study in 1970.

2256.   Minor, John A. "Teachers' Social Reinforcement Behavior
as a Discriminative Stimulus and Emitted Social
Reinforcement Behavior of Students." Ed.D. Dissertation,
West Virginia University. Dissertation Abstracts
International, 37 (4-A), 2081-2082. Order no. 76-22,438,
1976.

This study is concerned with the way in which social interaction patterns are developed. It explores the development
of affiliative relationship; more exactly, the concept of
"emitted social reinforcement" within the teacher-student
interaction situation. The investigation proceeded from an
operant conditioning theoretical position using behavior
modification technology as a methodological base. Research
questions were: 1) Is it possible to increase the frequency
of emitted positive social reinforcement by a student to a
teacher as a function of systematic programming of a
teacher's stimulus behavior within a social interaction
situation; and 2) What are the affects of different programs
of a teacher's stimulus behavior upon the student's emitted
social behavior? The study was conducted in an experimental
reading center located in a public elementary school. In
order to isolate a standard social response which would
occur with sufficient frequency to make analysis possible, a
"fun ticket" system was introduced. Students earned fun
tickets by correctly completing exercises. The results were
as follows: 1) The giving of fun tickets was demonstrated
to be a meaningful social response. 2) Use of the classroom
teacher as mediator to implement the experimental intervention program worked with 96 percent accuracy and observational evidence indicated that there was little or no disruption of classroom procedures. 3) No statistically significant difference in the giving of B portions to the teacher
was found between the period when she did and did not give
them to the two experimental subjects. 4) No statistically
significant difference was found between the contingent and
non-contingent giving of B portions by the teacher. These
results may be due to the fact that the experimental subjects earned so few fun tickets that they had only a few B
portions to give.

2257.   Mistur, R. J. "Behavioral Group Counseling with
Elementary School Children: A Model." Ph.D. Dissertation,
Case Western Reserve University. Dissertation Abstracts
International, 38 (12-A), 7156. Order no. 7809294, 1978.

It was the primary purpose of this study to develop a
behavioral group counseling model which was applicable with
children in an elementary school setting. Other objectives
included: 1) to identify those major learning theories
which serve as the underlying theoretical basis of the model
developed. b) to identify and define the basic learning
concepts and assumptions of the model. c) to evaluate the
model in terms of evaluative criteria as suggested in the
review of the literature. In the study, the term "model"
was defined as a symbolic analogy which simplifies
phenomena. The model for this investigation was postulated
to contain the following elements: a) answers to questions
concerning the child's nature and how his behaviors change,
b) well defined constructs which serve as a framework of the
model, c) assumptions accepted as true on a logical basis or
based on empirical data. d) a new system of relationships
among the theoretical constructs within the phenomena under
study. The behavioral group counseling model as developed
through this investigation will serve to assist those professionals who are dedicated to helping children through their
group counseling efforts.

2258.   Mittag, M. C. "Dogmatism and Attitudes Regarding
Discipline as Predictors of Selection of Elementary Level
Among Teacher Education Majors." Ph.D. Dissertation,
Fordham University. Dissertation Abstracts International,
39 (3-A), 1196. Order no. 7816594, 1978.

This study examined degree of dogmatism and attitudes toward
class discipline, as represented by Kounin's (1970)
categories of clarity, firmness, and roughness, of female
elementary education majors in order to determine whether
these variables could predict choice of elementary teaching
level (nursery through six). The sample consisted of 152
female elementary education majors from a northeastern
university. The subjects were administered the Rokeach
Dogmatism Scale, Form E, a Semantic Differential on
attitudes toward class discipline, as represented by
clarity, firmness, and roughness, and a checklist of choice
of elementary teaching level, nursery school through sixth
grade. Attitudes toward class discipline, as represented by
Kounin's (1970) discipline categories of clarity, firmness,
and roughness, were found not be be significant predictors
of choice of elementary teaching level. In addition, grade
point average was found to be unrelated to choice of elementary teaching level. Essentially, the vocational decision
theoretical model was supported in terms of the dogmatic
personality. Dogmatism was found to be a moderate predictor
for the criterion of choice of elementary teaching level.
Examination of the results showed a negative linear relationship between the two variables. Those education students
who chose to teach the lower grades had the highest mean
dogmatism scores, while those who chose to teach the higher
grades had the lowest mean dogmatism scores. Therefore, the
results of this study suggest that education students choose
particular grade levels because they believe certain

personality needs will be fulfilled by teaching at a particular level.

2259.   Monnig, F. R. "A Comparison of the Efficacy of Token Reinforcement and Dyad Competition to Increase Time on Task in a Remedial Reading Class." Ph.D. Dissertation, University of Wyoming. Dissertation Abstracts International, 35 (12-B), 6104-6105. Order no. 75-12,838, 1975.

The efficacy of token reinforcement and dyad competition to increase time on task in a remedial reading class was compared for the purpose of investigating the feasibility of introducing competition into token programs. The subjects were 16 elementary school students, average age eight years, eight months, with mean WISC IQ of 97.8. The dependent measure was the percentage of ampled 15 second intervals on task. The tasks were a variety of routine learning exercises whose purpose was to enhance reading and writing skills. These exercises included standard workbook exercises, independent reading and writing, and prescription type exercises designed by tutors to increase proficiency in specific skills. The result of a pilot study suggested the hypotheses that token reinforcement increases percentage of intervals on tasks and that competition increases percentage of intervals on task as much as, or more than, token reinforcememt. An ancillary study investigated the effects of competition on the social desirability of the competitors. The results indicate that no significant change occurred in the social desirability of competitors as a result of the introduction of competition conditions. Although the results of the main study are somewhat ambiguous, they suggest that 1) competition is a more powerful incentive than token reinforcement, 2) competition may have a more enduring learning effect, 3) competition may be a means of motivating some subjects who do no respond to token reinforcement, 4) competition can reduce the financial costs of token programs, 5) competition may furnish program designers with an added novelty to combat response fatigue and monotony.

2260.   Moore, Dennis R. "Determinants of Deviancy: A Behavioral Comparison of Normal and Deviant Children in Multiple Settings." Ph.D. Dissertation, The University of Tennessee. Dissertation Abstracts International, 36 (3-B), 1479. Order no. 75-18, 976, 1975.

Grade school children labeled normal or deviant by their teacher were observed thirty minutes a day for ten consecutive school days in both school (referral) and home (non-referral) settings. Ongoing activity was recorded by trained observers using a behavior coding system defining nineteen subject response behaviors and six environmental stimulus behaviors. Daily event records of negative behavior episodes and of adult attitudes toward child behavior was also taken. The observational data differentiated child behavior in both settings. Deviant children produced less appropriate behavior and more attention seeking behavior in both settings, more adult directed social behavior in the home, and more oppositional behavior in the school than their normal counterparts. Parents of deviant children engaged in more child directed social behavior and reported more negative behavior episodes than normal child parents. Teachers reported higher rates of negative behavior episodes and more negative behavior attitudes for the deviant children.

2261.   Moore, J. R.   "A Study of the Relationships Between the Trust Held by Students for Principals of Selected Ohio Senior High Schools and the Incidence Rate of Six Negative Behavioral Performances."   Ph.D. Dissertation, Bowling Green State University. Dissertation Abstracts International, 38 (9-A), 5169. Order no. 7800236, 1978.

The purposes of this study were to: 1) examine the relationship between high school seniors' perceptions of trust of the principal and selected variables reflecting negative behavior performances of students; 2) explore the trust perceptions of female students in contrast with male students; and 3) investigate the influence of the size of the school attended on student perceptions of trust of the principal. The study sample was composed of twenty-eight Ohio high schools. An average of fifty senior students from each school responded to an instrument designed for the study to measure perceptions of trust of the principal. Data supplied by school principals relative to study variables were converted to indices which were tested against mean student scores obtained on the study instrument. Schools where students hold a high degree of trust of the principal may be expected to have comparatively low rates of dropouts, suspensions, and court referrals. 2) High or low trust perceptions by students of the high school principal appear to have no effect upon the rates of disciplinary office referrals, vandalism, and absenteeism. 3) The sex of students does not seem to be a factor of consequence regarding their perceptions of trust of the principal. 4) Students in small schools can be expected to have a higher perception of trust of the principal than students in large schools.

2262.   Moore, M. G.   "Task-Oriented Classroom Behavior of Reflective and Impulsive Nine- and Eleven-Year-Old Children." Ph.D. Dissertation. The University of North Carolina at Chapel Hill, 1977.

Seventy-nine 9- and 11-year-old children were classified as reflective or impulsive during at least two of three successive years of Matching Familiar Figure (MFF) test administration. Reflective and impulsive groups at both age levels were comparable with respect to IQ and race. A five-second interval time-sampling procedure was used to code classroom child behavior for two, five-minute periods in each of three classroom settings: individual seat work, large group instruction and small group instruction. A total of 15 predetermined categories were devised that were hypothesized to index impulsive behavior in classroom settings. Observation categories were grouped into one of our categories: task-oriented, non-task-oriented, appropriate social and inappropriate social. With regard to race, black children were observed to be more distracted, to self-verbalize more, and to obtain lower SES, IQ and academic achievement scores than their white peers. The achievement differences between black and white children were larger than might be expected based upon measured IQ and were discussed in terms of the inter-relationsips between lower SES, deprivation, self-concept and underachievement. Order no. 77-27,283, DAI.

2263.   Morris, Mary J. "Contingency Contracting and Behavior Modification Techniques Applied in a Secondary School Setting." Ed.D. Dissertation, Brigham Young University, 1975. Dissertation Abstracts International, 35 (11-A), 7130. Order no. 75-5862.

This study sought to determine if contingency contracting with behavior modification techniques could imporve daily attendance, grade point average, self concept, and the reduction of discipline referrals in high school girls. The hypotheses stated that there would be no significant difference between girls subjected to contingency contracting with behavior modification techniques and girls receiving no such treatment. Ninety-seven girls were divided by grade and randomly assigned to one control or one experimental group. The control group and the experimental group were comprised of 30 girls each. A pre and post self concept scale was administered to all subjects along with a pre and post comparison of each subject's daily attendance, discipline referrals, and grade point average. To test the hypotheses the data was analyzed by analysis of variance. The results indicated that contingency contracting with behavior modification techniques can significantly improve daily attendance, grade point average, self concept, and positive behavior in high school girls.

2264.   Morris, N. J. "Contingency Contracting and Behavior Modification Techniques Applied in a Secondary School Setting." Ed.D. Dissertation, Brigham Young University, 1975.

The study sought to determine if contingency contracting with behavior modification techniques could improve daily attendance, grade point average, self-concept, and the reduction of discipline referrals in high school girls. Ninety-seven girls were divided by grade and randomly assigned to one control or one experimental group. The control in the experimental group were comprised of 30 girls each. The results of the study indicated that contingency contracting with behavior modification techniques can significantly improve daily attendance, grade point average, self-concept and positive behavior in high school girls.

2265.   Morrison, R. L. "In-Service Classroom Management Training: A Consultant Model." Ed.D. Dissertation, University of California, Los Angeles. Dissertation Abstracts International, 33 (12-A), 6736. Order no. 73-13,156, 1973.

A consultant model was developed and intensively studied in a teacher focused classroom mangement intervention program. Four interdependent factors (relationship, role-playing, instructional, and social reinforcement) were combined and systematically presented in the form of an in-service training program. The consultant conducted twenty-two 30-minute training sessions with the teacher during a twenty-five day intervention period. During this time the teacher was trained to role-play two fixed modes of behavior. It was concluded that the in-service training model operated effectively and predictably. The teacher expressed approval and stated expectations much more frequently. The students in the classroom, especially the target-students, became more attentive and task-oriented. Furthermore, the teacher's attitudes about the six target students became more favorable and her awareness of positive and negative teacher response contingencies was considerably improved. More importantly, in terms of training issues, the teacher completed the program feeling her effort was worthwhile and the gains developed during intervention appeared to be maintained six weeks later.

2266.   Motta, R. W. "An Investigation of Teacher Perceived Differences in Classroom Behavior." Ph.D. Dissertation, Hofstra University. Dissertation Abstracts International, 36 (4-B), 1906. Order no. 75-21, 599, 1975.

In light of studies such as those of Rosenthal and Jacobson (1966, 1968) in which favorable teacher expectancies were found to result in higher tested levels of achievement and IQ among otherwise "average" students, the present investigation was conducted in order to examine the relationship between teacher perceptions and the student characteristics of SES, grade and sex while statistically examining the variance in perceptions due to student IQ. Teachers rated the classroom behavior of 805 white children on a 32 item behavior rating scale. Among the major findings were: a) Girls were perceived as more dependent, creative and achievement oriented than boys. b) Boys were perceived as more aggressive than girls. c) In no case did the effect of grade or SES significantly reverse the trend of these findings. d) Significant SES effects were not found on the four major factors. e) IQ was shown to correlate higher with achievement related items than non-achievement items but IQ did not significantly alter the magnitude of factor loadings on any of the behavior rating items.

2267.   Moulton, Patricia A.   "The Effects of Filmed-Modeling and Vicarious Consequences on Counteracting the Influence of a Deviator."   Ph.D.   Dissertation, University of Kansas. Dissertation Abstracts International, 38 (12-B), 6166-6167. Order no. 7809370.

The purpose of the present study was twofold. First, it was designed to extend and examine the usefulness of imitative learning procedures with a simulated school-type activity for children in small group situations. These group situations included two types of behavioral designs: a) group modeling of appropriate task behavior prior to a child's opportunity to perform that task; and b) a behavioral contagion design in which children were exposed to deviant and non-deviant models while performing a task. The second purpose of the study was to determine if appropriate modeling prior to the performance of a task could be used to counteract the influence of a deviant model's behavior. Modeling procedures with and without the use of vicarious consequences were examined. Thirty-six boys and thirty-six girls from the fourth-grade classrooms of three elementary schools participated as subjects in this study. The results indicated that imitation of a task deviator's behavior (i.e., behavioral contagion) occurred in a small group situation, even when there were two children present who were attending appropriately to the task. The findings also demonstrated that the use of filmed-models attending appropriately to the task could counteract the behavioral contagion effect of the task deviator's behavior. The filmed-models were effective deterrents to the behavioral contagion effect whether or not the models received tangible consequences for their work. In the above situations there were no significant differences between the behavior of boys and girls.

2268.   Moye, N.   "An Investigation of the Relationship Between Student Perceptions of Pupil Control Behavior Orientation of Teachers and Student Alienation in Selected Secondary Schools."   Ed.D.   Dissertation, University of Georgia. Dissertation Abstracts International, 36 (9-A), 5705. Order no. 76-6432, 1976.

The purpose of this study was to determine whether a significant relationship existed between student perceptions of teacher pupil control behavior and student alienation within selected secondary schools. The personal variables of sex and race were also examined for their possible association with student alienation. The public school was regarded as an involuntary client-serving organization in which some form of client control must be imposed if organizational goals are to be attained. Seeman's multi-dimensional concept of alienation was used to distinguish five alternative meanings of alienation as subjectively felt states of mind. The five dimensions are normlessness, powerlessness, isolation, meaninglessness and self-estrangement. Kolesar's Pupil Attitude Questionnaire was used to measure each of

these five dimensions. The instrument also yields a total
alienation score which is the sum of the five subtests. The
general hypothesis guiding this study was as follows: total
alienation of secondary students, as measured by the Pupil
Attitude Questionnaire, is significantly predicted by a.
perceived teacher pupil control behavior of secondary
students; b. sex-class of secondary students; c. race of
secondary students. Five Georgia secondary schools
participated in the investigation. These schools had an
organizational pattern of grades 9-12, a minority population
of from 25-50%, and an enrollment of from 300-900 students.
Findings were generally contrary to the predicted directional relationships. Custodialism was negatively
correlated with total alienation, normlessness and self-
estrangement. No significant relationship existed between
PCB and powerlessness. Custodialism had a very low association with isolation. Meaninglessness received the strongest
directional support.

2269.   Muller, Gene E. "The Effects on Teacher Knowledge,
Attitude and Classroom Behavior of Simulated Practice Versus
Application of Behavior Management Techniques During
In-Service Instruction." Ph.D. Dissertation, The University
of Texas at Austin, 1980. Dissertation Abstracts
International, 40 (11-A), 5796. Order no. 8009901.

In-service workshops are frequently characterized by an
emphasis on the understanding of concepts and employ
simulated practice prior to their application in the classroom. Other approaches incorporate application of concepts
during the training. Both approaches have been employed to
train teachers in the area of classroom management and both
have been demonstrated to be effective when compared to
nontreatment controls. The present study attempted to
examine and compare both of the above approaches to in-
service instruction for teachers within the context of a
single study. A sample of regular public school teachers
was divided into two groups with one group being exposed to
a training approach which emphasized the learning of concepts prior to their application in the classroom setting.
The second group was exposed to a training approach which
supported application of the concepts in the participants'
classrooms in conjuction with the training. Posttest and
follow-up measures were compared to pretest measures of 1)
knowledge of the concepts, 2) attitude, and 3) in-class
performance by means of an analysis of covariance procedure.
An analysis of the data determined significant differences
(at the 0.05 level) existing between groups on follow-up
scores in the areas of 1) knowledge of principles and 2)
attitudes toward classroom management techniques. The
results indicated that participants benefited more from
learning concepts in conjuction with their application in
the classroom rather than learning the concepts prior to
their application. Conclusions reached suggested that the
application of techniques in conjunction with training of
those techniques leads to benefits not experienced when the

application is absent during training. In addition, the effects of the training may not be evidenced until a period of time has elapsed after the training has ended.

2270.   Multhauf, A. P. "Teacher Pupil Control Ideology and Behavior and Classroom Environmental Robustness." Ed.D. Dissertation, The Pennsylvania State University. Dissertation Abstracts International, 38 (12-A), 7291. Order no. 7808399, 1978.

This study was designed to examine the relationships between pupil control ideology, pupil control behavior, and classroom environmental robustness. The sample consisted of 32 fourth, fifth, and sixth grade teachers and their students. Thirty-two teachers completed the Pupil Control Ideology (PCI) Form, 797 students completed the Pupil Control Behavior (PCB) Form, and 787 students completed the Robustness Semantic Differential (RSD) Scale for the concept My Classroom. The first hypothesis proposed a direct relationship between teacher custodialism in pupil control ideology and student report of high classroom robustness. Based on the statistical analysis this hypothesis was rejected. The second hypothesis posited a direct relationship between teacher custodialism in pupil control behavior and student reports of high classroom robustness. The original hypothesis, proposing a positive relationship was rejected since a significant inverse relationship was found. The third hypothesis predicted a direct relationship between student reports of teacher custodialism in pupil control behavior and student reports of high classroom robustness. The original hypothesis was rejected since for the entire sample and for each grade level taken separately the results were significant and negative.

2271.   Murdoch, G. R. "The Relationships Between Family Environment, Children's Social Perception, and Classroom Behavior." Ed.D. Dissertation, University of Cincinnanti. Dissertation Abstracts International, 40 (12-B, PT 1), 5871. Order no. 8012241.

The purpose of this study was to explore the relationship between family environment, children's social perception, and classroom behavior. Subjects in the study were white, middle class children, in the fourth and fifth grades, and their parents. The family environment was measured by the Family Environment Scale which consists of ten scales measuring relationship dimensions, system maintenance factors, and personal growth factors of the family. Social perception was measured by the Paired Hands Test. The results of the data analysis suggested that the characteristic family environment that was related to positive classroom behavior was one in which children experienced a low level of conflict and felt encouraged to be assertive and self sufficient, in the context of warmth and support. This was also a family that worked at being effective by actively doing things together. The importance of the specific

variables of levels of conflict and active recreational
orientation was significant in that these are variables that
are not typically considered in family assessment. The
classroom behaviors most related to family influences were
immaturity, withdrawal, and distributed peer relations.
Immaturity was the behavior most significantly related to
family factors. The relationship between children's and
parents' perceptions of family environment was examined.
The results showed that children's perceptions were more
significantly related to classroom behavior. Children's
social perception and family environment were not significantly related. Children's social perception was perceived
as a developing personality factor in which more specific
influences needed to be examined. Children's social perception was not related to classroom behavior. It is possible
that behavior does not always reflect inner feelings
expecially negative feelings in which expression is effected
by impulse control.

2272.   Murphy, F. J. "A Study of the Effects of Group
Counseling on Attendance at the Senior High School Level."
Ed.D. Dissertation, The George Washington University.
Dissertation Abstracts International, 36 (5-A), 2549-2550.
Order no. 75-25,392, 1975.

The purpose of the study was to investigate the effects of
group counseling with chronically absent sophomores on the
variables of attendance, achievement and behavior. The
counseling was conducted by practicing high school counselors with similar training. The counselors worked within
time limitations imposed on the operational school situation
in four suburban Maryland high schools. Specifically, the
intent of the study was to see if group counseling would
significantly decrease the number of absences among
chronically absent sophomores between the second and third
grading periods. These absences were compared with absences
among a like number of control students. Of 1,400 10th
grade students enrolled in four Maryland county high schools
in January, 1974, 120 were identified from a comparison of
school attendance cards. From the 120 chronically absent
students identified, 30 students in each school were
randomly selected and assigned to one study and one control
group in each of four high schools. The testing of the
hypotheses and the analysis of the data revealed the
following findings: 1) Students with chronic attendance
problems who received group counseling had significantly
fewer absences than non-counseled students, at the .01
level. 2) On the basis of the present data, it is not
possible to state conclusively that the achievement level of
the study group improved. 3) It is not possible, on the
basis of this study, to state that the number of times a
chronically absent student was sent to the office for discipline was significantly decreased.

2273.   Murry, M. D. "The Relationship of Classroom Behavior to Academic Achievement and Aptitude." Ph.D. Dissertation, The University of Tennessee. Dissertation Abstracts International, 38 (12-A), 7156. Order no. 7807711, 1978.

The relationship of classroom behavior to academic achievement and general academic aptitude among 69 fifth-grade students was examined. Classroom behavior was observed during 10 arithmetic class sessions and coded in discrete categories according to a system developed for this study. The relationship of classroom behavior to achievement and aptitude was very similar for math, reading, and IA suggesting that a single group of behaviors is related to academic competence. The relationship of classroom behavior to over- and underachievement was examined by calculating a score to represent each subject's level of over- or under-achievement. Classroom behavior was found to have little relationship to over and underachievement because there was little range of the discrepancy scores. Results supported previous findings on the relationship of classroom behavior and achievement while suggesting that a very similar relationship exists between behavior and aptitude. The efficacy of posture and duration of study discriminations was also supported and the implications of including such categories in future research was examined.

2274.   Myers, M. H. "A Comparison of the Effects of a Group-Initiated Activity Program and a Leader-Directed Activity Program on the Maladjusted Social Behavior of Selected Fifth and Sixth Grade Students." Ed.D. Dissertation, University of Cincinnati. Dissertation Abstracts International, 37 (6-A), 3526-3527. Order no. 76-28,001, 1976.

The purpose of this study was to determine by controlled experimentation the effects of a group-initiated activity program and a leader-directed activity program upon certain psycho-social characteristics of students with behavior problems. The psycho-social characteristics, under investigation, were: 1) psychological sense of belongingness, 2) academic skills, 3) level of intellectual functioning, 4) verbal communication skills, 5) adaptive behavior, 6) peer-relationships. The subjects of the study were ten black male and female students assigned to regular fifth and sixth grade classrooms in an urban elementary public school. Although this investigation dealt with a relatively small sample, its findings were impressive. Considerable improvement was brought about in demonstrated characteristics of children labeled as "behavior problems" and thus demonstrated the efficacy of certain kinds of programs that can be introduced in urban school systems now.

2275.   Nagle, C. C. "The Effects of Alterations in Seating Arrangement on Distractibility of Kindergarten and First Grade Children." Ph.D. Dissertation. The University of North Carolina at Chapel Hill, 1979.

The purpose of this dissertation was to examine the effects of three seating arrangements on the distractibility of 26 dyads of kindergarten and first grade children. In examining the literature on distractibility, it became apparent that no generally accepted definition was available. Several behaviors have been used to measure distractibility. Researchers recently advocated a correlational analysis of all measure in order to formulate a more comprehensive definition. In this dissertation, distractibility was coded by two scales which incorporated measures suggested in the literature: off-task verbalization, off-task no verbalization, glances, quadrant changes, and total movement. The behavior of children was coded while the children completed an assigned task. The children were seated at desks positioned either side-by-side, face-to-face, or back-to-back, and at a diagonal to each other in a laboratory setting. The primary distractor was the presence of a second child of the same age and sex. The results indicated that the children, regardless of their sex or age, exhibited similar behaviors. Alterations in seating arrangement did not affect significantly distractibility. A consistent pattern within a setting between the five measures of distractibility was not indicated. Four out of the five measures of distractibility were significantly intercorrelated. Verbalization was highly correlated with off-task behavior. Order no. 8005061, DAI.

2276.   Nelson, Kenneth O. "The Effect of Two Parent Group Counseling Models on the Behavior of Educationally Handicapped Children." Ph.D. Dissertation, Arizona State University. Dissertation Abstracts International, 33 (5-A), 2110. Order no. 72-30,133, 1972.

The purpose of this study was to determine the effects of two parent group counseling models on the classroom behavior of educationally handicapped elementary school children. The two counseling models develop for this study (child-centered parent groups counseling model and the behavior modification parent group counseling model) represented two theoretically divergent viewpoints. The population for this study was composed of 17 elementary school children identified for inclusion in the Type I (engineered) Classroom in the Special Project Aimed at Reaching Children (SPARC) in the Tempe Elementary School. Parent involvement in two parent group counseling models indicated no statistically significant differences between groups on measures of classroom task attention behavior of their children, although there was a trend in favor of the group whose parents experienced the behavior modification parent group counseling model.

2277.   Nelson, M. A. P. "Attitudes of Intermediate School Children Toward Substitute Teachers Who Receive Feedback on Pupil-Desired Behavior." Ed.D. Dissertation, University of Oregon, 1972.

This study proposed to measure difference in pupil reactions to substitute teachers by systematically using pupil feedback to modify substitute teacher behavior. The hypothesis was that if two groups of substitute teachers frequently administered an attitudinal scale to intermediate grade (4-6) children, there would be more behavior modification on the part of the group that received feedback about the scale than on the part of the group that received no feedback. An underlying assumption of the study was that because substitute teachers are by professional training and experience generally as competent as regular classroom teachers, systematic feedback would be as effective for them as it has been proven to be for regular classroom teachers. The study was conducted in School District 48, Beaverton, Oregon. Ten schools were randomly selected for two groups, the one to be experimental, the other control. All intermediate grade children (1786) in the ten schools completed as a pretest a nine-item Likert-type attitudinal scale which measured satisfaction with teacher behavior. Educational implications of the study lie in the test of the hypothesis—pupils are most satisfied with the substitute teachers' behavior when the substitute teachers know both how pupils feel and how to modify their own personal behavior. On the basis of these findings, the investigator believes school districts could profitably conduct inservice training workshops for substitute teachers, using as a focus the types of behavioral items on the scale used in this study. Personnel coordinators could establish feedback loops to enable substitute teachers to benefit from evaluation available to classroom teachers. Substitute associations could modify existing handbooks to include interpersonal relationship techniques as well as district policy. Providing substitute teachers with systematic feedback should benefit all those involved in the substitute teacher experience. Order no. 73-7937, DAI.

2278.   Newman, D. G. "An Approach to Combat Student Misbehavior at the Ninth Grade Level: The Committee on Referral and Evaluation." Ed.D. Dessertation, Part 2, Nova University, 1979. 187p.

The Committee on Referral and Evaluation was the second phase of a practicum designed to improve the behavior of students identified as hard core discipline problems. The first phase was a computer discipline record keeping system used to identify problem students. This program combines school, community and state agencies in an effort to intervene at an early level, the ninth grade, to solve current discipline problems and prevent future problems. A student identified for this program was evaluated by the committee to determine the best prescription for treatment. Possible treatment included family counseling at a local agency, counseling by a teacher or student, a new program of study, a job experience program, a home study, correspondence or night school program, vocational rehabilitation, the Job Corp, a community college program, a mental hygiene clinic, private psychiatric care, or other community resources. The last resort was expulsion. Spin-offs of the program were a substance abuse prevention program for all ninth graders and a career counseling program. See ERIC Abstract ED 193766.

2279.   Newman, D. G. "Develop and Implement a Computerized System to Collate, Analyze and Maintain Records on All Student Discipline Infractions and Administrative/Teacher Punitive Actions in the Seaford Senior High School. Ed.D. Dessertation, Part 1, Nova University, 1978. 96p.

To comply with a 1975 memo from the office for civil rights, the Seaford Senior High School in Delaware was required to maintain records on all student discipline actions. These records consisted of student disciplinary case reports designated by case file members. Also discipline actions were to be logged by racial or ethnic designation, sex, school, offense, notice given, hearing authority, hearing sequence, time elapsed, testimony, findings, and disposition of the case. The purpose of this program was to develop a computerized system to record such data. The objectives of the program were to save time for administrators and clerical workers, to develop forms for the reporting of discipline offenses, and to develop information necessary for possible alternatives to suspension. The author judged the program to be extremely successful and urged that it be viewed as a foundation for other computerized systems for such functions. See ERIC Abstract ED 193765.

2280.   Newman, J. D. "The High-Risk Student: A Predictive Study." Ph.D. Dissertation, The University of Michigan. Dissertation Abstracts International, 36 (6-A), 3524. Order no. 75-29,298, 1975.

The motivation for this research was the need to develop a technique for predicting the "future level" of school success for a group of high-risk junior high school students. The research comprised two phases. Phase I involved collecting and analyzing data from the Coopersmith Self-Esteem Inventory, the Classroom Questionnaire, the Pupil Behavior Inventory, and individual interviews with each of the students as well as teachers and administrative and guidance personnel. The analysis of these data provided for the formulation of predictions about the individual high-risk student's "future level" of school functioning. Predictions were made for each of the students in one or more of the following areas: a) peer-relationships, b) authority figure relationships, and c) academic functioning. During Phase II, approximately 18 months later, follow-up data were collected, using the same research instruments. The purpose was to examine the predictions made during Phase I. The evaluation of these predictions required the use of statistical procedures appropriate for the single case, N of one. On the basis of the evaluation, 35 of the 50 verifiable predictions were accurate.

2281.   Norris, J. H. "Non-Attending Behaviors in First Grade
Students Under Three Fluorescent Lighting Conditions."
Ed.D. Dissertations, Texas Woman's University. Dissertation
Abstracts International, 40 (12-A, PT 1), 6232-6233, 1980.

The purpose of this study was to demonstrate effects of
different fluorescent lighting conditions on the degree of
non-attending behaviors exhibited by children in regular
school classrooms. Eleven first grade classrooms in three
elementary schools in three suburban school districts near a
large metroplex were used in the research. The statistical
method used the difference scores of group means in a one-
way analysis of variance. There was a decrease in the
frequency of all thirteen non-attending. Five of these
behaviors showing the greatest change were analyzed. These
five behaviors were: vocalizes without teacher permission,
eye contact to task broken without teacher direction, chair
balanced on two legs, out of seat without permission, and
teacher reprimands student (verbal or non-verbal). Eye
contact to task broken without teacher direction was significant at p 01. Behavior data collected was reliable due to
inner rater reliability correlations which ranged from .955
to .992.

2282.   Nussen, J. L. "Student Use of Behavioral Principles to
Control Their Classroom Behavior." Ph.D. Dissertation,
University of Virginia. Dissertation Abstracts
International, 40 (9-A), 5003. Order no. 8004681, 1980.

Discipline has been and continues to be a problem in public
schools. There is much written about "how-to" solve the
problem, but there are few experimental or quasi-
experimental studies in this area. This study was designed
to see if students could be taught to use appropriate
behaviors when responding to teacher's commands, and to
reinforce teachers by asking the teacher a question and
thanking him/her for help. A sample of eighth and ninth
grade students from a large, urban school were selected.
All the students were pre-tested in video-taped role-play
conflict situation with a confederate teacher. Following
the pre-test fourteen of the students were randomly selected
for training. The other students received no training. The
training consisted of three, fifty minute sessions during
which the youth were taught how to react to teacher's commands in an appropriate manner and how to positively reinforce teachers. After completion of training all students
were post-tested in a role-play situation identical to the
pre-test. The results show that students who received
training exhibited a significantly higher frequency of
appropriate behavior in the post-test. The total length of
time for the role-play interactions of the experimental
students was significantly less than for the controls,
indicating that use of appropriate behaviors ends the interaction quickly, before it escalates into a confrontation.
Two weeks after the training ended all students were
observed in their math and English classes in order to see

if the training generalized to the regular classrooms. Results did not support the hypothesis that the experimental youth would use a higher frequency of appropriate behaviors in the classroom.

2283.   Okeefe, K. J. "A Study of the Effects of an Operant In-Service Teacher Training Program on Behavioral Learning Principles and Classroom Management Procedures." Ph.D. Dissertation, The University of Iowa. Dissertation Abstracts International, 34 (6-A), 3151-3152. Order no. 73-30,965, 1973.

Research by behavioral psychologists in training teachers to become effective remediators of problem behaviors in the classroom has been extensive. However any specific, detailed training programs, with significant long-term effects in training groups of teachers, appears nonexistent. The experiment divided 17 elementary teachers, who had volunteered for an in-service program to be conducted by one of the school district's psychologist, into an experimental and control group. Teachers were informed that they could enroll for three hours of graduate credit at The University of Iowa and could earn up to the cost of tuition ($138.00) by fulfilling the requirements of the program. These requirements had previously been specified and a point value assigned to each of them by the experimenter. Prior to the training program, each teacher filled out a questionnaire to measure knowledge of and attitude toward behavioral learning principles, and rated every child in her class on a 12 question problem behavior checklist. Concurrently, each child rated both his teacher, and his schoolwork and class-room atmosphere. The training program followed a sequenced pattern proceeding from behavioral learning principles, to the theoretical basis for such a position, to more advanced and sophisticated procedures that could be used in class-rooms to individualize for children. Within the program, each teacher attempted to modify a behavior of her (rated) most problematic child. The classroom behavior of the five children whom she rated as most problematic, as well as that of the teacher, was recorded by trained, reliable observers at pre-treatment, post-treatment, and, for the experimental group, at a follow-up period two months after termination of the program (at that time the control group was involved in the same program). At post-treatment also, measures on teacher knowledge and attitude, teacher ratings of their most problematic students, most problematic students' ratings of teachers, and most problematic students' ratings of schoolwork and classroom atmosphere were again taken. Results analyzed by means of analysis of covariance proce-dures, showed that there was no significant difference between groups on the following measures: 1. total appro-priate, and inappropriate, teacher behavior; 2. inappro-priate behavior of the most problematic, and four next-most-problematic, students; 3. teacher ratings of both the most problematic, and four next-most-problematic, students; 4. the four next-most-problematic students' ratings of teacher behavior; 5. the most problematic, and four next-most-problematic, students' ratings of schoolwork and classroom atmosphere. There was a significant difference between groups (which favored the experimental group) on: 1. teacher knowledge and attitude toward behavioral learning principles; and 2. the most problematic students' ratings of teacher behavior.

2284.   Okon, Edet E. "A Descriptive Analysis of Classroom Management Approach Preferences." Ed.D. Dissertation, University of Houston. Dissertation Abstracts International, 38 (5-A), 2528. Order no. 77-24,436, 1977.

The purpose of the study was two-fold: 1) to design and develop an instrument which would serve as a reliable and valid operational measure of teacher classroom management approach preferences; and 2) to use that instrument to identify and describe the classroom management approach preferences of teachers who differed with regard to a variety of presage factors. The study posited a series of null hypotheses which allowed statistical tests to determine the extent to which the classroom management approach preferences of teachers possessing a particular presage factor differed significantly from those teachers possessing a different presage factor. Given the hypothesis the study was designed to test, the following presage factors were treated as independent variables: 1) sex of the teacher; 2) age of the teacher; 3) teaching experience of the teacher; 4) educational level of the teacher; 5) type of school in which the teacher teaches; and 6) location of school in which the teacher teaches. The dependent variables were teacher perceptions regarding seven classroom management approaches as measured by the Teacher Opinion Questionnaire: 1) authoritarian approach; 2) the behavior modification approach; 3) the group process approach; 4) the instructional approach; 5) the permissive approach; 6) the socio-emotional climate approach; and 7) the bag-of-tricks approach. The sample consisted of 1035 teachers from nine school districts in the Houston metropolitan area. The results of the study suggested the following conclusions: 1) female teachers are more positive toward the behavior modification, socio-emotional climate, and group process approaches than are male teachers; 2) male teachers are more positive toward the authoritarian and bag-of-tricks approach than are female teachers; 3) teachers of different ages and years of teaching experiences do not differ with regard to their approach preferences; 4) teachers with master's degrees are more positive toward the instructional approach than are teachers with bachelor's degrees; 5) primary elementary teachers are more positive toward the behavior modification, socio-emotional climate, and permissive approaches than are middle school junior high school and senior high school teachers; 6) intermediate teachers are more positive toward the socio-emotional climate approach than are middle school junior high school teachers; 7) rural teachers are less positive toward the socio-emotional climate approach than were either urban or suburban teachers; and 8) suburban teachers are less positive toward the bag-of-tricks approach than are either inner city or urban teachers.

2285.   Owen, T. L. "A Study to Determine the Effect of Selected Behavior Modification Techniques on Performance of Non Attending, Non Achieving Junior High School Students." Ph.D. Dissertation, University of Utah. Dissertation Abstracts International, 34 (10-A), 6318-6319. Order no. 74-8851, 1974.

The purpose of this study was to gain new insights into the kinds of programs necessary to provide meaningful academic and social progress within the normal school situation for the potential high school dropout. Specifically, a program was designed to assist students characterized by (1) unacceptable social classroom behavior, and (2) below grade placement academic achievement. Through a system of behavior modification based on tangible and intrinsic rewards, it was hoped the students studied would exhibit more desirable classroom behavior and improve their academic skills. Eighteen subjects characterized by school officials as (1) continually referred to the principal for infraction of school regulations, (2) lengthy periods of absenteeism, and (3) low academic achievement, participated in a program designed to emphasize tangible and intrinsic rewards as change agents toward the goal of increased academic achievement in the areas of math and reading. The same rewards were employed as change agents toward increased incidence of desirable social classroom behavior. Emphasis throughout the eight phases of the study (range, 1-12 weeks per phase) gradually changed from tangible reinforcement to that of intrinsic reinforcement as reward for acceptable academic achievement and/or desirable social classroom behavior. Phase I was designated as baseline and measured existing academic and social behaviors of the students studied. During Phase II and III reinforcement was primarily tangible (e.g., soft drinks, free time, candy). Phase IV was designed as a reversal period to measure the effect of the rewards of phases II and III. During Phase V the introduction of more intrinsic rewards (e.g., social praise, letter grades) were gradually substituted for tangible rewards. Phase VI served as a reversal period designed to measure the reward system to that point in the study. During Phases VII and VIII tangible rewards were replaced almost entirely by intrinsic rewards. Academic progress related to grade level placement in math and reading increased 1.8 (t-5.16) and 1.6 (t-5.14) respectively, both significant at the .001 level. Incidence of undesirable classroom behavior decreased from an average of 37.7 percent during Phase I to an average of 4.8 percent during Phase VIII (t-14.26, significant at the .001 level). Overall grade point average for the 18 studied increased from 1.142 at the beginning of the program to 1.498 during the first report period of the year following the program. The increase of .356 (t-2.10) was significant at the .05 level. It was believed that (1) increased academic skills, (2) more desirable classroom behavior, and (3) reduced pupil teacher ratio (2/18) would combine to result in increased school attendance for the 18 students studied. A 3.2 percent decrease in attendance, pre to post program, indicated the belief to be incorrect. The t score of 2.13 was significant at the .05 level.

2286.   Page, V. H. "The Effect of Encouragement Techniques by Teachers on the Disturbing Behaviors of Students." Ph.D. Dissertation, University of South Carolina. Dissertation Abstracts International, 36 (2-A), 713. Order no. 75-16, 493, 1975.

The present study was designed to determine whether the use of encouragement techniques by teachers would reduce the disturbing behavior incidents of students in the classroom. One half of the teachers (Group A) was trained to deal specifically with acting-out behaviors. The other half (Group B) was trained to deal specifically with negligent behaviors. The population in the study was 216 elementary school students and 169 secondary school students in 12 elementary classes and eight secondary classes in an urban public school system and the teachers of the 20 classes. Prior to the beginning of the study each teacher rated the class each day at the end of two one-hour sessions on 16 deviant behaviors. For ten consecutive days, each teacher rated the class each day at the end of two one-hour sessions on the 16 deviant behaviors, also. The teachers recorded a 38.9 percent decrease in acting-out and negligent classroom behavior for the total group subjects at the conclusion of the study. This decrease was statistically significant. Group A teachers recorded a 52.7 percent decrease in acting-out behaviors and a 46.9 percent decrease in negligent behaviors for the investigation. Both of the decreases were statistically significant. In Group B, the teachers recorded a 30.3 percent decrease in negligent behaviors and a 25.4 percent decrease for acting-out behaviors. Neither of the decreases was significant.

2287.   Paine, S. C. "The Effects of Repeated Treatment on the Maintenance of Social Behavior." Ph.D. Dissertation, University of Oregon. Dissertation Abstracts International, 39 (7-A), 4184. Order no. 7901086, 1979.

Nine elementary school children, each referred originally to his/her teacher due to low levels of peer interaction in free-play situations at school, participated in a study designed to assess the effects of treatment "booster shots" on the maintenance of social behavior. Five of these children previously had been involved in CORBEH's Program for Establishing Effective Relationship Skills (PEERS); none of the remaining four children had a previous history of treatment for social withdrawal. An intervention package, consisting of social skills tutoring and a recess-based point system, was alternated with treatment reversal periods to determine whether maintenance effects would accumulate with repeated exposure to the treatment procedures. Observational data collected during playground recess periods showed that four of the five previously treated subjects were interacting within normative levels of social behavior following a series of three treatment "booster shots". In general, these data appeared to be stable during final maintenance evaluations. Only one of the four previously untreated subjects evidenced a similar effect. Verbal behavior did not appear to be responsive to the treatment procedures. Teacher and parent ratings of child social behavior revealed general improvement for both treated and untreated subjects between pre- and post-treatment assessments to rating levels approaching those of their non-withdrawn peers. Peer social metric ratings also showed increases from pre- to post-treatment phases for both groups of subjects.

2288.   Paquet, Ronald A.   "Judicial Rulings, State Statutes and State Administrative Regulations Dealing with the use of Corporal Punishment in Public Schools." Ed.D. Dissertation, Northern Illinois University, 1980. Dissertation Abstracts International, 41 (3-A), 878. Order no. 8020776.

It was the purpose of this study to determine the extent to which selected areas of judicial concern regarding the use of corporal punishment in schools are reflected in guidelines found in state statutes and administrative regulations. In addition, the study has drawn implications for consideration by legislators and educators who review or formulate regulations in the future. An analysis of state and federal court rulings concerning the legality of corporal punishment generated five general areas of judical concern (cruel and unusual punishment, equal protection, due process, manner of administration and rights of parents). Only three of these areas were found to have produced guidelines for the use of corporal punishment (due process, manner of administration and rights of parents). These three areas of judicial concern became the basis for the analysis of guidelines found in state statutes and administrative regulations. Copies of statutes and administrative regulations were solicited from each of the fifty states and the District of Columbia. The full texts of these statutes and regulations are contained in the study and provide a valuable resource for legislators and educators. The analysis of state statutes and administrative regulations indicated variety among states as to whether they address the subject of corporal punishment, whether they permit it, how much they leave to local discretion and what terminology they use to define, describe or limit its use. Corporal punishment is permitted in thirty-six states. Four states and the District of Columbia prohibit it. Ten states are silent about corporal punishment in their statutes and regulations. Of the forty states that address the topic of corporal punishment, thirty-one use only statutes, five use only administrative regulatinos and four use both statutes and administrative regulations. Statutes dealing with corporal punishment were found in both educational and criminal codes.

2289.   Parashar, O. D. "Investigation of the Academically Relevant Disturbed Classroom Behaviors of the Clinically Diagnosed Mentally Retarded, Learning Disabled and Emotionally Disturbed Children as Measured by the Devereux Elementary School Behavior Rating Scale." Ed.D. Dissertation, University of Cincinnati. Dissertation Abstracts International, 34 (9-A, PT 2), 5758-5759. Order no. 73-29,458, 1974.

The study was designed to identify and measure the nature and prevalence of academically relevant disturbed classroom behavior (ARDCB) factors of the clinically diagnosed Mentally Retarded, Learning Disabled and Emotionally Disturbed children. It was also aimed at identifying those unique ARDCB factors which distinguish them from each other. The sample of the study consisted of 172 subjects; 56 M.R., 51 L.D. and 65 E.D. children who were diagnosed in the clinics during a period of eleven months. All the subjects were enrolled in educational programs and were between the ages of 80 to 142 months at the time of investigation. Results indicated that (1) Disrespect-defiance was the most dominant factor which discriminated the L.D. and the E.D. subjects, (b) External blame was the most dominant factor which discriminated the three groups, and the M.R. and the E.D. subjects, and (c) Achievement anxiety was the most dominant factor which discriminated the M.R. and the L.D. subjects.

2290.   Patterson, J. R. "Applied Behavior Analysis in the Classroom: Issues and Techniques." Ph.D. Dissertation, The University of Arizona. Dissertation Abstracts International, 38 (3-A), 1307. Order no. 77-18,662, 1977.

This dissertation is a report of the process of moving a body of knowledge, gleaned from prior research in applied behavior analysis, into a special education setting. These activities are conceptualized as the dissemination of the process of inquiry, that is, the application of the scientific method by the teacher in order to evaluate teaching activities and attain specified education goals. The groundwork necessary for setting goals and making an environmental assessment is described. The process of implementing a teacher training program, setting up a token economy, managing that economy, restructuring classroom curriculum, implementing record keeping systems, designing observational instruments, collecting observational data, and using that data for feedback and decision making are described. In addition, the experimental comparison of two group contingent procedures versus individually contingent token reinforcement in a multiple-baseline design is described and discussed in terms of data on student classroom participation, department, and social interaction.

2291.   Peltzman, B. R. "Dyadic Interaction in the Primary School Classroom: An Examination of the Effects of Young Children on the Behavior of Teachers." Ed.D. Dissertation, Columbia University. Dissertation Abstracts International, 36 (3-A), 1291. Order no. 75-20,218, 1975.

This study considered the ways in which the behavior of young children seems to affect the behavior of the teacher. The study focused upon the dyacid interaction which takes place between the teacher and students in the Early Childhood classroom. It was hypothesized that an examination of the dyadic interaction would reveal that behavior occurs in a reciprocal fashion; thus, the teacher may learn behavior patterns as a result of the quality and quantity of dyadic interaction with young children, as well as influence the behavior of the children. The study examined and described the relationship between teacher behavior responses to student behavioral cues as this might reveal evidence of socialization of the teacher by the children. The questions and findings were as follows: 1. Is there a significant difference between teacher-initiated activities in the fourth month of school as compared to the first month of school? Data for all 14 classes were tested for difference between Period I and Period II. A significant difference was found at the .01 level. 2. Will Early Childhood teachers ask significantly more product questions (questions requiring a short, simple statement of fact answer) than process questions (questions requiring a detailed description of the intellectual or mechanical process involved in reaching the answer)? In all 14 classes in both periods, the proportion of product questions was significantly higher than process questions. 3. Will teachers respond with a "warming" or negative behavioral contact following child-initiated activities during the fourth month of school significantly more times than they did in the first month of school? The proportion of warnings and the proportion of negative behavioral responses in each class were compared in Period I and Period II. No significant difference was found for warnings, but a significant difference was found for negative behavioral responses at the .01 level. Will there be a significant difference in the quantity of procedural responses by the teacher to child-initiated activities during the first month of school and the fourth month of school? The proportion of procedural responses was significantly lower at the .01 level in Period II than in Period I. Will there be fewer child-initiated activities during the fourth month of school than there were during the first month of school? The number of child-initiated activities for Period I and Period II for all 14 classes were compared. No evidence of a decline was found.

2292.   Petruzielo, F. R. "Organizing and Using Resource Personnel to Improve Student Behavior." Introductory Practicum submitted in partial fulfillment of the requirements of the National Ed.D. program for educational leaders, Nova University, 1976. 25p.

A plan was devised to improve the behavior and attitude of
selected junior high school students who, as a result of
continual classroom misbehavior had been frequently referred
by classroom teachers to the assistant principal. The
program involved organization and use of resource persons
already available in the school including guidance counselors, the work experience coordinator and the substance
abuse specialist. They worked with each student in the
target group on a regular basis for the first nine week term
of the 1975-76 school year. Discipline records from the
previous school year were used to identify participants.
Each student's cumulative guidance record was reviewed and a
personal visit to each residence was made by the assistant
principal. Each student was withdrawn from one of his
regularly scheduled classes to participate in the program
and the progress of each pupil was monitored through the use
of commercially available interum progress report forms.
Results indicated that disciplinary referrals to the assistant principal for each student were reduced by 50%. The
classroom conduct grades for each student in the overall
group improved markedly and the attitudes of participants
were generally more positive at the conclusion of the program than they had been at the outset.

2293.   Pines, M. B. "An Investigation of the Effectiveness of
Contingency Contracting Using Teachers and Peers as Contract
Managers." Ph.D. Dissertation, The University of
Connecticut. Dissertation Abstracts International, 38
(1-A), 184. Order no. 77-14,492, 1977.

The purpose of the present study was to investigate the
effectiveness of contingency contracting in a school environment using professionals (teachers) and paraprofessionals
(students) as contract managers. In addition, changes in
selected behaviors resulting from the contractual system,
were examined. Behaviors of concern included on-task and
passive and aggressive off-task behavior of target students
along with several interaction measures (no response,
inappropriate talking, praise, disapproval, appropriate
talking, and attention). Six target students (two each from
grades two, three, and four) were selected because of insufficient appropriate classroom social and academic behaviors.
The behaviors of the six targets were observed and recorded
by means of categories adopted from the Behavioral Observation Schedule for Pupils and Teachers. All observational
data were collected using a ten-second time sample. The
four treatment conditions consisted of the successive
presentation and removal of reinforcement contingencies in
the form of teacher and peer managed contingency contracts
negotiated with each target student. Peers were selected
because of their popularity with targets and high frequency
of appropriate behaviors, while teachers volunteered to
participate. A within-subjects design, typical of applied
behavior analysis research, was used. The targets' behavior
was modified by means of a contingency contract managed by
peers and teachers in which points were exchanged for small

toys and special privileges. Peers and teachers operated a kitchen timer which rang at various times during the first academic period. If the target was engaged in appropriate behavior when the timer went off, he earned a point. If the target was not engaged in appropriate bheavior, he earned nothing. Results of correlated t-tests showed that contracting was an effective behavior change tool since the percentage of on-task behavior was significantly higher during intervention conditions (teacher and peer contracts) than during nonintervention phases (baseline and reversal). Peer managers were shown to be equally effective as teachers in modifying appropriate and inappropriate target behaviors.

2294.   Pinkelton, Norma B. H. A Comparison of Referred Headstart, Non-Referred Headstart and non-Headstart Groups of Primary Public School Children on Achievement, Language Processing and Classroom Behavior." Ed.D. Dissertation, University of Cincinnati. Dissertation Abstracts International, 37 (3-A), 1459-1460. Order no. 76-21,451, 1976.

The purpose of this study was to evaluate the progress of children who had gone through Cincinnati Public School System's Headstart Program as a means of getting some feedback about a longer range impact of Headstart. It was considered that five years was an adequate length of time to test for concrete changes in the socio-emotional, language, perceptual-motor and behavior of the children enrolled in Headstart. It was concluded that the Headstart and Non-Headstart students used in this study did not demonstrate any significant differences in cognitive abilities or in achievement-related classroom behavior overall. This was inclusively true for all variable comparisons from the traditional and the non-traditional tests. There were more areas of significant behavior differences for the main effect of sex between the subgroups of Headstart: 1) Referred and 2) Non-Referred than specific cognitive subgroup differences.

2295.   Piotrowski, W. D. "A Study of the Effects of Classroom Environment on Student Behavior: Open Pod Versus Self-Contained." Ph.D. Dissertation, The Florida State University. Dissertation Abstracts International, 38 (6-A), 3389. Order no. 77-26, 985, 1977.

This study examined the effect of walling-off individual class units within an open school pod upon student and teacher behaviors. One second-grade and one fourth-grade class unit were observed under open pod (four class units sharing the same instructional area) and self-contained conditions. During the self-contained condition the target class units were partioned-off from the remaining class units in the pod by using visual barriers. The data indicate that self-containment of single-class units within the open pod setting may increase productivity (percent of students turning in assignments), on-task behavior, and student mobility. Teacher behavior was generally not effected excepting a slightly higher rate of one-to-one teacher-student contacts during closed conditions. These findings imply that classroom structure may help to increase certain desired teacher and student behaviors.

2296.   Plumb, G. B. "A Comparison of School Morale in Junior High School Students Before and After a Comprehensive Intervention Program." Ph.D. Dissertation, Southern Illinois University. Dissertation Abstracts International, 37 (9-A), 5575-5576. Order no. 77-6249, 1977.

There has been little experimental research done as to whether or not attitudes toward school and the behavioral indices of attitudes, namely discipline and attendance can be improved. If, as much of the literature suggests, attitudes toward school can affect learning, it is imperative that ways be found to enhance the attitudes of young people toward school. A Title III program was implemented including 500 junior high school students, approximately 150 community participants and parents, and 24 graduate students in psychology or a related field. Regular school was suspended for two weeks in favor of workshops in three priority areas: 1) career explorations, 2) leisure-time activities, and 3) affective discussion groups. School Morale was measured pre and post. Absenteeism and discipline contacts were measured pre, during, and post. In addition, sex, race, standardized achievement scores, and amount of concentration in the three program areas were used to predict school morale. Results showed that: 1) measured school morale went down significantly three weeks after program, 2) there was no difference in absenteeism pre, during, or post program, 3) there was a significant decrease in discipline contacts during program when compared to prior to or following program, 4) there was a significant increase in discipline contacts following program when compared with prior to and during program, and 5) the independent variables used in regression analyses did not individually or collectively predict measured school morale better than chance.

2297.   Poetter, Rodney A. "The Effects of Covert Negative Reinforcement on Students' Attending Behavior." Ph.D. Dissertation, Ohio University. Dissertation Abstracts International, 38 (8-B), 3901-3902C. Order no. 7730272, 1978.

Covert negative reinforcement is a cognitive modification procedure whereby termination of an imagined aversive event leads to an increase in probability of the target behavior imagined immediately following its termination. Experiment 1 examines the effectiveness of the procedure on students' attending behavior. Experiment 2 addresses the theoretical basis for the procedure, viz., the assumption that this covert technique obeys the same laws as its established overt counterpart. Sixth-, seventh-, and eighth-grade learning disability students served as subjects. An observer monitored both attending and disruptive behaviors during the daily 45-minute class periods throughout both investigations. The results of Experiment 1 demonstrate that attending behavior improves significantly during covert negative reinforcement sessions when treatment trials occur at the beginning of the class period. Continued acceleration of the target behavior during a return to baseline conditions suggests that improved on-task responding is not a result of the procedure per se. This is further emphasized by results of Experiment 2, which demonstate that regardless of treatment condition, all students significantly improve attending behavior. It is concluded that the avoidance contingency is an unnecessary element of the procedure, and that the procedure works due to other variables, e.g., demand characteristics, expectancy, self-monitoring of a target behavior.

2298.   Pollack, S. L. "Reactivity in the Classroom Observation of Hyperactive Children." Ph.D. Dissertation, University of Houston. Dissertation Abstracts International, 39 (11-B), 5578-5579. Order no. 7910233, 1979.

The study attempted to investigate the extent of focal reactivity in the classroom observation of hyperactive children. Four classes of causal factors can be identified yet naturalistic technologies have differed in the type and extent of dependent measure confounding which has been produced. A technology for investigating focal reactivity was proposed and involved eliciting intentional response distortions which were compared with measurements made under baseline or typical conditions. Four carefully selected hyperactive and matched normal first grade boys were chosen for this study. Beginning with four days of baseline observation, all subjects were videotaped for one hour on eight consecutive school days. Following the baseline period, teachers were asked to alternately produce two-day samples of target children's "best" and "worst" behavior. As expected, measures of social behavior were not vulnerable to focal confounding while motor activity measures were generally non-reactive. Although there were differences between dependent measures and subject groups, the estimates of focal response distortions typically relected a "fake good" response set during normal observation. Attentional behavior patterns also appeared inflated during baseline conditions, particularly for the hyperactive sample. Teachers used different tactics to influence the two types of children, though they were more successful with the hyperactives. A heightened sensitivity to the misbehavior of target children during baseline observations may have mediated teachers' efforts to create a favorable impression in observers.

2299.   Preston, L. B.   "The Real and Ideal Role of the High
School Disciplinarian."   Ed.D. Dissertation, The University
of Arizona.   Dissertation Abstracts International, 35 (4-A),
1929.   Order no. 74-21,151, 1974.

The main purpose of this study was to determine whether
significant differences existed among the perceptions of
high school administrators, disciplinarians, teacher's and
students concerning the real and ideal roles of the high
school disciplinarian.   Specifically, the following questions were answered: 1) Are there significant differences
among the perceptions of high school administrators,
teachers, and students concerning the real and ideal roles
of the high school disciplinarians?   2) Are there significant differences among the perceptions of high school
principals, assistant principals, disciplinarians, teachers,
and students concerning the real and ideal roles of the high
school disciplinarian?   3) Among the eight high schools in
the study, are there significant differences concerning the
real and ideal roles of high school disciplinarians?   4) Is
there a relationship regarding the amount of contact a
student has had with the disciplinarian and the manner in
which he responds to the questionnaire?   The total sample
included eight high schools, eight high school principals,
sixteen high school assistant principals, sixteen high
school disciplinarians, eighty high school teachers, and 160
senior high school students.   Findings include: 1) There
were significant statistical differences at the .01 level of
significance among administrators, teachers, and students on
the ideal and real parts of the questionnaire utilized in
the study.   2) There were significant statistical differences at the .01 level of significance among the principals,
assistant principals, disciplinarians, teachers, and
students on the ideal and real parts of the questionnaire.
3) There was no statistical relationship between students'
contact with the disciplinarian and the manner in which they
responded to the questionnaire.   4) There were significant
statistical differences at the .01 level of significance
between schools regarding the ideal role of the high school
disciplinarian.   5) There were significant statistical
differences at the .01 level of significance between schools
regarding the real role of the high school disciplinarian.
6) Of the five groups in the study, students and assistant
principals were most lenient and disciplinarians and principals, the most severe.

2300.   Primeaux, A. F.   "The Relationship Between Pupil Control
Ideology, Pupil Control Behavior and the Political Attitudes
of Elementary School Teachers."   Ed.D. Dissertation, The
Pennsylvania State University, 1979.

The basic purpose of this study was to determine whether
there was a relationship between elementary teachers' pupil
control ideology (PCI), pupil control behavior (PCB), and
their political attitudes.   Four hypotheses were tested in
this investigation: 1) Teacher custodialism in PCI will be

directly related to the teacher's conservative political attitudes. 2) Teacher custodialism in PCB will be directly related to the teacher's conserative political attitudes. 3) Teacher humanism in PCI will be directly related to the teacher's liberal political attitudes. 4) Teacher humanism in PCB will be directly related to the teacher's liberal political attitudes. The Pupil Control Ideology Form developed by Willower, Idell and Hoy was employed as the measure of teacher beliefs toward control on a humanistic-custodial continuum. The Pupil Control Behavior Form, a companion instrument to the PCI Form was completed by the students and measured teacher PCB on a humanistic-custodial continuum. The instruments were administered to 86 class-room teachers in selected public schools, contract schools and cooperative schools. These three school types were selected in order that Indian and non-Indian teacher PCI, PCB and political attitudes might be compared. Of the 86 teachers in the sample, 22 were Native American and 64 were Caucasian. The data collected on each instrument was coded, scored, key-punched and analyzed through computer programs. The major hypotheses were tested by the Pearson product-moment correlation coefficient formula. Multiple mean comparisons were tested by analysis of variance. Additional analyses using the t-test for differences between the means were computed for other major variables. It was found that the relationship between teacher custodialism in PCI and conservative political attitudes was significant at the .01 level. The tests of the three other major hypotheses failed to yield significant results. There were no significant differences among teachers by school type, age, sex or ethnic affiliation of PCI and PCB scores. However, on the variable of liberalism one comparison yielded differences that were significant beyond the .01 level. Indian teachers were more liberal in their political views than non-Indian teachers. No significant results were found for the vari-able of conservatism. Order no. 7922332, DAI.

2301.   Pritchett, Wendell. "The Relationship Between Teacher Pupil Control Behavior and Student Attitudes Toward School." D.Ed. Dissertation, The Pennsylvania State University, 1974.   Dissertation Abstracts International, 35 (4-A), 1929-1930. Order no. 74-21,022.

In this study, the relationship between student perception of teacher pupil control behavior and student attitudes toward school was examined. Data were secured from two paper and pencil instruments. 1) The Pupil Control Behavior (PCB) Form of Helsel and Willower, This instrument was designed to measure educators' behavior with regard to pupil control. 2) Coster's High School Student Opinion Question-naire (HSSOQ), Part I, provided data concerning student attitudes toward school. It was hypothesized that there is a positive relationship between custodialism in teacher pupil control behavior and unfavorable student attitudes toward school. The PCB Form and the HSSOQ were administered to students from metropolitan area secondary schools.

Correlations between each pupil's scores on measures of perceptions of teacher pupil control behavior and student attitudes toward schools were computed. Some of the conclusions of the study were: 1) Custodial teacher pupil control behavior was found to be positively related to negative student attitudes toward school. 2) Junior high school students perceived teacher pupil control behavior as somewhat more custodial than senior high school students perceived their teachers' pupil control behavior to be. 3) Student attitudes toward teachers were revealed to be a particularly dominant factor in determining student attitudes toward school. 4) The relatively high correlation between student attitudes toward teachers and teacher pupil control behavior emphasized the importance of interpersonal relationships in determining students' attitudes toward school.

2302.   Proctor, J. E. "The Attitudes of Elementary Principals and Teachers From Schools With Three Different Racial Student Populations Toward Student Behavior Problems and Principal Responses to Student Behavior Problems." Ed.D. Dissertation, Northern Illinois University. Dissertation Abstracts International, 40 (5-A), 2472. Order no. 7924403, 1979.

This study examined the attitudes toward discipline of elementary school principals and teachers from schools with three different racially integrated student populations in terms of what they considered serious student behavior problems, and what they considered appropriate principal responses to student behavior problems. Principals and teachers indicated how serious they considered each of 39 student behavior problems listed on The Student Behavior Elvauation Form. Elementary principals and teachers in three suburban school districts in Northern Illinois constituted the population for this study. 1) Principals from schools with three different racially integrated student populations were largely in agreement regarding their perceptions of serious student behavior problems. There was a significant difference in their responses of two of 39 items on The Student Behavior Evaluation Form. The two items were: no interest in classwork and daydreaming in class. 2) The attitudes of elementary principals from schools with three different racially integrated student populations were mixed in terms of what they considered appropriate responses for elementary principals to make to serious student behavior problems. There was a significant difference in the frequency that they selected as appropriate four of ten principals response items on The Principal Response Scale. The four responses were: talk to and/or warn the student (tell what will happen if problem continues), assign in-school suspension, suspend from school, and recommend expulsion. 3) There were differences in the attitudes of elementary teachers from schools with three different racially integrated student populations in terms of what they considered serious student behavior problems. There was a significant difference in their responses to ten of 39 itmes on The Student Behavior Evaluation Form. The ten items were: no interest in classwork, failure to turn in required work, immature behavior for student's age and grade, habitually lae to school, threatening other students (ex. "I'm going to beat you up at lunchtime."), fighting in school, gang threatens an individual or small group, lying or untruthfulness, calling other students names, and calling other students' parents names. 4) The attitudes of elementary teachers from schools with three different racially integrated student populations were mixed in terms of what they considered appropriate responses for elementary principals to make to serious student behavior problems. There was a significant difference in the frequency that they selected as appropriate three of ten principal response items on The Principal Response Scale. The three responses were: involve special service personnel (social worker, nurse, pyschologist, etc.), use corporal punishment (if the district permits), and assign in-school suspension.

2303.   Prosser, Ronald L. "The Effects of Teacher Consultation on the Nonproductive Behaviors of Elementary School Children." Ed.D. Dissertation, The University of Arizona. Dissertation Abstracts International, 37 (4-A), 1996. Order no. 76-22,471, 1976.

Many theorists have proposed that there is a functional relationship between the child's behaviors and the interactions with significant adults. They suggest further, that a most efficacious way to change the nonproductive behaviors of children is to educate parents and teachers in the use of principles and methods found to be effective in dealing with these behaviors. The present study investigated the effect of a teacher-consultation model based upon Adlerian principles by determining its impact on specific nonproductive behaviors of elementary school children. The sample consisted of six elementary school children that ranged in age from six to fifteen. With the use of a multiple baseline, data were recorded on the following behaviors: 1) teachers' positive responses directed to the selected students, 2) teachers' negative responses directed to the selected students, 3) selected students' productive behaviors, and 4) selected students' nonproductive behaviors. Following the collection of the baseline data by two independent observers in each of the three classrooms, a teacher-consultation session was held on a weekly basis with each teacher. An increase was noted in selected students' productive behaviors and the teachers' positive responses directed to the selected students. A decrease was observed in selected students' nonproductive behaviors and the teachers' negative responses directed to the selected students. The results suggested that a teacher-consultation model which focuses on Adlerian principles and methods would produce enduring changes in the nonproductive behaviors of elementary school children.

2304.   Puckett, R. B. "A Review of Selected Research Findings Pertaining to Classroom Discipline." Ed.D. Dissertation, Saint Louis University. Dissertation Abstracts International, 40 (04). Order no. 7923668, 1978.

The project involved an intensive and extensive search of the periodical literature and ERIC for research and review articles dealing directly and indirectly with aspects of discipline, both inside and outside of the classroom. The essence of the project involved an investigation and presentation of selected research findings and reviews of discipline in an attempt to relate such toward a meaningful discourse that might be employed by teachers in the disposition of their duties. Exactly 946 individual research studies pertaining to discipline were investigated, categorized, and utilized to support 114 generalized research findings. In addition, 114 reviews of various aspects pertaining to discipline were categorized and briefly referred to in the project. Articles involving opinions, testimonials, and/or editorials were omitted. The combined 1,060 individual research and review articles dealth with a variety of subjects. Such pertinent items as discipline research, rating devices, attitudes, social pressures, parent and teacher behavior, characteristics of behavioral problem children, environmental influences on behavior, punishment, aggression, school discipline, self control, and behavior modification procedures were included. The findings of the project were diverse and subject to individual scrutiny. A lengthy and detailed bibliography was provided for follow-up study.

2305.   Purgess, P. J. "Teacher Expectancy for Academic Success in Relation to Label, Sex, and Pupil Behavior." Ph.D. Dissertation. Fordham University, 1979.

The study investigated effects of labels ("educable mentally retarded", no label, "intellectually normal"), pupil behavior (adaptive or disruptive), and pupil sex on teacher expectations of academic success. Effects of these three variables on teachers' ratings of present academic success and likelihood of retention were also examined. Teacher Evaluation of Academic Success Scale (TEASS), developed by the present researcher, consisted of twelve behavioral descriptions of hypothetical children. A pilot study demonstrated the construct validity as well as the test-retest reliability of the TEASS. Childrens' behavior, sex, and educational label were varied in the twelve vignettes. Teachers rated the hypothetical child described as to his/her probable future academic success, present academic achievement, and likelihood of retention on a six point scale ranging from "excellent" to "very poor." Elementary school teachers ($\underline{N}$=1344) employed by the New York City public school system responded to the TEASS. Teachers were randomly assigned to experimental groups through a random distribution of one behavioral description. Teacher return rate was 38 percent. Results indicated that labels and pupil behavior affected teachers' expectations of academic success, ratings of present academic achievement, and ratings of likelihood of retention. However, pupil sex did not have a significant effect on any dependent variables. Thus, variables of label and pupil behavior were found to be more potent than pupil sex in explaining teachers' expectations. Results indicated that teachers rated disruptive children as less likely to be academically successful in both the present and future as well more likely to be retained than adaptively behaved children. Teachers were found to hold negative expectations for present and future academic success as well as for the likelihood of retention of hypothetical children labeled "educable mentally retarded" as compared to those labeled "intellectually normal." Unlabeled conditions posed problems for teachers. Teachers were not able to predict the future academic success or likelihood of retaining unlabeled children. A significant interaction effect was found between pupil behavior and educational label. Order No. 7920683, DAI.

2306.   Quesenbery, Billy G., Jr. "Contingency Management in the Classroom: A Demonstration of a No-Cost Plan and Investigation of Interval Reinforcement Effects on a Group Operant."   Ph.D.   Dissertation,   University   of   South Carolina, 1971.   Dissertation Abstracts International, 32 (10-B), 6038. Order no. 72-12,022.

A no-cost, contingency management plan utilizing tokens, free-time, and interval reinforcement of a group operant was applied to two fifth-grade classes to evaluate its effectiveness in reducing inappropriate verbalizing. Also of interest was whether reinforcement at the end of fixed vs. variable intervals (FI vs. VI) would differentially affect the rate of inappropriate verbalizaing in the two classes during conditioning and extinction. Inappropriate verbalizing, the dependent variable, was measured daily via continuous in-class observation and noted as the number of 10 sec. intervals in which unauthorized talk or obnoxious oral noise-making occurred. The design was a conventional reversal type using matched groups and replication. Variables on which the two classes were matched included a) grade level, b) subject matter, c) teaching style, d) age, e) sex, f) intelligence, g) socio-economic status, and h) level of inappropriate verbalizing. After a 10 day baseline period, during which behavioral equivalence of the two classes was ascertained, one class was assigned to an FI reinforcement condition and the other to a VI reinforcement condition. During a five day conditioning phase teams in each class were observed at fixed or vriable intervals by the teacher and awarded tokens (chalk marks on the board) for following a rule which prohibited unauthorized talking. Teams which earned five or all of the six possible points were granded 8 min. of free-time at the end of the class period; losing teams continued working. During extinction, the next phase, plan-specified contingencies were discontinued and classes conducted as they had been prior to the experiment. Replication consisted of observing the effects of reintroducing the plan and discontinuing after another five day conditioning period. Cumulative frequency functions generated by the classes during each conditioning and extinction phase were compared for the purpose of detecting differences in behavior effected by the use of VI vs. FI reinforcement schedules. None were found. Between-phase comparisons which consisted of comparing frequencies recorded for a class during one phase with those of the same class in all other phases, indicated that plan-specified contingencies reduced markedly the amount of inappropriate verbalizing in both classes. Evidence pointing toward possible loss in plan-effectiveness, however, was found when daily measures (absolute frequencies) recorded for the two classes in the first conditioning and extinction phases were totalled and compared with those in the second conditioning and extinction phases.

2307.   Quinn, A. R. "The effects of intrinsic and extrinsic reinforcement on the learning of paired associates as it relates to middle class boys with behavior problems who vary in their locus of control." Ph.D. Dissertation, the University of Connecticut, 1974.

In order to explore the relationship between locus of control and reinforcement effectiveness with boys who present behavior problems within the regular public school classroom, an experimental design was developed. One hundred and fifty six middle class boys in grades four through six were screened with the conduct disorder and personality problem items from the Behavior Problem Checklist. Hypotheses that were tested included 1) there would be no significant difference between conduct disorder and personality problem children in learning, 2) there would be no significant difference between the conditions of intrinsic and extrinsic reinforcement in learning, 3) there would be no significant difference between boys within an internal and an external locus of control in learning, 4) there would be no significant difference in the interaction between reinforcements and types of behavior problems in learning. These hypotheses were accepted. Trends with regard to the hypothesis that there would be no signficant difference in the interaction between reinforcements and locus of control in learning were found. In general, internals tend to do better with intrinsic reinforcement than with extrinsic reinforcement.

2308.   Ramage, R. L. "A Study of the Effects of Activity Group Counseling on the Self-Concepts, Teachers' Ratings of Student Behavior, and Achievement of Fourth and Fifth Grade Students with Learning Disabilities." Ed.D. Dissertation, The Medical College of Pennsylvania, 1979.

This study was designed to investigate the effects of Activity Group Counseling on the self-concepts, the classroom behavior patterns, and the achievement levels of fourth

and fifth grade students classified as "learning disabled."
The effectiveness of the model of intervention as conceptualized for this study, was evaluated by assessing: 1)
Self-concept as measured by the Piers-Harris Children's
Self-Concept Scale, 2) Behavior as measured by the Teacher's
Rating Scale of Student Behavior, and 3) Achievement in
arithmetic and reading as measured by the Wide Range Achievement Test. Subjects for this study were 63 fourth and fifth
grade students classified as "learning disabled," from six
public elementary schools in the South Area of Dade County,
Florida. The sample was predominately male, with ages
ranging from 9 to 12. For each school, the sample was
divided into three groups -- two treatment and one control.
Small groups of three to five subjects met 16 times for
30-minute sessions over an eight-week period. The three
instruments, Piers-Harris Children's Self-Concept Scale,
Teacher's Rating Scale of Student Behavior, and Wide Range
Achievement Test, were utilized in a pre- and post-test
experimental design. Subjects were randomly assigned to
three groups -- Activity Group Counseling, Arts/Crafts
Activity, and Control. Analysis of the data revealed no
statisically significant differences among the means of the
three groups. Each of the null hypotheses failed to be
rejected. it could not, therefore, be concluded that
Activity Group Counseling as defined in this study, does
influence: 1) Self-concept as measued by the Piers-Harris
Children's Self-Concept Scale, 2) Behavior as perceived by
classroom teachers, and 3) Arithmetic or reading achievement, as measured by the Wide Range Achievement Test. These
vairables are equally unaffected by Activity Group Counseling as a model of intervention for the particular population of children identified for this study. Order no.
7921769, DAI.

2309.   Rappaport, S. J. "Teacher-Student Questioning and
Approval/Disapproval Behavior in High School Social
Studies." Ph.D. Dissertation, Columbia University.
Dissertation Abstracts International, 35 (7-B), 3563-3564.
Order no. 74-28,524, 1975.

This study was designed to investigate, systematically, the
types and rates of questions asked by teachers and students
to determine whether the findings of previous research would
be replicated. Further, the types of responses to these
questions and the use of teacher verbal approval and disapproval were examined to investigate the role of reinforcement as a variable in maintaining the high frequency of
teacher "memory" or "fact" questions and the low frequency
of student questioning. The student sample for this study
consisted of 968 students from a suburban community outside
of New York City. Since there wre no observed instances of
students verbally approving or disapproving of teacher questions or responses, it was hypothesized that the type of
student response gave a teacher important information about
her teaching. Receiving correct responses from a student,
consequently, would be reinforcing to a teacher because it

implied that she was doing a "good job." This theory was supported as teachers in this study asked, in highest frequency, those types of questions (definition questions of non-instructional managerial items and isolated fact content) which had the highest probability of yielding a correct response as opposed to an incorrect or nonresponse.

2310.   Rautenberg, L. L. "Development of a School Attitude Scale and Its Relationship to Student Response Variables." Ph.D. Dissertation, The University of Nebraska. Dissertation Abstracts International, 39 (7-A), 4150-4141D. Order no. 7900345, 1979.

The purpose of this study was to test the relationship between students' attitudes toward school and several kinds of variables, in particular, students' school behavior. The procedures used in this study were 1) the development of a reliable instrument to measure high school students' general attitudes toward school and 2) the collection of data to test the relationship of pupils' school attitudes and several criterion variables. The instrument was piloted on a sample of 62 high school students attending a parochial school in Lincoln, Nebraska. The main investigation was carried out on a sample of 223 students attending a high school in Syracuse, Nebraska. 1) The pupils' school attitudes were moderately correlated to two aspects of their school behavior as was reported by the students: 1) the number of different types of extra-curricular activities participated in by the students, and 2) the number of times the students were punished or reprimanded by school personnel. The students' school attitudes did not accurately predict pupil lateness, tardiness, absenteeism, or class-cutting. 2) The students' general attitudes toward school were fairly highly correlated to the students' average or overall attitude toward all of their school subjects (physical education excluded), and were moderately correlated to the students' favorite and most disliked subjects. 3) The students' school attitudes were very highly correlated to the students' self-ratings of their own school attitudes. The pupils' school attitudes did not accurately predict: 1) students' grade point averages, 2) teacher ratings of their students' attitudes toward school, and 3) pupils' ratings of their classmates' attitudes toward school. 4) The pupils' attitudes toward school did not predict most indicators of parental involvement in their children's education, as reported by the students, when the variance attributed to the dependent variables was partialled out. 5) The students' general school attitudes did not predict most indicators of the socioeconomic status of the students' families as reported by the students, after the partialling out procedure.

2311.   Ree, George E. "The Relationship of Religiosity to School Behavior of Public High School Students." Ed.D. Dissertation, State University of New York at Albany, 1973. Dissertation Abstracts International, 34 (3-A), 1041. Order no. 73-19,696.

The purpose of this investigation was to compare the school related behavior of students judged by their pastors as possessing "high religiosity" with the behavior of other students within the same junior high and senior high school classes. The investigation was conducted in the six New York State public school districts of Worcester, Maryland (Schenevus), Milford, Unatego (Unadilla and Otego), Sidney and Afton. Each community was a relatively small rural village, located near the foot of the Catskill Mountains and along the Susquehanna River. After permission was granted by both the school and church authorities, the students of "high religiosity" were nominated by their pastors. The names of these students were taken to the school guidance counselors for a "best match" with other students in the school. The matching process was based on five criteria: Grade, Sex, Academic Quartile, Course of Study, and Warner Scale Socio-economic level based upon the occupation of the parents. Three teachers rated each matched pair of students on a seven point behavior scale. The teachers were not given any information as to the groupings or comparisons to be made. The Behavior Scale, developed for this study, included four major areas with six questions in each area. These major areas were: Classroom Conformity, Social Considerations, Personal Goal Seeking, and Controversial Matters. High positive correlations were obtained between "Classroom Conformity" and "personal Goal Seeking," and between "Social Considerations" and "Controversial Matters." High positive correlations (.820 to .872) were noted within each of the two groups of students compared but not between the groups.

2312.   Reynolds, Boyd. "Automatic Suspension as Preventive Discipline: A Procedure Designed to Eliminate Disturbing Behavior from the Classroom and the Child in Elementary Schools, United States Dependents Schools, European Area." Ed.D. Dissertation, University of Southern California, 1972. Dissertation Abstracts International, 33 (5-A), 2047. Order no. 72-27,689.

The purpose of the study was to investigate in a systematic manner the effectiveness of one special procedure, automatic suspension, in reducing or eliminating in a school of military dependents a child's recurring disturbing behavior from the child as well as from the classroom. A careful review of the literature, related research, and legal back- ground was undertaken to determine the nature and appro- priateness of the study and to determine the legality of the procedure. The opinions of five specialists were sought to learn the psychological soundness of automatic suspension.

Automatic suspension was used as a non-punitive consequences of disturbing behavior with children who had been identified by teachers as having chronically disturbing behavior. A record was kept of the dates and times of each child's suspensions. Interviews were conducted with the parents and teachers of each child. During the period September 1970 to March 1972, there were fifteen children who were placed on automatic suspension and for whom records of quantitative data were kept and for whom qualitative data were obtained from interviews. 1) Elimination of target behaviors for one day was achieved on the first day of automatic suspension by two children, on the second day by four children, and on the third day by five children. Elimination of the target behavior for one month was achieved in the third month of automatic suspension by two children, in the fourth month by four children, and by one child each in the fifth month, sixth month, and eighth month. 2) While automatic suspension was in effect, the percentage of days on which target behaviors were not performed by all subjects was 84.6, ranging between 41.4 percent and 94.9 percent. 3) Factors influencing the time required to reduce performance of target behaviors wre a) the amount of time that the child had remaining in school, b) parent and teacher consistency in fulfilling their roles, and c) parental mental set toward automatic suspension. 4) The latter two factors also were found to influence the effectiveness of automatic suspension in reducing the performance of target behaviors.

2313.   Rice, W. K., Jr. "Effects of Discipline Techniques on Children's Personality-Trait Inferences." Ph.D. Dissertation, The University of Oklahoma. Dissertation Abstracts International, 34 (12-A, Part 1), 7593-7594. Order no. 74-12, 322, 1974.

The effects of task-focused and approval-focused desists were investigated under conditions of limited information. Sixty-four eighth grade students heard one of two tape-recorded desists. They then rated the target of the desist and the teacher doing the desisting on: a. personality-trait scales and b. degree of confidence scales. The scripts for the tapes were developed from statements rated as task- or approval-focused by 35 graduate students. The words used in the personality-trait scales were selected from a larger group of personality-trait adjectives that had been rated by 50 students as to the desirability of either a teacher or child described by the word. The instruments were validated using stories designed to depict positive and negative personality-traits. These were presented to 32 students. A discriminant analysis revealed that the scores of the personality-trait scales accurately classified the individuals described. The instruments were then used to measure the effects of discipline techniques on children's personality-trait inferences. The use of approval-focused desists resulted in the target of the desists and the person doing the desisting being rated as having significantly less desirable personality-traits. No significant effects due to

the Sex of the rater or Sex of rater x Type of desist interaction were observed. No significant differences were
observed when the degree of confidence scales were analyzed.

2314.   Richburg, J. E. "A Descriptive Analysis of Pupils'
Perceptions of the Use of Reward and Punishment." Ph.D.
Dissertation, Michigan State University. Dissertation
Abstracts International, 37 (9-A), 5590-5591. Order no.
77-5874, 1977.

The purpose of this study was to analyze the effect of
certain reward and punishment techniques used by elementary
school teachers, when applied according to the moral development stage of the pupil with whom they are used. In addition, an attempt was made to determine whether it is
possible to derive from the Kohlberg model a more useful
procedure for analyzing descriptions of a teacher's approach
to rewards and punishments, and whether there is a reasonable basis for assuming that teachers who have a well-
conceived rationale for selecting a certain reward and/or
punishment for their individual pupils have more success in
social control in the classroom. It was felt to be
expecially important that educators fully understand the
concepts that underlie the use of reward and punishment and
why particular rewards and punishments are effective with
certain, but not all, pupils. Data were collected from all
teachers in grades 3, 4, and 5 at a single school in which
99 percent of the pupils were white, middle class, and whose
parents were predominantly college educated. There were two
teachers at each of the three grade levels mentioned--three
females and three males. The teachers involved in the study
were asked to provide the names of four students with whom
they felt they had in the past been successful in using a
reward or punishment to get the student to comply with the
teacher's standard of acceptable behavior. The teachers
were asked to describe, in a general way, the kinds of
rewards and punishments they used, which ones were effective
or ineffective, and what they thought were reasons for their
effectiveness or ineffectiveness. Each teacher was also
asked to name four different students with whom he or she
had been unsuccessful. Additionally, each teacher related
an episode that involved each of the eight pupils. The
teacher described each student's behavior in the episode and
told how he attempted to get the student to comply with his
standard of classroom behavior. Two judges decided whether
the teacher's approach in attempting to get the pupil to
comply would appeal to a child at Stage 1, 2, 3, 4, 5, or 6
of the Kohlberg model of moral development, which was
selected for use in analyzing the teachers' responses.
Students who had been mentioned by the teachers were questioned to determine their perceptions of the kinds of reward
and punishments their teachers used. Each pupil was asked
what he thought his teacher would and should do if he
behaved in a certain way described by the interviewer. The
same two judges were asked to decide whether the student's
suggested manner of handling the same episode his teacher

had earlier described would appeal to a child at Stage 1, 2,
3, 4, 5, or 6. Comparisons were then made between the moral
developmental stages of the teachers' and students'
responses. It was noted whether the moral developmental
stage appeal of each student's response was the same as,
lower, or higher than the developmental stage appeal of his
teacher's response. Teachers who attempted to make their
reward or punishment fit the child's characteristics were
referred to in this study as differentiators. Those
teachers who used the same reward or punishment for all
pupils, irrespective of individual characteristics, were
referred to as nondifferentiators. The results of this
study showed that more pupils of teachers who differentiated
(87.5 percent) reported that they liked the teacher; ways of
handling them than did pupils of teachers who did not
differentiate (68.8 percent). Generally, more successfully
managed pupils of both teachers who differentiated and of
those who did not (89.6 percent) reported that they liked
the way the teachers handled them than was true for the
unsuccessfully managed pupils (66.7 percent).

2315.   Richey, D. D. "Classroom Behavioral Styles of Learning
Disabled and Non-Learning Disabled Children: Implications
for the Stereotype and for Remediation." Ph.D.
Dissertation, The University of North Carolina at Chapel
Hill. Dissertation Abstracts International, 36 (6-A), 3569.
Order no. 75-29,065, 1975.

The purpose of the investigation was to examine the classroom behavioral style of learning disabled children as
compared to that of non-learning disabled children. The
research was conducted in two elementary schools in the
Durham County School System. Data were collected in a total
of 10, third or fourth grade classrooms, five classrooms at
each school. Fifteen learning disabled children from those
settings were matched on selected variables with non-
learning disabled children. Each of the 15 pairs was
observed simultaneously for a total of 30 minutes over a
three-day period. Two observers were used to collect time
sampling observational data. Behavior was coded every 10
seconds; each subject therefore had 180 behavior entries.
Behavior was observed in the morning (between 9:30 a.m. and
11:15 a.m.) predominantly during language arts activities.
The observation instrument employed provided for coding of
behavior into 12 discrete categories, including self-
directed activity, attending, constructive play, task-
oriented interaction, non-constructive activity, distractibility, passive responding, gross motor activity, social
interaction, dependency, aggression, and teacher interaction. It was discovered that the only classroom behavior
which differentiated learning disabled children from non-
learning disabled children was distractibility. There was
very limited support for the stereotyped cluster of negative
behaviors associated with learning disabilities. The group
difference finding on distractibility and the failure to
identify other behavioral style differences were discussed

regarding their relevance both for the stereotype and for remediation of learning disabilities.

2316.   Rife, F. N. "Modification of Student-Teacher Behavior and Its Effects Upon Pupil Behavior." Ph.D. Dissertation, The Ohio State University. Dissertation Abstracts International, 34 (8-A, PT 1), 4844-4845. Order no 74-3298, 1974.

In an effort to determine the extent to which a behavioral focus in physical education teacher training is effective in the acquisition of appropriate teaching behaviors, this study examined the changes in teacher behavior and its effects upon pupil behavior. Data for both teacher and pupils were analyzed as the differences between rates of teacher behavior and percentages of appropriate pupil behavior during baseline and after modeling intervention with accompanying feedback. Subjects were two male students of The Ohio State University enrolled in their student teaching experience in the Columbus Public elementary schools. The pupils observed were in these classes. Student teachers were observed for ten one-minute intervals of event recording. Pupils were observed for a ten-second period, termed placheck was used for determining the percent of pupils engaged in appropriate behavior. A time interval termed response latency was also taken on the students. This was utilized to see how much time it required for students to organize themselves into an activity upon cues from the teacher. Modeling consisted of the experimenter teaching the class and emphasizing a particular teaching behavior. Feedback came after a modeling intervention and consisted of instructions, cueing and reinforcement, and graphic feedback. Results of this study showed that modeling and feedback were effective in decreasing teacher behavior rates of negative feedback for skill attempts and negative reactions to off-task behavior. Modeling and feedback were also effective in increasing teacher behavior rates of positive feedback for skill attempts and negative reactions to on-task behavior. The teacher category of managerial behavior remained unaffected. The student behavior of response latency revealed a mixed effect as one teacher's class decreased its response latency while another showed an increase. Both classes had high percentages of appropriate behavior yet as teacher control shifted from negative to positive, appropriate pupil behavior went even higher.

2317.   Riley, M. G. "The Identification and Validation of Critical Incidents in Classroom Discipline and the Solutions Reported by First-Year Vocational Teachers in the State of Florida." Ph.D. Dissertations, The Florida State University. Dissertation Abstracts International, 40 (09). Order no. 8007501, 1979.

The purpose of the study was 1) to identify those discipline incidents that were both critical and frequent in occurrence

and the appropriate alternatives for handling the selected
incidents; 2) to identify the types of solutions used by the
first-year vocational teachers in resolving the discipline
problems and the types of solutions proposed by experts in
the field for resolving the discipline problems; and 3) to
compare the solution types used by the teachers with the
solution types proposed by experts in the field. The
selected sample included seventy-nine first-year vocational
teachers who were teaching in public secondary schools in
twenty-nine county districts in the state of Florida. The
findings of the study suggest the following: 1) first-year
vocational teachers in the state of Florida are experiencing
discipline problems that are both critical and frequent in
occurrence under the categories of a) class assignment, b)
disruptive personal habits, c) equipment safety, d) interpersonal conflicts, e) mainstreaming of slow learners, f)
mischievous actions, and g) racial misunderstanding; 2) the
types of solutions most frequently used by the teachers in
resolving discipline problems were classified as having a
short term effect and included external counseling, corporal
punishment, direct and academic strategies; 3) the types of
solutions most frequently proposed by experts in the field
were classified as having a short term effect and included
external counseling, corporal punishment, direct and
academic strategies; 4) the types of solutions most
frequently proposed by experts in the field were classified
as having a long term effect and included such strategies as
individual counseling, group counseling, the behavioral
approach and removal from the classroom; 5) when confronted
with a discipline problem, source assistance identified by
first-year vocational teachers were obtaining informal
assistance from colleagues and to a lesser degree, assistance from administrators; non specified in-service education as a source of assistance.

2318.   Risner, Roy L. "Student Attitudes Toward Corporal
Punishment." Ph.D. Dissertation, United States
International University, 1975. Dissertation Abstracts
International, 36 (3-A), 1181. Order no. 75-20,256.

The problem of the study was to determine the attitudes of
students toward corporal punishment, and its effectiveness
as a disciplinary process. The study was designed to
delineate those differences in attitudes attributed to age,
grade, sex, ethnic group, and socio-economic level. The
method was to conduct individual interviews with two hundred
students from Banning, California and Palmdale, California.
The selection of students included the 1974 summer school
enrollments of Coombs Intermediate School, every third
student at Banning High School, every tenth student from
Palmdale Intermediate School, and a Palmdale driver's education class. The interviews were conducted in seclusion and
on a one-to-one basis. Three interviewers were used. Each
interviewer asked the same questions and recorded the
answers on a duplicate record sheet. The results showed
that a majority of students (79 percent) were in favor of

corporal punishment both at home and school. Students perceived corporal punishment as 75 percent effective. The students interviewed were generally in favor of corporal punishment's continued use in the school (71 percent). Eighty-nine percent of the two hundred students interviewed felt that corporal punishment should be used at home. A majority of students in all categories (age, grade, sex, ethnic group, and socio-economic level) favored corporal punishment. The only exception was the seventeen year olds where only 44 percent favored the use of corporal punishment at school. Corporal punishment as perceived by the student seems to be effective. Seventy-seven percent said that experiencing corporal punishment stopped them from committing punishable acts, and 70 percent said that the threat of corporal punishment stopped them from committing punishable acts.

2319.   Roberts, S. M. "Race, Values and Pupil Control Ideology: An Analysis of the Relationship Among Some Variables Influencing Teachers' Perceptions of the Leadership Effectiveness of Black Principals." Ph.D. Dissertation, New York University. Dissertation Abstracts International, 38 (2-A), 582. Order no. 77-16,445, 1977.

The purpose of this investigation was to assess the impact of race, congruency of value orientation, and congruency of pupil control attitudes on teachers' perceptions of the leadership effectiveness of black principals. Social systems theory, the distinction between sacred and secular values, and pupil control ideology formed the theoretical bases of the study. Three instruments and a personal data form were administered to staff members of 33 elementary schools in Bergen and Essex Counties in northern New Jersey. The first instrument administered to teachers and principals was the Differential Values Inventory (DVI) to determine the respondents' values. The second instrument, the Executive Professional Leadership Scale (EPL), was administered to the teachers in the study sample in order to measure teacher ratings of the principal as as leader. The final instrument, the Pupil Control Ideology Form (PCI), was administered to teachers and principals to determine attitudes toward pupil control. Thirty-three black principals and a stratified random sample of 349 black teachers and 346 non-black teachers participated in the study. Differences between groups in the ratings of the effectiveness of the principals were subjected to t-tests. It was found that (1) black teachers rated black principals higher on EPL than did non-black teachers with an (emergent) traditional value system and (3) that black teachers with a (humanistic) custodial pupil control orientation rated black principals higher than did non-black teachers with a (humanistic) custodial pupil control orientation.

2320.   Robertson, J. C. "A Study of Principals' Perceptions of Discipline Problems in Tennessee's Middle Schools." Ed.D. Dissertation, Memphis State University. Dissertation Abstracts International, 41 (3-A), 926. Order no. 8020389, 1980.

This study investigated the perceptions of Tennessee middle school principals relative to selected variables that are concerned with discipline. Of primary concern in this study was the extent of the discipline problem and the major causes of discipline problems. These comparisons were made among male and female principals, principals of rural and urban schools, and principals of large, medium, and small schools, using the number of teachers on the faculty as the criterion to determine the size of the school. Additional areas of concern in this study included: change in the discipline problem; types of students according to sex, race, and achievement levels involved in discipline problems; use of expulsions; use of suspensions; use of corrective measures and the extent that these measures are effective; and administration of punishment on an equitable basis. This study utilized a mailed opinionnaire. Analysis of the data generated by this opinionnaire revealed that there were no statistically significant this study also indicated that the discipline problems had not increased during the past three years. The discipline problems that did exist were, according to these principals, attributable to the influences of society and the home. Disobedience to general rules and to the teacher was perceived to be the biggest discipline problem. These respondents indicated that no one particular type of student, according to sex or race, was most often involved in discipline problems. The principals did feel, however, that students making low grades were responsible for the greatest number of discipline problems. According to the respondents, corporal punishment was used most often to correct discipline problems, although it was not perceived to be the most effective method. Counseling was considered to be the most effective disciplinary practice.

2321.   Rose, J. S. "Relationships Among Teacher Locus of Control, Teacher and Student Behavior, and Student Achievement." Ph.D. Dissertation. University of South Carolina, 1978.

This study investigated the hypothesis that teachers' locus of control in the classroom setting causes variation in student performance through the mediating effects of their teaching behavior. Previous research suggested that internal teachers would produce greater achievement in mathematics than externals because they would exhibit teaching practices which maintain a more controlled classroom environment and promote greater student time-on-task. Specific behaviors predicted to be characteristic of internal teachers were a) more active engagement in instructional activities, b) use of less, but more effective controlling behaviors to maintain student discipline, and c) greater accountability for student performance. Furthermore, it was predicted that students in classrooms of internal teachers would spend more time in appropriate, on-task behaviors. A sample of 30 fourth grade teachers completed Rotter's I-E Scale and the Teacher Locus of Control (TLC) scale, an intrument developed by the investigator to measure teachers' internal vs. external control for various classroom and instructional situations. Overall, the TLC scale was found to be more predictive of classroom behavior than the I-E Scale. However, not all of the hypothesized correlations between teacher locus of control and behavior were found. Specific findings were as follows: High I+ teachers from low SES schools gave fewer disciplinary commands. Students in classrooms of high SES teachers who scored as internals for student success engaged in more productive work, while high SES students engaged less in inappropriate behavior in classrooms of high I- teachers. Several relationships for the I-E Scale were in the predicted direction but did not reach statistical significance. Order No. 7911856, DAI.

2322.   Rose, K. R. "Teachers' Sense of Power and Pupil Control Ideology and Behavior Congruence." Ph.D. Dissertation, The Pennsylvania State University. Dissertation Abstracts International, 36 (3-A), 1226-1228. Order no. 75-19,806, 1975.

The purpose of this study was to investigate the relationship between teachers' sense of power and pupil control ideology and behavior congruence. Sense of power ordered teachers on a unidimensional continuum, and determined their perceived ability to influence school policy directions. Pupil control ideology and pupil control behavior were conceptualized on continuums ranging from humanism to custodialism. The major hypothesis of the study was: Teachers' sense of power will be directly related to the congruence of teacher pupil control ideology and behavior. It was reasoned that a person who felt relatively secure and powerful in his position would be less susceptible to pressures and constraints on his behavior, and would behave in ways consistent with what he believed; that is, his ideology would be consistent with his behavior. Seventy-one teachers from 18 secondary schools selected from a large metropolitan area and its immediate suburban area were used in the study. The analysis empirically supported the hypothesized relationship between teacher SOP and PCI-PCB congruence at the .05 level of significance; a high sense of power was associated with a high behavior-ideology congruence, and a low sense of power was associated with a low behavior-ideology congruence. Thus, a teacher who felt that he had some control over school policy decisions acted in ways that were consistent with his beliefs. No significant relationship was found between teacher SOP and PCI, or teacher SOP and PCB. Partial correlations showed that no teacher characteristic predicted teacher PCI-PCB congruence.

2323.   Rosenberg, R. I.   "The Relationship Between Moral
Judgment and Classroom Behavior Among Emotionally Disturbed
Elementary School Children." Ph.D. Dissertation, Fordham
University. Dissertation Abstracts International, 37 (5-A),
2753. Order no. 76-25,791, 1976.

The purpose of this study was to determine whether a relationship exists between moral judgment and nine aspects of
classroom behavior among emotionally disturbed elementary
school children. The nine variables of classroom behavior
were: persistence, honesty, courtesy, generosity, cooperation, aggression towards peers, classroom disturbance,
disrespect-defiance, and aggressiveness vs. withdrawal. The
sample consisted of 76 children between the ages of 9 and 12
years, attending classes for emotionally disturbed children
in a large urban public school system. The analysis of the
data revealed significant correlations between moral judgment and six of the classroom variables: persistence, honesty, courtesy, generosity, cooperation, and disrespect-
defiance. There were no significant correlations between
moral judgment and two of the classroom variables: aggression towards peers and classroom disturbance. It was concluded that moral judgement, as defined by Kohlberg and
other recent researchers, can be viewed as a somewhat
broader trait than has been previously thought.

2324.   Roth, H. J. "The Earliest Childhood Recollection as One
Method of Attempting to Understand Classroom Behavior in
School for Male Fifth- and Sixth-Grade Students with Reading
Problems." Ph.D. Dissertation, Duke University. Dissertation
Abstracts International, 38 (8-A), 4697. Order no. 7731687,
1978.

The purpose of the research was to utilize earliest childhood recollections as one method of attempting to understand
classroom behavior in school. The classifications arrived
at from a judge's analysis of a student's earliest childhood
recollection and the classifications arrived at by a teacher's perception of the same student's behaviors and attitudes were analyzed to determine the extent of teacher and
judge agreement. The researcher obtained a total of 100
earliest childhood recollections during a personal interview
with each subject. Subjects were male fifth-and sixth-grade
students whose reading scores were at least one year and not
more than three years below grade level as measured by the
Iowa Tests of Basic Skills (Hieronymous & Lindquist, 1971).
The major conclusions of the research were: a) The classification system presented in the research can be used by
different judges for the purpose of classifying subjects
into the same one of ten possible categories: and b) the
classification system presented in the research can be used
by judges and teachers for the purpose of obtaining statistically significant agreement between the classifications
arrived at from a judge's analysis of a student's earliest

childhood recollection and the classification arrived at by a teacher's perception of the same student's behaviors and attitudes.

2325.   Rothberg, C. I.   "Ethnic Factors and the Effectiveness of Individual and Group Contingencies Upon Performance."   Ph.D. Dissertation, The University of New Mexico.   Dissertation Abstracts International, 34 (6-A), 3157.   Order no. 73-27, 776, 1973.

The study was designed to determine 1) whether reward is more effective when based upon group rather than individual achievement, and 2) whether children of different ethnic backgrounds (Anglo vs. Mexican-American) respond differently to group and individual reinforcement contingencies.   Nine classes of fifth grade students of the Albuquerque public schools participated in a two-week study of the effects of individual reinforcement, group reinforcement, and group reinforcement plus individual recognition on academic and cooperative behavior.   The following hypotheses were tested: 1) Mexican-American children will have higher mean academic scores under group than under individual reinforcement contingencies and Anglo children will achieve higher mean academic scores under the individual contingency.   2) There will be a significantly greater amount of helping or cooperative behavior under group as compared with individual reinforcement contingencies.   3) Under group contingencies as compared with individual contingencies there will be a greater increase in the size of choices made by subjects on a sociometric post test as compared to the size of choices on the pre-test.   The data failed to support these three hypotheses.

2326.   Russell, J. B.   "Corporal Punishment: A Study of the Attitudes of Parents, Students, and Teachers in the Imperial Valley, California, Toward Its Use as a Disciplinary Technique in the Junior High School."   Ed.D. Dissertation, Brigham Young University.   Dissertation Abstracts International, 39 (8-A), 4604-4605A.   Order no. 7903626, 1979.

The purpose of this study was to determine the attitude of parents, students, and teachers toward corporal punishment from each of five different junior high schools in Imperial County, California, during the 1976-1977 school year.   The data were collected by means of a twenty-eight item rating scale.   The results indicated that corporal punishment is believed to be an effective way of making students behave in school.   Corporal punishment should be given by a member of the administrative staff and only after other methods of discipline have been tried and proven ineffective.   The only method of corporal punishment acceptable to the three groups surveyed is the spanking of a student on the buttocks with a wooden paddle leather belt, or palm of the hand.   Types of behaviors found to be deserving of corporal punishment are: being disrespectful to the teacher, fighting with another student, using vulgar language in the classroom, writing or carving on the top of a student desk, and stealing things from the teacher's desk or from other students.

2327.   Ryabik, J. E.   "A Practical Machine to Measure and to Reduce Random Movement of Hyperactive and Normal Children." Ed.D. Dissertation, University of Northern Colorado. Dissertation Abstracts International, 37 (7-B), 3627-3628. Order no. 76-29,780, 1977.

It was the purpose of this exploratory study to coordinate a mechanical apparatus with behavior modification procedures to determine the effects on treating hyperactive and normal children. Comparisons were made between the baselines and the treatment effects of both the hyperactive and normal groups.   Two groups of subjects were used in this study: one was hyperactive, the other was normal as determined by teachers and parents. The Ryabik-Farrall Activity Chair was used to measure random in-seat activity rates in both hyperactive and normal children.   This exploratory study was conducted to determine if this device might have practical classroom value for measurement and treatment. The findings from the statistical analysis warranted the following conclusions which supported the three major hypotheses. There were no statistical differences manifest when the inseat random activity rates of the hyperactive and normal, demonstrated a remarkable reduction in activity when a treatment technique of auditory feedback and reward were coupled. This treatment technique was significant at the p .0001 level of significance. Finally, both groups of subjects appeared to decrease their activity at a similar rate in that there were no statistically significant differences when the improvement rates of the two groups were compared. The Ryabik-Farrall Activity Chair proved to be a viable apparatus for measuring and reducing random in-seat activity of both hyperactives and normals.

2328.   Ryan, Robert G.   "An Evaluation of a Program for Modification of Disruptive Student Behavior."   Ed.D. Dissertation, University of Southern California. Dissertation Abstracts International, 36 (11-A), 7309-7310.

The purpose of the study was: 1) to determine the effect of a comprehensive, school-wide behavior modification program on disruptive student behaviors; 2) to provide a workable model for school personnel for fostering positive student behavior.   The 725 subjects were students in the first through sixth grades of Lexington School, Pomona Unified School District, Pomona, California, during the 1972-73 school year.   The treatment consisted of a comprehensive school-wide program of behavior modification using positive reinforcers with individuals and class units.   The entire staff was responsible for the development and the implementation of the program. Disruptive student behaviors were monitored daily and tabulated every tenth day to provide 17 observation periods. An opinionnaire was administered to all school personnel at the conclusion of the school year. The tabulated data were presented in terms of percentage gains or losses. The tabulations of the daily reports of student behavior revealed a 38.7% decrease in the total amount of disruptive student behavior, a 40.5% decrease in the amount of infractions of school rules, a 25.4% decrease in aggressive behavior among peers, and a 40.7% decrease in the amount of defiant behavior toward school personnel. The proportional amount of disruptive behaviors cause by infractions of school rules, by aggressive behavior among peers, and by defiance of school personnel varied minimally during the course of the year. Third and fourth grade students were responsible for a disportionate amount (49.8%) of the disruptive behavior. The opinionnaire responses revealed strong agreement among staff members that the behavior modification program had been successful, that student behavior had improved, that the daily reporting of student infractions helped to identify problems and that student behavior had become increasingly motivated by reward incentives as opposed to fear of punishment.

2329.   Saba, Robert G. "The Effects of Two Behavior Modification Techniques on Behavior, Attitudes and Grade Point Averages of Fifth and Sixth Grade Pupils Identified as Consistently Off Task." Ph.D. Dissertation, University of Southern Mississippi. Dissertation Abstracts International, 33 (9-A), 4848-4849. Order no. 73-5579, 1973.

This study was conducted to evaluate and compare the effects of: 1) Model-reinforcement group counseling with consistently off-task fifth and sixth grade pupils, and 2) Model-reinforcement group counseling in combination with classroom behavior management with consistently off-task fifth and sixth grade pupils. The sample population was chosen from three elementary schools in Hattiesburg, Mississippi and two elementary schools in Forrest County, Mississippi, which had a combined enrollment of approximately 1,100 pupils in the fifth and sixth grades. The administrations of the school systems of Forrest County, Mississippi and Hattiesburg, Mississippi indicated schools which contained a large number of pupils with consistently off-task behavior. The schools which were chosen to participate were from predominantly lower socio-economic areas. From these schools, a total of sixteen teachers of fifth and sixth grade pupils were randomly assigned by groups of four to one of four experimental groups: model-reinforcement, model-reinforcement in combination with classroom behavior management, placebo control group, and no treatment control group. From the results of this study it appears that when consistently off-task fifth and sixth grade pupils of predominantly lower socio-economic areas are 1) given the opportunity to participate in model-reinforcement groups or 2) given the opportunity to participate in model-reinforcement groups in combination with classroom behavior management, on-task behavior increases. Further, when given the opportunity to participate in the combination technique, grade point averages also increase.

2330.   Sanders, D. M. "The Influence of Teacher Use of the Verbal I-Message on Disruptive Behavior in Primary Grade Classrooms." Ph.D. Dissertation, Texas Woman's University. Dissertation Abstracts International, 38 (9-A), 5407. Order no. 7801777, 1978.

One hundred ten students in four second-grade public school classrooms served as experimental subjects in a study designed to gather evidence concerning the possible effectiveness of a teacher's use of the verbal skill called the "I-Message" to reduce disruptive student behavior. Three of the classroom teachers, selected at random, were trained to deliver the I-Message in response to disruptive student behavior. Students and teacher in the fourth classroom served as controls. The I-Message consisted of a description by the teacher of the student's or students' disruptive behavior, the teacher's feelings in reaction to such behavior, and an explanation of the tangible effects or consequences of that behavior on the teacher. It was concluded that: 1) In the three classrooms in which the teachers attempted to use the I-Message there was no increase in the percentage of intervals of disruptive student behavior. All changes in categories favored the use of the I-Message. 2) The patterns of teacher response changed in the experimental classrooms. The three teachers who attempted to use the I-Message reduced the number of verbal responses they gave to disruptive student behavior and were able to either reduce or eliminate their typical responses. 3) The three teachers who attempted to use the I-Message reacted positively to its use as an effective way to deal with students on a one-to-one basis.

2331.   Sandercock, J. M. "The Development And Implementation Of A Program Of Open Campus." Doctor of Education Degree Nova University, 197679P.

The purpose of this practicum was to develop and implement a workable program of open campus for the Harriton High School of Lower Merion, Pennsylvania. The first phase of the practicum defines needs and shortcomings, defined objectives, developed a model program of open campus, and evaluated the program. In the second phase a refined program was implemented into the school and the open campus program was evaluated. The evaluation indicated that the model program was successful in terms of fostering student self-discipline in an atmosphere conducive to academic achievement. See ERIC Abstract #ED 133830.

2332.   Sanderson,   R.   A.   "Psychosituational   Classroom
Intervention: An   Exploratory   Study   of   the   Model."   Ed.D.
Dissertation, Rutgers University The State University of New
Jersey   (New   Brunswick).   Dissertation   Abstracts
International, 39 (5-A), 2843-2843P. Order no. 7820343,
1978.

The   study   explored   an   intervention-in-context   approach,
Psychosituational Classroom Intervention (PCI), as applied
in   elementary   school   classrooms.   The   PCI   approach
emphasizes aiding children who are experiencing adjustment
difficulties   in   the   classroom   through   intervention   techniques implemented within the normal class environment. The
study involved four second and third grade children, three
boys and one girl, who served as their own controls. Data
were   collected   on   specific   behaviors   observed   by   teachers,
and teachers supplied information in regards to their perceptions of the PCI approach and to the progress of each target
child.   Case   selection   was   based   on   children   referred   after
a   specified   date   who   met   the   following   criteria: displayed
adjustment   difficulties   with   peers,   presented   behavioral
concerns to their teachers, and showed a negative attitude
towards classwork.   Interventions were conducted by a school
psychologist   over   a   ten   week   period.   Each   child   was   seen
one hour each week in her/his classroom or in school-based
areas with her/his classmates, e.g., library, gym class.
The teachers recorded frequencies of the target children's
specified behaviors on an average of three periods weekly.
Evaluation   of   each   child's   progress   also   was   based   on:
teacher   questionnaires,   ongoing   teacher   and   investigator
reports, and final teacher interviews.   Measures to examine
changes in self-concept and academic achievement also were
employed.   Behavior frequencies over the intervention period
suggested that behavioral gains were made by three of the
four children.   In two cases, behaviors viewed by teachers
as negative decreased markedly, while, generally, increases
in positive behaviors were inconsistent or minimal.   In a
third case, a similar pattern was noted though frequency
changes were slight and suggestive at best.   In a fourth
case, positive behaviors increased markedly while negative
behaviors showed no substantial change.   Teacher reports and
questionnaires supported the data concerning the behavioral
changes of the target children.   Based on behavior frequencies and teacher reports, marked improvement in peer interaction was suggested in two cases.   In the other two cases,
gains related to not disturbing peers as frequently and to
developing one positive peer relationship in class were
noted.   In general, though the sources of data were not
viewed as highly reliable there was a trend towards gains in
self-concept   in   three   cases   and   improvement   in   areas   of
academic achievement and in attitude towards classwork in
all four cases.

2333.   Sandler, P. S.   "Male and Female Teachers' Ratings of
Children's Behavior."   Ed.D. Dissertation. University of
Georgia, 1979.

This study investigated how male and female teachers rated twelve behaviors of male and female pupils. These behaviors were: physical aggression toward peers, physical aggression toward teachers, verbal aggressiveness toward peers, withdrawal from peers, autism, learning disability, gifted, mental retardation, underachievement, child abuse, divorce, and excessive absence. All of these behaviors were presented to the teachers in a written form. Six items followed each behavior and all the teachers rated these items on a five point scale from strongly disagree to strongly agree. The 60 male and 60 female middle school teachers who participated in the study were randomly chosen from school systems in Georgia, Maine and Massachusetts. The two independent variables for each of the twelve behaviors of the study were the sex of the teacher (male and female). The six dependent variables were the ratings for each behavior. These ratings were based upon the teachers' responses to the following six items: the child has a problem and requires help, the child can best be helped by the classroom teacher, the child should be referred to the school psychologist, the child should be referred to the school principal, the parents should be informed of the situation, and the child will outgrow the situation if it is ignored. The only sex bias between teachers' ratings occurred in gifted behavior. Female teachers rated this behavior more severely than did the male teachers. No other differences occurred between the ratings of the teachers. There were strong sex biases for several of the behaviors. Males were rated more severely for learning disability, verbal aggression, and gifted behaviors. The female pupils were rated more severely for physical aggression toward both peers and teachers, autistic, divorce, and excessive absence behaviors. The most severe overall ratings were given for the behaviors of child abuse, underachievement, and mental retardation. Parents were the most often chosen referral source while school principals were the least frequently chosen. Teachers and school psychologists were chosen with the same frequency. Order No. 7923145, DAI.

2334.   Saudargas, R. A. "Setting Criterion Rates of Teacher Academic Approvals: The Effects of Videotape Feedback with Behavior Analysis Follow Through Teachers." Ph.D. Dissertation, The Florida State University. Dissertation Abstracts International, 33 (7-A), 3405. Order no. 73-222, 1973.

The present study was designed to analyze the effects of videotape feedback on setting criterion rates of teacher praise. An additional part of the research design was a partial assessment of the procedural components of counting and counting and graphing rates of approvals from vidotape recordings. The study was conducted in three Behavior Analysis Follow Through Classrooms. Each classroom was characterized by four teaching adults, a token reinforcement system, and an individualized instructional program. The school day was divided into "Earn Periods" during which the children received tokens for academic work, and "Spend Periods: during which the children exchanged tokens for reinforcing activities. The data indicated that having teachers count, graph, and meet two different criterion rates of Academic Approvals was effective in both increasing and decreasing the observed rates of Academic Approvals. The rate changes appeared to have been most reliably produced during the time period when the teacher was being videotape recorded and during the observation time period immediately following the videotape recording.

2335.   Schlottman, K. B.   "The Relationship Between the Means of Control of the Elementary School and Student Involvement: A Test of Etzioni's Compliance Thesis."   Ph.D. Dissertation, University of Southern California.   Dissertation Abstracts International, 40 (10-A), 5393. 1980.

The purpose of the study was to determine if there is a relationship between the means of control employed by a school and the involvement of its students. The theoretical basis for the investigation was provided by Etzioni's compliance thesis which posits a relationship between the organizational means of control and the kind of involvement of participants.   The thesis holds that organizations use three types of power to control participants: coercive, remunerative, and normative.   Involvement of participants concerns their orientation to the organizational power system, i.e., directives or rules, sanctions, and persons in power.   The orientation is held to range from commitment (associated with normative control) to alienation (associated with coercive control).   Two major hypotheses were investigated along with four additional hypotheses formulated in the course of the study; each hypothesis has three subhypotheses concerning participants' orientation to rules, sanctions, and persons in power.   In addition, four research questions concerned with student control were investigated.   The study sample consists of all of the elementary schools (N=8) of a unified school district.   The faculty sample (N=71) consists of all principals, vice principals, counselors, and fifth-and sixth-grade teachers. The student sample (N=594) consists of all sixth-grade students (and in one school, also fifth-grade students). The methodology included the development and administration of faculty and student questionnaires to provide measures of school means of control and student involvement, respectively; interviews with all principals and counselors; analyses of the questionnaire data with Spearman rho correlation coefficient and chi-square statistic.   Tests of the hypotheses reveal the following significant relationships between school means of control and student involvement: 1) a positive relationship between normative control and student overall commitment and commitment to rules and sanctions; 2) an inverse relationship between normative control and student alienation to sanctions; 3) a positive relationship between coercive control and alienation to sanctions; 4) an inverse relationship between coercive control and student overall commitment and commitment to rules, sanctions, and persons in power.

2336.   Segal, Marie S. "The Influence of a Mainstream Vocational Placement on Achievement, Self-Esteem and Behavior." Ed.D. Dissertation, Lehigh University, 1980. Dissertation Abstracts International, 41 (3-A), 1023. Order no. 8019725.

The major concern of this research was to determine whether a difference exists in academic achievement, self-esteem, and behavior for educable mentally retarded adolescents and learning disabled adolescents in a mainstream vocational shop placement and those in a special class vocational shop placement. Subjects for the study consisted of 100 high school age students enrolled in a full-time vocational high school program in a southern county in New Jersey. Fifty students had been placed in a mainstream vocational shop placement, and 50 had been placed in a special class vocational shop placement. Subjects were tested on the Gray Oral Reading Inventory, the Key Math Diagnostic Arithmetic Test, the Coopersmith Self-Esteem Inventory and the Coopersmith Behavior Rating Form. The teachers were surveyed on the Teacher Attitude Form. This study revealed that a student in a mainstream vocational shop placement scored significantly higher than a student in a special needs shop placement in math achievement (p. .05) and behavior (p .05). Students in a special needs vocational shop placement scored higher than students in a mainstream shop placement in school and academic self-esteem (p. .05). This study revealed that learning disabled students scored significantly higher than educable mentally retarded in reading (p. .01) and mathematics (p. 01) achievement; total (p. .01), social (p. .05), school and academics (p. .05), and general (p. .01) self-esteem. White students scored significantly higher than non-white students in total (p. .05), home parents (p. .05) and lie-defensiveness (p. .05) self-esteem. Students in the mechanic shop cluster scored higher than building or service in general (p. .05) self-esteem. Students academically mainstreamed in reading achieved higher than non-academic mainstreamed in reading (p. .01) and students academically mainstreamed in mathematics (p. .05) achieved higher than non-academic mainstreamed in mathematics. Teachers of the mainstream vocational shops scored significantly higher than teachers of special needs shops in attitude (p. .01) toward mainstreaming.

2337.   Seipel, Richard M. "A Study of the Effects of Behavior Modification, Using a Program of Positive Reinforcement, on the Attendance Rate of Selected Junior High School Students." Ed.D. Dissertation, University of Kansas, 1977. Dissertation Abstracts International, 38 (12-A), 7240. Order no. 7809445.

The problem was to determine whether a program of behavior
modification using a lottery system of positive reinforcement with monetary rewards would be effective in significantly reducing the absenteeism rate of participating junior
high school students. 1) Two junior high schools, as
similar as possible in size, socioeconomic makeup, geo-
graphic proximity, etc., were selected for the study. The
experimental group was at one school, and the control group
at the other, to avoid any effect of the intervention on the
control group. 2) An attendance problem was defined, and
then students with attendance problems at each school were
identified. From this population of students with attendance problems the experimental group was randomly selected
at one school, and the control group was randomly selected
at the other. 3) The attendance of students in the experimental and control groups were monitored for one quarter to
determine a base line and to see whether there was any
significant difference in the absenteeism rate of the two
groups. 4) The attendance of students in the experimental
group was positively reinforced for one quarter while the
control group was again only monitored. The absenteeism
rate of the two groups was then compared again to see
whether there was any significant change in the absenteeism
rate between the groups. 1) During the quarter of observation, students selected to participate in the experimental
group missed a total of 174 student school days, and
students in the control group missed a total of 163.5
student school days out of possible 980 student school days.
There was no significant difference in the absenteeism rate
of the two groups during the observation period at the 0.10
level of significance. 2) During the quarter of intervention, student participating in the experimental group missed
a total of 133.5 student school days, and students in the
control group missed a total of 195.5 student school days
out of a possible 960 student school days. There was a
significant difference in the absenteeism rate of the two
groups, during the intervention period, at the 0.05 level of
significance.

2338.   Sesow, P. A. "Effects of an Educational Development for
Growth and Effectiveness Seminar on Self-Concept, Behavior
and Achievement." Ed.D. Dissertation. Arizona State
University, 1978.

The problem of this study was to determine what effects a
specially designed Educational Development for Growth and
Effectiveness seminar had on the self-concept, behavior and
achievement of Title I students in a high school. Major
hypotheses were: 1. The self-concept self-criticism, total
conflict, total positive, total variability, distribution
scores, disciplinary referrals, suspensions, absentee rate,
dropout rate, second semester grade-point average, and
reading scores of Title I students who participate in an ED
GE seminar are not significantly different from Title I
students who do not participate in an ED GE seminar. 2.
There is no positive correlation between the total positive

self-concept scores and the number of disciplinary referrals, suspensions, absentee rate, dropout rate, grade-point
averages, and reading scores of the Titel I students who
participate in an ED GE seminar. Data were collected on a
pre posttest basis utilizing the Tennessee Self Concept
Scale, Nelson Reading Test, attendance, grade-point average,
and behavior records. Analysis revealed the following: 1.
Significant increases were found in the total positive
self-concept scores, decreases in total conflict scores
among females, and lower absentee rates of the experimental
group. 2. No significant differences were found in disciplinary referrals, suspensions, dropout rate, grade-point
average, self criticism, total variability, distribution
scores, and reading achievement between the experimental and
control groups. 3. There was no correlation between total
positive self-concept, achievement and behavior. Order No.
7911135, DAI.

2339.   Shaffmaster, L. D. "A Descriptive Study of the Relation-
ships Between Teachers' Verbal and Nonverbal Behaviors and
Children's Prosocial and Antisocial Behaviors." Ph.D.
Dissertation, The Pennsylvania State University.
Dissertation Abstracts International, 37 (11-A) 7050. Order
no. 77-9757, 1977.

This study was designed to examine the relationships between
teachers' verbal and nonverbal behaviors and children's
prosocial and antisocial behaviors. The general purpose of
the study was to validate a proposed teaching competency
regarding teachers' use of verbal and nonverbal behaviors to
foster prosocial learning. It was hypothesized that children would respond prosocially to supportive teacher behaviors and antisocially to restrictive teacher behaviors.
Furthermore, it was hypothesized that when verbal and nonverbal behaviors communicated inconsistent messages (one
supportive, the other restrictive) the nonverbal message
would be more powerful. Therefore, it was expected that
child behavior subsequent to inconsistent messages would be
more related to teachers' nonverbal behavior than to verbal
behavior. This descriptive study was based on a multidimensional system for recording and coding teachers' verbal and
nonverbal behavior in naturalistic settings. The observational system used for collecting data was based on checklists, developed as part of the study, for coding teacher
and child behavior. The system was designed to provide
information regarding the extent of learner-supportive
and/or learner-restrictive verbal and nonverbal behaviors
used by teachers in response to disruptive classroom incidents. The subjects of this study were 15 female teachers
of children aged five to nine (kindergarten to third grade).
Data were collected during classroom observations in four
different primary schools. Subjects were observed for four
35 minute sessions each or 140 minutes per teacher. Analysis of data indicated significant positive correlations
between supportive verbal and nonverbal teacher behavior and

prosocial child responses and between restrictive verbal and
nonverbal teacher behavior and antisocial child responses.

2340.   Shaw, C. C. "The Effects of Classroom Management
Techniques of Students' Choice Status and Self Concepts."
Ph.D. Dissertations, North Texas State University.
Dissertation Abstracts International, 33 (12-A), 6740, 1973.

The purpose of this study was to determine the effects that
certain classroom management techniques would have on the
self concepts and choice status of sixth grade students and
to assess the potential of these techniques. All sixth
grade students (86) enrolled in one elementary school
participated in this study. There were four class sections,
two of which made up the experimental group and two of which
made up the control group. The IPAT Children's Personality
Questionnaire, What You Do and What You Think (1963)
provided a measurement of self concept. It was concluded
that role playing and sociometric techniques were not
effective ways of significantly changing students; self
concepts and choice status.

2341.   Shaw, Elizabeth S. "The Relationship of Expressed
Problems and Classroom Behaviors on the Part of Children
Referred for Intensive Counseling." Ph.D. Dissertation, The
Ohio State University. Dissertation Abstracts International,
35 (8-A), 5039. Order no. 75-3191, 1975.

This study was motivated by the need for improved and
feasible ways of describing and understanding the behaviors
that emerge in the classroom, behaviors that are of concern
to the teacher because they interfere with the learning
process; to investigate how youngsters behave in class and
how behaviors interrelate. The general hypothesis of this
study is that concerns expressed by children referred for
counseling in grades K through 6 will be related systematically to the patterns of behavior which they show in the
classroom. Therefore, two instruments were used to assess
children's concerns and overt behavior in the classroom
setting.

2342.   Shearn, Donald F. "The Effects of Glasserian Classroom
Methods of Children's Self-Concepts and Behavior." Ph.D.
Dissertation, University of Southern Mississippi.
Dissertation Abstracts International, 35 (10-A), 6468-6469.
Order no. 75-9603, 1975.

The problem was to explore the use of Glasserian guidance
techniques as an instrument of change in self-concepts and
observed task behavior of fourth-grade children. The basic
objectives of the study were: 1) What changes in self-
concept, if any, can be affected by use of the Glasserian
classroom approach with elementary school children? 2) What
changes in observed on-task behavior can be affected by use
of Glasserian classroom approach with elementary school
children? 3) If a change does occur in the elementary

school child's self-concept or on-task behavior, can it be attributed to the Glasserian classroom approach and not such factors as the artifact of testing, the passage of time, or the anticipation of prestigious treatment? The following conclusions were derived from this study: 1) Results of this study seem to indicate that, while improvement in self-concept and behavior by use of Glasserian techniques is possible, no short range significant changes were discernible by the evaluative techniques used in this research. 2) It was found that Glasserian Classroom Guidance Activities are a popular guidance tool with teachers and children. 3) It was recommended that further studies covering different periods of time, different individual changes, and different means of evaluation be made.

2343.   Sheldon, K. L. "The Relationship Among Internal-External Locus of Control, Classroom Behaviors, and Cognitive and Affective Development." Ed.D. Dissertation. University of Georgia, 1978.

The present. study was designed to assess the relationships among internal-external locus of control, the classroom behaviors, task persistence, self-esteem, and positive effect, and cognitive and affective decentration. The five null hypotheses were that there would be no differences among the three locus of control groups, internal, mixed, external, in: the frequency of occurrence of task persistence, self-esteem; positive affect behaviors in the classroom: the ability to conserve, cognitive decentration; and the ability to role-take, affective decentration. A total of 130 children from three southeastern communities enrolled in grades one through four served as subjects. They were part of a larger sample of children used in another study conducted by the Mathemagenic Activities Program-Follow Through based at the University of Georgia, Athens. The smaple charateristics were approximately equal in regard to sex, race, income, and grade level. All of the children were administered the Stephens-Delys Reinforcement Contingency Interview (locus of control), Purdue conservation film, Role-taking Task, and were observed in the classroom using the Classroom Observation Instrument. The subjects were divided into three locus of control groups (internals, mixed, and externals) based on their total internal scores. The statistical analyses consisted of computation of alpha reliability coefficients for each of the variables and five one-way analyses of variance to test the null hypotheses. Results of the computation of the reliability coefficients indicated that the locus of control, conservation, and role-taking tasks were quite acceptable. The reliabilities for the three classroom observation variables were low. Results of the analyses of variance indicated that three of the null hypotheses could not be rejected. There were no differences among the three locus of control groups on task-persistence, self-esteem, and conservation. Statistically significant results were found for the classroom variable, positive affect, and role-taking. Order No. 7914056, DAI.

2344.   Shigley, Ralph H. "A Comparison of Group Administered Punishment and Individually Administered Punishment to Suppress Inappropriate Classroom Behavior." Ph.D. Dissertation, University of Georgia. Dissertation Abstracts International, 34 (8-B), 4028. Order no. 74-4881, 1974.

This study was concerned with the effects of Group Administered Punishment and Individually Administered Punishment on the inappropriate talking-out behavior of elementary school children. Included within the review of the relevant literature was a discussion of: the general effectiveness of behavior modification in classroom settings; token systems; the effects of teacher attention; the effects of punishment; group contingencies and peer influence; and behavior contrast. Four second grade teachers served as the primary experimenters in their own classrooms. Both punishment procedures were studied in all four classes, and the punishment conditions were preceded and followed by baseline (non-punitive) conditions in order to study the effects of the punishment. Findings for each of the hypotheses were presented along with tables and graphs of the corresponding data. Two of the three null hypotheses received support or partial support from the data. The results indicated that the teachrs were able to effectively implement the experimental contingencies and reliably measure and record the corresponding changes in children's behavior. In addition it was demonstrated that both Group Administered and Individually Administered Punishment were extremely effective in suppressing inappropriate talkout behavior. In addition, there was partial support for the prediction that Group Punishment was more effective than Individual Punishment. There was a lack of support for the prediction that there would be a contrast effect after Group and Individual Punishment were removed, and that the relative talkout rate would be greater after Group Punishment than after Individual Punishment.

2345.   Short, B. L. "Investigation of the Effects of the Ecological Setting of the Public School Classroom on Student Behavior." Ph.D. Dissertation, University of California. Dissertation Abstracts International, 36 (10-B), 5238. Order no. 76-8247, 1976.

This study combined theory and methods from ecological and experimental psychology to investigate the effect of ecological settings on the behavior of setting inhabitants. The settings were one open-space and two self-contained sixth grade public school classrooms matched on all salient variables. The second self-contained classroom was included to provide an internal replication of results. In all settings, the student/teacher ratio was the same, and there was no difference in population density among the classrooms. The study examined eight hypotheses derived from the education literature regarding the differential effect of open-space and self-contained classrooms on student behavior. The hypotheses tested claims regarding differential frequencies of a) interaction between the teacher and the total class, b) interaction between the teacher and individual students, c) overall student-student interaction, d) work action and interaction among students, e) student non-work action and interaction, f) student work-related behavior directly supervised by the teacher, g) student work-related behavior initiated but not directly supervised by the teacher, and h) student work behavior initiated by the student and not supervised by the teacher. The results show that the two different types of settings had markedly different effects on specific types of student behavior, although not consistently those reported in the education literature. The results provided strong empirical support for hypotheses that a) teachers in open-space classrooms both direct and reprimand large groups of students less often than do self-contained teachers, b) open-space students engage in work behavior (specifically, work interaction) more than self-contained students.

2346.   Siggers, Walter W. "Intervention in an Elementary School with Adversive and Positive Contingencies: The Effect Upon Disruption and Teacher Correcting Behavior." Ph.D. Dissertation, University of Pennsylvania. Dissertation Abstracts International, 37 (7-A), 4246. Order no. 77-879, 1977.

This study investigated the effects of an implementation program that utilizes both positive and adversive consequences to reduce disruption in schools. Presented is a procedure that incorporated behavioral principles to 11 volunteering, elementary teachers in a suburban school through a series of 10 workshop meetings. Essentially, the focus of this study was upon the problem of disruption in classrooms, which persists despite the extensive and varied attempts to curtail it. The data yield evidence that teachers can change disruptive children's behavior using such techniques. Further, the data show that teachers, having participated in workshops which trained them in the application of a contracting system which incorporated both positive and aversive contingencies, seemed to change their general correcting behavior.

2347.   Silber, C. L. "The Academic and Behavioral Characteristics of Successful Versus Nonsuccessful Learning Disabled Students." Ph.D. Dissertation, North Carolina State University at Raleigh. Dissertation Abstracts International, 34 (3-A), 1481-1482C. Order no. 7811627, 1978.

The purpose of this study was to investigate systematically some of the academic and behavioral characteristics of learning disabled children who were categorized as "successful" or "nonsuccessful" by their learning disability teachers. The subjects were 61 students with identified, learning disabilities and 30 control students attending six elementary schools. PIAT's, student self ratings, and LAR's were administered to all subjects. Demographic information and previous test scores were obtained from the school files. A Learning Disability Severity Index was completed by the learning disability teachers. The overall results of this study indicated: (1) There were no differences between "successful" and the "nonsuccessful" groups at the beginning of the intervention program by age, entering academic achievement, race or sex. The "successful" group had a mean IQ of 94 compared to a mean IQ of 89 for the nonsuccessful" group. (2) More third and fourth graders were selected as "non-successful" LD students whereas the "successful" group was evenly distributed throughout the six grades. (3) SES differences were found between LD students categorized as "successful" and "nonsuccessful." (4) There were no significant differences between "successful" and "nonsuccessful" students on the behavior codes in either the resource or regular classroom. (5) There were no differences on task-oriented behavior between the resource and regular classroom. In the resource room, LD students engaged in more interaction with teachers and peers about academic matters and less nonproductive behavior than in the regular classroom. (6) The LD students' behavior was found to be significantly different from normal controls in the regular classroom. They were less task oriented, engaged in more nonproductive activity, conferred more with teachers and peers about academic matters and were slightly more socially disruptive. (7) The learning disability teachers did not spend more time in remediation or make more parental contact with the "successful" group compared to the "nonsuccessful" group. (8) There were no significant differences found between the two LD groups on locus of control. (9) LD students as a group rated themselves as making significantly more inprovement in the resource room than in the regular classroom.

2348.   Silverstein, J. M. "Individual and Environmental Correlates of Pupil Problematic and Nonproblematic Classroom Behavior." Ph.D. Dissertation, New York University. Dissertation Abstracts International, 40 (5-A), 2567. Order no. 7925292, 1979.

The present study utilized ecological and traditional methodologies to examine the relation between classroom environments, pupil learning characteristics, and levels of problematic behavior in self-contained, teacher centered classrooms. Since this relationship appears to be relatively unexplored, the present study was exploratory, with two major purposes: a) documenting environmental structures (learning formats) and pupils' behaviors during arithmetic and reading lessons, and b) identifying environmental and pupil variables for future research. Three hypotheses were presented, Hypothesis 1 concerned the effect of pupil learning characteristics on levels of classroom problematic behavior. Hypothesis 2 concerned the effect of environmental characteristics on levels of problematic behavior. Hypothesis 3 concerned the effect of the interaction between pupil learning characteristics and environmental characteristics on levels of problematic behavior. Two sets of independent variables were studied: pupil learning characteristics (skill and interest levels in reading and arithmetic, combined into skill-interest levels in reading and arithmetic, combined into skill-interest categories), and learning format characteristics (perceptual and task demands of pupil activity, teacher leadership pattern, pupil role, pacing, accountability, and group quality). The dependent variable was pupil behavior, with each behavior's "problematic" or "nonproblematic" quality determined by the nature of the activity, and the teacher's conception of the appropriateness of the behavior. Findings indicated that pupils in both classrooms behaved differently during different parts of the classroom day, with significantly higher proportions of problematic behavior occurring during seatwork than during small group formats. No significant differences were found between proportions of problematic behavior exhibited by pupils in different skill-interest categories, when these categories were considered alone or in interaction with learning format characteristics. Further post hoc observation indicated a trend toward higher proportions of pupils with lower skill levels being involved in higher proportions of problematic behavior during seatwork.

2349.   Smith, Douglas K. "Development and Validation of the Classroom Management Questionnaire." Ph.D. Dissertation, Georgia State University - School of Education. Dissertation Abstracts International, 38 (8-A), 4590. Order no. 7731049.

The purpose of this study was to develop and validate an instrument for effective measurement of teachers' styles of classroom management (Classroom Management Questionnaire), based upon Aronfreed's induction-sensitization model of socialization. Additional studies examined teacher classroom management styles as a function of grade level, nature of student behavior, sex of student, socioeconomic status of school, training of teacher and experience of teacher. Subjects for this study included 200 teachers and non-teachers. All subjects completed the Classroom Management Questionnaire and a subsample completed the Rokeach Dogmatism Scale, the Rotter Internal-External Locus of Control Scale, the Taylor Manifest Anxiety Scale and the Christie-Gein Machiavellianism Scale V. Statistical analyses of the data collected in the study indicated that: 1) Classroom management styles of teachers varied by nature of student behavior with inductive techniques used more frequently in response to academic behavior and sensitizing techniques used more frequently in response to dependent behavior. 2) Classroom teachers utilize inductive techniques more frequently with female students than with male students. 3) Female teachers utilize inductive techniques to a greater degree with both male and female students than do male teachers. 4) Special education teachers utilize inductive techniques more frequently than regular classroom teachers. 5) Relationships between socioeconomic level, grade level, teacher experience and teacher degree with respect to classroom management style were nonsignificant. 6) The use of inductive classroom management styles correlates positively with an internal locus of control and negatively with dogmatism and Machiavellianism. No relationship was established between style of classroom management and the Taylor Manifest Anxiety Scale.

2350.   Smith, J. A. "The Effect of Self-Instructional Training on Children's Attending Behavior." Ph.D. Dissertation, The University of Toledo. Dissertation Abstracts International, 36 (10-B), 5285. Order no. 76-8364, 1976.

Meichenbaum and Goodman (1971) devised a training program to teach impulsive children to talk to themselves as a means of self-control. These investigators found that such training enabled children to reduce errors and increase performance scores on a number of psychomotor performance tasks. The present study was a attempt to extend these findings to another target behavior, that of attending to a teacher. It was hypothesized that normal first-grade children who received self-instructional training would increase the amount of time they spent attending in a classroom analogue situation. It was also predicted that the children would increase the amount of material they retained in such a situation and increase their belief that reinforcement was contingent on their own behavior. In order to test these hypotheses, 27 children, in groups of three, observed a videotaped story presentation while they were being videotaped. They then answered questions on the story and a locus of control questionnaire.

2351.   Smith, R. E. "Teacher Characteristics, Observations of Classrooms, and Recommendations for Action." Ph.D. Dissertation, Washington University, 1979.

The impetus for the study has been the work of Kounin who showed that elementary school teachers who intervene decisively when misbehaviors occur and who do so before the mis-conduct has progressed very far have pupils with relatively low rates of deviancy and relatively high rates of involvement in the work. Kounin's study did not consider the characteristics of teachers who do, or who do not, perceive and respond appropriately to misbehavior. This study attempts to determine whether teachers' demographic characteristics and attitudes are related to their observations of, and reactions to, pupil classroom behavior. The possible effects of the context were checked as well. The sample contains forty subjects. Thirty subjects taught in the middle school of a suburb of a large midwestern city. Ten subjects taught in the junior high school of the same

school district. A five-minute videotape of a staged class
session provided the stimulus for observations and recommendations. During the viewing of the videotape and
continuing through the interview which followed, the observations, recommendations, and other remarks of each subject
were captured on audiotape. Demographic variables included
Sex, Age, and Years of Teaching. Attitudes were measured by
the Minnesota Teacher Attitude Inventory and the Pupil
Control Ideology Form. Context variables were the School in
which the subject taught and Minutes per Day with Students.
The latter is an indication of the type of organization of
classes -- either elementary or secondary type. Types of
Misbehavior Seen, Incidents Talked About, and Average Time
Difference are the observation variables. The value of the
first variable is the number of the twelve types of misbehavior which the subject reported seeing. The value of
the second is the number of the twenty-six incidents of
misbehavior about which the subject talked. The value of
the third variable is the average delay from the beginning
of a misbehavior incident till the subject stopped the
videotape to talk about it. Percentage of Words Recommending Change the Teacher is a general recommendation
measure. Seven more specific recommendations complete the
set of variables. Both correlation analysis and regression
analysis were completed with the final set of fifteen
variables. The correlation analysis revealted significant
relationships between the variables within each category and
significant relationships between variables across
categories. Significant correlations within a category
support the belief that the variables are measuring the same
concept. Significant correlations across categories suggest
effects of variables of one category on variables of the
other. These suggested effects were examined by regression
analysis. Order no. 8002467, DAI.

2352.   Smith, Y. E. "The Relationship of Skin Color and Teacher
Perception of Pupil Behavior in the Classroom." Ph.D.
Dissertation, University of California, Berkeley.
Dissertation Abstracts International, 37 (9-A), 5669-5670.
Order no. 77-4604, 1977.

This study investigated the relationship of pupil skin color
and teacher perception of pupil classroom adaption and
adjustment in the classroom and whether the teacher's
opinion about the student's future success and adjustment
was influenced more by skin color than by the student's
present behaviors and reading ability. The subjects were
second-grade male students and their teachers from urban
school districts in the Far West. The students were divided
into four groups according to skin tone, white (N=75), and
three classifications of black skin tone, yellow (light,
N=30), brown (medium, N-54) and black (dark, N=77). The
teacher subjects were black (N=8) and white (N-12). The
students were individually administered The Gray Oral
Reading Test which provided a means to equate their reading
abilities. During the administration of the test of skin

color of the student was appraised and judged against the Index of Skin Color. Teachers were asked to complete the Pupil Behavior Rating Scale, an objective measure consisting of scale values for descriptors of behavior defining anchored points along a continuum for each of eleven non-intellectual attributes. Teachers were also asked to nominate three male students (a subjective measure) they though were most and least likely to become professional people and to be happy and well-adjusted in later life. Both procedures for obtaining teacher ratings were administered with disclosing the findings from the reading test or the skin color assessment. It was hypothesized that there would be no significant differences among the pupil groups in reading ability, that students would be judged to have increasing classroom behavior problems as the skin tone changed from white to yellow to brown to black, that students would be nominated most likely to be future professionals and to be happy and well-adjusted in decreasing numbers as the skin tone changed from white to black, that students would be nominated least likely to be future professionals and to be happy and well-adjusted in increasing numbers as the skin tone changed from white to black, and that black and white teachers would not differ in their perceptions of pupil behavior or in their nomination of students according to skin color. Overall, the results indicated that there were significant differences in reading ability among the pupil groups and that skin color is an important pupil variable in teacher perception of the students, but it is a variable vulnerable to the student's level of achievement and behavior difficulties. The brown-skinned and black-skinned students were found to have significantly more adjustment and adaptation problems than the white students. Teacher nominations for future success and adjustment were influenced more by actual behavioral differences than by prejudicial attitudes about skin color.

2353.   Sobel, N. J. "A Study in Teaching Frustration Management to Disruptive Students." Ed.D. Dissertation. The American Univeristy, 1978.

This experimental study investigated the effects of the Self-Control Curriculum: Curricular Area, Managing Frustration, upon disruptive students. This study was premised upon the fact that vast amounts of human potential are wasted by disruptive students. Once cause of their disruption was assumed to be frustration. The intervention, Self-Control Curriculum: Curricular Area, Managing Frustration identified objectives which were translated into activities for teaching the experimental subjects to manage frustration constructively. The study investigated these four hypotheses: Hypothesis 1: There will be a significant decrease in the intensity of disruptive behavior as rated by teachers for students in the experimental group over students in the control group; Hypothesis 2: There will be a significant increase in attention to tasks by the students in the experiemntal group over the students in the control

group;   Hypothesis 3:   There will be a significant decrease
in the Aggression Inventory scores of the students in the
experimental group over students in the control group; and
Hypothesis 4:   There will be a significant increase in the
self-esteem ratings of the students in the experimental
group over the students in the control group. The sample
population of 30 were eighth and ninth grade students
attending George Mason Junior-Senior High School in suburban
Falls Church, Virginia.   The duration of the intervention
was ten weeks.   Groups met twice weekly for 35 minute sessions.   The experimental gruops received instruction in
managing frustration.   The activities were derived from the
Self-Control Curriculum: Curricular Area, Managing Frustration.   The three units were: Accepting Feelings of Frustration; Building Coping Resources; and Tolerating Frustration.
The control groups did not receive instruction in managing
frustration.   Three of the four results of hypothesis
testing were found to be significant.   Order No. 7904990,
DAI.

2354.   Solis, J. S.   "An Analysis of Teacher Perceptions of
Chicano and Anglo Students' Misbehavior and Teacher-Assigned
Grades."   Ed.D.   Dissertation,   University   of   Houston.
Dissertation Abstracts International, 38 (5-A), 2534. Order
no. 77-24,438, 1977.

The purpose of the study was to explore the relationships
between overt classroom behavior characteristics of fifth
grade Chicano and Anglo students as perceived by the classroom teacher and the grades assigned them by teachers in
reading, spelling, English, mathematics, and social studies,
as well as total achievement.   Two groups of students were
utilized in this study.   One group was composed of 87
Chicano fifth grade students while the other group was
composed of 78 Anglo fifth grade students.   Both groups
utilized were enrolled in public schools located in the
Lower Rio Grande Valley of Texas.   Using the Devereux
Elementary School Behavior Rating Scale (Devereux), the
teachers rated each of their respective students.   The
Devereux provided 47 behaviors defining 11 behavior
categories plus three additional items as follows: 1) Classroom Disturbance, 2) Impatience 3) Disrespect-Defiance, 4)
External Blame 5) Achievement Anxiety, 6) External Reliance,
7) Comprehension, 8) Inattentive-Withdrawn, 9) Irrelevant-
Responsiveness, 10) Creative Initiative, 11) Needs Closeness
to Teacher 12) Unable to Change, 13) Quits, 14) Slow Work.
As a result of the study, it was concluded that the greater
the extent of misbehavior perceived by the teacher was
related to lower grades assigned by the teacher across all
subject areas.   Further, for Chicano students, lower grades
assigned by the teacher across all subject areas and total
achievement were related to greater impatient, externally
reliant, inattentive-withdrawn, quitting and working slow
behavior, while higher grades were related to comprehension.
At the same time, for Anglo students, lower grades were
related   to   greater   classroom   disturbance,   impatience,

disrespect-defiance, external blame, external reliance, inattentive-withdrawn, irrelevant responsiveness, unable to change, quitting and working slow. Additionally, higher grades for Anglo students were related to comprehension and creative initiative.

2355.   Solomon, C. E. "Pupil Control Ideology and Selected Personality Factors of Administrators in Custodial and Humanistic-Type Intermediate Schools." Ed.D. Dissertation, Fordham University, 1979.

The purpose of this study was to determine and compare the responses of school administrators in custodial and humanistic-type intermediate schools in New York City with respect to the variables of their pupil control ideology and their selected personality factors; and, to determine and compare the responses of those teachers who were classified as custodial and those teachers who were classified as humanistic with respect to the variable of their pupil control ideology. Too, an attempt was made to ascertain whether significant interrelationships existed amongst the responses of the school administrators in custodial and humanistic-type intermediate schools with respect to their pupil control ideology and their selected personality factors and the variables of the school administrators' age, education, experience, sex and number of pupil suspensions. The subjects of the study consisted of 48 school administrators and 432 teachres. The instruments used were the Pupil Control Ideology Questionnaire Form (PCI) and the 16 Personality Factor Questionnaire (16PF). The major conclusions of the study were: 1) The PCI of the administrators was centered near the mid-point of the conceptual custodial-humanistic control continuum. 2) Personality factor subdimension variances occurred more for administrators in custodial-type schools than for administrators in humanistic-type intermediate schools. 3) There were significant differences between the responses of those teachers classified as custodial and those teachers who were classified as humanistic with respect to their PCI. 4) There were no significant differences between the responses of administrators in custodial and humanistic-type intermediate schools with respect to their PCI. 5) The school administrators differed most with respect to the personality factor subdimensions of: emotional-emotionally stable; practical-imaginative; and, forthright-shrewd. 6) The personality factor subdimension of shyventuresome was slightly correlated with the pupil control ideology dimension of school administrators in custodial-type intermediate schools. Order no. 7920688, DAI.

2356.   Solomon, R. W. "Peers as Behavior Modifiers for Problem Classmates." Ed.D. Dissertation, The University of Tennessee. Dissertation Abstracts International, 33 (8-A), 4189. Order no. 73-2497, 1973.

Peer and teacher interactions with five "disruptive" children were studied within an elementary school classroom.
The intent of the study was to analyze experimentally peer
reinforcement control of the disruptive children's problem
behaviors. Social attention provided by all peers was found
to be directed exclusively to the problem behaviors during
baseline. Following baseline, several manipulations of
selected peer social attention contingencies demonstrated
the reinforcement function of the stimulus class, and
supported the hypothesis of behavior maintenance from
related environmental events. Children were taught to
provide differential social attention to the reduction of
classroom problem behaviors and the individual level of
problem behaviors were demonstrated.

2357.   Spencer, H. D.   "A Grounded Theory of Aligning Actions in
an Elementary Classroom."   Ph.D. Dissertation, University of
Missouri.   Dissertation Abstracts International, 38 (2-A),
1049.   Order no. 77-15,551, 1977.

The purpose of this dissertation was to develop a grounded
theory for understanding the processes of alignment which
occurred between teachers and children in an individualized
elementary school over issues of classroom management. The
processes of classroom management included the types of
responses teachers and children had to one another in disruptive situations, the nature of negotiations between teachers
and children over disruptive situations. The symbolic
interactionist perspective was utilized in this study as an
analytic framework because it was useful in discerning the
world views of actors in social situations--in this study,
the perspectives of teachers and children in classroom
situations. Qualitive methods were used to gather data for
this study. Westwood School was chosen as the setting for
the research, where the researcher spent several months as a
nonparticipant observer in the classes of teachers, student
teachers and children in the fourth, fifth and sixth grade
unit. Further insight was gained into the perspectives of
the actors through formal and informal interviews. Information about teachers' labels of children was gained from
sociometric questionnaires. Children's abilities at impression management fell into four types. Children whose self-
presentation in the front and back stage regions was good,
were likely to be labeled cooperative. (The labels teachers
placed on children--cooperative or uncooperative, were
obtained from the sociometric data.) Children who had a
poor self-presentation in both the front and back stage
regions were likely to be labeled uncooperative. Children
who presented a good front to the teachers but were disruptive behind their backs, were likely to be labeled cooperative, while children who called teachers into account or
defied them to their faces (yet were cooperative with peers)
were likely to be labeled uncooperative.

2358.   Stahl, J. R. "The Comparative Effects of Behavioral
Contracting, Behavior Rehearsal and Self-Evaluation Training
on the Classroom Behavior of Problem Youth." Ph.D.
Dissertation, University of Vermont. Dissertation Abstracts
International, 36 (7-B), 3628-3629. Order no. 76-1268,
1976.

The effects of three forms of behavioral intervention of the
classroom behavior of problem youth were compared. Each
intervention aimed to devleop appropriate classroom
behaviors by reinforcing these behaviors with the activities
available in a youth center. School behaviors were targeted
via a behavior rating card system, and the youth center
reinforcers were mediated through a token economy point
system. The subjects were 40 seventh- and eighth-graders
who were judged by guidance counselors to display school and
family or community adjustment problems. The youth
contracted to carry cards on which their behavior was rated
by teachers. After four weeks of baseline each subject was
assigned to one of three treatment groups. Subjects in the
conventional behavioral contracting group earned youth
center points according to teachers' ratings of classroom
performance; subjects in the behavior rehearsal group earned
points for practicing desirable classroom behaviors at the
youth center and for describing in writing their experiences
in performing these behaviors at school; and subjects in the
self-evaluation group earned points for monitoring their
behavior and matching teachers' ratings. The points were
exchangeable at the youth center for access to a variety of
activities which were of reinforcing value to the youth.
Classroom behavior was measured by teacher ratings, grades
and classroom observations. Economic and behavioral problem
characteristics of the subjects were examined. Teacher
ratings of classroom behavior were high during baseline (4.3
on a 5-point scale). However, mean teacher ratings
increased during intervention in all three treatment groups.
There was a trend ($p = .21$) for teacher ratings of participation to increase and a statistically significant increase
in attitude ratings. The project demonstrated that
clinically relevant behaviors occurring in the school setting could be targeted employing youth center activities as
reinforcers.

2359.   Stallworth, R. L. "The Effect of Suspension as a
Disciplinary Technique in the Classroom of the 1970's."
Ph.D. Dissertation, The University of Michigan.
Dissertation Abstracts International, 38 (7-A), 3871. Order
no. 77-26,366, 1978.

This study was an appraisal of the disciplinary technique of
suspension in one large city public school system. One
school district in the State of Michigan served as the
target area of this study. Suspension in elementary
schools, junior high schools, and senior high schools was
examined. Among the findings, the following were reported:
Suspension is used more often as a disciplinary technique in

the junior high school than in elementary school or in senior high school. Suspension is used less often to punish infractions of school regulations and more to discipline students who engage in violent or illegal behavior. Suspension is considered a positive disciplinary measure by both beachers and administrators. Permanent suspension was found to be a powerful disciplinary tool for educators to maintain proper control of the classroom environment.

2360.   Starr, L. H. "The Relationship of School Functioning and Contextual Cues to Four Cognitive Styles." Ed.D. Dissertation, Rutgers University, The State University of New Jersey. Dissertation Abstracts International, 36 (2-A), 797-798. Order no. 75-17,367, 1975.

The primary concern of this study was to investigate the concept of cognitive style. Much of the literature is concerned with the styles of impulsivity and reflectivity. The variables which are used to define cognitive styles, response time, and error score, yeild two other possible styles. These proposed styles were labeled as incisive and withdrawn. There is no mention of these styles in the literature, and their absence provided the impetus for the study. The study dealt with two major hypotheses. The first part focused on comparisons of the performance of impulsive, reflective, incisive, and withdrawn subjects on the school-related variables of intelligence, reading, and arithmetic achievement, visual-motor development, auditory discrimination, and classroom behavior. The second part of the study was concerned with the effects of contextual cues on cognitive styles. Subjects were tested under conditions defined as anxiety-free and anxiety-provoked. Data were derived from 100 children, 25 subjects for each of the four cognitive styles. An equal number of subjects was taken from kindergarten, first, second, third, and fourth grades. The Matching Familiar Figures Test (MFF) was used to make the cognitive style classifications. The only differences between styles occurred for the variables of intelligence and visual-motor skills. Reflective and incisive subjects scored higher than impulsive subjects on the intelligence test, and reflectives scored higher than impulsives on the visual-motor test. A number of explanations were proposed for these results: a criticism of the measuring instruments, the effects of cognitive styles on performance, the nature of the data analysis, and the dissimilarity between the subjects reported in the literature and those in the study.

2361.   Stein, Sharon A. "Selected Teacher Verbal and Nonverbal Behaviors as Related to Grade Level and Student Classroom Performance." Ph.D. Dissertation, Northwestern University. Dissertation Abstracts International, 37 (7-A), 4246-4247. Order no. 77-1359, 1977.

Teacher verbal and nonverbal behaviors were analyzed in light of the factors: grade level taught, student classroom performance, and teacher preference for a high or low ability group of students. The relationship between teacher verbal and nonverbal behaviors was studied in a preliminary analysis. Following this analysis, the principle questions examined were: 1) Do teacher verbal and nonverbal behaviors differ according to the classroom performance of their students? 2) Do teacher verbal and nonverbal behaviors differ according to the grade level they teach? 3) Do teacher verbal and nonverbal behaviors differ according to their preference for a high or low ability group of students? The sample used included 27 teachers and 341 students from grades one to three in 12 of the 17 elementary schools. A discriminant analysis was used to analyze data related to the factor, teacher preference for a high or low ability group of students. No significant results were found.

2362.   Sterman, A. "Student Perceptions of Democratic/Non-Democratic Teacher Behavior in the Classroom." Ed.D. Dissertation, The University of Arizona. Dissertation Abstracts International, 37 (8-A), 5022-5023. Order no. 77-2309, 1977.

This study focused upon the perceptions of certain secondary school students regarding their teachers' classroom behavior. The investigator attempted to find the answer to the following question: Among a selected group of secondary school students, what perceptual patterns regarding democratic non-democratic teacher classroom behavior will emerge? The high school in this study was one of nine high schools in a large district in a rapidly growing urban community in the southwestern part of the United States. Sixty students, selected randomly from all grade levels, participated in the study. Utilizing the theory of Democratic Processes developed by Barnes and Tidwell and Bishop and a theory of Non-Democratic Processes developed by the investigator, an instrument was formulated to gather the data. It consisted of the following categories: 1) Contact/Avoid, 2) Consul/Ignore, 3) Find/Disregard, 4) Share/Exclude, and 5) Accompany/Abandon. The data gathered in this study tended to suggest that students generally perceived their teachers' classroom behavior to be relatively non-democratic. On the forced choice scales of the questionnaire, the students indicated a high degree of teacher behavior was somewhat democratic in the categories of "Contact," "Consult" and "Accompany." In the categories of "Find" and "Share" the students responded that teacher behavior was considerably less democratically oriented.

2363.   Stewart, I. S. "Cultural Differences in the Attributions and Intentions of Anglos and Chicanos in an Elementary School." Ph.D. Dissertation, University of Illinois at Urbana-Champaign. Dissertation Abstracts International, 34 (1-A), 520. Order no. 73-17,439, 1973.

The purposes of this study were 1) to identify the differences between Anglo teachers, children, and parents, and Chicano children and parents in their view of the appropriateness of child behavior in a classroom context, 2) to study the perceptions of Anglo teachers, children, and parents, and Chicano children and parents of the behavioral patterns of Chicano children in a public school context, 3) to explore the desirability of using attribution theory as a means of studying cultural conflict situations in an educational setting, and 4) to develop procedures which might facilitate the collection of significant information on the education of young children who are culturally different from their teachers. The study was an exploratory investigation of cultural differences in a classroom context. The subjects were Anglo teachers, children, and parents, and Chicano children and parents (N=52) from one school in a small midwestern town. The basic design was a multi-step design which began from the framework of attribution theory, proceeding to verbal elicitation procedures from which incidents exemplifying critical behavioral conflicts were extracted. These behavioral incidents were used, in turn, to elicit attributes and intentions. The primary results of the study were the following: 1) There were no clear, uncomplicated differences between how Anglos and Chicanos deal with children in a classroom context. In order to ascertain cultural differences between Anglos and Chicanos, the responses of the respondents had to be across incidents and not tied to individual incidents. Thus, the interrelation of the ethnicity and age of the respondent, ethnicity of the stimulus person, and the use of attributes and intentions identified cultural differences between Anglos and Chicanos in a classroom setting. 2) Certain specific incidents were associated with differential use of attributes and intentions, while others were not. The specific incidents for which use of attributes was differentiated were not always the ones on which use of intentions was differential. 3) Anglos and Chicanos were more similar in their use of attributes, than they were similar in their use of intentions. 4) Generally, all the groups similarly perceived the Anglo stimulus person, but differed in their perception of the Chicano stimulus person.

2364.   Stiltner, B. L. S. "The Effects of Interaction Activities on Group Development in Junior High School Classes. Ph.D. Dissertation, University of Colorado. Dissertation Abstracts International, 34 (10-A), 6393. Order no. 73-32, 596, 1973.

This study was designed to assess changes in the classroom atmosphere and interpersonal relationships in junior high school classes in order to detect the stages of group development which evolved in these classes. A sample of twenty volunteer teachers was recruited from five junior high schools in Jefferson County, Colorado. These teachers represented the following subject matter areas: language arts, social studies, mathematics, science, and home economics. The teachers were trained in a one-day workshop in the use of a series of exercises designed to develop the discussion and interaction skills of their pupils. Each teacher was provided with a packet of these exercises to use with his or her students in the classroom to train the students to conduct effective classroom discussion and to interact positively with other group members. The changes in the classroom atmosphere and interpersonal relationships were assessed through the use of student inventories of classroom climate and teacher-pupil and pupil-pupil relation-ships, a sociometric questionnaire, and planned observation. Eleven of the twenty teachers were observed. The teacher's conception of the ideal teacher-student relationship was also examined as a possible intervening variable through the use of teacher inventories. The relationship of these test scores to the dependent variables was evaluated using simple correlations. Highly significant differences between the teachers and the schools participating in the study were found on many of the thirty-five dependent variables. A number of significant differences between the treatment groups and across the four measurement times occurred. These findings led to the conclusion that the use of the sequence of activities resulted in different stages of group development being experienced in the experimental classes than occurred in the control classes.

2365.   Strohl, Darle A.   "The Effects of Consultee-Centered Case Consultation on Disruptive Classroom Behavior and Teacher Perception of Disruptive Students."   Ed.D. Dissertation, Boston University School of Education, 1979.   Dissertation Abstracts International, 40 (6-A), 3128. Order no. 7923900.

The purpose of this study was to develop, provide and test a model of consultee-centered case consultation with elemen-tary teachers which was a modification and extension of Carkhuff's "core dimensions of a helping relationship" (Carkhuff, 1969). This model was described in the "eight core deminsions of a consulting relationship" and was measured by using the Scales for the Assessment of Consultee-Centered Case Consultative Effectiveness which was a modification and extension of Carkhuff's (1969) Scales for the Assessment of Interpersonal Functioning. The treatment consisted of a series of four, five or six weekly meetings with three different elementary teachers. Each meeting lasted forty-five minutes. The treatment was tested as to its effects on the percentage of disruptive classroom behavior, number of students engaged in disruptive behavior, and teacher perception of two students selected by the teacher as most disruptive of the classroom. A case study of the process of consultation is also provided. Another purpose of this study was to provide an experimental design that was appropriate and feasible for use by both researchers and practitioners to test the effectiveness of consultee-centered case consultations. The Categories of Disruptive Classroom Behavior was used weekly by observers to measure the percentage of disruptive classroom behavior and to calculate the number of students engaged in such behavior. Teachers' perceptions of the two most disruptive students were obtained by utilizing the Coopersmith Behavior Rating Form. This measure was administered once before and once following the end of the study. A case study of the process of consultation with the three teachers was also provided. A visual analysis of the results showed what appeared to be a decrease in percentage of disruptive classroom behavior and a decrease in number of students engaging in such behavior in two classrooms and an increase in both measures in the third classroom. Teachers' perceptions were more positive at the end of consultation for the third classroom but stayed the same or became more negative for the first two classrooms. However, these results must be interpreted with caution due to the lack of experimental control and the limitations of the study.

2366.   Stumme, J. M. "An Approach to Changing Teachers' Positive and Negative Verbalization, and Its Effect on Student Attending Behavior." Ed.D. Dissertation. Drake University, 1979.

The purpose of this study was to analyze experimentally the effects on an elementary school principal's cueing technique on the number of positive and negative teacher verbalizations, and to measure the effect that this verbalization change had on the total number of students involved in on-task behavior in the classroom. This research was conducted in two adjoining second grade classrooms in a rural elementary school in mid-Iowa. The elementary school principal served as the primary observer/experimenter, while the school psychologist functioned as an observer for reliability purposes. The two teachers who particpated in this investigation had twenty-four and twenty-three students respectively in their classrooms ranging in age from seven years, six months, to eight years, eleven months. To analyze the treatment procedures a multiple-baseline design was employed for the two classrooms. This involved four sequential conditions consisting of: condition I (baseline), condition II (treatment one), condition II, (treatment two), and condition IV (reversal). The baseline rate was taken for the number of positive, negative, and neutral teacher verbalizations, as well as the number of students involved in on-task behavior. The principal recorded the baseline for a duration of four consecutive days in Classroom A and for nine consecutive schools days in Classroom B. During treatment one, which as applied for five consecutive days in each classroom, the principal recorded and cued the teachers each time they emitted a negative verbalization. Upon being cued the teachers were instructed to find four students engaged in attending behavior and praise them individually. Treatment two immediately followed with the only difference being that it was applied twice a week for a duration of three weeks rather than five consecutive days. At the conclusion of treatment two the principal returned to baseline and recorded only. The results demonstrated that the systematic application of the cueing technique by the principal substantially increased the number of positive teacher verbalizations and conversely decreased the number of negative teacher verbalizations. In Classroom A there was a positive teacher verbalization increase of 129 percent and a negative teacher verbalization decrease of 88 percent. In Classroom B there was a positive teacher verbalization incrase of 344 percent and a negative teacher verbalization decrease of 88 percent. The results also demonstrated that this verbalization change effected an increase in the total number of students involved in on-task behavior. In Class-room A 16 percent more students were involved in on-task behavior, while in Classroom B 7 percent more students were involved in on-task behavior in posttreatment. Order No. 7923335, DAI.

2367.   Sudduth, R. S. "The Relative Efficacy of Three Methods of Presenting Psychoeducational Test Data To Teachers." Ed.D. Dissertation, University of Georgia. Dissertation Abstracts International, 36 (12-A), 7965. Order no. 76-14,023, 1976.

This study compared the effects of a psychoeducational report and school psychologist-teacher consultation, a psychoeducational report only, school psychologist-teacher consultation only, and no psychological services on (1) quantity of change in teachers' understanding of children; (2) the direction of change in teachers' understanding of children; (3) teachers' ratings of children's behavioral maturity; (4) children's ratings of their behavioral maturity; and (5) teachers' satisfaction with psychological services. The following hypotheses were tested: 1. There will be no significant differences in the quantity of change in teachers' understanding of children as a result of the treatment utilized. 2. There will be no significant differences in gains in teacher-psychologist agreement in understanding of children as a result of the treatment utilized. 3. There will be no significant differences in gains in teachers' ratings of children's behavioral maturity as a result of the treatment utilized. 4. There will be no significant differences in gains in children's ratings of their behavioral maturity as a result of the treatment utilized. 5. There will be no significant differences in teachers' ratings of satisfaction with psychological ser-vices as a result of the treatment utilized. Participants were eight school psychologists employed in Northeast Georgia. Each used 12 male referrals from grades 2-5 who were having classroom adjustment problems of an academic, emotional, or interpersonal nature. Three treatment groups and a control were used. One group received a psycho-educational report and consultation, one group received a report only, one group received consultation only, and the control received no services. The findings were as follows: 1. There were no significant differences in quantity of change in teachers' understanding. Hypothesis one was retained. 2. There were no significant differences in gains in teacher-psychologist agreement. Hypothesis two was retained. The report and consultation group increased significantly (P .01) in agreement from pre to post. 3. There were significant differences in gains in teachers' ratings of children's behavioral maturity. Significant differences at the .01 level were found between the report and consultation group and the consultation group, and between the report group and the consultation group, and between the report group and the consultation group. Hypothesis three was rejected. The report and consultation group increased significantly (P .05) in gains in teachers' ratings of children's behavior maturity. 4. There were no significant differences in gains in children's ratings of their behavioral maturity. Hypothesis four was retained. No groups increased significantly from pre to post. 5. There were no significant differences in teachers' ratings of satisfaction with psychological services. Hypothesis five was retained.

2368.   Sullenger, R. V. "The Relationship of Selected Personality Factors to Disruptive Behavior of High School Students." Ph.D. Dissertation. Southern Illinois University at Carbondale, 1978.

The primary purpose of this study was to determine whether disruptive behavior of high school students is related to certain personality factors, the rationale being that if there is a significant relationship, this knowledge would be useful for appropriate school personnel to assist these young people in making positive adjustments. Subjects included 490 students in the 1977-78 sophomore class of Parkview High School of Little Rock, Arkansas, which is considered to be a typical urban integrated high school similar to many others in the United States. Early in the school year these subjects were administered the nationally known and standardized High School Personality Questionnaire (HSPQ) which is designed to give the maximum information in the shortest time about the greatest number of dimensions of personality. At the end of the first semester these subjects were classified by their teachers and appropriate administrative personnel into a category of being disruptive or non-disruptive based on predetermined criteria. Of the 490 subjects, 72 were classified as disruptive. Four hypotheses were tested. The main conclusion was that the HSPQ could be useful as a predictor of disruptive behavior among sophomore students of the Little Rock Parkview High School, which is relatively representative of urban integrated high schools in many parts of the United States. Order No. 7908087, DAI.

2369.   Sutherland, E. A. "Teacher Expectancy Effects." Ph.D. Dissertation, McGill University. Dissertation Abstracts International, 34 (10-B), 5212. 1974.

The study, a series of related experiments conducted over a three-year period, investigated certain aspects of the

establishment, transmission and effects of teacher expectation as it becomes naturally established during normal,
ongoing classroom interactions. The main subject pool was
109 Grade 1 and 2 pupils in an average socioeconomic area of
Montreal. Results indicated some specific behaviors on the
part of both pupils and teachers which are associated with
varying levels of teacher expectation and further indicated
that a relationship exists between negatively discrepant
teacher expectations and lowered I.Q. gain. The use of I.Q.
testing in the primary grades was discussed and suggestions
were advanced concerning both teacher training and inservice
training programs in the light of these findings.

2370.   Swanstrom, C. R.   "An Examination of Structured Learning
Therapy and the Helper Therapy Principle in Teaching a
Self-Control Strategy to School Children with Conduct
Problems."   Ph.D.   Dissertation,   Syracuse   University.
Dissertation Abstracts International, 40 (1-B), 434-435.
Order no. 791426, 1979.

The investigation had two purposes. The first was to
examine the efficacy of Structured Learning Therapy (SLT)
consisting of modeling, role playing, and systematic social
reinforcement, in promoting the acquisition and generalized
usage of a verbally-mediated self-control strategy in
elementary-school children with behavior problems. SLT has
been found to be an effective means of fostering therapeutic
skill acquisition with diverse populations. It was predicted that SLT would produce greater acqusition and generalization in the usage of the self-control strategy than a
didactic Structured Discussion (SD) procedure which
presented the strategy in the same content terms as with
SLT, but without the components of model role playing, and
systematic social reinforcement. It was futher predicted
that SLT and SD would both be more effective in promoting
treatment goals than a Brief Instruction Control (BIC)
condition in which children received only brief instruction
in the strategy just prior to posttesting. Results
indicated that while children in both the SLT and SD conditions displayed significant cognitive acquisition of the
strategy than the BIC condition. However, neither SLT nor
SD children demonstrated clear superiority to BIC children
in their posttreatment ability to cognitively generalize the
use of the strategy to hypothetical problematic situations
not encountered in training. The second pupose of this
study was to examine the Help Therapy Principle in enhancing
the treatment goals of SLT and SD training. Research investigating this principle has demonstrated that various
therapeutic-like changes, e.g., increased academic learning,
positive emotional changes, have accrued to individuals
placed in diverse roles in which they have helped others.
It was predicted that children who helped teach another
child the self-control strategy following their own training
would demonstrate greater acquisition and generalized usage
of the strategy than children without such helper-role experience. It was also predicted that the expectation during

training that one would later be helping teach the strategy to another ("helper structuring"), without actual helper-role experience, would be sufficient to foster greater enhancement of treatment goals than training alone. Results indicated that, contrary to predictions, neither helper structuring, nor helper structuring plus actual helper-role experience, increased the effectiveness of the training methods.

2371.   Taber, F. M. "Videotapes: An Aid in Teaching Behavior Identification and Techniques for Behavior Management." Ed.D. Dissertation, Western Michigan University. Dissertation Abstracts International, 37 (6-A), 3555. Order no. 76-28,095, 1976.

Teacher trainees in Western Michigan University's Special Education Department, who were about to enter the student teaching phase of their programs, were selected to be subjects for a study in the instruction of classroom management skills. The study was divided into two experiments. During Experiment One the trainees were observed while in a student teaching situation, given treatments in classroom management skills, and then observed again in their student teaching situations. During Experiment Two the trainees were given treatments in classroom management and then observed in their student teaching situation on a post-treatment observation basis only. The results indicated that both the lecture/discussion method and the traditional method, with the addition of the videotape as a teaching tool, were significantly effective for instructing teacher trainees in the identification of unacceptable pupil behaviors and in the determination of alternative strategies for dealing with these behaviors on a short-term basis.

2372.   Tefft, B. M. "Underachieving High School Students as Mental Health Aides with Maladapting Primary Grade Children: The Effect of a Helper-Helpee Relationship on Behavior, Sociometric Status, and Self-Concept." Ph.D. Dissertation, The University of Rochester. Dissertation Abstracts International, 37 (7-B), 3635. Order no. 76-24,026, 1977.

This study evaluated the effectiveness of a school-based, nonprofessional mental health program which recruited alienated, underachieving high school students as help agents with maladapting primary grade children. The program was conceived in recognition of serious inadequacies in traditional therapeutic approaches and widespread school maladjustment problems. Based on the "helper therapy" principle, it attempted to promote more satisfactory school adjustment in both groups by establishing cross-age, helper-helpee relationship. Prospective high school helpers were nominated by teachers and assessed on objective school indices of academic underachievement. Volunteering helpers were divided into matched experimental (N=24) and control (N=12) groups. In addition, a random control group (N=15) of average achievers was selected. Classroom behavior, sociometric status, and self-concept ratings were obtained for all three groups. Primary grade helpees were nominated by teachers as experiencing behavioral and learning diffi- culties, and were divided into matched acting-out (N=11) and shy-anxious (N=11) problem types based on teacher-rated classroom behavior. Helpers attended six weekly, hour-long training sessions, during which appropriate helping roles and basic concepts of psychological adjustment in children were discussed. A social learning approach stressing different interventions with acting-out and shy-anxious children was presented. Pre-post change scores revealed that both helpers and helpees improved significantly overall in classroom behavior. Moreover, helpers tended to improve in school attitude and involvement. The program was differentially effective for acting-out and shy-anxious children. Contrary to previous outcome findings, acting-out helpees evidenced significant overall and problem-specific gain relative to a control group while shy-anxious helpees did not. This discrepancy was attributed in part to high visibility of acting-out problems and helper characteristics and life experiences.

2373.   Thomas, A. K. "The Comparative Effects of Structured Group and Group-Individual Counseling on Self-Concept, Study-Habits and Attitudes, Academic Achievement, and Observed Classroom Behavior of Low-Motivated Male High School Juniors. Ph.D. Dissertation, Michigan State University. Dissertation Abstracts International, 37 (6-A), 3431-3432. Order no. 76-27,157, 1976.

The purpose of this study was to test the effects of two types of group counseling on the self-concept, study habits and attitudes, academic achievement, and change in observed classroom behavior of low-motivated male eleventh grade students. The design of the study was a post-test-only with control group model. The treatments were: 1) group coun- seling only, and 2) group plus individual counseling. Eighteen group sessions were conducted by a counseling team made up of one male and one female counselor. The coun- selors were active participants in the group discussions. Combined affective and structured techniques were used in each session. Three major findings that emerged from this study were: 1) The Conformity Scale scores from the Minnesota Counseling Inventory (MCI) indicated a significant difference between treatment groups, but not in the direc- tion predicted. The other six scales did not yield signifi- cant results. 2) The grade point average changes were not significantly different between treatment groups. However, the GPA means of the counseled groups increased each grading period. The mean GPA of the control group decreased. 3) The group counseling was effective with or without the addition of individual counseling when counselor time was held constant.

2374.   Thomas, Bruce A. "A Study of the Attitudes of Educators Relative to the Use and Value of Corporal Punishment." Ph.D. Dissertation, University of Pittsburgh, 1973. Dissertation Abstracts International, 34 (6-A), 2999. Order no. 73-29,377, 1973.

The major focus of this study was to measure the relationship between teachers' attitudes toward corporal punishment and specific principles relating to punishment drawn from the literature. A secondary purpose of the study was to determine attitudinal differences toward corporal punishment among certain groups of teachers in one school district. In order to determine what attitudes various segments of a district's teaching population have toward the use of corporal punishment a questionnaire, with emphasis on eight principles from current educational literature, was developed, tested, and then administered to the teachers in the Gateway School District, Monroeville, Pennsylvania. The questionnaire consisted of 24 objective type items and six open-ended questions. A score of 1 to 4 was possible for each item. A high score indicated a favorable attitude toward the principle opposing the use of corporal punishment, in relation to that particular item. The following results and conclusions were obtained: 1) A plurality (41 percent) of the teachers believe that corporal punishment tends to increase student respect for the teachers. 2) The majority of teachers do feel that corporal punishment of one student either positively or negatively affects the behavior of other students. 3) Thirty-eight percent of the teachers feel that corporal punishment enhances the attainment of their objectives. 4) A majority of the teachers do not feel that elimination of corporal punishment would alter their effectiveness. 5) The majority of teachers do feel that the use of corporal punishment does have an effect, either positive or negative, on the future beahvior of the student upon whom it is administered. 6) The majority of teachers do feel that they should have the right to administer corporal punishment. 7) Sex, tenure status, and family status are not major factors in the attitude of teachers toward the use of corporal punishment. 8) The level at which a teacher works does have a relationship to his attitude toward corporal punishment.

2375.   Thomas, Carroll R. "Systematic Desensitization as a Self-Control Technique for Developing Socially Relevant Behavior in Children." Ph.D. Dissertation, The University of Arizona. Dissertation Abstracts International, 38 (3-B), 1425-1426. Order no. 77-18,592, 1977.

The present study investigated the effectiveness of a program based on systematic desensitization designed to eliminate non-assertive behavior and to develop assertiveness and self-control in eight and nine year old children in the third grade classroom after training a regular classroom teacher in the procedures. Twenty-one children served as subjects and were exposed to the treatment: however, more precise and continuous data were collected on six target children identified as non-assertive. Results of behavioral observations indicated that assertive behavior of all target children increased substantially once the treatment was introduced. Treatment gains were maintained at the post-treatment and follow-up phases of the program. Conclusions of the study indicated that the program clearly resulted in positive effects on the target children as well as all other children in the class.

2376.   Thomas, G. M. "The Use of Modeling in Elementary School Guidance in the Meridian Separate School District in Mississippi. Ed.D. Dissertation, The University of Alabama. Dissertation Abstracts International, 34 (10-A), 6395. Order no. 74-9398, 1973.

The purpose of this investigation was to determine the effect of modeling on the attending behavior of disadvantaged first grade pupils. The subjects were pupils in the Meridian Separate School District of Mississippi. The 69 pupils involved in the study were selected from those referred by their teachers as having significant difficulty in paying attention in class. All subjects were observed daily for four weeks by trained aides. The aides recorded either attending or nonattending behavior at one minute intervals for a fifteen minute time span. Following one week of observations with no treatment, the experimental groups were treated on Monday, Wednesday, and Friday of the next two weeks. Observations and recordings continued daily for pupils in all three groups through the treatment period and for an additional week. Hypotheses were tested for difference in mean pre-treatment levels between groups, difference between pre and post-treatment means for each group, and difference between post-treatment mean levels for the two experimental groups. There was no statistically significant differences among groups in pre-treatment tests. Both of the experimental groups had a significantly higher posttreatment than pre-treatment means but no significance was determined between posttreatment means for the experimental groups. The control group had no significant difference between pre and posttreatment means. The investigation substantiated the statements in the literature concerning the effectiveness of modeling on modifying the behavior of subjects. The pupils who viewed the models exhibited a higher level of the desired attending behavior following their viewing. The different instructions given the two experimental groups did not affect a significant difference in behavior.

2377.   Tomlin, S. L., Jr. "An Analysis of the Effects of Superintendent Initiated Procedures on Office Referral Rates in a Junior/Senior High School." Ph.D. Dissertation, University of Kansas, 1979.

This study tested the effects of superintendent initiated procedures to reduce office referral rates of a suburban junior/senior high school. Ten teachers with the highest number of office referrals were divided into four groups. Each group contained teachers whose combined total of office referrals was approximately the same at the end of baseline. An ABC AAA design was used to 1) assess the frequencies and types of office referrals, 2) decrease the number of inappropriate referrals, 3) reduce administrative time to handle inappropriate referrals, and 4) assure the decreases in the number of inappropriate referrals were directly related to increases in the number of inappropriate behaviors handled by the classroom teacher. The procedures analyzed were superintendent/principal conferences and principal/teacher conferences with feedback. The results of this study demonstrated that superintendent initiated procedures were significantly effective in reducing the number of inappropriate office referrals. Order no. 8002767, DAI.

2378.   Tropp, N. D. "Behavior Change Through Self-Control Compared With Group Therapy and a Control Group." Ph.D. Dissertation, University of Washington. Dissertation Abstracts International, 37 (5-B), 2532. Order no. 76-25,466, 1976.

This study compared the therapy techniques of behavior change through self-control and supportive group therapy. The present study attempted to partially fill these needs by gathering certain information on associated personality and behavioral changes following therapy and two months after therapy. It further tried to assist school personnel in finding effective ways to work with ninth, tenth, eleventh, and twelfth graders who are achieving only marginally at school. Subjects were 31 high school students identified by notices of failing or near-failing grades. These subjects agreed to participate in a study and were randomly assigned by sex and grade to one of three groups. Group 1 (n = 11) learned the skill of behavior change through self-control; Group 2 (n = 11) received supportive group therapy; Group 3 (n = 9) was a no-treatment control. Group 1 members tended to receive fewer discipline slips at posttreatment and to have a higher self-concept a follow-up. They also tended to feel they had learned additional skills, studied more, and succeeded better at school. Both Group 1 and 2 subjects tended to feel better able to attack school problems. The therapy group members felt the groups were generally helpful. Groups 1 and 3 received more internal locus of control scores at follow-up while Group 2 scores were less internal at that time. Group 2 tended to have more absences at posttreatment. Members of all three groups had a significantly lower dropout rate than did other students with two or more notices of failing or near-failing grades.

2379.   Tshionyi, M. B. "The Effect of an Instructional Program in Pupils' Simulated Misbehaviors on Student Teachers' Cognitive Achievement of the Intended Outcomes." Ph.D. Dissertation, University of Oregon. Dissertation Abstracts International, 37 (6-A), 3389. Order no. 76-27,690, 1976.

The purpose of this pilot study was to develop an instructional program that could be used in pre-service training to equip prospective teachers with pre-classroom experience in disruptive behaviors. Four specific objectives were investigated: 1) the ability to probe conditions that seem to provoke misbehavior, 2) the ability to formulate hypotheses about misbehaviors, 3) the ability to generate long range plans for constructive behavior changes, and 4) the ability to select a course of action to remediate misbehaviors. Findings revealed that seven student teachers made gains between pre- and post-test scores: one student teacher's score remained unchanged, and three student teachers' reported negative results. Regarding the objectives, greatest cognitive gains were noted for objective one, the ability to investigate conditions that seem to provoke misbehaviors, and objective three, the ability to generate long range plans for correcting misbehaviors. The lowest cognitive achievement was reported for objective two, the ability to formulate hypotheses. Objective four, the ability to select a course of action recorded a negative result.

2380.   Turner, A. J. "An Analysis of the Relationship Between Student Codes of Conduct and Student Behavior." Ph.D. Dissertation, The University of Michigan. Dissertation Abstracts International, 39 (6-A), 3507-3508S. Order no. 7823025, 1978.

The primary purpose of this study was to investigate the relationship between student codes of conduct and student behaviors. The perceptions and observations of classroom teachers provided the study data. Ten public high schools in Wayne Country, Michigan were randomly selected to participate in this study. The participants included all members of the following departments at the selected schools: (1) Language, (2) Social Studies, (3) Vocational and (4) Mathematics and Science. All participants were given the self-administered questionnaire at faculty meetings by a school official. The questionnaires, developed especially for this study, were returned via first-class mail in the pre-addressed, stamped envelopes. A number of relevant findings were revealed by the study data. There was general agreement among the teachers concerning the low level of influence student codes of conduct were having on student behavior at their schools. The mean score rankings consistently indicated that student codes of conduct were having very little impact on specific types of student behaviors. Behaviors such as tardiness and smoking on school property were regularly ranked ahead of other behaviors as the most observed student conduct. The data revealed that the codes of student conduct appeared to be somewhat more effective in regulating the most serious types of student behaviors.

2381.   Tursini, J. G. "The effects of parent and teacher training on the generalization of behavior change in children." Ph.D. Dissertation, Arizona State University, 1974.

The purpose of this study was to measure the effects that training of parents, teachers, and a combination of both parents and teachers in behavioral techniques may have in modifying maladaptive or undesirable behavior in children. Specifically the study sought to ascertain whether behavior intervention brought about through the training of teachers in school to generalize to the home setting, and whether behavior change brought about by parental intervention in the home to generalize to school setting. The subjects were randomly assigned to four groups and a pre-test post-test experimental design was utilized. It was concluded that training of parents of teachers in behavioral intervention techniques is a highly effective method to promote behavior change in maladaptive children both at home and at school. There were generalization effects from training teachers that indicate that be- havior change in maladaptive children is produced not only in the school but also generalizes to the home setting. There are also generalization effects from training parents that indicate that behavior change in maladaptive children is produced not only in the home but also generalizes to the school setting.

2382.   Upton, Charles C. "Television Violence 'Effects' Reevaluated: Use of a Two-Factor Theory of Emotional and Personality Traits to Predict Adolescents' Aggressive Responses in a Classroom Setting." Ph.D. Dissertation, Ohio University, 1978. Dissertation Abstracts International, 39 (2-A), 528-529. Order no. 7812004.

The major purpose of this experiment was to test three sets of variables as predictors of adolescent aggressive behavior and to evaluate a paradigm which was desigend to approximate "real life" conditions. The paradigm involved test taking activities in a classroom setting, with a criterion measure based on covert sabotage of the test answers as retaliation against the experimenter. The hypothesis tested was that varying levels of aggression would be obtained by manipula- ting the arousal and cue components of emotion, and would be mediated by 11 personality traits with increased retaliation predicted for subjects who 1) were aroused (viewed violent/exciting television), 2) were cognitively cued by verbal attack, and 3) were characterized by relatively lower scores on the 11 selected personality traits. High school students ($\underline{n}$ = 177) tested in a classroom setting completed the California Psychological Inventory (measuring personality traits); a lengthy series of questions to provide a ruse that the study concerned television viewing habits and program preferences, and to tire the subjects of test taking; and the School Morale Scale (to permit pre-post test comparisons). A television segment (very violent,

violent, nonviolent) was shown (to proivde arousal/excitation) but viewing was interrupted on the pretext that the School Morale Scale answer form were incorrectly completed. The findings of the experiment were: 1) That from among a variety of aggressive-cooperative responses, there exists a means of selectively eliciting retaliatory aggressive behavior by varying the arousal and cuing components of emotion in adolescent subjects tested in a classroom setting. 2) The violence and excitement content of a television segment provided sufficient arousal intensity to interact with environmental cues and to elicit aggressive behavior from adolescent subjects tested in a classroom setting. 3) Verbal attack provided sufficient cue properties to interact with heightened arousal and to elicit aggressive behavior from adolescent subjects tested in a classroom setting. 4) Three personality traits mediated the elicitation of retaliatory aggressive behavior from properly excited and cued adolescents in a classroom setting. Those subjects who had low scores on Socialization, Self-Control, and Communality were most likely to be retaliators. 5) Aggressive behavior in general (as opposed to the special arousal and cue conditions of retaliation) was identified with adolescent subjects scoring lower on Communality, Intellectual Efficiency, Psychological Mindedness, and Responsibility, when tested in a classroom setting. 6) Grand Sum (total) scores from the School Morale Scale were predictors of general aggressive behavior (as opposed to retaliation) in adolescent subjects tested in a school setting; however, this difference was also explainable by personality triat differences.

2383.   Vanian, D. J. "Attitudinal and Behavioral Changes Through Semantic Desensitization." Ph.D. Dissertation, University of Southern California. Dissertation Abstracts International, 33 (7-A), 3313-3314. Order no. 73-782, 1973.

The purpose of the study was to investigate the semantic conditioning technique as a means of altering the attitudes and behavior of elementary school students who have exhibited negative, maladjustive classroom behavior. The problem under investigation posed the following questions: (1) Can the meaning of the verbal label "teacher" be altered by the use of semantic counter-conditioning techniques for students who exhibit negative, maladjustive behavior and a high degree of anxiety toward the teacher? (2) If the meaning of the verbal label "teacher" can be altered, will this alteration generalize to other teacher-related labels such as "school" and "studying?" (3) Can the use of semantic counter-conditioning techniques affect the level of anxiety provoked by the verbal label "teacher?" (4) If the level of anxiety provoked by the verbal label "teacher" can be altered, will this generalize to other teacher-related variables such as "school" and "studying?" (5) Can the use of semantic counter-conditioning with the verbal label "teacher" affect the degree of maladaptive pupil behavior toward the nonverbal significate "teacher?" The results show the semantic conditioning technique to be an effective means of altering verbal behavior of pupils.

2384.   Vernot, G. G. "A Study of the Effectiveness of Group Counseling Using a Human Relations Treatment Program with Disruptive Tenth Grade Boys." Ph.D. Dissertation, The Florida State University. Dissertation Abstracts International, 36 (6-A), 3420. Order no. 75-26,825, 1975.

The purpose of this study was to design, implement, and evaluate a human relations training program for disruptive 10th-grade boys. This study was conceived because of an increasing need to deal effectively with the behavior problems of the disruptive student. A one semester group counseling program using a human relations treatment format was proposed as a means of effectively helping these students change their behavior. This program included a variety of exercises designed to build skills in communication, problem solving, conflict resolution, and decision making. Fifty-two 10th-grade boys as a large urban high school were selected for this study by meeting at least one of the following criteria: a) students who had received at least one suspension over the past school year, b) students who had shown a high rate of absenteeism without cause (20 or more days) over the past school years, c) students who were on record two or more times for conduct detrimental to the operation of the school, such as fighting. These students were randomly assigned to one of three groups: experimental (N=19), control (N=17), or placebo (N=16). The effectiveness of the treatment program was evaluated through group comparisons on the following variables: school conduct grade, attendance rate, and teacher ratings of student behavior obtained from the Bristol Social Adjustment Guides (BSAG). Statistical analysis of the data revealed that no significant differences were found among the three groups on any of the variables involved in hypotheses testing. However, the control group was found to have made the most improvement on the conduct variable while the experimental group showed the most gain in attendance. Results obtained from BSAG scores indicated that subjects in the experimental group were seen by teachers as becoming more passively disruptive. In contrast, students in the control and placebo groups increased in their acting out behaviors by the end of the study.

2385.   Wagner, N. A. "Teacher's Judgment of the Social Competency of a First Grade, First-Born Student and the Student's Sex, Socioeconomic Status, Academic Grades and Classroom Behavior." Ph.D. Dissertation, Case Western Reserve University. Dissertation Abstracts International, 38 (3-A), 1313, 1977.

This study investigated whether the sex and socioeconomic status of a first born, first grade child influenced a teacher's judgment of that child's level of social competence. This study further investigated whether a teacher's judgment of the academic competence of a child varied as a function of the teacher's judgment of the child's level of social competence. Finally, this study investigated whether the nature of the teacher-student classroom interactions was related the the teacher's perception of the student's level of social competence. This study involved 82 first born, first grade students and thirty teachers. The Harvard Preschool's Social Competence Rating Scale (Shapiro, 1972), Brophy-Good Dyadic Interaction Observation Schedule (1969), and the Hollingshead Two Factor Index provided measures of the teacher's judgment of a student's level of social competence, teacher-student interactions, and the student's socioeconomic status, respectively. Analysis revealed no significant difference in the teacher's judgment of a student's level of social competence as a function of the student's sex. However, the results indicated a trend for students of a middle socioeconomic status to be judged as more socially competent than students from a lower socioeconomic status.

2386.   Wall, S. M. "Behavioral Self-Management: An Effective Classroom   Technique."   Ph.D.   Dissertation,   Columbia University. Dissertation Abstracts International, 38 (5-A), 2678. Order no. 77-24, 351, 1977.

The effects of two different self-reinforcement procedures on children's test performances were investigated and compared to each other and to external reinforcement. In one self-reinforcement procedure, children set points in a contingency in advance of performance while in another procedure children determined a total number of contingent points after performance. Subjects were 167 fourth-grade children in eight classes in the same suburban public school district. Three contingency conditions resulted in significant and comparable increases in total test performance over controls, as well as significant increases from baseline to contingency sessions: externally determined contingencies, self-determined contingencies with training, and self-determined contingencies with training, and self-determined contingent points after performance. All other non-control conditions showed small but significant increases from their baseline to contingency sessions but were not significantly different from controls in contingency scores adjusted for baseline and IQ.

2387.   Wallin, Kenneth R. "The Comparative Effects of Two Behavioral Treatments on the Behavior, Grade-Point Average and Attitudes of Fifth and Sixth Grade Students who are Classified as Highly Distractible." Ph.D. Dissertation, University of Southern Mississippi. Dissertation Abstracts International, 33 (9-A), 4859-4860. Order no. 73-5591, 1973.

This study was conducted to evaluate and compare the effects of Classroom Behavior Management and the pairing of Classroom Behavior Management with Model-Reinforcement on classroom behavior, grade-point average and attitudes of fifth and sixth grade students who are classified as highly distractible. The sample population was chosen from four elementary schools located in Forrest County, Mississippi. From a total of twenty fifth and sixth grade classrooms, twelve classes were selected for the study. A total number of twelve fifth and sixth grade classrooms, and their respective teachers, were randomly assigned in groups of four to each of the following groups for a period of twelve weeks: 1) Classroom Behavior Management Group. 2) Classroom Behavior Management with Model-Reinforcement Group. 3) Control Group. The following findings are indicated from this study. 1) Classroom Behavior Management and the pairing of Classroom Behavior Management with Model-Reinforcement have differential effects on on-task behavior and grade-point average of children identified as highly distractible. When teachers utilize a Classroom Behavior Management approach or when they pair this method with Model-Reinforcement, on-task behavior and grade-point averages of highly distractible children increase. 2) In comparing the two behavioral techniques, the method of pairing Classroom Behavior Management with Model-Reinforcement appears more effective in improving on-task behavior than using Classroom Behavior Management alone.

2388.   Walter, G. H. "The Relationship of Teacher-Offered Empathy, Genuineness, and Respect to Pupil Classroom Behavior." Ph.D. Dissertation, The University of Florida. Dissertation Abstracts International, 38 (11-A), 6629-6630. Order no. 7806767, 1978.

The purpose of this study was to investigate the relationship between teacher-offered empathy, genuineness, and respect and pupil classroom behavior. A significant positive correlation was expected between teacher-offered empathy, genuineness, and respect and pupil supportive classroom behavior. A significant negative correlation was expected between teacher-offered empathy, genuineness, and respect and pupil deviant classroom behavior. The data analyses led to the following conclusions: 1) Teacher-offered empathy, genuiness, and respect were significantly related to pupil supportive classroom behavior. 2) There did not appear to be any significant negative correlation between teacher-offered empathy, genuineness, and respect and pupil deviant classroom behavior. 3) There was a significant difference between the correlations of teacher-offered empathy, genuineness, and respect and pupil supportive behavior, and the correlations of teacher-offered empathy, genuineness, and respect and pupil deviant behavior. Findings from this study suggest that training teachers to improve their interpersonal skills in the classroom may results in increases in pupil supportive behavior.

2389.   Walter, Timothy L.   "Classroom Management: Intervention by Feedback."   Ph.D.   Dissertation,   The University of Michigan.   Dissertation Abstracts International, 32 (11-A), 6231.   Order no. 72-15,035, 1972.

Feedback of performance information is widely used to modify the behavior of teachers, students, and various institutional personnel.   Research of behavior modification has shown that feedback may be manipulated both to increase correct student responses and to reduce inappropriate student behavior.   In this study, a feedback intervention strategy was developed which focused on the acceleration of positive (task) behaviors with small and then large groups during the first half of intervention.   During the second half of intervention the focus of accelerating negative (nontask) behaviors was incorporated, first with small groups and then with large groups.   The studies were undertaken in three classrooms which varied widely in age level of the students, community setting, and experience of the teacher.   The intervention strategy consists of four steps: 1) provide information feedback on task responses to a small group of students;   2) extend information feedback to the entire class;   3) avoid responding to the inappropriate behavior of a small group of students; and 4) extend non-responding to the entire class.   During the first half of the intervention, with a focus on acceleration of task behaviors, two of the three teachers achieved significant increases in task behavior and all three teachers were successful in decelerating inappropriate behavior.   During the second half of intervention, when the focus shifted to the deceleration of nontask behavior, one of the two teachers who had achieved significant increases in task behavior began to see a deceleration in task behavior while the rate of inappropriate behavior continued to decrease. The second teacher continued to see significant increases in the rate of task behavior while the reate of inappropriate behavior remained the same.   The third teacher remained unable to accelerate task behavior although inappropriate behavior continued to decrease.   Thus, the shift to the second half of intervention resulted in the deceleration of inappropriate behavior for two of the teachers, but adversely affected the rate of task behavior for the third.

2390.   Waple, C. C.   "Relationship Between the Existence of 'Ressentiment,' Student Perception of Internal-External Control and Pupil Control Ideology of Certificated High School Staff, In selected Ohio Public Schools."   Ph.D. Dissertation, Bowling Green State University.   Dissertation Abstracts International, 35 (4-A), 1939.   Order no. 74-23,344, 1974.

The purpose of this study was to discover: 1) the relationship between the differences in levels of "Ressentiment" among high school students and schools; and 2) the relationship between the existence of "Ressentiment" and student perception of Internal_External control and pupil control ideology of certified staff. Schools were divided into five average daily memberships (ADM) ranges as of October 10, 1972, in grades 10, 11, and 12. The instruments used in the study were: 1) Friedenberg-Nordstrom "Essentiment" Characteristics Index, 2) Custodialism-Humanism Scale (Form CI) Developed by Terry Eidell, and 3) the Modified Rotter Internal-External Scale. Supplemental Data to Assist in describing the schools and from the 1970 U.S. Census data for Ohio was provided. Usable responses were received from 975 students and 323 teachers. 1) Statistically significant rated "Ressentiment" was found in all schools. 2) The basic assumption that higher levels of teacher custodialism is present, was supported at the .01 level of confidence for hypothesis one. 3) The hypothesis that the level of "Ressentiment" is related to the level of students perception of internal control over their destiny in school was also supported at the .01 level of confidence. 4) There appears to be no statistical relationship between schools in the form of interaction between level of "Ressentiment," student feelings of internality, and teacher control ideology.

2391.   Wegman, T. J. "Reinforcement Schedules and Social Maturity in an Inexpensive Token Motivation Program." Ph.D. Dissertation, United States International University. Dissertation Abstracts International, 34 (10-B), 5178. Order no. 74-8909, 1974.

The problem of the study was threefold: 1) How can the effects of a token economy practically and inexpensively be extended over a long period of time? 2) Do different schedules for back-up reinforcement have different effects upon behavior? 3) What effect does a token economy have upon variables other than target behaviors, e.g., social maturity? Corresponding to these questions, there were three purposes: 1) to determine the effects of an inexpensive token economy upon "learning about peers," "paying attention," and "handing in homework on time" in a classroom of second grade children; 2) to determine the effects of two schedules for back-up reinforcers (fixed interval and variable interval); 3) to determine whether there was a temporal relationship between the token economy and significant changes in social maturity. The rationale of the study was that answers to the above questions could be valuable to users of token economies. Research hypotheses were: 1) "Learning about peers," 2) "Paying attention," and 3) "Handing in homework on time: will be significantly greater when contingently reinforced than when not contingently reinforced. 4) "Learning about peers," 5) "Paying attention," and 6) "Handing in homework on time" will be significantly greater under the variable interval than under the fixed interval schedule for back-up reinforcement. 7) There will be a significant increase in social maturity during the time the token economy is in effect. Subjects were thirty-nine, "normal" (no exceptional handicaps, liabilities, or assets, no behavioral problems), second grade boys and girls in one classroom. There was one female teacher and no teaching assistant. The first, second, third, and seventh research hypotheses were accepted; and the fourth, fifth, and sixth research hypotheses were rejected.

2392.   Weinrott, Mark R. "Observation Training and Practice: Effects on Perception of Behavior Change." Ph.D. Dissertation, McGill University (Canada), 1976. Dissertation Abstracts International, 36 (10-B), 5291.

This study examined the relationship between behavior change in children and teacher perception of that change. It was hypothesized that the extent to which an individual is trained in observation skills, practices them, and is monitored by others is related to the accuracy of his ratings of child behavior. A laboratory test of this hypothesis (Experiement I) showed that teachers who were trained to record discrete responses and collected data on a daily basis were quite accurate in their judgements of distractibility. Ratings by teachers who received little or no training without practice were considerably less accurate. A naturalistic test of the same hypothesis was also performed (Experiment II). Teacher ratings of a selected child were compared with independently obtained observation data. Results showed that the effects of observation training, data collection, and monitoring were not significant in improving the accuracy of perception.

2393.   Weinstein, C. R. S. "The Effect of a Change in the Physical Design of an Open Classroom on Student Behavior." Ed.D. Dissertation, Harvard University. Dissertation Abstracts International, 36 (11-A), 7315. Order no. 76-10, 571, 1976.

The present study had several goals: 1)to develop a category system and an observation technique that could be used to investigate the relationship between the physical setting of an open classroom and student behavior; 2) to observe and record the spatial and temporal distribution of activity in such a classroom; and 3) to investigate the effects of a change in the physical design of the classroom on the students' behavior. The subjects of the study were 25 second and third graders in a self-contained open class-room which the teacher had divided into five areas: mathematics, reading, games, art, and science. The category system developed for the study consisted of 48 overt, "common-sense" classroom behaviors, such as "arts and crafts," "play with animals," and "reading." The observation technique itself used two approaches--time-sampling and continuous recording. In the first approach, each child was assigned a letter of the alphabet. At the scheduled time, the observer entered the classroom, visually located Child A, and coded on a floor plan of the room the child's letter, his location, and the number of the behavior category in which he was engaged. The observer then repeated this process with the remaining children, taking about ten minutes in all. The major goals of the room changes were:

1) to increase the use of areas that were insufficiently visited by children and to decrease the use of areas that were too crowded, and 2) to increase the frequency of several specific categories of behavior, such as "manipulation of objects." Specific hypotheses were formulated to test each goal. The results of the time series analysis conducted on the time-sampling data indicated that most hypotheses were confirmed beyond the .05 level. One surprising finding of the continuous observations was the extremely short attention span exhibited by the children, even those designated "least active."

2394.   Weis, H. M. "Classroom Management Training Project Social Skill Training for Teachers of Problem Classrooms at the Secondary Level." Ph.D. Dissertation, The University of Rochester. Dissertation Abstracts International, 40 (01). DAI no. 7914506, 1978.

Teacher training utilizing the Classroom Management Training Project social skill "package" was employed in four suburban junior high school classrooms noted for high levels of disruptiveness largely under the instigation of several of the school's leading "troublemakers." A role-playing procedure identical to that used in previous Classroom Management Training Project research was used to help teachers master and integrate a large number of specific classroom management skills. These skills focused upon both limit-setting and differential reinforcement of on-task behavior in classes using either a seatwork or group discussion format. Teacher training reduced disruptiveness by over 50% in three of the four classrooms with three classrooms showing a significant change (p .05) based upon a t statistic corrected for serial dependence among observations. Measures of percent time on-task for the three most disruptive members of each class were inconsistent.

2395.   Wells, James N. "Status and Substance of Missouri School Districts' Policies Dealing with Corporal Punishment." Ed.D. Dissertation, University of Missouri - Columbia, 1979. Dissertation Abstracts International, 40 (8-A), 4346. Order no. 8002408.

There were three major purposes of this study. They were: 1) To determine the percentage of Missouri School Districts in this study that allow the use of corporal punishment. 2) To determine whether or not the school districts have written board policies concerning corporal punishment. 3) To identify the elements in the policies that limit, govern, or control the use of corporal punishment and the frequency by which they occur. 1) The large majority of school districts in Missouri allow the use of corporal punishment (98%). 2) Most school districts in Missouri have written policies concerning corporal punishment (66.5%). 3) Small school districts are less likely to have written policies than the larger schools. 4) A large majority of the school districts revise or amend their policy every five years or less, but a few have gone as long as fifteen years before revision.

2396.   Wells, M. L. "The Effect of a Behavioral Contract Upon the Academic Performance and Self-Concept of Failing Middle School Students." Ed.D. Dissertation, The Florida State University. Dissertation Abstracts International, 41 (2-A), 469-470. Order no. 8016681, 1980.

The purpose of this study was to determine the effect of a behavioral contract upon the academic performance and self-concept of failing middle school students. These students were selected by random sample from failing sixth, seventh, and eighth grade students of approximately the same socio-economic level in one school in Northwest Florida. The California Test of Basic Skills, the grade point average as determined by percentage scores, and the Piers-Harris Children's Self-Concept Scale were used to obtain data. Thirty-five cases each were selected for experimental and control cases. Significant differences at the .05 level were found in achievement test scores and grade point averages in all cases (except the language subtest gain score at the completion of the treatment). The self-concept scores were found to be significant at the .05 level; the subtest scores, Intellectual and School Status were also found to be significant at the .05 level.

2397.   Wentzel, E. M. "Teacher Ratings of Classroom Behavior and Its Relationship to Student Anxiety and Reading Achievement." Ph.D. Dissertation, Case Western Reserve University. Dissertation Abstracts International, 38 (8-A), 4706. Order no. 7731016, 1978.

The purpose of this study was to investigate the relationship between student anxiety, teacher judgments of classroom behavior, and reading achievement; and how this relationship is affected by student intelligence quotient, sex and grade level. The sample for this study consisted of 248 students ranging from grade five through eight, attending a private school in what is described as a low-middle socio-economic suburb of a large midwestern city. The students were administered the Iowa Test of Basic Skills to determine reading achievement; the Cognitive Abilities Test to determine the intelligence quotient and the General Anxiety Scale for Children and the Test Anxiety Scale for Children to determine student self-reported anxiety. To assess classroom behavior, each of the nine homeroom teachers participating completed the Devereux Elementary School Behavior Rating Scale for the subjects of the study who were in their classrooms. The results of this study indicated that there was a significant linear relationship between the teachers' perception of student's classroom behavior and the students' reading achievement.

2398.   West, R. C. "Responses of Internal and External
Maladjusted Third Grade Children to Individual and Group
Reinforcement." Ed.D. Dissertation, Columbia University.
Dissertation Abstracts International, 35 (9-A), 5976-5977.
Order no. 75-6478, 1975.

The purpose of this study was to compare the way in which
group and individual reinforcement affected behavior, mutual
liking, self-esteem and group performance in internal and
external third grade children who were maladjusted. In
group reinforcement rewards are dependent on responses of
all group members. In individual reinforcement rewards are
dependent on responses of individuals. External children
see consequences of behavior as externally determined.
Internal children see consequences of behavior as determined
by personal action. Hypotheses of the study proposed more
powerful consequences of group reinforcement with positive
results in adaptive behavior, mutual liking, self-esteem and
performance in group tasks. The hypotheses also predicted
stronger effects of group reinforcement with external
children. In comparing group and individual reinforcement
it was found that group and individual reinforcement were
equally effective in reducing maladaptive behavior,
promoting mutal liking among peers, and in stimulating
performance in group problem-solving tasks. Group reinforcement was less effective than individual reinforcement in
stimulating self-esteem. In comparing external and internal
children, external children were better behaved with group
reinforcement, liked their peers equally well under both
conditions, but had lower estimated of peer liking for self
with group reinforcement. Conclusions were that group
reinforcement has potential uses with maladjusted children.
Social skills and methods of working together in groups
should be developed in such children. They also appear to
need additional support to develop self-esteem in group
settings.

2399.   Whitmore, J. S. "A Leadership Program Designed to
Improve the Attitudes and Behavior of Black Elementary
Students: An Action-Research Project." Ph.D. Dissertation,
Stanford University. Dissertation Abstracts International,
34 (6-A), 3164. Order no. 73-30,493, 1973.

This study was part of an in-service education project
conducted by the Stanford Center for Research and Development in Teaching. The subjects were low-income Black
elementary students in grades 4,5,6. The intervention, a
Leadership Program, was constructed in response to teacher
and pupil reports that rewarding outcomes were lacking for
educationally desired behaviors; teachers believed they were
most rewarded professionally for coercive control of pupils
and students felt most rewarded socially for disruptive or
non-compliant behavior. A lack of school or professional
pride and low morale had resulted. Specific aims of the
intervention were to reduce the disruptive, negative
behavior of some socially powerful students while increasing

the rewards for more appropriate models and for teacher efforts to improve classroom climate. Eight teachers identified 64 male and female social leaders, classifying each as usually positive or negative in attitudes and behavior. Thirty-two Leaders, four from each class, comprised the Leadership Group; thirty-two served as control subjects. The Leaders met twice a week and daily implemented projects to improve interpersonal relations in the school in order to develop a more harmonious and productive learning environment. They studied the school's problems, gathering information from peers and adults through class discussions, interviews and observations. Leaders designed a Good Citizen Program and projects involving monitoring of students, assisting administrators, and helping in Kindergarten-Primary classrooms. Effects of the intevention upon attitudes were determined by measure of self-concept, perceived locus-of-control and social efficacy, and attitude toward school. Although results of ANOVA revealed few statistically significant changes in attitude toward self which were clearly related to the intervention, definite trends in the predicted directions were evident. Significant gains in self-concept did not occur but participation as Leaders did reduce the "normal" trend of females and Negatives becoming increasingly negative. Leaders, especially Negative males, increased their sense of efficacy and internal acceptance of responsibility. Attitudes toward school were not significantly affected. Teacher support was found to be critically important. Negative Leaders with teachers more supportive of the Program often showed significant changes in attitudes but benefitted most regarding behavior. They increased their constructive behavior markedly and decreased destructive behavior more than 50 percent while control S̲s increased disruptiveness.

2400.   Wiesner, David E. "A Comparative Study of the Effects of Cross-Discipline Team Teaching and Departmentalized Teaching on the Classroom Behavior of Eighth Grade Pupils. Ph.D. Dissertation, St. Louis University. Dissertation Abstracts International, 31 (8-A), 3795. Order no. 71-3297, 1971.

The volume of literature concerned with team teaching is rapidly growing, but little scientific research has been conducted with respect to the effect of team teaching on pupil classroom misbehavior. This study was concerned primarily with this heretofore neglected area. The following questions were considered and an effort made to test what appeared to be reasonable hypotheses as to their answers: 1) Do classes organized for team teaching generally have pupil classroom behavior problems that are significantly different in nature and frequency from those occurring in classes not so organized? 2) To what extent are pupil behavior problems associated with the subject matter taught in the classes, the sex, the intelligence, the chronological age, and the socio-econominic background of the pupils? An experimental approach was used to gather objective evidence regarding the pupil classroom misbehavior

of two groups of eighth grade pupils. Two hundred eighty-
one of these pupils constituted the traditionally organized
control group. The experimental group consisted of three
hundred four pupils in team organized classrooms. The
findings of the study revealed that: 1) The frequency and
nature of pupil behavior problems which required office
referral arising in academic classes using a cross-
discipline team teaching plan of organization did not differ
significantly from those arising in traditional academic
classes. 2) Differences between the team organized classes
and traditionally organized classes in the frequency and
nature of classroom behavior problems referred to the office
did not appear to be associated with the content area of the
classes or such pupil characteristics as intelligence, age,
and socio-economic background. Differences were, however,
associated with sex.

2401.   Wiggins, M. M. "The Opinions of Elementary Teachers in
Open-Spaced Schools and Self-Contained Classrooms Toward
Punishment, Management and/or Control, and Trust of
Elementary School Students." Ed.D. Dissertation, Oklahoma
State University. Dissertation Abstracts International, 34
(10-A), 6527. Order no. 74-8143, 1974.

The central problem of this study was to determine if there
is a difference in the opinions of elementary school
teachers teaching in open-spaced schools and self-contained
classrooms toward punishment, management and/or control, and
trust of students. The Punishment, Management and/or
Control, and Trust Opinionnaire, a 57 item summated rating
scale form with a response time of approximately 20 minutes,
designed, validated and found reliable by the researcher for
this study, was administered to 280 teachers in eight
elementary open-spaced schools and eight self-contained
classroom schools in four southwestern cities of varying
sizes. Sixty-seven percent of the teachers responded to the
opinionnaire. The PMT Opinionnaire consisted of statements
about student behaviors in planning, evaluating, decision
making, movement, voicing personal opinions, and interaction
with fellow students. The statements are categorized into
the instrument's component parts: punishment, management
and/or control, and trust of students. The teachers'
responses to the Opinionnaire were used to determine differences in the opinions between the two groups. Individual
school scores were not analyzed. Four hypotheses were
tested: Hypothesis One stated that there is no significant
difference between the opinions of elementary school
teachers teaching in open-spaced schools and self-contained
classrooms toward punishment of students as measured by the
PMT Opinionnaire. Hypothesis One was rejected. Hypothesis
Two stated that there is no significant difference between
the opinions of elementary school teachers teaching in open-
spaced schools and self-contained classrooms toward management and/or control of students as measured by the PMT
Opinionnaire. Hypothesis Two was rejected. Hypothesis
Three stated that there is no significant difference between

the opinions of elementary school teachers teaching in open-spaced schools and self-contained classrooms toward trust of students as measured by the PMT Opinionnaire. Hypothesis Three was rejected.

2402.   Wilcox, L. C. "Effects of a Dramatic Activity on Self-Concept and Behavior of Fifth-Grade Students." Ed.D. Dissertation, Brigham Young University. Dissertation Abstracts International, 36 (8-A), 5066. Order no. 76-2564, 1976.

This study was conducted to determine whether six weeks of dramatic activity would affect significantly the self-concept and behavior of fifth-grade students. Five classes were each divided by random assignment into an experimental and a control group. Each experimental group rehearsed and presented two one-act plays with each student portraying two or more characters. The Piers-Harris Children's Self Concept Scale and the Donaldson Student Behavior Rating (Elementary) were used in pre- and posttests. Analyses of covariance on the posttest gains using the pretests as covariates indicated no significant difference between experimental and control groups. However, teacher comments cited observations of improvement in self-concept and behavior of thirteen of the experimental subjects. Nine of the 60 experimental and thirteen of the 53 control subjects made individual gains in total self-concept scores near or exceeding one standard deviation. Increased teacher attention in the remaining half of the class with drama students away for rehearsal may have benefited control subjects.

2403.   Wilde, Evelyn P. "An Analysis of the Effects of Instructing Selected Student Teachers in the Use of a Reinforcement Technique for Classroom Behavior Management." Ed.D. Dissertation, University of Southern Mississippi, 1972. Dissertation Abstracts International, 33 (9-A), 4862. Order no. 73-5594.

The study was designed to determine if the classroom behavior of a group of student teachers trained in the use of a reinforcement technique for classroom behavior mangement would differ significantly from the classroom behavior of a group of student teachers who had not been trained in the technique. The study also attempted to determine whether the trained group would have a more positive self concept after the completion of the student teaching experience than they had before the student teaching experience began. The experimental group received training and a supervised practicum in behavior modification and the control groups received no training. In order to analyze the differences in the classroom behaviors of the groups, the experimental group and one control group were observed three times by two trained observers. These observations included the tabulation of responses designated as approval, disapproval, error of approval, and error of disapproval. The experimental group were observed additionally, and were provided with immediate feedback information as to the frequency of their classroom responses of approval, disapproval, and errors of approval and disapproval. The data collected during the study supported the belief that, as compared to untrained student teachers, the observations of the trained student teachers would indicate a higher frequency of approval responses following appropriate student behavior and a lower frequency of disapproval responses following inappropriate student behavior. The data did not support the belief that observations of trained student teachers would indicate a lower frequency of errors of approval and errors of disapproval responses than the untrained group. Also, the data did not support the belief that the trained student teachers would have a more positive self concept at the end of the student teaching experience.

2404.   Wilde, John W. "The Effects of Modeled Punishment on Disruptive Junior High Classroom Behavior." Ph.D. Dissertation, Southern Illinois University. Dissertation Abstracts International, 37 (6-A), 3557. Order no. 76-28,786, 1976.

The purpose of this study was to determine the efficacy of punishing video taped models as a means of decreasing disruptive student behavior in two junior high school classes. A total of six target subjects identified by school personnel as being disruptive were exposed to a video tape of adolescents punished for disruption in the classroom. Independent observers rated the subjects, three from two classes, and four behaviors defined as being disruptive. The observers' ratings were subsequently plotted according to baseline measurements. A comparison of the target subjects' behavior prior to the treatment condition was made with their behavior after the treatment condition. Both from a traditional baseline evaluation and a statistical analysis it appeared that the experimental condition had no effect upon the number of disruptive behaviors emitted by the target subjects. Within the limitations of this study, modeled punishment had no effect upon the target subjects in this investigation.

2405.   Wilkinson, R. L. "Measures of Behavior and Attitude as Early Indicators of Reading Potential." Psy.D. Dissertation, Rutgers University The State University of New Jersey. Dissertation Abstracts International, 39 (1-B), 366. Order no. 7800213, 1978.

The purpose of this study was to investigate the relationships among reading readiness, personality traits, behavior ratings and reading achievement. It was hypothesized that reading readiness scores and favorable self-ratings would be positively related to reading achievement while unfavorable teacher ratings would be negatively correlated with reading ability. The research sample consisted of 113 first grade boys and girls at four central New Jersey parochial schools. The Lee Clark Reading Readiness Test, Early School

Personality Questionnaire and SRA Assessment Survey Reading Achievement Test were administered to each subject. Teachers completed the Burks' Behavior Rating Scale for a subsample of 88 students. The results of this study, which are in accord with the position that readiness scores can be used to predict reading achievement, suggest that such information accounts for only a small part of the variance. Therefore, readiness scores are of limited value when used as the sole predictive variable. Findings also suggest that emotional maturity and persistence as well as ability to conform to a prescirbed set of behaviors, think abstractly and relate to others are correlated with reading achievement. Although individual correlations as of a low order, there is evidence of a relationship between positive self-ratings and reading ability.

2406.   Williams, Edward W. "Teacher and Student Behaviors in Multiethnic High School Classrooms: An Analysis Using Socioeconomic Stratification of Students." Ph.D. Dissertation, The University of Texas at Austin. Dissertation Abstracts International, 37 (1-A), 50. Order no. 76-14,533, 1976.

The purpose of this study was to determine the differences 1) between teachers teaching low-level socioeconomic classes and teachers teaching high-level socioeconomic classes and 2) between students from low-level socioeconomic families and those from high-level socioeconomic families in multiethnic high school classrooms. Questions to be answered as a result of the study were: 1) Do Black and Mexican American high school students from upper socioeconomic levels behave differently in the classroom than do those from lower socioeconomic levels? 2) Do teachers instructing classes in which the majority of the students are Blacks and Mexican Americans from homes in the upper socioeconomic levels show a more positive attitude and a greater degree of job satisfaction than those teaching Blacks and Mexican Americans from the lower socioeconomic level? 3) Do teachers whose students are primarily Blacks and Mexican Americans from the upper socioeconomic levels exert more influence on student behavior and motivation than those instructing Blacks and Mexican Americans from the lower socioeconomic level? 4) Is there a significant difference in teacher-student instruction in classes with Blacks and Mexican Americans in the upper socioeconomic levels than those with Blacks and Mexican American students in the lower socioeconomic levels? 5) Does the socioeconomic level of Blacks and Mexican American students affect their self-concept? Significant differences were found in the classroom behaviors of teachers as well as Mexican American and Black students from high- and low-socioeconomic levels. These differences favored the students from the higher socioeconomic levels. No significant differences were found between the groups with respect to self concept and attitude toward school.

2407.   Williams, Russell A.   "A Study to Determine the
Effectiveness of a Behaviorally Oriented Staffing Plan for
Upgrading Rural Utah Elementary Schools."   Ph.D.
Dissertation, Brigham Young University.   Dissertation
Abstracts International, 35 (11-A), 7138.   Order no.
75-11,273, 1975.

The purpose of this study was to determine the effectiveness
of a differential staffing plan and a behavioral oriented
teaching approach for upgrading of rural Utah elementary
schools.   The experimental model was successful in providing
an overall (multivariate) significantly better attitude
toward learning and a significantly higher level of achievement among students employed in this experiment.   The
specific areas of significance of attitude toward learning
for the students engaged in the experimental model were:
class content, career development, multiple talent, enjoyment of school and individual instruction.

2408.   Willoughby, J. N.   "The principal as a change agent in
teacher utilization of positive reinforcement techniques in
the classroom."   Ed.D. Dissertation, University of Southern
Mississippi, 1974.

The study was designed to investigate the effect an in
service program conducted by the principal could have on
teacher utilization of verbal approval reinforce-ment, non
verbal approval reinforcement and task oriented positive
reinforcement in the classroom.   Behavioral observations
were recorded on six subjects who are teachers in the fifth
and sixth grade in an elementary school.   Each teacher was
observed for ten minutes daily for a period of ten days in
order to obtain base line data.   Observers recorded three
types of positive reinforcement behavior demonstrated by the
teacher.   These types were verbal approval reinforcement,
non verbal approval reinforcement and task oriented positive
reinforcement.   The results indicated that the principal, by
conducting an in service program using the Behavior Management in the Classroom Kit and the Praise-Criticism Ratio
Kit, can act as a change agent in teacher utilization of
positive reinforcement techniques in the classroom.

2409.   Wilson, E. L.   "A Study of the Relationship Between
Student Perceptions of Teachers' Classroom Behaviors and
Teachers' Classroom Management Preference."   Ed.D.
Dissertation, University of Houston.   Dissertation Abstracts
International, 39 (04).   DAI no. 7818226.

The purpose of this study was to examine the relationship
between students' perceptions of their teachers' classroom
behavior and their teachers' preference for classroom management behavior.   The teacher Opinion Questionnaire is a self-
report questionnaire which was used to determine teachers'
preference of classroom management behavior.   The Pupil
Observation Survey provided a total measure of students'
perceptions of teachers' classroom behavior.   Both teacher

and student instruments were administered during a regular
class period. Data were collected during a six-week period
of the first semester of the 1976-77 school year. The
sample consisted of 80 teachers and students in their
classes (one class for each teacher participating in the
study) of inner-city and Title One schools in the Houston
Independent School District. Each teacher was classified
into one of five groups of teachers based on his or her
response to the Teacher Opinion Questionnaire. Using the
student responses from the Pupil Observation Survey, a
median score was determined for each teacher, on factor of
the Pupil Observation Survey, and used in the analysis. One
global hypothesis and five related hypotheses were
formulated. A final conclusion which may be stated at the
risk of serious oversimplification is that on the average
(inspection of median scores) students' perception of
teachers' classroom behavior relative to teacher preference
of classroom behavior did not show an appreciable descriptive difference relative to factors such as: friendly,
admired, cheerful; knowledgeable, poised; interesting,
preferred: strict control; and democratic procedure.

2410.   Wilson, J. C. "Spalding Junior High, Unit One Dropout
Prevention Program." ED .D. Dissertation, Nova University,
1976.

The purpose of this practicum was to develop strategies to
reduce the dropout rate at a Junior High School in Griffin,
Georgia. Potential dropouts were identified and specific
strategies were used to assist students in solving problems
which caused them to become potential dropouts. Some of the
strategies developed were: 1) Faculty intervention with
dropout prevention plans, 2) Positive identification of
potential dropouts, 3) Personal counseling of selected
students, 4) Parental counseling, and 5) Placement of
students in alternative schools. See ERIC Abstract ED
134915.

2411.   Winston, A. S. "Experimental Analysis of Cheating and
Admission of Cheating in a Classroom Setting." Ph.D.
Dissertation, University of Illinois at Urbana-Champaign.
Dissertation Abstracts International, 36 (5-B), 2508. Order
no. 75-24,440, 1975.

When a child admits wrongdoing, adults use a variety of
consequences in hopes of reducing future transgressions. It
is possible that such consequences merely alter the tendency
to admit or deny prohibited behavior with changing the
proability of the behavior itself. This problem was
investigated using within subjects, reversal designs. In
Experiment 1, a technique was developed for obtaining a
precise measure of academic cheating. Grade school boys in
a behavior modification classroom worked arithmetic problems
using a special aparatus that allowed cheating and errors to
be recorded. The procedures were found to yield a stable
measure of cheating over sessions and to be sensitive to

manipulations of task difficulty, adult monitoring, and the contingencies for corresponding. In Experiment II, these procedures were used to investigate the effect of social and material consequences on both admission of cheating and subsequent cheating. Adult praise increased admission of cheating only when it was accompanied by extra token reinforcement. When the adult uses a combination of praise and punishment the children continued to cheat on nearly all trails but no longer admitted doing so. The consequences also affected the children's tendency to admit or deny without being asked, but were ineffective in reducing subsequent cheating. The implication of the findings for traditional conceptions of children's moral behavior were discussed.

2412.   Wodarski, John S. "The Effects of Different Reinforcement Contingencies on Peer-Tutoring, Studying Disruptive, and Achievement Behaviors: A Study of Behavior Modification in a Ghetto School." Ph.D. Dissertation, Washington University. Dissertation Abstracts International, 32 (2-A), 683. Order no. 71-19,837, 1971.

The present study was undertaken in order to determine what type of reinforcement contingencies lead to optimal levels of peer tutoring, the point beyond which group contingencies are useless in the development of peer tutoring, and what effect the employment of the different contingencies has on the occurrence of studying, nonstudying, disruptive, and achievement behaviors. It was hypothesized that as more incentives were made contingent upon the group's performance, more peer-tutoring behaviors would occur, achievement and studying behaviors would increase, and nonstudying and disruptive behaviors would decrease. The study employed four reinforcement contingencies: individual, group, and two contingencies composed of combinations of the individual and group reinforcement contingencies at different times in four groups of fifth-grade ghetto children to assess which contingencies lead to: a) the greatest occurrence of peer-tutoring behaviors, b) the greatest increase in the number of problems worked correctly, c) the greatest occurrence of disruptive behaviors, d) the greatest incidence of studying behaviors, and e) the greatest incidence of nonstudying behaviors. Data indicated that there was a linear relationship between acquisition in the number of problems worked correctly and the proportion of group reinforcement composing a contingency, acquisition being greater as the proportion of group reinforcement increased. The linear relationship was significant at the .05 level for the bottom-four pupils and the class as a whole and at the .10 level for the top-four pupils. Concurrently, the data indicated that as the proportion of group reinforcement increased the incidence of peer tutoring increased. Data provided by the achievement tests indicated that the pupils in the experimental groups had a higher grade level change during the experimental period than the pupils in the two comparison groups.

2413.   Wolfolk, A. E. "Increasing Student Attention: A Learning Theory Approach With an Emphasis on Transfer to the Regular Classroom." Ph.D. Dissertation, The University of Texas at Austin. Dissertation Abstracts International, 33 (9-A), 4961. Order no. 73-7680, 1973.

Fifty-four elementary school children who had been identified as consistently inattentive to classroom activities were involved in a four-week treatment program. Attention was assessed using a time-sampling observational instrument developed for the study, based upon Hewett's (1969) technique. Subjects were assigned randomly to either an experimental (E), out-of-class (OC), or stay-in-class (SC) condition. Subjects in the E And OC conditions left their regular classrooms each day for 30 minutes to meet with a specially-trained teacher in a small group lesson. In the E condition, attention to a standard lesson series was reinforced by making the earning of token points contingent upon appropriate responses to a signal-detecton task embedded in the lessons. Token points were exchanged for back-up reinforcers on an increasingly delayed schedule. OC subjects participated in the same lesson series without the token reinforcement system. SC subjects remained in their regular classrooms. Four of the nine participating classroom teachers received three house of inservice training in operant conditioning techniques of maintaining student attention. Subjects were observed in the treatment lessons and in their regular classrooms before, during, and after the treatment period, and their attention was assessed using the observational instrument. Analysis of variance tests revealed that the attention and vigilance scores of subjects in the E condition were significantly higher than scores of subjects in the OC condition during the treatment lessons (p .01). In-class attention scores of the E, OC, and SC groups were not significantly different during or after the treatment period, however. Inservice training for teachers did not affect the in-class attention scores of the subjects.

2414.   Woolever, R. M. "Expanding Elementary Pupils' Occupational and Social Role Perceptions: An Examination of Teacher Attitudes and Behavior and Pupil Attitude Change." Ph.D. Dissertation, University of Washington. Dissertation Abstracts International, 37 (3-A), 1394. Order no. 76-20,741, 1976.

This study examined the outcome, on elementary teachers and their pupils, of a federally funded innovative project, Project Equality, designed to change sex stereotyped attitudes regarding appropriate roles and social behavior for males and females. Project Equality was carried out in Highline School District, Seattle, Washington. Pilot teachers (n = 91) volunteered to participate after they had attended an informational workshop. A Pilot teacher was expected to attend workshops, to pretest and posttest pupils, and to attempt, during the approximately five month interim between pupil pretest and posttest, to change pupils' sex steretyped attitudes. Sixteen Comparison teachers were selected by building principals. This investigation included a measure of teacher attitudes regarding the personality traits of ideal adult males and ideal adult females. Pilot teachers were not significantly different than Comparison teachers in the amount of discrepancy between the traits by which they described their adult females as compared to their ideal adult male. As a group, neither the Pilot nor the Comparison teachers stereotyped their ideal adult on the basis of sex. Both Pilot and Comparison teachers described their ideal adult as characterized by a combination of stereotypic "masculine" and "feminine" traits and by a combination of socially valued and not socially valued traits, as determined in previous studies of widely held attitudes.

2415.   Workman, Edward A. "The Effect of a Covert Behavioral Self-Control Procedure on the On-Task Behavior of Elementary School Children: A Time Series Analysis." Ed.D. Dissertation, The University of Tennessee. Dissertation Abstracts International, 38 (9-B), 4495. Order no. 7802048, 1978.

In this investigation, five students in each of three groups were used to investigate the effect of instructions to engage in Covert Positive Reinforcement (CPR) on the on-task behavior (OTB) of elementary school children. The effect of a covert modeling control procedure was also investigated. The results of this investigation indicated no clear effect for any of the CPR or covert modeling control conditions. The results were discussed in terms of several factors which might have resulted in the lack of significant changes in OTB due to CPR. Suggestions were made as to how these factors might be controlled in subsequent CPR studies.

2416.   Yoshinaga, Myrtle E. "Teachers' Judgment in the Area of Classroom Management." Ph.D. Dissertation, Michigan State University. Dissertation Abstracts International, 35 (6-A), 3538. Order no. 74-27,507, 1974.

The purpose of this investigation was to determine the responses and confidence levels of teachers, with varying amounts of experience and in-service training, to specific classroom incidents of an acting-out youngster and a withdrawn youngster. The choices from which the teachers decided were behavior formation strategies (reinforcement and modeling) and behavior elimination strategies (extinction and punishment). This study was conducted with eight third, fourth, and fifth grade teachers without in-service training (group 2), and six student teachers (group 3), from the Highland Park City Schools. The eight teachers of group 1 attended seven or more behavior modification in-service training sessions. Total in-service sessions were 18. The eight experienced teachers who comprised group 2 were from another elementary school and had no previous contact with the in-service program or the investigator. The six student teachers were also housed in this elementary school. The questionnaire administered consisted of two case-studies, that of an acting-out youngster and of a withdrawn youngster. Each of the case-studies was divided into five distinct sections: classroom incident, psychological history, school history, social history and a follow-up classroom incident. The psychological, school and social histories were systematically varied, for the study was interested in the increments of information and not whether particular information would bring about a change in the responses. This study hypothesized that generally the group of experienced teachers with in-service training would choose behavior formation strategies more frequently, and be more confident about the appropriateness of their decision, than the contrast experienced group without in-service training and the inexperienced group without in-service training and the inexperienced group of student teachers. It was also hypothesized that for all groups, the initial choice of strategy, based only on the classroom incident, would remain stable despite increasing amounts of information. The confidence level for all groups would increase as information increased. A final hypothesis involved the comparison of responses observed in the classroom and the questionnaire responses of the experienced group without in-service training. It was hypothesized that there would be a high degree of correspondence between the questionnaire responses after all the information was given and the most frequent classroom management strategy used by the teacher. The results indicated that there were significant differences in the confidence levels between groups. These differences were found 1) in the acting-out case study with increasing increments of information and 2) comparing the acting-out and withdrawn cases after all the information was given. Comparisons using the Scheffe post-hoc method revealed no significant comparisons. No significant differences across repeated measures of the choice of strategies were obtained. Because of this finding, the hypothesis of the stability of the initial response across increments of information was confirmed. Increasing levels of confidence with increasing increments of information was not supported. The teachers with in-service training did not differ significantly in their choices of strategies in either the acting-out case or the withdrawn case. After all the information was given, there were no significant differences in the choices the three groups made in either case.

2417.   Yoshinaga, N. E. "Teachers' judgment in the area of classroom management." Ph.D. Dissertation, Michigan State University, 1974.

Teachers, both beginning and experienced, have felt frustrated and uncertain in handling discipline concerns of the acting out youngster and the withdrawn youngster. The acting out youngsters in pairs both the group's progressed and his own functioning, while the withdrawn youngster only impedes his own classroom functioning. The purpose of this investigation was to determine the responses and competence levels of teachers, with varying amounts of experience and in service training, to specific classroom incidents of an acting out youngster and a withdrawn youngster. The choices from which the teachers decided were behavior formation strategies and behavior elimination strategies. The questionnaire used consisted of two case studies, that of an acting out youngster and of a withdrawn youngster. Each of the case studies was divided into five distinct sections: classroom incident, psychological history, school history, social history and a follow up classroom incident. After each increment of information, the teacher was asked to make a choice from behavior formation strategies and behavior elimination strategies. The results indicated that there were significant differences in the confidence levels between groups. These differences were found 1) in the acting out case study with increasing increments of information, and 2) comparing the acting out and withdrawn cases after all the information was given.

2418.   Young, K. R., Jr. "The Comparative Effectiveness of Individual Versus Group Token Reinforcement Contingencies." Ph.D. Dissertation, University of Utah. Dissertation Abstracts International, 34 (10-A), 6472. Order no. 74-8152, 1974.

Two groups of students at the Jordan Resource Center were used as subjects in an experiment designed to compare the effectiveness of individual versus group token reinforcement contingencies. Group I consisted of 5 students in the secondary class (grades 7-10). Group II consisted of 5 students in the elementary class (grades 4-6). Both Groups experienced the same experimental conditions (Baselines, Individual Points, and Group Points) but in a different sequence. The conditions were arranged in an A B A B design. The comparison was made on the basis of four criteria: 1) the effectiveness of the systems in controlling classroom behavior, 2) the effectiveness of the systems in motivating the completion of academic assignments, 3) the amount of token reinforcement earned during the two different systems, 4) the amount of social reinforcement received during the two different systems. In comparing the effectiveness of an individual token reinforcement program and a group token reinforcement program the data indicate the following conclusions: 1) there is no significant difference between the two methods in controlling classroom behavior, 2) the individual token reinforcement method was slightly more effective in producing academic output, 3) the subjects earned significantly more points during the individual conditions, 4) no clear conclusion can be drawn about social reinforcement in relationship to these two methods.

2419.   Zinar, E. H. "Intervention Procedures for Classroom Management Using the Guided Inquiry Mode and Programmed Materials: A Consultant Model." Ed.D. Dissertation, University of California, Los Angeles. Dissertation Abstracts International, 36 (11-A), 7225. Order no. 76-11,542, 1976.

This investigation examined the impact of an instructional mode of counseling combined with programmed materials on the behavior of teachers of educationally handicapped pupils in the elementary school setting. The counseling mode, derived from cognitive learning theory and behavioral counseling, was specified by controlling the verbal behavior of the counselor; the content of sessions was specified through the use of programmed materials based on learning and reinforcement theory. The intervention model was initially applied in the regular classroom by Horowitz (1972) who used the original programmed booklets. The purpose of intervention was to teach teachers to apply a problem-solving sequence to classroom problems and to provide a replicable model for in-service training by the counselor and other appropriately trained school personnel. The research design was a planned time-series framework using a case study approach replicated in two classrooms. The investigator served as counselor with the first counselee; a teacher trained by the counselor counseled the second counselee. The project extended over a twelve-week period for each counselee. The logistics and activities of the program were reviewed at a preliminary meeting. Intervention consisted of four 60-minute counseling sessions and one 90-minute counseling session. There was a weekly interval between the first four sessions; a two-week interval, recommended by the structure of the booklets, between the fourth and fifth session. Each counseling session focused on one booklet or step of the problem-solving sequence. At a final meeting, the counselor was provided with additional teacher evaluation of the program, and the teacher, with summary feedback on classroom observations. In consideration of the time requirements of intervention, each counselee paid fifty dollars. The program operated effectively and as predicted. Outcome behaviors were assessed in the cognitive, affective, and behavioral domains. Cognitive growth was indicated by the teachers' performance on the cognitive post test, their completion of the problem census questionnaire, and analysis of the tapes. Behavioral change was demonstrated by an increase in teachers' use of expectational statements, their positive interactions with pupils, and their ability to apply the problem-solving sequence in the classroom. Reports by teachers and observers also noted improvement in pupil behavior and in the classroom atmosphere. Affective reaction, derived from the tapes and post meeting reaction forms, was favorable. Teachers found the program worthwhile but demanding. Gains demonstrated were maintained three and five weeks after the last counseling session.

2420.   Zockle, M. A. "Student Behavior Adjustment Through Self-Management Applications." Ph.D. Dissertation, The Ohio State University. Dissertation Abstracts International, 37 (11-A), 7018. Order no. 77-10,633, 1977.

The study measured self-control in two fourth-graders and two sixth-graders selected from two classes in a Midwestern school. Self-control, whether implicit or explicit, is an important product of the educational system. Self-control has been researched from a variety of perspectives, such as self-assessment, self-administration or reinforcement, etc. These various studies have shown that self-control methods are effective in altering behavior. This study focuses on the potential efficacy of simple self-control methods to decrease inappropriate interactional behaviors in fourth- and sixth-grade students. Classroom teachers--one fourth-grade and one sixth-grade--identified inappropriate or undesirable behaviors, using a Student Behavior Rating Scale with all of their students. Those behaviors listed most frequently were verbal provocation, physical provocation on peers as an initiating or reactive behavior, and lack of compliance to authority. The students were then trained in self-control methods through role playing, principles of self-control, and mediation training methods. Four target students were observed by a trained observer. Change scores were computed with pre- and post-test ratings. Ratings of behavior were made on a seven-point scale, with F indicating the worst behavior and I the best. All of the students involved in the study showed a decrease in the amount of inappropriate behaviors; however, one sixth-grade boy did not do as well as the other three children. It should also be remembered that ratings were the result of teacher perceptions and were open to bias, pro or con, on the actual behavior of the student. Further, all four subjects showed a decrease in appropriate behaviors during the intervention period of this study. It is possible that the decrease in appropriate behaviors may be dealt with by a longer period of training the subjects.

3.

JOURNAL ARTICLES

3001.   Aaron, R. et al. "Computer-Managed Instruction for Behaviorally Disordered Adolescents." Reading Improvement, 12, 2 (Summer, 1975): 103-107.

Author concludes that computer assisted instruction can improve student achievement among behaviorally disordered adolescents with reading problems. See ERIC Abstract EJ 119165.

3002.   Abikoff, H., Gittelman, R. and Klein, D. F. "Classroom Observation Code For Hyperactive Children: A Replication Of Validity." Journal Of Consulting and Clinical Psychology, 48, 5 (October, 1980): 555-565.

Researchers replicated the validity of a modified state university of New York at Stoneybrook classroom observation code to distinguish normal children from children evaluated as hyperactive by their teachers. Sixty-one six - twelve year olds were observed using the code. This study gives strong support to the realiability and discriminative validity of the code and documents its utility in studies of hyper-active children. See ERIC Abstract 1340464-6.

3003.   Acker, L. E., Oliver, P. R., Carmichael, J. A. and Ozerkevich, N. J. "Inter-Personal Attractiveness and Peer Interactions During Behavioral Treatment Of The Target Child." Canadian Journal of Behavioral Science, 7, 3 (July, 1975): 262-273.

In an attempt to evaluate the consequences of operant techniques in addition to changes in the target behavior of a ten year old boy, an individual-contingent, group-reinforcement program was implemented in a regular classroom containing fifth and sixth graders. Periods of on-task behavior by the target child were reinforced by the provision of special activities in which all class members participated. Major results included: 1) The effective control of the target child's on-task behavior, 2) An observed decrease by peers of social interactions with the target child as the study progressed and see an initial decrease and subsequent recovery in the popularity of the target child following implementation of the contingency program. See ERIC Abstract 0146655-1.

3004.   Adams, W. "Mental Help in the Schools: Parent Training." Paper presented at the Annual Convention of the American Psychological Association, Toronto, Canada, August, 1978.

A training program by teachers for parents of school children who were creating problems at school was investigated. Ten couples rated their child's at-home behavior by means of a checklist, participated in group sessions lead by the teachers with a focus on means for dealing with student behavioral problems, and then rated child's at-home behavior after the completion of the group sessions. The control group of six parental couples completed only the behavior checklist at the beginning and end of the final grading period of the school year. A correlated T-test between parental ratings before and after group involvement indicated significant subjective positive changes by the parents. While no significant changes occured among the control group. Additionally, teachers rated children whose parents attended the group sessions more positively in overall classroom behaviors whereas control group children's ratings were unchanged. See ERIC Abstract ED 166589.

3005.   Ainsworth, L. and Stapleton, J. C. "Discipline at the Junior High School Level." NASSP Bulletin, 60, 397 (February, 1976): 54-59.

This article explores current attitudes, situations and plans for improvement relating to discipline. Much of the data were attained through research gathered from a junior high school, grades seven through nine, during the previous school year. See ERIC Abstract EJ 144087.

3006.   Aitchison, R. A. et al. "Training Paraprofessionals Counselors to Treat Behavioral and Academic Deficits in Elementary Classrooms." Paper presented at the Annual Conference of the Western Psychological Association, San Francisco, California, April, 1974.

Current and projected manpower shortages within the field of mental health suggest a greater role for paraprofessionals. But, without careful evaluation and precise training, added manpower would not solve any of the problems facing psychology in overcoming the limits to the delivery of services. These two papers review several attempts to evaluate the effects of an existing paraprofessional training package on several specific behaviors of the volunteers. The initial training procedure was used with 12 college students who volunteered to work with elementary school students having behavior or academic problems. A pre-test, post-test research design was used, with counselor training taking place in five weekly one hour meetings during which reading assignments were discussed, and triadic role playing employed with the observer giving feedback to the others following five minutes of role playing. Data from the study showed that college students could be trained to emit specific counseling behaviors. Several other case studies of training paraprofessionals are also presented. See ERIC Abstract ED 105316.

3007.   Alberti, C. E. "Due Process and Discipline." Clearinghouse, 51, 1 (September, 1977): 12-14.

The enjoyment of the right of attending school is conditioned necessarily on compliance by pupils with the reasonable rules, regulations and requirements of the school authorities. Discusses the legal decision that set the foundation for developing school discipline and responsibilities of administrators, educators, as well as school districts in maintaining discipline policy. See ERIC Abstract EJ 169086.

3008.   Alexander, R. N. and Apfel, C. H. "Altering Schedules Of Reinforcement For Improved Classroom Behavior." Exceptional Children, 43, 2 (October, 1976): 97-99.

Researchers implemented a VI reinforcement schedule during a one-hour day communicative skills period in an effort to improve attending and study behaviors of five seven-thirteen year olds who have been on a token economy for four months. Baseline data for attending behaviors and daydreaming, motor, and verbal non-attending behaviors were recorded for eight days. During the baseline phase, token reinforcement was given at the end of the hours; during the first experimental phase tokens were given on a three minute schedule for two days and then on the three minute VI Schedule. Comparisons indicated that the frequencies of attending behaviors were higher during the two experimental phases and the frequencies of non-attending behaviors were higher during the baseline phases. Five general guidelines are offered for the implementation of VI Schedules during less structured classroom activities. See ERIC Abstract 1151257-5.

3009.   Algozzine, R. "The disturbing child: what you see is what you get." Alberta Journal of Educational Research, 22, 4 (December, 1976): 330-333.

Researcher compared the ratings of 25 special education teachers, 25 regular education teachers, and 25 teachers-in-training with regard to the relative "disturbingness" of certain behaviors. A modified version of the behavior problem checklist was used. Regular teachers found the

behaviors more disturbing than either of the other groups.
See ERIC Abstract #0614658-3.

3010.   Alper, Kermit T. and Kranzler, G. D.   "A Comparison of
the Effectiveness of Behavioral and Client Centered
Approaches for the Behavior Problems of Elementary School
Children."   Elementary School Guidance Counseling, 5, 1
(October, 1970): 35-42.

Researchers view the nonsignificant results obtained in the
study described as one more indicator that new directions
need to be taken to make more effective the work of the
elementary school counselor. New directions can and should
be taken because the old ones have not stood the test of
experimental evaluation. See ERIC Abstract EJ 026549.

3011.   Alschuler, A., et al.   "Social Literacy: A Discipline
Game Without Losers."   Phi Delta Kappen, 58, 8 (April,
1977): 606-609.

The social literacy approach attempts to determine the
systemic causes of discipline problems.   See ERIC Abstract
EJ 156990.

3012.   Alvord, J. B.   "Male/Female Dynamics and Student
Discipline."   NASSP Bulletin, 63, 428 (September, 1979):
55-58.

Results of a study show that male teachers refer male
students to the administration for disciplinary action 2 1/2
times more often than they refer female students, while
female teachers refer 1.3 times more often. Both male and
female staff refer girls in nearly the same number. See
ERIC Abstract EJ 206328.

3013.   American Friends Service Committee. "A Report on Short
Term, Out of School Disciplinary Suspensions in the Junior
High/Middle and High Schools of Richland County School
District #1, 1075-1976 and 1974-1975."   Columbia, South
Carolina: South Carolina Community Relations Program, 1976.

Short term suspensions are a severe disciplinary tool that
can be dispensed by school officials for one to five days at
their own discretion. In addition to the negative impact of
suspension on students, districts lose some state financial
aid when students are not in school because they have been
suspended. A continuing assessment of suspensions in the
Richland County School District #1 had occurred in the last
few years primarily because of the differential application
of suspension on black and white students. In 1975-76,
there were 3.4 suspensions among blacks for every one
suspension among whites. This represents only a fractional
reduction from the previous year when the ratio was 3.6
black suspensions to one white. The report contains basic
data over a two year period on seven high schools, two
junior high schools, and nine middle schools. The name of

the school, number of suspension by grade, number of suspensions by race, and number of suspension days are listed for all the schools. Entries of percent black students are available for all but one school. Reasons for suspensions are not complete for some of the middle schools. See ERIC Abstract ED 127663.

3014.   Andam, K. and Williams, R. L. "A Model for Consultation with Classroom Teachers on Behavior Management." _School Counselor_, 18, 4 (March, 1971): 253-259.

A contract, formulated by the teacher and her students at the suggestion of a consultant, was designed to encourage less disruptive classroom behavior. The arrangement permits the student to learn or not to learn without having to cope with nagging by the teacher. See ERIC Abstract EJ 06433.

3015.   Anderson, L. M. et al. "Dimensions in Classroom Management Derived from Recent Research. Research and Design Report No. 6006." Washington, D.C.: National Institute of Education. Paper presented at the annual meeting of the American Educational Research Association, San Francisco, California, 1979.

A year long study of 28 third grade teachrs yielded extensive data describing their classroom management practices. The seven most effective and the seven least effective teachres were compared to determine what dimensions of management discriminated between them. Teachers who qualified as better managers had a firm preconceived notion of acceptable behaviors and fashioned their classroom structures in such a way as to actively discourage intolerable behaviors. They also exhibited superb task anaylsis and an expertise in coordinating teacher and student activities in the most efficient manner. The less effective managers appear to suffer from the lack of a clear set of expectations regarding student behavior and student work level. They considered student activity primarily on the basis of discouraging refractory deportment and in not displaying an adequately aggressive disposition toward positive student involvement. See ERIC Abstract ED 175860.

3016.   Anderson, L. M. and Evertson, C. M. "Classroom Organization at the Beginning of School: Two Case Studies." Washington, D.C.: National Institute of Education. Paper presented at the Annual Meeting of the American Association of Colleges for Teachers of Education, Chicago, Illinois, February, 1978.

Observation of two third grade teachers during the opening of school revealed different approaches to organizing their classes and instructing their classes on correct classroom behavior. The results of observation are given in narrative form and analyzed. Five principles that characterized the most teacher are presented: 1) the teacher who was better organized demonstrated an ability to analyze the task of the first week of school and presented them to students in small easily understood steps, 2) before the morning began, the better organized teacher had clear expectations about what she would accept in the students' behavior and what would be encouraged, 3) the better organized teacher communicated her expectations clearly to the students, 4) the better organized teacher remained sensitive to the students' concerns and needs for information, and 5) the better organized teacher monitored her students closely in order to give immediate feedback. See ERIC Abstract ED 166193.

3017.   Anderson, L. S.   "The Aggressive Child." Children Today, 7, 1 (January/February, 1978): 11-14.

The role of anger is discussed in young children and its relationship to learning and suggestions are made for specific approaches and techniques for managing aggression in young children. Sited in the article are over a dozen strategies for teaching children more effective mastery of their anger feelings. See ERIC Abstract EJ 178096.

3018.   Ascare, D. and Axelrod, S.   "Use of a Behavior Modification Procedure in Four Open Classrooms." Psychology in Schools, 10, 2 (April, 1973): 243-248.

Author discusses the British Primary System with open classrooms and a behavior modification procedure which worked effectively in these open classrooms.

3019.   Axelrod, S.   "Comparison of Individual and Group Contingencies in Two Special Classes." Behavior Therapy, 4, 1 (Janaury, 1973): 83-90.

The study tested two behavior modification treatments with 28 eight to ten year old predominantly black students. An undesirable behavior was tabulated whenever a subject distrubed a classmate or left his seat without permission. During group contingencies the number 25-0 were listed on the blackboard. Following each undesirable behavior, by any subject, the teacher crossed out the highest remaining number on the board. After each session, all subjects received the number of tokens which corresponded to the highest remaining number. During individual contingencies, the teacher wrote each subject's name on the board with the numbers 25 to 0 below each name. Following an undesirable act, the teacher crossed off the highest number under the responsible subject's name. After each session, each subject received the number of tokens corresponding to the highest remaining number under his name. The group contingencies system produced more non-target behavior incompatible with academic progress. See ERIC Abstract 0367350-2.

3020.   Ayllon, T., Garber, S. and Pisor, K.   "The Elimination of Discipline Problems Through a Combined School-Home Motivational System." Behavior Therapy, 6, 5 (October, 1975): 616-626.

Authors describe a new procedure that include children's homes as a powerful source of reinforcement to eliminate discipline problems in school. The procedure consists of linking the child's daily classroom behavior to consequences provided at home by the parents. An entire third grade class of 23 black students was observed for 1.5 hours daily. Baseline measures indicated that the average level of disruption was 90%. To give the child feedback regarding classroom conduct, a good behavior letter was sent home with the child if he met criteria for good conduct. Results indicated that a school-home-based motivational system can be effective in reducing disruptive behavior and maintaining appropriate conduct in the classroom. See ERIC Abstract 0283956-2.

3021.   Ayllon, T. and Rainwater, N. "Behavioral Alternatives to the Drug-Control of Hyperactive Children in the Classroom." School Psychology Digest, 5, 4 (Fall, 1976): 33-39.

Authors discussed and illustrated with several case studies involving hyperactive children acting out in school classroom situations. In each case, a tangible prize such as money or candy was used to reward the children for limiting their disruptive behavior. The programs were found to be effective in reducing the incidence of disruptive behavior. Recommendations for using behavioral modification strategies in the classroom include: 1. providing a structured classroom environment at all times by stating and applying all rules clearly, 2. providing reinforcement only for correctly completed academic work, and 3. basing rewards on the wants of the student. See ERIC Abstract 0479162-2.

3022.   Ayllon, T. and Roberts, M. D. "Eliminating Discipline Problems by Strengthening Academic Performance." Journal of Applied Behavior Analysis, 7, 1 (Spring, 1974): 71-76.

Authors observed five fifth grade boys identified by their teachesr as discipline problems. The teacher conducted 15 minute performance sessions in her reading class during which written academic performance and disruptive behavior were recorded. The subjects' average level of disruption was 34%, while the reading performance was below 50%. When systematic token reinforcement was applied to reading performance, the rate of disruption fell drastically. Reading performance increased. See ERIC Abstract 0858452-4.

3023.   Bach, L. "Of When, School Administration, and Discipline." Phi Delta Kappan, 57, 7 (March, 1976): 463-466.

According to the author, if the educational leader is a woman who has overcome her usual acculturation, yet preserved her ancient heritage of empathy and nurturements, she would be an educator in the finest sense of that term: disciplined yet creative, logical yet emphatetic, directive yet supportive. See ERIC Abstract EJ 132531.

3024.   Bach, N. "Selected Problems of Student Disruptive
Behavior in the State of Wisconsin," _Journal of
International Association of Pupil Personnel Workers_, _22_, 3
(June, 1978): 161-171.

The relationship between identified disruptive students
enrolled in the educational support program and data
recorded on their guidance cummulative folders is examined
to justify early childhood intervention as a mens of prevention. Disruptive students tended to have lower IQ scores,
come from large families, and be from minority groups. See
ERIC Abstract EJ 184535.

3025.   Balch, R. W. and Kelly, D. H. "Reactions to Deviance in
a Junior High School: Student Views of the Labeling
Process." _Journal of Instructional Psychology_, _1_, 1
(Winter, 1974): 25-38.

Researchers conducted a questionnaire study of 105 ninth
graders to examine key aspects of the labeling process.
Results showed that subjects believed that the same deviant
act would evoke different reactions from their teachers
depending on the character of the offending student.
Subjects also believed that their teachers tended not to
offer constructive help to boys defined as trouble-makers.
Subjects believed that troublesome students were subjected
to various practices which could probably further alienate
them from the educational system. See ERIC Abstract
0609453-3.

3026.   Bardon, J. I. et al. "Psychosituational Classroom
Intervention: Rationale and Description." _Journal of
School Psychology_, _14_, 2 (Summer, 1976): 97-103.

Based on consideration of the environmental role in
determining behavior, an approach to direct intervention
with a pupil in the classroom is described. Assumptions
underlying the intervention approach, examples of the
method, and cautions in its use are presented. See ERIC
Abstract EJ 140946.

3027.   Barkley, R. A., Copeland, A. P. and Sivage, C. "A Self-
Controlled Classroom for Hyperactive Children." _Journal of
Autism and Developmental Disorders_, _10_, 1 (March, 1980):
75-89.

Researchers investigated the effectiveness of a package of
self-controlled procedures in a classroom with six hyperactive boys aged seven to ten years. Measures of on-task
behavior and class misbehavior, as well as measures of
activity level, were recorded. Results indicate that the
self-controlled package was effective in improving misbehavior and attention to tasks during the individual seed
work but not during group instruction. Activity level was
not affected by the treatment. See ERIC Abstract 0419264-2.

3028.   Barth, R. S. "Discipline: If You do that Again, --."
Phi Delta Kappan, 61, 6 (February, 1980): 398-400.

A school discipline system modelled after the adult legal
system is described. It serves two critical purposes. It
establishes discipline, allowing teachers to continue class
instruction unimpeded, and it constitutes an important part
of the curriculum. See ERIC Abstract EJ 215958.

3029.   Baruth, L. G. "The Incident (Case Analysis)." Elementary School Guidance and Counseling, 8, 3 (March, 1974):
227-232.

The author presents a case study describing the way one
elementary school counselor, with assistance from parents
and teachers, helped solve a behavioral problem of a
student. See ERIC Abstract EJ 095855.

3030.   Baxley, G. B. and Ullmann, R. K. "Psycho Active Drug
Effects in a Hyperactive Child: A Case Study Analysis of
Behavior Change and Teacher Attention." Journal of School
Psychology, 17, 4 (Winter, 1979): 317-324.

Researchers analyzed the effects of Methylphenidate on the
behavior and teacher interactions of a nine year old hyperactive female. Observations of subject's task-related and
disruptive behaviors and of interactions between subject and
her classroom teacher were made when subject received the
active drug and a placebo. Results show that, when subject
was receiving Methylphenidate, she engaged in task-related
activities a greater percent of the time, had a higher
percent of teacher interactions that were instructional in
quality, and received lower behavior ratings by the teacher
than when she was receiving a placebo. Results suggest that
the use of medication may enable the hyperactive child to
profit both behaviorally and academically. See ERIC
Abstract 0382165-2.

3031.   Beeken, D. and Janzen, H. L. "Behavioral Mapping of
Student Activity In Open- Area and Traditional Schools."
American Education Research Journal, 15, 4 (Fall, 1978):
507-517.

Article discusses the comparison of activity recordings from
open- area and traditional schools which indicated that
social behavior, travel and housekeeping activities were
more frequent in the open- area school. Interaction between
peers was greater in open-space at some expense, apparently
to individual contact with the teacher. See ERIC Abstract
1283163-6.

3032.   Bell, M. E. and Scott, C. C. "An Analysis of Instruction
Derived from Gagne's Domains of Learning." Journal of
Instructional Psychology, 5, 2 (Spring, 1978): 23-26.

Article describes the evaluation of teaching strategies using an instrument derived from Gagne's Domains of Learning. Implementation of the instructional sequence inventory for nine days in seven classrooms with five teachers and 105 high school students indicated a difference between observed and desirable types of instructional events. Observations revealed that a majority of classroom instruction was spent in teacher-initiated verbal information. See ERIC Abstract 1465762-6.

3033.   Bernal, M. E. et al. "Cross-Validation of Excuses and Cooperation as Possible Measures for Identification of Clinic Dropouts and Continuers." Bethesda, Maryland: National Institute of Mental Health, June, 1974.

This report deals with parents who are the dropout of continue to cooperate with procedures for identification of problem children. Some suggestions are made regarding measures for identifying dropouts and continuers in mental health agencies. These suggestions are based on data collected over two years of time while families were being recruited during the conduct of a clinical research project involving the identification of young discipline-problem boys. The results of a preliminary report were combined with results of data collected furing the project's second year. Dropping out for cooperative behavior by parents was predicted from early reactions to the project, particularly excuses made in contacts with agency staff. See ERIC Abstract ED 087548.

3034.   Bernal, N. E. et al. "Excuses and Cooperation as Possible Measures for Identification of Clinic Dropouts." Paper presented at the Annual Convention of the American Psychological Association, Montreal, Canada, August, 1973.

This report concerns parents who contact a mental health agency to obtain help for children and do not cooperate with agency procedures. Some suggestions are made regarding measures for identifying cooperative and uncooperative parents. These suggestions were based on data collected while cooperation of mothers was being solicited during conduct of a secondary prevention project involving that identification of antisocial kindergarten age boys. A normal control group was included. Number of excuses given by mothers predicted their lack of cooperation with the identification procedures, and cooperation with subsequent ones. See ERIC Abstract ED 087547.

3035.   Berry, C. "Effects of a Resident Outdoor Experience Upon Behavior of Selected 5th Grade Students." University Park, Pennsylvania: Pennsylvania State University, January, 1978.

Fifteen fifth grade students designated disruptive by their classroom teachers in the State College Area School District of Pennsylvania were divided into three groups and exposed to three weeks of differing lead-up activities followed by a week of residential outdoor education activities at Pennsylvania's Stone Valley Outdoor School. Pre and post tests data were collected by classroom teachers, an outside observer, and counselor-teachers via the Devereux Elementary School Behavior Rating Scale. The Peterson-Quay Behavior Problem Checklist and informal taped interviews with the teacher-counselors on the final night of the outdoor school experience. Data were analyzed in terms of total and individual test scores in the lead-up approaches. Major findings were: the media/discussion oriented group demonstrated significant behavioral improvements ways: achievement anxiety, decision making abilities, attention span, relevant characteristics of a person who is not nervous, withdrawn or attentive; the field experience could positively influence certain problem behaviors and the type of lead-up methods used did influence behavioral outcomes. See ERIC Abstract ED 143463.

3036.   Besalel, A. V., Azrin, N. H. and Armstrong, P. M. "The Student-Oriented Classroom: A Method of Improving Student Conduct and Satisfaction." Behavior Therapy, 8, 2 (March, 1977): 193-204.

Reinforcement procedures have been affective in remedying classroom problems. The present method used many of these reinforcement procedures in a program that maximized student responsibility and included behavioral contracting, self-correction, positive practice for mistake, token economy, individualized codes of conduct, parental feedback, self-selection of extensive reinforcers, and frequent student-teacher conferences. Ten fifth graders were given the new program and ten were used as a control group for one month. The new program resulted in fewer problems and it is concluded that greater student and teacher satisfaction can be achieved by a behavior reinforcement program that emphasizes the role of the student. See ERIC Abstract 1028358-5.

3037.   Bien, N. Z. & Bry, B. H. "An Experimentally Designed Comparison of Four Intensities of School-Based Prevention Programs for Adolescents With Adjustment Problems." Journal of Community Psychology, 8, 2 (April, 1980): 110-116.

Forty urban seventh graders were assigned to one of three prevention programs or to a no program group. Half of the subjects participated for one hour on two mornings per week throughout the school year. The other half participated in the afternoons. Results show that program intensity had a significant effect on grades and observed classroom behavior in the morning programs. No such effect occurred in the afternoons. The effects in the morning were preventive in nature. Only the most intense program, which included parent contact, had a greater effect than no program at all. Implications for school - based interventions are discussed. See PSYC Abstract 1125165-5.

3038.   Biestman, M. and Peckman, J. "Limits." San Francisco, California: Far West Laboratory for Educational Research and Development, 1980.

This paper provides introduction for a teacher workshop on the importance of teacher clarity in controlling disruptive behavior in young students. The main thrust in that a teacher must set forth his or her limits on behavior clearly and simply in order for a student to begin setting his or her own limits and thus become self-directed. Sample lesson plans from the workshop are included.

3039.   Billings, C. "Decorum and Discipline: The Politics of Black Exclusion in Secondary Schools." Paper presented at the annual meeting of the National Association Black Political Scientists, Washington, D.C., March, 1979.

Data concerning the reported offenses of suspended students in a school district in the southeastern United States are examined to determine whether the disproportionate number of black student suspensions is due to ordinary problems of decorum or to actual challenges to the authority of the school. Offenses attributed to males and to females of both races are described. It is pointed out that the racial pattern of these offenses differs, with blacks being involved in a wider range of authority defiance than whites. This nonconsent posture taken by blacks is held accountable for their higher suspension rates. Attached tables provide data, by race and six, on 1) suspension rates for three academic years, 2) exclusion rates, rates based on the actual number of suspensions minus the expected number, 3) most frequently occurring suspendable offenses, 4) student fighting, 5) suspensions for refusing discipline, and 6) a rank ordering of offenses. See ERIC Abstract ED 178659.

3040.   Birkimer, J. C. and Brown, J. H. "The Effects of Student Self Control on the Reduction of Children's Problem Behavior." Behavior Disorders, 4, 2 (February, 1979): 131-136.

Researchers investigated whether accurate self-rating and lower level of children's self-destructive behaviors could be maintained in the absence of teacher social reinforcement or punishment and whether a self-evaluation procedure would be more effective than a teacher-administered point system in reducing disruptive behaviors. Nine and ten year old children showed moderate reductions in disruptive behavior when rules were introduced, little or no improvement with the point system, a further reduction when self-rating with bonus points for matching the teachers rating were introduced and deterioration when returned to the teacher-administered point system. See ERIC Abstract 1118164-5.

3041.   Blanchard, E. B. and Johnson, R. A. "Generalization of Operant Classroom Controlled Procedures." Behavior Therapy, 4, 2 (March, 1973): 219-229.

Researchers applied several previously reported operant procedures for changing classroom behavior in a study with behavior problem seventh graders. Frequency of target behaviors of the ten subjects in the class in which the operant procedure were applied were recorded. Concurrent measures of the same behaviors was made in a second, different class. Procedures conducted in the same usual manner. Tangible rewards and punishments were effective in improving behavior, whereas the efficacy of teacher attentional variables was specific to the teacher. See ERIC Abstract 0384751-2.

3042.   Block, J. "Effects of a Rational-Emotive Mental Health Program on Poorly Achieving, Disruptive High School Students." Journal of Counseling Psychology, 25, 1 (January, 1978): 61-65.

Failure and misconduct prone and Hispanic high school students were given five weekly sessions of rational-emotive education. Comparisons were made with alternate treatment and on treatment controls. The rational-emotive groups showed greatest improvement on all dependent variables over an extended period of time. See ERIC Abstract EJ 177353.

3043.   Blunden, D. et al. "Validation of the Classroom Behavior Inventory." Journal of Consulting and Clinical Psychology, 42, 1 (February, 1974): 84-88.

Factor-analytic methods were used to assess construct validity of the classroom behavior inventory, a skill for rating behaviors associated with hyperactivity. The classroom behavior inventory measures three dimensions of behavior: hyperactivity, hostility, and sociability. Significant concurrent validity was obtained for only one classroom inventory category: impulsiveness. See ERIC Abstract EJ 099136.

3044.   Boegli, R. G. and Wasik, D. H. "Use of the Token Economy System to Intervene on a School Wide Level." Psychology in the Schools, 15, 1 (January, 1978): 72-78.

It has been suggested that professionals dealing with psychological problems in school settings need to consider procedures for consulting on a system level, rather than on an individual or group level. This report discusses a token economy system which was implemented for all 459 students in a kindergarten to grade six elementary school. Managing an intervention program at the system level requires comprehensive procedures for staff training and program modification. A major decrease in classroom disruption and a decrease in negative teacher interactions were found during the token economy system compared with baseline data. Analysis in the next summer on system wide variables demonstrated that the number of suspended students and number of days of suspension decreased, that the rate of gain on achievement tests in reading and mathmatics increased and that the teacher turnover rate decreased. See ERIC Abstract 0183861-1.

3045.   Bogle, N. W. "Relationship Between Deviant Behavior and Reading Disability: A Retrospective Study of the Role of the Nurse." Journal of School Health, 43, 5 (May, 1973): 312-315.

The results of this study support the hypothesis that 1) there is a behavioral difference between children with reading disabilities and children without reading disabilities, 2) a high risk population can be identified and helped so that both deviant behavior and reading disability can be averted, 3) multi-disciplinary resources are necessary to provide identification and positive change. See ERIC Abstract EJ 080143.

3046.   Bolstad, O. D. and Johnson, S. M. "Self-Regulation in the Modification of Disruptive Classroom Behavior." Journal of Applied Behavioral Analysis, 1972.

This study compared self-regulation and external regulation procedures in the treatment of children's disruptive behavior following the collection of baseline data, three of the four most disruptive children in each of the ten first and second grade classrooms were reinforced by the experimentor for achieving low rates of disruptive behavior. The fourth child served as a control subject throughout the experiment. Two of the three experimental subjects were taught to self-observe their own disruptive behavior. In the final reinforcement period, these subjectives were given control over dispensing reinforcement to themselves, based on their self-collected behavioral data while subjects in the other experiemental group continued with the externally managed reinforcement. In extinction, reinforcement was discontinued for all subjects, but one of the self-regulation subjects in each of the classroom continued to overtly self-observe. Results indicated that both reinforcement programs produced a considerable reduction in disruptive behavior. The self-regulation procedures were slightly more effective in reducing disruptiveness than was the external regulation procedures and this advantage persisted into extinction. These results suggest that self-regulation procedures provide a practical, inexpensive, and powerful alternative in dealing with disruptive behavior in children. See ERIC Abstract ED 065195.

3047.   Bolstad, O. D. and Johnson, S. P. "The Relationship Between Teachers' Assessment of Students and the Students' Actual Behavior in the Classroom." Child Development, 48, 2 (June, 1977): 570-578.

Authors examined the relationship between the descriptions that teachers gave of sixty of their students and the behavior that these students exhibited. Teachers were asked to select from their classroom boy and girl pairs whom they would lable as "best, average, and least well behaved" in classroom conduct. Both retrospective teacher ratings and immediate behavioral observation data were collected for each of these students. Results indicated that teachers' rating were convergent with assessments of their students' observed behavior. See ERIC Abstract 0187960-1.

3048.   Bongiobamni, A. F. et al. "Leviton is Wrong on the Use of Corporal Punishment." Psychology in the Schools, 15, 2 (April, 1978): 290-292.

A recent article by Leviton develops a texonomy for individualized school discipline including use of corporal punishment with conduct disordered pupils. Research shows corporal punishment does have a negative affect on some types of behavior disrodered children, but it may not be wholly inappropriate for all types of misbehavior. See ERIC Abstract EJ 182974.

3049.   Borg, W. R. "Changing teacher and pupil performance with protocols." Journal of Experimental Education, 45, 3 (Spring, 1977): 9-18.

Researcher examined whether training teachers with the Utah State University Protocol Modules brought about significant changes in teaching performance and related pupil outcomes. 28 in-service kindergarten through 6th grade teachers were randomly assigned to two groups. Group A was trained in the classroom management modules, Group B in the self-concept modules. Teachers and the 641 pupils in both groups were observed in their own classrooms on performance variables related to both sets of modules. Results indicate that Group A teachers had significantly more favorable post treatment means than Group B on 7 of the 13 classroom management skills. Group B teachers had significantly more favorable post treatment means on 11 of 12 behaviors covered in the self-concept modules. See ERIC Abstract #1238658-6.

3050.   Borg, W. R. and Ascione, F. R. "Changing on-task, off-task and disruptive pupil behavior in elementary main-streaming classrooms." Journal of Educational Research, 72, 5 (May/June, 1979): 243-252.

Study involved nine 4th through 6th grade teachers who were trained with the Utah State University Classroom Management Program, while a comparable control group of 8 received no training. Teachers in the training program made significant improvements in about one-half of the classroom management skills. 99 pupils in experimental classrooms and 77 in control classrooms were observed. Pupils in experimental classrooms made significantly greater improvements in reducing off-task and deviant behaviors than controls. See ERIC Abstract #0875564-4.

3051.   Borg, W. R., Langer, P. and Wilson, J. "Teacher classroom management skills and pupil behavior." Journal of Experimental Education, 44, 2 (Winter, 1975): 52-58.

An experimental group of 20 in-service elementary teachers were trained using the Utah State University Classroom Management Protocol Modules. Teachers were trained and compared before and after training with a control group of 9 teachers. The level of work involvement and deviant behavior of pupils of the experimental group teachers was compared before and after the teachers had been trained. In recitation situations, pupil work involvement increased and deviant behavior decreased significantly. In seat work situations, pupil work involvement increased significantly. See ERIC Abstract #0131256-1.

3052.   Bostow, D. and Geiger, O. G. "Good Behavior Game: A Replication and Systematic Analysis with a Second Grade Class." S.A.L.T.: School Application of Learning Theory, 8, 2 (January, 1976): 18-27.

Researchers studied a method used with a second grade class of 31 pupils to develop behaviors desirable in a living-learning situation. The method consisted of easily replicated models, minimal change in teacher behavior and neglible cost reinforcers. Target behaviors were "out of seat", "talking out", "lack of attention to assigned task", and "bothering one's neighbors." The class was divided into two teams and each time a member broke a rule the teacher stated the rule and placed a mark after the subjects name. Reinforcement was lining up first for lunch plus for a cookie for each winning team member. Results indicate that the game significantly reduced incidence of target behaviors. See ERIC Abstract 0432358-2.

3053.   Bostrom, B. and Thunder, S. "Dealing with the Angry Ones." Today's Education, 65, 4 (November-December, 1976): 60-61.

Self-achievement and growth through education is a brief intervention program for behavioral disturbed adolescents designed to develop coping skills so that they may return to a regular class as soon as possible. See ERIC Abstract EJ 157748.

3054.   Bourgeois, D. "Positive Discipline: A Practical Approach to Disruptive Behavior." N.A.S.S.P. Bulletin, 63, 428 (September, 1979): 68-71.

A program designed for the handling of student disruptions uses the basic concepts of Berne's Transactional and Alice's in an inservice program to help teachers to understand better what is happening in transctions betwen two people. William Glasser's Reality Therapy is used as a vehicle for attempting to change student behavior. See ERIC Abstract EJ 206331.

3055.   Bradley, R. H. and Gaa, J. P.   "Domains Specific Aspects of Locus of Control: Implications of Modifying Locus of Control Orientation."   Journal of School Psychology, 15, 1 (Spring, 1977):   18-24.

Authors studied 36 tenth graders to see if locus of control orientation with respect to intellectual achievement could be changed and to determine whether the change generalized to other types of situations.   Goals setting conferences were employed to improve locus of control orientation for academic achievement situations.   Results support doman specific aspects of locus of control and implied that educators can design programs to modify locus of control orientation with less fear that a more internal orientation for academic situation will lead to maladaptive responses in other types of situations.   See ERIC Abstract 1248058-6.

3056.   Bradley, R. H. and Teeter, T. A.   "Perception of Control Over Social Outcome and Student Behavior."   Psychology in the Schools, 14, 2 (April, 1977):   230-235.

Locus of control and classroom behavior data were gathered from 223 randomly selected students in 75 senior and junior high school classrooms.   The intent of the study was to examine the relationship between locus of control orientation regarding social outcome and two types of classroom behaviors.   Considerate versus hostile and task-oriented versus distractible.   Results show moderate positive correlation between internality and both considerable and task oriented behavior.   The strongest relationship observed was that between perceptions about the teachers control over negative outcome and the subjects behavior.   See ERIC Abstract 0206159-1.

3057.   Bratter, T. E.   "From Discipline to Responsibility Training: A Humanistic Orientation for the School."   Psychology in the Schools, 14, 1 (January, 1977):   45-54.

Author believes that angry, alienated and affluent high school students are no longer motivated or contained by the more traditional "care, custody, controlled, conformity" curriculum.   These adolescents will respond positively to humanistic, relevant and realistic educational philosophy which stresses the worth and dignity of students, an appreciation of individual differences, and a recognition of their inherent rights regarding self-determination and freedom of choice.   A nine step discipline process, which can become a profound learning experience for potentially disruptive students, is outlined and discussed.   See ERIC Abstract 0619858-3.

3058.   Breyer, N. L. and Pollack, B.   "Behavioral Consultation Within the Existing Public School System."   S.A.L.T.: School Application of Learning Theory, 4, 1 (October, 1971): 2-13.

Authors used the services and resources of existing school personnel to establish a behavioral consultative approach to effective classroom management. The experiment aimed to increase the class' appropriate on task behavior, to increase the teacher's verbal attention to appropriate student behavior, to decrease the teacher's attention to inappropriate behaviors and to train teacher clerical aides as observer's and students' behavior. Twenty-three fourth graders were used to test the system. Positive effects were evident after nine school days with off task behaviors decreasing from 41% to 9% of total class time. See ERIC Abstract 0986149-5.

3059.   Briskin, A. S. and Anderson, D. M. "Students as Contingency Managers." Elementary School Guidance and Counseling, 7, 4 (May, 1973): 262-268.

Authors describe the successful use of six sixth grade boys as contingency managers for two disruptive third grade boys. The sixth graders administered time out for inappropriate classroom behavior and along with the teacher, positive reinforcement for appropriate behavior. See ERIC Abstract 0182151-1.

3060.   Briteon, P. R. and Stallings, J. W. "Changing a Climate-Weary Warrior to Hardy Hunters." N.A.S.S.P. Bulletin, 65, 441 (January, 1981): 58-64.

The successful program to reduce discipline problems described here emphasizes four areas. An effort was made to change the erroneous thinking of students, parents, and teachers; to reward and punish students systematically; to clean up the campus; and to increase cooperation and responsibility. See ERIC Abstract EJ 238674.

3061.   Broadbelt, S. "Effective Discipline: A Consideration for Improving Inner-City Schools." Clearinghouse, 54, 1 (September, 1980): 5-9.

Analyzing the serious discipline problems existing problems in inner-city secondary schools plus teacher and administors preceptions of it, the author tells educators that they cannot expect to alter the home-school psychio-economic clash which generates the problem, but they can create a positive learning climate which will raise student achievement. See ERIC Abstract EJ 231404.

3062.   Broadbelt, S. "The Epidemic of School Violence." Clearinghouse, 51, 8 (April, 1978): 383-388.

The problem of violence in the school is explored, related to research, historical viewpoints are presented and the peculiar difficulties are examined by utilizing interviews with the chief of security and five junior high and two senior high principals in the Baltimore City Public Schools. See ERIC Abstract EJ 182787.

3063.   Brody, C., Plutchiuk, R., Reily, E. and Peterson, M. "Personality and Problem Behavior of Third Grade Children in Regular Classes." Psychology in the Schools, 10, 2 (April, 1973): 196-199.

Authors studied the relationship between personality traits of 60 third graders and the extent to which they showed proper behavior in the classroom. Subject were randomly selected from various classrooms and were rated by their teachers on the emotion profile index and problem inventory. Analysis was in the form of boy-girl comparisons of the various variables. Conclusions were stated in terms of proportion of difficulties to be expected at the third grade level. See ERIC Abstract 0977950-5.

3064.   Brokowski, W. W. and Dempsey, R. A. "Attendance Policies in Student Performance." Clearinghouse, 53, 3 (November, 1979): 129-130.

A study of the impact of a new restrictive and punitive attendance policy is reported in relation to high school students' attendance, scholastic achievement, behavior, and extra-curricular participation. Variables of student age, I.Q., and sex were analyzed. The Punitive attendance policy was considered effective for certain students. See ERIC Abstract EJ 22764.

3065.   Brooks, R. "Contrast Between Teachers' and Clinicians' Perceptions of Secondary School Children's Behavior." Educational Research, 21, 1 (November, 1978): 63-65.

Questionnaire data from 180 teachers in 70 clinicians suggest that teachers' perceptions of student behavior were conditioned by the effects of certain conduct on the rest of the class: were escalation by contagion was feared, the presented behavior was rated as "more serious." Clinicians were much more concerned by behavior reflecting personality disorders. See ERIC Abstract 1280663-6.

3066.   Brophy, J. E. and Colosimo, J. "Applying a Contingency Management System to all Students in Each Classroom in an Entire Elementary School." Catalog of Selected Documents in Psychology, 5, 340 (1975): 1123.

An experiment, during the second semester of the school year that involved mandated implementation of a contingency management program in a school that had previously run tradi- tionally is described. Although teachers were required to participate whether or not they wanted to, implementation of the desired procedures was excellent and teacher attitudes toward contingency management imporved following experience with it. Attendance increased compared to the previous year, and achievement increased in two out of three grades for which data were available. Other results were either mixed or insignificant. In addition to these evaluation data, research data bearing on a variety of questions concerning the implementation and individualization of contingency management programs in typical school settings are discussed.

3067.   Brophy, J. E., Colosimo, J. and Carter, T. "Applying a Contingency Management System To All Students in Each Classroom in An Entire Elementary School." JSAS Catalog A Selected Documents in Psychology, 5, 340, 1975.

An experiment, during the second semester of the school year, that involves mandated implementation of a contingency management program in a school that had previously been run traditionally is described. Although teachers were required to participate whether or not they wanted to, implementation of the desired procedures was excellent and teacher attitudes toward contingency management improved following experience with it. Attendance increased compared to the previous year, and achievement increased in two out of three grades for which data were available. Other results were either mixed or insignificant. In addition to these evaluation data, research data varying on a variety of questions concerning the implementation and individualization of contingency management programs in typical school settings are discussed.

3068.   Brophy, J. E. and Rohrkemper, M. M. "The Influence of Problem Ownership on Teachers' Perceptions of and Strategies for Coping with Problem Students. Research Series No. 84." Paper presented at the annual meeting of the Educational Research Association, Boston, Massachusetts, April, 1980.

Elementary teachers read vignettes dipicting incidents involving students who represented chronic behavior problems, and then told them how they would respond if the incidents occurred in their classrooms. Responses were coded for attributions about the students and about the teacher's rolls in causing and remediating the problem. Teachers attributed control ability and intentionality to students presenting teacher-owned problems, but not to teachers presenting student-owned problems. Students presenting shared problems often were seen as able to control their behavior, but not as misbehaving intentionally. The contrasting patterns of attributions seen in their three levels of problem ownership were also associated with contrasting patterns of goals and strategies. The data bear out expectations based on attributional analyses of helping behavior, but raise questions about teachers' preparedness to cope with problem students. See ERIC Abstract ED 196884.

3069.   Brophy, J. E. and Rohrkemper, M. M. "Teachers' Specific Strategies for Dealing with Hostile, Aggressive Students. Research Series No. 86." Paper presented at the annual meeting of the American Educational Research Association, Boston, Massachusetts, April, 1980.

Elementary teachers' free response self-reports of how they respond to students' hostile, aggressive behavior were transcribed, coded and analyzed for relationships to the teachers' grade level, school location, and rating by their principals and by classroom observers. In general, most teachers were poorly prepared to cope with student aggressiveness, and many, especially inner-city teachers, did not wish to even try to do so, preferring instead to refer the students to the principal. Teachers rated higher in ability to cope with problem students were more likely than teachers rated lower to try to settle the incident themselves and to try to socialize the aggressive students more effectively rather than to just punish them. See ERIC Abstract ED 196885.

3070.   Broughton, S. F. "The Unwitting Behavior Modifier." Elementary School Journal, 75, 3 (December, 1974): 143-151.

Article suggests that many teachers develop control over unmanageable pupils through conditioning processes which they use unconsciously. They overlook the conditioning mechanisms which are continually found to some degree in all behavior of all learning organisms. Positive reinforcement, punishment, bicarious consequences, and extinction are discussed. Teachers are constantly conditioning their pupils, who in turn condition their teachers. Few individuals have such a catholic view of their own behavior that they are aware of their own conditioning patterns and how they are conditioned by others. Author includes several studies which illustrate the results of the conditioning processes among pupils. See ERIC Abstract 1240653-6.

3071.   Browder, D. "The Critical Need for In-Service Training in Behavior Management." Education Unlimited, 2, 5 (November-December, 1980): 49-53.

Components of an effective in-service plan are pointed out and models for behavior managemenet in-service to deal with behavior problems are described. See ERIC Abstract EJ 240536.

3072.   Browder, L. H., Jr. "Bergen County Battle Plans: What to do Before Students Demonstrate." Nation's Schools, 85, 4 (April, 1970): 86-87.

Specific plans are outlined for coping with potential student disorder submitted by secondary school in a New Jersey county. See ERIC Abstract EJ 020854.

3073.   Brown, J. A. & MacDougall, M. A. "Teacher Consultation For Improved Feelings Of Self-Adequacy In Children." Psychology In The Schools, 10, 3 (1973): 320-326.

Authors studied the impact of teacher examination, discussion and behavior modeling opportunities on the reported self-perceptions of their pupils. Four hundred elementary school pupils and their fourteen teachers were used in the study. The teachers received twelve hours of in-service training on classroom management problems. The test instruments were the Peer Acceptance Index and Self--Perception Index. Results indicate that the teachers' in-service training program had a positive influence on the self-concept of the children they taught. See ERIC Abstract 0586451-3.

3074.   Brown, J. H., Frankel, A., Birkimer, J. C. & Camboa, A. M. "The Effects Of The Classroom Management Workshop On The Reduction Of Children's Problematic Behaviors." Corrective And Social Psychiatry And Journal Of Behavior Technology, Methods And Therapy, 76, 22 (2) (1976): 39-41.

Reasearchers measured the comparative effectiveness of a workshop to teach behavior-change techniques versus teacher observation alone and teacher attitudes before and after the workshop toward specified children and the relationship of these attitudes to student behavior change. The 25 experimental and 16 control subjects were mainly black males with a median grade level of three. Data included observations by the teachers and the school behavior check list. Results suggest that teachers can be taught to produce significant changes in childrens problematic behaviors through a large group or workshop format. See ERIC Abstract 1354757-6.

3075.   Browne, J. A. "We Want a Meeting." Orbit, 7, 1 (February, 1976): 20-21.

A program is described in which children in primary grades solve problems involving class difficulties, attitude and behaviors in groups with their teachers. See ERIC Abstract EJ 143836.

3076.   Brownell, K. D. et al. "Self-Control in School Children: Stringency and Leniency in Self-Determined and Externally Enclosed Performance Standards." Behavior Therapy, 8, 3 (June, 1977): 442-445.

Researchers investigated the capacity of stringent and lenient performance standards to illicit and maintain academic performance when self-determined or externally imposed. The ability of stringent instructions and self-reinforcement to prompt the enduring the self-selection of stringent standards was examined. Thirty-four third and six fourth graders served as subjects. Subjects in two contingent reinforcement conditions were allowed to self determine performance standards while one group given stringency instructions and social reinforcement while the same requirements were externally imposed on subjects in two other conditions. Controls performed without reinforcement. Stringency instructions and social reinforcement were effective in illiciting and maintaining the self selection of stringent standards. See ERIC Abstract 0655659-3.

3077.   Bruiniks, V. L. "Patterns and Personality Correlates of Teachers' Interactions with Students." Psychological Reports, 42, 1 (February, 1978): 239-242.

One hundred and nine elementary and secondary teachers were found to give more positive feedback to students for work products than for ideas or for personal/social behaviors in the classroom. Inverse relationships were found between the amount of positive feedback provided for work products and that provided for ideas and personal/social behaviors. The teacher's need to express control was related to this pattern of classroom interaction with students. See ERIC Abstract 0960261-4.

3078.   Brumbaugh, R. D. and Skinkus, J. R. "Organizational Control and the Middle School Principal: Man/Woman in the Middle Period." Paper presented at the annual conference of Concerned Leaders in Educational Administration and Research, Alexandria, Virginia, November, 1978.

Recent imperical research identifies a potential area of both a role and organizational conflict for the middle school principal and perhaps all principals. Findings from a role norm inventory revealed that middle school principals do not perceive the realtive importance of disciplining pupils, while teachers -- significant members of their role sector -- accord this particular role behavior considerable weight. While differing significantly in their rankings of a general listing of pupil personnel role behaviors, middle school principals, teachers and counselors demonstrated a degree of concensus on selected items relating to the principal's authority in matters of organizational control. Implications for administrative practice, research and theory are explored. See ERIC Abstract ED 180053.

3079.   Bryan, T. H. "Social Relationships and Verbal Inter-actions of Learning Disabled Children." Journal of Learning Disabilities, 11, 2 (February, 1978): 107-115.

Author describes a series of research studies which investi-gated the psyciometric status, social behavior and social relationships of learning disabled children in classroom observations and laboratory studies. Over time, the sample varies from 80 to 100 elementary school children, of whom about 40% were black and 25% were elementary girls. Control groups matched with subjects on sex and race were used. Results indicated that a significant number of learning disabled children are experiencing difficulty in illiciting positive responses from others and in establishing friend-ships with peers. The source of difficulty for learning disabled children's interpersonal problems seem to rest in their comprehension of non-verbal communication, their affective involvement with others and their expressive language abilities. It is suggested that social relation-

ships be considered in academic area worthy of the development of intervention strategies to train social skills. See
ERIC Abstract 1194061-5.

3080.   Buckley, P. K. and Cooper, J. N. "Classroom Management:
A Rule Establishment and Enforcement Model." Elementary
School Journal, 78, 4 (March, 1978): 254-263.

Describes a model for classroom rule establishment and
enforcement and which has been utilized to assist observers
or teachers themselves in evaluating the classroom management system. Rule enforcement is illustrated by eight
different examples of the effect of reward and punishment on
appropriate and inappropriate behaviors. Questions and
issues concerning the interaction of teacher/student
behavior are discussed. See ERIC Abstract 1056063-5.

3081.   Burnett, L., McLaughlin, T. F. and Hunsaker, D. "Instruc-
tion Following Behavior of an Entire Third Classroom:
Effects of a Timing Device, Public Posting and Teacher
Praise." Behavioral Engineering, 5, 2 (1978): 37-40.

The effects of the timing device, public posting, and
teacher praise were examined in a changing criterion design
on the instruction following behavior of a 24 member third
grade class. Results indicated that such a treatment procedure decreased the number of seconds that it took the entire
class to follow teacher directions. Follow-up data taken 3,
5, and 7 days after the formal termination of the study
indicated that the behavior was maintained. See ERIC
Abstract 0201464-1.

3082.   Burress, C. B. "Group Workshops to Eliminate Self-
Defeating Behavior as an Alternative to Suspension in the
Secondary School." Together, 3, 1 (Spring, 1978): 32-36.

Group workshops are described which illuminates self-
defeating behavior as an alternative to suspension in the
secondary school. Students who worked at understanding that
process reported they had better communication with their
teachers and received fewer, and in many cases, no more
disciplinary referrals. See ERIC Abstract EJ 177428.

3083.   Buys, C. J. "Effects of Teacher Reinforcement on
Elementary Pupils' Behavior and Attitudes." Psychology in
the Schools, 9, 3 (July, 1972): 278-288.

Author reports results of two investigations examining the
effects of teacher reinforcement on elementary pupils'
behavior and attitude. Study 1 reports on the reduction of
deviant classroom behavior by means of specific public and
private teacher reinformcement contingencies. Study 2
reports on the degree to which the reinforcement contingencies altered the subjects' evaluations of themselves, the
target behaviors and their teachers. See ERIC Abstract
0533449-3.

3084.   Camp, W. G. "Educator Perceptions of Student Discipline." Paper presented at the annual meeting of the American Educational Research Association, Boston, Massachusetts, April, 1980.

This paper reports on a survey of Indiana Public Secondary Educator perception of student discipline problems. An extensive list of specific student misbehaviors are rated by respondents answering the following four questions. Which misbehaviors are problems in the area of discipline? How often does each occur? How serious would it be when, or it, it occurs? How much would it interfere with the learning environment? Comparisons are made between the responses of teachers and administrators. A second set of comparisons are made among urban, suburban and rural respondents. Major findings were that most serious problems occur only rately and that the least serious behaviors occur most frequently. See ERIC Abstract ED 187006.

3085.   Camp, W. G. and Bourn, L. P., Jr. "Student Discipline: An Analysis of Teacher and Administrator Perceptions." Paper presented at the International Congress on Education, Vancouver, British Columbia, June, 1979.

This paper discusses research findings concerning student discipline problems in the Indiana Secondary Schools. Issues explored attempted to determine: 1) what specific student behaviors are perceived by teachers and administrators to be discipline problems, 2) how frequently these problems occur, 3) how serious teachers and administrators perceive the problems to be, and 4) how much the identified discipline problems interfere with the learning environment. Questionnaires were mailed to a sample of secondary school teachers and administrators in Indiana. Of the 101 student misbehaviors listed, only 47 were perceived to be discipline problems by a majority of the teachers responding. The paper concludes, that teachers who deal with the individual classroom work of the students hold different perceptions of student discipline than administrators who must be concerned with the problems of the school at large. Related literature on the subject of student discipline is reviewed in detail. See ERIC Abstract ED 173971.

3086.   Campbell, N. J. "The Relationships Between Students' and Teachers' Perceptions of Teacher Behaviors in the Junior High Classroom." Journal of INstructional Psychology, 5, 1 (Winter, 1978): 16-20.

Author examined the relationships between junior high teachers' perception and their students' perceptions of the teacher's classroom behaviors. Seventy-three junior high teachers in 28 public schools and one class of students of each of the teachers (1,602 students) participated. Significant but very low relationships were found between teacher and mean student perceptions of only 25% of the teacher behaviors. See ERIC Abstract 0722661-3.

3087.   Canter, L. "You Can Do It -- Discipline." Instructor, 89, 2 (September, 1979): 106-108, 110-112.

Classroom discipline is discussed and suggestions are presented on how teachers can become more assertive in their classroom. See ERIC Abstract EJ 213028.

3088.   Carberry, H. "Behavioral Block Busters." Instructor, 88, 8 (March, 1979): 73-74.

A psychologist provides helpful suggestions for teachers having trouble with negativistic, impulsive, passive-dependent, and anxious children. See ERIC Abstract EJ 199919.

3089.   Carey, N. F. "Four Principals Reshape Their Educational Perspective." NASSP Bulletin, 64, 436 (May, 1980): 104-106.

A New Jersey principal-initiated program to change the undesirable beahvior of disruptive, under-achieving youngsters is described. Although the anticipated 80% success rate was not realized, results showed the positive growth recorded in most areas was impressive. See ERIC Abstract EJ 221626.

3090.   Cates, J. T. and Gang, N. J. "Classroom Discipline Problems and Reality Therapy: Research Support." Elementary School Guidance and Counseling, 11, 2 (December, 1976): 131-137.

Methods are reported and results listed of two studies ont he successful application of reality therapy to classroom discipline problems. Results indicated that reality therapy is an effective humanizing approach for solving problems. See ERIC Abstract EJ 151103.

3091.   Cates, W. M. "Organized Non-Activity: A Proposed Solution to Some Common Classroom Problems." Clearinghouse, 51, 5 (January, 1978): 220-222.

Compulsory attendance laws seem to assure each teacher a fair share of students who are less than enthusiastic about being in the classroom. Experience has shown teachers that many students in this less than enthusiastic state present discipline and learning problems. Here is a method designed to minimize classroom discipline problems while stimulating students to learn. See ERIC Abstract EJ 178711.

3092.   Chapman, E. B. "An Analysis of Opinions About the Behavior of Disruptive High School Students and a History of Their Earlier School Behavior." Journal of the International Association of Pupil Personnel Workers, 23, 4 (September, 1979): 196-204.

Anecdotal records are analyzed of students who have presented behavioral problems in previous schools, and comparisons are made of opinionnaires of students, parents and faculty regarding attendance, attitudes, and communication. The students' records and opinionnaires are compared with their eleventh grade records to ascertain if these problems could have been detected earlier. See ERIC Abstract EJ 209251.

3093.   Chapman, R. B. "Academic and Behavioral Problems of Boys in Elementary School." Counseling Psychologist, 7, 4 (1978): 37-40.

The behaviors implicit in many boys' sex roles are oppositional to the behaviors required in the student role. The conflict results in the inability of the boy to assume the student role, and may result in his being identified as having an academic and/or behavioral problem. See ERIC Abstract EJ 193720.

3094.   Chernick, E. "Effects of the Feingold Diet on Reading Achievement and Classroom Behavior." Reading Teacher, 34, 2 (November, 1980): 171-173.

A study is described that examined the classroom behavior and reading achievement of elementary school children placed on the Feingold Food Additive Elimination Diet. It was concluded that children who remained on the diet for six months became less impulsive but did not raise the reading scores significantly. See ERIC Abstract EJ 234063.

3095.   Churchill Films. "Keep Fit, Study Well, Work Hard." 1973.

In this film schooling is contrasted with China, where the stress is on discipline and group activities. Schools in the United States are compared to China's methods. The film uses an admonition of Mao Tse Tung's "Keep Fit, Study Well, Work Hard." Twelve minutes. 16mm film. See NICEM 0873626.

3096.   Cipani, E. "Measuring the utility of a classroom intervention procedure: effects on student behavior and continued voluntary use of procedure by teacher." Corrective and Social Psychiatry and Journal of Behavior Technology, Methods and Therapy, 25 2 (1979): 56-63.

An experiment with twenty-four first graders and their teachers is described to demonstrate the effectiveness of free time, independent, group oriented contingency procedure for reducing off task behavior. The effects were maintained during follow-up, and the teacher continued to use the procedure after the experiment was over. See ERIC Abstract 0407165-2.

3097.   Clark, K. & Miller, C. "Points/Counterpoint: Should Corporal Punishment Be Abolished in the Elementary School?" Instructor, 89, 8 (March, 1980): 22.

Kenneth Clark asserts that corporal punishment is an anachronism and that it is applied arbitrarily and sometimes sadistically, teaching children to use violence to solve problems. Miller replies that both common-law and common sense support the use of corporal punishment, when all other disciplinary approaches have failed. See ERIC Abstract EJ 220461.

3098.   Colyer, M. J. "Behavior analytic procedures for reducing disruptive classroom behavior in the elementary school: a review." Behavioral Engineering, 4, 3 (1978): 67-87.

Behavior analysis strategies describe procedures that alter the form and timing of the consequences that a child receives in the classroom. This paper reviews the different behavior analytic procedures that have been applied to decrease disuptive behaviors within the elementary school classroom. The author discusses the need for future strategies to change the dependent variables and provide children with academic motivation and better teaching methods as the primary way of reducing disruptive behaviors. See ERIC Abstract 1446161-6.

3099.   Committee on Education and Labor. "Safety and Violence in Elementary and Secondary Schools." Hearings before the Sub-Committee on Elementary, Secondary and Vocational Education, Washington, D.C.: U.S. Government Printing Office, 1975.

Included in this publication are statements, letters and supplemental materials presented to the Committee on Education and Labor of the House of Representatives in June of 1975.

3100.   Committee of the Judiciary United States Senate. Challenge for the Third Century: Education in A Safe Environment--Final Report of the Nature and Prevention of School, Violence and Vandalism. Report of the Sub Committee to Investigate Juvenile Delinquency by Senator Birch Bayh, Washington: U.S. Government Printing Office, 1977.

This report is the result of an intensive investigation of school violence and vandalism conducted over the past several years by the Sub Committee to Investigate Juvenile Delinquency. Its primary purpose is to suggest to the educational community various models and strategies which were examined by the Sub Committee in the course of its investigation and were found to be particularly helpful in reducing and preventing this phenomenon. The report is divided into several sections, the first of which is the concise over-view of the extent of school-related violence and vandalism on a nationwide basis. In the second section, several of the factors influencing the nature and development of these problems including intruders, disciplinary and suspension policies, learning disabilities, truancy and school size are discussed. The third section of the report sets out the various strategies and models useful to schools in reducing violence and vandalism. The fourth section of the report contains the series of suggested initiatives which the community may undertake to help implement the strategies discussed in the previous section. The sixth section presents a list of suggested readings and a bibliography.

3101.   Cone, J. D.   "Assessing The Effectiveness of Programmed Generalization." Journal Of Applied Behavior Analysis, 6, 4 (Winter, 1973): 713-718.

Issues related to assessing change and retention of change are discussed. An alternative analysis is suggested for the data of the 1972 study by Walker and Buckley. They found that peer reprogramming, equating stimulus conditions, teacher training and control groups maintained seventy-seven, seventy-four, sixty-nine and sixty-seven percent respectively of appropriate behavior produced in a token economy. See ERIC Abstract 0396052-2.

3102.   Congress of the United States. "Federal Involvement in the Use of Behavior Modification Drugs on Grammar School Children of the Right to Privacy Inquiry. Hearing Before a Sub Committee on Government Operations, House of Representatives, 91st Congress, Second Session." Washington, D.C.: Superintendent of Documents, U.S. Government Printing Office, 1970.

This publication consists of the contents of a hearing before a subcommittee of the committee on government operations of the U.S. House of Representatives. The hearing was conducted during the second session of the 91st Congress. The primary purpose of this hearing was to investigate federal responsibility in promoting the use of amphetamines to modify the behavior of grammar school children. Such investigation was stimulated by the indications that these days are being widely employed to ameliorate the effects of what is called minimal brain disfunction in children. Statements were presented by several recognized authorities in the fields of education, child psychology, neuropharmacology, nursing and chemistry. Supplemental statements in correspondence received by the subcommittee subsequently to the hearing are presented. In addition, supplemental newspaper and magazine articles pertaining to federal involvement in the use of behavior modification drugs on grammar school children are appended. See ERIC Abstract ED 064636.

3103.   Conway, A.   "An Evaluation of Drugs in the Elementary Schools: Some Georgraphic Considerations." Psychology in the Schools, 13, 4 (October, 1976): 442-444.

The relationship between type of educational institution and the prescription of medication to elementary age children with behavioral problems was examined with questionnaire data obtained from school psychologists, administrators, and mental health professionals. The conclusion discusses how urban systems vary from rural ones in their approach to correcting problems in pupil management. See ERIC Abstract EJ 146251.

3104.   Conway, A.   "Therapeutic Drugs in the Elementary Schools: An Urban Phenomenon."   Education, 97, 3 (Spring, 1977): 299-301.

The relationship between type of educational institution and the prescription of medication to elementary school children with behavioral problems was examined via questionnaire data obtained from school psychologists, administrators, and mental health personnel in rural New York, and this data was then compared against urban data compiled by others. See ERIC Abstract EJ 162844.

3105.   Cooper, A. J. et al.   "The Development of Behavior Control Competency in Pre-adolescence: A Case Vignette." People Watching, 1, 1 (Spring, 1972):   32-36.

The utility of a crisis intervention approach for helping pre-adolescents build competency in behavior control is demonstrated.   The following dimensions are highlighted: immediacy of intervention, trust relationships, structural interventions, facilitating vs. controlling, problem-solving orientation, and mobilization of group membership sanctions. See ERIC Abstract EJ 055273.

3106.   Cooper, C. & Walker, C.   "Peer Dynamics Final Evaluation Report.   1979/1980, Part I."   Lincoln, Nebraska: Nebraska State Commission on Drugs, June, 1981.

This is Part I of a final evaluation of a program designed to reduce the incidence of destructive risk-taking behavior among school-age youth.   Background research indicates that peer group pressure is the single most important factor in dictating the presence or absence of juvenile delinquency behavior.   The peer dynamics program trains and supervises students who participate in the group interaction plan with other students to develop self-esteem and better communication skills.   Peer modeling takes place.   Some past discrepancies in figures reported by schools previously involved are discussed.   Currently, distinctions are made between the schools with active programs, schools with inactive programs, and programs deleted due to staff turnover.   Time tables are provided for the school years 1979-1981, and several changes are suggested in the areas of organization, distribution of activities, newsletters and in staff training.   Limiting the program to junior high school grades is suggested because that age group appears to benefit most from the program.   New evaluation tools have been selected because the earlier tests were seen as nonfunctional on several levels. See ERIC Abstract ED 197278.

3107.   Cooper, C. and Walker, C.   "Peer Dynamics 1979-1980
Evaluation Report, Part II." Lincoln, Nebraska: Nebraska
State Commission on Drugs, June, 1981.

This is Part II of a final evaluation of a program to reduce
destructive risk-taking behavior in school-age youth.   The
program uses peer counseling in schools to develop self-
esteem and better communication skills in students.   An
analysis of attitude tests is performed and factors
affecting the outcomes of the tests are discussed.   Anxiety
level, setting and rapport between facilitator and peer
groups are discussed.   Overall, school evaluation results
indicate that there has been a positive attitude change
among peer group members due to their participation in the
peer dynamics program.   A significant positive change in
overall self-attitude was seen in all grade levels, with the
greatest in grades eight, ten, and eleven.   A control group
at one junior high showed no significant change in their
attitudes toward self or others.   See ERIC Abstract ED
197279.

3108.   Copeland, A. P. & Weissbrod, C. S.   "Effects of Modeling
on Behavior Related to Hyperactivity."   Journal of Educational Psychology, 72, 6 (December, 1980):   875-883.

Differences between hyperactive and non-hyperactive boys in
their play and responses to models were assessed.   Hyperactive boys behaved differently during play even before
viewing any model, and generally responded more to the
guidelines suggested by the model, especially the fast one,
than did the hyperactive boys.   See ERIC Abstract EJ 239638.

3109.   Copeland, R. E., Brown, R. E. and Hall, R. V.   "The
effects of principal-implemented techniques on behavior of
pupils."   Journal of Applied Behavior Analysis, 7, 1
(Spring, 1974):   77-86.

Researchers conducted three investigations on the effects of
procedures initiated by a principal on the behavior of
elementary school children.   Included were seventy-five
subjects in kindergarten, first, third, and fifth grade.   In
the first experiment when three chronically absent subjects
attended school, the principal entered their classroom and
praised them for being present.   In experiment two, three
low achieving subjects were sent to the principal's office
to receive praise when they met criteria in word-recognition
and addition tutoring sessions.   Experiment three assessed
the effects of a procedure implemented by a principal on the
academic functioning of seventy-four third graders.   Twice
weekly in two classrooms the principal recognized both
improving subjects and the highest performing subject for
their work on addition study sheets.   In every experiment,
target behaviors increased when the principal applied the
treatment contingencies.   See ERIC Abstract 0859052-4.

3110.   Corbeh, E. "Deviant Classroom Behavior as a Function of Combinations of Social and Token Reinforcement and Cost Contingency." Behavior Therapy, 7, 1 (January, 1976): 76-88.

A series of program variables was evaluated in modifying deviant classroom behavior. Experiment one, with four male and one female 6-9 year old problem children evaluated combinations of one setting variable and three treatment variables in modifying behavior. Experiment two, with five male subjects similar to the subjects in experiment one, evaluated combined effects of the variables over an extended period of 45 days. Combinations of variables were less effective in controlling behavior than in simultaneous application of all treatment variables. Relationships were found between increases in appropriate behavior and both token reinforcement and cost contingency. See ERIC Abstract 0140756-1.

3111.   Cossairt, A., Hall, R. V. & Hopkins, B. L. "The Effects Of Experimenter's Instructions, Feedback And Praise On Teacher Praise And Student Attending Behavior." Journal Of Applied Behavior Analysis, 6, 1 (Spring, 1973) 89-100.

The authors use E's instructions, feedback and feedback plus social praise to increase teacher praise for student attending behavior of third and fourth grade teachers. The verbal interactions with teachers, teacher's verbal praise of student behaviors and pupil attending behavior were recorded during base line conditions. The entire package of E's instructions, feedback, and feedback plus social praise was introduced to teacher C in a experimental condition. Introduction of the package produced more teacher praise for student attending behavior. See ERIC Abstract 0980550-5.

3112.   Cote, R. W. "Behavior modification: some questions." Elementary School Journal, 74, (October, 1973): 44-47.

Discussed in this article are the problems of a program of behavior modification among behaviorally atypical pupils. The authors raises the question with respect to reconciling the goals of developing free and open minded children versus applying measures that modify their freedom-seeking behavior. Another question concerned the interpretation of the atypical behavior. Does the behavior of such a child need modification or does the pattern of the milieu in which the child is placed need drastic reform in the direction of accommodating atypical children? It is concluded that behavior modification was not intended as remedial work for large groups of children who perform at or below the normal grade levels but to generate intrinsic motivation for such children whom the school has little power to motivate to comply with the acceptable pattern behavior. See ERIC Abstract 0176852-1.

3113.   Cowen, E. L., Orgel, A. R., Gesten, E. L. and Wilson, A. B. "The Evaluation of an intervention program for young school children with acting out problems." Journal of Abnormal Child Psychology, 7, 4 (December, 1979): 381-396.

Authors described the rational and nature of a program to train fifteen non-professional children's aides for helping interactions with two hundred and thirty-four young acting out school children. Pre-post program teacher measures of children's problems and competencies, aide measures of problem behavior, and school mental health professionals' change-in-behavior estimates were used to evaluate program effectiveness. Children showed significantly greater reductions both in acting out problems and in over all maladjustment when being seen by ten trained aides then similar children seen by comparable aides who did not have additional training. See ERIC Abstract 0367965-2.

3114.   Cowen, R. J., Jones, F. H., & Bellack, A. S. "Grandma's rule with group contingencies: a cost efficient means of classroom management." Behavior modification, 3, 3 (July, 1979): 397-418.

This study involved using a stop watch and a stop clock in two versions of a classroom incentive program designed to reduce student disruptions and increase on task behavior during a small group instructional format. Twenty-five six-nine year olds were studied to investigate whether the two procedures would be effective in reducing disruptions and increasing task orientation among those students outside the reading circle who were relatively unsupervised by the teacher without intruding into the teacher's conducting his or her lesson and whether the more expensive stop clock would be incrementally effective compared to the stop watch in order to justify the additional cost of the stop clock. Results indicated that both techniques reduced disruptions and that there was no systematic difference in effectiveness. See ERIC Abstract 110964-5.

3115.   Cox, W. B. "Crime and punishment on campus: an inner city case." Adolescence, 13, (Summer, 1978): 339-348.

The article describes an experience in performance of discipline in a large, metropolitan area, with a predominately black high school. The opinions and preceptions of teacher, administrators and students were solicited. It is recommended that students have a more active role in the administration of justice and other areas of decision making. See ERIC Abstract 0444962-2.

3116.   Craigie, F. C. and Garcia, E. E. "Effects of child behavior change on teacher verbal behavior and rating of student behavior." Journal of Applied Behavior Analysis, 11, 2 (Summer, 1978): 308.

This study examined the relationship between student behavior change and its effect on teacher behavior in two multiple base line experiments with a total of six fourth grade boys and their two teachers. As student behavior improved, daily teacher ratings of children improved moderately, and the percentage of teacher vocalizations in response to appropriate child behavior increased. See ERIC Abstract 1221262-5.

3117.   Csapo, M. "Parent teacher intervention within appropriate behavior." Elementary School Guidance and Counseling, 7, 3 (March 1973): 198-203.

Twelve six-eight year olds who exhibited emotionally disturbed behavior both at home and in school were assigned to one of four behavior modification conditions: school intervention, home intervention, home and school intervention, or no intervention. Results show that inappropriate behavior decreased for the three experimental groups used during and after intervention sessions, with subjects in the combined parent-teacher intervention group showing the greatest mean reduction in inappropriate behavior over days. See ERIC Abstract 0980950-5.

3118.   Cummings, C. H. "Consistency is the Key." Kappa Delta Pi Record, 17, 1 (October, 1980): 28-30.

The author suggests several techniques for improving secondary school discipline which emphasize cooperation between teachers and principals, consistent application of the rules, and positive attitudes that promote school morale and reward good student behavior. See Eric Abstact EJ 231449.

3119.   Damico, S. B. and Purkey, W. W. "Class clowns: a study of middle school students." American Educational Research Journal, 15, 3 (Summer, 1978): 391-398.

This study examined the class clowns who were identified by peer nominations, teacher ratings and self-esteem in school attitudes in a group of eighth grade students. See ERIC Abstract 0414163-2.

3120.   Damico, S. B. et al. "A Comparison Between the Self-Concepts as Learner of Disruptive and Non-Disruptive Middle School Students." Paper presented at the annual meeting of the American Educational Research Association, San Francisco, California, April, 1976.

The purpose of the study was to compare the scores of disruptive and non-disruptive middle school students on professed and inferred academic self-concept. The Florida Key and the School Academic sub score of the Coopersmith Self-Esteem Inventory were used to obtain scores on a population of 3,254 students enrolled in four middle schools in north Florida. From this group, 208 students were identified as disruptive on a basis of having to be removed from the learning environment two or more times during the first six months of the 1973-74 school year. Significant differences were revealed between inferred and professed self-concept as learner scores of disruptive and non-disruptive students. A significant interaction was found on the Self-Esteem Inventory. Those students identified by their behavior as disruptive had significantly lower inferred and professed academic self-concepts than did students identified as non-disruptive. See ERIC Abstract ED 128710.

3121.   Darch, C. B. and Thorpe, H. W. "The principal game, a group consequence procedure to increase classroom on-task behavior." Psychology in the Schools, 14, 3 (July, 1977): 341-347.

The effect of school principal attention was examined; contingent on team on task performance in an unruly fourth grade class. Subjects were ten boys who had been judged by their regular classroom teacher as being most devient. The experiment involved a reversal technique with multiple phases and was conducted for one month. In condition one, principal attention was delivered through a game-like group-consequence procedure referred to as the principal game. During condition two, principal attention was delivered to individual subjects contingent on each individual's behavior. Results show that the principal attention was a strong reinforcer in both experimental conditions but percentage of on task behavior during team consequences was higher than during individual consequences. See ERIC Abstract 1310159-6.

3122.   Darst, T. W. "Effects Of Competency-Based Intervention On Student-Teacher And Pupil Behavior." Research Quarterly, 47, 3 (October, 1976): 336-345.

Four female and three male elementary physical education students teachers were observed along with one class of pupils from each teacher's assignment during base line and intervention conditions. Nine categories of teacher behavior and three categories of pupil behavior were observed. Findings revealed that the competency-based intervention had a significant effect on teacher behavior and a slight effect on pupil behavior. See ERIC Abstract 0615458-3.

3123.   Davidson, C. W. and Bell, M. L. "Relationships between pupil-on-task-performance and teacher behaviors." Southern Journal of Educational Research, 9, 4 (Fall, 1975): 230-235.

Authors studied the relationship between specific teacher behaviors and pupil on-task-performance using twenty-four fourth through sixth grade teachers and their students. It was found that there were no significant relationships between any of the teacher behavior variables and the pupils on task performance. See ERIC Abstract 0559755-3.

3124.   Davis, D. H. "Facilitating Developmental Guidance Through Behavioral Management." Elementary School Guidance and Counseling, 15, 2 (December, 1980): 104-113.

The counselor, facilitating classroom development guidance lessons, may experience conflict and difficulty. The management system presented here allows for flexibility and provides sufficient behavioral structure, while encouraging individual expression from students. This behavioral management approach is supportive of, but necessary to, developmental guidance goals. See ERIC Abstract EJ 236250.

3125.   Dawson, D. "Some Mental Health Concerns of School Psychologists." School Guidance Worker, 35, 6 (August, 1980): 19-23.

The article focuses on the implications that children's excessive attention-seeking behavior, lonliness, and low self-esteem have for counselors. Early intervention is essential. Provision of counseling services in all elementary schools is recommended to ensure children's mental health. See ERIC Abstract EJ 227260.

3126.   Day, B. and Brice, R. "Academic Achievement, Self Concept Development, and Behavior Patterns of Six-year Old Children in Open Classrooms." Elementary School Journal, 78, 2 (November, 1977): 132-139.

One hundred six-year old children were compared in four classrooms, varying in degree of openness, as established by the Walberg-Thomas Scale on three variables: achievement, self concept development, and classroom behavior. The four classrooms included one three-teacher team, one two-teacher team and two one-teacher classrooms. The size of the teaching team was positively correlated with degree of openness. Results indicate no significant differences for a) academic achievement by classroom setting or sex and b) self concept development by sex, setting or socioeconomic status. Significant differences were found on several dimensions of classroom behavior favoring the more open settings. Implications of results to increased use of open settings are discussed. See ERIC Abstract 1466862-6.

3127.   Dean, R. S. "Teachers as Raters of Aberrant Behavior." Journal of School Psychology, 18, 4 (Winter, 1980): 354-360.

The behavior of pre-adolescent males was rated by two teachers using the Devereux Child Behavior Rating Scale. Interrater teacher realiability estimates were not significantly different than those reported with mental health professionals, but differentiated significantly between diagnostic categories. See ERIC Abstract EJ 240094.

3128.   Dececco, J. P. & Shaeffer, E. A.   "Using Negotiations to Resolve Teacher-Student Conflicts." Journal of Research and Development in Education, 11, 4 (Summer, 1978): 64-77.

Reasons are presented using negotiation to resolve school conflicts, using a model based on the understanding of conflict and the cognitive and affective response to conflict. A description is presented on the research upon which the model is based, how school personnel may be trained to use negotiation, and the author discusses briefly the relationship of negotiation and discipline. See ERIC Abstract EJ 189892.

3129.   Dee, V. D.   "Contingency Management in a Crisis Class." Exceptional Children, 38, 2 (April, 1972): 631-634.

Article describes a contingency management program for first through eighth graders who are unable to function in regular classes but are considered potentially responsive to short-term intervention. The cases of two boys illustrate how the program operates. A guideline is included for the use of contingency management systems. See ERIC Abstract 068150-4.

3130.   Deesch, J. B.   "Group Counseling With Disruptive Students." Paper presented at the annual convention of the American Personnel and Guidance Association, Atlanta, Georgia, March, 1980.

The counseling profession must provide therapeutic opportunities that help disruptive and alienated youth addressed to the realities of society in a manner that is psychologically helpful to the individual, the school, and the community. A therapeutic group counseling model which focused upon the definition and implementation of specific goals identified by individual members during an intake interview was used to determine if disruptive students could assume responsibility for their own effective and active involvement in their educational experience and psychological development. Ninety-seven students were randomly assigned to seven controlled and seven treatment groups. Treatment groups met for nine to twelve weeks and ranged in size from five to seven members. Results indicated that group counseling decreased school conflict and improved the self-concept of the disruptive youth. The counseled groups decreased their referrals to the discipline office and improved their academic achievement. See ERIC Abstract ED 192234.

3131.   Deesch, J. B.   "Group Counseling With Disruptive Students." Journal for Specialists in Group Work, 4, 3 (Summer, 1979): 117-122.

A model of group counseling was thought to provide therapeutic atmosphere in which disruptive students had the opportunity to gain responsibility for effective and active involvement in their educational experience and psychological development. Results indicated the process helped disruptive students acquire thinking and behavior patterns to interact more successfully. See ERIC Abstract EJ 209151.

3132.   Deibert, J. P. & Hoy, W. K. "Custodial High Schools and Self-Actualization of Students." Educational Research Quarterly, 2, 2 (Summer, 1977): 24-31.

The relationship between the pupil control orientation of schools and the personal development of students were investigated. Data were collected from teachers and students in forty high schools. Results indicated that the more custodial the pupil control orientation of the school, the less inner directed, time competent, and self-actualized the students. See ERIC Abstract EJ 174759.

3133.   Deitz, S. M. and Repp, A. C. "Differentially Reinforcing Low Rates of Misbehavior With Normal Elementary School Children." Journal of Applied Behavior Analysis, 7, 4 (Winter, 1974): 622.

Researchers used a modified differential reinforcement of low rates procedure with three students in normal classrooms to eliminate talking out and out-of-seat behaviors. See ERIC Abstract 1042353-5.

3134.   Deno, S. L. "Direct Observation Approach to Measuring Classroom Behavior." Exceptional Children, 46, 5 (February, 1980): 396-399.

Included is a description of an observation system that is based on the assumption that any label applied to a child identifying him or her as a conduct problem implies that the behavior differs significantly from that of the peer group. The system includes the recording of the frequency of four key target behaviors (noise, out-of-place, physical contact/destruction, and off task) emitted by the referred student and by a normative peer sample. Data were obtained by observing three elementary school students from different classrooms who were identified as socially deviant by their teachers. Variations in the levels of behavior observed among classrooms emphasized the importance of sampling both target and peer behavior. The data also indicate that multiple observations are essential to avoid drawing erroneous conclusions. See ERIC Abstract 1069863-5.

3135.   Den Houtter, K. "Alternatives to Drug Treatment for Hyperactivity." Elementary School Guidance and Counseling, 14, 3 (February, 1980): 206-212.

Results from recent studies on the effectiveness of Ritalin for hyperactivity showed that this treatment is dubious, at best. The article presents an alternative treatment approach, placing emphasis on devising an appropriate learning situation that meets the needs of the so-called hyperactive child. See ERIC Abstract EJ 217340.

3136.   Dennison, D. "An Alcohol Education Model to Reduce
Alcohol-Disruptive Behaviors." High School Journal, 64, 6
(March, 1981): 269-272.

This ten classroom hour instructional model for alcohol
education focuses on cognitive information, affective
instruction, and selected field activities to assist
students in establishing physiological and psychological
relationships in alcohol areas. This integration is
organized to clarify values and instill responsible alcohol
behaviors in the students. See ERIC Abstract EJ 241776.

3137.   Derevensky, J. L. & Rose, M. I. "Teacher Preferences For
Various Positive Reinforcements." Psychology In The
Schools, 15, 4 (October, 1978): 565-570.

Researchers investigated the relationship between applied
behavioral training and reinforcement preferences of 294
classroom teachers. Data obtained from the positive
reinforcement observation schedule, a paired comparison
task, indicated minimal differential reinforcement preferences for classroom teachers with no training, limited
training, or extensive training in applied behavioral
analysis. Results are discussed with reference to the
educational implications of existing behavioral training
programs and classroom practice. See ERIC Abstract
0628363-3.

3138.   Devine, V. T. and Tomlinson, J. R. "The 'Work Clock':
An Alternative to Token Economies in the Management of
Classroom Behaviors." Psychology in the Schools, 13, 2
(April, 1976): 163-170.

Described in this article is a set of procedures for
modifying the behavior of an entire class. The procedures
involved a five-day work clock phase in which free time is
contingent on attending behavior of the entire class while
non-attending behaviors are consequented by a strike and
time-out procedure. The second phase retains the time-
on room behavior for both referred and non-referred
students. See ERIC Abstract 0191957-1.

3139.   Devoe, N. & Sherman, T. M. "Microtechnology: A Tool for
Elementary School Counselors." Elementary School Guidance
and Counseling, 10, 2 (December, 1975): 110-115.

Microtechnology is the maintenance of specific skills
identified and taught under controlled conditions. Desirable behaviors are taught through modeling, letting the
child initate the model, and providing feedback on the
child's performance. Microtechnology can also help in
problem-solving, career education, and in coping with
behavior problems. See ERIC Abstract EJ 129223.

3140.   Dickerman, W. "Toward An Efficient Technique for Teacher Conducted Behavior Modification Program for Disruptive Classroom Behavior." Paper presented at the Education Research Association Convention, New York, New York, February, 1971.

Because training teachers to collect observational data and to use operant techniques has frequently been found to be time consuming, the author attempts to develop similar, simplier, more efficient training procedures. This report presents the results of a study in which these procedures were implemented. Teachers followed a three-step training process to learn to observe a disruptive child's behavior, to observe their own interactions with a child, and to initiate more frequent contact with the child when he is on-task in order to increase his on-task behavior. Observers recorded children's behavior as well. Reliability of observations by both teachers and observers was found to be adequate. Two teachers successfully used the procedures to change the behavior of disruptive children. Two were not successful because they failed to change their own behavior. See ERIC Abstract ED 047328.

3141.   Dielman, T. E. et al. "Dimensions of Problem Behavior in the Early Grades." Journal of Consulting and Clinical Psychology, 37, 2 (1971): 243-249.

A behavior problem checklist was administered to the teachers of six to eight year old children. Eight factors were identified as hyperactivity, disciplinary problems, sluggishness, paranoiac tendencies, social withdrawal, acting out, speech problems, and anti social tendencies. Three sets of order factors were identified as neuroticism, sociopathic behavior, and autism. See ERIC Abstract EJ 046876.

3142.   Diem, R. A. "Conflict and Conflict Resolution: Teacher Education to Improve the Teaching Environment." Paper presented at the annual meeting of the National Council for the Social Studies, Atlanta, Georgia, November, 1975.

The general purposes of this study were to determine what constitutes conflict situations in a suburban high school and how these situations are viewed by parents, teachers, and students. The high school used in this study was one of four high schools within a large shcool district located in the northwest corner of Cook County, Illinois. The research study consisted of non-participant behavior observations and administration of statistical instruments. The questionnaires consisted of identifying information and posing questions about conflict, conflict situations, and conflict-solving mechanisms. The major conclusions drawn both from the behavior observation and the questionnaires were that conflict was caused by four distinctive types of behavior: cutting classes, using drugs, smoking cigarettes, and drinking alcoholic beverages. Teachers and parents accepted the authoritarian role given them. However, it was found that some parents would not use this role in certain situations, yet they expected the school to enforce the rules against these behaviors and sought stringent rules against them. The author suggests that efforts to under-stand and deal with conflict which takes place when teachers are preparing for the new role. See ERIC Abstract ED 115521.

3143.   Diem, R. A.   "Social Deviance--A Student Perspective." Paper presented at the annual meeting of the Southwest Educational Research Association, Austin, Texas, January, 1978.

This paper describes a study of deviant behavior among students attending a high school in Texas. All students in the study attended a Sociology class taught by a very strict teacher whose rules of behavior conflicted with students' peer group behavior expectations. Participant observation of student behavior in class and interviews with individual students were conducted to identify daily behavior patterns and students' attitudes toward the patterns. Deviant behavior included skipping class, unauthorized smoking, use of drugs, school vandalism and stealing. It was found that very few students skipped class, and that peers would not report students who did. Smoking restrictions were violated by all students who smoked, and they felt students should have smoking privileges equal to those of teachers. Almost all students had used marijuana and alcohol, and admitted that it was deviant, but would not report the use of drugs to authorities. Vandalism occurred in only a few cases and was condoned by students as long as it did not interfere with individual rights. However, stealing personal property angered the students, and they reported they would prosecute someone who took their property. Conclusions are that students do not disapprove of deviant behavior unless it directly affects them. Students identified the major cause of deviant behavior as lack of parental control over their children. See ERIC Abstract ED 150063.

3144.   Dietz, S. M. and Repp, A. C.   "Decreasing Classroom Misbehavior Through the Use of DRL Schedules of Reinforcement."

Three experiments are reported on in which reinforcing low rates of responding reduced inappropriate behaviors are described. In the first experiment, the talking-out behavior of an 11-year old trainable mentally retarded boy was reduced when the teacher allowed five minutes of free time for a talk-out rate of less than .06/minute. In the second experiment, the talking-out behavior of an entire class was reduced when reinforcement was delivered for a response rate of less than .10/minute. In the third experi-ment successively decreasing the differential reinforcement of low rates reduced the off-task verbalizations of 15 female high school students. See ERIC Abstract 1197651-6.

3145.   Di Giulio, R. "The 'Guaranteed' Behavior Improvement Plan." Teacher, 95, 8 (April, 1978): 22-26.

Author suggests that there is no rule that guarantees appropriate classroom behavior, yet, to control the class, a teacher must control himself. Thirteen tenets are given for helping elementary teachers to maintain a controlled classroom, and twelve guides are included for improving student behavior. See ERIC Abstract EJ 184373.

3146.   David W. Parker Professional Arts, Inc. "Discipline and the School Bus Passenger." Lawren Productions, Inc., 1976.

Film presents the school bus drivers with practial solutions to discipline problems in all age groups. It emphasizes prompt, firm handling of problem behavior from fist fights to vandalism. Twenty-four minutes. 16mm film. See NICEM 0881937.

3147.   Dobson, J. E. & Campbell, N. J. "The Relationship of Teacher's Philosophy of Human Nature and Perception and Treatment of Behavioral Problems." Humanist Educator, 18, 1 (September, 1979): 23-31.

Research reveals that teachers with a positive view of human nature seem to be more open toward and accepting of acts considered to be typical behavioral problems of elementary school children. This group also seemed more concerned with the child's personal adjustment than with proper behavior and department. See ERIC Abstract EJ 210623.

3148.   Dodge, E. R. "High School Classroom Control." Today's Education, 64, 2 (March/April, 1975): 58-60.

A high school teacher discusses ways to control a high school classroom. See ERIC Abstract EJ 131700.

3149.   Dodson, D. W. "Student Power As a Means to Educational Change." Integrated Education, 8, 6 (November/December, 1970): 32-39.

This is a speech by a New York University School of Education professor at the Consultation for Education Justice sponsored by the New York City National Council of Churches. High school unrest is discussed as indicating the need for redistributing power throughout the schools, and the crisis of legitamacy of the schools is discussed. See ERIC Abstract EJ 028000.

3150.   Doleys, D. M. and Williams, S. C. "The Use of Natural Consequences and a Makeup Period to Eliminate School Phobic Behavior: A Case Study." Journal of School Psychology, 15, 1 (Spring, 1977): 44-50.

The school-phobic behavior of a seven year old male was modified through restructuring of natural consequences and the use of a makeup period. Full-time school attendance was achieved on the 16th day of the program. Discussed are the advantages of using school personnel as monitors and not as disciplinarians of a school-phobic child's behavior. See ERIC Abstract 1249358-6.

3151.   Doob, H. S. "Codes of Student Discipline and Student Rights. E.N.R.S. Report." Arlington, Virginia: Educational Research Service, Inc., 1975.

Basic information, positive suggestions, and examples pertaining to student codes are included. Presented are findings of a recent inquiry regarding written codes of student discipline and replication of examples of selected codes. 76% of the 538 responding school systems indicated that they had developed written codes of discipline for secondary level pupils. Large districts with enrollments of 25,000 or more were the most likely to have such codes. Very small districts with enrollments of 200 - 3,000 were the least likely. Written codes of student rights were much less prevalent. 34% of all respondents reported having a written code of student rights. See ERIC Abstract ED 108341.

3152.   Doss, D. A. & Ligon, G. D. "The ERC: A Practical Economical, Reliable and Valid Measure of Student Classroom Behavior. Publication No. 78." Paper presented at the annual meeting of the American Educational Research Association, San Francisco, California, April, 1979.

The Behavior Rating Checklist was developed in the Austin Independent School District to evaluate the counseling component in the Elementary Secondary Education Act Title I Compensatory Education Programs for students in kindergarten through grade five. The ERC was developed by: defining the behavior on which the counseling activities focused, studying other behavior rating scales, drafting items for pilot testing, pilot testing, analyzing the pilot test, conferring with program staff and parent advisory committees, and finalizing the instrument. The final instrument was comprised of ten items to be rated on a nine-point scale. Five items measured students' on-task readiness, willingness, and ability to participate. Five items measured students' in-class discipline or disruptive behavior. The evaluations of the ERC were conducted 1) item by item analysis to check factor, structure and realiability and 2) a check of the validity. Conclusions were reached indicating that ERC is practical, economical, reliable, and valid. See ERIC Abstract ED 177212.

3153.   Dougherty, E. H. and Dougherty, A. "The Daily Report Card: A Simplified and Flexible Package for Classroom Behavior Management." Psychology in the Schools, 14, 2 (April, 1977): 191-195.

Article stresses that there is a growing need for rapid, low cost and proven behavior management techniques for classroom teachers. Often, and uncomplicated system of feedback to pupils at frequent intervals, backed by reinforcers delivered at home by cooperating parents, is sufficient to decease problem behavior and excelerate homework and class-work completion. The paper presents a system consisting of report cards and instructions for students, parents, and teachers which is designed to accomplish these objectives. One application of the daily report cards in a regular fourth grade classroom is presented. In this case, a behavior problem, talk-outs, and homework assignment completion were targeted and recorded during a baseline period. Results indicate a rapid improvement of a minimum of teacher time and effort. See ERIC Abstract 0195159-1.

3154.   Dowd, E. T. "Interpersonal Process Recall as a Classroom Management Technique." Elementary School Guidance and Counseling, 11, 4 (April, 1977): 296-299.

Author assessed the effectiveness of Kagan's interpersonal process recall system as a technique for managing student disruption in a fifth grade and 2 second grade classrooms. Two video playbacks of classroom behavior combined with follow-up verbal interchange were used. Teacher reports indicate that the system followed by some moderate decline in pupil disruption occurred. See ERIC Abstract 1056863-5.

3155.   Downing, C. J. "Teaching Children Behavior Change Techniques." Elementary School Guidance and Counseling, 11, 4 (April, 1977): 277-283.

Investigated in this study was the effectiveness of a group counseling program designed to teach elementary school children to make positive changes in their own behavior. Thirty-seven 6th graders, previously identified by their teachers as classroom disruptive, we assigned to an experi-mental behavioral change learning group or to a group of delayed treatment controls. The subjects were exposed to ten weekly hour counselor-lead group sessions stressing value clarification, problem identification, goal setting, behavior change, and contracting. Comparison achievement tests, school attendance records, and teacher observation showed that the experimental group made greater academic achievement gains, was absent from school less frequently, and experienced a higher rate of improvement in classroom behavior. See ERIC Abstract 1069963-5.

3156.   Draba, R. E. et al. "The Impact of the Goss Decision: A State Survey." Viewpoints, 52, 5 (September, 1976): 1-19.

Results of this survey indicate that the Goss versus Lopez decision, concerning notice and hearing requirements in school suspension incidents, does not represent an over-whelming administrative burden in Illinois, since many principals have long provided the safeguards that the decision mandates. See ERIC Abstract EJ 150804.

3157.   Drabman, R. S. and Lahey, B. B. "Feedback in Classroom Behavior Modification: Effects on the Target and Her Classmates." _Journal of Applied Behavior Analysis_, _7_, 4 (Winter, 1974): 591-598.

A behavior modification program is described that employed feedback with no additional contingencies. It was initiated and withdrawn in an ABAB design on a ten year old child. The disruptive behavior of the target child, as well as that of her peers was monitored. The sociometric status of the target child was recorded. The positive and negative comments made to the target by her teacher and her peers were related to initiation and withdrawal of the feedback contingencies. The results show that 1) feedback alone may be an effective behavior modification procedure 2) the disruptive behavior of the target's classmates changed 3) sociometric status of the target was altered by behavioral contingencies 4) positive comments by classmates to the target increased and 5) negative comments from the teacher to the target child decreased. See ERIC Abstract 1039053-5.

3158.   Drabman, R. and Spitalnik, R. "Social Isolation as a Punishment Procedure: A Controlled Study." _Journal of Experimental Child Psychology_, _16_, 2 (October, 1973): 236-249.

Evaluated in this study was the use of social isolation as punishment for disruptive behavior of five 9 to 11 year old emotionally disturbed children. Trained student observers rated the frequency of disruptive behavior in the classroom. Baseline behavior was observed before and after the 16 day period of contingent social isolation. Disruptive behavior was significantly decreased during the period of contingent social isolation. During the last baseline observation period, disruptive behavior did not significantly increase over the first baseline period. It is concluded that contingent social isolation is an effective, although specific, punisher. See ERIC Abstract 1197751-6.

3159.   Drabman, R. S., Spitalnik, R., and O'Leary, K. D. "Teaching Self-Control to Disruptive Children." _Journal of Abnormal Psychology_, _82_, 1 (August, 1973): 10-16.

Eight, nine and ten year old disruptive males were taught in after school remedial classes to match teachers' evaluations of their behavior in the context of a token reinforcement program. During the time when teaching of self evaluation was initiated and after all point loss or gain was removed for over evaluation or under evaluation, subjects maintained very low levels of disruptive behavior and high rates of academic output. See ERIC Abstract 0586651-3.

3160.   Drabman, R., Spitalnik, R., and Spitalnik, K.   "Sociometric and Disruptive Behavior as a Function of Four Types
of Token Reinforcement Programs." Journal of Applied
Behavior Anaylsis, 7, 1 (Spring, 1974): 93-101.

Twenty-three 1st graders were divided into four groups and
compared with four types of token economies as to there
effectiveness in changing target behavior, preference by
subjects, ease of use, and cost.   The four types were
individual reinforcement determined by individual performance, group reinforcement determined by the behavior of the
most disruptive child, group reinforcement determined by the
behavior of the least disruptive child, and group reinforcement determined by the behavior of a randomly chosen child.
Responses were taken on questions of responsibility, friendship, and funniness.   Results show a significant decrease of
inappropriate behavior for the disruptive subjects and no
difference between the effectiveness of the four types of
token economies in producing behavior change.   Other differences indicated that the system in which group reinforcement
was determined by a randomly selected child would be desirable for most teachers.   See ERIC Abstract 0859252-4.

3161.   Dragoon, N. & Klein, R.   "Preventive Intervention to
Reduce Conflicts Among Students." School Counselor, 27, 2
(November, 1979): 98-103.

An intervention program is described at Lehman High School
in Bronx, New York.   A Conflicts Class was introduced to
reduce violence and tensions among students.   Trust and
openness increased, and fear of the loss of control was
allayed through counseling, interpersonal relationships, and
activities, and video tape feedback.   See ERIC Abstract EJ
217312.

3162.   Draper, W.   "In-Out Group: An Alternate Approach to
Classroom Structure." Creative Child and Adult Quarterly,
4, 2 (Summer, 1979): 106-110.

Article describes a classroom structure that allows a child
to chose to be in the "in group" for the day and participate
in class activities or to be in the "out group" and not
participate.   Rules for implementing the in-out group
approach are suggested, beginning with the agreement by
pupils in the out-group that they will not disturb the in-
group.   This approach is intended to benefit failing and
truant students and reduce competition and negative feelings
about school.   See ERIC Abstract 0876965-4.

3163.   Drawbaugh, C. C. & Schaefer, C. J.   "Traveling Seminars
on Student Behavior." Journal of Industrial Teacher
Education, 14, 2 (Winter, 1977): 43-48.

The use of a traveling instructional team to provide local
inservice workshops to assist New Jersey Vocational Teachers
and Administrators in reducing and dealing with discipline

problems is described and the effectiveness of the training seminars evaluated. See ERIC Abstract EJ 156628.

3164.   Drury, R. L. and Robbins, C. A. "Behavioral Outcomes for Pre-Delinquents Receiving Behavioral, Generic, or No Counseling." Paper presented at the Annual Meeting of the Western Psychological Association, San Francisco, CA, 1974.

Thirty-six students at a continuation high school were identified as pre-delinquents and selected as subjects on the basis of their poor attendance and academic records. Pre-treatment and post-treatment data were collected on the following variables: attendance figures and academic credit. Following preliminary assessment the subjects were randomly assigned to one of three conditions: treatment by a behaviorally trained counselor, treatment by a generically trained counselor, or no treatment. Counselors were new careerists who were divided into two matched groups. The groups received one month of either behavioral or generic counselor training. After a time limited treatment period, the assessment procedure was readministered so that the relative efficacy of the differentially trained counselors could be evaluated. Significant differences favoring the behaviorally trained counselors were found for both dependent variables. See Eric Abstract ED 106676.

3165.   Dubey, D. R. et al. "Reactions of Children and Teachers to Classroom Observers: A Series of Controlled Investigations." Behavior Therapy, 8, 5 (November, 1977): 887-897.

Three experimental investigations were conducted on the effects observers in the laboratory classroom. In each study, classroom observers were systematically introduced and withdrawn, while additional observers collected data surreptitiously on the behavior of 24 disruptive first graders. It was revealed in the studies that little systematic effect on the behavior of children or their teachers was evidenced. See ERIC Abstract 0825260-4.

3166.   Dubner, M. A. "The Effect of Modeling and Vicarious Reinforcement Upon the Subsequent Imitation of a Socially Approved Response." Journal of School Psychology, 11, 2 (Summer, 1973): 132-138.

Forty-eight female fourth graders were assigned to three experimental and one controlled group. The experimental groups watched a video tape of a peer model drawing. In one condition the model was praised; in the second, no praise was given and a short interval elapsed before the subject could model the behavior. In the third, no praise was given and the subject could model the behavior immediately. The controlled group watched a blank screen. Significant modeling effects occurred among those subjects exposed to the tapes. Discussed in this article are the practicality and feasibility of using modeling procedures in schools. See ERIC Abstract 0790651-4.

3167.   Duff, C. F. "Helping the Middle School Student in Trouble." NASSP Bulletin, 63, 424. (February, 1979): 50-54.

A group approach is described with parents, teachers, and students, which worked in helping students who have problems in school. See ERIC Abstract EJ 196065.

3168.   Duke, D. L. "Adults can be Discipline Problems Too." Psychology in the Schools, 15, 4 (1978): 522-528.

Observational data and survey information were collected on student behavior problems and discipline policies in a large suburban high school. Analysis of the data indicated that many of the concerns of teachers and administrators centered more around adult behavior than student behavior. See ERIC Abstract EJ 192000.

3169.   Duke, D. L. "How Administrators View the Crisis in School Discipline." Phi Delta Kappan, 59, 5 (January, 1978): 325-330.

School administrators in California and New York share views on what are the most pressing discipline problems -- skipping class, truancy, and tardiness -- but those views do not seem to be shared by teachers and students. The administrators are taking steps to resolve the problems. See ERIC Abstract EJ 169845.

3170.   Duke, D. L. "Making School Discipline Policy in the Eighties: Options, Illusions, and Dreams." Contemporary Education, 52, 1 (Fall, 1980): 24-29.

Five options for the improvement of discipline in the public school system in the eighties include more rules and harsher punishments, better teacher training in classroom management, relaxation of student suspension guidelines, increased campus security personnel and equipment, and changes in the Juvenile Justice System. See ERIC Abstract EJ 237733.

3171.   Duke, D. L. "Who Misbeahves? -- A High School Studies Its Discipline Problems." Educational Administration Quarterly, 12, 3 (February, 1976): 65-85.

This study compares an entire population of high school discipline problem students with a control group of students who were not involved in acts of misconduct. Significant differences were found to exist in intelligence, scholastic achievement, scholastic abilities, vocational aptitude, and personality characteristics in elementary school. See ERIC Abstract EJ 150170.

3172.   Duke, D. L. "Why Don't Girls Misbehave More Than Boys in School." Journal of Youth and Adolescence, 7, 2 (June, 1978): 141-157.

In reviewing the research, the author speculates on six reasons why girls misbehave less than boys, despite the fact that girls have more personal problems during adolescence. The author concludes that a combination of personal characteristics and external pressures inhibit misbehavior in girls. See ERIC Abstract EJ 193424.

3173.   Duke, D. L. and Perry, C. "Can Alternative Schools Succeed Where Benjamin Spock, Spirol Agnew, and B. F. Skinner Have Failed?" Adolescence, 13, 51 (Fall, 1978): 375-392.

This study sought to determine if student behavior was as great a problem in 18 California alternative high schools as it is reported to be in regular high schools. Results showed that discipline was rarely a major concern in the alternative schools. Fourteen possible reasons were hypothesized. See ERIC Abstract EJ 199093.

3174.   Durlak, J. A. "Description and Evaluation of a Behaviorally Oriented School-Based Preventive Mental Health Program." Journal of Consulting and Clinical Psychology, 45, 1 (February, 1977): 27-33.

An adaptation of a school-based preventive mental health program are described and evaluated. Teachers at one school and college student volunteers at another used behavioral reinforcement techniques to work with groups of maladaptive second graders. Evaluation of the eight week intervention program included a seven month follow-up. Experimental subjects improved significantly more than controlled in classroom adjustment. The results support a school-based model of preventive intervention and the effectiveness of the behavioral treatment strategies in such a program. See ERIC Abstract 0164758-1.

3175.   Dustin, R., and Burden, C. "The Counselor as a Behavioral Consultant." Elementary School Guidance and Counseling, 7, 1 (October, 1972): 14-19.

Guidelines are presented for the counselor to serve as the behavioral consultant who works with a consultee to help clients. The consultant is not in direct contact with the client, the student. Procedural steps are suggested: 1) determination by the consultant of who has the problem, 2) identification of the problem behavior by the consultee, 3) identification of desired client behaviors by the consultant and consultee, 4) observation of the client by the consultant, 5) development of a remedial program by the consultant and the consultee, and 6) evaluation of the outcome. See ERIC Abstract 0174550-1.

3176.   Eckbreth, C. "Discipline in the Secondary Classroom." Social Education, 42, 2 (February, 1978): 109-112.

Suggestions are offered to Junior High School teachers regarding discipline policy. Suggestions are: explain basic rules during the first week of school, vary teaching techniques to avoid boredom, deal with discipline problems as they arise, and demonstrate personal interest in students whenever possible. See ERIC Abstract EJ 174507.

3177.   Ebel, R. L. "The Case for Corporal Punishment." Paper presented at the annual meeting of the American Educational Research Association, Washington, D. C., March, 1975.

A young child who has not been taught to obey the directives of his parents or his teachers is libel to suffer serious consequences in a sometimes hostile environment. Teacher organizations tend to support retention, or reinstitution, or the possibility of using corporal punishment as one means of correction or control. Ultimately, the case for or against corporal punishment must rest on the effect it has on pupil achievement of whatever goals society has set for it's schools. See ERIC Abstract ED 105596.

3178.   Eder, S. C. "The Effect of group counseling upon the classroom behavior and on the manifest anxiety of elementary school student teachers. Final Report." Office of Education, Washington, D.C., Bureau of Research, 81p, 1971.

The purpose of this study was to assess the effectiveness of a group counseling treatment on the classroom behaviors and on the manifest anxiety levels of elementary school student teachers. 44 volunteer student teachers were randomly assigned to 1) an experimental counseling group, 2) a Hawthorne seminar control group, and 3) a control group. The counseling group received 8 weekly treatments with the problem identification model, which includes psycho-dramatic techniques. The seminar group met for the same amount of time. A post-test only design was used to measure classroom behavior. Two twenty minute samples of each subject's teaching behavior were obtained using Flanders Interaction and Analysis categories. Results showed no significant differences between groups in percentages of restricting classroom behavior or in decrements of state anxiety over time. See ERIC Abstract #ED 052170.

3179.   Edlund, C. V. Reading: A Behavior Modification Approach. SCFC Corporation, Sioux City, Iowa. 90p, 1975.

This report includes illustrations of practical applications of behavior modification to a variety of reading skills and is intended for implementation in all reading classrooms. Chapter 1 presents a brief orientation to behavior modification. The subsequent chapters deal with the application of respondent conditioning, operant conditioning, and modeling to selected reading skills. A positive reinforcement program is presented for academic and social behavior. The concluding section presents a reporting system for reinforcing reading and other academic behaviors in elementary schools.   A bibliography is included.   See ERIC Abstract #ED 147786.

3180.   Educational   Products   Information   Exchange   Institute. "In-Service Teacher Training Materials: Individualizing Instruction,   Classroom   Mangement/Discipline,   Motivation." Washington, D.C.:   National Institute of Education, January, 1979.

This report contains detailed descriptions of 49 sets of materials designed to be used for in-service teacher training in individualizing instruction, classroom manage- ment, and discipline, and motivation.   The report attempts to   provide   consumer   information   for   teachers   chosing materials for in-service training.   Each entry consists of a summary of the materials, as well as a detailed description. The summary includes the following information: title, publication date, intended users, grade levels, number of participants,   primary   focus,   in-service topics covered, activities and resources involved in using the materials and a describer critique.   See ERIC Abstract ED 158874.

3181.   Eisenhart, M. "Maintaining control: teacher competence in the classroom." Paper presented at the Annual Meeting of the American Anthropological Association, Houston, Texas, 19p, December 2, 1977.

To insure competent teaching, the school environment must be organized to preserve a system of student behavior and group functioning which allows a teacher to select activities in which the group will engage.   Means of organizing the school context   to   affect   student   behavior   are   examined   in   this paper.   Thse means include: 1) the arrangement of the physical environment and the people in it, 2) the use of time, and 3) a system of rewards and recognition.   The ways in which teachers utilize these means are discussed in terms of their differential success in maintaining control.   See ERIC Abstract #ED 154098.

3182.   Elardo, R.   "Behavior modification in an elementary school: problems   and   issues."   PHI   DELTA   KAPPA,   59 (January, 1978): 334-338.

This article describes the implementation of a token economy as a method of controlling student behavior in an elementary school setting.   Student participation is stressed and broad issues,   such   as   teacher   resistance   to   the   program   and evaluation questions are presented.   See ERIC Abstract #EJ 169847.

3183.   Elardo,   R.   "Implementing   Behavior   Modification Procedures in an Elementary School: Problems and Issues." Office of Child Development, Washington, D.C., 27p, 1977. Paper presented at the Annual Meeting of the American Educational Research Association, New York.

This report describes a year-long case study of the implementation of a token economy in an entire elementary school. The effort was intended to provide teachers with an alternative to corporal punishment as a form of school discipline. In this report, both the successful and unsuccessful procedures are described in chronological fashion. This provides insights into the process of implementing laboratory-derived principles of behavior management into the regular public school environment. See ERIC Abstract #ED 135762.

3184.   Ellis, R. S. "Student-parent activities center." New York City Board of Education, Brooklyn, New York. Office of Educational Evaluation, 39p (1976).

This report discusses a student-parent activities center, a program designed to involve parents in the educational process of their children, improve parental knowledge and participation in the school, and improve parental influence on student attendance. 50 parents and 150 students were included in the study. The parents all had children in the fifth through eighth grades who were truant or whose attendance records were poor. The parent participants were organized into two groups composed of up to 20 participants each. The groups met weekly and discussed mathematics, reading and school attendance. The evaluation of the program concluded that parents were made aware of pupil academic and discipline requirements of the school. See ERIC Abstract #ED 141487.

3185.   Emmer, E. T., et al. "The First weeks of class ... and the rest of the year." Research and Development Center for Teacher Education Report #6005, 29, 1979.

Classroom observation of 28 third grade teachers illustrated the management and planning strategies that differentiate effective teachers from less effective teachers. Effective teachers communicated a workable system of rules and procedures, monitored students carefully, and were consistent in treating inappropriate behaviors. Less effective managers did not establish their credibility at the outset of the year and were inconsistent in their feedback and discipline techniques. Discipline and organizational procedures were delineated during the first weeks of the school year by the more effective teachers. See ERIC Abstract #ED 175861.

3186.   Englehardt, Leah, et al. "The Counselor as a consultant in eliminating out-of-seat behavior." Elementary School Guidance and Counseling, 5, 3 (March 1971): 196-204.

Article discusses the study results showing that investment of time by a counselor in working with a teacher to help reduce disruptive classroom behaviors is time well spent. The teacher is better able to cope with the specific behavior problem of the moment, and she has insights for future handling of classroom problems. See ERIC Abstract #EJ 032662.

3187.   Epstein, M. H., et al. "Decreasing obscene language of behaviorally disordered children through the use of a DRL schedule." Psychology in the School, 3, 15 (July, 1978): 419-22.

During the DRL procedure, reinforcement was made available for inappropriate language that was less than a prescribed limit for each day. Data indicated that reinforcing low rates of behavior may be an effective alternative to the use of aversive contingencies to reduce the misbehavior of children. See ERIC Abstract #EJ 183047.

3188.   Epstein, R. and Goss, C. M. "A Self Control Procedure for the Maintenance of Non-Disruptive Behavior in an Elementary School Child." Behavior Therapy, 9, 1 (January, 1978): 109-117.

Following self evaluation training and the establishment of reinforcer effectiveness, a ten year old boy with a history of high rates of disruptive classroom behavior was provided with a self-control procedure designed to ensure honesty, peer support, a high level of appropriate behavior, and his continued adherence to the regimen for an indefinite period, with little teacher intervention. The subject adhered to this regimen until his school year ended, and a high level of appropriate behavior was maintained. See ERIC Abstract 0203861-1.

3189.   Erickson, E. L., et al. "Final report of the evaluation of the 1971-72 school home contact program." Teaching and Learning Corporation. New York, New York. 52p, 1972.

Report discussed the school-home contact program, which was designed to send paraprofessional workers who are familiar with the community into the homes of students who show serious problems in attendance, adjustment and achievement. The purpose of the program was to establish rapport between school and parents, anticipating that better communication would prevent problem students from dropping out of school. Family assistants contacted parents of students referred to them by school personnel. They communicated to the parent the nature of the problem, kinds of assistance available from the school, and what they might do to help their children. They also arranged appointments with professional school staff when indicated. The major conclusion of this study, which included 1,000 students, 180 parents, 48 high school teachers, and 2 supervisors, is that this contact program has been associated with lower absenteeism, tardiness and school dropping out. See ERIC Abstract #ED 072129.

3190.   Estep, L. E., et al. "Teacher pupil control ideology and behavior and predictors of classroom robustness." High School Journal, 63, 4 (January, 1980): 155-59.

This study hypothesized that confrontations between a strict teacher and misbehaving students added drama and robustness to the classroom. 88 secondary classrooms were used for the study, and in each robustness and teacher control ideology and behavior were measured. The hypothesis was rejected; humanistic control behavior related to high robustness. See ERIC Abstract #EJ 224771.

3191.   Esveldt, K. C., Dawson, P. C., and Forness, S. R. "Effect of Video Tape Feedback on Children's Classroom Behavior. Journal of Educational Research, 67, 10 (July-August, 1974): 453-456.

Video tape feedback was used in a classroom setting with three ten year old boys who had exhibited disruptive behavior. Observable classroom performance was a dependent variable, and comparison was made of the effects of the standard teacher conference, video feedback and video feedback accompanied by discussion. Results indicated that viewing their own performance in the classroom provided an effect on subjects' classroom behavior beyond that expected from teacher discussion alone. See ERIC Abstract 0397253-2.

3192.   Evertson, C. M. "Relationships of Teacher Praise and Criticism to Student Outcomes." Report #75-7. National Institute of Education, Washington, D.C., 25p, 1975. Paper presented at the Annual Meeting of the American Educational Research Association, Washington, D.C., April, 1975.

This study discussed praise and criticism data which were collected during a two year correlational study of a selected sample of second and third grade teachers chosen for their consistency in producing a student learning gain averaged over four years. These data were analyzed to determine the effect that praise, criticism, rewards, and punishment have on learning gains. Data on motivations, incentive, and punishment, differed considerably by socio--economic status. The most effective way of dealing with misbehavior was through an individual conference with the student. The main factor was the teacher's ability to motivate students to become actively engaged in a learning process, to the point that he or she would answer questions in public response situations and work consistently at seat work. Successful teachers communicated high expectations. See ERIC Abstract #ED 146155.

3193.   Fairchild, T. N. "Home-school token economies: bridging the communication gap." Psychology in the Schools, 13, 4 (October, 1976): 463-467.

Article discusses how school token economy systems are being employed with a variety of children in a variety of settings. Additional benefits accrue when token systems are used. These benefits are discussed, as well as the steps necessary toward implementation of these systems. Two case studies are shared as practical examples. See ERIC Abstract #EJ 146256.

3194.   Farber, H. and Mayer, G. R.   "Behavior Consultation in a Barrio High School." Personnel and Guidance Journal, 51, 4 (December, 1972): 273-279.

A study was conducted to determine whether behavior modification techniques developed by a counselor and a teacher would improve the assignment completing behavior 14-19 year old inner city students in a tenth grade English class. Oral praise, tangible rewards, and school privileges were used to reinforce desirable behaviors, and directions, prompts, and models were used to help students learn the conditions under which behavior would be reinforced. Results reflect they typical characteristics of a reversal procedure, showing a low level of student productivity during baseline and a subsequent rise, fall, and rise of productivity for treatment one, reversal and treatment two phases respectively. Conclusions support the hypothesis that a secondary school counselor can function effectively as a behavioral consultant to an inner city teacher. See ERIC Abstract 0984150-5.

3195.   Farran, D. C. and Yanofsky, S. M.   "Change in junior high schools: two case studies."   Pennsylvania Advancement School, Philadelphia.   1972, 277p.

This report presents the mini-school approach used by the Advancement School to improve the quality of education in two Philadelphia school district junior high schools. Considerable attention is given to the development of relationships between the administrative teams of the school in each of the two schools. Topics included are: the instructional program developed, team functioning, the effects of mini-schools on the students. Problems in the junior high schools of Philadelphia, such as discipline, are analyzed. The role of the Advancement School as an external change agent in dealing with these problems is discussed. See ERIC Abstract #ED 169165.

3196.   Feldhusen, J. F.   "Behavior problems in secondary schools. Final Report. National Institute of Education, Washington, D.C., 29p, June, 1979.

This paper reviews the problems of anti-social student behavior in schools, identifies causes, and examines programs and procedures for remediating and preventing such behavior. The report deals with junior and senior high schools and all forms of anti-social, aggressive, disruptive behaviors that interfere with school functioning. The report states that the problems of school discipline, violence, crime, vandalism and truancy have grown to large proportions in many American high schools and junior high schools. Principals and school boards often are reluctant to admit the problems that begin or are caused by forces outside the school. Poor home conditions, television violence, a climate of crime in the community, gangs, and peer crime influences are all initial contributors to the problems that surface in schools. The author states that the school also contributes, with poor teaching, a negative school climate, a dose of failure for many students, and irrelevant curricula. A set of recommendations for action by educators is presented. See ERIC Abstract #ED 165253.

3197.   Feldhusen, J. F. "Behavior problems in secondary schools." Journal of Research and Development in Education, 4, 11 (1979): 17-28.

The article clarifies the problems of anti-social student behavior in schools, ranging from talking out of turn to violent attacks upon fellow students and teachers. It focuses on the high school and junior high school, and attempts to identify causes while examining programs and procedures for remediating or preventing such behavior. See ERIC Abstract #EJ 189888.

3198.   Filipczak, J., Archer, M. B. and Friedman, R. M. "In-school social skills training: use with disruptive adolescents." Behavior Modification, 4, 2 (April, 1980): 243-263.

A group oriented social skills training program is described which was conducted in urban, suburban, and rural junior high schools. The research is related according to the objectives defined for each setting, the specific curriculum that resulted from these objectives, the means by which both cognitive and behavioral features of the program were implemented, and the measures that were applied for assessment of effects. Problems encountered in program development, conduct, and evaluation are highlighted. Program results indicate both short and long range cognitive and behavioral change across a number of obtrusive and unobtrusive measures. Several implications are noted for the further development and conduct of cost effective social skills training in the schools. See PSYC Abstract 1115065-5.

3199.   Filipczak, J., Archer, M. B. and Neals, M. S. "Issues in multivariate assessment of a large scale behavioral program." Journal of Applied Behavior Analysis, 12 4 (Winter, 1979): 593-613.

Several social and research issues directed affected the development and implementation of multivariate assessment in a large community based applied research program. Examples are drawn from experiences of the preparation through a responsive educational programs project for disruptive and skill deficient adolescents in suburban, rural, and urban junior high school settings, focusing on the assessment of academic and social skill development and long term skill maintenance. The social context altered both project treatment and follow up plans, requiring assessment of potentially unintended effects and decreasing consistency across sites. Community acceptance of such programs may depend on a) the investigators' adaptation to diverse community pressures for program conduct and assessment and b) the measurement of phenomena that are not always directly observable.

3200.   Fincham, F. "A comparison of morale judgement in learning disabled and normal achieving boys." Journal of Psychology, 96, (May, 1977): 153-60.

Study finds no group differences in morale judgement between learning-disabled children and normal achievers. Discusses the results in terms of behavior problems associated with the learning-disabled. See ERIC Abstract #EJ 173449.

3201.   Fink, A. H. "Behavior Management Training Through Simulation And Role Playing." Viewpoints, 49, 6 (November, 1973): 71-84.

Discusses the questions of how one trains teachers to become managers of behavior and considers what should be the subject of this training. Simulation is suggested as a solution, and several advantages of simulation techniques are outlined together with a description of modules providing a systematic presentation of management strategies. See ERIC Abstract 0986951-5.

3202.   Flowers, J. V. "Behavior Modification Techniques to Reduce the Frequency of Unwarranted Questions by Target Students in an Elementary School Classroom." Behavior Therapy, 5, 5 (October, 1974): 665-667.

Eight fifth graders, after a three week token reinforcement treatment, significantly decreased their unwarranted questions and significantly increased their warranted questions. Twenty-one subjects not in treatment also significantly increased their frequency or warranted questions, indicating that the change in the target subjects actually changed the entire classroom system. See ERIC Abstract 0615153-3.

3203.   Foley, W. J. and Brooks, R. "Pupil control ideology in predicting teacher discipline referrals." Educational Administration Quarterly, 3, 14 (Fall, 1978): 104-12.

Study concludes that humanism in teachers is related to reporting fewer unresolvable conflicts with pupils and that pupil control ideology and subsequent teacher control behavior, the referring of pupils to the administration for disciplinary action, are related. See ERIC Abstract #EJ 209458.

3204.   Fontein, H. "Weight discipline: an ounce of prevention." Social Education, 2, 42 (February, 1978): 105-8.

Author maintains that most discipline problems arise when students are asked to perform beyond their capabilities. She outlines several techniques for teaching social studies to slow learners, with such techniques as group reading, simulations, math drills, neighborhood surveys, and art projects. See ERIC Abstract #EJ 174506.

3205.   Forehand, R., et al. "An examination of disciplinary procedures with children." Journal of Experimental Child Psychology, 1, 21 (February, 1976): 109-120.

Two experiments are discussed in this article. The first examined the effect of negative attention and repeated demands on the non-compliant behavior of children. Experiment two studied the relative effectiveness of negative attention, isolation, ignoring, and a combination of procedures in reducing non-compliance in children. See ERIC Abstract #EJ 141683.

3206.   Forman, S. G. "A Comparison of Cognitive Training and Response Cost Procedures in Modifying Aggressive Behavior of Elementary School Children." Behavior Therapy, 11, 4 (September, 1980): 594-600.

Thirty aggressive 8-11 year olds were assigned to cognitive restructuring, response cost, or controlled conditions. Assessment included teacher ratings (the classroom disturbance in disrespect-defiance subskills of the Bevereaux Elementary School Behavior Rating Skills), teacher records of aggression, and independent observations. Results show that cognitive restructuring and response cost were significantly more effective than control, although response cost decreased disruptive behavior to a greater extent. See ERIC Abstract 1297564-6.

3207.   Forness, S. E., et al. "Follow-up and high-risk children identified in kindergarten through direct classroom observation." Psychology in the Schools, 1, 13 (January, 1976): 45-49.

Sixty-one children, identified at the beginning of kindergarten on the basis of four distinct clusters of observable classroom behavior, were evaluated at completion of first grade. Children in the non-risk cluster continued to do well, while children in the high-risk cluster were still doing poorly in many areas.

3208.   Forness, S. R., Guthrie, D., and Hall, R. J. "Follow-up of High-Risk Children Identified in Kindergarten Through Direct Classroom Observation." Psychology in the School, 13, 1 (January, 1976): 45-49.

Sixty-one children identified at the beginning of kindergarten on the basis of four destinct clusters of observable classroom behavior, were evaluated at the completion of first grade to determine the validity of the original clusters in predicting educational risk. Teacher ratings and individual achievement test scores partially confirmed the predictive validity of the original clusters. Subjects in the non-risk cluster continued to do well, while subjects in the high-risk cluster were still doing poorly in some areas. Concerns about specific aspects of observable behavior are discussed. See ERIC Abstract 0684456-4.

3209.   Friedling, C. & O'Leary, S. G. "Effects of Self-Instructional Training on Second and Third Grade Hyperactive Children: A Failure to Replicate." Journal of Applied Behavior Analysis, 12, 2 (Summer, 1979): 211-219.

Bornstein and Quevillon demonstrated generalization from a two hour self instructional training session to on-task behavior in the classroom with four over-active four year olds. In an attempt to replicate this work with older children, eight hyperactive seven and eight year olds were assigned to either a self-instructional training group or an attention practice control group. On task behavior in the classroom and performance measures in reading and arithmetic were assessed. The level of difficulty on these tasks varied. Bornstein and Quevillon's results were not replicated, although the subsequent introduction of a token program significantly increased on-task behavior. See PSYC Abstract 1123165-5.

3210.   Frith, G. H. et al. "An Alternative Approach to School Suspension: The Folthan Model." Phi-Delta Kappan, 61, 9 (May, 1980): 637-638.

The thirteen components of the Folthan Model, a program to reduce the number of school suspensions are listed. Among components are eligibility criteria, Behavior Guidelights and Evaluation Design. See ECER 125141.

3211.   Fuller, G. and Friedrich, D. "Predicting Potential School Problems." Perceptual And Motor Skills, 37, 2 (October, 1973): 453-454.

A battery of tests were used to compare intellegence, reading, personality, achievement, and visual-motor skills in two groups of rural sixth graders. Seventy-seven subjects who were referred for psychological services and one hundred and twenty-six normal controls were used. With twenty-two variables, a stepwise multiple regression analysis for predicting potential school problems yielded significant differential factors in the areas of vocabulary, average reading abilities, intellegence, and visual-motor skills. See ERIC Abstract 0991751-5.

3212.   Fullerton, S. "Self-Concept Changes Of Junior High Students." Journal Of Counseling Psychology, 20, 5 (September, 1973): 493-494.

Previous studies have identified a relationship between self-concept and school behavior. This study investigated whether self-concept and school behavior of problem Junior High school students could be changed by participation in a teacher-helper program in an elememtary school. Subjects matched on grade, sex, and grade point average were randomly assigned to an experimental or control group. Self-concept ratings of experimental subjects who participated in the teacher-helper program for eight weeks significantly increased during this period, while controls did not change. Neither group changed significantly changed in attendance or grade point average. See ERIC Abstract 0988651-5.

3213.   Gallagher, P. A. "Structuring Academic Tasks For Emotionally Disturbed Boys." Exceptional Children, 38, 9 (May, 1972): 711-720.

Researchers structured the procedures of scheduling and reinforcement into two teaching methods designed to guide 16 disturbed 7-11 year old boys in the acquisition of vocabulary word learning and attentional work time. Results indicate a strong affirmation of the positive influence of the highly structured rather than a modified structured approach on the subjects' performances. See ERIC Abstract 0570350-3.

3214.   Gansmeder, B. M. et al. "An Analysis Of The Association Between Teachers' Classroom Objectives And Activity." Journal Of Educational Research, 70, 4 (March-April, 1977): 175-179.

For three days 67 elementary school teachers maintained a record of their major objectives and corresponding activities. The resulting 1470 objectives were classified as belonging to the cognitive, affective or psychomotored domain and to specific within the domain. Each of the activities was classified using an adaptation of Dale's "Cone Of Experiences." Percentages of various types of objectives and activities resembled those reported in observational studies. It was found that teachers selected differential type activities to accomplish different types of objectives. It was suggested that the first step in changing teachers' behavior in the classroom is not to change the behaviors but to change the objectives with which these behaviors are associated. See ERIC Abstract 1240958-6.

3215.   George, T. W., Coleman, Juanita, and Williams, P. "The Systematic Use Of Positive And Negative Consequences In Managing Classroom Encopresis." Journal Of School Psychology, 15, 3 (Fall, 1977): 250-254.

The treatment by classroom teachers of an eleven year old boy with a history of chronic encopresis is described. Through the contingent application of a combination of positive and negative consequences the subject's behavior was reduced from an eighty percent occurance level during baseline to just two occasions during the final five month treatment base. The investigation utilized an ABACD type behavior modification design. See ERIC Abstract 1023760-5.

3216.   "Get More Out of Teaching." Instructor, 90, 1 (August, 1980): 7-11, 152, 154, 156.

Tips are presented to teachers on preserving their enthusiasm, organizing their time, maintaining class control, boosting school morale, and maintaining public support. See ERIC Abstract EJ 229458.

3217.   Gibbons, T. J. and Lee, M. K. "Group Counseling: Impetus To Learning." Elementary School Guidance And Counseling, 7, (October, 1972): 32-36.

A group counseling experience with eight male average fifth grade volunteers referred for exhibiting or responding to disruptive classroom behavior is described. A recurring theme in the sessions was the subjects' feeling of powerlessness over the environment. This feeling decreased when the subjects made suggestions which were followed by their teacher, or were given concrete reasons why certain rules could not be changed. As the sessions progressed, the counselor and the teacher established better communication with each other, subjects began to show progress in reading and assignment completion, and classroom disciplinary incidents decreased. See ERIC Abstract 0177350-1.

3218.   Giesselmann, W. T. "A Legal Guide for Development and Administration of Pupil Personnel Policies." Birmingham, Ala.: Southern Region School Board Research and Training Center, Inc., 1976.

The purpose of this publication is to provide a reliable and practical digest of useful information about the overall governance of pupil personnel as effective precedents. It examines the constitutional parameters and the governance of pupil conduct in view of there parameters. Pupil conduct, which interferes substantially with the maintenance in the school of a proper atmosphere for learning, is subject to disciplinary action. Disciplinary actions which are fair and reasonable, and thus comply with the due process clause are legally defensible. Included are the following chapters: 1) Table Of Cases; 2) Introduction; 3) Defensible Codes Of Conduct; 4) Substative Due Process; 5) Other Precedents and Guidelines for Substative Areas; 6) Procedural Due Process In The School; 7) The Law And Student Records; 8) Title VIIII Regulations; 9) Legally-Based Policies And Regulations.

3219.   Giles, A. "Organization and discipline in the comprehensive school." Educational Review, 3, 9 (June, 1977): 213-20.

The author discusses his study of school organization and discipline in a large number of comprehensive schools. The article summarizes his findings about the way in which school organization can influence student behavior and teachers' coping skills. See ERIC Abstract #EJ 162764.

3220.   Gillespie, J. and Wright, J. "Student assessment service: model of assessment of learning and behavior problems in the high school." 20p, 1976.

Author states that there is little provision in the average high school for the evaluation of students with learning and behavior problems. Article discusses the new master plan for special education in California which calls for at least two levels of assessment, one to be implemented in a school appraisal team, including teachers, program and resource specialists, and administrator. Serious problems should be referred to an educational assessment service that provides specialized evaluation by psychologists, physicians, and other professionals. Author states that this is the first time that a real consideration is being given toward providing a built-in system at the school level for assessment of student academic skills as the need becomes apparent. See ERIC Abstract #ED 140157.

3221.   Glaser, E. N. and Sarason, I. G. "Reinforcing productive classroom behavior: a teacher's guide to behavior modification." Final Report. Office of Education, Washington, D.C., 48p, 1970.

This guide is designed to be of assistance to classroom teachers who may not be trained in the application of operant conditioning methods to classroom behavior. It attempts to provide practical suggestions which have been validated in research studies. The guide contains descriptions of some common elementary classroom problems, the principles and ethical considerations in the use of behavior modification, suggestions for creating a better learning climate in the classroom, examples of practical applications of behavior principles, and illustrative case studies based upon research investigations. A glossary is included with behavioral terms and an annotated bibliography. See ERIC Abstract #ED 049469.

3222.   Glasser, W. "Disorders in our schools: causes and remedies." Phi Delta Kappan, 59, 5 (January, 1978): 331-3.

Author states that the answer to better discipline is giving students a stake in the school, caring for them, and teaching them without failure. See ERIC Abstract #EJ 169846.

3223.   Glazer, N. T. "Reading deficiency and behavior problems: a study." Reading Horizons, 18, 4 (Summer, 1978): 282-4.

Article describes a study on the relationship between reading deficiency and disciplinary problems; relating the original data to the same student population status with regard to high school graduation four years later. See ERIC Abstract #EJ 186592.

3224.   Glennon, C. A. and Nason, D. E. "Managing the behavior of the hyperkinetic child: what research says." Reading Teachers, 27, 8 (May, 1974): 815-24.

Authors review some of the issues involved in diagnosing and treating the hyperkinetic child. See ERIC Abstract #EJ 097718.

3225.   Glickman, C. D. and Wolfgang, C. H. "Conflict In the Classroom: An Eclectic Model Of Teacher-Child Interaction." Elementary Guidance And School Counseling, 13, 2 (December, 1978): 82-87.

Reviewed are three contrasting theoretical models of class-room conduct management: 1) The noninterventionist, 2) The interactionalist, 3) The interventionist. An eclectic approach combining the best techniques from each model is more efficacious than reliance on any single method. See ERIC Abstract 0834863-4.

3226.   Glickman, C. D. and Wolfgang, C. H. "Dealing with student misbehavior: an eclectic review." Journal of Teacher Education, 30, 3 (May-June, 1979): 7-13.

Author states that a combination of principles drawn from the current major theories of behavior discipline often are more effective than the use of any single theory. See ERIC Abstract #EJ 208603.

3227.   Glowacki, L. "Effect Of Spatial Titration On Task Performance." Psychology In The Schools, 13, 3 (July, 1976): 350-355.

A reinforcement schedule and spatial titration method was used with two third grade boys to determine the most preferred and effective taskreinforcement area separation. The separation was decreased by errors in task performance and increased by correct responses. Zero separation was the most preferred and effective in producing high-task perfor-mance. See ERIC Abstract 0193057-1.

3228.   Gnagey, W. J. "Attitudes, values and motives of class-room facilitators and inhibitors." Illinois, 16p, 1979.

In an effort to isolate personal characteristics which might influence the behavior of disruptive students, high school teachers were asked to identify disruptive students (inhibitors) and well behaved students (facilitators). 59 inhibitors and 86 facilitators were selected for the study. Each subject was administered the Quality of School Life Instrument, the Inventory of Values, and the Motivation Inventory. Results showed that facilitators, as compared to inhibitors, perceived school life as more satisfying, their classes as more interesting, and their teachers as more affective. A large difference between the two groups' scores on the National Education Development Test suggested

a strong connection between classroom behavior and achievement. The results of the study showed that classroom
inhibitors are comparatively unhappy, frightened group of
students, with less than average achievement records. See
ERIC Abstract #ED 173731.

3229.   Gnagey, W. J. "Locus of Control, Motives and Crime
Prevention Attitudes of Classroom Facilitators and
Inhibitors." Paper presented at the Annual Meeting of the
American Educational Research Association, Boston,
Massachusetts, April, 1980.

The author states that it is time to stop blaming the rise
in serious student youth behavior on families, peers,
teachers, school systems and society, and to begin to hold
students responsible for their own actions. This study
compared the personal characteristics of disruptive and
normal students. Teachers in a small high school identified
69 inhibitors (desruptive students) and 92 facilitators
(well behaved students) who subsequently completed the
Intellectual Achievement Responsibility Questionnaire, the
Rotter Internal/External Control Scale, the Motivation
Inventory, and the Crime Prevention Attitude Inventory. The
study revealed that compared to inhibitors, facilitators
were more internal, more strongly motivated by needs higher
on the Maslow Hierarchy, and more law and order oriented
with respect to crime prevention. Results were discussed in
terms of their salience for classroom teachers and the
probably effects of attribution retraining upon inhibitors.
See ERIC Abstract #ED 186806.

3230.   Goldstein, J. M. and (Weber, W. A.) "Teacher Managerial
Behaviors and Student On-Task Behavior." Paper presented at
the Annual Meeting of the Southwest Educational Research
Association, Houston, Texas, February, 1979.

The researchers hypothesized that teacher managerial
behavior may have a greater effect than teacher instructional behavior on ultimate student academic achievement.
It is supported through the explication of seven major
approaches to class management. Forms of teacher managerial
behavior examined are: 1) authoritarian, 2) behavior
modification, 3) common sense, 4) group process, 5) instructional, 6) permissive, and 7) socioemotional climate. The
relationship between the seven clusters of teacher behaviors
and student on-task behaviors are extended to infer
causality between the teacher behaviors and the students'
academic achievement levels. Included is a bibliography.
See ERIC Abstract #ED 178484.

3231.   Good, T. L. and Brophy, J. E. "Changing Teacher and
Student Behavior: An Empirical Investigation." Journal of
Educational Psychology, 66, 3 (June, 1974): 390-405.

In this study, modified teacher behavior toward two
different groups of students, a total of 49 first graders,

by presenting teachers with information about their previous interaction with the target children. Forty hours of pre-treatment and forty hours of post-treatment data were collected in eight classrooms drawn from three different schools. Treatment procedures marketly altered both quantitative an qualitative aspects of teacher interaction with target students, and the behavior of the target students changed reciprocally. Changes in specified teacher behavior toward target children were accompanied by many additional changes in unspecified teacher behavior toward both target and non-target children. See ERIC Abstract 1091452-5.

3232.   Goodman, G. and Hammond, B.   "Seat Belts Control Hyper-activity." Academic Therapy, 11, 1 (Fall, 1975): 51-52.

Sixteen highly distractible and impulsive primary school children with learning problems were tied to their seats with an easily unfastened string. The technique was non-punitive. The children approved of the apparatus and hyperactivity was reduced. See ERIC Abstract 1392457-6.

3233.   Goodman, G. and Timko, N. G.   "Hot Seats and Aggressive Behavior." Academic Therapy, 11, 4 (Summer, 1976): 447-448.

The success of a Gestalt Therapy devise was described, The Hot Seat, in solving problems of disruptive peer relations in a fourth grade inner-city classroom. In three months of feeling verbalization and role exchange by this method, need to use the hot seat technique diminished from two to three times a day, to about three times a week, with numerous pheripheral benefits. See ERIC Abstract 0198357-1.

3234.   Goodman, J. C. "Group Counseling with Seventh Graders." Personnel and Guidance Journal, 54, 10 (June, 1976): 519-520.

Nine 7th Grade students whose classroom behavior was unacceptable were selected for a group counseling program. The group was later divided into two similar groups for better interaction. Positive behavioral changes in the classroom are reported for seven of the nine students. See ERIC Abstract 0846563-4.

3235.   Goodwin, D. "School Bureaucracy and Political Conflict," Paper presented at the Annual Meeting of the American Educational Research Association, San Francisco, California, April, 1976.

The findings of this paper raised questions about the validity of educational assumptions underlying efforts to reform bureaucratic dysfunctions in the schools. Although specific reforms are not examined, there is a tenuous con-nection between bureaucratic organization of schools and the kinds of teacher attitudes toward clients so often cited as the justication for changes. The ability of teachers to interact with parents and students without conflict, and to accept pedagogical and organizational reforms, appears enhanced by the reliance on clear and concise rules for teacher behavior in areas such as student discipline and relatinos with parents. Organization strategies that enabled teachers to make difficult decisions, sort out ambiguous situations, and reaffirm frequently challenged authority are often well received. Extensive school rules for teacher behavior are compatible with teacher expectations and a reasonably successful administrative strategy. See ERIC Abstract #ED 125116.

3236.   Gorton, R. A.   "Responding to student misbehavior." National Association of Secondary School Principles Bulletin, 61, 405 (January, 1977): 18-26.

Nonpunitive approaches to discipline (changing the student, remediating learning problems, changing the school environment, and implementing alternative programs) can eventually reduce student misbehavior and should be considered as alternatives to punitive approaches for working with students who are discipline problems. See ERIC Abstract #EJ 158811.

3237.   Goshko, R. "Self-determined behavior change." Personnel and Guidance Journal, 51, 9 (May, 1973): 629-632.

Article discusses a project in which children were found to be capable of learning the basic skills of behavior identification and behavior modification. Author states that counselors can help children solve seemingly complex problems by breaking the problems down into simple behaviors that can be worked on one by one, providing children with an opportunity to determine what will happen. See ERIC Abstract #EJ 080799.

3238.   Gottesman, R. "Due process: Are we going too far?" National Organization on Legal Problems of Education, Topeka, Kansas, 6p, 1974.

School authorities will have to yield some of their discretionary power in discipling students in cases that merit a hearing. What must be aimed at is a more equitable balancing of the interests of all parties involved. The school's interest in using disciplinary measures is to prevent the interruption of the normal school routine. The teacher's interest is to use discipline to enable him to carry out a lesson plan. The student's interest in disciplinary measures is that discipline be enforced so that his interests not be interrupted and that discipline be meated out fairly. These interests must be weighed carefully before determining whether due process has gone too far. See ERIC Abstract #ED 090627.

3239.   Gottlieb, J.   "Attitudes Toward Retarded Children: Effects of Labeling and Behavioral Aggressiveness." Journal of Educational Psychology, 67, 4 (August, 1975): 581-585.

Effects of the label "Mentally Retarded" on attitudes of peers among forty-eight third graders was examined. Half of the subjects were shown a videotape of an actor to explain acting-out behavior, while the remaining half were shown a videotape with the same actor engaging in passive behavior. Half of the subjects in each of these two groups were told that the actor was a fifth grader, and the other half were told that he was a mentally retarded boy in special class. Analysis of variance results revealed a significant inter-action between label and behavior, which indicated that the subjects responded more negatively to the mentally retarded actor who displayed acting-out behavior than to the same actor who exhibited identical behavior but was not labeled. It is concluded that labels should be considered only if they interact with specific behavior. See ERIC Abstract 1258154-6.

3240.   Graff, P. R. "Student discipline--is there a bag of tricks?   Or is organization the solution?" National Association of Secondary School Principals Bulletin, 65, 441 (January, 1981): 1-5.

Article outlines the five items that one administrative team has stressed in promoting a workable, understandable, and realistic discipline program. One important step has been to make administrators and counselors visible. See ERIC Abstract #EJ 238662.

3241.   Grantham, M. L. "The Herbert Marcus Elementary School Model for Classroom Management Provided by Alternatives in Discipline." Doctor of Education, Nova University, 233p, 1975.

The purpose of this study was to see whether a model program utilizing alternative disciplinary actions as a means to improve the discipline problems at an elementary school would be successful in 1) reducing the number of student misbehaviors, 2) providing more appropriate learning situa-tions for the needs of individual students, and 3) reducing the apparently racially biased disproportion of disciplinary actions against minority students. Staff development ses-sions were held for one year with the assistance of the principal and visiting professionals who taught teachers methods of identifying student problems and averting potential discipline problems. Faculty answered question-naires before and after the program, rating themselves on a variety of skills indicative of classroom control. The Fink Interaction Analysis System was used to chart teacher behavior in the classroom in terms of numbers of positive and negatives behaviors related in interacting with students. An analysis of the data indicated that the program was effective in improving teacher competencies,

while at the same time, student academic achievement
improved as disciplinary behavior decreased. See ERIC
Abstract #ED 115587.

3242.   Grantham, M. L. and Harris, C. S., Jr.   "A faculty trains
itself to improve student discipline." Phi Delta Kappan,
57, 10 (June, 1976): 661-664.

The Marcus Elementary School staff felt that the best
approach to discipline was a preventive one--a provision of
a variety of educational and environmental alternatives that
will interest, challenge, and motivate the pupil. See ERIC
Abstract #EJ 138344.

3243.   Granum, R. A.   "Teachers Study Groups: Do They Make A
Difference." Elementary School Guidance And Counseling, 9,
3 (March, 1975) 210-217.

Study attempted to determine whether or not teacher participation in study groups, using an orientation toward understanding and applying individual or Adlerian psychology, can
alter teachers' abilities to manage behavior-adjustment
problems.   Thirty-four subjects including twenty-seven
teachers, six aides and a school principal participated in
10 one hour sessions. It was concluded that the Adlerian
study groups in schools can aid teacher-pupil interaction.
See ERIC Abstract 1246560-6.

3244.   Gray, F., Graubard, P. S. and Rosenberg, H.   "Little
Brother Is Changing You." Psychology Today, 7, 10 (March,
1974):   42-46.

Seven twelve to fifteen year olds were selected from a class
of incorrigible students and were taught behavior modification principles in order to have more positive relations
with teachers.   After a baseline period during which the
subjects learned how to recognize positive and negative
interpersonal relations, the subjects began reinforcing
pleasant teacher contact by praise and discouraging negative
contact.   It was important for the subjects to maintain
records of positive and negative interactions in order to
obtain adequate feedback.   These records showed a marked
increase in positive interactions and a drop to near zero in
negative interactions. See ERIC Abstract 0626552-3.

3245.   Green, J., et al.   "What's going on around here?"
National Elementary Principals, 56, 4 (March/April, 1977):
9-19.

Article includes a discussion by nine principals of their
problems and what they see as the most critical issues
confronting principals today. See ERIC Abstract #EJ 157038.

3246.   Green, K. D., et al. "Accuracy of Teacher Nominations of Child Behavior Problems." National Institute of Mental Health, Bethesda, Maryland. 1980. Paper presented at the Annual Meeting of the Western Psychological Association, Honolulu, Hawaii, May, 1980. 16p.

The purpose of this study was to examine the accuracy of a teachers' abilities to identify problem children. The subjects included 95 3rd grade children. Teachers designated each child as conduct problem, withdrawal problem, or normal, resulting in 16, 14 and 65 children being assigned to the three groups. Behavioral observations, peer sociometric ratings, and academic achievement scores were collected. The results of the study indicated that conduct problem children differed from normal children on behavioral, sociometric, and academic measures, whereas withdrawn children differed from normals on the latter two measures. Conduct problem and withdrawal problem children did not differ on any of the outcome measures. The results suggested that teachers can identify children who are having difficulties in class, but may be less accurate in differentiating between different types of problem children. See ERIC Abstract #ED 191579.

3247.   Greenberg, J. S. "The Use of Drugs to Calm Kids." Paper presented at New York State Federation of Chapters of the Council for Exceptional Children, Buffalo, New York, November, 1974. 19p.

Through an extensive review of the literature, the author describes the present state of knowledge regarding hyperkinetic syndrome. The review is organized into several categories: 1) hyperactive child syndrome, 2) the child's behavior, 3) treatment for the syndrome, and 4) the role of schools and school personnel. Suggestions pertaining to administration of drugs to treat hyperkinesis and to appropriate responses of school personnel are offered. A conclusion reached is that hyperkinetic child syndrome is a complex condition whose problems persist long after the hyperactivity ceases. Examples of these problems are low self esteem, despair, parental rejection, socially inappropriate behavior, and a bad reputation. The author suggests a team, consisting of physician, parent, teacher, and siblings, organized to respond to these problems. See ERIC Abstract #ED 101268.

3248.   Greene, D. and Lepper, M. R. "The Intrinsic Motivation: How to Turn Play into Work." Psychology Today, 8, 4 (September, 1974): 49-54.

The hypothesis was investigated that extrinsic rewards for an activity will lower the value for an intrinsic reward. A replicated study showed that nursery school children used magic markers less often after being rewarded for using them then they did before the reward, and less often than other children who were not rewarded. The use of mass related activities by grade school children was similarly affected. Since there appears to be some sort of trade off between extrinsic and intrinsic motivation, extrinsic motivation should be used only when there is no intrinsic motivation to lose or when the fundamentals are being learned. See ERIC Abstract 0618153-3.

3249.   Greene, D., Sternberg, B. and Lepper, M. R. "Over-Justification in a Token Economy." *Journal of Personality and Social Psychology*, 34, 6 (December, 1976): 1219-1234.

A classroom token economy was designed to discover demon-stratably effective reinforcement procedures would also produce an over-justification effect, indicated by a signifi-cant decrement in post-treatment engagement with previously reinforced activities, in the absence of preceived tangible or social rewards. Three different experimental token economy groups formed with 33 fourth and fifth graders were compared with a single control group of 11 subjects. Fine baseline observations, a treatment phase was initiated, during which differential reinforcement was made contingent on time spent with designated target activities. During this phase, subjects in all three experimental groups spent significantly more time with these activities than did the non-differentially reinforced controls. Subsequently, after differential reinforcement was withdrawn, subjects in two of the three experimental groups spent significantly less time with their target activities than controls did, demonstra-ting that multi-trial contingent reinforcement procedures are capable of producing over-justification effects. The relationship between these findings and the problems of achieving generalization of treatment effects from token economies is discussed. See ERIC Abstract 1252960-6.

3250.   Greenwood, C. R. et al. "Standardized classroom manage-ment program: social validation and replication studies in Utah and Oregon." *Journal of Applied Behavior Analysis*, 12, 2 (Summer 1979): 235-253.

A validation study was conducted of the program for academic survival skills, a consultant based, teacher mediated program for student classroom behavior. Program satisfac-tion ratings of students, teachers, and consultants were uniformly positive, and continued use of the program was reported one year later. See PSYC Abstract 115365-5.

3251.   Greenwood, C. R., Hops, H. and Delquadri, J. "Group contingencies for group consequences in classroom management: a further analysis." *Journal of Applied Behavior Analysis*, 7, 3 (Fall, 1974): 413-425.

The relative effects of rule, rules plus feedback, and rules plus feedback plus group and individual consequences for appropriate behavior were investigated in three classrooms containing a total of 68 children in grades one through three during reading and mathematics periods. The consequences were individual and group praise, and group activities. The total intervention package was most effective in increasing appropriate behavior. Rules plus feedback produced increased appropriate behavior in two of the three classrooms. Rules alone produced no change in classroom behavior. Maintenance of appropriate classroom behavior was noted approximately three weeks after the program ended. See ERIC Abstract 0610453-3.

3252.   Greenwood, C. R., Hops, H. and Walker-Hill, M.   "The durability of student behavior change: a comparative analysis at followup." Behavior Therapy, 8, 4 (September, 1977): 631-638.

The maintenance of classroom behavior was investigated in a program for academic survival skills. The study was conducted in ten classrooms in a rural primary school with six people from each of the ten classes. Six classes were designated experimental and four control. Approximately 30 trained observers collected a minimum of eight minutes of data of each subject in both mathematics and reading periods. The past program only and two maintenance enhancement conditions were contrasted to a no treatment control group at one week following the program, three weeks following the enchancement conditions, and at six weeks following termination of all procedures. Results indicate the procedures contained in the past programs were sufficient to produce maintenance over a nine-week period. See ERIC Abstract 0395760-2.

3253.   Greenwood, C. R., Hops, H. and Walker-Hill, W.   "The program for academic survival skills: effects on student behavior and achievement." Journal of School Psychology, 15, 1 (Spring, 1977): 25-35.

The effects of the program for academic survival skills was investigated. It is a group behavior management program. The Wide Achievement Test was used as the primary achievement measure for reading and mathematics. Fifty-four of the 96 selected low-achieving, low survival skill, first through third graders of normal I.Q. were assigned to an experimental condition in which their teachers used the program. The remaining 42 were assigned to a control condition. The program produced significant gains in survival skills during its operation and one week following program termination in both reading and mathematics periods. Findings for achievement indicated a significant gain for first grade experimentals only in reading, with a similar but non-significant gain for first grade mathematics. See ERIC Abstract 1250558-6.

3254.   Gresham, F. M. and Nagle, R. J.   "Treating School Phobia Using Behavioral Consultation: A Case Study." School Psychology Review, 10, 1 (Winter, 1981): 104-107.

This case study illustrates how behavioral consultation can be integrated by the school psychologist using a modification and expansion of the rapid treatment procedure in eliminating school phobia. The importance of including teachers, parents, and administrators as consultees and participants in the decision-making process is demonstrated. See ERIC Abstract EJ 243239.

3255.   Grieger, R. N. and Richards, H. C. "Prevalence and structure of behavior symptoms among children in special education and regular classroom settings." Journal of School Psychology, 14, 1 (Spring, 1976): 27-37.

This project studied the factor structure of the behavior problem checklist, determined the extent to which factors generated from children in regular classrooms approximated those from children in special education, and examined the effects of class placement, sex, and the interaction of these variables on the average rating children received. See ERIC Abstract #EJ 134339.

3256.   Griepenstroh, G. and Miskel, C. "Training groups and student teachers' pupil control ideology." Planning and Changing, 6, 3-4 (1976): 177-184.

Author states that on-going t-group training can work as an effective intervention in the socialization of student teachers' pupil control ideology; those teachers in such groups were scored humanistic in their pupil control ideology; those teachers in such groups were scored humanistic in their pupil control ideology than those in a controlled group. See ERIC Abstract #EJ 146409.

3257.   Griggs, M. B. "Discipline: Managing behavior in the classroom." Illinois Teacher of Home Economics, 21, 1 (September/October, 1977): 17-20.

Author defines discipline problems and discipline and discusses why discipline problems exist within the schools. Article includes Harvey Clarizo's four steps that teachers can take to minimize these problems. See ERIC #EJ 171076.

3258.   Gueringer, G. "The 'stop program' (school treatment of problems)." Journal of the International Association of Pupil Personnel Workers, 19, 2 (March, 1975): 65-67.

Article presents an experimental stop program centered around a regular equipped classroom which provides containment of pupils on a temporary basis due to misbehavior. Goals are to contain the child in school by removing him from his regular classroom, on a temporary status. See ERIC Abstract #EJ 113956.

3259.   "Guide to Sanity Saving Discipline." Instructor, 88, 4 (November, 1978): 59-61.

Article describes seven detailed approaches to effective classroom discipline including: teacher assertiveness training, effective limit setting, priority problems approach, those games kids play, the eye contact method, the paradox response, and the use of letters to parents as a discipline device. See ERIC Abstract EJ 190978.

3260.   Guilford, B. J. "Junior high school in a democracy: enforcement of discipline without representation." New Voices in Education, 2, 2 (Spring, 1972): 8-9.

Article discusses the use of a democratic process for junior high school students in which they enforce discipline without teacher or administrative assistance.

3261.   Gulyas, P. A. "Improving the Behavior of Habitually Disruptive High School Students." Revised Individual Practicum Report, Nova University. 52p, 1979.

A means was developed to reduce the necessity for discipline among 25 students who were the most chronic discipline problems at Thomas Jefferson High School, a 1500 student school in suburban Pittsburgh. The students were identified by assigning point values to various disciplinary measures administered to students. These students met with a vice-principal weekly for a minimum of five minutes to discuss any school problems, potential discipline problems they felt might arise, or recent discipline they had received. The premise was that the talks would help prevent more serious problems or additional disciplinary measures. Weekly sessions were scheduled during each study hall. The student could arrange conferences if an immediate problem could not wait until the next session. Result of this preventive maintenance approach revealed that compared with the same semester a year earlier, total suspension days were reduced 50%, instances of corporal punishment were reduced 24%, and detention hours were reduced 54%. See ERIC Abstract #ED 130075.

3262.   Gump, P. V. and Good, L. R. "Environments are Parading in Open Space and Traditionally Designed Schools." Journal of Architectural Research, 5, 2 (1976): 20-26.

Behavior setting observations were conducted of 700 students and interviews of 50 teachers were made in two open and two traditional schools for grades 1-2 and 5-6. Operating segments of behavior were followed for their duration. Comparisons were made for a variety of environmental sites and teachers, nonsubstance time, group size, external stimulation and guidance, student behavior differences, and teacher reaction. Results show that in the open space schools, in comparison with the traditional schools, children entered more learning sites, more teachers worked in a wider variety of group sizes, consumed more nonsubstance time, spent slightly less time on substative tasks, and were externally stimulated and guided more by teachers. See ERIC Abstract 0825760-4.

3263.   Guralnick, N. J. "Early Classroom Based Intervention and the Role of Organizational Structure." Exceptional Children, 42, 4 (September, 1975): 25-31.

The role of organizational structure in classroom based early childhood intervention programs is explored. Nine characteristics are identified as necessary components for an effective system. The operation of a curriculum evaluation feedback model which incorporates these nine components is described and discussed in terms of the interrelationships among the elements of the system.

3264.   Hakanen, L. J. "Combating student truancy: a working plan." Illinois School Journal, 59, 4 (Winter, 1980): 25-28.

Article describes the administrative policy developed to deal with student truancy at Harlem South High School in Rockford, Illinois. The policy calls for intensive monitoring of attendance and involves parents, as well as school officials. See ERIC Abstract #EJ 222737.

3265.   Halatyn, T. V. "Logic -vs- Reality: prospects of facing school crime legislation upon research." Contemporary Education, 52, 1 (Fall, 1980): 36-41.

The legislative actions taken by California from 1977 through 1979 are discussed in detail. The purpose behind this legislation is to help prevent and identify criminal and violent behavior in schools. See ERIC Abstract #EJ 237735.

3266.   Hall, V. C., Huppertz, J. W. and Levi, A. "Attention and Achievement Exhibited by Middle and Lower Class Black and White Elementary School Boys." Journal of Educational Psychology, 69, 2 (April, 1977): 115-120.

In-class behaviors of 80 7 and 8 year old boys equally divided by race and social class were recorded. Subjects were administered a vocabulary test, the Test of Basic Experience and Raven Colored Progressive Matrices. The three observers compiled and used a list of behaviors judged to be all-inclusive of what occurs in normal classroom activity. No differences were found between groups in percentage of time attending. Although there were social class and race differences in achievement and intelligence test scores, no relationship was found between attending and these variables. There was a significant correlation between the intelligence and achievement test scores but no evidence that the relationship was different for the different groups. See ERIC Abstract 1259858-6.

3267.   Halperin, M. S. "First Grade Teachers' Goals and
Children's Developing Perceptions of School." Journal of
Education Psychology, 68, 5 (October, 1976): 636-648.

A longitudinal design was used to investigate how goals and
practices of first grade teachers influenced students'
perceptions of school and their classroom behaviors. Before
school began, the goals and classroom structure of 13
teenagers were assessed. Seventy-seven children were then
interviewed and tested prior to first grade and again seven
months later. Observations were conducted to corroberate
self-report data. Results suggest that teachers' beliefs
influenced classroom activities, chiildren's behaviors, and
children's perceptions of school. Certain combinations of
the identified ideologies produced classroom environments
which children found anxiety arousing. See ERIC Abstract
1070256-06.

3268.   Halpin, W. Gerald, et al. "Case analysis: consultation
and counseling." Elementary School Guidance and Counseling,
6, 4 (May, 1972): 273-277.

Article describes the way in which the counselor works
successfuly with a group of troublemakers bent on changing
their image around the school. Activities are discussed.
See ERIC Abstract #EJ 057108.

3269.   Halverson, C. F., Jr. and Victor, J. B. "Minor physical
anomalies and problem behavior in elementary school
children." Child Development, 47, 1 (March, 1976): 281-285.

Article describes behavior in elementary school-aged
children in relationship to their physical problems.

3270.   Hannum, J. W., et al. "A Comparison of Desensitization
and Behavior Training with Two Teachers." 18p, 1976.

Two elementary teachers were given systematic desensitization and behavior modification training to help them manage
their feelings of anxiety and establish classroom control.
Changes in teacher and student classroom behavior were
recorded through daily observations by trained observers.
The observers recorded teacher praise and criticism, as well
as student talk-outs and out-of-seats. A single subject
design using back to baseline reversals was used to test the
effectiveness of each intervention. The data indicates
desensitization was effective in changing all observed
behaviors in one teacher's class, but none in the other
teacher's class. Behavior modification training, on the
other hand, was generally effective in changing the
behaviors in both classes. See ERIC Abstract #ED 155567.

3271.   Hanson, J. Merrell. "Discipline and Classroom Manage-
ment: Different Strokes for Different Folks." National
Association of Secondary School Principals Bulletin, 63, 428
(September, 1979): 40-47.

This is a review of the major schools of thought related to disciplinary techniques. See ERIC Abstract EJ 206325.

3272.   Harbach, R. L. & Asbury, F. R. "Some Effects Of Empathic Understanding On Negative Student Behaviors." Humanist Educator 15, 1 (1976): 19-24.

Eleven teachers enrolled in a human relations training class received 15 hours of human relations training emphasing empathic response skills in addition to training and observing, defining and recording student behavior. Results indicate that teachers need to focus empathically on individual students in addition to their classes in general and that teacher-facilitators must be persistent in their efforts so that students will perceive their efforts as genuine. See ERIC Abstract 0936361-4.

3273.   Hardesty, Lorraine. Pupil Control Ideology of Teachers as it Relates to Middle School Concepts. Paper presented at the annual meeting of the American Educational Research Association, Toronto, Ontario, March, 1978.

The purpose of this study was to test the hypothesis that there will be a statistically significant main effect and interaction effect for school level assignment (elementary, junior high, and senior high) and support for middle school organizational concepts on pupil control ideology. 252 teachers served as subjects. A two way analysis of variance partially supported the hypothesis. A one way analysis of variance revealed that junior high teachers were significantly more custodial than either elementary or senior high teachers. See ERIC Abstract ED 150722.

3274.   Hardy, R. E. "Measuring the common factor variance between perceptual and behavioral measures of behavior." Pupil Personnel Services Journal, 3, 3 (1974): 37-41.

Thirty-six high school students in three psychology courses were administered the Brown Holtzman Survey of Study Habits and Western Michigan University Teacher Image Questionnaire and observed for voluntary student hand-raising and verbal responses. Results show that common factor variance between perceptual and behavioral measures of behavior was not systematic. See ERIC Abstract 06329254-3.

3275.   Hargrave, G. E. and Hargrave, N. C. "A peer group socialization therapy program in the school: an outcome investigation." Psychology in the Schools, 16, 4 (October, 1979): 546-550.

An outcome study of a 14-session pre-adolescent peer group therapy program conducted in an elementary school with 12 fourth through sixth graders is discussed. Two school psychologists and one teacher served as therapists. Group structure and activities designed to facilitate the acquisition of social skills with peers are presented. Teachers completed the classroom behavior inventory before and after students were enrolled in the program. A comparison of the scores showed that group members improved significantly in task-oriented classroom behaviors, but the relationship between this improvement and improved social skills was unclear. See ERIC Abstract 0408365-2.

3276.   Harper, G. F., Guidubalvi, J. and Kehle, T. J. "Is Academic Achievement Related to Classroom Behavior?" Elementary School Journal, 78, 3 (1978): 202-207.

The correlates of achievement is 70 children, kindergarten through grade two, were investigated in an open elementary school. Predictor variables included intelligences and behavioral indices of distractibility, passive responding, dependency, and constructive play. Sixteen trained observers collected the behavioral data. Regression analysis indicated that intelligence significantly predicted achievement, but no consistent patterns across grade levels were found for the four behavioral indices. Reasons for inconsistencies with prior research are discussed. See ERIC Abstract 0412863-2.

3277.   Harris, A. & Kapche, R. "Problems Of Quality Control In The Development And The Use Of Behavior Change Techniques In Public School Settings." Education And Treatment Of Children, 1, 3 (Spring, 1978): 43-51.

Authors discuss behavior modification in school settings from the perspective of a psychologist attempting to train students and coordinate students and school personnel. Part 1 examines the problems encountered in the training setting (college) and Part 2 examines difficulties encountered when the 12 trainees went into the elementary schools. Training involved four phases: 1) preintervention training and observation and data collection, 2) preintervention training and classroom contingency training management, 3) intervention strategy training, 4) implementation training. Problems were encountered in the following areas: students not completing required reading, students needing more feedback, video tape observation training taking too much time, camera-shyness in video taping of role playing, and students and classroom teachers each viewing the other group as incompetent. See ERIC Abstract 0628663-3.

3278.   Harris, Merril. "Children With Short Fuses." Instructor, 90, 4 (November, 1980): 52-54.

Advice is included in this article to the classroom teacher for dealing with a child subject to explosive temper tantrums. It discusses why such outbursts occur and gives a sequence for controlling the tantrum and calming the child. It also considers long-term methods for helping the child curb anger and aggression. See ERIC Abstract EJ 233443.

3279.   Harris, V. W. and Sherman, J. A. "Use and Analysis of the Good Behavior Game to Reduce Disruptive Classroom Behavior." Journal of Applied Behavior Analysis, 6, 3 (Fall, 1973): 405-417.

This study was a replication of the procedures of the good behavior game developed by Barrish to reduce disruptive classroom behavior. Twenty-two fifth and 28 sixth graders were observed. Results show that the techniques to be effective in reducing disruptive talking and out-of-seat behavior. Further analysis indicated that the effective components of the game were division of the class into teams, consequences for a team winning the game, and criteria set for winning the game. Although disruptive behavior was markedly reduced by the game, the reductions were correlated with only slightly improved accuracy of academic performance in the one classroom when academic performance was measured. See ERIC Abstract 1190451-6.

3280.   Harshbarger, Mary E. "The Role of Drugs, Diet, and Food Additives in Hyperactivity." Paper presented at the annual meeting of the International Reading Association Great Lakes Regional Conference, Cincinnati, Ohio, October, 1978. 17p.

Author states that a variety of causes have been suggested for hyperactivity: anoxia and other adverse birth conditions, genetic factors, delayed maturation, interaction of temperment and environment, lead poisoning, allergy and food additives, and deprivation of required stimulation. Treatments includes drug treatments, especially with ratalin or dexedrine; the Feingold diet restricting sugars and artificial colorings; administration of megavitamins; behavior therapy; differential reinforcement procedures; modeling; role playing. Possible educational involvement with a hyperactive includes developing minimal stimulation programs, developing structured, predictable, consistent, and logical programs; behavior modifications programs; and bio-feedback. Cooperation between parents, teachers and physicians is important in treating children who are hyperactive. See ERIC Abstract ED 163439.

3281.   Hart, Stuart N. "The Others -- Concept in Children With Special Needs." Paper presented at the annual meeting of the American Psychological Association, Chicago, Illinois, September, 1975. 18p.

Subjects in this study were 669 fourth grade students in a suburban middle class school. They were given the Paired Hands test, measuring the others-concept, in conjuction with special needs screening process. This process requires that fourth grade teachers identify all children having a significant learning-behavioral problem of a specific type and then judge each student's functioning for each of 23 specific behavioral-learning problem characteristics. In general, students identified as having special needs had lower-others concepts than those not so identified. See ERIC Abstract ED 122197.

3282.   Harvey, Donald L. and Moosha, William G.   "In-School Suspension: Does it Work."   National Association of Secondary School Principals Bulletin, 61, 4057 (January, 1977): 14-17.

Article describes a program which reduced the total number of students suspended in the high school by approximately 29 percent and in the junior high school by approximately 42 percent. See ERIC Abstract EJ 158810.

3283.   Hautala, L. W. & Mason, G. E.   "In Search of Success." Southern Journal of Educational Research, 12, 4 (Fall, 1978): 235-248.

Descriptive data is presented on actual classroom behaviors of 24 primary teachers whose students had averaged 1¼ academic year's gained in reading achievement per eight months instruction over the past three to five years. Each teacher was observed for a total of one hour and her behaviors were reported on a teacher observation/interview guide. The results indicate that while many of the behaviors demonstrated by these teachers adhered to advocated practices, several behaviors that they demonstrated have been strongly criticized in the literature. See ERIC Abstract 0198664-1.

3284.   Haviland, J. M.   "Teachers' and Students' Beliefs About Punishment."   The Journal of Educational Psychology, 71, 4 (August, 1979): 563-570.

Three hundred and sixty (360) first, third and fifth graders and their 16 teachers from three school systems were interviewed in the Fall and Spring of the same school year, to assess the developing relationship between teachers' and students' beliefs about punishment. Older children were less punitive than younger children. Teachers remained relatively punitive compared with fifth graders. Teachers with more punitive beliefs had students whose beliefs were more punitive when compared with students whose teachers had less punitive beliefs. Children and teachers thought the teachers should give more punitive responses than peers for the same misbehavior. The school systems that allowed corporal punishment had students with more punitive beliefs than the school system without corporal punishment. Results indicate that the school environment is perceived to be authoritarian and punitive by students and teachers. See ERIC Abstract 0189963-1.

3285.   Hawley, H.   "Steps To Establish Classroom Discipline." Montana Schools Office Of Public Instruction, 22, 5 (January, 1979).

Discipline problems in schools have ranked high in teacher and parent polls across the nation in recent years. There are a number of approaches professional educators can take. The author states several principles regarding discipline. And then ask four questions first, the teacher must ask "What am I, the professional, doing--and, is it working?" Second the teacher must remember to be personal in dealing with students. The third step involves democratically establishing classroom rules. The fourth step enables the teacher to deal with misbehavior. If misbehavior recurs the fifth step which varies for elementary and secondary students includes when misbehavior recurs in an elementary school age child, that student should be isolated from the class. With secondary students they should be sent out of the classroom to a in-school suspension room.

3286.   Hay, W. H., Hay, L. R., and Nelson, R. O. "Direct and Collateral Changes in On-Task and Academic Behavior Resulting From On-Task vs. Academic Contingencies." Behavior Therapy, 8, 3 (June, 1977): 431-441.

Compared in the study was the relative efficacy of on-task and academic classroom contingencies on the dependent measures of on-task behavior and rate and accuracy of academic performance. Five male elementary students experienced baseline 1, the on-task contingency, baseline 2, and the academic contingency. Five other subjects experienced baseline 1, the academic contingency, baseline 2, and the on-task contingency. The academic contingency was the more parsimonious intervention strategy, producing increments in both on-task behaviors and academic achievement. The on-task contingency increased on-task behaviors without concomitant academic improvements. See ERIC Abstract 0660759-3.

3287.   Hay, L. R., Nelson, R. O. and Hay, W. M. "The Youth of Teachers as Behavioral Observers." Journal of Applied Behavior Analysis, 10, 2 (Summer, 1977): 345-348.

The effect of using teachers as behavioral observers on both pupil and teacher behavior was examined with eight male teachers and 32 pupils. The frequencies of prompts to those pupils observed by the teacher increased signigicantly from non-observered to teacher observed experimental phases. In addition, pupils observed by the teacher showed more change in appropriate behavior than those not observed. See ERIC Abstract 1324659-6.

3288.   Hayes, M. L. "A Technique For Presenting Behavior Modification To Groups." SALT: School Applications Of Learning Theory, 7, 4 (June, 1975): 1-4.

Graduate students in secondary education were trained in techniques for demonstrating effectiveness of behavior modification in groups. See ERIC Abstract 1362157-6.

3289.   Hecht, L. W.   "Measuring Student Behavior During Group Instruction."   Journal of Educational Research, 71, 5 (May-June, 1978): 283-290.

If teacher behaviors and learning conditions have an influence on student achievement the authors felt it seemed likely that student behavior must mediate this relationship. An instrument designed to assess the physical and mental behaviors and activities of students during group instruction is described.   The instrument was employed in a study of five 10th grade mathematics classrooms with 166 students. Findings indicate that scores from the activities checklist correlate highly with more general measures of student participation obtained from direct observation and from the stimulated recall procedure.   The student behavior measures were shown to be highly predictive of achievement, adding support to the notion that student behavior during instruction is strongly linked to student learning.   See ERIC Abstract 1486962-6.

3290.   Hegerle, Dana R. and others.   "A Behavior Game for the Reduction of Inappropriate Classroom Behavior."   School Psychology Digest, 8, 3 (Summer, 1979): 339-343.

A group-contigency behavior game significantly decreased disruptive classroom behavior after five weeks in this study.   The classroom observers gradually phased themselves out of the program, while training the teacher to continue the game unaided.   See ERIC Abstract EJ 211842.

3291.   Heller, J. and Kiraly, J.   "Behavior Modification: A Classroom Clockwork Orange."   Elementary School Journal, 74, 4 (January, 1974):   196-202.

The implications are presented of the increasing non-identity of the individual with social institutions and movement in the problem of behavior modification of youth. This non-identity is characterized by the inability to feel and to establish close relationships with others.   A description of this non-identity is a coolness on the part of the individual.   The reinforcement to that coolness is the promise of freedom and power.   That coolness produces apathy which permits violence which in turn promotes apathy.   This increasing feeling of non-identification has important implications for the problem of behavior modification. Shall techniques be used to develop compliant, unassuming, faithful, inquiring, and intelligent and who do not comply with the authoritarian devices of rule-of-thumb teachers? It must be emphasized that behavior modification should be one of the devices of the teacher to promote empathy and care for others, which produces a sense of purpose and meaning.   See ERIC Abstract 0191052-1.

3292.   Helsel, A. Ray and Willower, Donald J.   "Toward
Definition and Measurement of Pupil Controlled Behavior."
Paper presented at the annual meeting of the American
Educational Research Association, New Orleans, Louisiana,
February, 1973. 19p.

The purpose of this study was to define and measure pupil
controlled behavior. An instrument called the Pupil Control
Behavior form was developed and tested. 31 custodial and 34
humanistic items were randomized, and the initial version of
the form was administered in 20 schools in Illinois.
Students described the pupil controlled behavior of their
teacher, counselor, and principal; teachers, counselors, and
principals completed the Pupil Control Ideology form and a
Personnel Data Sheet. The general hypothesis was supported.
See ERIC Abstract ED 074073.

3293.   Henning, Joel F.   "Student Rights and Responsibilities
and the Curriculum." Phi Delta Kappa, 56, 4 (December,
1974): 248-250,256.

Author suggests that student behavior could be the subject
matter in social studies classes. See ERIC Abstract EJ
107313.

3294.   Henson, Kenneth.   "A New Concept of Discipline."
Clearinghouse, 51, 2 (October, 1977): 89-91.

Author states that by examining some of the recent changes
in adolescents and in school environment, some insights into
desirable methods for coping with discipline problems may be
gained. See ERIC Abstract EJ 170985.

3295.   Hewitson, M. T.   "The Context of Secondary School
Discipline: Discipline as Control." Unicorn, 3, 1 (March,
1977): 5-18.

Author believes that discipline is viewed in its broad
organizational context as control of behavior. The context
of secondary school discipline is analyzed in both its
theoretical and practical aspects. See ERIC Abstract EJ
160415.

3296.   Hibbard, K. Michael.   "Improving Decision - Making Skills
Through Open Space Education." National Association of
Secondary School Principals Bulletin, 61, 411 (October,
1977): 61-66.

Articles describes a student center program that sets the
stage for daily decision making by students and faculty.
Priorities for the use of lesuire time, fulfilling academic
responsibilities, relating to authority, establishing
friendships, in getting along with peers prepare students
for life after high school. See ERIC Abstract EJ 167808.

3297.   Hickok, Angelina B.   "Search and Seizure in Schools." Tennessee Education, 10, 1 (Spring, 1980): 21-23.

Even though problems such as drug abuse, bomb threats, theft, and concealed weapons at times make search and seizure necessary, students rights must be protected through proper legal procedures. Articles presents guidelines for conducting locker and personnel searches and for educating students, teachers, and administrators on student rights. See ERIC Abstract EJ 226191.

3298.   Hightower, Toby E.   "The Role of the Principal." Clearinghouse, 52, 8 (April, 1979): 373-377.

This article presents a description of problems principals face, along with suggestions with solving them. The main focus in on discipline in dealing with student misconduct. See ERIC Abstract EJ 199162.

3299.   Hillman, B. W.   "The Family Constellation: A Clue to the Behavior of Elementary School Children." Elementary School Guidance and Counseling, 7, 1 (October, 1972): 20-25.

Adler's theory is discussed, that is, that family constellation, the dynamic relationships between siblings and other family members, is a major factor in the development of the individual. Central to this theory is the concept that the basic force behind all human activity is a striving to move from feelings of inferiority to a position of status and adequacy. The need for status may lead to competitive or cooperative relationships between siblings, with adjacent siblings tending to present more mutual threat than alternate siblings. Adlerian views on the characteristics of children in various sibling positions are described, and it is emphasized that the child's personality developement is influenced by his interpretation of his position rather than birth order. By using this concept, elementary school counselors can better understand the indiviual child, help the child understand his own behavior, either through individual or group counseling, and help parents and teachers become aware of family relationships and their effects on specific children. See ERIC Abstract 0181350-1.

3300.   Hiltzheimer, N. B. and Gumaer, J.   "Behavior Management and Classroom Guidance in an Inner City School." Elementary School Guidance and Counseling, 13, 4 (April, 1979): 272-278.

A six-week program is described of behavior change designed to reduce classroom disruption and improve academic performance among twenty-five fourth grade pupils in a predominantly black inner city school. Positive reinforcement, in the form of praise and candy, was used along with guided affective discussions. The frequency of disruptions was reduced and teacher perception of self and students improved. See ERIC Abstract 1057863-5.

3301.   Hinely, P. M. and Dolly, J. P.   "The Effect of Locus of Control on Teacher Perception of Reinforcement and Time On Task."   Journal of Instructional Psychology, 5, 3 (Summer, 1978):   15-18.

It was investigated whether there were significant differences in the way internal and external teachers perceived their own reinforcement behavior and their students' time on task.   Twelve teachers were selected from a middle school in South Carolina.   Subjects were asked to indicate how often they reinforced their students and how much time their students spent on task in the classroom.   Subjects' statements were compared with classroom observations of reinforcement and time on task.   Results indicate that both external and internal teachers significantly over-estimated the amount of reinforcement used in the classroom.   See ERIC Abstract 0628863-3.

3302.   Hinkley, Ed.   "An Instructional Program for Dropouts." National Association of Secondary School Principals Bulletin, 63, 424 (February, 1979): 59-64.

Author identifies the characteristics of students who are likely to dropout and introduce several techniques to help the students.   See ERIC Abstract EJ 196058.

3303.   Hipple, Margorie L.   "Classroom Discipline Problems? Fifteen Human Solutions."   Childhood Education, 54, 4 (February, 1978): 183-187.

Articles presents solutions to common classroom discipline problems and suggestions for way to implement them.

3304.   Hoffman, F. J.   "Use of the Adlerian Model in Secondary School Counseling and Consulting."   Individual Psychologist, 12, 2 (November, 1975):   27-32.

Several Adlerian principles were presented to high school teachers at a faculty meeting.   Teachers were asked to list students who exhibited attention seeking behaviors; and six teachers volunteered to take part in a group whose dynamics include change, collaboration, consultation, confrontation, communication, caring, and commitment consultation.   The students listed were divided into four groups A) subjects receiving Adlerian group counseling who had a teacher in the consultation group, B) subjects receiving Adlerian counseling, C) subjects with teachers in the counseling group, and D) subjects with no counseling and no teachers in the counseling group.   Counseling groups of both students and teachers met for one and one half hours a week for ten weeks.   Students' attention seeking behavior was rated by three trained observers at the beginning and end of the experiment.   The relative effectiveness of the various conditions for reducing the behavior studied was, in decreasing order, A) counseling of both teacher and student,

B) counseling of teacher only, C) counseling of student only, and D) no counseling. See ERIC Abstract 0402163-2.

3305.   Hoffman, Jacob and Stranix, Edward. "A Lunchroom Survival Guide." National Association of Secondary School Principals Bulletin, 61, 405 (January, 1977): 30-33.

Author suggests useful strategies to improve discipline in secondary school lunchrooms.

3306.   Holborow, P., Elkins, J. and Berry, P. "The Effect of the Feingold Diet of 'Normal' School Children." Journal of Learning Disabilities, 14, 3 (1981): 143-147.

Three-hundred and forty-four five to twelve year old children in seven elementary schools followed the Fiengold Diet for Hyperactivity for two weeks. Teachers rated subjects before and after the Diet using a questionnaire that incorporated Connors' Hyperactivity Factor Items related to the normal or average child. Of the total sample, 8.5% improved by 5 points or more. Before diet mean scores of subjects who improved were below the cut-off value for hyperactivity, indicating hyperactivity itself is not a necessary condition for improvement. Item by item analysis of the response shows that the behavior problems most likely to show improvement were distractibility, attention span, fiddling, and demands for attention. Subjects who ingested a great deal of additive rated significantly higher in behavioral problems then subjects receiving little additive. See PSYCH Abstract 1331765-6.

3307.   Hollomon, John W. "Dealing With Children's Unacceptable Classroom Behaviors." 1976. 26p.

The purpose of this investigation was to determine unacceptable classroom behavior and how teachers deal with them. 114 female through third grade teachers with 3 or more years of classroom experience were asked 1) to list and describe in descending order no more than three behaviors each preceived to be most unacceptable in the classroom and 2) to describe in descending order no more than 3 techniques they judge to be most effective in dealing with these behaviors. The results revealed 19 unacceptably behaviors and 12 techniques. Both were analysed and arranged in a descending order, based on the frequency with which they were listed and described. See ERIC Abstract ED 138370.

3308.   Holman, Truman. "Prescriptive Pre-punishment: Panacea for Pupil Problems." National Elementary Principal, 49, (May, 1970): 59.

This article is a tongue-in-cheek suggestion that the normal type of punishment for discipline problems be replaced by pre-punishment, a philisophical innovation advocating that children who are justly punished for being naughty before the fact, are obviously less likely to be repeating offenders. See ERIC Abstract EJ 022451.

3309.   Hom, Harry L., Jr. and Maxwell, Frederick R. "Individual Patterns in Intrinsic Motivation." Paper presented at the annual meeting of the Southwestern Psychological Association, Oklahoma City, Oklahoma, April, 1980. 22p.

The purpose of this study was to investigate the effects of extrinsic reward on students' intrinsic interest by using a single subject design in a behavior disorders classroom. Baseline measures of the interest level of five children ages 9 through 11, were collected for academic and non-academic paths. Assessment was then made of each subject's response hierarchy or level of interest in each of four activities: math, reading, coloring, and a spirograph game. Subsequently, children were instructed that if they were working when a timer went off, they would then receive a token which could be exchanged for erasers. Children were rewarded for work on their most preferred activity. Following this phase, rewards were withdrawn. While the effect of reward withdrawal was highly variable across the children there was little evidence of any long-term losses in intrinsic interests. See ERIC Abstract ED 188782.

3310.   Hops, Hyman, et al. "Class: A Standardized In-Class Program for Acting Out Children: II. Field Test Evaluations." Journal of Educational Psychology, 70, 4 (August, 1978): 636-644.

Two experiments evaluated the effects of a packaged teacher-consultant mediated intervention program for modifying acting out behavior in the regular classroom. Consultants were instructed as part of an eight-week course by two college instructors or a two four-day workshop by the program's developmentors. Twenty-seven experimental and twenty-seven control subjects from three school districts were involved. Results indicates the experimentals, in contrast to the controls, significantly increased their proportion of appropriate behavior post-intervention in the next academic year, and required fewer remedial services and special class placements up to three years later. See ERIC Abstract 0462162-2.

3311.   Horak, Willis J. and Roubinek, Darrell L. Dimensions of Elementary Education Students' Attitudes About Classroom Management, Student Trust, and Teacher Discipline. Arizona.

The purpose of this study was to investigate the possibility of identifying groups of basic educational attitudes of pre-service elementary education majors who had few field experiences prior to their taking upper level education courses. The attitudes investigated pertained to beliefs about classroom management, student trust, and teacher discipline. Eight basic factors were delineated. These factors concerned 1) attitudes about social influences on discipline, 2) student responsibilities in school, 3) influences on disciplinary options, 4) teacher respected order, 5) student classroom behavior, 6) school rules enforcement, and 7) student punishment procedures. See ERIC Abstract ED 190499.

3312.   Horne, N. D. and Larrivee, B. "Behavior Rating Scales: Need for Refining Normative Data." Perceptual and Motor Skills, 49, 2 (October, 1979): 383-388.

An attempt was made to generate normative data by grade and sex to accompany behavior rating scales. Teachers rated 483 males and females in grades one through four. Findings suggest that rating scales should be re-examined, since norms by grade level and sex may be desirable attributes. See Eric Abstact 0642465-3.

3313.   Houck, Don. "The Discipline Ladder -- A Strategy for Managing Disruptive Behavior." National Association of Secondary School Principals Bulletin, 65, 441 (January, 1981): 25-28.

This approach emphasizes that each successive offense of the same type should result in punishment made more uncomfortable by designed increments. See ERIC Abstract EJ 238666.

3314.   Howard, Eugene R. and Jenkins, John M. "Improving Discipline in the Secondary School. A catalogue of alternatives to repression." An occasional paper. C.F.K., Limited. (Denver, Colorado) 1970. 15p.

Authors state that the usual approach to improving discipline in schools is the repressive approach -- more rules, stricter enforcement, more efficient pupil surveillance, suspension of privileges, or additional rules imposed by boards of education. School administrators, faced with increased public concern and lacking well-defined alternatives to such repressive measures, tend to accede to public pressure, thereby making matters worse. This paper is designed to serve the educator who wants to take positive rather than negative steps toward improving school discipline. The projects add up to a comprehensive effort to modify the learning environment. Three major parts of the environment are considered in this paper -- the belief in the value system of the school, the communication system of the school, and the manner in which decisions are made within the institution. Significant changes in these important components of the institution should do much to remedy the causes of discipline problems. See ERIC Abstract ED 087090.

3315.   Howard, Judith S. "Systems Intervention and School Psychology." Paper presented at the International Colloquium in School Psychology, Jerusalem, Israel, June, 1980. 32p.

Paper presents an ecological model derived from family systems theory and stategies borrowed from family therapy which are effective substitutes for the medical model and clinical methods traditionally used by school psychologists to help children with behavior problems. Author states that behavior is an outgrowth of inter-personal processes in a particular system rather than the product of a child's interapsychic processes, attitudes, physical defects, or history. The ecological model focuses on problem resolution in the classroom; behavioral changes are promoted through the restructuring of inter-personal transactions in the school environment. Deviant classroom behavior results from and is maintained by the system within the school, which assigns roles and defines behavioral expectations to preserve its own homeostasis. Author proposes that sessions involving the child, teacher, administrator and parents transform adversarial relationships into relationships marked by shared responsibility for mutually desired outcomes. School psychologists are encouraged to abandon their traditional linear approach, which focuses on why behaviors occur, and adopt a systems approach that looks at the what and when of behavior during the conference session to increase their effectiveness in promoting system changes. See ERIC Abstract ED 195879.

3316.   Howard, Rose A. "Middle School Discipline. What Do Teachers Prefer." Clearinghouse, 54, 4 (December, 1980): 155-57.

A study during 1978 involving 194 teachers identified as effective in 21 Kentucky middle schools surveyed techniques that these teachers would use to deal with 15 discipline problems. Agreement on prefered technique was highest for serious infractions. Individual attention was preferred for minor annoyances. Existence of a district discipline code affected teachers' responses.

3317.   Hudgens, John H. "Two Successful Methods for Dealing with Discipline." National Association of Secondary School Principals Bulletin, 63, 430 (November, 1979): 113-114.

Article describes the Richland Northeast High School in Columbia, South Carolina, which has an after school detention program and a Student Supreme Court. Author states that this method is very successful in handling discipline problems. See ERIC Abstract EJ 210896.

3318.   Huff, T. N. and Schnelle, J. F. "Discrimination Between Appropriate and Inappropriate Classroom Behavior by Well-Behaved and Poorly-Behaved Students." Perceptual and Motor Skills, 39, 3 (December, 1974): 1247-1253.

Fourteen well-behaved male fifth, sixth, and seventh graders were compared with sixteen poorly-behaved subjects in ability to point out inappropriate behaviors on a video tape. The subjects' responses were compared to responses made by four teachers who saw the same video tape. Well-behaved and poorly-behaved groups were defined by two different categorization methods: teachers' judgment and behavioral ratings by independent observers. See ERIC Abstract 1236353-6.

3319.   Hughes, Jan. "A Case Study in Behavioral Consultation: Organizational Factors." School Psychology Review, 9, 1 (Winter, 1980): 103-107.

Author states that the external behavior consultant should address several concerns: reducing the threat of outside intervention; meeting staff and administration expectations; supporting school philosophies; maintaining impartiality; and establishing credibility. A case study is presented which illustrates the importance of these organizational factors. See ERIC Abstract EJ 224611.

3320.   Hume, N., O'Connor, W. A. and Lowery, C. R. "Family Adjustment and the Psycho-Social Echo System." Psychiatric Annals, 7, 7 (July, 1977): 32-49.

Families of sixth grade boys rated as either high adjusted or low adjusted in classroom behavior were compared on eleven categories of family environment activity. Results indicate group similarity with regard to constrained time categories but major differences in unconstrained activity. Specifically, low adjusted boys and their fathers spent significantly more time viewing television, while high adjusted boys and their fathers spent significantly more time in interpersonally demading forms of recreation and social activity. See ERIC Abstract 0544764-3.

3321.   Hummel, John H.; and others. "Misbehavior in the Classroom: A Comparison of Two Reinforcement-Based Behavior-Reducing Procedures." Paper presented at the Annual Meeting of the American Educational Research Association, New York, New York, April, 1977. 11p.

Two methods of scheduling reinforcement, differential reinforcement of other behaviors, and differential reinforcement of low rates of responding were investigated in two experiments that demonstrated each procedure's effectiveness in reducing misbehavior when used by teachers in school settings. See ERIC Abstract ED 139513.

3322.   Humphrey, L. L., Karoly, P. and Kirschenbaum, D. S. "Self-Management in the Classroom: Self-Imposed Response Cost Versus Self-Reward." Behavior Therapy, 9, 4 (September, 1978): 592-601.

In the study with eighteen seventh graders, the effects of self-imposed fines were contrasted with effects of self-administered rewards on academic and social classroom behavior. Within the context of a classroom token economy, baseline assessments were followed by the first

self-management phase during which subjects either fined or
rewarded themselves contingent on their academic performance. After a period of program withdrawal, subjects who
had self-rewarded then self-imposed response cost and vice
versa. Results showed that, during self-management phases
relative to baselines, participants improved their reading
rates, engaged in less disruptive behavior, maintained
accurate work on reading papers, and generalized performance
increments to workbook reading. Both self-management
procedures were effective, although self-reward improved
reading rates and workbook performance to a somewhat greater
extent. See ERIC Abstract 0462262-2.

3323.   Hurley, L. "Alternative Education: Another Way." The
NJEA Review, 54, 7 (March, 1981): 18-20.

Author argues for small alternative schools as the solution
for dealing with disruptive, alienated youth. He presents
an outline of basic ingredients necessary to the success of
such a program. He addresses six possible objections to
alternative schools for disaffected students. See ERIC
Abstract EJ 239787.

3324.   Hutt, M. L. and others. "The Predictive Ability of HABGT
Scales for a Male Delinquent Population." Journal of
Personality Assessment, 41, 5 (October, 1977): 492-496.

The Adience-abience and Psychopathology Scales of the Hutt
Adaptation of the Bender-Gestalt Test were administered to
120 adolescent male delinquents. Significant correlations
were obtained between the two scales and recidivism.
Neither scale was high enough though to warrant their use in
prediction. See ERIC Abstract EJ 176591.

3325.   Hyman, I. A. "An Analysis of Studies on the Effectiveness of Training and Staffing to help schools manage student
conflict and alienation. A report." Washington D.C.:
National Institute of Education, 1979.

A search of the literature was made on the effectiveness of
recruitment and selection procedures for identifying and
retaining administrators and school staff who are effective
in managing student conflict and alienation. A classification scheme devised to fit approaches to school discipline
within a theoretical framework includes 1) the psychodynamic-
interpersonal model, 2) the behaviorally model, 3) the
sociological model, 4) the eclectic-ecological model, and 5)
the human potential model. At least one approach within
each model is reviewed. In the first section of the report,
each model is explained and available research studies are
sited. The limitations of the research and applications of
the model are discussed followed by a bibliography. The
next section contains summaries selected programs from 52 of
the largest city districts. The concluding section
discusses the lack of data on both the inservice training
and school administrators and the area of problems of

recruitment, selection, and retention of school staff who
can manage student conflict and alientation. The report
concludes with a summary of the findings, methodological
problems, and suggestions for further research. See ERIC
Abstract ED 176378.

3326.   Hyman, I. A. et al. "Discipline in American Education:
An Overview and Analysis." Journal of Education, 161, 2
(Spring, 1979): 51-70.

This paper integrates information from several areas
regarding the use of discipline in American schools. The
material provides a framework for conceptualizing what
happens when children misbehave. See ERIC Abstract EJ
204026.

3327.   Imber, S. C. "Cooperative Parent-Teacher Strategies for
Managing Behavior Problems of Special Needs Children: A
College Workshop for Parents and Teachers of Exceptional
Children and Youth." Paper presented at the Annual Inter-
national Convention of the Council for Exceptional Children,
Philadelphia, Pennsylvania, 1980.

The author reviews literature supporting the importance of
cooperative parent-teacher relationships for exceptional
children and describes a graduate level course offered at
Rhode Island College on behavior management for parents and
teachers of exceptional children and youth with behavior
problems. Both advantages and problems with offering a
college course on behavior management for parents and
teachers of exceptional children are considered, including
that parents and teachers can explore their feelings about
positive and negative and negative parent-teacher conferences and that special administrative arrangements need to
be made so parents and teachers can take the same course.
See ERIC Abstract ED 187078.

3328.   "Ingraham v. Wright, 498F.2D248 (5th Circuit, 1974)."
Federal Reporter, 2D. Series; 498; 248-291, 1974.

This is a text of a federal appeals court case in which
parents sought damages and injunctive relief as to use of
corporal punishment in a county school system. The evidence
established that use of corporal punishment at one school
violated due process in the constitutional prohibition
against cruel and unusual punishment. See Eric Abstract EJ
105816.

3329.   Jacob, B. and Studer, J. "Secondary Discipline--Where do
Your People Come From." Thrust for Education Leadership, 6,
5 (May, 1977): 16-17.

Author states that the fundamentals of sound secondary
student discipline are embodied in six concepts. He suggests that recognition of these concepts and in enthusiastic

to implement them will have a positive impact on schools. See ERIC Abstract EJ 163707.

3330.   Janis, M. G. and Costello, J.   "The Discovery Room -- Developing an Approach for Teachers to Help Children with Problems in Primary School."   Paper presented at the annual meeting   of   the   American   Orthopsychiatric   Association, Atlanta, Georgia, 1976. 26p.

The discovery room is a mental health oriented primary school   intervention   for   children   with   learning   and behavioral difficulties in the classroom which have been steadily modified over a four year period through accom- modation to real life needs of an inner city school.   A special teacher assigned to the discovery room works with children alone or in pairs for two half hour sessions a week.   Improvement in academic and social functioning is fostered by strengthening child's self image throughwork with varied materials and imaginative play in the context of a close, supportive relationship between the teacher and the child, and positive communication with parents and classroom teacher. See ERIC Abstract ED 137691.

3331.   Jason, L. A. & Ferone, L.   "Behavioral Versus Processed Consultation   Interventions   In   School   Settings."   Americal Journal Of Community Psychology, 6, 6 (December 1978): 531-543.

Teachers who were experiencing difficulties in managing disruptive, acting out children in two parochial first grade classes were provided either behavioral or process consulta- tion.   The behavioral intervention included discussions of behavior   modification   principles,   feedback   concerning contingent   praise,   and   individualized   behavior   interven- tions.   In contrast, the process consultant used clarifying, supportive,   and   reflective   responses   to   help   the   teacher better   understand   classroom   difficulties   and   enhance   the ability   to   work   with   problem   children.   Results   indicated that   during   consultation   sessions   and   followup,   problem behaviors were significantly reduced and attention to desir- able behaviors significantly increased.   See ERIC Abstract 1053363-5.

3332.   Jason, L. A. & Nelson, T.   "Investigating Relationships Between   Problem   Behaviors   and   Environmental   Design." Corrective and Social Psychiatry and Journal of Behavior Technology, Methods and Therapy, 26, 2 (1980):   53-57.

The effects of three physical design variables were investi- gated on problem and non-problem children in a first grade classroom.   Two main hypothesis were that A) Rates of mis- behaviors of problem children increase with larger group size and less teacher supervision and B) the non-problem child's misbehavior rates increase less when group size increases and teacher supervision decreases.   Subjects were two problem males with serious acting out problems and one

non-problem male.   Desirable behaviors included talking with
recognized by teacher, focusing on-task, and leaving seat
with teacher's permission.   Problem behaviors included
emitting a non-permitted sound, focusing off-task, and
leaving seat without permission.   Results support the
hypothesis.   Different children are differentially affected
by organizational - environmental subunits.   Several
methodological shortcomings are noted.   See PSYC Abstract
1120365-5.

3333.   Jason, L. A. and others.   "Evaluating Ecological,
Behavioral, and Process Consultation Interventions."
Journal of School Psychology, 17, 2 (Summer, 1979):
103-115.

This study evaluated differential effectiveness of
conceptually distinct consultation programs (ecological,
behavioral, and process) in inner city elementary schools.
Problem children, evidence seen acting out problems, were
monitored through baseline treatment, and follow-up phases.
Significant reductions in observed and rated behavioral
problems occurred only in classes which provided behavioral
consultation.   See ERIC Abstract EJ 202837.

3334.   Jefferies, D.   "Should We Continue to Deradicalize
Children Through the Use of Counseling Groups."   Educational
Technology, 13, 1 (January, 1973):   45-48.

Author discusses the counseling method used to help students
adjust in school situation.   She presents the pros and cons
to use of counseling groups.

3335.   Jensen, R. E.   "Cooperative Relations Between Secondary
Teachers and Students: Some Behavioral Strategies."
Adolescence, 10, 40 (Winter, 1975):   469-482.

Strategies for classroom control with secondary students,
which are aimed at reciprocal teacher-student cooperation
rather than obedience to teacher authority, are considered.
Group norms, optimizing teacher reinforcement value, and
reducing dysfunctional teacher emotions, are discussed as
the foundation of behavior control.   Basic interventions,
including differential reinforcement, precise communication
and adversive intervention, are presented.   Relational
structuring and re-directing relational process are offered
as advanced strategies.   See ERIC Abstract 1386057-6.

3336.   Jenson, W. R.   "Behavior Modification in Secondary
Schools; Review."   Journal of Research and Development in
Education, 11, 4 (Summer, 1978):   53-63.

Reviews that use of behavior modification to control
behavior problems in secondary schools.   The literature
reviewed demonstrates the effectiveness of behavior modification with average and very difficult students.   It describes
behavioral techniques, such as group contingencies, home

based reinforcement systems and contingency contracting. See ERIC Abstract EJ 189891.

3337.   Jenson, W. R. and Sloane, H. N. "Chart News and Grab Bags: A Simple Contingency Management." Journal of Applied Behavior Analysis, 12, 3 (Fall, 1979): 334.

A record keeping system is described for classroom contingency management proceudres that is neither complex nor time consuming, but that is maintained by the child and gives him or her constant feedback. The teacher randomly allows the child to draw a line between dots on a dot chart when appropriate target behavior is exhibited, thus comprising the first intermittent schedule. Second, only chart news ending on the randomly placed larger dots allow the child to dip into the grab bag, thus programming a schedule. See ERIC Abstract 0206465-1.

3338.   Jett, D. L. and Platt, M. L. "Pupil Attendance: The Bottom Line." National Association of Secondary School Principals Bulletin, 63, 424 (February, 1979): 32-38.

The addition of an attendance clerk and the implementation of a system that stresses the importance of attendance have worked well to reduce absenteeism at North Harford Senior High School in Pylesville, Maryland. See ERIC Abstract EJ 196053.

3339.   Jirak, I. L. "Cool, One School." Education Digest, 37, 6 (February, 1972): 11-14.

The author, an assistant principal of a racially troubled high school, describes means by which administration, teachers, and students worked to eliminate black-white tension. See ERIC Abstract EJ 051177.

3340.   Johnson, C. and others. "Improving Learning Through Peer Leadership." Phi Delta Kappa, 59, 8 (April, 1978): 560.

The peer leadership program decreased student absences, the dropout rate, physical attacks, and vandalism costs, and increased student involvement. See ERIC Abstract EJ 175654.

3341.   Johnson, J. L. & Sloat, K. C. "Teacher Training Effects: Real or Illusory." Psychology in the Schools, 17, 1 (1980): 109-114.

Teachers participated in a course on behavioral approaches in the classroom. Training was conducted in phases: information, instructions to practice, guided practice, coding practice, and performance feedback. Significant increases in positive teacher behaviors and decreases in negative teacher behaviors were observed but were not maintained. See ERIC Abstract EJ 217304.

3342.   Johnson, S. M. "Self-Reinforcement vs. External Reinforcement   in   Behavior   Modification   with   Children."
Developmental Psychology, 3 (1970): 147-148.

The purpose of this study was to examine self-reinforcement
as an agent of behavior change with children who were
deficient and desired attention behaviors. Twenty-three
first and second grade school children were taught through
external reinforcement procedures to raise their level of
attention on a simple discrimination task. One group of
subjects were taught to manage their own reinforcement
contingencies and their performance was compared with that
of a group continued on external reinforcement in a group
for which reinforcement in a group for which reinforcement
was discontinued. Results showed that groups receiving
reinforcement performed at higher levels than the no reinforcement group. Self reinforcement maintained discrimination behavior at a high level and external reinforcement
with no decrement in discrimination accuracy. See ERIC
Abstract ED 065196.

3343.   Johnson, S. O. "Better Discipline for Middle School
Students." Clearinghouse, 53, 2 (October, 1979): 86-89.

The author outlines four causes of classroom discipline
problems: lack of administrative leadership; poor teacher
organization; lack of a basic set of principles for avoiding
disruption; and failure to identify the characteristics of
potentially disruptive students. For each factor, successful practices are identified. See ERIC Abstract EJ 220568.

3344.   Johnson, S. O. "Minorities and Discipline Games." High
School Journal, 63, 5 (February, 1980): 207-208.

Author describes disruptive games that black students play
which lead to fighting. He suggests that these games are
played so students can gain status with their peers. If the
teacher recognizes these games and can learn how to termi-
nate them, some discipline problems can be prevented or
eliminated. See ERIC Abstract EJ 226865.

3345.   Johnson, R. W. "Can Schools Cope with the Chronically
Disruptive Student?" National Association of Secondary
School Principals Bulletin, 63, 428 (September, 1979):
10-15.

An alternative educational program that is highly structured, closely supervised, and appropriately staffed is
proposed for the chronic disruptive student. See ERIC
Abstract EJ 206320.

3346.   Jones, B. T. and Starkey, K. T. "Redefinition of
Counseling Roles in an Alternative School: A Case History."
Paper presented at the annual meeting of the American
Educational Research Association, Washington, D.C. March,
1975.

This paper discussed an alternative school in which the roles of teachers have been redefined to include counseling functions. The counselor is a staff developer for the teachers, a community resource person, and an advocate for students in police court procedures. The psychologist is a staff developer for special techniques, a definer of individualized curricula for students, and an interpreter of test results. Community resources are an integral part of the school. Socially maladjusted youth are helped to build self esteem, a sense of self worth and of interdependence. Group counseling and group projects serve as the basis for the school curriculum. See ERIC Abstract ED 108062.

3347.   Jones, E. Editor. "Joys and Risks in Teaching Young Children as Experienced in Nursery/Kindergarten/Primary Programs at Pacific Oaks." Pacific Oaks College and Childrens School, Pasadena, California. 1978. 167p.

The papers in this collection discuss ideas about children, teachers, and environments for learning which resulted from participation in the "yards" at Pacific Oaks Friends School, an open education environment established by Quakers for preschool, and elementary aged children. Each of the eight articles focuses on either the problem of clarifying the goals of the open classroom or the risks entailed in learning by discovery. The first four papers discuss the meaning of open education, suggest planning and communicating as an emergent curriculum and present results of a follow-up study of the primary students and their transition to other schools. The second group of four papers presents an open education teacher role as an authority with power and explores the teacher intervention used with children's activities. It also presents implications of Piagetian for the development of social consciousness. See ERIC Abstract ED 182005.

3348.   Jones, F. H., Fremouw, W. & Carples, S. "Pyramid Training of Elementary School Teachers To Use A Classroom Management Skill-Package." Journal of Applied Behavior Analysis, 10, 2 (Summer, 1977): 239-253.

Three regular elementary teachers were trained in the use of a classroom management skill-package. Subsequently each of the three teachers trained three more teachers to use the same skill-packet. Direct behavioral measures of student disruptiveness were taken in the classrooms and permanent product measures of student productivity in arithmetic were taken. Student disruptiveness decreased at least as much in the classrooms trained by the second group of teachers as those in the classroom of the first. Also, serving as trainers benefited the teachers who had profited least from the original training by producing further reductions in disruptiveness in their respective classrooms. See ERIC Abstract 1305659-6.

3349.   Jones, N. M. and others. "The Hyperkinetic Child: What do Teachers Know?" Psychology in the Schools, 12, 4 (October, 1975): 388-392.

This article discusses the identification of hyperactive children. Author suggests that if school personnel use their expertise to identify hyperactive children in the classroom and begin behavioral intervention programs at the earliest possible time, medical referral and treatment will be unnecessary. See ERIC Abstract EJ 127407.

3350.   Jones, P. and Garner, A. E.   "A Comparison of Middle School Teachers' Pupil Control Ideology." Clearinghouse, 51, 6 (February, 1978): 292-294.

Authors compare pupil control ideology -- discipline policy -- of middle school classroom teachers with the intent of finding what attributes are needed for middle school teachers and the particular type classroom environment that facilitates optimum learning conditions for middle school children. See ERIC Abstract EJ 180781.

3351.   Jones, R. T. and Evans, H. L.   "Self-Reinforcement: A Continuum of External Cues." Journal of Educational Psychology, 72, 5 (October, 1980): 625-635.

Following trials in which children self administered prizes, subjects in the stringent-demand group perform significantly better, during both the incentive and the extinction conditions, on time on-task, number of correct problems, and number of problems attempted, than did subjects in lenient demand and control groups. See ERIC Abstract EJ 237876.

3352.   Jorgenson, G. W.   "Relationship of Classroom Behavior To The Accuracy Of The Match Between Material Difficulty and Student Ability." Journal of Educational Psychology, 69, 1 (February, 1977): 24-32.

Examined in this study were the level of difficulty of material used for reading instruction with seventy-one second through sixth graders, and the relationship between the material difficulty and student ability level difference scores and classroom adjustment. Readability formulas determined material difficulties; individual reading tests determined ability levels. Subjects tended not to receive instruction in material at a level of difficulty equal to their tested ability. Material difficulty/ability level difference scores were significantly related to classroom adjustment: Behavior improved as the material became easier for the subjects. Less accurately matched material therefore tended to be related to improve behavior. Unexpected relationships thus exist between classroom behavior and level of difficulty of instructional material. See ERIC Abstract 0613558-3.

3353.   Joseph, P. B. "Parents and Teachers: Partners in Values Education." Social   Education, 43, 6 (October, 1979): 477-478.

Author considers how elementary social studies teachers view the earlier values development their students receive in the home. She discusses the influence of parents, the modeling process, discipline, parents as teachers, and proposes a cooperative parent-teacher project for values education. See ERIC Abstract EJ 208595.

3354.   Jury, L. E., Willower, D. J. and Delacy, W. J. "Teacher Self Actualization and Pupil Control Ideology." Alberta Journal of Educational Research, 21, 4 (December, 1975): 295-301.

The prediction that level of teacher self actualization would be directly related to humanism in teacher pupil control ideology was supported by data gathered from 272 public school teachers. Subjects were administered the Personal Orientation Inventory and the Pupil Control Ideology Form. Expected differences in the pupil control ideology of elementary and secondary teachers were found, but level of self actualization was not significantly different for teachers grouped dichotomously according to sex, grade levels taught, or experience. See ERIC Abstract 0145156-1.

3355.   Kaczmarek, M. A. and Levine, E. S. "Expansion Training: A Counseling Stance for the Withdrawn Rigid Child." Elementary School Guidance and Counseling, 15, 1 (October, 1980): 31-38.

Authors explain expansion training which is a modeling technique for counseling withdrawn children, using behavioral and humanistic principles. The child in the case study learned assertive behavior to cope with frustration and mistakes. Good rapport between child and counselor are necessary for success. See ERIC Abstract EJ 233767.

3356.   Kafry, D. "Fire Play and Fire Setting of Young Children." Paper presented at the Annual Convention of the American Psychology Association, Montreal, Canada, September, 1980. 24p.

Variables related to children's interest in and play experiences with fire and fire producing materials were explored. Information was obtained from samples of public school children and their parents. Seventy boys and sixtynine girls took part in the study. Data were assembled through interviews and evaluations. Findings indicate that 37 children had played with fire and had burnt different items. One half of the burning behavior was done intentionally. In order to analyze fire play in detail, five categories of reported involvement in these episodes were formed. The five groups were then compared in terms of

family background, child characteristics and child preference. Findings indicate that fire playing, fire setting,
accident prone, hyperactive and delinquent children show
very similar behavioral and personality patterns to each
other, as well as similar family conditions and that playing
with matches was found to be related to problem areas in
children's lives. See ERIC Abstract ED 196524.

3357.   Kaltsounis, B. and Higdon, G. "Black Teachers; Perceptions of the Ideal Pupil." Perceptural and Motor Skills,
45, 3, Part II (December, 1977): 1071-1075.

The Ideal Child Checklist was administered to seventy-six
black elementary school teachers. A comparison of their ten
most and least valued traits with those of experts on the
creativity personality showed that the two groups agreed
only once on the ten most valued traits and three times on
the ten least valued traits. See ERIC Abstract 0193461-1.

3358.   Kamp, B. W. "Stability of Behavior Ratings." Perceptual
and Motor Skills, 43, 3 (December, 1976): 1065-1066.

Significant correlations were obtained between teachers'
ratings of behavior on the school behavior checklist in two
consecutive primary grades for 246 males. The Boehm Test of
Basic Concepts was also administered. Ratings on the aggressive subscale of the checklist were significantly higher
than for other subskills. See ERIC Abstract 0432658-2.

3359.   Kaplan, B. L. "Classroom Discipline is More Than
Technique." Elementary School Journal, 73, 5 (February,
1973): 244-250.

The social psychology of discipline in the classroom is
discussed in this article. According to the role theory of
behavior, the individual child acts fairly consistently in a
number of specific situations in his or her environment to
establish a certain role. When inconsistencies or conflicts
occur in the role, the subject develops some form of
activity to make that role as consonant as possible. Reinforcement of that role is crucial to its continuance. The
misbehaving child usually considers, at least partially, the
social reinforcement to his behavior. Misbehaviors can be
frequently interpreted as a bid for a certain form of leadership in the group processes. A chart is presented illustra-
ting pupils' feelings in term of positive, ambivalent, and
negative orientations. Corresponding active performances
are: being an initiator and seeking out successful actions,
being a competitor and fluctuating between success and
failure, and being a disrupter. Corresponding passive
performances are: being a compliant follower, being a fence
sitter, and being a withdrawer. See ERIC Abstract
0574550-3.

3360.   Kaplan, P. J. "Sex, Age, Behavior, and School Subjects as Determinants of Report of Learning Problems." <u>Journal of Learning Disabilities</u>, <u>10</u>, 5 (May, 1977): 314-316.

Researcher asked 280 undergraduates to establish priorities for assigning tutorial help to children failing in school. Subjects were administered a questionnaire on which they rated the children on the basis of various combinations of sex, age, kind of behavior problems and subject of school difficulty. Results who the variable selected for top priority were boys, the older child, acting out behavior, and difficulty in reading. Variables of lowest priority were girls, the younger child, withdrawn behavior and difficulty in arithmetic. The child's sex interacted with type of behavior in such a way that withdrawn boys and acting out girls -- both deviations from the norm -- were considered to need more help than children whose behavior conformed to the norm for their sex. See ERIC Abstract 0668359-3.

3361.   Kaplan, William. "Rebellion Against Authority in High Schools." National Council of Crime and Delinquency, Hackensack, New Jersey. Newgate Resource Center, Department of Health, Education and Welfare, Washington, D.C. 1978. 37p.

This paper examines rebellion against authority in high school from the perspective of school status theories. Extending such theories beyond concern with the immediate response to academic status and structural inequality, this paper addresses the broader issue of legitimacy of authority in high school. Using data from a state wide sample of 3,100 adolescents in Illinois, the paper also examines the process of peer support for rebellious behavior. See ERIC Abstract ED 157185.

3362.   Karpowitz, D. H. "Reinstatement as a Method to Increase the Effectiveness of Discipline in the School or Home." <u>Journal of School Psychology</u>, <u>15</u>, 3 (Fall, 1977): 230-238.

In this study, 90 first grade boys who left their seats and played with toys in a tempting situation were assigned randomly to one of three conditions of reinstatement: minimal reinstatement, verbal reinstatement, or verbal and behavior reinstatement. Half of each group received mild discipline, the other half, no discipline. Discipline was defined as the withdrawal of physical resource (a marble) and a verbal rebuke. Reinstatement was defined as the detailed rehearsal of the undesirable behavior sequence. After an intervening task, the subjects were placed in the tempting situation again, and time before playing with some toys was recorded. Results confirmed two hypotheses and do not confirm two others: A) discipline was significantly more effective than no discipline, B) reinstatement significantly increased the effectiveness of discipline, C) discipline with verbal and behavioral reinstatement was no more effective than discipline with verbal reinstatement alone. Verbal reinstatement and verbal plus behavioral reinstatement were no more inhibiting than minimal reinstatement when followed by no discipline. See ERIC Abstract 1025760-5.

3363.   Kaufman, Alans and others. "Dimensions of Problem Behaviors of Emotionally Disturbed Children as Seen by Their Parents and Teachers." Psychology in the Schools, 16, 2 (April, 1979): 207-217.

This study compared the factor structure of parents' and teachers' ratings of childrens' behavior problems. Data were analyzed for heterogeneous group of 194 emotionally disturbed boys and girls age 3-13 years. Three factors emerged based on parent ratings, and highly similar factors were obtained from teacher ratings. See ERIC Abstract EJ 200810.

3364.   Kelley, E. A. "Developing a Lesson Plan for Classroom Discipline." Action in Teacher Education, 1, 2 (Fall-Winter, 1978): 41-45.

Preventing classroom discipline problems requires planning and a willingness to seriously examine and change regularized classroom and school policies and procedures. Specific, practical steps to provide teachers with more control in a positive learning environment are offered. See ERIC Abstract EJ 197175.

3365.   Kelton, D. "Confrontation Resolution Without Sacrifice." Academic Therapy, 11, 4 (Summer, 1976): 481-484.

A strategy is described for teachers to use in a crisis type confrontation with a student, which every teacher experiences at one time or another. There are two obvious alternatives in such a situation, neither satisfactory: the child may be sacrificed to the teacher's authority or the teacher's authority may be sacrificed. A third alternative is suggested, in which the teacher offers an objective, non-emotional reply designed to alleviate tension and deflate hostility. Diverting the class back to work, the teacher then manages as quickly as possible a brief, private conversation with the student; depending on his response, he is returned to the classroom and the incident is followed up later, or he is sent to a third party not emotionally involved in the situation. See ERIC Abstract 0198557-1.

3366.   Kennedy, J. J., Cruickshank, D. R. and Myers, B. "Problems of Beginning Secondary Teachers in Relations to School Location." Journal of Educational Research, 69, 5 (January, 1976): 167-172.

The perceived problems of beginning secondary teachers were examined, grouped on the basis of school location, inner city, outer city, suburban, and rural. One hundred and fifty-nine beginning teachers indicated whether certain specific classroom problems occurred frequently and if such problems were bothersome. These responses were factor analyzed, producing six factors for both frequency and bothersomeness data. Factor scores associated wition, professional authonomy, and control. See ERIC Abstract 0132956-1.

3367.   Kennedy, James and others. "A Day School Approach to Aggressive Adolescents." Child Welfare, 55, 10 (December, 1976): 712-724.

In day school for aggressive adolescents organized coopera- tively by a school system, a youth guidance center and a state hospital in providing an alternative to institution- alization. Education and therapy are combined in a suppor- tive setting. See ERIC Abstract EJ 155512.

3368.   Kent, R. N. and O'Leary, K. D. "A Controlled Evaluation of Behavior Modification With Conduct Problem Children." Journal of Consulting and Clinical Psychology, 44, 4 (August, 1976): 586-596.

A behavioral intervention program was evaluated for conduct problem children with both behaviorial and academic difficulties in elementary school. Sixteen subjects were assigned to either a treatment or a no contact control group. A standardized twenty hour treatment program involving the child, parents, and the teacher was provided by clinical psychologists. Both observational recordings and teacher ratings of social and academic behavior demon- strated that significantly greater behavioral improvement occurred for treated than for controlled children. However, at a nine month follow-up, the controlled group had improved sufficiently that these differences were no longer signifi- cant. See ERIC Abstract 0840356-5.

3369.   Kent, R. N. & O'Leary, K. D. "Treatment of Conduct Problem Children: B.A. and/or Ph.D. Therapists." Behavior Therapy, 8, 4 (September, 1977): 653-658.

A treatment program successfully implemented by clinical psychologist was evaluated when that model was implemented with a B.A.-Ph.D. team versus Ph.D.'s alone. Twenty-three second through fourth graders with conduct disorders were treated during a 20-hour consultation program designed to produce change in classroom behaviors. Evaluation measures included classroom observations, teacher ratings, the California Achievement Tests, reading and math sections, and school grades. Results indicate that treated children improved more than non-treated children, although the treat- ment effects were not different whether the treatment was implemented by the B.A.-Ph.D. team or the Ph.D.'s alone. See ERIC Abstract 0415260-2.

3370.   Kerlin, M. A. and Latham, W. L. "Intervention Effects of
a Crisis Resource Program." Exceptional Children, 44, 1,
(September, 1977): 32-34.

Twenty-one eight through twelve year old low socio economic
black males exhibiting problem behaviors were randomly
assigned to one of three groups. Pre and post crisis
resource intervention scores on observed classroom behavior
and the Walker Problem Behavior Identification Checklist
showed significant differences in social behavior among
subjects in the experimental groups. See Eric Abstact
0396260-2.

3371.   Kern, C. R. "Discipline for the 80's -- Techniques for
the rocky road ahead." National Association for Secondary
School Principals Bulletin, 64, 436 (May, 1980): 121-123.

Author emphasizes that parent and educators must join forces
if school discipline in the 1980's is to improve. See ERIC
Abstract #EJ 221634.

3372.   Kersten, T. A. "Focus on discipline: an in-service
program." National Association of Secondary School
Principals Bulletin, 63, 428 (September, 1979): 59-62.

In-service programs can help teachers learn to deal more
effectively with classroom discipline problems. See ERIC
Abstract #EJ 206329.

3373.   Kidder, S. J. & Guthrie, J. T. "The Training Effects of
a Behavior Modification Game." Washington, D.C.: Office of
Education, Department of Health, Education and Welfare,
1971.

A game designed to teach some of the skills used in behavior
modification with slow learners was evaluated. The game,
called "modifying," was developed to increase the range of
experience for students preparing to be special education
teachers. A randomized, posttest only design was employed.
The design incorporated 3 treatments: conventional lecture,
game and short discussion, and game with longer discussion
and replay of the game. Two measures of the treatments;
effects were utilized: a situation test of a special
education classroom and a performance test which required
each subject to teach a special education child a simple
paper construction task using behavior modification. See
Eric Abstact ED 057613.

3374.   Kilburn, J. "Better for both -- thoughts on teacher-
pupil interaction." Education, 6, 2 (October, 1978): 3-13.

Presented in this article is a simple model to remove the
adversary emphasis from pupil-teacher interactions. It
shows how an intervention can protentially make a situation
better, worse, or unchanged for the pupil and the teacher.
A sample scenario is provided by two teachers dealing with a

misbehaving child.   See ERIC Abstract #EJ 199008.

3375.   Kilmann, P. R.; et al.   "The impact of affective
education on elementary school under-achievers." Psychology
in the Schools, 16, 2 (April, 1979): 217-223.

The purpose of this study was to examine the impact of
affective education on elementary school under-achievers who
were referred by their teachers for behavior problems or
randomly selected for treatment.   The experimental subjects
showed a greater increase in readying skills, and were more
warm hearted, emotionally stable, venturesome, and vigorous
after the group experience. See ERIC Abstract #EJ 200811.

3376.   Kincaid, W. H.   "Tips for a student discipline program."
National   Association   of   Secondary   School   Principals
Bulletin, 63, 428 (September, 1979): 16-18.

An effective discipline program requires times, effort, and
commitment   from   school   administrators.   Guidelines   are
presented. See ERIC Abstract #EJ 206321.

3377.   King, A. J. C. and Ripton, R. A.   "The school in
transition: A profile of a secondary school undergoing
innovation."   The   Ontario   Institute   for   Studies   in
Education, Toronto, Ontario. 1970. 52p.

The impact of four school innovations is examined from the
students' point of view, the teachers' reaction, and the
changes wrought in guidance services and administrative
functions.   Teacher and student reaction was generally
favorable to the individualization brought about by personal
timetabling, subject promotion, a credit system, and a more
student-centered   approach   to   discipline   policy.   Most
dissatisfaction expressed by teachers, guidance personnel,
and administrators stemmed from the increased clerical work
and from changes in their respective roles necessitated by
the new procedures. See ERIC Abstract #ED 040502.

3378.   Kingston, A. J. and Gentry, H. W.   Discipline problems:
then and now. University of Georgia. 1974, 14p.

This paper compares data collected in a 1974 survey of
discipline problems in Georgia secondary schools with data
from a similar survey conducted by the same investigators in
1961.   The earlier survey looked at 20 types of student
misbehavior that had been identified in earlier studies.
The later study included those 20 plus 13 additional items.
341 Georgia secondary school principals received the
questionnaire. 78% of those responded.   The most common
types of student misbehavior in 1961 were also the most
common in 1974.   This paper includes a number of data tables
that summarize responses to both surveys and facilitate
comparisons between them. See ERIC Abstract #ED 117811.

3379.   Kingston, A. J. and Gentry, H. W. "Discipline problems in Georgia secondary schools -- 1961 and 1974." National Association of Secondary School Principals Bulletin, 61, 406 (February, 1977): 94-99.

Article compares data on discipline in Georgia secondary schools that were gathered in similar surveys of secondary school principals in 1961 and 1974. See ERIC Abstract #EJ 160396.

3380.   Kirschenbaum, D. S.; et al. "The effectiveness of a mass screening procedure in an early intervention program." Psychology in the Schools, 14, 4 (October, 1977): 400-406.

Mass screening consisted primarily of teachers rating the frequency of all primary grade childrens' acting-out, moody-withdrawn, and learning problem behaviors. The mass screening procedures that were employed is discussed as an effective procedure and suggestions are offered which could increase its utility. See ERIC Abstract #EJ 169369.

3381.   Kirschner, N. M. and Levin, L. "A Direct School Intervention Program for the Modification of Aggressive Behavior." Psychology in the Schools, 12, 2 (April, 1975): 202-208.

This article presents an intervention program for modifying aggressive behavior by elementary school children. It includes positive reinforcement, behavioral rehearsal, and modeling. It also reports a study that measured the effectiveness of these techniques. See ERIC Abstract 0137155-1.

3382.   Klein, A. R. and Young, R. D. "Hyperactive Boys in Their Classroom: Assessment of Teacher and Peer Perceptions, Interactions, and Classroom Behaviors." Journal of Abnormal Child Psychology, 7, 4 (December, 1979): 425-442.

A comparison using multi-variables analysis and plan comparisons was made on teacher ratings, peer perceptions, peer interactions, and classroom behaviors of 17 hyperactive and 17 active first, second, and third grade boys, nominated by their teachers. Hyperactive subjects were significantly different from active subjects on measures from all data sources in that they perceived and interacted more negatively. Cluster analysis of teacher ratings of 90 hyperactives from a clinical sample and 17 hyperactives from the current sample were used to discriminate among different types of hyperactives. Four types were identified: anxious, conduct problem, inattentive, and low problem hyperactives. See ERIC Abstract 0348665-2.

3383.   Knafle, J. D. "The relationship of behavior ratings to grades earned by female high school students." Journal of Educational Research, 66, 3 (November, 1972): 106-110.

A study was made of the relationship of classroom behavior to grades in specific subject areas. Four hundred and forty-one tenth and eleventh grade black girls served as subjects. Good behavior ratings were found to accompany good marks in all subjects areas studied and unsatisfactory behavior ratings were found to accompany failing marks in all subject areas except foreign language. Teachers who gave favorable behavior ratings also tended to give higher rades than teachers who gave unfavorable behavior ratings. Social studies teachers gave the highest proportion of excellent behavior ratings, and English teachers gave the highest proportion of unsatisfactory behavior ratings. See ERIC Abstract 1197149-6.

3384.   Knaus, W. "Rational, emotive education." _Theory into Practice;_ 16, 4 (October, 1977): 251-255.

Rational, emotive education -- an outgrowth of theories developed by Albert Ellis -- is a teaching design of mental health concepts and problem solving activities designed to help students to approach and cope with their problems through experiential learning, via a structured, thematic sequence of emotive education lessons. See ERIC Abstract #EJ 178623.

3385.   Knight, C. W. II and Dunkleberger, G. E. "Early adolescence." _Science and Children,_ 18, 3 (November-December, 1980): 38-39.

Authors discuss several teacher leadership strategies which may be used to circumvent disruptive pupil behavior and maintain effective student control in the science classroom. Strategies include starting and closing procedures for each class period and late assignment policies. See ERIC Abstract #EJ 235175.

3386.   Koch, L. and Breyer, N. L. "A token economy for the teacher." _Psychology in the Schools,_ 11, 2 (April, 1974): 195-200.

The researchers explored the effects of a simple token economy that used a group contingency in a regular class setting. Subjects included twenty-eight fifth graders in a language arts section. Points were given to a group if all the subjects were doing on task behaviors at the time of the observation. It is concluded that the intervention condition was functionally related to higher percentages of appropriate classroom behaviors. See ERIC Abstract 1314752-6.

3387.   Koester, L. S. and Farley, F. H. "Arousal and hyperactivity in open and traditional education." Paper presented at the Annual Convention of the American Psychological Association, San Francisco, California, August, 1977.

Farley's theory of arousal and stimulation-seeking proposes specific educational alternatives for high and low arousal

and hyperkinetic children. This study tested the prediction
that open classrooms provide children at the lower end of
the physiological arousal continuum with enough external
stimulation to reduce their overt seeking of stimulation.
The reduced level of external stimulation in traditional
classrooms was predicted to be more suitable for high
arousal children. 98 subjects were used in 3 open and 3
traditional classrooms. They were observed and tested on
both physiological and performance measures at the beginning
and end of their first year of school. Results indicated
that observers and teachers identified behavior problems
more readily in traditional classrooms, with clearly
differentiated norms, than in open classrooms, in which a
wider range of behavior is tolerated. Children in the open
classrooms took longer to complete tasks and made fewer
errors at both times of testing. Data analyzed for subgroups of children representing extremes of the arousal
level continuum revealed an interesting pattern: high
arousal children showed performance decrements over time in
the open classroom. See ERIC Abstract #ED 155543.

3388.   Kohl, H. "Insight: crime and punishment." Teacher, 97,
4, (January, 1980): 8,12,16.

Author describes a jury trial involving intermediate grade
students as defendents, lawyers, and jury, with an adult as
judge. It is suggested that it is important to deal with
serious offenses at school in a democratic way that involves
students in decision making. See ERIC Abstract #EJ 226823.

3389.   Kohl, H. "Insight: a fair trial." Teacher, 97, 8
(May-June, 1980): 12-16.

In the January, 1980 issue of Teacher, the author proposed
handling discipline problems through classroom trials. In
this article, he expands on that scenario in response to
critics worried about the civil rights of the child on
trial, guarantees of fairness, and the role of the
defendent's parents. See ERIC Abstract #EJ 229355.

3390.   Kohl, H. "Insight: limits and symbols." Teacher, 98, 2
(September, 1980): 22-24.

The author states that metaphorical, physical examples can
sometimes help children understand psychological situations,
particulary those concerned with limits, more effectively
and with less embarrassment than a direct discussion of
behavior. See ERIC Abstract #EJ 229476.

3391.   Kohut, S. "Defining Discipline in the Classroom."
Action in Teacher Education, 1, 2 (Fall-Winter, 1978):
11-15.

A definition of school discipline and the dilemma faced by
teachers in making decisions about school behavior are
presented. The problem and dilemma are complex; and several

alternative philosophies and practices are available. See ERIC Abstract EJ 197172.

3392.   Kok, M, E.D.; et al. "Team leadership training in vocational special needs." Proceedings: Annual Statewide Conference on Vocational Special Needs, College Station, Texas, April, 1979. 79p.

These proceedings of a statewide Texas conference focus on the need for cooperation between the leadership from the fields of special and vocational education in order to meet the needs of handicapped students. Many sessions reported cover practical approaches in training dealing with safety, learning opportunities for teachers in mainstreaming, motivation, attitudes, and discipline. See ERIC Abstract #ED 194787.

3393.   Konarski, E. A., Johnson, M. R. and Crowell, C. R. "Response Deprivation and Reinforcement in Applied Settings: A Preliminary Analysis." Journal of Applied Behavior Analysis, 13, 4 (Winter, 1980): 595-609.

Two experiments are discussed in this article. In each, two first graders engaged in seat work behaviors under reinforcement schedules based on the Premack principle and the response deprivation hypothesis. Schedules were presented in a counter balanced fashion that fulfilled the conditions of one, both, or neither of the hypothesis. Duration of on-task math and coloring in experiment one and on-task math and reading in experiment two were the dependent variables. A modified A-B-A withdrawal design, including a control for the non-contingent effect of the schedule, indicated an increase of on-task instrumental responding only in those schedules were response deprivation was present regardless of the probability differential between the instrumental and contingent responses. Results were consistent with laboratory findings supporting the necessity of response deprivation for producing the reinforcement effect in single response instrumental schedules. See ERIC Abstract 0633065-3.

3394.   Kourilsky, M. and Hirshleifer, J. "Mini society versus token economy: an experimental comparison of the effects of learning in autonomy of socially emergent and imposed behavior modification." Journal of Educational Research, 69, 10 (July-August, 1976): 376-381.

Researchers compared the effects of two teacher training programs designed to emphasize one of two forms of behavior modification in teaching economics to three hundred and eight-seven students in grades four, five, and six. Twenty teachers were trained in the mini society techniques (socially emergent behavior modification); while half were trained to prevent such conversion. Three tests measured effects of the different techniques upon improvements in economic understanding and upon autonomy. While both techniques of instruction yielded significant improvements in economic understanding, the results of the socially emergent behavior modification were significantly superior to those achieved by the imposed behavior modification. See ERIC Abstract 0194357-1.

3395.   Krajewski, R. J. "Implications of a rank ordering process by elementary principals." Paper presented at the Annual Meeting of the National Association of Elementary School Principals, Las Vegas, Nevada, April, 1977.

To obtain a realistic understanding of the supervisory role perception of the elementary principal, a ten-item questionnaire was sent to 400 elementary principals and teachers in Texas. They rank ordered both real and ideal role dimensions and agreed that the role is not what it should be. Principals served mainly as disciplinarians, but do not wish to do so. Both principals and teachers want the principal's role as instructional and curriculum supervisory to be more pronounced than it presently is. See ERIC Abstract #ED 140468.

3396.   Krippner, S. "The Churchill school: an alternative to drug treatment for hyperactive children." Paper presented at the Annual Meeting of the College Reading Association, Bethesda, Maryland, October, 1974. 13p.

This paper presents a discussion of the Churchill School, which is an alternative approach to serving the educational needs of children diagnosed as hyperactive, hyperkinectic, brain-damaged, neurologically impaired, or suffering from minimal brain dysfunction. The program attempts to be wholistic in nature, utilizing three programs which present alternatives to drugs for the treatment of hyperactive children. The first program, perceptual-motor training, is eclectic in nature and includes several components. The second program, orthomolecular medicine, is described and reference is made to research in mega-vitamin therapy. The third program, the open classroom approach, is described as an attempt to channel each pupil's hyperactivity into constructive pursuits. See ERIC Abstract #ED 103751.

3397.   Kritek, W. J. "Teachers' concerns in a desegregated school in Milwaukee." Integrated Education, 17, 1-2 (January-April, 1979): 19-24.

The concerns of teachers in a recently desegregated elementary school include: 1) problems from busing, 2) unfamiliar behavior among black children, with whom white teachers have not had previous experience, 3) disadvantaged family and educational background, 4) maintanance of discipline, and 5) wide range of achievement levels among students. See ERIC Abstract #EJ 218831.

3398.   Kupietz, S. S. and Richardson, E. "Children's vigilance performance and inattentiveness in the classroom." Journal of Child Psychology and Psychiatry and Allied Disciplines, 19, 2 (April, 1978): 145-154.

Authors tested the hypothesis that vigilance performance is related to children's attentiveness in a classroom setting. Sixteen children with the mean age of ten years, were administered an auditory and visual vigilance task, and their performance was assessed in relation to their off-task behavior in a classroom. In addition, the relationship of vigilance performance to teacher ratings of the children's behavior and reading achievement scores was also assessed. Vigilance errors were significantly, positively correlated with off-task behavior. Findings support the general hypothesis. See ERIC Abstract 0203163-1.

3399.   Kurdek, L. A. "Relationship between cognitive perspective taking and teachers' ratings of children's classroom behavior in grades one through four." Journal of Genetic Psychology, 132, 1, (March 1978): 21-27.

Explored in this study was the relationship between cognitive perspective taking and teachers' ratings of classroom behavior of ninety-six first through fourth graders. Good cognitive perspective taking skill was related to classroom behaviors that involved active peer interactions, particularly fighting and quarreling. It is suggested that although the present evidence suggests that cognitive perspective taking may be a cognitive pre-requisite for various social behaviors, the investigation of the length between social cognition and social behavior would proceed more fruitfully if the motivational systems underlying the social behavior of interest were identified and assessed.

3400.   Ladd, E. T. and Walden, J. C. "Students' rights and discipline." National Association of School Principals, Arlington, Virginia. 1975. 74p.

This book clarifies what one should keep in mind and to describe what courses of action are open when one confronts a particular situation. It is stated that teachers and principals encounter discipline problems not because they are deficient in skill or in virture, but because they have inherited misleading definitions of their respective roles. What schools must do, may do, and may not do about disciplining is a matter of the governing of children. Chapters deal with the legal basis for student governance, fundamentals of governance -- definitions, norms and influence measures; the application of norms and compliance devices to different situations; the leadership role of the principal in the governance, governance tasks that trouble teachers and how principals can help, the ways to talk with students when there has been trouble, major offenses, and some considerations in building a governance program. The appendices provide a list of students rights, a suggested list of important elemental norms for public elementary schools, and a list of basic influence procedures. See ERIC Abstract #ED 109773.

3401.   Lagreca, A. N. and Santogrossi, D. A. "Social skills training with elementary school students: a behavioral group approach." Journal of Consulting and Clinical Psychology, 48, 2, (April, 1980): 220-227.

Skills training children demonstrated increased skill in a role/play situation, a greater verbal knowledge of how to interact with peers, and more initiation of pure actions in school compared to children in the attention-placebo and waiting-list control. See ERIC Abstract #EJ 225024.

3402.   Lahey, B. B.; et al. "On the independence of ratings of hyperactivity, conduct problems, and attention deficits in children: a multiple regression analysis." Journal of Consulting and Clinical Psychology, 48, 5 (October, 1980): 566-574.

Findings from this study argue against the existence of a separate diagnostic category of hyperactivity. Hyperactivity and conduct-problem scales should be combined for purposes of rating child behavior problems. A category of "attention deficit disorder without hyperactivity" should be considered as a separate rating scale factor. See ERIC Abstract #EJ 233781.

3403.   Lahey, B. B., Green, K. D. and Forehand, R. "On the independence of ratings of hyperactivity, conduct problems, and attention deficits in children: a multiple regression analysis." Journal of Consulting and Clinical Psychology, 48, 5 (October, 1980): 566-574.

Teacher ratings, direct observational measures, and peer evaluations were obtained on a hundred and nine third grade children. Factor scores on the Conners Teacher Rating Scale were correlated with the following measures: observation of time on task; frequency of teacher interaction; positive and negative peer interaction; peer ratings of acceptance, rejection, and dislike; and three measures of academic performance. Arguments were made for combining hyperactivity and conduct problem scales in rating child behavior problems. See ERIC Abstract 1342664-6.

3404.   Lahey, B. B., McNees, M. P. and McNees, N. C. "Control of an obscene "Verbal Tic" through timeout in the elementary school classroom." Journal of Applied Behavior Analysis, 6, 1 (Spring, 1973): 101-104.

In this experiment the behavior of a ten year old boy was modified. He had a high rate of obscene vocalization accompanied by facial twitches. In the first phase, the teacher instructed the subject to repeat rapidly the most frequent obscene word in four daily fifteen minute session.

This procedure reduced the frequency of obscene vocalizations but not to an acceptable level. Subsequently, the
teacher was able affectly to control the target behavior
using a timeout procedure. See ERIC Abstract 0991950-5.

3405.   Lamb, P. H. and Jacobi, C. L. "Taking Action Toward
Better Discipline: Shared Role for the Schools and
Universities." Kappa Delta Pi Record, 17, 3 (February,
1981): 83-84.

The authors suggest that teachers, colleges and schools
should cooperate in putting some emphasis on discipline
training for perspective and new teachers. Objectives for
such training are listed. See ERIC Abstract EJ 241693.

3406.   Lambert, B. G. "Behavior clinics: A method to change
attitudes." Paper presented at the Annual Convention of the
National Association of Student Personnel Administrators,
Dallas, Texas, March, 1976. 7p

Paper discusses behavior clinics which are now being used in
a urban-rural area of five secondary schools as substitutes
for suspension. Infractions of school rules, which can lead
to placement in the behavior clinic are: truancy, fighting,
use of obscene language, smoking, disrespectfullness, and/or
suspension. During the 1975-76 school year, a random sample
of 50 students in Junior and Senior high school were
studied. The rating scale SPAT (school-pupil-attitude-
teacher) and SPAS (school-pupil-attitude-student) were
constructed. Results indicate that both teachers and
students feel that behavior clinics are worthwhile and
beneficial. See ERIC Abstract #ED 140129.

3407.   Landis, D., Triandis, H. C., and Adamopoulos, J. "Habit
and behavioral intentions as predictors of social behavior."
Journal of Social Psychology, 106, 2 (December, 1978):
227-237.

Researchers assessed the relative impact of habit and
behavioral inattentions in predicting classroom teacher
behavior, using a model proposed by Triandis. Responses
from a behavioral differential and two hours of classroom
observations were taken on seventy-seven male and female
black and white junior high school teachers. Results
indicate that habit was the more potent predictor of classroom behavior than intentions. See ERIC Abstract 0641764-3.

3408.   Lane, J. and Muller, D. "The effect of altering self-
descriptive behavior on self-concept and classroom
behavior." Journal of Psychology, 97, 1 (September, 1977):
115-125.

Researchers examined the impact of operant reinforcement of
positive self-descriptive behavior on the self-concepts and
classroom behavior of sixty fifth graders. Three groups of
ten male and ten female low self-concept students wrote a

series of eight essays describing their school performance. The first group received written reinforcement for positive self-descriptions of their school performance. The second group received an equal number of reinforcements for general statements. The third group received no reinforcement for written statements. Three areas of self-concept were measured with the primary self-concept inventory: personal-self, social-self, and intellectual-self. A frequency count was also made of nine classroom behaviors thought to be influenced by self-concept. See ERIC Abstract 1314559-6.

3409.   Laneve, R. S. "Presentation: Disruptive Students." A paper presented at the National Association of Secondary School Principals, Miami, Florida, January, 1980.

This paper discusses how to deal with disruptive students. Aspects considered include the role of schools in America, a look through the student's eyes, the parents, and family, and the educator's role. Several techniques that have been successful in working with disruptive students are described, including defining what can and cannot be changed, determining what else is going on in the student's life, communicating with the student, teaching the student to deal with conflict, extending special school privileges to disruptive students and setting a firm commitment for the student. See ECER 124257.

3410.   Langhorne, J. E. Jr., et al. "An alternative teacher consultation model: a case study." School Psychology Digest, 8, 2 (Spring, 1979): 235-240.

The case history presented in this paper describes intervention techniques used with a nine year old male with behavior problems. The procedures used were classroom observation and teacher consultation, drug withdrawal, direct consulted intervention, and class change and follow-up. See ERIC Abstract #EJ 207368.

3411.   Lansdorf, R. et. al. "Ethnicity, social class, and perception of hyperactivity." Psychology in the schools, 16, 2 (April, 1979): 293-298.

Studied by these researchers was the relationship between ethnicity and hyperactivity, an area largely neglected in research on hyperactivity. The assumption that hyperactivity in uniformly distributed among ethnic groups is challenged, based on the sample of one thousand seven hundred and nineteen white, black, and hispanic elementary school children. The Abbreviated Conners Teacher Rating Scale was used to identify the hyperactive group. Two important findings resulted: A) The fifteen overall incidence rate was substantially higher than previously reported in a literature for large samples. B) In schools with non-white majorities, teachers rated black children as significantly more often hyperactive and Mexican American children as significantly less often hyperactive than would

be expected, based of their representation in the general
student body. See ERIC Abstract 0650264-3.

3412.   Lasley, T. J. "Classroom misbehavior: some field
observations." High School Journal, 64, 4 (January, 1981):
142-149.

Researchers observed one urban and one suburban junior high
classroom, recording misbehavior incidents, teachers'
response, and student's reaction to teacher control techniques. Two categories emerged for student misbehaviors and
one category for teacher responses. See ERIC Abstract #EJ
239791.

3413.   Lasley, T. J. "Misbehavior: challenging, coping with
the classroom system." National Association of Secondary
School Principals Bulletin, 63, 428 (September, 1979):
48-51.

Author believes that most student behavior is either a way
of challenging or coping with the classroom system.
Examples of and suggestions for dealing with coping and
challenging behaviors are given. See ERIC Abstract #EJ
206326.

3414.   "The Last Resort." Newsletter of the Committee to End
Violence Against the Next Generation, Inc. Berkeley,
California, 9, 4 (March-April, 1981).

Included in this letter are articles on child advocacy,
department of social services, radical education reforms,
the report of a working party on corporal punishment in
schools, a report on The Fifth National Conference on Child
Abuse and Neglect, court decisions, and articles on banning
corporal suspension, in school suspension, questions about
corporal punishment, and book reviews.

3415.   Laughlin, N. T. "Athletic participation and the grade
point average, absences, cuts, and disciplinary referrals of
high school athletes." International Journal of Sports
Psychology, 9, 2 (1978): 79-89.

Examined in the study were the relationships between participation in athletics by two hundred and forty five high
school athletes and four indices of their in-season and
out-of-season behavior: GPA, absences, cuts, and referrals
for disciplinary infractions. The total sample had significantly more absences out-of-season than in-season. Junior
varsity athletes had fewer cuts and more referrals than
varsity athletes, and engaged in fewer sports. More junior
varsity athletes quit a sport. Varsity athletes had higher
grade point averages in-season than out-of-season. See ERIC
Abstract 1279563-6.

3416.   Lavergne, F. A. "The Development and Testing of a Systematic Observation Instrument with a Focus on Academic Disruption in the Classroom." Paper presented at the annual meeting of the Southwest Educational Research Association, Dallas, Texas, February, 1981.

The system of identifying teacher and student interactions as they relate to discipline problems are developed and validated as a method of resolving disruptive classroom behavior. It involves the use of trained observers who code and record student and teacher interactions according to ten validated behavior categories: 1) transition, 2) teacher or student instructional activity, 3) non-instructional student talk, 4) non-instructional student action, 5) confusion, 6) disruption of academic mode not initiated by teacher or student, 7) criticism, 8) unnoticed disruptive behavior, 9) redirection, and 10) praising non-academic behavior. A 20-hour training program for three trainees tested the reliability of the system. It is suggested that the system be discussed in teacher or administrator in-service training and in teacher preparation programs. See ERIC Abstract ED 199236.

3417.   Lavoie, J. C. and Adams, G. R. "Teacher expectancy and its relation to physical and interpersonal characteristics of the child." Alberta Journal of Educational Research, 20, 2 (June, 1974): 122-132.

Investigated in the study were the effects of physical attractiveness, sex of child, and conduct of the child on teacher expectations. Four hundred and four male and female teachers in the primary and elementary grades were presented with a student progress report of a boy or girl of low, moderate, or high physical attractiveness who's conduct evaluation was either acceptable or unacceptable; and asked to predict academic ability, level of aspiration, and leadership potential. A colored photograph was attached to the report. Conduct level of the child influenced teacher predictions on all measures, while level of attractiveness and sex of child appeared to exert little effect. See ERIC Abstract 1309752-6.

3418.   Leviton, A., Shulman, J., Yaney, P., and Strassfeld, R. "Psychometric test scores and school behavior of girls identified as daydreamers by their teachers." Perceptual and motor skills, 42, 3, Part two (June, 1976): 1307-1313.

In this study fourteen daydreaming nine year old girls were compared to fourteen non-daydreaming girls. According to the results obtained from psychometric tests and school questionnaires, the daydreamers scores were more variable than those of the non-daydreamers. According to the teachers of these girls, daydreamers who are more likely to have problems with flexibility, distraction, ability to persist at a task, peer relations, and arithmetic. Findings suggest that daydreaming does not occur as an isolated entity. See ERIC Abstract 0689057-3.

3419.   Leviton, Harvey S. "The Counselor As Disciplinarian: Some Unconventional Thoughts." Counseling and Values, 21, 4 (July, 1977): 253-258.

Subjects in the study included 66 parents, 77 teachers, and 550 students. Each group seemed to agree that student supervision and discipline are low priority counseling functions. The teachers' ratings of guidance attitude statements did not suggest that these additional responsibilities made counselors too busy to meet the other needs of their counselees. See ERIC Abstract EJ 161885.

3420.   Leard, H. M. "The elementary counsellor and discipline." Canadian Counsellor, 8, 2 (April, 1974): 126-136.

Elementary school counseling is in need of a new image. The counselor must have a thorough understanding of the many problem areas in which he will be involved. Many aspects of school functioning, teacher behavior as it pertains to classroom management and individual psychology are related to the entire question of discipline. See ERIC Abstract #EJ 102371.

3421.   Leblanc, P. H. "Learning problems." Journal of the International Association of Pupil Personnel Workers, 20, 3 (June, 1976): 137-143.

Paper examines the problems parents and teachers face when dealing with a hyperactive child. See ERIC Abstract #EJ 141002.

3422.   Lecompte, Margaret D. "The Civilizing Of Children: How Young Children Learn To Become Students." Journal of Thought, 15, 3 (Fall, 1980): 105-127.

This study presented material dealing with a group of kindergartners who anticipated an actually experienced school. Interviewed in the summer, before starting kindergarten, and then again in April, the children were asked to describe their own and the teacher's role, activities they engaged in, and what rules or constraints on child behavior existed. See ERIC Abstract EJ 239702.

3423.   Lecompte, Margaret D. "Establishing A Workplace: Teacher Control In The Classroom." Education and Urban Society, 11, 1 (November, 1978): 87-106.

This study of teacher behavior in four separate classrooms reveals that, concerning management, teachers looked rather alike. Where differences did exist, they seemed to be determined by the individual personality and philosophy of the teacher rather than by institutional constraints, which dictated the management core. See ERIC Abstract EJ 193519.

3424.   Lee, Beverly A. "Mental Health in the Adolescent In The Eighties: A Perspective." School Guidance Workers, 35, 6 (August, 1980): 30-36.

Adolescent difficulties include preoccupation with food and weight, low levels of physical activity and fitness, and moving patterns. Educational alternatives to meet adolescent needs include: integrated studies, multi-disciplinary approaches to critical issues, cooperative education and work-study programs, and community and self-help groups. See ERIC Abstract EJ 227262.

3425.   Lee, J. "Some treatment techniques with disruptive aggressive children." Association of Educational Psychologists Journal, 5, 1 (Summer, 1979): 29-32.

Presents a description of individual and situational treatment techniques used with six disruptive children aged 5-13 years where one or more teachers were partners in the treatment. The aim was to enable the child to examine the alternative behaviors and different strategies for dealing with situations. The use of both individual and situational treatment provided a powerful combination. A side benefit is that the direct involvement of teachers may raise their threshhold of tolerance and encourage them to accept the long wait for change. See ERIC Abstract 0887065-4.

3426.   Lee, Jung. "Groups As A Method of Counseling And Staff Development." Paper presented at the annual meeting of the Canadian and Counseling Association, Vancouver, British Columbia, June, 1975.

Many secondary schools, because they encompass youth who are obliged to remain in school regardless of their suitability, have many problems. Groups are designed to enable some of these students to adjust better within school systems and within society and to get along better with their families. In order to do this, the group experience must aim to increase the self-esteem and the sense of direction of its members. These groups are characterized by the presence of many unruly, poorly disciplined, impulsive, talkative youngsters. They have the potential for very honest and meaningful conversation with each other. Most are capable of benefiting from and contributing to the group experience. Honesty, self-awareness, and acceptance plus the capacity to discipline a small group are essential qualities for the group leader. If the leader cannot discipline the group no meaningful conversation or expression of feeling can take place. See ERIC Abstract ED 122177.

3427.   Licata, Joseph W. "Custodial Teacher Social Types." University of Ohio, 1980.

Two types of teacher behavior were elicited from student responses to the Pupil Control Behavior Form. Two custodial teacher types emerged from the data: the screamer type, described as a teacher who controlled pupil behavior with verbal methods that expressed anger or frustration and the cold fish type, a teacher who controlled students by withholding praise and acceptance of their behavior. See ERIC Abstract ED 109518.

3428.   Licata, Joseph W. and Willower, Donald J. "Student Brinkmanship And The Schools As A Social System." Educational Administrative Quarterly, 11, 2 (Spring, 1975): 1-14.

Article examines student and teacher attitudes toward student brinkmanship, behavior that challenges the authority system of the school while avoiding negative sanctions, and discusses possible consequences of student brinkmanship for the school's social system. See ERIC Abstract EJ 119191.

3429.   Lietz, Jeremy J. and Gregory, Mary K. "Pupil, Race and Sex Determinants Of Office And Exceptional Educational Referrals." Educational Research Quarterly, 3, 2 (Summer, 1978): 61-66.

In a naturally integrated public elementary school, significantly more black children were referred to the office than white children, but no differences between races were observed for exceptional education referrals. A higher proportion of males than females were referred to the principal's office for disciplinary reasons. See ERIC Abstract EJ 193479.

3430.   Ligon, Jerry. "How To Run A Needs Meeting." Clearing House, 52, 7 (March, 1979): 336-339.

The author describes the meeting where he and his students jointly set classroom roles agreeable to everyone. He used the no-lose method of problem solving, developed by Thomas Gordon, author of "Parent Effectiveness Training". The six steps in this method are presented. See ERIC Abstract EJ 199154.

3431.   Lindholm, Byron W.; and Others. "A Canonical Correlation Analysis of Behavior Problems and School Achievement for Different Grades, Sexes, and Races." Journal of Educational Research, 70, 6 (July, August, 1977): 340-342.

Article discusses behavior problems that are occur for children in various grades, students of both sexes, and students from several different racial groups. He analyses behavior problems as related to these groups.

3432.   Lindholm, Byron W.; and Others. "Influence of Family Structure and School Variables On Behavior Disorders Of Children." Psychology in the Schools, 13, 1 (January, 1977): 99-103.

The purpose of this study was to examine the influence of family structure in school variables on behavior disorders of 1,162 children. Results indicated that grade in school, sex, social class, ordinal position in the family and teacher were important variables in the determination of behavior disorders. See ERIC Abstract EJ 153318.

3433.   Lindholm, Byron W.; and Others. "Racial Differences In Behavior Disorders of Children." Journal of School Psychology, 16, 1 (Spring, 1978): 42-48.

614 black children and 162 white children were compared on the behavior problem checklist. Blacks were judged to have a greater frequency of behavior disorders than whites. A number of interactions of race with other variables were found, and their meanings are discussed.

3434.   Lintula, P. and Miezitis, S. "A Classroom Observation-Based Consultation Approach to Early Identification." Ontario Psychologists, 9, 4 (October, 1977): 29-38.

Article includes a discussion of the limitation of test-based screening programs and the advantages of classroom observations in teacher strategies for children who are at risk educationally. A school consultant makes six classroom observations in each of two first grades and noted children at risk for various reasons. The two teachers were then interviewed to obtain their perceptions. There was 94% agreement between the consultant and the teachers as to which children were at risk and which were not. Only two of 17 at-risks required psychological assessment before remedial educational plans could be formulated. The approach was felt to be superior to the usual test-based programs. See ERIC Abstract 1487862-6.

3435.   Lipsitz, Joan S. "Public Policy and Early Adolescent Research." High School Journal, 63, 6 (March, 1980): 250-56.

The author discusses research needs for children aged ten to fifteen. The article highlights areas in which federal policy concerns intersect with developmental research, and presents ideas in six areas: social equity, basic skills, school discipline, parent participation and school effectiveness. See ERIC Abstract EJ 226973.

3436.   Litt, Iris F. "The Role Of The Pediatrician In Management of Secondary School Behavior Problems." Journal of Research and Development in Education, 11, 4 (Summer, 1978): 92-100.

This article presents various ways in which teachers faced with student behavior problems can learn from and collaborate with pediatricians. See ERIC Abstract EJ 189894.

3437.   Littky, D. & Bosley, L. "A Contingency Management
Program in Urban School Classrooms." Paper presented at the
Eastern Psychological Association Convention, April, 1970.

The project described in this study was implemented in the
Ocean Hill Brownsville Demonstration School District,
Brooklin, to train teachers and paraprofessionals to work
within their present structures, using the principles of
behavior analysis as a means for teaching children to read,
for controlling behavior problems and for conducting more
efficient classrooms. The project was conducted in an
innercity elementary school whose population was 85% black,
10% Puerto Rican, and 5% white, the subjects being from five
second grade classes. In experimental and control classes,
data were collected by observation of the children for 20
minutes per day, five days per week. Five one-hour workshops were conducted for the teachers and paraprofessionals
to introduce a motivational and behavioral management
program, and to teach a contingency management system.
Further training was provided by bi-weekly meetings to
discuss progress and problems. Results showed an increase
in the experimental classrooms of the average percentage of
children working on their programmed reading books, compared
to no increases in the control classroom. See ERIC Abstract
ED 041966.

3438.   Lobietz, W. C. and Burns, W. J. "The 'Least Intrusive
Intervention' Strategy for Behavior Change Procedures: The
Use of Public and Private Feedback in School Classrooms."
Psychology in the Schools, 14, 1 (Janaury, 1977): 89-94.

Many classroom behavior modification procedures have failed
to be adopted by practicing teachers because the procedures
are overly intrusive into the regular classroom routine. A
strategy for teachers and consultants which moves from less
to more intrusive interventions is described and demonstrated with a case example. Private feedback was ineffective in reducing a nine-year-old male fourth grader's
inappropriate behavior, but the introduction of public
feedback resulted in a decrease in inappropriate behavior to
below the class average. See ERIC Abstract 0632258-3.

3439.   Long, J. D. & Williams, R. L. "The Comparative Effective-
ness Of Group And Individually Contingent Free Time With
Inner-City Junior High School Students." Journal Of Applied
Behavior Analysis, 6, 3 (Fall, 1973): 465-474.

Researchers accessed the relative effects of group versus
individually contingent free time in modifying student
behaviors. The effectiveness of well planned lesson
activities and tokens without backup reinforcers was also
studied. Eight students in an inner city seventh grade
class of thirty-two blacks served as subjects. Well
organized lesson activities and success feedback via tokens
did not produce high levels of desirable behavior. In
contrast, group and individually contingent free time

produced substantially higher levels of appropriate behavior than did the base line conditions. The group reinforcement procedure appeared to be slightly more effective than individual reinforcement. See ERIC Abstract 1192151-6.

3440.   Loos, F. M., Williams, K. P. & Bailey, J. S. "A Multi-Element Analysis Of The Effect Of Teacher Aides In An 'Open Style' Classroom." Journal Of Applied Behavior Analysis, 10, 3 (Fall, 1977): 437-448.

Accessed in this study were the effects of three types of teacher aides on student achievement and on-task behavior by comparing each with a standard no-aide condition. Subjects were fifty-four third graders in two open style classrooms. The three types of aides--helping adult, disciplinary adult, and helping fifth grade aide--were compared in a multi-element design with a no-aide control. Results show that the helping-adult aide significantly affected the academic output of the class when compared with a no-aide condition. All aide conditions produced more academic work and on-task behavior than did the standard no-aide condition. See ERIC Abstract 0820160-4.

3441.   Lorion, R. P. & Cowen, E. L. "Referral To A School Mental Health Project: A Screening Note." American Journal Of Community Psychology, 6, 3 (June, 1978): 247-251.

Evaluated in this study was the screening efficiency of two measures of school adjustment, the AML form and the Class-room Adjustment Rating Scale, used to refer fifty first graders to a school mental health program. The implications for using a cut off score procedure to determine referrals are discussed. See ERIC Abstract 0986562-4.

3442.   Lorton, Larry. "Operant Control of Misbehavior: Coun-selor Intervention." 1977.

The major idea of this paper is that elementary counselors can become the most behavioral change agents in the school. First, certain aspects of behavior modification are discussed. Second, trends in elementary school counseling are reviewed and a synthesis is presented, including a model around which an effective behavior change program can be built and instituted in a school or school system. See ERIC Abstract ED 130176.

3443.   Lovitt, T. C. & Smith, D. D. "Using Withdrawal Of Positive Reinforcement To Alter Subtraction Performance." Exceptional Children, 40, 5 (February, 1974): 357-358.

In a multiple base line design, an eleven year old girl who showed erratic arithmetic performance was required to complete three sheets of different problems. A withdrawal contingency was successively scheduled for each type of problem. Performance increased markedly on the problems on which the contingency was scheduled; after completion of the six experimental phases in which the contingency was placed on various problem type combinations, performance remained adequate even when the contingency was removed. See ERIC Abstract 0397852-2.

3444.   Luce, S. C., Delquadri, J., & Hall, R. V. "Contingent Exercise: "A Mild But Powerful Procedure For Surpressing Inappropriate Verbal And Aggressive Behavior." Journal Of Applied Behavior Analysis, 13, 4 (Winter, 1980): 583-594.

Two single subject experiments were conducted in public school classrooms for severely emotionally disturbed children. Investigated were the effects of a treatment requiring a child to exhibit a simple exercise task after a verbal or aggressive response. Reversal and multiple-base line designs were used. The subjects were seven and ten year old boys. The independent variable, contingent exercise, required standing up and sitting on the floor five to ten times contingent on inappropriate behavior. The exercise was easy to carry out, and following it, the child quickly returned to the learning task that had been interrupted by the inappropriate behavior. This procedure required a minimum of prompting or manual guidance. Although the contingent exercise was not topographically related to the inappropriate response, it decreased those responses dramatically. Results suggest that the contingent exercise was not only more powerful but also could be administered independently. This exercise may be an alternative procedure for therapists confronted with severely abnormal behaviors, particularly in settings where procedures such as time out and painful consequences find restricted use. See ERIC Abstract 0639665-3.

3445.   Lufler, Henry S., Jr. "Discipline: A New Look At An Old Problem." Phi Delta Kappa, 59, 6 (February, 1978): 424-426.

Author believes that increasing the severity of punishment, ignoring the non- school origin of discipline problems, and failing to consider the role of the schools themselves are all contributing factors to discipline problems. See ERIC Abstract EJ 171616.

3446.   Lupiani, D. A. "The Classroom As A Political Microcosm: An Observation." Journal Of School Psychology, 14, 3 (Fall, 1976): 235-241.

Article describes an outbreak of aggressive behavior involving an entire second grade class. Fifty-seven percent of the pupils were Jewish and it was observed that at that time--November 26, 1973 to December 7, 1973--the public news was full of the Arab/Israeli conflict, as well as the threatened impeachment of President Nixon, inflation, and the decline in the public's trust in institutions. A meeting with the parents of these children confirmed that their dinner table conversation was strained as a result of national and international developments. An observation of other classes in the school revealed that other teachers freely discussed news events with their students, while the second grade teachers felt that such discussions were inappropriate at that level. The aggressive behavior ceased after the teacher began responding with open discussion whenever issues were raised and when a kind of classroom debate was organized. A hypothesis of a relationship between national affairs and classroom behavior is proposed. See ERIC Abstract 0440157-2.

3447.   Mace, Jane. "Teaching May Be Hazardous To Your Health." Phi Delta Kappa, 60, 7 (March, 1979): 5-12, 13.

Author believes that our schools today are institutionalized and archaic and that there is no peace and order, nor are students given the love and attention they deserve as individuals. The atmosphere in huge school plan is a cross between a factory, and a prison, and is massively inhumane. See ERIC Abstract EJ 197908.

3448.   Macekura, Joseph. "Building Discipline In A 'Tough' School." Social Education, 42, 2 (February, 1978): 100-104.

Author describes methods adopted by a Virginia Junior High School to ease racial tensions following a desegregation decree in 1965. Methods include in-service programs for teachers, development of special learning opportunities, and school-community interaction. See ERIC Abstract EJ 174505.

3449.   Mack, Jean. "Report Card on a Teacher." Journal of Teacher Education, 30, 4 (July-August, 1979): 37-38.

Authors explores the gaps between educational policy regarding discipline techniques and the reality of the classroom. See ERIC Abstract EJ 210271.

3450.   MacPherson, E. N., Candee, B. L., & Hohman, R. J. "A Comparison Of Three Methods For Eliminating Disruptive Lunchroom Behavior." Journal Of Applied Behavior Analysis, 7, 2 (Summer, 1974): 287-297.

Compared in the study were three methods of controlling disruptive lunchroom behaviors of 221 elementary school children. Basic modification procedures, basic modification procedures plus punishment essays, and basic modification procedures plus mediation essays were used. During an in-service workshop, six paraprofessional lunch aides received training in these methods to modify three classes of disruptive lunchroom behaviors. They then apply the methods in a counter-balanced design. Fourth and fifth grade elementary school pupils were observers and made reliability counts of the target misbehaviors under the various methods. Results indicate that during the periods when aides have been directed to use basic modification procedures plus mediation essays, target misbehaviors were almost totally eliminated and occurred significantly less often than during the periods when they had been directed to use basic modification procedures alone or basic modification procedures plus punishment essays. See ERIC Abstract 1315352-6.

3451.   Madsen, C. H. et al. "Classroom RAID (Rules, Approval, Ignore, Disapproval): A Cooperative Approach for Professionals and Volunteers. Journal of School Psychology, 8, 3 (February, 1970): 180-184.

Comparisons between trained and untrained teachers demonstrated that trained teachers were substantially higher in teacher approval following appropriate student behavior and much lower in frequency of disapproval directed at inappropriate student behavior, and they had no errors or approval errors of approval or disapproval. Inappropriate student behavior was significantly lower for trained teachers. See ERIC Abstract EJ 025798.

3452.   Macmillan, Donald L. and Morrison, Gale, M. "Correlates Of Social Status Among Mildly Handicapped Learners In Self-Contained Special Classes." Journal of Educational Psychology, 72, 4 (August, 1980): 437-444.

In this study combined teacher-ratings of perceived cognitive competence and misbehavior accounted for the most variance in peer acceptance or rejection of educable mentally handicapped children. Ratings of academic competence were associated with both acceptance and rejection of educationally handicapped children. See ERIC Abstract EJ 235501.

3453.   Main, G. C. & Munro, B. C. "A Token Reinforcement Program in a Public Junior High School." Journal of Applied Behavior Analysis, 10, 1 (Spring, 1977): 93-94.

Article described a program initially used with emotionally disturbed nine year olds and then modified for use with 6 behavior problem ninth graders. The program involves a token system used in conjunction with educational structure and praise of appropriate behaviors. It produced a dramatic decline in inappropriate behavior. Tokens were gradually thinned and this condition removed, yet a four week follow-up showed maintena course entitled "Personal Growth" included 12 high school students with histories of destructive behavior, conflicts, academic failure, truancy, and drug abuse. One hour sessions were held daily with students for one semester. Antisocial behavior in early classes led to a new procedure. Each session began with the whole group sitting in a circle. Members who began to be disruptive were sent to other tables. The procedure led the subjects to realize how they were spending their time, in class and in other classes, and to want to spend more and more time in the circle with other students. See ERIC Abstract 0848063-4.

3454.   Major, Robert L. "A Perspective On Discipline." High
School Journal, 63, 5 (February, 1980): 203-206.

The author discusses eight insights concerning discipline.
Topics covered include: philosophy, respect, student-
teacher relationships, matching discipline with the student
and the incident, classroom rules, classroom environment and
parent involvement. See ERIC Abstract EJ 226864.

3455.   Manley Casimir, Michael E. "The Exercise of Administra-
tive Discretion in Secondary School Discipline: Grounded
Hypotheses." Paper presented at the annual meeting of The
American Educational Research Association. New York, New
York, April, 1977.

This study used ethnographic research methods to generate
hypotheses about the exercise of administrative discretion
on secondary school discipline. The study investigated the
exercise of discretion by the school disciplinarians in an
integrated high school in Chicago. Participant observation
focused interviews, and administrative statistics yielded
the data. Simple statistical analysis of the quantitating
data yielded three hypotheses about the pattern of selective
enforcement: 1) The more prominent the discipline administrator's concern with order maintenance, the greater the
likelihood students will be suspended; 2) The more prominent
the discipline administrator's concern with individual
treatment, the greater the likelihood students will be
treated leniently and not suspended; and 3) Boys, posing as
they seem to do a greater threat to the security and good
order of the school, will be suspended systematically more
frequently than girls. See ERIC Abstract ED 136383.

3456.   Manley Casimir, Michael E. "Procedural Due Process In
Secondary School Discipline." Theory Into Practice, 17, 4
(October, 1978): 314-20.

This article uses the Supreme Court decision in Goss vs.
Lopez for describing and assessing the discipline procedure
in one public high school. See ERIC Abstract EJ 198794.

3457.   Mannarino, Anthony P; and Others. "Evaluation of Social
Competence Training In The Schools." Paper presented at the
annual meeting of the Midwestern Psychological Association,
St. Louis, Missouri, May, 1980. 21P.

The usefulness of problem-solving training with emotionally
troubled students and of peer ratings as an index of change
was investigated to determine the success of an early intervention program. During a fourteen week period, advanced
undergraduates conducted a small group intervention program
focused on social skills training for thirty-two maladaptive
students. Children in the program made significantly
greater gains in classroom adjustment and in peer acceptance
than did a control group. The results suggest that an
interpersonal problem-solving model can be used effectively

as an intervention strategy with high-risk primary grade children. See ERIC Abstract ED 188088.

3458.   Marandola, P. & Imber, S. C. "Glasser's Classroom Meeting: A Humanistic Approach to Behavior Change With Pre-Adolescent Inner-City Learning Disabled Children." Journal of Learning Disabilities, 12, 6 (June-July, 1979): 383-387.

This study evaluated the effects of Glasser's classroom meetings are the argumentative behavior of ten 11 and 12 year old inter-city, learning disabled boys. Baseline data for frequency and duration of verbal argument and physical confrontations among subjects were gathered and recorded for two weeks prior to 8 daily problem solving classroom meetings. The data were compared to the number of arguments and confrontations that occured during the intervention period. Considerable decreases in argumentative and physical confrontation were noted during the intervention period, suggesting that the method may be affectively used with a learning disabled population. See ERIC Abstract 1470662-6.

3459.   Marchase, Gail H. "Generalization Of Reinforced Behaviors In A Game Situation." John Hopkins University, Baltimore, Maryland, 1971.

Conflicting evidence as to the presence or absence of generalization in classroom behavior modification programs prompted this study of the conditions of generalization. During the experiment, behaviors operationally defined as competitive or cooperative were reinforced in certain game situations. The generalization of this training over variable of task, type of response, and time periods was measured. It was predicted that generalization of the reinforced response would occur most strongly in the testing situation most like the original one. Experimental results confirmed these expectations. Results showed, in addition that there was no significant difference in competiveness between boys and girls. See ERIC Abstract ED 060648.

3460.   Marcus, B. Jerry. "Discipline And The School Calendar." N.A.S.S.P. Bulletin, 61, 406 (February, 1977): 88-90.

Author suggests that before secondary principals can deal effectively with discipline problems, they should grasp disciplinary incidents according to the school calendar in order to indentify peak behavioral problem periods. See ERIC Abstract EJ 160394.

3461.   Margolis, H., Brannigan, G. G. & Poston, N. A. "Modification of Impulsivity: Implications For Teaching." Elementary School Journal, 77, 3 (January, 1977): 231-237.

Reviewed is the research on different strategies to assist impulsive children to perform more reflectively in terms of response time and/or response accuracy. Research findings demonstrate that impulsivity can be modified by using the following techniques: a) Peer models acting reflectively, b) Self-instruction and covert and overt rehearsal of strategies, c) Increasing concern over being correct, and d) Training and scanning strategies for visual discrimination. Suggestions for classroom remediation of impulsivity are included. See ERIC Abstract 0896161-4.

3462.   Marin, Glenn H. "Coping With The Chronic Disruptive Student." Illinois School Research and Development, 17, 1 (Fall, 1980): 35-38.

Looking at the emotional and academic needs of the chronically disruptive student, the author suggests a temporary alternative class which emphasises self-esteem development and individualized instruction. He feels that this is the best programmatic solution. See ERIC Abstract EJ 231392.

3463.   Marlowe, R. H. et al. "Severe Classroom Behavior Problems: Teachers or Counsellors." Journal of Applied Behavior Analysis, 11, 1 (Spring, 1978): 53-66.

The relative effectiveness was determined of teaching and counseling approaches in the reduction of disruptive and inappropriate classroom behavior in 12 academically low achieving, seventh grade, black male students. Three groups with nearly equal mean inappropriate behaviors, were randomly assigned to one of three treatment conditions: behavioral, client centered, or no counseling. Each experimental group received 15 30-minute counseling sessions, at a rate of two to three times a week. In addition to counseling, all subjects subsequently received teacher approval in the classroom. Results indicate that the teacher was able to reduce inappropriate behavior more than any counseling group. See ERIC Abstract 0979561-4.

3464.   Martin, R. "Student Sex and Behavior As Determinants Of The Type And Frequency Of Teacher-Student Context." Journal of School Psychology, 10, 4 (December, 1972): 339-347.

Five second grade teachers ranked their eighty students according to the extent to which they exhibited problem behaviors in a classroom. Boys and girls who exhibited few behaviors and children who exhibited many problem behaviors were observed in their dyadic interactions with their teachers. Boys who were behavior problems were found to interact with their teachers significantly more than boys who were not behavior problems, and more than girls, regardless of their classroom behavior. Results indicate that the high rate of student-teacher interaction for boys found by other investigators is probably characteristic of only a small percentage of boys. See ERIC Abstract 0382950-2.

3465.   Marvelle, J. D. Compiler, et al. "Impact Parent Program Workshop Leader's Manual." Washington, D.C.: Bureau of Elementary and Secondary Education, 1978. 271p.

This program manual provides a series of eight two-hour sessions designed to further parents' abilities to teach and communicate with their young children and to build supportive family-school relationships. Session 1 introduces the series and emphasizes the important roles parents have as teachers of their children. In Session 2, an overview of child growth and development is presented. Session 3 discusses how children learn and includes an exercise in task analysis. Session 4 discusses the curriculum. The last are sessions that focus on the importance of affective communication, children's behavior and techniques for coping with unacceptable behavior. Session 5 stresses the importance of communication in understanding children and Session 6 emphasizes the importance of a child's subconcept and provides guidelines for discipling children. Session 7 discusses the basic principles of behavior. Parents learn how to define behavior specifically and also learn three techniques for solving behavior problems. In Session 8 parents discuss their implementation of a technique for changing child's behavior. See ERIC Abstract ED 184691.

3466.   Masters, J. R. and Laverty, G. E. "The effects of a School Without Failure Program Upon Classroom Interaction Patterns, Pupil Achievement and Teacher, Pupil and Parents Attitudes (Summary Report of First Year of Program)." Washington, D.C., National Center for Educational Research and Development, 1974. 25p.

The purpose of this document is to present the evaluation of the Schools Without Failure Program carried out during the programs first year of operation in Newcastle, Pennsylvania. Ten elementary schools were pared on the basis of size, socioeconomic status, and pupils' past achievement. One school of each pair was randomly assigned to begin teacher training and implementation. The other school of each pair became a control school. Instructional session and schools without failure schools classroom meeting interactions were measured by the expanded category system and the reciprocal category system. Results indicated that the program had its major impact on teacher and little difference existed in the achievement of pupils in schools without failure and control schools. Some positive changes in Schools Without Failure schools primary people attitudes toward being in school and toward doing difficult work were found. Positive changes occurred in Schools Without Failure school intermediate pupil attitudes toward the importance of doing assignments and learning and in these schools the number of pupils referred to principals for disciplinary reasons was reduced. See ERIC Abstract ED 107690.

3467.   Masters, J. R., et al. "The Effects of a Schools Without
Failure Program Upon Classroom Interaction Patterns, Pupil
Achievement and Teacher, Pupil and Parent Attitudes (Summary
Report of a Two Year Study)." Final report. Washington,
D.C., National Institute of Education, 1975. 31p.

Presented in this report is a two year evaluation of William
Glasser's Schools Without Failure Program. The study was
carried out in the Newcastle school District in
Pennsylvania. Ten elementary schools were paired on the
basis of five, socioeconomic status, and past achievement of
pupils. During the first year one school of each pair was
randomly assigned to begin teacher training and implementation of the program. In the second year both groups
received training in Glasser's methods and implemented the
program. Data were collected and analyzed to determine
whether the second year or the first year produced stronger
changes and how schools that received two years of training
differed from traditional schools. See ERIC Abstract ED
111099.

3468.   Matas-Lark, A. "Spontaneous Behavior in a High School
Classroom." University of Maryland Counseling and Personnel
Journal, 3, 1 (1972-1973): 25-33.

The effectiveness of the use of positive verbal reinforcement by a teacher in increasing the incidents of spontaneous
behavior was studied in 28 tenth graders. The training of
the observer who recorded the behaviors during the baseline
and test period is detailed. Results indicate that the
verbal reinforcement procedures did effectively increase the
spontaneous behavior and teacher talking time decreased by
approximately 50%. See ERIC Abstract 1096552-5.

3469.   Mathey, K. B., Anderson, G. L. and Blue, F. R. "Development of Effective Behavior in School Through the Use of
Models." Journal of Psychology, 99, 1 (May, 1978): 75-81.

Sixteen 12th graders were used as models to encourage
certain desirable school behaviors in eighth graders. It
was hypothesized that these eighth graders would show
greater gains in grades, study skills, leadership participation behaviors, self-expectations for academic success, and
confidence in their ability to influence what happens to
them then would their control counterparts. One hundred
ninety-two male and female subjects were randomly assigned
to experimental and control groups. Criterion measures were
grade point average, participation index, Self-Concept of
Academic Ability Scale, Rotter Internal-External Locus of
Control Scale and the Survey of Study Habits and Attitudes.
Pre and post test differenct scores suggested their experimental subjects showed a significant gain the skills over
the controls. These results suggested that 12th grade
models can encourage certain desirable changes in eighth
grade students. See ERIC Abstract 0463662-2.

3470.   Matson, J. L. and Cahill, T. "Overcorrection: A
Technique for Eliminating Resistant Behaviors." Washington,
D.C.: American Psychological Association, 1976. 11p.

Overcorrection is a mild punishment technique that provides
for logical consequences of inappropriate behaviors. The
method has two components--restitution, during which a
disruptive environment is reinstated to a state vastly
superior to the original one, and positive practice, during
which more appropriate responses are taught to replace the
misbehavior. A number of studies are reported that demonstrate the effectiveness of overcorrection in eleminating
highly resistant behaviors. A possible application of the
technique is the school is described, and a comparison is
made of how overcorrection differs from more traditional
techniques such as writing sentences. See ERIC Abstract ED
131386.

3471.   Mayer, G. R. and Butterworth, T. W. "A Preventive
Approach to School Violence and Vandalism: An Experimental
Study." Personnel and Guidance Journal, 57, 9 (May, 1979):
436-441.

The researchers employed strategies that would attack
identified perpetrators of school violence and vandalism
existing within schools. Results indicated that the costs
of vandalism in terms of dollars and frequency of inappropriate student behavior decreased more in experimental than
in controlled schools. See ERIC Abstract EJ 200919.

3472.   Mayron, L. W., Ott, J., Nations, R. & Mayron, E. L.
"Light Radiation, and Academic Behavior: Initial Studies On
The Effects of Full-Spectrum Lighting and Radiation
Shielding On Behavior And Academic Performance Of School
Children." Academic Therapy, 10, 1 (Fall, 1974): 33-47.

Four first grade classrooms were equipped with various
lighting arrangements and were photographed by hidden camera
which recorded their motor activity. SCORE, a Student
Performance Objectives Test, was administered three times
during the semester. Full-spectrum fluorescent lighting and
radiation shielding decreased hyperkinetic behavior relative
to normal, cool, white fluorescent light, and there were
significant changes in academic performance. See ERIC
Abstract 0403054-2.

3473.   McCann, E. "Children's Perception of Corporal Punishment." Educational Studies, 4, 2 (June, 1978): 167-172.

Author explores views of children in English schools who
have received corporal punishment from teachers. The
findings indicated that most children accpeted firm and
non-excessive punishment as an integral part of their
relationship with adults. See ERIC Abstract EJ 185991.

3474.   McCarthy, M. M., et al. "Five Questions You Ask Most About Teaching." Instructor, 78, 2 (September, 1977): 71-94.

Authors provide suggestions on how teachers can best manage their classroom, how they can plan more effective lessons, and how they can develop procedures for fostering creative thinking and the art of imagining in their students. They discuss student behavior and provide some ideas for keeping track of student skills. See ERIC Abstract EJ 169098.

3475.   McCullough, J. P. "An Investigation of the Effects of Model Group Size Upon Response Facilitation in the High School Classroom." Behavior Therapy, 3, 4 (October, 1972): 561-566.

The response facilitation effect of peer modeling groups among a high school population of students was tested following two weeks of treatment. Analysis of 185 14 through 18 year old subjects in eight English classes showed that the facilitation effect did not occur. Target behavior rates generally declined once treatment was applied and increased when treatment was terminated. It is concluded that the inhibitory responses were strengthened in the observers as they observed models being reinforced. The high school teacher appears to have less reinforcing significance to his students than does his elementary school colleague. See ERIC Abstract 0999649-5.

3476.   McCullough, J. P., Cornell, J. E., McDaniel, M. H. and Mueller, R. K. "Utilization of the Simultaneous Treatment Design to Improve Student Behavior in a First Grade Classroom." Journal of Consulting and Clinical Psychology, 42, 2 (April, 1974): 288-292.

A brief discussion is presented of timed series designs and outlines the methodological limitations of the ABAB Design, one of the most representative and widely used time series. The simultaneous treatment is discussed as one means to avoid the serious limitations of the ABAB. A single case study is presented to demonstrate the utility of the simultaneous treatment design to modify the behavior of a first grade boy. One teacher and her aide recorded data and administered the program. The simultaneous treatment design allowed for statistical comparison of the treatment effects of two contingency programs administered simultaneously. The more effective program was successfully maintained. See ERIC Abstract 08650952-4.

3477.   McCurdy, B., et al. "Human Relations Training with Seventh-Grade Boys Identified as Behavior Problems." School Counselor, 24, 4 (March, 1977): 248-252.

Twelve boys who identified as constituting behavior problems in a class of underachievers, were given group human-relations training. Self esteem was improved by training procedures including video tape, as well as facilitating communication. Group experiences seemed to affect classroom behavior positively, as evidenced by a decrease in behavior problems. See ERIC Abstract EJ 156744.

3478.   McDaniel, T. R. "Identifying Discipline Problems: a Self-Evaluation Exercise." Childhood Education, 57, 4 (March-April, 1981): 223-225.

Article provides teachers with a chance to select the most severe discipline problems from among a set of ten illustrations. It points out the areas of tolerance and intolerance teachers' choices reflect. See ERIC Abstract EJ 242855.

3479.   McKee, N. "Socratic Suggestions for the Mind Set of Teaching." A Manual for Those New to the Profession of Teaching Concerning the Establishment of Classroom Organization During the First Days of School. Research and Development Report #4102." Washington, D.C.: National Institute of Education, 1978. 35p.

Twenty-eight third grade teachers were observed by a team from the Research and Development Center for Teacher Education at the University of Texas in order to identify discipline in teaching strategies most conducive to the establishment of a successful student-teacher relationship. See ERIC Abstract ED 185026.

3480.   McKinney, J. D. "Teacher Perceptions Of The Classroom Behavior Of Reflective and Impulsive Children." Psychology In The Schools. 12, 3 (July, 1975): 348-352.

Four second grade teachers completed the Classroom Behavior Inventory for 101 students. Thirty-two subjects were classified as reflective and thirty-two as impulsive by using the matching "M", familiar "F", figures "F" tests "T". Teachers rated impulsive boys as less task-oriented and considerate than reflective children of either sex. On the other hand, impulsive girls and reflectives were rated comparably on these scales. Differences were not observed among the four groups in teacher ratings of hostility, extroversion or introversion. See ERIC Abstract 1250354-6.

3481.   McLaughlin, N. W. Innovation in Classroom Organization. Paper presented at the American Education Research Association Meeting, Washington, D. C., March 31, 1975.

In this paper the author discusses several cases of attempts to implement fundamental change in classroom organization by local school districts. These cases were examined as part of the Rand Change Agent Study. The author focuses on the problems particular to this sort of innovation, and suggests what lessons these efforts have for the implementation of educational innovations generally. Included are sections on components of a successful implementation strategy, local material development, staff training, planning and staff meetings, general lessons. The researcher found that successful innovation was characterized to a greater or lesser extent in all innovative projects by a process of mutual adaptation. Since this adaptive process is essential to classroom organization projects, these innovative efforts provide a particularly good opportunity to identify the components of an adaptive implementation strategy and to observe the way particular strategies work together to promote adaptation and change. The data suggests that successful implementation does not simply involve the direct application of a technology and that it is neither an automatic nor a certain process.

3482.   McLaughlin, T. F. "The Comparative Effects of Token-Reinforcement With and Without a Response Cost Contingency With Special Education Children." Educational Research Quarterly, 2, 1 (Spring, 1977): 34-41.

Affects of the academic and disruptive behavior of special education pupils after adding a cost contingency to a token reinforcement procedure were examined. Response rates were higher when response cost was added than during either the baseline or token reinforcement contingency. See ERIC Abstract EJ 172821.

3483.   McLaughlin, T. F. and Malaby, Jr. "Intrinsic Reinforcers in a Classroom Token Economy." Journal of Applied Behavior Analysis, 5, 3 (Fall, 1972): 263-270.

An inexpensive, easily managed token economy was used for one year in a normal combined fifth and sixth grade class-room with 25 to 29 pupils. Data were collected for the entire academic performance in spelling, language, hand-writing, and math. During a baseline period, assignment completion was variable. Introduction of a token economy with a point exchange every five days increased assignment completion and decreased variability of performance. An application of a token economy that had a point exchange averaging four days was accompanied by an assignment comple-tion rate that approximated 100%. A reinforcement contin-gency for quiet behavior rather than for assignment comple-tion was accommpanied by a marked diminution or assignment completion. A reintroduction of the token reinforcement for assignment completion again increased that behavior. See ERIC Abstract 0549749-3.

3484.   McLaughlin, T. and Malaby, Jr. "Reducing and Measuring Inappropriate Verbalization in a Token Classroom." Journal of Applied Behavior Analysis, 5, 3 (Fall, 1972): 329-333.

A procedure was employed that enabled a teacher to bring inappropriate verbalizations under control in a classroom of approximately 25 fifth and sixth graders. Contingent point loss for inappropriate verbalizations was correlated with a low but steady rate of such verbalizations. Point gain contingent upon quite behavior produced a marked decrease in inappropriate verbalizations. A return to contingent point loss was accompanied by an increasing rate of inappropriate verbalizations. Verbalizations decreased when quiet behavior was reinforced again. A note worthy feature of the study was the utilization of subjects from within the class to act as data recorders. See ERIC Abstract 0549649-3.

3485.   McNamara, E. "Pupils Self-Management in the Secondary School: The Goal of Behavioral Intervention." Association of Educational Psychologists Journal, 5, 1 (Summer, 1979): 26-29.

In this article it is suggested that educational psychologists working with teacher colleagues in the secondary schools are ideally placed to implement research oriented treatment programs based on a self-management model of behavior modification. The model presented could lead to a more wide spread use of behavioral counseling techniques by the helping teams of secondary schools. See ERIC Abstract 0887465-4.

3486.   McPartland, J. M. and McDill, E. L. "High School Rules and Decision Making Procedures as a Source of School Stability. A Report." John Hopkins University, Baltimore, Maryland, Center for the Study of Social Organization of Schools. Washington, D.C.: National Institute of Education, 1974. 143p.

The School Organization Program of the Center for Social Organization of Schools is currently concerned with authority-control structures, task structures, reward system and peer group programs in schools. This report examines one aspect of authority-control structures in high schools -- content of school rules and procedures for deciding them -- to determine their relationship to school stability. The analysis of the survey data from 3,450 students in 14 urban high schools show that a school's stability in terms of truancy, vandalism and protests, is related its procedures for deciding rules, as well as to the content of the school rules. See ERIC Abstract ED 091870.

3487.   McPartland, J., Epstein, J. L. and McDill, E. L. "Student Reactions to the Transition from Open Elementary School to Junior High School: A Case Study." Center for Social Organization Schools Reports, John Hopkins University, 139, 1 (October, 1972).

A survey questionnaire was administered to sixth graders in 63 open elementary schools and in 88 traditional elementary schools. One year later 21 subjects from the open and 26 subjects from the traditional school completed a similar measure after attendance at the same junior high school. After controlling for student background and previous academic performance, no significant differences were found between the two groups in adjustment to junior high school as measured by grades, attendance, discipline, and satisfaction with school. Before entring junior high, the open school subjects showed a stronger preference for open school organization than the traditional subjects. Differences disappeared during the first year of junior high, with the open school subjects retaining their preferences and the traditional subjects increasing their accpetance of the open school concept. This finding, in addition to the general finding that open schools subjects found greater similarities between elementary and junior high schools than the traditional school subjects, suggests that the open elementary school may be closer to junior high in selective organizational properties that are stallient to students. School corganizational variables and family influence on student transition are discussed. See ERIC Abstract 0790049-4.

3488.   McWilliams, S. A. and Finkel, N. J. "High School Students as Mental Health Aides in the Elementary School Setting." Journal of Consulting and Clinical Psychology, 40, 1 (February, 1973): 39-42.

Fifteen underachieving high school students were offered more relevant experiences by training them to work with 23 maladapted primary graders. Teachers' rating of childrens' behavior indicated program children improved more than 27 matched controls, a finding supported by aides' ratings of improvement in program children. Aides felt the program helped their understanding of children, and they preceived it as better than other school activities. These findings, together with the positive reaction of personnel to the program, testified to the effectiveness and its feasibility. See ERIC Abstract 1087850-1.

3489.   Media V Film Distributors. "Dare to Discipline." 1978.

The importance of teachers establishing and maintaining their authority in the classroom is explained. The film emphasizes the building of self-esteem and responsibility in the students, as well as refining the leadership skills of the teacher. It is based on the book Dare to Discipline by Dr. James Dobson. Twenty-nine minutes. 16mm film. See NICEM 0886353.

3490.   Media V. Film Distributors. "Dealing with Discipline Problems." Media V Film Distributors, 1973.

Demonstrates proven techniques for handling many of the most common school discipline problems. Twelve real life situations are featured in which individual teachers reveal how they achieved discipline by putting the success concepts of reality therapy into everyday practice. The film shows how to get problem students to evaluate their behavior and commit themselves to a better way, how to handle children who continually make and break commitments, and how to reach a child who is unwilling to make any self-judgement. Thirty minutes. 16mm film. See NICEM 0872841.

3491.   Media V Film Distributors.   "Glasser on Discipline."
1972.

Dr. William Glasser discusses a successful new approach to
the old problem of school discipline. Included are five
basic steps to achieving effective discipline in any school.
Twenty-eight minutes. 3/4 inch video cassette. See NICEM
0123914.

3492.   Media V Film Distributors. "Humanity of Teaching."

A study is presented of positive relationships in the
classroom and an explanation given on how teachers can
strengthen the climate for effective, natural discipline,
which rewards both teachers and students with a mutually
satisfying, productive existence.   Twenty-nine minutes.
16mm film. See NICEM 0807492.

3493.   Media V Film Distributors.   "The Reality Therapy
Approach."

Teachers are documented who have successfully used concepts
developed by Dr. William Glasser to achieve effective school
discipline, along with a full explanation by Glasser of his
five-part approach to discipline and the seven steps of
reality therapy.   Twenty-nine minutes.   16mm film.   See
NICEM 0813301.

3494.   Media V Film Distributors.   "School Discipline -- A
Series."

A thorough re-examination is provided of the meanings and
functions of discipline, authority, control, power and
responsibility including special concern of minorities. See
NICEM
0814083.

3495.   Media V Film Distributors. "Starting Tomorrow." Media V
Film Distributors.

A thought-provoking of practical suggestions, and workable
classroom approaches is presented.   Helpful tips and several
new ideas are presented that every teacher can use to
improve human relations and school discipline.   Interviews
are featured with such therapists as William Glasser, Thomas
Gordon, and others.   Twenty-nine minutes.   16mm film.   See
NICEM 0815292.

3496.   Media V Film Distributors.   "What is Discipline, Anyway?"
Media V Film Distributors.

Film seeks to answer question "What is Discipline?"   A
montage of viewpoints are revealed around the central theme
of school discipline, what it is and how to achieve it
within a framework of realistic enforceable rules.   A

differentiation is made between discipline and punishment. Twenty-nine minutes. 16mm film. See NICEM 0817848.

3497.   Media V Film Distributors. "Why Human Relations?" 1974.

The film identifies the basic need for good human relationships in schools and re-examines goals of public education. It shows how discipline and human relations are closely interwoven and presents documentary scenes of several schools where human relationships have been consciously improved. Twenty-nine minutes. 16mm film. See NICEM 0878314.

3498.   Medway, F. J. and Forman, S. G. "Psychologists' and Teachers' Reactions to Mental Health and Behavioral School Consultation." Journal of School Psychology, 18, 4 (Winter, 1980): 388-348.

School psychologists and elementary school teachers were shown videotapes of a psychologist consulting with a teacher, with the psychologists using either behavioral or mental health consultation techniques. Teachers preferred behavioral consultation, while psychologists rated the mental helath consultation as better suiting their needs. See ERIC Abstract EJ 240092.

3499.   Meichenbaum D. and Burland, S. "Cognitive Behavior Modification with Children." School Psychology Digest, 8, 4 (Fall, 1979): 426-433.

The shift in behavior therapy towards more cognitively oriented interventions in the treatment of behavior disorders in school children is presented. Recent applications of cognitive behavior modification have dealt with traditional academic concerns. See ERIC Abstract EJ 217075.

3500.   Meisels, L. "The Disturbing Child and Social Competence in the Classroom: Implications for Child Care Workers." Child Care Quarterly, 4, 4 (Winter, 1975): 231-240.

Article describes a residential school program which emphasizes a behavioral orientation which enables adults to increase their consistency and individualization for behaviorally disordered children. See ERIC Abstract EJ 134936.

3501.   Mellinger, M. and Rachauskas, J. A. "Quest for Identity: National Survey of the Middle School, 1969-1970." Illinois: Chicago State College, 1970. 35p.

The purpose of this survey was to determine the characteristics that distinguish the middle school from other types of academic organization. One section deals with the primary responsibility for discipline by grade organization. Samples were drawn from a questionnaire sent to 1,988 schools who's names included the word middle school. Two hundred seventy five elementary and 91 junior high schools were added to furnish a basis for comparing middle school with non-middle schools. See ERIC Abstract ED 044776.

3502.   Mendez, R. "School Suspension--Discipline Without Failure." NASSP Bulletin, 61, 405 (January, 1977): 11-13.

Author stresses that in-school suspension programs can combine efforts to help students succeed with the administration of discipline. See ERIC Abstract EJ 158809.

3503.   Meridian Public Schools, Mississippi. "Using Video Tape Modeling to Increase Attending Behavior." Elementary School Guidance and Counseling, 9, 1 (October, 1974): 35-40.

Studied were the use of videotape models in teaching attending behavior to first graders from disadvantaged families. Sixty-nine subjects with the lowest scores on the standardized rating scale of attending behavior were observed in the classroom to establish base levels of attending behavior. Subjects were divided into a control group and two experimental groups in which films were shown of children paying attention in classrooms and subjects were given either neutral or directive verbal instructions. It was found that attending behavior increased significantly in both experimental groups, and it is suggested that elementary students can learn learning skills through imitation of appropriate models. See ERIC Abstract 0632454-3.

3504.   Metz, M. H. "Clashes in the Classroom: The Importance of Norms for Authority." Education and Urban Society, 11, 1 (November, 1978): 13-47.

The author discusses the nature of authority as found in the literature, the character of authority between teacher and student within the classrooms in four segregated junior high schools and discusses the implications. See ERIC Abstract EJ 193516.

3505.   Metz, M. H. "Classrooms and Corridors: The Crisis of Authority in Desegregated Secondary Schools." Washington, D.C.: National Institute of Education, 1979. 285p.

Sociological perspectives are employed in this study of two desegregated junior high schools with racially and socio-economically similar student bodies. The different ways that teachers, students, and administrators in the two schools address the task of pursuing education while maintaining safety and order are analyzed. Situations and incidents indicative of authority and control are described in terms of social structures and processes which shape behavior, tension, conflict and crisis. A comprehensive bibliography is included. See ERIC Abstract ED 159288.

3506.   Metz, M. H. "Order in the Secondary School: Variations
on a Theme." Paper presented at the annual meeting of the
American   Sociological   Association,   Chicago,   Illinois,
September, 1977. 22p.

The sources of the chronic precariousness of order in public
secondary schools are examined. The means of control available to principals and teachers are analyzed and the consequences of strategies of control are considered as they
ineract with strategies for academic education. Order and
academic education as goals often require mutually contradictory actions supported by different organizational
structures. The need for opposing practices to meet these
two basic goals is greatest when incoming students are
skeptical or challenging the usefulness of the schools goals
or its good faith in pursuing them. See ERIC Abstract ED
150754.

3507.   "Mid-Year Conference on Classroom Management. From
Hickory Stick to Human Relations." Provo, Utah: College of
Education, Brigham Young University, 1976.

This publication outlines significant findings and methods
presented at the first annual mid-year conference at the
College of Education at Brigham Young University. The area
covered is on classroom management and it is hoped that
those ideas, techniques and methods which are presented may
be used effectively in our concerted efforts toward more
efficient classroom management. Included are presentations
by the following authors: William Glasser, Charles H.
Madsen, Jr., Dennie Butterfield, James Dunn, Ruel Allred,
Marvin Tolman, R. Carl Harris, Stan Knight, Floyd Sucher,
Rex Wadham, Lori Crnkovich, Ray Wilcox, Larry Arnoldsen,
Reed Bradford, Jean Larsen, and Lance Lanport.

3508.   Migenes, J. R. et al. "A Federally Funded Program to
Reduce the Incidence of Delinquent Acts in the Syracuse, New
York, Adolescent Population." Symposium given at the North
Atlantic Regional Association for Counselor Educators and
Supervisors, Kiamesha Lake, New York, October, 1975. 55p.

A multi-focal pilot program is described in which the goals
of primary, secondary, and tertiary prevention of delinquent
acts are approached by a multiple intervention strategies.
The primary and secondary prevention strategies are focused
on the junior high school. All school personnel undergo
training in those skills which create prositive emotional
climate at the school, as well as those skills which screen
out adolescents who are at high risk for acking out
behavior. Specific differential responses are taught to the
trainees which they are encouraged to implement in their
work with troubled adolescents in school. Continuous on-
sight consultation at the school is provided to the
trainees. Tertiary prevention efforts are focused upon
refining the skills of the county's juvenile probation
workers in their work with adolescents whose behavior has

already brought them into contact with the courts. See ERIC Abstract ED 123512.

3509.   Milliman, H. L. and Schaefer, C. E. "Behavioral Change: Program Evaluation and Staff Feedback." Child Welfare, 54, 10 (December, 1975): 692-702.

Authors review four recent books which focus on disruptive teenagers in schools. The general orientation of the book is micro-sociological. Reviewers suggest that some conflict in schools is unavoidable and that pervasive, severe school disruption is an index of fundamental social change. See ERIC Abstract EJ 131395.

3510.   Miranty, T. J. & Ryckman, D. B. "Classroom Behavior Inventory: Factor Verification." Journal of Research and Personality, 8, 3 (October, 1974): 291-293.

Three factors of the eighteen item inventory-task-oriented versus distractibility, extroversion versus introversion, and considerateness versus hostility loaded perfectly, according to the a'priori structure of the instrument, on data from second graders. See ERIC Abstract 0840053-4.

3511.   Mitchell, D. W. & Crowell, P. J. "Modifying Inappropriate Behavior In An Elementary Art Class." Elementary School Guidance and Counseling, 8, 1 (October, 1973): 34-42.

The researchers conducted a behavior modification program with three nine year old males who tended to be hyperactive in classroom groups and exhibited varying degrees of learning disabilities. Counselor baseline observations revealed that two of the subjects had problems with motor activity and one subject had verbal-behavior difficulties. Subjects were told they would be observed during their art class and rewarded for good behavior using a point system. This reinforcement period was followed by a return to baseline and a second reinforcement period. All subjects maintained good behavior during the first reinforcement period, two subjects behaved reasonably well during the second baseline period, and all subjects remained on-task during the second reinforcement period. Both the art teacher and the counselor felt the improved behaviors of the subjects had a positive effect on classmates' behaviors. See ERIC Abstract 0588451-3.

3512.   Mitchell, M. "Assistant Principals can be Effective Counselors, and Mediators." NASSP Bulletin, 64, 436 (May, 1980): 29-32.

Author stresses that assistant principals must function as both counselors and mediators if they hope to succeed in mollifying disruptive students. See ERIC Abstract EJ 221614.

3513.   Moracco, J. and Kazandkian, A. "Effectiveness of Behavior Counseling and Consulting with Non-western Elementary School Children." Elementary School Guidance and Counseling, 11, 4 (April, 1977): 244-250.

Behavioral counseling and consulting may be less value laden than other orientations to changing behavior. It appears the principles of behavior modification are not as directly derived from a particular culture as other orientations may be. Behavioral counseling and consulting have definate applicability across different cultural settings. See ERIC Abstract EJ 158407.

3514.   Morales, C. A. "Discipline: Applicable Techniques for Student Teachers." Education, 101, 2 (Winter, 1980): 15-17.

Author discusses what is being done at one teacher training institution to train pre-service teachers in the area of classroom management. See ERIC Abstract EJ 237306.

3515.   Morris, J. D. and Arrant, D. "Behavior Ratings of Emotionally Disturbed Children by Teachers, Parents and School Psychologists." Paper presented at the annual meeting of the American Educational Research Association, Toronto, Canada, March, 1978. 15p.

Emotional disturbance was rated by teachers, parents and the school psychologist for a group of 104 children diagnosed as severely emotionally distrubed. Black and white, as well as male and female students were included. Teachers were found significantly more severe in their judgements than the school psychologists on the behavior and socialization skills of the REFERRAL CHECKLIST, but not on communication. The teacher rating profile was also found to deviate from parallelness from the other raters with increased severity in the behavior skill. None of the nine correlations between judges on the same scales were significant. The results suggest a reappraisal of the referral process. See ERIC Abstract ED 174628.

3516.   Morrison, T. L. "The Classroom Boundary Questionnaire: An Instrument to Measure One Aspect of Teacher Leardership in the Classroom." Educational and Psychological Measurement, 35, 1 (Spring, 1975): 119-134.

Author discusses the implications and uses for the classroom boundary questionnaire. He then goes on to describe how it worked with teacher leadership in the classroom.

3517.   Morrison, T. L. "Classroom Structure, Work Involvement, and Social Climate in Elementary School Classrooms." Journal of Educational Psychology, 71, 4 (August, 1979): 471-477.

Author identified two behavioral dimensions of classroom structure, amount of child activity in proportion of activity controlled by the teacher. Four thirty minute observations were conducted in 32 fourth, fifth and sixth grade classrooms with 267 children and administered was a social climate questionnaire and the Test Anxiety Scale for children. High structured classrooms had the most work involvement. Both high activity and low control were related to more active deviancy. High control classrooms had more friction. See ERIC Abstract 0203363-1.

3518.   Moskowitz, G. and Hayman, J. L. "Success Strategies of Inner-City Teachers: A Year Long Study." Journal of Educational Research, 69, 8 (April, 1976): 283-289.

In a replication and expansion of an earlier study by the authors, the classroom interaction of 10 best and 11 first year teachers in two urban junior high schools was analyzed over the course of a school year. Differences between groups at the start of the year related to climate setting behaviors; at midpoint to reinforcing behaviors; and the end of the year, to control, discipline, and immediate feedback behaviors; and throughout the year to motivating behaviors. New teachers had discipline problems which continued to grow as the year progressed. They used more direct behaviors than the best teachers, who maintained control all year and used more indirect behaviors. See ERIC Abstract 0133956-1.

3519.   Mosley, W. J. and Sitko, M. C. "A Model Program for Training Teachers of the Mildly Handicapped." Teacher Education Form; Vol. 4, No. 4. Washington, D.C.: Bureau of Educational Personnel Development, 1976. 24p.

The development, operation and evaluation of an experimentally based teacher training program, the Mildly Handicapped Program is described in this report. The main concern of the program is to develop teachers who, in the real world public school classroom setting, obtain the best possible results from elementary age children in special and/or regular classroom settings. The program enables students to obtain a degree in elementary education with 1. major certification in elementary education and 2. special education endorsement in two areas -- mental retardation and emotional disturbance/behavior disorders. The program is a teaching teacher training program designed to prepare teachers to provide educational services to regular class students and to child who are thought to be mildly handicapped in the exceptional child areas of mental retardation and behavior disorders. The major objective of the program is to prepare teachers who can efficiently deal and teach a wide range of cognitive abilities and behavioral styles. See ERIC Abstract ED 128299.

3520.   Mowder, B. A.   "Pre-Intervention Assessment of Behavior
Disordered Children: Where Does the School Psychologist
Stand."   School Psychology Review, 9, 1 (Winter, 1980):
5-13.

Assessment of behavior disorders and emotional disturbances
in children is difficult to achieve because a generally
recognized classification system does not exist, definitions
of emotional disturbance are not clear, incidents figures
vary, and many hypotheses are available.   The author
recommends a multidimensional approach.   See ERIC Abstract
EJ 224601.

3521.   Moyer, D. H.   "Discipline in the Urban Middle School: A
Rehabilitative Process."   NASSP Bulletin, 62, 416 (March,
1978):   68-74.

Discipline in the urban middle school is a rehabilitative
process requiring accurate adult perception of the kind of
behavior problems which interfere with student achievement.
See ERIC Abstract EJ 173581.

3522.   Multhauf, A. P., Willower, D. J. and Licata, J. P.
"Teacher Pupil-Control Ideology and Behavior in Classroom
Environmental Robustness."   Elementary School Journal, 79, 1
(September, 1978):   41-46.

Investigated in the study was the relationship between
teacher pupil-control ideology, teacher pupil-control
behavior, and classroom robustness.   Using a sample of 17
female and 15 male teachers in grades 1-6, teacher ideology
was measured by questionnaire, while teacher behavior and
classroom robustness were measured by pupil ratings.   No
significant relationship between teacher pupil-control
ideology and classroom robustness was found.   However,
humanistic control behavior was significantly associated
with more robust classrooms.   See ERIC Abstract 0643664-3.

3523.   Muro, J. J., Brown, J. C., and Kelley, J. D.   "Research
and Innovation in Elementary School Guidance and Counseling:
Students and Teachers as Co-Clients."   Elementary School
Guidance and Counseling, 9, 3 (March, 1975):   249-251.

A description is given of the help given by counselor-
consultant to an experienced teacher who is having classroom
problems, using behavior modification methods.   After two
weeks of baseline observation and the establishment of two
target behaviors (inappropriate talking and failure to
complete assignments on time), students and teacher
discussed and agreed on rules for both sides.   Social reinforcement of the desired behavior by students, in the form
of praise for individuals and for the class as a whole, was
furnished by the teacher, and reinforcement for the teacher
herself was furnished by the counselor-consultant and by the
principal in consequence of observed improvement on the part
of the teacher.   Assessment of classroom behavior after two

weeks of this procedure show significantly less inappropriate talking and better fulfillment of assignments, and much more feelings positively expressed by the teacher toward her work. See ERIC Abstract 1256860-6.

3524.   Murphy, M. C. et al.   "School Desegregation and the Role of the Urban Counselor."   Journal of Black Psychology, 3, 1 (August, 1976):   87-99.

Authors states that the urban counselor has to be prepared and become acutely aware of the functions that take place in the desegregated school.   His allegiance must go out to all students and participate totally in a changing and progressing educational system.   Authors make suggestions and recommendations which should be considered by counselors and educators.   See ERIC Abstract EJ 152541.

3525.   Musgrove, W. J. & Harms, R. A.   "Teachers' Attitudes Toward Behavior Modification."   Humanist Educator, 13, 3 (March, 1975):   133-137.

Measured in the study were attitudes toward behavior modification held by 303 elementary school teachers who were surveyed by the author.   The skill yielded a neutral attitude score of 60.   The subjects; average score was 64.82, which indicated a mildly favorable attitude toward behavior modification techniques.   Subjects who held a masters degree or who had completed fifteen credits beyond their masters degree favored the behavior modification techniques to significantly greater degree than subjects who had completed only a baccalaureate degree or fifteen credits beyond that degree.   It is suggested that teachers develop positive attitudes toward behavior modification during exposure to college classes, and additional training and practice in behavior modification techniques during undergraduate teacher training is recommended.   See ERIC Abstract 1172661-5.

3526.   National Education Association.   "Management of Disruptive Surface Behavior: Prescriptive Learning Package Five. Description of Teacher In-Service Education Materials." Washington, D.C.:   National Institute of Education, May, 1979.

Described is a prescriptive learning package for in-service teacher education.   The package seeks to aid the teacher in developing and implementing individualized intervention techniques suitable for children whose learning situations result in disruptive behavior; knowledge and application of terms and principles of behavior management are highlighted. Information is provided on the purposes and content of the package, activities and resources necessary for implementation, history development, and ordering information.   See ERIC Abstract ED 164536.

3527.   National   Education   Association.   "Reality   Therapy.
Description   of   Teacher   In-Service   Education   Materials."
Washington,   D.C.:   National   Institute   of   Education,   May,
1979.

Described   is   a   programmed   text   for   in-service   teacher
education   focusing   on   Reality   Therapy   as   a   technique   to   help
students   change   their   unacceptable   behavior.   The   text
covers   techniques   of   classroom   management,   discipline,   and
control   of   student   behaviors.   Information   is   provided   on
the   purposes   and   content   of   the   programmed   text,   as   well   as
descriptions   of   activities   and   resources.   See   ERIC   Abstract
ED   164535.

3528.   National   Education   Association.   "Teaching   1:   Classroom
Management.   Description   of   Teacher   In-Service   Education
Materials."   Washington,   D.C.:   National   Institute   of
Education,   May,   1979.

Presented   in   this   learning   module   is   a   description   of   an
in-service   teacher   education   package.   The   module   focuses   on
systematic   principles   of   behavior   modification,   and   emphasises   the   procedures   underlying   effective   social   development
and   the   use   of   positive   motivational   methods   with   children
and   young   adults.   Information   is   provided   on   the   purposes
and   content   of   the   module,   as   well   as   the   activities   and
resources   necessary   for   its   implementation.   See   ERIC
Abstract   ED   164538.

3529.   National   Education   Association.   "The   L.E.A.S.T.   Approach
to   Classroom   Discipline.   Description   of   Teacher   In-Service
Education   Materials."   Washington,   D.C.:   National   Institute
of   Education,   June,   1979.

The   in-service   teacher   education   program   focuses   on   a   system
of   employing   minimum   action   in   order   to   attain   and   maintain
effective   classroom   discipline,   and   offers   a   survival
strategy   for   the   classroom   teacher.   The   product   title   is   an
acronym   for   the   five   steps   or   options   outlined   for   achieving
classroom   discipline: 1)   leave   things   alone   because   no
problems   are   likely   to   occur,   2)   end   the   action   indirectly
because   behavior   is   disrupting   the   classroom,   3)   attend   more
fully   because   more   information   or   communication   is   needed,
4)   spell   out   directions   because   disruption   or   harm   will
occur,   and   5)   track   student   progress   to   evaluate   and   reinforce   student   behavior.   Information   is   provided   concerning
program   purposes,   content,   activities,   resources,   and
history   of   development.   See   ERIC   Abstract   ED   166143.

3530.   Nay,   W.   R.,   Schulman,   J.   A.   and   Bailey,   K.   G.   "Territory
and   Classroom   Management: An   Exploratory   Case   Study."
Behavior   Therapy,   7,   2   (March,   1976):   240-246.

In   this   study   an   alternative   to   the   token   approach   was   used,
territory   as   a   reinforcer   within   the   classroom.   A   teacher
in   a   suburban   school   had   considerable   difficulty   in

controlling 24 fourth graders. Using a multiple baseline approach, the intervention program included two phases, the first to control out-of-seat behavior, and the second, inappropriate verbalizations. A one square yard area was marked off on each subject's desk with heavy tape, subjects were then allowed to select an area to be seated and to name their territory. During the first phase, violations of clearly communicated rules regarding out-of-seat behavior resulted in an immediate twenty minute loss of territory. During this period, the subject was seated in a desk chair at the side of the room which was not defined by tape boundaries. While out-of-seat behavior immediately declined, inappropriate verbal behavior remained at baseline levels. When occupation of subjects' territory was made contingent upon following rules for verbal behavior, inappropriate verbalization showed a marked detriment. See ERIC Abstract 0679156-4.

3531.   Neill, S. B. "Crisis Counseling." American Education, 13, 1 (January-February, 1977): 17-22.

Each year according to the author most school districts spend any where from $1 to $13 per student repairing damage caused by vandals. The Yerba Buena High School in San Jose, California, spends less than $1,000 per year in total, and attributes the success to a project called "crisis counseling." See ERIC Abstract EJ 161506.

3532.   Nelsen, E. A. and Uhl, N. P. "The Influence of Racial Composition of Desegretated Secondary Schools Upon Black Students' Perceptions of the School Climate." Paper presented at the AA project called "Crisis Counseling." See ERIC Abstract EJ 161506.

A questionnaire describing 87 environmental characteristics of schools is administered to entering freshman at a predomi- nantly black university to study the relationships of racial composition to various dimensions of school environment and social climate. Both racial and nonracial aspects of school environments are examined. Correlation of the student responses with a racial composition index generally reveals perception of predominantly white schools. Results indicate that black students of both sexes who attend predominantly white schools are more likely to report better care for their school building, more clubs and extra curricular activities, and more inter-racial friendships and inter- racial dating. See ERIC Abstract ED 123316.

3533.   Nelson, R. O., Hay, L. R. and Hay, W. M. "The Reactivity and Accuracy of Teachers' Self-Monitoring of Positive and Negative Classroom Verbalization." Behavior Therapy, 8, 5 (November, 1977): 972-985.

In the first experiment, two fourth grade teachers self- recorded positive and negative classroom verabliations during different phases of the study. In the second

Telos

experiment, four fifth and sixth grade teachers self-recorded positive or negative classroom verbalizations and/or received experimental instructions to increase positive statements or to decrease negative statements. Observers also recorded verbal responses and the classroom behaviors of students during both experiments. Self-recording tended to increase positive statements but was less effective in decreasing negative statements. See ERIC Abstract 0820860-4.

3534.   Nelson, R. O., Kapust, J. A. and Dorsey, B. L. "Minimal Reactivity of Overt Classroom Observations on Student and Teacher Behaviors." Behavior Therapy, 9, 5 (November, 1978): 695-702.

A multiple baseline design across four normal junior high school classrooms was employed. Obtained was data from five observers for each of seven categories of student behavior and five categories of teacher behavior. There was little evidence of reactivity for any category of teacher or student behavior in any of the classrooms observed. See ERIC Abstract 0950662-4.

3535.   Newman, J. "From Past to Future: School Violence in a Broad View." Contemporary Education, 52, 1 (Fall, 1980): 7-12.

Two explanations for school violence are evaluated from a historical viewpoint. One approach assumes an inherent relationship between the behavior of students and the disciplinary practices of the schools. The second approach attributes school disorders to characteristics of the students. See ERIC Abstract EJ 237730.

3536.   Newton, R. R. "Models of Schooling and Theories of Discipline." High School Journal, 63, 5 (February, 1980): 183-190.

Four educational models are presented, then the implications of these models for discipline are explored and explicated. The aim is to promote a greater awareness of the theoretical assumptions which motivate different attitudes toward discipline, thereby creating a more solid basis both for understanding and for intelligent action. See ERIC Abstract EJ 226860.

3537.   Narholin, D. and Steinman, W. M. "Stimulus Control in the Classroom as a Function of the Behavior Reinforced." Journal of Applied Behavior Analysis, 10, 3 (Fall, 1977): 465-478.

Researchers attempted to demonstrate a means by which the academic and social behavior of children can become less dependent on the teacher's direct supervision. Eight fifth and sixth graders with behavior problems performed in a classroom under three conditions: A) unreinforced baseline,

B) reinforcement for being on task, and C) reinforcement for the accuracy and rate of math problems solved. The teacher was absent for a protion of the class session under each of these conditions. In the teacher's absence, on task behavior declined significantly and disruption increased significantly, regardless of reinforcement. In addition, the teacher's absence resulted in significantly fewer problems attempted and significantly decreased accuracy. The extent to which the subjects became disruptive was significantly reduced and the number of problems increased when reinforcement was contingent on academic accuracy and rate, instead of being contingent on being on task. See ERIC Abstract 0820260-4.

3538.   Nickel, J. et al. "The Confrontation Meeting: Identifying First Year Junior High Teachers' Problems." Clearinghouse, 49, 8 (April, 1976): 358-360.

If communication problems in the resulting feelings of power-lessness are concerns for experienced teachers, what must the problems and concerns of first year teachers be? A workshop designed to gather information about the concerns and problems of 25 first year junior high school teachers is discussed. See ERIC Abstract EJ 144206.

3539.   Nielsen, A. and Gerber, D. "Psycho-Social Aspects of Truancy in Early Adolescence." Adolescence, 14, 54 (Summer, 1979): 313-326.

The authors investigated truancy in junior high school students by the means of structured interviews with 22 truants. Truancy at this age was commonly associated with difficulties at home, at school, and with peers. Two types of truants were delineated, authority defined and peer phobic. See ERIC Abstract EJ 211985.

3540.   Nielsen, L. "Successful In-School Suspension Programs: The Counselor's Role." School Counselor, 26, 5 (May, 1979): 325-333.

Article describes the problems which were encountered in establishing eight in-school suspensions centers. She believed that the benefits for students in these centers were overwhelmingly positive. She hopes that the specific suggestions formulated in this study can help counselors sponsor effective in-school suspension centers in their own schools. See ERIC Abstract EJ 204225.

3541.   Niensted, S. "Discipline for Today's Different Chil-dren." Phi Delta Kappan, 60, 8 (April, 1979): 575-576.

The author is a teacher who returns to the classroom after eleven years of absence. She notes that discipline is much more a problem now than before and attributes much of the change to the way parents excuse their children's behavior. See ERIC Abstract EJ 197947.

3542.   Noble, C. G. and Nolan, J. D.   "Effect of Student Verbal Behavior on Classroom Teacher Behavior." _Journal of Educational Psychology_, 68, 3 (June, 1976): 342-346.

The functional relationship between individual student rates of volunteering in the classroom was investigated as compared to the differential rates of teacher questions directed to the individual students and the percentage of student volunteering approved by the teacher in 12 high school classrooms with 90 subjects during the 1st and 3rd month of the term. Teachers did not differentially approve different rates of volunteering. However, those students who volunteered more were more likely to receive a directed question. During the third month, the rate of directed questions correlated with student volunteering for those who did volunteer. Results imply that student control whether they receive a directed question and, as the term progresses how frequently the teacher addresses them. See ERIC Abstract 0299356-2.

3543.   Noblit, G. W. and Collins, T. W.   "Order and Disruption in a Desegregated High School." _Crime and Delinquency_, 24, 3 (July, 1978): 277-289.

It has been assumed that schools play a dramatic role in creating school crime. This paper, by using ethnographic data from a desegregated high school in the south demonstrates the interrelationships among administrative styles, deterrents, commitment, and disruption. It appears that legitimacy of rules even within a school's beauracy needs to be developed through negotiating order with students. See ERIC Abstract 1195862-5.

3544.   Noblit, G. W. and Collins, T. W.   "Order and Disruption in a Desegregated High School." Washington, D.C.: Department of Health, Education and Welfare, 1978. 37p.

This is one of theoretical papers on school crime and its relation to poverty. By utilizing ethographic data the reader develops an understanding of the inter-relationships among administrative styles, deterrence, commitment, and disruption. The effect of change of administrative styles on the character of order and disruption in a desegrated southern high school is examined. The purpose of this paper is to examine the control systems and their effects. The paper concludes that a highly representative governance system foster commitment in the vast amjority of school participants. The participants have a major role in making and revising the rules, and, thus, when caught violating them, they are hard pressed to question the legitimacy of those rules.

3545.   Noll, R. L., Willower, D. J. & Barnette, J. J.   "Teacher Self-Actualization and Pupil Control Ideology-Behavior Consistency." _Alberta Journal of Educational Research_, 23, 1 (March, 1977): 65-70.

The hypothesis was tested that the teacher's level of self-actualization would predict the consistency between the teacher's pupil control ideology and behavior. Data were gathered on a) the level of self-actualization and pupil control ideologies of 84 teachers, and b) the pupil control behavior of these teachers. The hypothesis was not rejected. Previous research that showed a positive relationship between teachers self-actualization and humanism in pupil control ideology was replicated. However, teachers self-actualization was not associated with humanism in pupil control behavior. See ERIC Abstract 0421759-2.

3546.   Nolte, M. C. "Due Process and its Historial Development in Education." Paper presented at the National Acadey of School Administrators Seminar, Denver, Colorado, April, 1974. 16p.

Due process of law has never been defined by the Supreme Court in so many words, the court choosing to define the term on a inclusiong-exclusion basis as it goes along. The author presents the historical development of the due process concept, and discusses cases where due process has affected the rights of those involved in the educational process. The author notes that the most pressing problems which involve due process of law are of two varieties: 1) those in which students claim lack of due process where punishment and explusions are involved, and 2) those in which the classification system used by schools to troup children for instructional and other purposes are being challenged. See ERIC Abstract ED 088186.

3547.   Noonan, J. R. and Thibault, R. "Primary Prevention in Appalachian Kentucky: Peer Reinforcement of Classroom Attendance." Journal of Community Psychology, 2, 3 (July, 1974): 260-264.

Ten elementary and 25 high school students who are identified as chronic absentees participated in a contingency management program in which a equal number of popular students were selected as reinforcing agents and assigned to each absentee. These monitors were required to observe when the target absentee did or did not attend school. When the target did attend, the monitors communicated that this was appreciated. When they were absent, the monitor contacted the target and sympathetically asked the reason for the absence and when they would return. The effects of this peer reinforcement were analyzed in a one and two month baseline treatment and follow-up assessment. Attendance rates of both the elementary and high school targets increased significantly between treatment and follow-up phases, and between baseline and follow-up phases. See ERIC Abstract 0190153-1

3548.   O'Brien, D. M. "In-School Suspension: Is it the new way to Punish Productively." American School Board Journal, 163, 3 (March, 1976): 35-37.

Author describes a successful in-school suspension program in four suburban Minneapolis schools. See ERIC Abstract EJ 132549.

3549.   O'Keefe, M. and Smaby, M. "Seven Techniques for Solving Classroom Discipline Problems." High School Journal, 56, 4 (January, 1973): 190-199.

Authors present seven different ideas for solving common classroom discipline problems.

3550.   Olivero, J. L. "Discipline. Number One Problem in the Schools? Forty Positive, Preventive Prescriptions for Those Who Care." Burlinghane, California: Association of California School Administrators, 1977.

The purpose of this paper is to help school administrators look seriously at one of the biggest school problems -- discipline. The author examines those factors that seem to cause student misbehavior -- factors having no origin in both the home and the school. Believing that the best way to handle discipline problems is through prevention rather than remediation, the author does not discuss punishment as a suspension or expulsion. Instead, he offers forty preventative prescriptions to help keep discipline problems from becoming so overwhelming that productivity and satisfaction isn't possible. These prescriptions fall into three categories: logististics/materials, processes, and programs. The author emphasizes the importance of parent education and participation in solving discipline problems. See ERIC Abstract ED 145566.

3551.   Olivero, J. L. "Rights, Respect, Responsibility: Those Three R's are Important Too." Thrust for Educational Leadership, 8, 3 (January, 1979): 8-10.

Several currently functioning techniques are noted for improving school climate and reducing the atmosphere of stress and conflict which leads to violence. Ideas include celebrating learning, providing cool down rooms or sustained silent reading periods to relieve tension during the school day, and implementing conflict resolution curriculum. See ERIC Abstract EJ 207504.

3552.   Omiza, M. M. "The Effects of Relaxation and Bio-Feedback Training on Dimensions of Self-Concept Among Hyperactive Male Children." Educational Research Quarterly, 5, 1 (Spring, 1980): 22-30.

The effects of relaxation training and bio-feedback on five factors of self concept among hyperactive male elementary school students are investigated: levels of aspiration, anxiety, academic interest and satisfaction, leadership and initiative, and identification versus alienation. Findings suggest that relaxation training/bio-feedback warrant inclusion in the curriculum. See ERIC Abstract EJ 231262.

3553.   O'Neal, E. et al. "Territorial Invasion and Aggression in Young Children." Environmental Psychology and Non-Verbal Behavior, 2, 1 (Fall, 1977): 14-24.

Forty black first and second grade students were given instructions intended to induce possessiveness for a designated toy and a play area. Each subject then surreptitiously observed an experimental confederate dressed in a clown costume playing with either the designated toy or another toy. Results are presented. See ERIC Abstract EJ 171284.

3554.   Osborne, D. L. "Discipline in the High School." 1978. 7p.

The high school has paradoxically undergone a loss in status while gaining in importance for young people. Education has become essential to survival in today's world. Along with the goernment's financial neglect of public high schools in favor of the development of post-secondary institutions, the high school's educational task has become more difficult due to rapid social change affecting particular adolescents. School discipline problems, such as vandalism, truancy, and violence have been on the increase nationwide. Studies support the idea that students that are not doing well academically are the ones having discipline problems and also problems coping with social pressures and responsibilities. Author believes that federal funding should be available at the individual school level for educational programs which will provide students with opportunities to develop both academically and socially. See ERIC Abstract ED 154095.

3555.   Osmund, P. J. "Authority in the Secondary School." A Trend in Education, 3, (September, 1975): 32-39.

Authority depends upon a complex form of negotiations between the parties involved. Author discusses which tactics our teachers employ in day-to-day school management. See ERIC Abstract EJ 128864.

3556.   Page, D. P. and Edwards, R. P. "Behavior Change Strategies for Reducing Disruptive Classroom Behavior." Psychology in the Schools, 15, 3 (July, 1978): 413-418.

The effect of independent and interdependent group contingencies for academic work on the disruptive classroom behavior of junior high school students was studied. Using a multiple baseline design, the disruptive classroom behavior in five mathematics classes was measured under baseline, independent group, and interdependent group contingencies. Group contingencies consisted of free time contingent on completion and accuracy of daily assignments. Free time was delivered either individually, contingent on individual performance or to the class as a whole, contingent on group performance. In all classes the level of disruptive behavior was reduced when treatment was initiated. Both independent and interdependent group contingencies resulted in lowered rates of disruptive behavior, with the interdependent contingency being slightly more effective. See ERIC Abstract 0964562-4.

3557.   Page, F. M. and Page, J. A. "Mission Impossible: The Pre-Service Teacher and Discipline." 1980. 8p.

Authors state that student-teachers need specific guidelines for classroom discipline that include preventive techniques, direct techniques, and techniques for dealing with severe or consistent misbehavior. This guide gives examples for each technique along with the proper situationfor their use. See ERIC Abstract ED 190524.

3558.   Panush, L. "One Day in the Life of an Urban High School Principal." Phi Delta Kappan, 56, 1 (September, 1974): 46-49.

This article is a minute-by-minute account of one Friday in the work day of a principal who has taught and been an administrator in schools for the past 40 years. See ERIC Abstract EJ 104204.

3559.   Parashar, O, D. "Disturbed Classroom Behavior: A Comparison Between Mentally Retarded, Learning Disabled, and Emotionally Disturbed Children." Journal of Mental Deficiency Research, 20, 2 (June, 1976): 109-120.

Researchers attempted to identify and measure the nature and prevalence of disturbed classroom behavior in fifty-six mentally retarded children and to compare them with fifty-one learning disabled and sixty-five emotionally disturbed children. Eleven types of disturbed classroom behaviors were studied. Subjects were rated by their teachers on the Devereux Elementary School Behavior Rating Scale. Results shows that the three groups exhibited significant differences on their profiles of the cumulative eleven disturbed classroom behavior factors. They also differed on the individual factors of classroom disturbance, disrespective-defiance, external blame, achievement anxiety, comprehension disorders, irrelevant responsiveness, and lack of creative initiative. See ERIC Abstract 1115359-5.

3560.   Parish, T. S., Maly, J. and Shiraci, A. "Use of Classical Conditioning Procedures to Control Aggressive Behaviors in Children: A Preliminary Report." Perceptual and Motor Skills, 41, 2 (October, 1975): 651-658.

It was hypothesized that classical conditioning would reduce children's aggression in the classroom. Twenty-five fourth and fifth graders who were shown pictures of aggressive scences pared were the presentation of negatively evaluated words subsequently displayed significantly fewer aggressive responses than forty controls who had not experienced these conditioning procedures. A significant teacher classroom effect was also found, which appeared to be a function of the level of the three teachers' permissiveness. Specifically, subjects' aggressive behaviors occurred more frequently in the classrooms where a permissive atmosphere prevailed than in a classroom where a more restrictive atmosphere was maintained. In those classrooms where a permissive atmosphere prevailed, the subjects who were the same sex as their teacher tended to display more aggressive responses than those who were the opposite sex than their teachers. See ERIC Abstract 0825255-4.

3561.   Parker, F. C. and McCoy, J. F. "School Based Intervention for the Modification of Excessive Absenteeism." Psychology in the Schools, 14, 1 (January, 1977): 84-88.

Three procedures to modify excessive absenteeism were implemented by an elementary school principal and assessed with an across subjects multiple baseline design. Intervention with parents, approval for attendance, and disapproval for absences produced sustained increases in attendance and parents-initiated contacts with the school. See ERIC Abstract EJ 153315.

3562.   Parker, H. C. "Contingency Management and Concomitant Changes in Elementary School Students' Self-Concept." Psychology in the Schools, 11, 1 (January, 1974): 70-79.

The effects of a positive reinforcement oriented contingency management program was evaluated on students' total and school-related self-concepts and on their personal and social adjustment. Subjects were twelve second and sixteen fourth graders. The Pictorial Self Concept Skill, the California Test of Personality and classroom observations were used to measure the effects of contingency management. Results indicate that the subjects gained significantly on total and school-related sub concepts but manifested little gain on the personal and social adjustment scales of the California Test of Personality. See ERIC Abstract 0629152-3.

3563.   Paschal, B. J. and Treloar, J. H. "A Longitudinal Study of Attitude Change in Perspective and Beginning Elementary School Teachers." Teacher Educator, 15, 1 (Summer, 1979): 2-9.

This longitudinal study of 78 undergraduate students reveals that in an individual's attitudes toward variables associated with teaching change as those individuals gain classroom experience. See ERIC Abstract EJ 213490.

3564.   Patterson, J. "Projects Succeed." Paper presented at the annual convention of the California Personnel and Guidance Association, Anaheim, California, February, 1979. 12p.

Project Succeed is a program for helping failure and drop-out oriented pupils to improve their school achievement. Attendance and assignment completion are the key behaviors for enchancing achievement. Behavior modification and communications procedures are used to bring the desired changes. Treatment procedures include current assessment information initial contact with teachers, students and parents and daily school notes and regular communications between teachers, counselors, students and parents. This document includes copies of the data sheets for daily reports, and communication with counselors, students, parents, and teachers. See ERIC Abstract ED 179848.

3565.   Patterson, L. B. "The Principal, the Student and the Law: A Prosecuting Attorney's View." Paper presented at the National Association of Secondary School Principals, Washington, D.C., February, 1976. 53p.

The relationship between a school principal and the student and the functions and responsibility of each, are being controlled and dictated by the continuing involvement of the courts. Many complex and confusing legal questions have arisen because of this judicial intervention. Issues discussed include school violence and vandalism, student rights, due process, and the distrinction between substantive due process and procedural due process. Guidelines are offered administrators in the form of a handbook and a compilation of ideas to help deal with a variety of school problems through the legislature, and with community apathy. See ERIC Abstract ED 123748.

3566.   Patton, T. L. "A Model for Teaching Rational Behavior Therapy in a Public School Setting." 1977. 12p.

Described in this paper is a training model for the use of Rational Behavior Therapy with emotionally disturbed adolescence in a school setting. Five basic rational behavior therapy techniques are discussed. These sessions which last ten weeks are described and also presented is an organizational for the actual classroom activities including content, materials and methods appropriate for each session. See ERIC Abstract ED 169415.

3567.   Payne, C. M. "Who Runs this Chicago High School." Integrated Education, 17, 1-2 (January-April, 1979): 9-14.

Author discusses the lack of discipline which allows large numbers of students to stay in the hallways rather than attend classes at a Chicago all black westside high school. He suggests that the administration does not enforce teacher discipline and that teachers, thus, do not fulfill their own duties to control students. See ERIC Abstract EJ 218829.

3568.   Pearson, C. "Resolving Classroom Conflicts." Learning, 3, 9 (May-June, 1975): 26-31.

Author presents a variety of techniques used to resolve classroom conflicts for the classroom teacher in the elementary school.

3569.   Peed, S. and Pinsker, M. A. "Behavior Change Procedures in Junior and Senior High Schools." Education and Urban Society, 10, 4 (August, 1978): 501-520.

While behavior change procedures should not be viewed as a panacea, they do offer an attractive alternative for addressing many of the problems faced by secondary school teachers and administrators. See ERIC Abstract EJ 188061.

3570.   Peoples, F. B. "Edmond S. Meany Junior High School and the Teacher Corps." College Education Recorder, 36, 3 (March, 1979): 46-48.

The teacher corp program at the Edmond S. Meany Junior High School is discussed and ways for other people to incorporate such a program is included.

3571.   Peretti, P. O. "Perceived Personality Impressions in Student Acceptance and Rejection Interaction Patterns in the Classroom." Research Quarterly, 46, 4 (December, 1975): 457-462.

The researchers attempted to determine the group structure of a sixth grade class of 30 students, the acceptance-rejection interaction patterns, and words or terms most frequently associated with personality impressions of students related to their classmates. Students were given A) an open ended questionnaire on which they indicated three students they would and three they would not like to sit next to and why, B) a forced choice questionnaire on which they indicated which of ten personality features were characteristic of their selections, C) another open ended questionnaire similar to the first and D) another forced choice questionnaire on which subjects indicated which of 20 characteristics were applicable to their selections. A sociogram of group structure was constructed from these sets of data. Among acceptance students, relationships tended to be reciprocal. See ERIC Abstract 0486556-3.

3572.   Perry, C. L. and Duke, D. L. "Lessons to be Learned about Discipline from Alternative High Schools." Journal of Research and Development in Education, 11, 4 (Summer, 1978): 78-91.

Attempts to determine whether behavior problems were as great a concern in schools-within-a-school as they were preceived to be in regular high schools were the purpose of this study. The authors use student and teacher ratings as critera for evaluating behavior problems. See ERIC Abstract EJ 189893.

3573.   Perry, J. D., Guidubaldi, J. and Kehle, T. J. "Kinder-
garten Competencies as Predictors of Third Grade Classroom
Behavior   and   Achievement."   Journal   of   Educational
Psychology, 71, 4 (August, 1979): 443-450.

To investigate the relationships between preschool competencies and later academic functioning, multiple regression
analyses were conducted using kindergarten intellectual,
academic and social variables, teacher ratings of academic
readiness, and the Sells Teacher Rating Scale a Peer
relations to predict third grade behavior. A random sample
of 184 third grade children evaluated during the 1973-74
kindergarten year and a second sample with additional time
one social and background variables were included. A social
competence measure of initiative was a particularly successful predictor of achievement. See ERIC Abstract 0200963-1.

3574.   Persons, W. S., Brassel, W. R. and Rollins, H. A.   "A
Practical Obsrvation Procedure for Minitoring Four Behaviors
Relevant to Classroom Management." Psychology In The
Schools, 13, 1 (January, 1976): 64-71.

A simple procedure is presented for observing four behaviors
relevant to classroom management: student disruption,
student attention, and the teacher's use of both positive
and negative events. Five paraprofessional teacher aides
observed twenty-eight elementary and middle school teachers
and their classes on ten occasions both at the beginning and
at the end of the school year. The aides manifested higher
inter-rater realiabilities. Stable estimates of all four
target behaviors were obtained by averaging the data. The
procedures yielded reliable, stable measures of four
important classroom behaviors. See ERIC Abstract 0679456-4.

3575.   Peterson, R. F. et al. "The Effects of Teacher Use of
I-Messages on Student Disruptive and Study Behavior."
Psychological Records, 29, 2 (Spring, 1979): 187-199.

Investigated in this study were the influences of
I-Messages, statements describing the effects of a child's
behavior on the teacher, on disruptive and study behaviors
in the classroom. In the first experiment, fifth grade
teachers were taught to use I-Messages in response to disruption. Four students with behavior problems served as
subjects. Three of the subjects showed systematic decreases
in disruption and increases in study behavior as a result.
In the second experiment, different levels of teacher
verbalization were controlled which had been observed in
experiment one. Two sixth grade teachers were taught to use
I-Messages if response to disruption. The teachers received
feedback in order to maintain appropriate levels of verbalization throughout the study period. Results showed
decreased disruptions in six of eight subjects. See ERIC
Abstract 1113564-5.

3576.   Pickhardt, C. E. "Fear In The Schools: How Students Make Teachers Afraid." Educational Leadership, Thirty-Six, 2 (November, 1978): 107-12.

Article includes a summary of the art of teacher intimidation and suggested teacher behavior learned from interviews from some student "experts." See ERIC Abstract EJ 190508.

3577.   Piersel, W. C. and Kratochwill, T. R. "Self-Observation and Behavior Change: Applications To Academic and Adjustment Problems Through Behavioral Consultation." Journal of School Psychology, 17, 2 (Summer, 1979): 151-161.

Self-observation as a behavior change technique was implemented through behavioral consultation with four children ages seven to fifteen, in a public elementary school system. The self-observation procedures were introduced to two subjects with academic problems and two subjects with behavioral problems. Subjects get daily charts on which they recorded instances of unwanted behavior or assignments completed. In all cases, self-observation resulted in improved behavior and academic achievement, succeeding when other planned interventions by school staff had failed. See ERIC Abstract 0886564-4.

3578.   Platte, J. S. and Kroth, R. L. "The Behavioral Cue Sort as an Aid in Responsible Modification of Adolescents' Behavior." Adolescence, 14, 53 (Spring, 1979): 241-246.

The effectiveness of a cue sort/behavioral intervention procedure in modifying off-task behavior, swearing, and excessive talking was examined in three junior high school students in a class for the emotionally disturbed. The cue sort allows the subject to distinguish between his or her real self and concept of ideal self; through resulting discrepancy is analyzed to determine the intervention target behavior. In these cases, the reward for three days of decreased target behavior was a trip to a hamburger stand. Tabular data are presented to show the decreases in target behavior obtained after the three day cue sort/intervention procedure. See ERIC Abstract 0845063-4.

3579.   Polirstok, S. R. and Greer, R. D. "Remediation of Mutually Aversive Interactions Between a Problem Student and Four Teachers by Training the Student in Reinforcement Techniques." Journal of Applied Behavior Analysis, 10, 4 (Winter, 1977): 707-716.

The effect of a social reinforcement training procedure for a female eighth grade problem student was tested on the verbal and nonverbal approval and disapproval of four of the student's teachers. A design using aspects of a multiple baseline within an extended reversal design was employed. Data were taken on the four teachers' approval and disapproval of the student, who was regarded as a major discipline problem, and the target student's approval and disapproval of the four teachers during baseline one, experimental condition one, baseline two, experimental condition two, and a post-check or baseline three condition six weeks after experimental condition two. Results show that increased student approval and decreased disapproval were attributable to training procedures. The increased student approval increased three of the four teachers' approval and decreased the disapproval of all four teachers. See ERIC Abstract 0210661-1.

3580.   Pooley, R. C.   "An Intergrated, Community-Based Approach To The Diagnosis And Treatment Of Disturbing Behaviors Shown By Children And Families." Washington, D.C.: Department of Health, Education and Welfare, 1978. 62P

This is one of fifty-two theoretical papers on school crime and its relation to poverty. It describes an interdisciplinary treatment program called the Pendelton Project. Certain salient dimensions of the problems and its treatment are developed in detail. The diagnosis and treatment of learning disabilities and methods to establish attachment between the disturbing child, his family, and the social order in general is presented. Strategies to extend innovation approaches to problem-solving are presented in the discussion of the practice of behavioral treatment and research activities associated with the practice. Topics include: 1) The Community Based Treatment Of Behavior Disorders, 2) Theoretical Consideration Of Delinquency, 3) Theoretical Considerations Of Treatment, Program Development And Staff Development. These topics are discussed in terms of principles of treatment, educational goals and deficits, short-term residential treatment, out client treatment, and research associated with such treatment. See ERIC Abstract ED 157196.

3581.   Popham, W. J.   "Discipline in the Classroom." VIMCET Associates, 1967.

A translation is described of operant methods to problems of classroom control. The film teaches the basic rules of contingency management, identifies instances when operant measures are being used, and presents solutions to common classroom behavior problems according to a reinforcement paradigm. Forty-five frames. Sound film strip. See NICEM 0730511.

3582.   Poppen, W. A., Thompson, C. L., Cates, J. T. & Gang, M. J. "Classroom Discipline Problems and Reality Therapy: Research Support." Elementary School Guidance and Counseling, 11, 2 (December, 1976): 131-137.

Recent research support for the application of reality therapy to the resolution of classroom discipline problem areas in the elementary school is described. Data confirmed that counselor-trained teachers can successfully use Reality Therapy to reduce the frequency of undesirable pupil behavior and to increase the frequency of desirable behavior. See ERIC Abstract 0204662-1.

3583.   Powell, T. H. "Help Teachers with Mainstreaming Now: Training in Behavior Management." Education Unlimited, 2, 5 (November-December, 1980): 11-13.

In-service teacher education on specific behavior management skills will enhance efforts to mainstream handicapped children. Among motivators for learning and applying such skills is graduate credit for completing the in-service training objectives. A table lists suggested modules and objectives for an In-Service Training Program in behavior management.

3584.   Powers, S. M. "The Vane Kindergarten Test: Temporal Stability And Ability To Predict Behavioral Criteria." Psychology In The Schools, 14, 1 (January, 1977): 34-36.

The Vane Kindergarten Test is judged to have limited usefulness in the early detection of learning handicaps for two reasons. 1) Its reliability is to allow discrimination between individuals. 2) The ability of the test to predict problem behaviors is quite limited. See ERIC Abstract EJ 153306.

3585.   Pritchett, W. and Willower, D. J. "Student Perceptions of Teacher/Pupil Control Behavior and Student Attitudes Toward High School." Alberta Journal of Educational Research, 21, 2 (June, 1975): 110-15.

In this study, the Helsel and Willower Pupil Control Behavior Form and the Coster High School Students' Opinion Questionnaire was administered to 852 junior and senior high school students. A significant relationship between student perceptions of custodial teacher/pupil control behavior and negative attitudes towards school was found. This relationship pertained to overall student attitudes and to each of six factors resulting from a factor analysis of the Coster Questionnaire. See ERIC Abstract 0150155-1.

3586.   "Problem Students." USA Today, 108, 2411 (August, 1979): 8.

Article reports on a large scale study which found that 60% of students are labeled as behavior problems by their teachers at least once during their elementary school careers. Author discusses the questions this raises about teacher judgments, school behavior standards, and the impact of student self-concept. See ERIC Abstract EJ 213641.

3587.   Project Head Start. "Discipline and Self-Control." New York University Film Library.

Film suggests how to prevent discipline problems and how to deal with them when they arise. It explains that such problems can be minimized if the teacher establishes warm, but firm relationships with the children. It discusses adequate supervision and shows children how to accept control. Twenty-four minutes. 16mm film. See NICEM 0804053.

3588.   Pulvino, C. J. and Hossman, C. "Mental Imagery in Counseling: A Case Analysis." School Counselor, 24, 1 (September, 1976): 44-47.

A case report is described of a male seventh grader who was referred for counseling because of slipping grades and classroom disturbances. The successful use of mental imagery in the counseling process is described. See ERIC Abstract 0237061-1.

3589.   Punch, K. F. and Rennie, L. "Some Factors Affecting Docility in Primary School Children." British Journal of Education Psychology, 48, 2 (June, 1978): 168-175.

The relationship between docility and age, sex, and the social structure of the school and a family was examined for 1,184 children in primary schools of differing social structure. Two docility measures were developed, based on the notions of an uncritical accepting attitude toward the pronouncements of authority figures, a disposition to obey instructions without regard to there merit, and a tendency to condemn behavior that is openly critical of authority figures. See ERIC Abstract 0415663-2.

3590.   Purl, M. C. and Dawson, J. "An Analysis Of Some Of The Effects Of "Schools Without Failure" Seminars On Participating Schools." Paper presented at American Educational Research Association Annual Meeting, New Orleans, Louisiana, February, 1973. 17P.

Written questionnaires were completed by the teachers, principals, and students of those elementary schools participating in the 1970-71 seminars based on Glasser's concept of "Schools without Failure." The questionnaires were designed to determine what changes had occurred since the seminars began and whether or not the schools were still following the practices contrary to Glasser's concept. Teachers and principals were asked to indicate the changes that had occurred in grading, testing, grouping, discipline, classroom meetings, parent conferences, curriculum and homework. Responses indicate that the seminar program apparently had positive effects on students and on teachers. Findings revealed that students have become more responsible for their own behavior and have learned to express themselves better and to listen to and respect the opinions of others. See ERIC Abstract ED 078535.

3591.   Quay, H. C., Glavin, J. P., Annesley, F. R. and Werry, J. S. "The Modification of Problem Behavior and Academic Achievement in a Resource Room." Journal of School Psychology, 10, 2 (June, 1972): 187-198.

This is a report of the second year of research on an experimental resource room program for classroom behavior problem children. The program emphasized academic remediation utilizing behaviorally oriented principles. Modification of both social behavior when in the resource room and academic gains in reading and arithmetic were significant for 69 second through sixth grade experimental subjects. Attentive behavior however, while in the regular classroom was not different from the 48 controls. See ERIC Abstract 0793249-4.

3592.   Rainwater, N. and Ayllon, T. "Increasing Academic Performance By Using A Timer As Antecedent Stimulus: A Study of Four Cases." Behavior Therapy, 7, 5 (October, 1976): 672-677.

Data from four first graders show that when a timer was introduced preceding math performance, math rate increased for all subjects. When the timer was also introduced preceding reading performance, the reading rate increased for all subjects. Results suggest that the teacher does not have to be limited to contingency management in the class-room. See ERIC Abstract 0904457-4.

3593.   Randolph, D. L. and Hardage, N. C. "Behavioral Consulta-tion and Group Counseling With Potential Dropouts." Elementary School Guidance and Counseling, 7, 3 (March, 1973): 204-209.

Fifteen fifth and sixth grade teachers were asked to identify potential dropouts on the Dropout Rating Scale. The obtained 90 children either A. were exposed to class-room behavior management by the teacher, who was given guidance in techniques of classroom behavior management by a doctoral level counselor B. participated in a weekly six member, client centered group counseling sessions or C. received no treatment. During the 12 week treatment period, the subjects' on-task behavior and the appropriateness of teacher behaviors were assessed by trained counselors. See ERIC Abstract 0998650-5.

3594.   Randolph, D. L. and Wallin, K. R. "A Comparison of Behavioral Consultation and Behavioral Consultation With Model Reinforcement Group Counseling for Children Who are Consistently Off-Task." Journal of Educational Research, 67, 3 (November, 1973): 103-107.

Seventy-five consistently inattentive pupils in 12 fifth and sixth grade classes were randomly assigned to one of three groups: classroom behavior management via behavioral consultation, classroom behavior management with model-reinforcement group counseling, and no treatment control group. Significant differences were found between the groups on on-task behavior and grade point average; no significant differences were reported for school attitudes. See ERIC Abstract 0792651-4.

3595.   Ransom, L. B. "Procedural Due Process In Public Schools: The "Thicket" Of Goss Versus Lopez." Wisconsin Law Review, 3, (1976): 934-74.

Consideration in this article is given to the extent to which the Supreme Court's decision in Goss versus Lopez opens the door to procedural requirements for historically discretionary in-school decisions by the boards, adminis-trators, and teachers in public elementary and secondary schools. See ERIC Abstract EJ 159034.

3596.   Rapport, M. D. et al. "The Effects Of A Response Cost Treatment Tactic On Hyperactive Children." Journal Of School Psychology, 18, 2 (Summer, 1980): 98-111.

Researches tested a response cost procedure, compared with Ritalin treatment on hyperactive elementary school children to determine effectiveness in reducing hyperactive behavior and in increasing academic performance. The cost program alone and combined with medication were effective in reducing off-task behavior and increasing academic perfor-mance. See ERIC Abstract EJ 227447.

3597.   Rawson, H. E. "Academic Remediation and Behavior Modification in a Summer School Camp." Elementary School Journal, 74, 1 (October, 1973): 34-43.

A ten day program of academic remedial work and behavioral rehabilitation is described in a summer camp for 24 disrup-tive pupils. Subjects were six to fourteen year old children, were below the seventh grade level, had IQs of 85, and were labeled as underachievers. Groups of six subjects each were assigned to a man and a woman who supervised their groups for the entire day. The goals of the program were to improve academic skills, modify disruptive behavior, and improve negative attitudes toward the school program. Without exception, subjects felt that the camp helped them with school adjustment. See ERIC Abstract 0180052-1.

3598.   Reese, S. C. and Filipczak, J. "Assessment of Skill Generalization: Measurement Across Setting, Behavior, and Time, in an Educational Setting." Behavior Modification, 4, 2 (April, 1980): 209-224.

Assessment of skill generalization was conducted within a large scale junior high school behavioral treatment program for 98 disruptive and academically deficient adolescents. Generalization was measured both within and between subjects. Results indicate that improved academic skills of the treatment group transferred across settings to non-treatment classes. Analysis of individual behavior programs indicated a transfer of skills across time for specific behaviors as well as across behaviors that were not the focus of the specific behavioral program. Generalization of the later types occurred within minimal programming. See PSYC Abstract 1116265-5.

3599.   Reiss, S. "Transfer Effects of Success and Failure Training From Reinforcing Agent to Another." Journal of Abnormal Psychology, 82, 3 (December, 1973): 435-445.

In this study the transfer effects of behavior changes in the presence of one reinforcing agent on behavior in the presence of another reinforcing agent was determined. Thirty-six six to ten year old boys in grades one through three who were judged to have poor attention span and low achievement in arithmetic were used as subjects. The experimental task consisted of a series of counting problems. Each session included two 12 minute sub-sessions during which the subject could earn token reinforcement only by attending to the task in solving problems. The experimenter conducted one sub-session and a second experimenter conducted the other. Following the establishment of stable, intermediate baseline levels of counting, experimenter A introduced a more favorable reinforcement schedule for some subjects and a less favorable schedule for other subjects, but continued baseline schedules for subjects in the control condition. The effects of success training produced generalization of greater counting behavior while the effects of failure training produced no transfer of less counting behavior and generalization of greater inappropriate classroom behavior. See ERIC Abstract 0990151-5.

3600.   Resnick, R. J. "The Primary Teacher And The Emotionally Disabled Child." Education, 98 4 (Summer, 1978): 387-91.

This article describes and discusses commonly seen problem children, delineates information into the causes of the emotional and behavioral problems, explores strategies for teachers working with a child on a daily basis, and provides antidotal data to help detect the emotionally disabled child and to illustrate the recommended interventions. See ERIC Abstract EJ 185368.

3601.   Reynolds, W. M. "Self-Esteem and Classroom Behavior in Elementary School Children." Psychology in the Schools, 17, 2 (April, 1982): 273-277.

The relationship between self-esteem and classroom behavior was investigated using 54 fifth and sixth graders, equally divided by class level and sex. Results indicate a significant relationship between self-esteem and classroom behavior. In addition, the demographic variables of age, sex, and grade, also related to classroom behavior in a summative manner. See PSYC Abstract 1120765-5.

3602.   Rich, D. and Jones, C. "The Home-School New Educational Partnership: A Handbook of Teacher-Tested Techniques And Activities For Parent-Home Involvement In Children's Learning." Washington, D.C.: Home And School Incorporated. 25P.

The purpose of this handbook is to help teachers promote parent-home involvement in children's learning by providing them with specific techniques and materials to use in working with parents. It begins with a general article discussing why parent-home involvement is important in the educational process and goes on to present ten ideas for parents on how to cooperate with the school and ten ideas for teachers on the school child at home. Specific guidelines and send home sheets are provided on various topics including one on discipline. See ERIC Abstract ED 113054.

3603.   Rich, J. M. "Glasser And Kohl: How Effective Are Their Strategies To Discipline." M.A.S.S.P. Bulletin, 63, 428 (September, 1979): 19-26.

Authors surveys the ideas of William Glasser and Herbert Kohl on discipline and then evaluates them by reviewing both their strengths and weaknesses. See ERIC Abstract EJ 206322.

3604.   Rich, Y. and Rothchild, G. "Personality Differences Between Well and Poorly-Behaved Adolescents In School." Psychology Reports, 44, 3, Part II (June, 1979): 1143-1148.

Sixty chronically misbehaving adolescents in special Israeli educational setting were compared with one hundred and twelve well-behaved schoolmates on a series of cognative, social, and personality instruments. Differences between the two groups were apparent on the self-concept and family relations measures indicating more positive development among the well-behaved subjects. The relationship between misbehavior in school and the various personality constructs is discussed. See ERIC Abstract 1120964-5.

3605.   Richey, D. D. and McKinney, J. D. "Classroom Behavioral Styles of Learning Disabled Boys." Journal of Learning Disabilities, 11, 5 (May, 1978): 297-302.

Compared in the study was a classroom behavior of 15 third and fourth grade learning disabled boys to that of 15 matched normal boys in order to determine differences in behavioral style and to examine learning disabled children's behavior in different classroom environments. Results indicate that of 12 discrete kinds of classroom behavior only one, distractibility, differentiated the two groups. There was very limited support for the sterotyped cluster of negative behavior often associated with learning disabilities. The study also supports the position that character-istics of the classroom environment may exert much influence in fostering or minimizing specific behavior related to academic achievement and competence. See ERIC Abstract 0229602-5.

3606.   Richman, J. S. "Increasing Class Appropriate Behavior Through Feedback Assisted Teacher Training Period." Behavioral Engineering, 3, 2 (Fall, 1975): 43-52.

Two approaches to teacher training in which a component of classroom-based, individual feedback assistance was delivered contingently or non-contingently upon a teacher's performance. The feedback was facilitated by an electronic communications device utilized by the instructor from an observation room. A class taught by each of four innercity sixth, seventh, and eighth grade teachers was observed twice a week. Class behavior was coded by trained observers as appropriate, inappropriate and other. Two subjects received each treatment. Results indicated the training with instructional feedback contingent upon performance was more effective. Data also suggests that a dichotomy exists between the school scheduled class-length-teaching-duration of a class and the actual delivered class-length-teaching-duration. See ERIC Abstract 1306055-6.

3607.   Riley, M. G. "Identification And Validation Of Critical Incidents In Classroom Discipline And Their Solutions As Reported By First Year Vocational Teachers In The State Of Florida." Paper presented at the annual convention of the American Vocational Association, Anaheim, California, December, 1979. 12P.

In response to the need for realistic materials for training in-service and/or pre-service teachers in classroom discipline, 79 first year vocational education teachers in public secondary schools in Florida were studied. The purpose of the study was to identify critical and frequent discipline incidents and the appropriate alternatives for handling them; to identify discipline problems which should be included in pre-service and/or in-service education and to compare the solutions used by the teachers where the solutions proposed by expects in the field. Data were collected by means of a critical incident form derived from McFadden's model, then screened by two panels of experts. The study revealed that 1) There was a discrepancy between what the first year teachers did to resolve discipline problems and what experts felt ought to be done, where the teachers more likely to use short term solutions, 2) The two panels of experts disagreed on effective solutions for a given critical incident, 3) Obtaining specific solutions to specific discipline problems was not feasible, 4) First year teachers had needs for training and handling discipline problems that had not been met by pre-service or in-service education, 5) Student placement in the laboratory setting were factors in discipline problems, 6) Students' disruptive personal habits were most often perceived as causes of critical discipline incidents. See ERIC Abstract ED 193448.

3608.   Ringer, B. N.   "The Use Of A 'Token Helper' In The Management   Of   Classroom   Behavior   Problems   and   In Teacher-Training Period."   Journal of Applied Behavior Analysis, 6, 3 (Winter, 1973): 671-677.

A teacher of thirty-seven fourth graders was trained in the use of token and verbal reinforcement.   An experienced "token helper" demonstrated the procedures in the classroom. Introduction of a simple token system resulted in signifi- cant decreases in the disruptive behavior of ten pupils in two morning periods.   When the token helper withdrew from the classroom, the teacher managed the token system and maintained disruptive behavior at lower than baseline levels. See ERIC Abstract 0398752-2.

3609.   Rist, R. C.   "On The Social And Cultural Milieu Of An Urban Black School: An Ethnographic Case Study."   Paper presented to the Sociology of Education panel of the Pacific Sociological Association meeting, Portland, Oregon, April, 1972.

To understand the phenomena of academic success or failure among black children in urban ghetto schools, the author feels that one must look beyond the boundaries of the individual classroom and examine the social and cultural milieu of the school itself.   Both the milieu of the class- room and the milieu of the school appear to sustain one another in a pattern of reinforcement of the presently accepted values and modes of behavior. Thus, the factors which help to establish the atmosphere of the school affect that of the individual classroom as well.   Thus, an effect occurs whereby the milieu of the school influences the learning experiences of the children, which in turn help to define the behavior and responses of the teachers and principal who have major responsibility for the general social themes present in the school.   It is contended that such conditions as the negative expectations for the chil- dren, the utilization of violence on the children, the exchange of information among the teachers which allows the development of stereotypes as to performance and behavior, and the norms governing the use of classroom discipline are destructive of a humane and supportive learning milieu.   See ERIC Abstact ED 066523.

3610.   Rist, R. C.   "The Milieu Of A Ghetto School As A Precipitator   Of   Educational   Failure."   Phylon,   33,   4 (Winter, 1972): 348-360.

Author elucidates several of the major social and cultural themes of a black urban elementary school, arguing that the milieu of the school influences the desire and willingness of the children to learn. See ERIC Abstract EJ 067928.

3611.   Ritter, D. R.   "Effects Of A School Consultation Program Upon Referral Patterns Of Teachers."   Psychology In The Schools, 15, 2 (April, 1978): 239-42.

Author reviews the effects of a school consultation program through an analysis of referral patterns of teachers over a seven year period. The provision of consultation services was found to result in a pattern of decreasing referrals on the part of teachers over time. See ERIC Abstract EJ182966.

3612.   Ritterband, P. and Silverstein, R.   "Group Disorders In The Public Schools." American Socialogical Review, 38, 4 (August, 1973): 461-467.

Authors examine several alternative models to account for the distribution of group disorders in New York cities 56 comprehensive academic high schools. They advance the thesis that, while disorders occur in the schools, their roots lie in the larger society. See ERIC Abstract EJ 100945.

3613.   Robertshaw, C. S. & Hiebert, H. D.   "The Astronaut Game: A Group Contingency Applied To A First Grade Classroom." Salt: School Applications of Learning Theory, 6, 1 (October, 1973): 28-33.

Studied was the use of token reinforcement on team competition as a method of raising the output of twenty-four first graders and the attemptive behaviors of one male member of the class. Baseline data were recorded for two weeks on attention-to-task behavior of the single subject and the average number of worksheets completed by the whole class. During the three week intervention phase, one of four teams was considered winner for the day, based on the number of tokens obtained contingent on desired behavior, and permitted choice of free activity. See ERIC Abstract 0861552-4.

3614.   Robertson, S. J., Dereus, D. M. and Drabman, R. S.   "Peer and College-Student Tutoring as Reinforcement in a Token Economy." Journal of Applied Behavior Analysis, 9, 2 (Summer, 1976): 169-177.

Sixteen second graders who initially received feedback in the form of nonredeemable tokens for reducing their disruptive classroom behavior were used as subjects in this study. Four types of tutoring were then introduced: noncontingent or contingent tutoring from one of five trained fifth graders, or noncontingent or contingent tutoring from one of four college students. No significant difference was found in the level of disruptive behavior of those subjects tutored by fifth graders or college students, but contingent tutoring was significantly effective in reducing disruptive classroom behavior. See ERIC Abstract 0673456-4.

3615.   Robin, A. et al.   "The Turtle Technique: An Extended Case Study Of Self-Control In The Classroom." Psychology In The Schools, 13, 4 (October, 1976): 449-453.

A preliminary investigation of the Turtle Technique, a procedure for helping emotionally disturbed children control their own impulsive behavior, is described. Eleven children were instructed in the use of the technique for self-control of aggression. Results revealed significant decrement in aggressive behavior in both classrooms. See ERIC Abstract EJ 146253.

3616.   Rogeness, G. A., Stokes, J. P., Bednar, R. A. and Gorman, B. L. "School Intervention Program to Increase Behaviors and Attitudes that Promote Learning." _Journal of Community Psychology_, 5, 3 (July, 1977): 246-256.

A two year intervention program attempted to work with the school as a social unit so that behaviors and attitudes that promote learning could be consistently reinforced throughout the school. The school contained kindergarten and first through eighth grades and had 21 classrooms and a bilingual program to serve the approximately 700 pupils of which over 60% were Latins. The intervention used both behavior modification and counseling techniques. See ERIC Abstract 0182460-1.

3617.   Rohrkemper, M. M. and Brophy, J. E. "Classroom Strategy Study: Investigating Teacher Strategies With Problem Students." "Research Series Number 50." Paper presented at the annual meeting of the American Educational Research Association, San Francisco, California, April, 1979. 15P.

A methodology for conducting research on managing the disruptive student based on identifying successful teacher strategies is described in this paper. The subjects were teacher selected as being outstanding or average in their ability to cope with behavior problems. Data collection included two half day classroom observations, a structured interview in which each teacher responded to a series of written vignettes depicting student behavior problems and a open ended interview in which the teacher discussed general strategies for dealing with each of the 12 types of problem behaviors. The data indicated that student disobedience and disruptive behavior provoked more intense and less effective teacher responses than do instructional problems. Also significant difference and responses to problems seems to favor teachers who view themselves as both instructors and socializers over those who view themselves as just instructors. See ERIC Abstact ED 175857.

3618.   Rohrkemper, M. M. and Brophy, J. E. "Influence Of Teacher Role Definition On Strategies For Coping With Problem Students." "Research Series Number 51." Paper presented at the annual meeting of the American Educational Research Association, San Francisco, California, 1979. 27P.

Paper discusses an investigation concerned teacher styles and strategies for coping with problem students and suggest role definition may not be as important teacher varabile as originally postulated. Thirty-seven experienced elementary school teachers were observed to determine overall management skill level and actual response to problem behavior. Teachers were divided into two role orientations: one group stressed the instructional role and the other the socialization role. While both teacher role emphasis and ability did affect teacher responses, the most powerful factor was the type of student behavior depicted. The research suggests that socialization problems (disobedience or disruption) provoke more intense and less effective teacher responses than do instructional problems. See ERIC Abstract ED 179522.

3619.   Rohrkemper, M. M. and Brophy, J. E. "Teachers' General Strategies For Dealing With Problem Students." "Research Series Number 87." Paper presented at the annual meeting of the Americal Educational Research Association, Boston, Massachusetts, April, 1980. 34P.

Elementary teachers' responses to vignettes depicting 12 types of student problem behavior (instructional concerns: failure syndrone, perfectionist, underachiever, and low achiever; aggression problems: hostile aggressive, passive aggressive, and defiant; activity issues: short attention span, hyperactive, and immature; and peer relation difficulties: shy/withdrawn and rejected by peers) were analyzed for points of agreement across the 12 types of problem behavior concerning problems solving strategies that involved rewards, punishments, supportive behaviors and threatening/pressuring behaviors. In general, teachers' responses to the vignettes involved more punishment than reward, and supportive behavior more than threatening or pressuring behavior. See ERIC Abstract ED 196886.

3620.   Rollins, H. A., McCandless, B. R., and Thompson, N. "Project Success Environment: An Extended Application of Contingency Management in Inner-City Schools." Journal of Educational Psychology, 66, 2 (April, 1974): 167-178.

Sixteen black and white inner-city public school teachers were trained to use positive behavior contingencies for one academic year with a total of 730 Afro-American disadvantaged first through eighth graders. Compared with matched-controlled teachers and classes, these sixteen teachers showed higher incidences of positive reinforcement and lower incidences of punishment. The experimental classes were less disruptive and more on task. They gained more in both I.Q. and school achievement. It is concluded that inner-city teachers can be trained to employ positive techniques of behavior management, they like and use such training, and public school pupils profit dramatically from restructuring their learning environment. See ERIC Abstract 0855152-4.

3621.   Rosenbaum, A., O'Leary, K. D. and Jacob, R. G.
"Behavioral Intervention with Hyperactive Children: Group
Consequences as a Supplement to Individual Contingencies."
Behavior Therapy, 6, 3 (May, 1975): 315-323.

In this study group reward and individual reward for
individual behavior was compared during a four week treatment and a four week maintenance period with two groups of
male hyperactive elementary school children, with a mean age
of 10 years. Each subject was rated four times daily on
individually determined target behaviors, and at the end of
the school day the subject exchanged his cards for candy,
either for himself or for himself plus his classmates.
Standardized teacher ratings of hyperactivity and weekly
ratings of problem behaviors both indicated a significant
treatment effect although no difference was found between
the two groups. The treatment effects were maintained
during a one month treatment withdrawal. A teacher questionnaire designed to assess teacher satisfaction with the
treatment programs indicated that the group reward program
was significantly more popular than the individual reward
program. The experiment results indicate that behavioral
intervention can be successfully applied to hyperactive
children, producing changes in behavior similar to those
reported with drug related therapies. See ERIC Abstract
1261054-6.

3622.   Rosenfield, S. "Introducing Behavior Modification
Techniques to Teachers." Exceptional Children, 45, 5
(February, 1979): 334-339.

Article cautions that teachers wishing to employ modification techniques must first be taught the behavioral
principles and engage in guided practice with feedback and
support. Sustained contact with a consultant is often
important because of the questionnaire asking whether or not
they had found a nine-week training program beneficial even
in circumstances where they could not use the technology on
any extensive basis. All subjects except one saw the
approach as useful in overcoming almost all academic and
behavioral problems in either normal or special classrooms.
See ERIC Abstract 0668756-4.

3623.   Ross, J. A. & Lubine, B. A. "Identification of Reinforcement For Talking Out In The Classroom." Psychological
Report, 38, 2 (April, 1976): 363-367.

Talking out in the classroom has been subjected to applied
behavioral analysis. An open implicit assumption has been
that peers' attention serves as a powerful reinforcer in
this natural setting, although there is little imperical
evidence. In this present study, with a special class
comprised of seven emotionally disturbed nine through eleven
year olds, tokens were removed when children responded to
verbal outbursts directed at them by peers. As a result,
such specifically directed verbal behavior decreased in

frequency, while verbal outbursts of a more general nature did not. Such findings lend experimental support to the hypothesis that talking out, of one variety at least, is maintained by peers' attention. See ERIC Abstract 0487356-3.

3624.   Rubenstein, G., Fisher, L. & Iker, H. "Peer Observation of Student Behavior In Elementary School Classroom." Developmental Psychology, 11, 6 (November, 1975): 867-686.

The purpose of this study was to assess the nature of conceptual schemas used by elementary school children in observing the behavior of peers and a comparison was made of the dimensions to those derived from teachers are sensitized to the difference in classroom events reflecting academic achievement, and those reflecting conformity to rules, students are more sensitive to phenomenon reflecting social behavior. See ERIC Abstract 0826355-4.

3625.   Rubin, R. A. and Balow, B. "Prevalence of Teacher Identified Behavior Problems: A Longitudinal Study." Exceptional Children, 45, 2 (October, 1978): 102-111.

In this longitudinal study from kindergarten through sixth grade, teachers annually rated the behavior of 1,586 children who were normally distributed on measures of IQ, socio-economic status, and school achievement. In any single year, from 23 to 31 percent of the subjects were judged by their teachers as manifesting behavior problems. Long-term cumulative prevalence rates were much higher. Among subjects receiving three or more annual ratings, 59% were considered as having a behavior problem by at least one teacher, and 7.4% were considered as having behavior problems contemporary expectations regarding children's behavior in school. See ERIC Abstract 0730562-3.

3626.   Rubin, R. A. and Krus, P. H. "Validation Of A School Behavior Rating Scale." Paper presented at annual meeting of Educational Research Association, New Orleans, Louisiana, February, 1973. 15P.

The pupose of this study was to validate a school behavior rating scale on a sample of 1153 elementary school children. Results indicate stable means and bariances over grades kindergarten through fifth grade and a stable factor structure. Sex differences on behavior ratings favored females over males at all grade levels. School behavior ratings obtained by subjects for whom special action such as special placement or receipt of special services, have been taken by the schools were significantly lower than the mean score of those from whose no such action have been taken. See ERIC Abstract ED 076656.

3627.   Ruchkin, J. P. "Silent Classrooms in Violent Schools." Action in Teacher Education, 1, 2 (All-Winter, 1978): 61-65.

This study of school violence presents data establishing the extent of deviant behavior, a theory explaining deviance in the schools, and some policy variables. See ERIC Abstract EJ 197178.

3628.   Rude, B. D. "A Baker's Dozen Of Educational Fallacies." Elementary School Journal, 78, 1 (September, 1977): 59-66.

A critique of 13 commonly held ideas concerning student-teacher relationships, discipline, goals and methods of instruction, and student motivation are presented in this article. See ERIC Abstract EJ 172336.

3629.   Rundberg, C. W. and Fredrickson, R. H. "The Prescriptive Counselor In The Elementary School." 1973. 13P.

This Prescriptive Counselor Model, as proposed for the elementary school, focuses on changing specific student behaviors through a particular prescription of materials, activities, and suggestions for teachers, parents, and the child himself. The emphasis is on dealing with behaviors by observing, conferring, setting goals, developing prescriptions, providing materials, and follow-up on the success on the prescriptions. The goals of the model are to increase the ability of teachers and parents to work with students and to permit the services of the counselor to have greater effect with more students. The prescriptive counselor translates his concern and care through the concreteness and specifics of the prescriptive process. See ERIC Abstract ED 092838.

3630.   Rusnock, M. and Brandler, N. "Time Off-Task: Implications For Learning." Paper presented at the annual meeting of the American Educational Research Association, San Francisco, California, April, 1979. 14P.

The purpose of this study was to investigate questions concerning the incidence of student off-task activities, which interrupt learning, in different academic activities, within different activity formats and among students differing in achievement growth. Achievement growth was defined as a pattern of continuous growth during the previous two ys were identified in each classrooms and 30 observations of four target students were 30 minutes each were made in four subject areas. Student behavior was coded on a minute by minute basis. Six off-task activity types were found. Among the significant findings the high achievement group students were more likely than the low achievement group students to go off-task during creative activities. Low achievement growth students were more likely to go off-task during resitation. High and low achievement group students spent nearly equal amounts of time off-task. See ERIC Abstract ED 171407.

3631.   Ryback, D. and Connell, R. H. "Differential Racial Patterns of School Discipline During the Broadcasting of 'Roots'." Psychological Reports, 42, 2 (April, 1978): 514.

Two southern high schools were surveyed as to the frequency of after school detentions occurring two weeks before, during and one week after the TV broadcast of "Roots." Although more blacks than whites served detentions during all periods, the proportion of blacks was greatest during the week long broadcast. See ERIC Abstract 0225862-1.

3632.   Ryckman, D. B. and Mirante, T. J. "Reliabilities of Schaefer's Classroom Behavior Inventory." Psychological Report, 41, 3, Part 2 (December, 1977): 1054.

In a suburban open concept school, two teachers rated their first and second graders on Schaefer's classroom behavior inventory. During the first week in May, teacher X rated 71 cases, and teacher Y independently rated 59 cases. Both factor structure and reliability were found satisfactory for an instrument a teacher can complete in two to three minutes. See ERIC Abstract 0487061-2.

3633.   Sagotsky, G., Patterson, C. J. and Lepper, M. R. "Training Children's Self Control: A Field Experiment in Self Monitoring and Goal Setting in the Classroom." Journal of Experimental Child Psychology, 25, 2 (April, 1978): 242-253i.

The effects of training in self-monitoring and goal setting skills on classroom study behavior and academic achievement was investigated among 67 fifth and sixth graders in an individualized mathematics program. In the self-monitoring conditions, subjects were shown a simple system for observing and maintaining daily records of their own study behavior during their math classes. In the goal setting conditions, subjects were shown a simple method of setting and recording daily performance goals during their math classes. Exposure to self-monitoring procedures produced significant increases in both appropriate study behavior and in actual achievement in the mathematics program, while exposure to goal setting procedures had no effect on either study behavior or academic achievement. See ERIC Abstract 0950561-4.

3634.   Saklofske, D. H. "Antisocial Behavior and Psychoticism in Adolescent School Boys." Psychological Reports, 41, 2 (October, 1977): 425-426.

Four groups were formed of twenty 13-14 year old males each on the basis of self reporting ratings of antisocial behavior and teachers' ratings of classroom misbehavior. Subjects were then administered the Junior Eysenck Personality Inventory. Significant differences on the psychoticism scale were obtained between both high vs. low antisocial behavior groups and well-behaved vs. badly behaved teacher rated groups. The interaction was not significant. See ERIC Abstract 0650860-4.

3635.   Saklofske, D. H. "Personality and Behavior Problems of School Boys." Psychological Reports, 41, 2 (October, 1977): 445-446.

The relationship of the Junior Eysenck Personality Inventory dimensions to two specific factors of school behavior was examined. Eighty-four 10 and 11 year old boys were grouped according to high or average scores obtained on the Devereux Elementary School Behavior Rating Scale measures of disrespect-defiance in classroom disturbance. Thirty-seven high scorers on the Devereux also scored significantly higher on the Eysenck scale and six significantly lower on the extra version and Lie scales than 37 well behaved subjects. See ERIC Abstract 0650960-4.

3636.   Salzberg, B. and Smith, N. E. "Program For Peer Relationship Development." Paper presented at the annual meeting of the Rocky Mountain Psychological Association, Salt Lake City, Utah, May, 1975. 18P.

Children, ages 10 to 12, were referred to an out-patient mental health center because of behavior problems, some involving social skill deficits, others not so involved. Children asknowledging a social skill problem, and a desire to do something about it were chosen pending parent approval and cooperation. Children and parents were interviewed to determine what goals each wanted to pursue within the program. The group met once a week for an hour and a half. Specific social skills deficits were pinpointed for each child and deficits common to all children were also identified. Techniques used were relaxation training, modeling, rehearsal, and game playing. Social and non-social reinforcement were utilized. This setting allowed children to practice newly-social skills in a non-threatening atmosphere and to become aware of behaviors which were turning off their peers. A prescriptive program was worked out with the family of each child in order to provide maximum generalization for newly-acquired social skills. See ERIC Abstract ED 122190.

3637.   Samuels, D. D. et al. "The Development And Analysis Of An Elementary Comprehensive Lunchroom Management Program." Education, 101, 2 (Winter, 1980): 123-26.

Authors present a case study detailing how para-professionals, acting as lunchroom supervisors, have been trained to utilize behavior management techniques to effectively reduce the incidence of disruptive behavior. See ERIC Abstract EJ 237308.

3638.   Sanders, S. G. & Yarbrough, J. S. Bringing Order To An Inner-City Middle School. Phi Delta Kappa, 58, 4 (December, 1976): 333-334.

Authors discuss the reorganization of a school and the training of teachers which has resulted in a program that has been effective in developing constructive, orderly, and acceptable behavior in students. See ERIC Abstract #EJ 148062.

3639.   Sandoval, J. "The Efficacy Of School-Based Consultation." Paper presented at the annual convention of the American Psychological Association, San Francisco, California, August, 1977. 10P.

This presentation discusses the concept of school-based consultation and contrast it with other consultation models. The validity of this model for the professional talking relationships of school psychologists is assessed first by examining 1) the likelihood that inter-professional interchange will take place, 2) the likelihood that case study information will be communicated effectively, 3) the nature of the models assumptions about teacher knowledge of individual differences in children, 4) the likelihood that school based consultants will serve as a model for principals and teachers to follow in collaborating with parents. See ERIC Abstract #ED 151616.

3640.   Sattler, H. E. & Swoope, K. F. "Teacher As Token Dispenser: Effect of An Observer." Psychology In The School, 13, 1 (January, 1976): 97-100.

Investigated in this study was whether the observer presence versus absence in the classroom results in the differential rate of token delivery by the teacher. Subjects included seven second grade teachers enrolled in a graduate behavior modification course. Data were obtained from record cards maintained by pupils for tokens received during an observer-present condition and for an observer-absent conditon. Comparison of reinforcement rates for observer-present versus absent indicated significantly higher rates of token delivery in the observer-present condition. The observer effect has important implications for those programs in which assessment procedures introduce an observer into the classroom to collect data on changes in teacher behavior. See ERIC Abstract 0679856-4.

3641.   Sawin, D. B. "The Child's Role In Sparing The Rod." Paper presented at the annual meeting of the American Psychological Association, Chicago, Illinois, 1975. 11P.

The impact of children's reactions to punishment on subsequent adult disciplinary actions was assessed in a study in which adult women administered rewards and punishments contingent on the behavior of a child viewed on a television monitor. Following an aggressive act by the target child and punishment administered by the adult subject, the adult saw the child react to being disciplined in one of four ways (plead, reparation, ignore or defiance). The adult subjects were given a subsequent opportunity to reward or punish the child by offering or taking away points that the child could ostensibly trade for free play time. The findings are discussed in terms of a bi-directional model of childhood socialization wherein recognition is given to the active role the child plays in controlling the disciplinary practices of socializing agents. See ERIC Abstract #ED 119839.

3642.   Sawin, D. B. & Parke, R. D. "Empathy And Fear As Mediators Of Resistance-To-Deviation In Children." The Merrill-Palmer Quarterly, 26, 2 (April, 1980): 123-34.

This article discusses the techniques of using empathy and fear as mediators of resistance to deviation in children. They present examples of this method of working with children with behavior problems.

3643.   Sawin, D. B. & Parke, R. D. "Inconsistent Discipline Of Aggression In Young Boys." Journal Of Experimental Child Psychology, 28, 3 (December, 1979): 525-38.

Two studies were conducted to assess the effects of inter-agents, inconsistent discipline on aggression in young boys. See ERIC Abstract #EJ 22223.

3644.   Schaefer, C., Baker, E., and Zawel, D. "A Factor Analytic and Reliability Study of the Devereux Elementary School Behavior Rating Scale." Psychology in the Schools, 12, 3 (July, 1975): 295-300.

In this study with 153 7-13 year old boys in a residential treatment center for the emotionally disturbed, the inter-rater and test-retest reliability of the Devereux Elementary School Behavior Rating Scale were found to be satisfactory when averaged over two raters. Two separate factor analyses of the 11 sub-scales revealed three broad-band factors: classroom management problem, self-reliant learner, and seeks teacher approval. See ERIC Abstract 106654-5.

3645.   Schlosser, L. and Algozzine, B. "The Disturbing Child: He or She." Alberta Journal of Educational Research, 25, 1 (March, 1979): 30-36.

Ratings by classroom teachers of behaviors that were more prevalent in boys than in girls with regard to their rela-tive effect on teachers' attitudes were compared. The results with 30 experienced elementary school classroom teachers, indicate that those behaviors more prevalent in boys were significantly more disturbing to teachers. See ERIC Abstract 0643864-3.

3646.   Schmidt, W. E. and Tyler, V. O. "The Pinpointing Effect vs. the Defusion Effect of Peer Influence." Psychology in the Schools, 12, 4 (October, 1975): 484-494.

In the study 12 six through eighth grade students were selected from six classes. Each entire class was rewarded for increased ignoring of the target behavior which was whispering; in the three pinpointed classes, for ignoring the whispering of a designated student; in the three defusion classes, for ignoring whispering by all class members. Results suggest that a peer group can decrease reinforcement of the disruptive behavior and thereby decelerate it in a singled out child with equal effectiveness. However, data suggests that peers ignored the pinpoint students most, defusion students next most, and a pinpoint designated subject the least and this pattern of ignoring was mirrored in the pattern of deceleration of the target behaviors in the three groups. These patterns suggest that the pinpointing effect may be stronger than the defusion effect. See ERIC Abstract 1094555-5.

3647.   Schumaker, J. B., Hovell, M. F. and Sherman, J. A. "An Analysis of Daily Report Cards and Parent-Managed Privileges in the Improvement of Adolescents' Classroom Performance." Journal of Applied Behavior Analysis, 10, 3 (Fall, 1977): 449-464.

A daily report card system, involving home privileges administered by parents, for it was developed for use with problem junior high school students. In the first experiment, when home privileges and parent praise were contingent on improved school conduct, classwork, daily grades, and teacher satisfaction, the school performance of the three male seventh graders improved. In experiment two, a similar system was employed with two similar subjects, except only parent praise was contingent on improved school performance. Under these conditions, one of the subjects did not bring the report card home, and class performance did not improve until contingent home privileges were added. The school performance of the second subject improved with the card and praise alone. However, there appeared to be a slow decline in classwork performance over time. For experiment three, an instructional manual describing the program was written for school guidance counselors. Two guidance counselors used it with two eighth graders and found that the school performance of both improved. Results suggest that the daily report card program with home consequences administered by parents can improve the school performance of students having difficulty in school. See ERIC Abstract 08211360-4.

3648.   Schwebel, A. I. and Cherlin, D. L. "Physical and Social Distancing In Teacher-Pupil Relationships." Journal of Educational Psychology, 63, 6 (December, 1972): 543-550.

The behavior of pupils who have been assigned to seats in the front, middle and back rows of their fourteen grade school classrooms was assessed through observation and teacher interview. New seats were then assigned to the subjects, and a second set of measures, which also included pupil questionnaires, was taken. Data indicated that teachers assigned in seats in ways that would best minimize classroom disruption, children assigned by teachers to the front row were more attentive to classroom activities then classmates in the middle and back rows, and occupancy of seats in the front, in contrast to those in the middle and back, positively affected the way in which pupils were perceived by their teachers and peers, and the way in which pupils evaluated themselves. See ERIC Abstract 0193850-1.

3649.   Schweisheimer, W. and Walberg, H. J. "A Peer Counseling Experiment: High School Students As Small Group Leaders." *Journal of Counseling Psychology*, 23, 4 (July, 1976): 398-401.

Sixteen high school juniors who were peer counselors were trained in human relations techniques, group dynamics, and decision-making skills applied to 122 potential dropouts. Peer counseling was conducted in small groups at approximately twenty one-hour meetings. Gain scores on sixteen variables were analyzed using a five-way factorial multivariate analysis. Although the counselees improved significantly in attendance and decisiveness over the controls, results are inconclusive in demonstrating the efficacy of their program on counselees. See ERIC Abstract 0686256-4.

3650.   Scott, J. W. and Bushell, D. "The Length of Teacher Contacts and Students' Off-Task Behavior." *Journal of Applied Behavior Analysis*, 7, 1 (Spring, 1974): 39-44.

The relationships between a teacher's contact durations and the off-task behavior of students not in contact with the teacher was investigated. Contact durations were defined as the amount of time the teacher spent working individually with each student. Off-task behavior was recorded for six third graders who comprised a small instructional group in mathematics. After baseline established that contact durations averaged approximately thirty-eight seconds, the teacher was instructed to hold contacts for at least fifty seconds. During this phase, the students' off-task behavior increased. The teacher was then instructed to hold contacts for only twenty seconds. During this phase, the students' off-task behavior decreased. See ERIC Abstract 0861952-4.

3651.   Scott, W. C. "A Middle School's Plan For An After-School Detention Program." *National Association Of Secondary School Principals Bulletin*, 63, 424 (February, 1979): 55-58.

This program was developed to help students increase their self-awareness, to understand and respect the rights of others, and to increase their ability to relate to their peers, teachers and other adults. See ERIC Abstract #EJ 196057.

3652.   Seidman, E. et al. "Assessment of Classroom Behavior: A Multi-Attribute, Multi-Source Approach to Instrument Development and Validation." <u>Journal of Educational Psychology</u>, <u>71</u>, 4 (August 1979): 451-464.

The simultaneous development and validation of three parallel instruments for the multi-dimensional assessment of a young child's classroom behavior is described. Skills were constructed to depict teacher, peer and self-rated behavior, including positive as well as negative attributes. The scales were continually refined over the course of three successive years, with the total sample size approaching one thousand first and second grade school children. The multi-dimensional nature, internal consistency, and test retest properties of each device are explicated. Higher order principal-components analyses are presented highlighting the convergent and divergent characteristics in this battery. See ERIC Abstract 0213163-1.

3653.   Sellers, J. "Found: A Neat Little Way To Improve Lunch Time Discipline." <u>American School Board Journal</u>, <u>7</u>, 29 (July, 1978): 165.

Described in this article are several elementary schools that feed students after recess instead of before which has resulted in reduced student discipline problems and food waste. See ERIC Abstract #EJ 183250.

3654.   Seyfarth, J. T. "Achieving Equity And Restraint In In-Schools Suspension." <u>High Journal</u>, <u>63</u>, 5 (February, 1980): 200-202.

In this article the author cautions against the overuse or misuse of in-school suspension as a disciplinary measure and suggests rules that incorporate principles of equity in order to avoid abuse of in-school suspension policies. See ERIC Sbstract #EJ 226863.

3655.   Seyfarth, J. T. "Discipline As A Cooperative Adventure: Where We Are." <u>Urban Review</u>, <u>12</u>, 2 (Summer, 1980): 87-90.

A survey was conducted with principals and assistant principals in 345 secondary schools regarding 1) the quality of discipline in their schools, 2) student behaviors perceived to be of most concern to administrators and teachers, 3) the extent and ways that parents, teachers, counselors, administrators, and students them- selves are involved in discipline. See ERIC Abstract #EJ 235589.

3656.   Shada, M. & Winger, J. "<u>Peer Dynamics 1977-78 Evaluation Report</u>." Lincoln: Nebraska State Commission On Drugs, 1978.

This is an evaluation of the second year of a program designed to reduce the incidence of destructive risk-taking behavior among school age youth. Background research indicated that peer group pressures was the single most important factor in dictating the presence or absence of juvenile deliquency behavior. The Peer Dynamics Process, involving 56 schools in Nebraska, trained and supervised students who participated in a group interaction plan with other students to develop self-esteem and better communication skills. Individual school evaluation results are reported along with student testimonies. Recommenations for program improvement are included. See ERIC Abstract #ED 197276.

3657.   Shanahan-Delaney, E.   "A Memory Of A Student."   English Journal, 69, 6 (September, 1980):   57-58.

Article relates the interactions between an English teacher and a problem student, showing how each learned to compromise. See ERIC Abstract #EJ 231953.

3658.   Shapiro, S.   "Some Classroom ABC's: Research Takes a Closer Look."   Elementary School Journal, 75, 7 (April 1975):   436-441

Efficiency in seventeen elementary schools is discussed. When the pupils in a classroom number less than sixteen, a significant reduction occurs in the social complexity of child behavior. Non-involvement by a pupil was highest when the pupil space was less than thirty or more than fifty square feet per pupil. See ERIC Abstract 0213163-1.

3659.   Shearburn, D.   "What To Do When You See Red."   Teacher, 95, 1 (September, 1977):   90-1.

A description of ten affirmative actions is presented with suggestions on how to implement them, for handling behavior and learning problems in the classroom. See ERIC Abstract #EJ 170926.

3660.   Shearn, D. F. & Randolph, D. L.   "Effects of Reality Therapy Method Applied in the Classroom."   Psychology in the Schools, 15, 1 (January, 1978):   79-83.

Reality Therapy Methods were examined via a four-group experimental design. Subjects were one hundred and fifty fourth graders in an overseas dependent school system in Japan. The groups were as follows: a) Pre-tested Reality Therapy   b) Unpre-tested Reality Therapy   c) Pre-tested Placebo and   d) Unpre-tested Placebo. No significant differences were obtained for self-concept and on-task behavior. Findings did not support Reality Therapy Methods as applied in the classroom. See ERIC Abstract 0238061-1.

3661.   Shecket, S. M. & Shecket, W. C.   "Behaviors Of Children Referred By Classroom Teachers As Hyperactive."   February, 1977.

In the study, a classroom observation technique was employed to examine the behaviors of a group of teacher-referred hyperactive children in order to determine the frequency of specific behaviors exhibited. The purpose was the further investigation of behavioral observation and intervention techniques used by other researchers as alternatives to prolonged medication therapy for hyperactive children. Subjects included eleven elementary school children in kindergarten, first and second grade. The control group consisted of all classroom peers who, because of their non-referral, were identified as not hyperactive. Subjects and controls were observed in the classroom and their behaviors charted using a time sampling procedure that recorded behavior frequency of nineteen categories of behavior. Significant differences were found between groups on behaviors in seven categories: approval, volunteers, initiation to teacher, physical negative, play, inappropriate locale, and self-stimulation. The control group had lower frequencies of occurance in all categories except volunteers. The authors suggested a behavioral intervention program be implemented to decrease or extinguish targeted behaviors. See ERIC Abstract #ED 129440.

3662.   Sheppard, C. "The Use of a Response-Cost Punishment Technique to Decrease the Disruptive Classroom Behaviors of a Group of Seventh and Eighth Graders." SALT: School Application of Learning Theory, 4, 1 (October, 1971): 22-26.

A point system was employed to effectively eliminate a high degree to undesirable classroom behavior. Four seventh and eight grade mathematics classes evaluated their own behavior which they themselves found to be unacceptable. Gym time was deducted in proportionate amounts as a function of number of punitive points accumulated over a period of a week. Results showed a significant improvement in classroom behavior, inproved class performance in mathematics, and increased sense of responsibility on the part of the students, who voluntarily bore the entire burden for class behavior. See ERIC Abstract 1006049-5.

3663.   Sherman, C. F. & Anderson, R. P. "Modification Of Attending Behavior In Hyperactive Children." Psychology In The Schools, 17, 1 (1980): 372-79.

A modified operant design demonstrated the effectiveness of a feedback procedure. Significant changes were evidenced by all groups of subjects. Initial results and follow-up observations indicated that the attending behavior of the experimental subjects increased and was maintained, without the use of tangible reinforcers. See ERIC Abstract #EJ 229837.

3664.   Shiffler, N., Lynch-Sauer, J. & Nadelman, L.   "Relationship Between Self-Concept and Classroom Behavior in Two Informal Elementary Classrooms." Journal of Educational Psychology, 69, 4 (August, 1977): 349-359.

Study investigated the relationship between self-concepts and classroom behaviors, in two combined grade informal classrooms using naturalistic observation and psychometric and sociometric techniques. Fifty-three children were observed in a first through third grade class and in a fourth through a sixth grade class. Subjects were given a self-concept test using three reference forms (self, teachers, peers), and a sociometric questionnaire. Profile analysis indicated significantly different patterns of classroom behaviors for differing self-concept levels. The highest self-concept group showed the greatest percentage of task oriented behaviors. The lowest self-concept group had the largest percentage of non-directed behaviors. See ERIC Abstract 0881759-4.

3665.   Shrigley, R. L.   "Strategies In Classroom Management." National Association Of Secondary School Principals Bulletin, 63, 428 (September, 1979): 1-9.

Authors suggest that forces within and outside the profession have made teachers vulnerable in dealing with disruptive student behavior. He presents six strategies that constitute a basic plan for coping with student behavior that interfers with learning. See ERIC Abstract #EJ 206319.

3666.   Shuttlesworth, J. & Evans, N.   "Why A Principal Must Be A Supervisor." School Management, 18, 5 (May, 1974): 46, 50, 64.

Discussed in this article is the relationship between administrative supervision and total school discipline. See ERIC Abstract #EJ 099376.

3667.   Sieber, R. T.   "School Rooms, Pupils, And Rules: The Role Of Informality In Bureaucratic Socialization." Human Organization, 38, 3 (Fall, 1979): 273-82.

Author suggests that classroom informality helps attune pupil behavior to the demands of bureaucratic life by contributing to pupil learning of formal social behavior. The paper presents various concepts of school and pupil roles and characterizes and analyzes the function of the apparently paradoxical nature of student rules. See ERIC Abstract #EJ 208467.

3668.   Silverman, L. E.   "Masculinity-Femininity in Children's Self-Concepts: The Relationship to Teachers' Judgments of Social Adjustment and Academic Ability, Classroom Behavior, and Popularity." Sex Roles, 4, 6 (December, 1978): 929-949.

The response of peers and teachers to children who differed in the extent to which their self-concepts was explored including traits that children that view as masculine and feminine. It was hypothesized that teachers would judge relatively more masculine children to be inferior in academic ability and social adjustment compared to more feminine children, and that these relationships would be independent of IQ. Relationships between masculine-feminine self-concept and observable classroom behaviors of popularity were examined. Subjects included 64 middle class 4th and 5th graders. For boys, the hypotheses were supported for evaluations made by seven female teachers. Evaluations made by one male teacher did not support the hypotheses. Neither hypotheses was supported for girls. Among boys, relative masculinity was associated with a distinctive pattern of classroom behavior, and this statistically accounted for women teachers' negative evaluations of the more masculine boys. For boys, the relationship between popularity and masculine-feminine self-concept differed significantly between classroom setting; for girls trhere were no significant relationships. See ERIC Abstract 1054763-5.

3669.   Silverman, M. "The Achievement Motivation Group: A Counselor-Directed Approach." Elementary School Guidance and Counseling, 11, 2 (December, 1976): 100-106.

The impact of an achievement motivation program on the academic achievement of thrid through sixth grade under-achievers is discussed. Within a behavioral modification framework, participants are counseled in small groups for one half hour sessions over an eight week period. Students meeting pre-set academic goals and are making visible efforts to complete assignments successfully receive verbal praise, prizes, recognition and other reinforcement. From 1973 to 1976, 90 southern Florida students completed the program, 78 demonstrated some improvement in grades. This type of program is an effective means of motivating under-achievers at the elementary school level. See ERIC Abstract 0236962-1.

3670.   Silverman, S. and Silverman, H. "Reducing Verbal and Physical Aggression in a Ninth Grade Class Using a Group Contingency." SALT: School Applications of Learning Theory, 7, 4 (June, 1975): 20-26.

The effects of behavior modification on aggressive physical and verbal behavior of 32 ninth graders was studied. After determining baseline rates of aggressive behavior, the following conditions were established: a) visible counting, b) reinforcement of physical aggression, c) reinforcement of verbal and physical aggression, and d) reinforcement of less than 5 total aggressive acts. In each case, reward was 10 minutes of free time daily. Results indicate significant reductions from each period beyond the baseline. It is suggested that behavior can be modified by simply making students immediately aware that behavior has occured; larger reductions may be obtained when reinforcement contingencies are available. See ERIC Abstract 1150457-5.

3671.   Silverman, S. H. and Miller, F. D.   "The Use of the Premack Principal and a 'Buddy' System in a 'Normal' Eighth Grade Class."   SALT: School Application of Learning Theory, 4, 1 (October, 1971): 14-19.

The use of preferred activities as reinforcers combined with use of student work peers was investigated. Five American History classes with a total of 160 eighth graders were studied over a seven week period employing one or more of the following techniques: a) priviledged use of preferred activities upon reacing the criterian weekly grade,   b) pairing of students who engaged in preferred activities upon the pair reaching criterian, and c) a buddy system with advanced work as a reward for criterian. Results show that a combination of preferred activities as reinforcers in a buddy system effectively increase learning. It is noted that no funds, programmed materials, or restructured classes were necessary. Lateness and absence decreased, less time was spent with discipline, and more time assisting students on an enjoyable one to one basis. See ERIC Abstract 1006549-5.

3672.   Simmons, J. T. & Wasik, B. H.   "Grouping Strategies, Peer Influence, and Freetime as Classroom Management Techniques with 1st and 3rd Grade Children." Journal of School Psychology, 14, 4 (Winter, 1976):   322-332.

The effects of different procedures on classroom behaviors were investigated, including teaching designated seating groups, seating groups based on sociometric data, peer encouragement, and freetime reinforcers. Subjects were 31 first and 25 3rd graders in classrooms using a follow through program model. Data were taken on the attending behavior of the children in small groups arranged by the teacher. The level of appropriate attending behavior was low and did not increase when the groups were restructured based on sociometric data. The introduction of instructions to the peer groups to help the child with his or her work brought about a major increase in the 3rd graders' appropriate behavior. Appropriate attending behavior for 1st graders did not increase to the predetermined acceptable level until a free time period for each peer group was made contingent upon the appropriate behavior of the subject in each group. See ERIC Abstract 0435658-2.

3673.   Simms, R. L. & Boger, D.   "Classroom Management That Works In Inner-City Schools." Contemporary Education, 15, 1 (Fall, 1978): 24-28.

A description is presented of several discipline problems frequently found in inner-city schools. Suggestions are presented for dealing constructively with them based on organization and classroom structure. See ERIC Abstract #EJ 195480.

3674.   Simpson, R. L. & Swenson, C. R. "The Effects and Side-Effects of an Over Correction Procedure Applied by Parents of Severely Emotionally Disturbed Children in a Home Environment." Behavioral Disorders, 5, 2 (February, 1980): 79-85.

Investigated in the study were over correction procedures applied by teachers and parents to parent self-stimulatory behavior of 2 autistic elementary school age children. The experimental design had 4 conditions during which observations were collected in the home. Following baseline, over correction was implemented in a public school classroom by a teacher, in the home by parents, and in both environments simultaneously. This permitted a) examination of the effects of treatment on the target behaviors across environments and b) determination of whether over correction would lead to desirable side effects. For this purpose, proximity to others and plane appropriately were identified as positive behavioral correlates for both subjects. Three behaviors were identified for each subject as negative behavioral correlates. Results show that in each setting, over-correction procedures were associated with statistically significant differences in the target behaviors. However, 2/3 of untreated behaviors changed into desirable and significant directions. Lowest levels of target behaviors were attained when the procedures were applied simultaneously at school and at home. See ERIC Abstract 0181265-1.

3675.   Sinclair, E. "Relationship Of Cycle Educational Diagnoses To Educational Placement." Journal Of School Psychology, 18, 4 (Winter, 1980): 349-53.

Investigated in this study was the relationship between diagnostic classifications and educational placement recommendations utilized by educational psychologists in the evaluation of psycho-educational reports evaluated for clinical consensus in five input areas: developmental history, school history, cognitive functioning, sensorimotor-perceptual functioning, and academic achievement. See ERIC Abstract #EJ 240093.

3676.   Sinner, G. & Sinner, J. L. "Options In High School Discipline." Phi Delta Kappan, 59, 6 (February, 1978): 407-409.

Seven alternatives to the traditional offerings in one high school are described. These programs are designed to counteract student boredom, frustration, anxiety, and related causes of discipline problems.

3677.   Sklarz, D. P. "Behavorial Teacher." Clearinghouse, 52, 9 (May, 1979): 429-430.

The author, a junior high school principal, describes how his teachers participate in the discipline process. They share duty in a small room and act as a behavioral teacher, using a Glasser Reality-oriented approach. Mildly disrupted pupils are sent to the behavioral teacher instead of to the assistant principal. See ERIC Abstract #EJ 202538.

3678.   Slavin, R. E. "Classroom Reward Structure: An Analytical and Practical Review." Review of Educational Research, 47, 4 (Fall, 1977): 633-650.

At various times in the history of social psychology, interest has arisen in the reward structure of the class-rooms, particularly in the idea of using the reward structures that place students in mutual dependence for rewards--cooperative reward structures. Some high points in the study of classroom reward structure were publications by Deutsch which presented a comprehensive theory of coopera-tion and competition, Miller and Hamblin and Johnson, V.W. & Johnson, R.T. Of these, only Johnson and Johnson reviewed the large body of research that has been done on coopera-tive, competitive, and individual reward structures, but their review was lacking in analysis of these findings. The present paper attempts to fill this gap by drawing theoretical and practical conclusions from the research on reward structures.

3679.   Slavin, R. E. "Separating Incentives, Feedback, and Evaluation: Toward a More Effective Classroom System." Reprinted from Educational Psychologists, 13, (1978): 97-100.

Grading is among the most controversial aspects of classroom practices. This paper seeks to answer why have grades been so hearty when they have been found so unpopular among significant groups of educators. The author discusses the possibilities for operationalizing separate incentive-performance feedback as evaluation systems in classrooms. What is important is not so much the particular system used, but the commitment to investigate incentive-feedback-evaluation systems that achieve their separate goals as effectively as possible. The paper argues that incentives, feedback and evaluation should not be combined in a single form through the grade, but should be treated both by researchers and by educational practitioners as separate issues to be pursued on parallel courses.

3680.   Slawski, E. J. & Scherer, J. "The Rhetoric Of Concern: Trust And Control In An Urban Desegregated School." Anthropology And Education Quarterly, 9, 4 (Winter, 1978): 258-271.

Although the rhetoric of concern which surrounds talk about desegregation in the southern urban public high school works to some degree in balancing the demands associated with controlling student behavior and developing trust amoung the

community, it seems to be dysfunctional for efforts in
dealing with race relations in the school. See ERIC
Abstract #EJ 195578.

3681.   Slawski, E. J. & Scherer, J.   "The Rhetoric Of Concern:
Trust And Control In An Urban Desegregated School."   Paper
Presented At The Annual Meeting Of The American
Anthropological Association, Houston, Texas, November 30,
1976.

Various sets of actors in an urban desegregated high school
are found to use a rhetoric of concern to discuss school
operation and events. This rhetoric is based upon the
accepted understanding that schools do what is best for
students. Since the rhetoric appeals to diverse segments of
the community in which the school is located, it enables
school officials to manage the conflicting demands of maintaining control and gaining the confidence of the community.
The rhetoric of concern allows school people to talk about
control in ways which build trust. Although this kind of
language is useful in gaining a consensus, in the high
school described the rhetoric is dysfunctional for dealing
with the persistant problems of race relations between
Blacks, Hispanics, and Southern Whites. See ERIC Abstract
#ED 156739.

3682.   Sloat, K. C., Tharp, R. G. & Gallimore, T.   "The
Incremental Effectiveness of Classroom-Based Teacher-
Training Techniques."   Behavior Therapy, 8 5 (November,
1977): 810-818.

Five female elementary teachers were trained to use praise
in the classroom during a series of 6 one week in-service
workshops over a period of 16 weeks. The training
components (didactic instruction, modeling and role-playing,
videotape feedback, direct coaching, graph feedback, and
graph feedback with goals) were ordered by several criteria,
with the primary aim of trying to identify the point beyond
which there were no further teacher-performance improvements
with further training. All subjects were observed and coded
daily during regular teaching activities. Use of praise was
not affected by didactic instruction, increased marketly as
a result of the modeling and role-playing component, further
decreased for 3 of the subjects during videotape feedback,
declined the next 2 components, and increased dramatically
during graphed feedback with goals. See ERIC Abstract
0815660-4.

3683.   Smith, J. K. and Laplante, D. A.   "Student and Teacher
Perceptions of Fair v. Unfair Teacher Activities and the
Problems Legitimacy."   High School Journal, 64, 3 (December,
1980): 108-114.

A questionnaire was administered to 180 students and 53
teachers in a rural and an urban high school. Results
indicate a fairly wide "shared perception" of the fairness

of teacher actions in general discipline, but significant differences on control of the academic process and content. See ERIC Abstract EJ 237969.

3684.   Smith, M. "The Secondary School Administrator and Student   Disruption   in   the   Desegregation-Integration Process."   Paper presented at the American Educational Research Association Annual Meeting, Chicago, Illinois, April, 1974.

In this report information is presented on whether or not students attending disruptive or nondisruptive schools and black or white students within those schools differ in whether or not these differences contribute to general disruption and conflict. Significant relationships were found between students attending disrupted or nondisrupted and between black and white students. Disruption was related to the race of students, their grade placement, and age grade differential, but not to the type of academic program in which they enrolled. Conclusions are based on data collected from 15 senior high schools in New York. See ERIC Abstract ED 090698.

3685.   Snider, S. J. & Cooper, L. J. "Classroom Conduct Theory Into Practice System." _Action in Teacher Education_, 1, 2 (Fall, Winter, 1978): 47-53.

Systematic analysis of classroom disruption and discipline problems can frequently correct undesirable behavior. The approach presented uses outside observers to help analyse problems and construct solutions. See ERIC Abstract EJ 197176.

3686.   Snow, D. L. and Brooks, R. B. "A School Consultation Program In Behavior Modification." _Journal of School Health_, 44, 3 (March, 1974): 130-135.

The role of the consultant and the consultant-teacher relationship is discussed in establishing an on-going behavior modification program on a school-wide basis. A major goal of the consultation program is to develop effective means to communicate with teachers and other school personnel. Several approaches to achieve the goal are the introduction of weekly conferences with teachers, meetings with small groups of teachers, staff meetings, or workshops. In addition to training teachers to be competent in their use of behavior modification techniques these approaches are also useful in helping to ensure the on-going youth of behavior modification principles. The need for effective follow-up procedures is emphasized. See ERIC Abstract 1257353-6.

3687.   Solomon, D. and Kendall, A. J. "Dimensions of Children's Classroom Behavior, as Perceived by Teachers." _American Educational Research Journal_, 14, 4 (Fall, 1977): 411-421.

Teachers described the classroom behavior of 205 third and fourth grade children with a 30 item rating scale. Factor analysis of the scale produced four factors: democratic, cooperative behavior; autonomists intellectual orientation; responsible perseverant striving behavior; and involvement in class activities. Correlations of factor scores with measure of achievement test performance, creativity, inquiry skill, and various orientations, motives, attitudes and values were investigated. Patterns of correlations with the two achievement related factors suggest that teachers that validly discriminate between "perserverant" and "autonomus, intellectural" approaches to achievement. See ERIC Abstract 1249460-6.

3688.   Solomon, D. and Kendall, A. J. "Individual Character-istics and Children's Performance in Open and Traditional Classroom Settings." Journal of Educational Psychology, 68, 5 (October, 1976): 613-625.

The performance of 56 boys and 36 girls was assessed with different motivational and cognitive characteristics in three open and three traditional classrooms. Claustro-analysis of factor scores representing child orientations, motives, and prior achievement produce six types. Three way analyses of variance investigated the effects child type, classroom type, sex of child, and various interactions on several outcome measures, including academic achievement, creativity, inquiry skill, social-educational attitudes, and teaching ratings of children's classroom behavior. Main effects appeared from ech of the three independent vari-ables, along with several child class interactions. An approach using child types of clusters rather than abstracted dimensions may facilitate further attribute treatment interaction research. See ERIC Abstract 1064756-6.

3689.   Solomon, D. and Kendall, A. J. "Teachers' Perceptions of and Reactions to Misbehavior in Traditional and Open Classrooms." Journal of Educational Psychology, 67, 4 (August, 1975): 528-530.

Teachers' disciplinary activities in traditional and open classrooms was compared. Measures of teachers' discipline and criticism and children's misbehavior were derived from observations of three traditional and three open elementary school classrooms. The teachers' discipline and criticism scores were significantly higher in traditional classrooms, while the child misbehavior category did not show a signifi-cant difference between class types. It is suggested that the two settings may create different norms and standards which cause teachers to perceive and act differently to objectively similar behaviors. See ERIC Abstract 1054754-5.

3690.   Solomon, R. and Tyne, T. F. "A Comparison of Individual and Group Contingency Systems in a First Grade Class." Psychology in the Schools, 16, 2 (April, 1979): 193-200.

With the use of a multi-element design, individual and group contingency systems were found to significantly reduce disruptive, unacceptable behaviors in a first grade classroom, compared to baseline-reversal conditions. Teacher control statements also were significantly decreased within the treatment programs. See ERIC Abstract 0646964-3.

3691.   Spaulding, R. L.   "Control of Deviancy in the Classroom as a Consequence of Ego-Enhancing Behavior Management Techniques." Journal of Research and Development in Education, 11, 4 (Summer, 1978): 39-52.

Some of the benefits of systematic behavior modification at the elementary level are described. Elementary school discipline is examined, not as a set of responses to deviancy and delinquency, but as an integral part of generic concepts of classroom amangement and instruction. See ERIC Abstract EJ 189890.

3692.   Speed, W. K.   "Project MAS -- QUE ESTA PASANDO?" NEATE Leaflet, 71, 1 (February, 1972): 31-37.

Project MAS was designed to offer more alternatives to students. The program, developed for the Hartford Public High School, Connecticut, is intended not only to reduce the phenomena known as dropping out but also to reduce the phenomenon known as pushing out. The progrm's background, development, objectives, and evaluation are discussed. Three major components of the project are: staff development, instruction, and supportive services. The problems epitomize those of urban American. Social, economic, and educational problems are common to almost every urban community. The project attempts to discover strategies that will identify the problems, the factors involved, and prescribes actions that lead to solutions. See ERIC Abstract ED 063298.

3693.   Speidel, G. E., and Tharpe, R. G.   "Teacher-Training Workshop Strategy: Instructions, Discrimination Training, Modeling, Guided Practice and Video Feedback." Behavior Therapy, 9, 5 (November, 1978): 735-739.

A three-day training program was designed to increase the use of positive verbal feedback by six experienced classroom teachers. Training components included lecturing, discrimination training, modeling, guided practice, and feedback. Observations of the trainees' academic and management praise rates in their home classrooms before and after the workshop and a five month follow-up indicated that the training effects were significant, specific to the trained behaviors and maintained for five months. See ERIC Abstract 0956962-4.

3694.   Sperry, L. & Carter, T. "Non-reactive Measures of Behavior Change Following Human Relations Training." Paper presented at the annual meeting of the American Educational Research Association, Chicago, Illinois, April, 1974.

The effects of a structured in-service human relations training program on Teacher Coping Behaviors in response to student misbehaviors are reported. Sixty teachers from Title 10 Elementary, Junior and Senior high schools were randomly assigned to three experimental and three controlled groups. Changes in coping behavior were assessed by three non-reactive measures: discipline cards, psychological, and counseling referrals four weeks before and four weeks after the training program. Results showed significantly fewer psychological and counseling referrals at the elementary and junior levels and fewer discipline cards at the elementary level for the experimental groups as compared to the controlled groups. See ERIC Abstract ED 090258.

3695.   Spillman, C. V. "Classroom Management: Mystery or Mastery." Education, 101, 1 (Fall, 1980): 41-45.

Some basic principles underline success or failure in classroom management are examined and activities are suggested to promote cooperative awareness among students. See ERIC Abstract EJ 234920.

3696.   Stabler, B. and Frazier, J. R. "The Use of Video Tape Self-Confrontation in the Acquisition of Behavior Management Skills by Elementary Special Education Trainees." Bulletin of the North Carolina Psychological Association, (Fall, 1973): 12-18.

The purpose of this study was to examine the use of video tape self-confrontation as a method for training 14 graduate students in behavior management. Subjects were randomly assigned to three groups for training: A) an experimental group using video tape recordings of their teaching performance, B) a control group, receiving coded feedback of their teaching performance, and C) a second control group, not receiving feedback of any kind but given information on principals of reinforcement. The classes with which the groups worked consisted of four moderately retarded children. Findings indicate a statistically significant increase in the use of punishment sequences by the experimental group. The advantages of video tape self-confrontation are discussed. See ERIC Abstract 1128657-5.

3697.   Starr Commonwealth for Boys. "Doorway to Hope." Davis Productions, 1966.

This is a public relations film about the Starr Commonwealth for Boys, a privately endowed school for troubled boys. It explains that the academic, homelife and treatment programs of the school emphasize self-discipline and individual responsibility. Fourteen minutes. 16mm film. See NICEM 0849750.

3698. Steinberg, J. A. & Hall, V. C. "Effects of Social Behavior on Inter-Racial Acceptance." Journal of Educational Psychology, 73, 1 (February, 1981): 51-56.

To test children's use of race and social behavior as cues in social acceptance, one hundred and twenty-eight black and white male kindergartners and first graders rated six unknown video taped target children for likability. Targets varied factorially on race and exhibited either positive, negative or neutral classroom social behavior. Across age, socioeconomic status, and race, subjects used behavior as a cue, accounting for 50% of likability variance. Positive targets were liked equivalently, but black, neutral and negative targets were liked less than white counterparts. See ERIC Abstract 0881665-4.

3699. Stetter, D. "Into the Classroom with Behavior Modification." School Counselor, 19, 2 (November, 1971): 110-114.

One female and ten male eighth graders who were receiving unsatisfactory academic and behavior grades in four math classes were selected. The subjects were reinforced with tokens for following regular classroom procedures for a period of four weeks. Pre and post reinforcement grades in math and science were examined. Math and behavior grades for all eleven subjects improved; science grades were improved for only two subjects. In a second study, three teachers of language and social studies classes for poor readers were instructed in an reinforcement program where subjects earned chances to win prizes by following classroom procedures. While the effects could not be directly assessed, both the teachers and students indicated that teaching and learning became more enjoyable. See ERIC Abstract 1007549-5.

3700. Stevens, M. L. "The Workclock: A Means of Establishing and Maintaining Classroom Control." Scandanavian Journal of Behavior Therapy, 6, 1 (1977): 1-8.

A practical workclock program was tested rather as an alternative to the time consuming token economy system. A clock was started whenever a pupil broke one of the rules stipulated, and it was stopped when rule-breaking ceased. The primary reinforcer for not making interruptions during the working periods was free time. Results show a great decrease in interruptions during both the formal work plot period and the follow-up period. See ERIC Abstract 0432159-2.

3701. Stone-Brandel Center. "The Healthy Relationship." Modern Talking Picture Services.

A new technique in teaching is presented which uses discipline problems in schools to teach younger children. It
emphasizes the grammar school's problem. Twenty-eight
minutes. 16mm film. See NICEM 0806928.

3702.   Struble, J. B. "The Application of Positive Social
Reinforcement to Behaviors of Getting Ready to Work." SALT:
School Application of Learning Theory, 4, 1 (October, 1971):
34-39.

This study improved the latency of the in-seat, ready-to-
work responses of a fourth grade class using praise as a
positive social reinforcement. The class frequently, in the
beginning, took more than four minutes to prepare for classroom activity. Tests were conducted over thirteen school
days with realiability checks made several times. Immediate
reinforcement was given to individual subjects who were
ready in less than one hundred and twenty seconds. Subjects
also reinforced and prompted each other and performed self-
checks. The procedure generated an immediate decrease in
time taken to get ready, and illustrates the ease in which
minor problems of classroom order and discipline can be
solved. See ERIC Abstract 1007949-5.

3703.   Stuart, R. B. "Behavior Modification Techniques For The
Education Technologist." In R.C. Sarfi and F. F. Maple
(Eds.), The School In The Community, Washington, D.C.:
National Association of Social Workers, 1972.

In this article, it is suggested that the traditional model
of the school social worker offering individual counseling
to troubled children is archaic. The first client of the
education technologist is the teacher, and the presenting
problems of students are regarded as reasonable reactions to
deficient environments. Among the techniques that are
detailed are analysis of the behaviors and their antecendent
and consequent conditions, positive and negative reinforcement, time-out, maintenance of learned behavior, and
generalization of behavior to other situations. See ERIC
Abstract 0787650-4.

3704.   Sucher, F. "Factors Contributing to Misbehavior and
Underachievement Among Elementary School Boys." Paper
presented at the Annual Meeting of the International Reading
Association Southeastern Regional Conference, Jacksonville,
Florida, February, 1976.

Often times boys have been identified as the primary source
of misbehavior by teachers and administrators. Boys constitute the greatest percentage of those students who are
underachieving and failing. This paper discusses the
problems of misbehavior, underachievement, and the related
conditions; it explores the two major factors contributing
to boys' school-related problems -- the home and the school,
and considers what can be done to rectify the problems,
including specific ways in which schools and teachers can

adjust to the learning styles, misbehavior patterns, and interests of boys. The paper concludes that what is needed most is teachers who are open, flexible, and fair with all students, regardless of their sex or behavior patterns. See ERIC Abstract ED 131440.

3705.   Sultana, Q. & Saunders, M. K. "Teacher Competencies With Behavior Disordered Students." Education Unlimited, 2, 2 (March, 1980): 26-29.

Twenty-eight elementary education teachers were asked to classify competencies and skills for dealing with behavior problems into three categories: those not addressed in their training program, those addressed minimally, and those addressed adequately. See ERIC Abstract EJ 230370.

3706.   Supreme Court of the United States. "Supreme Court of the United States: Gos et al. v. Lopez et al. Appeal from the United States District Court for the 7th District of Ohio. No. 73-898. Argued October 16, 1974 -- Decided January 22, 1975." Washington, D.C., 1975.

On January 22, 1975, the Supreme Court decided that students facing temporary suspension from a public school have property and liberty interest that qualify for protection under the due process clause of the 14th Amendment. Having chosen to extend the right to an education for two students, the state may not, without due process, withdraw that right on grounds of misconduct. Further, due process requires, in connection with a suspension for up to ten days, that the students be given oral or written notice of the charges against him. If he denies the charges, the student is due an explanation of the evidence the authorities have, and he must be given an opportunity to present his version of the case. See ERIC Abstract ED 100020.

3707.   Supreme Court of the United States. "Supreme Court of the United States: Wood et al. v. Strickland et al. Certiorari to the United States Court of Appeals for the Eight Circuit, No. 73-1285. Argued October 16, 1974 -- Decided February 25, 1975." Washington, D.C., 1975.

Three Arkansas high school students were expelled for violating a school regulation prohibiting intoxicating beverages at school activities. The students brought suit in the United States District Court claiming violation of their rights to due process. The District Court directed verdicts for the school board on the ground that school officials are immuned from damage suits except in cases of proved malice or ill will. The Court of Appeals reversed the District Court ruling on the ground that the school board had not acted in good faith, since there was no evidence that the regulation had actually been violated. Although the students admitted spiking punch with malt liquor, there was no evidence that the alcoholic content of the punch met the Arkansas definition of intoxicating beverage. The Supreme Court agreed with the Court of Appeals that school officials are immuned only if they act in good faith and with proper regard of students' constitutional rights. However, the Court also found that the school regulation forbidding intoxicating beverages did not hinge on the percentage of alcohoic content and that there was ample evidence that the students had knowingly violated the regulations. The judgment of the Court of Appeals was therefore vacated, and the case remanded for consideration of possible procedural violations of the students' rights to due process. See ERIC Abstract ED 101464.

3708.   Swift, M. & Back, L. "A Method for Aiding Teachers of the Troubled Adolescent." Adolescence, 8, 29 (Spring, 1973): 1-16.

Several common classroom behavior problems are described for academically troubled adolescents along with alternative teaching techniques suited to each. The behavior patterns were derived from the Hahnemann High School Behavior Rating Scale and the teaching techniques from the authors' experience. See ERIC Abstract 0589251-3.

3709.   Switzer, E. B., Deal, T. E., & Bailey, J. S. "The Reduction of Stealing in Second Graders Using a Group Contingency." Journal of Applied Behavior Analysis, 10, 2 (Summer, 1977): 267-272.

Three classes of 26 second graders were subjects in a study of the effects of two types of intervention programs on stealing: an anti-stealing lecture with no specific contingency implied, and a direct group contingency applied, whereby children were rewarded with a) extra free time for no thefts, b) allowed normal free time if stolen items were returned and c) punished with loss of free time if stolen items were not returned. See ERIC Abstract 1318259-6.

3710.   Tacke, G. & Hofer, M. "Behavioral Changes in Teachers as a Function of Student Feedback: A Case for the Achievement Motivation Theory." Journal of School Psychology, 17, 2 (Summer, 1979): 172-180.

This study tested whether forty-four seventh through tenth grade teachers would change their behavior when they received student ratings as feedback on their own behavior and on the behavior of a fictitious ideal teacher. Achievement motivation theory has been considered as an explanation for such behavioral changes and provided the basis for a series of hypotheses. The major one was that discrepant feedback induces achievement motivation, and the increased effort connected with achievement motivation leads to behavioral changes. Results were inconclusive; subjects improved only slightly. See ERIC Abstract 0876964-4.

3711.   Taylor, W. F. and Hoedt, K. C. "Classroom-Related Behavior Problems: Counsel Parents, Teachers, or Children." Journal of Counseling Psychology, 21, 1 (January, 1974): 3-8.

Compared was the effectiveness of group counseling with significant adults, parents or teachers, and of group counseling with elementary school children in reducing classroom behavior problems. Subjects were three hundred and seventy-two children of average socio-economic backgrounds. Results of an analysis of variance following a ten-week treatment period indicated that the indirect approach was more effective than the direct approach, regardless of grade level. See ERIC Abstract 0640252-3.

3712.   Teeter, T. A. and Teeter, C. R. "Teaching and Discipline." High School Journal, 63, 1 (October, 1979): 12-16.

The authors draw specific guidelines for the high school teacher on creating a productive classroom environment and preventing discipline problems. Four approaches to behavior management are outlined. See ERIC Abstract EJ 220505.

3713.   Thacker, J. "Teaching Students: Teaching Teachers." Association of Educational Psychologists Journal, 4, 3 (Christmas, 1976): 23-25.

An inservice course is described in behavior modification for teachers for severely mentally handicapped children which was offered by student educational psychologists as part of their own training. Problems and possible alternative presentations are discussed. See ERIC Abstract 0647259-3.

3714.   Thiagarajan, S. "Make Protocol Films: An Exercise in Concept Teaching." Educational Technology, 15, 9 (September, 1975): 38-40.

A procedure for making protocol films is described. Protocols are records of real or realistic segments of educationally relevant human interactions. Specific examples of behaviors occuring in such films provide a base from which a trainee may learn to identify, relate, and interpret different types of interactions and induce a conceptual framework. The first step in making a protocol film begins with an ascending of divergent positive and negative examples of each interactional concept. These examples are analyzed for the presence of common elements which specify attributes critical for membership in the concept class and the presence of irrelevant attributes. A hypothetical example of a film being made on disruptive behaviors is discussed. The second step consists of preparing a story board. A range of positive examples is worked out by varying the dimensions of each irrelevant attribute, and a set of negative examples requiring finer discriminations on the part of the viewer is generated by eliminating one critical attribute at a time. The examples then are arranged in a sequence according to guidelines for instructional effectiveness. See ERIC Abstract 0174560-1.

3715.   Thomas, J. W. "Agency and Achievement: Self-Management and Self-Regard." Review of Educational Research, 50, 2 (Summer, 1980): 213-240.

Studies of self-management, attribution, and achievement and motivation challenge the view that basic skills instruction requires strong teacher control, structure, convergence on learning activities, less pupil freedom, and less experimental teaching activities. Student-managed instruction yielded the greatest achievement gains and heightened achievement motivation and self-control. See ERIC Abstract EJ 229097.

3716.   Thompson, C. L. "Counseling Elementary School Students: Techniques and Proposals." Elementary School Guidance Counseling, 4, 3 (March, 1970): 164-171.

Studies sought to 1) identify pupil learning, behavior and adjustment problems for which teachers feel they need remediation strategies, 2) present rationale for behavior change strategies, 3) test two strategies for working with representative problems identified by teachers. See ERIC Abstract EJ 015448.

3717.   Thompson, C. L. and Cates, J. T. "Teaching Discipline to Students: An Individualized Teaching-Counseling Approach." Paper presented at the Annual Convention of the American Personnel and Guidance Association, Chicago, Illinois, April, 1976.

The purpose of this study was to determine whether or not the treatment process of individualized lesson plans for teaching discipline to children was effective in reducing time-off-task and disruptive behaviors, while increasing time-on-task and appropriate social behaviors. The study was conducted at a primary school in Knoxville, Tennessee. Each of six teachers selected their most serious problem student as subjects for the study. Three students from the Department of Educational Psychology and Guidance of the University of Tennessee were employed and trained as observers. It was hypothesized that the individualized approach to teaching discipline would result in an increase in the students' appropriate behavior and decrease in their inappropriate behavior. The hypothesis was supported. See ERIC Abstract ED 127507.

3718.   Thomson, S. and Stanard, D. "Student Attendance and Absenteeism. The Practitioner, Volume I, No. 1." Reston, Virginia: National Association of Secondary School Principals, 1975.

Excessive absenteeism is a complex and continuing secondary school problem with personal, institutional, economic, and social causes. Issues of excused or unexcused absences and age of majority are complex and largely ignored by research. Research indicate absenteeism is positively correlated with the second semester, boys, older students, one parent families, low grades, and students with low personality ratings by teachers. Cohesive families, college preparatory programs, high grades, and extracurricular activities positively correlate with better attendance. Exemplary programs relfect strong policies that are cooperatively and consistently developed in well publicized schools. Nine schools with positive attendance policies are described. See ERIC Abstract ED 102682.

3719.   Tisdale, P. C. and Fowler, R. E. "Incidence of Behavior Disorders in Children in South Carolina: Teachers' Perceptions." Paper presented at the University of South Carolina Conference on Educational Research, December 6, 1980.

The purpose of this study was to determine the incidence of behavior disordered children in selected elementary class-rooms as perceived by the regular classroom teacher. Two hundred four elementary teachers categorized students according to their perceptions of their students' needs for special services. The categories were defined as mild, moderate, or severely behavior disordered. The data when analyzed by perceived disorder and by sex and race of the students. The results were discussed, and it was found that the total mean of children thought to require special ser-vices was 16%. It was concluded that the needs of behavior disordered children are not being adequately met. Implica-tions for teacher competencies and administrative arrange-ments are made. Changes in three areas are suggested: preservice teacher preparation, inservice teacher training, and the provision of self contained in resource classes for behavior disordered students.

3720.   Toby, J. "Crime in American Public Schools." _Public Interest_, 58, (Winter, 1980): 18-42.

Article reviews the National Institute of Education's 1978 study of school crime. Several social trends are offered as possible causes for recent increases in school crime. Methods are suggested for reducing violence in the schools. See ERIC Abstract EJ 218798.

3721.   Tombari, M. L. and Bergan, J. R. "Consultant Cues And Teacher Verbalizations, Judgments And Expectancies Concerning Children's Adjustment Problems." _Journal Of School Psychology_, 16, 3 (Fall, 1978): 212-219.

The verbalizations of sixty college seniors majoring in education were studied. These verbalizations dealt with children's classroom problems as a function of medical-model or behavioral-model cues. These cues illicited descriptions of problem behavior congruent with their respective assumptions about human behavior. In addition, medical-model cues illicited more pessimistic expectancies about an instructor's ability to solve classroom problem behavior in the classroom setting than did behavioral cues. See ERIC Abstract 0833263-4.

3722.   Toner, I. J. et al. "The Effect of Serving as a Model of Self-Control on Subsequent Resistance to Deviation in Children." Paper presented at the Biennial Meeting of the Society for Research in Child Development, New Orleans, Louisiana, March, 1977.

The effect of having a child serve as a rule following model for other children on the model's own subsequent rule-following was investigated in a resistance to deviation situation. Forty-five middle class boys in grades one and two were assigned to one of three experimental conditions randomly following instruction not to touch a set of attractive but prohibited toys. In the model condition, boys performed as models of resistance to deviation before a TV camera for children at another school. In the no model condition, boys were told they sould serve as models for others but, through a mechanical failure, were unable to do so. Control subjects were not told they were to be models. When alone with the prohibited toys, boys in the model condition touched less often and for less time than did boys in the control condition. Boys in the no model condition did not touch significantly less than control subjects. Model boys touched less quickly than no model and control subjects. Boys in the model condition spontaneously reproduced the idosyncratic resistance behaviors they modelled more than boys in the other conditions who also practiced this behavior. Thus, having a child serve as a model for good behavior for other children appears to be an effective disciplinary technique that avoids some of the undesirable side effects associated with punishment, such as increases in the child's aggression, resentment and alienation. See ERIC Abstract ED 135492.

3723.   Touliatos, J. and Lindholm, B. W. "Teachers' Perceptions of Behavior Problems in Children from Intact, Single-Parent, and Step Parent Families." Psychology in the Schools, 17, 2 (April, 1980): 264-269.

In this study results indicated that, compared to children from intact homes those living with mothers only had more problems on all scales; those with fathers only, more socialized delinquency; those with mothers and step fathers, more conduct problems and socialized delinquency; and those with fathers and step mothers, more conduct problems. See ERIC Abstract EJ 231725.

3724.   Trahan, D. and Stricklin, A. "Bender-Gestalt Emotional Indicators and Acting-Out Behavior in Young Children." Journal of Personality Assessment, 43, 4 (August, 1979): 365-375.

The relationship between 15 emotional indicators on the Bender-Gestalt Test and the acting-out behavior of 93 chldren, ages 5-12, as rated by their teachers, was investigated. Use of the Bender-Gestalt Test as a projective measure was seriously questioned. See ERIC Abstract EJ 210279.

3725.   Travers, P. D. "A Historic View of School Discipline." Educational Horizons, 58, 4 (Summer, 1980): 184-187.

Article surveys educational environments and philosophies of school discipline from the colonial era through the 20th century to illustrate that students have always been considered difficult to control. See ERIC Abstract EJ 231434.

3726.   Travis, C. B. "Social Behavior of Children in a Classroom Setting." Contemporary Educational Psychology, 2, 4 (October, 1977): 373-383.

Twenty-five male and seventeen female second graders in two traditional classrooms were videotaped during normal classroom activity, until approximately fifty minutes of tape was accumulated for each subject. A variety of behaviors was then coded on an event recorder, including subject-subject interactions, general behaviors, and subject-teacher interaction. Teacher evaluations expressed as ratings between by-polar adjectives were also obtained. A principal components analysis revealed six distinct factors. The strongest factor was composed of teacher-subject interactions. It was indicated that defects and birth-order differences were limited. Compared to males, females engaged in significantly more verbalization with same sex peers and significantly more cooperation with same sex peers. Teacher's evaluations were not significantly influenced by the sex of the subjects. Favorable teacher evaluations were clearly associated with the extent to which a subject approached and remained in proximity to the teacher. See ERIC Abstract 0407660-2.

3727.   Trumble, L. D. and Thurston, P. "Improving Classroom Management: A Systematic Application of Dreikurs' Theory of Misbehavior in the Elementary School." Planning and Changing, 7, 2 (Summer, 1976): 29-34.

A theoretical framework is presented which was developed by Rudolf Dreikurs in tabular form that can be easily used in suggesting appropriate action for a particular type of misbehavior. See ERIC Abstract EJ 150201.

3728.   Tsoi, D. J. et al. "Group Counseling with Nonverbalizing
Elementary Students: Differential Effects of Premack and
Social Reinforcement Techniques." Journal of Counseling
Psychology, 18, 5 (September, 1971): 437-440.

In terms of the criterion measure, the social reinforcement
group differed in this study significantly from the teacher
expectation and the control group. Differences in mean
response gains between Premack and social reinforcement
groups approached significance with the greatest changes in
client behavior favoring the social reinforcement group.
See ERIC Abstract EJ 043763.

3729.   Tymitz, B. S. and Omark, D. R. "A Naturalistic Observation Of Verbal Discipline Modeling In A First Grade
Classroom." Instructional Science, 7, 1 (January, 1978):
81-94.

In order to illustrate three observational techniques verbal
disciplinary techniques as used by a regular classroom
teacher and a student teacher were compared. Managing,
threatening and describing behaviors were observed since
these were used as attempts by the teachers to stop inappropriate behaviors, and presumably, to return the children to
on-task behaviors. Since discipline is frequently a student
teacher's most difficult task, some modeling of the classroom teacher's behaviors were expected to occur. This was
found for discipline directed at individual children, but
not for total group disciplinary attempts. While the
regular teacher produced more decists and was more effective
in returning the children to on-task behavior, when disruptive children's sequential patterns of behaviors were
examined, the most frequent response was something other
than on-task behaviors. Questions are raised about what
should be modeled, and when any sequence of behaviors a
teacher should intervene. See ERIC Abstract 0227361-1.

3730.   Umana, R. F. and Schwebel, A. I. "Academic And
Behavioral Changes In tutored Inner-City Children."
Community Mental Health Journal, 10, 3 (Fall, 1974):
309-318.

A study was conducted of sixty fourth, fifth, and sixth
grade children to determine the effectiveness of short-term
tutoring in producing improvement in tutored children's
academic performance and classroom behaviors; the rolls of
tutor support and supervision and volunteering on the part
of tutored children were also examined. Subjects were
divided into four groups: Group One subjects were tutored
by undergraduates fulfilling a psychology course requirement; Group Two subjects were tutored by undergraduates who
volunteered as part of a community project; Group Three
subjects requested but were not assigned tutors; and Group
Four subjects were those who most closely matched subjects
assigned to the previous groups. The improvement by Group
One children in the three academic areas assessed by the

Wide-Range Achievement Test suggest that with support undergraduates can be effective tutors for inner-city children. See ERIC Abstract 0831753-4.

3731.   Unger, K. V. et al. "A Behavior Curriculum: Skills Training Can Reduce Problems." NASSP Bulletin, 63, 428 (September, 1979): 72-76.

In a program designed to teach students specific behavior skills that will help them to function better in the classroom, appropriate behaviors are systematically monitored and reinforced. See ERIC Abstract EJ 206332.

3732.   U.S. Bureau of Education for the Handicapped. "One Hour a Week." U.S. National Audio-Visual Center, 1973.

The home training program of the League School for seriously disturbed children is described. The film shows how it helps parents to cope with their child's emotional handicap by demonstrating techniques in behavior modification that they can practice at home. Eighteen minutes. 16mm film. See NICEM 0874115.

3733.   U.S. Bureau of Education for the Handicapped. "That's What It's All About." U.S. National Audio-Visual Center, 1973.

All aspects of the Regional Intervention Program for unmanageable children are depicted. It begins with the initial intake through the various behavior modification modules through the child's return to a normal public school within the community. Twenty-nine minutes. 16mm film. See NICEM 0847770.

3734.   U.S. Office of Economic Opportunity. "Discipline and Self-Control." U.S. National Audio-Visual Center.

Film discusses the problems of discipline from a teacher's perspective and a parent's perspective. It explains the means by which a teacher can establish control and maintain a good climate in the classroom. Twenty-five minutes. 16mm film. See NICEM 0804054.

3735.   Unks, G. "The Front Line: The Real Discipline Problem." High School Journal, 63, 5 (February, 1980): 179-182.

The author contends that discipline problems are not caused by television, family problems, drugs or integration, but by the teacher and the administrator due to their absurd rules and ridiculous activities. See ERIC Abstract EJ 226859.

3736.   Unruh, A. "Teachers and Classroom Discipline." NASSP Bulletin, 61, 406 (February, 1977): 84-87.

Eight categories of teacher weakness that contribute to classroom discipline problems are discussed, as identified by 61 junior high and high school teachers who participated in a series of seminars on discipline. See ERIC Abstract EJ 160393.

3737.   "The Use of Observational Data in Elementary Counseling." Canadian Counselors, 11, 2. (January, 1977): 93-96.

A proposal is made for dealing with problems of underachievement within the elementary classroom. It entails collection of behavioral data within the classroom by the consultant and the development of intervention stategies to be implemented by the classroom teacher. See ERIC Abstract EJ 167372.

3738.   Uslander, A. S. "Hey, Look . at Me." Teacher, 97, 1 (September, 1979): 22, 24, 26, 28.

Article discusses the child who never manages to succeed, who always falls short of his or her personal or academic goals. Consideration is given to causes of failure in the child's over or under expectations of self and to the behavior problems that can result from continuous frustration. See ERIC Abstract EJ 219125.

3739.   Usova, G. M. "Reducing Discipline Problems in the Elementary Schools: Approaches and Suggestions." Education, 99, 4 (Summer, 1979): 419-422.

Teachers should think in terms of preventing discipline problems by carefully analyzing their own behavioral expectations, treating children in an adult like manner, and being thoroughly organized for instruction. See ERIC Abstract EJ 206937.

3740.   Vaal, J. J. "The Decrease of Unintelligible Verbal Responses Through the Use of Operant Conditioning Techniques." Psychology in the Schools, 9, 4 (October, 1972) 446-450.

The article describes attempts to decrease the unintelligible verbal responses of two fifth grade girls to their teachers. In the behavior modification process, the attention of the teachers was used as the reinforcer. Analysis of the data indicates that the treatment was successful in modifying the girls' behavior.

3741.   Valenti, R. D. "Some Principles for Secondary School Principals." NASSP Bulletin, 61, 406 (February, 1977): 91-93.

Article outlines basic management principles intended to aid secondary school principals in dealing with school discipline problems. See ERIC Abstract EJ 160395.

3742.   Valentine, C. F. "A Program to Reduce Vandalism and to Improve Student Behavior at Vineland High School North." Paper presented at the Annual Meeting of the National Association of Secondary School Principals, Houston, Texas, February, 1979.

New Jersey's Vineland High School North faced many behavioral and vandalism problems during its first year of operation and adopted a program to improve this situation during its second year. This effort involved adoption and thorough dissemination of student rules, a series of parent orientation meetings, a new community information program, the creation of a parent teacher association, an inservice program in humanistic education, a peer leadership program, and the hiring of paraprofessionals to improve communication between home and school. During the program's initial year, vandalism dropped substantially and most student behavior improved. Suspension figures were higher due to greater attention to the problems that remained. The need for police intervention was greatly reduced although arrest levels remained near the original level. The problems, their causes, the program designed to solve them, and the results of that program are described. See ERIC Abstract ED 173899.

3743.   VanHevel, J. and Hawkins, R. P. "Modification of Behavior in Secondary School Students Using The Premack Principle and Response Cost Technique." Salt: School Applications of Learning Theory, 6, 4 (July, 1974): 31-41.

A simple, economical, self-contained token reinforcement system was applied which increased the amount of time that junior high school students spent attending to their work. During baseline, a record was made of the percentage of time each student spent attending to his work. When points, backed up by free time, were delivered contingent upon attending behavior, the percentage of time spent attending increased. When the experimental contingencies were discontinued for a short time, attending behavior decreased. Reinstatement of the procedure again increased the time spent attending. Performance was maintained as reinforcement was delivered less often, and was also maintained on checks made several weeks after the experimental contingencies were gone from the classroom. See ERIC Abstract 06170153-3.

3744.   VanHouten, R. "The Performance Feedback System: Generalization of Effects Across Time." Child Behavior Therapy, 1, 3 (Fall, 1979): 219-236.

Direct and generalized effects were assessed of a performance feedback system introduced sequentially in two elementary classrooms with sixty subjects during two daily story-writing periods. Following baseline, a treatment package consisting of explicit timing, self-recording, and public posting was instituted only during the first story-writing period, the target behavior being words-per-minute. Next, the target was changed to the number of different action words written. After a return to baseline, several follow-up assessments were made. The treatment package produced a sustained increase in both target behaviors which generalized to the second story period. Results are more equivalent for the percentage of action words. See ERIC Abstract 0634765-3.

3745.   VanHouten, R., Morrison, E. and Jarvis, R. "The Effects Of Explicit Timing And Feedback On Compositional Response Rate In Elementary School Children." Journal Of Applied Behavior Analysis, 7, 4 (Winter, 1974): 547-555.

The effects of several variables were studied on compositional response rate in three second and fifth grade classrooms. After establishing baseline composition rates in each classroom, an experimental phase was introduced that consisted of explicit timing of the children's composition period with a stopwatch, immediate feedback on the number of words each child produced, public posting of the greatest number of words written by each child to date, and instructions to try to exceed their highest score. In all cases, introduction of the experimental conditions led to a doubling of rate of words written by students and an increase in subjective quality ratings of compositions made by independent judges. See ERIC Abstract 1046953-5.

3746.   Vannote, V. G. "A Practical Approach to Behavior Modification Programs." School Counseling, 21, 5 (May 1974): 350-355.

A description is presented of a design to be implemented in providing a behavioral modification program in the Junior High School. The model focuses on the checklist which serves two fundamental pruposes: 1) Providing timely reinforcement and 2) Eliminating the necessity of teaching behavior modification to all teachers. It also facilitates daily teacher-student interaction. Earned points, derived and accumulated from checklists scoring, are used by students to buy rewards in the community. In one study, the behavior of three-fourths of the students participating improved. See ERIC Abstract 1317252-6.

3747.   Vassar College. "Discipline and Self-Control." New York University Film Library.

The problem of discipline is stated as one of teaching and living with young children. The film illustrates how a teacher can establish control in a friendly climate and prevent disciplinary problems. It discusses adequate supervision and the danger of over and under control. It demonstrates how to help a child accept control. Twenty-five minutes. 16mm film. See NICEM 0804055.

3748.   Victor, J. B. et al. "Objective Behavior Measures of First and Second Grade Boys' Free Play and Teachers' Rating on a Behavior Problem Checklist." Psychology in the Schools, 10, 4 (1973): 439-443.

This behavior problem checklist was seen as a useful way qualified teacher judgments of first and second grade hyperactive boys' classroom behavior. The activity recorder score and vigor of play ratings were seen as salient variables in the behavior judgment that their teachers made of these boys. See ERIC Abstract EJ 089270.

3749.   Von Baeyer, C. "Effectiveness of Volunteer Adult Companions in Helping School Children with Adjustment Problems." Canada's Mental Health, 23, 1 (March, 1975): 6-7.

This study involved ten boys and eight girls, eight to twelve years old, who were paired with eighteen volunteers (housewives and students), in comparison to other children in the same classes, rated as having the same degree of maladjustment but not referred for companionship help. Teacher ratings, clasroom observations by a trained observer and a sociometric test were employed as indicators of adaptation to school; ratings were based on classroom behavior and peer acceptance. Volunteers were assessed by interview and personality tests. Results indicate that experimental subjects did not benefit from companionship. Subjects with companions were warm, nurtured volunteers experienced a drop in peer esteem. Greater improvement in subject behavior was associated with higher scores on an assertive scale for the volunteer. It was concluded that very few volunteers engaged in companionship programs are likely to really help the children. See ERIC Abstract 0449657-2.

3750.   Wade, B. E. "Highly Anxious Pupils in Formal and Informal Primary Classrooms: The Relationship Between Inferred Coping Strategies and: II--Classroom Behavior." British Journal, 51, 1 (February, 1981): 50-57.

Using a behavior observation schedule, classroom behavior was investigated in relation to pupils' level of anxiety and achievement need, which were hypothesized to be indicative of coping strategies. Subjects were 104 British students ages 10-11 in formal and informal classrooms. See ERIC Abstract EJ 241783.

3751.   Wagner, C. A. "Meeting the Perceived Needs of Children and Parent." Elementary School Guidance and Counseling, 13, 4 (April, 1979): 232-42.

This article reviews some of the major findings of two recent national surveys and discusses their implications for counselors' work in the areas of discipline and limit testing, learning, television, and mental and emotional health. See ERIC Abstract EJ 199269.

3752.   Wagner, P. F. "Teaching in America, Proceedings of the Annual Conference, Washington, D.C., April, 1967.

The proceedings of the annual conference included presentations on such topics as 1) Teaching in America, 2) Education via poetry, 3) Improving the quality of education, 4) Classroom behavior management, 5) Creating the right learning environment, 6) Improving training of guidance counselors, 7) Aspects of teaching the disadvantaged, 8) Characteristics of the good teacher, 9) Teacher persistence. See ERIC Abstract ED 013232.

3753.   Waksman, S. A. "An Evaluation of Social Learning Procedures Designed to Aid Students With Conduct Problems." Psychology in the Schools, 16, 3 (July 1979): 416-421.

Researchers used a multiple outcome measures to assess treatment effects of a social learning-based intervention program. Reports by teachers on behavior checklists and daily ratings of targeted behaviors indicated improvement with nine of the twelve consecutively referred students who were aged ten to fourteen. A more conservative criterion of improvement on measures from two independent sources indicated improvement with seven subjects. All subjects received improved scores on at least one outcome measure and the program was well received by teachers. See ERIC Abstract 1333364-6.

3754.   Walberg, H. J. & Heise, K. "The Distribution of Misbehavior: A Research Note." Psychology in the Schools, 16, 2 (April, 1979): 306-08.

The numbers of disciplinary referrals to the principal's office for 202 boys and 202 girls from a middle class, suburban junior high school, were obtained from student records and fitted to a highly skewed negative binomial distribution. The fitted and observed distributions do not significantly differ. See ERIC Abstract EJ 200824.

3755.   Walden, J. C. "The Student Press. Law and the School Principal." National Elementary Principal, 53, 3 (March, April, 1974): 69-71.

Several court cases were examined dealing particularly with censorship and discipline issues arising out of student publications. Proposals are made for prior submission rules. See ERIC Abstract EJ 096031.

3756.   Walker, H. M. and Buckley, N. K. "Programing Generalization and Maintenance of Treatment Effects Across Time and Across Settings." Journal of Applied Behavioral Analysis, 5, 3 (Fall, 1972): 209-224.

In this study the effects of one control and three experimental strategies in facilitating generalization and maintenance of treatment effects was investigated on four thrid through sixth grade problem children after two months in a token economy classroom. At the conclusion of treatment, subjects were randomly assigned to one of three maintenance strategies or a control group and returned to their regular classroom. Maintenance strategies were peer reprogramming, equating stimulus conditions betwen the experimental and regular classrooms, and teacher training in behavioral management techniques. Strategies were implemented in the regular classroom for a two month classroom and then terminated. Results indicate a power treatment effect produced by the token economy. Behavior maintenance effects following treatment were also obtained. The mean percent appropriate behavior for the peer reprogramming and equating stimulus conditions strategies were significantly greater than the mean for the control subjects. See ERIC Abstract 0557249-3.

3757.   Walker, H. M. & Holland, F. "Issues, Strategies, and Perspectives in the Management of Disruptive Child Behavior in the Classroom." Journal of Education, 161, 2 (Spring, 1979): 25-50.

This paper focuses on disruptive child behavior in the classroom. The goals of the paper are to give information about the dynamics of disruptive child behavior and to present practical, cost-effective behavior management strategies that teachers can use in remediating such behavior. See ERIC Abstract EJ 204025.

3758.   Walker, H. M. and Hops, H. "The Class Program for Acting Out Children: Research and Development Procedures, Program Outcomes and Implementation Issues." School Psychology Digest, 8, 4 (Fall, 1979): 370-381.

Article describes a class (contingencies for learning, academic and social skills), a comprehensive, self contained behavior management package designed for remediation of the behavior problems of disturbed, acting out children in kindergarten through third grade. The research and development process used to develop, test and validate the package is described; an overview of the package is presented; and guidelines for application and implementation problems are provided. It is concluded that Class is a highly valuable and cost effective program for remediating disruptive child behavior in mainstream settings. See ERIC Abstract 0633363-3.

3759.   Walker, H. M. and Hops, H. "The Use of Group and Individual Reinforcement Contingencies in the Modification of Social Withdrawal." L.A. Hamerlynck, L.C. Handy and E.J. Mash (Ed.S.) Behavioral Change: Methodology, Concepts and Practice. Champaign, Illinois: Research Press, 1973.

Twelve subjects with a low rate of social interaction with classroom peers were studied based on social withdrawal scores on the Walker Problem Behavior Identification Checklist. Three subjects were selected on the basis of classroom observation for lowest rate of social interaction, and three experiments using individual and/or group token reinforcement were conducted. All three interventions were effective but combined individual-group procedures produced the most traumatic change. See ERIC Abstract 0185551-1.

3760.   Walker, H. M., Hops, H. and Greenwood, C. R. "Competency Based Training Issues in the Development of Behavior Management Packages for Specific Classroom Behavior Disorders." Behavioral Disorders, 1, 2 (May, 1976): 112-122.

In this article competency based behavior management packages are described for teachers of mainstreamed behaviorally disordered children. Packages for acting out behavior and work and study skills are described as to consultant training, teacher training, and assessment of teacher competency. See ERIC Abstract 0647659-3.

3761.   Walker, H. M., Hops, H. and Johnson, S. M. "Generalization and Maintenance of Classroom Treatment Effects." Behavior Therapy, 6, 2 (March, 1975): 188-200.

Two experiments were conducted with a total of nine first through third graders were behavior problems to study A. the maintenance of appropriate classroom behavior following treatment in an experimental classroom and B. cross situational consistency and generalization of treatment effects. In experiment one, two groups of four subjects were observed after treatment in a token economy operated classroom. Procedures to facilitate maintenance of treatment produced behavior changes were successfully implemented for one group of subjects in their respective regular classrooms. The effects of the combined treatment generalized to a significantly greater degree in the subsequent academic year than did the treatment effects for subjects who were involved in only one experimental classroom procedure. In experiment two, five children from the first study were observed in family interaction to determine whether there were also behavior problems at home. Only one subject was deviant in the home setting. Further observations following experimental classroom treatment showed more child deviancy and parental negativeness than before school intervention. See ERIC Abstract 0189254-1.

3762.   Wallbrown, J. D. & Wallbrown, F. H. "Classroom Behaviors Associated With Difficulties in Visual Motor Perception." Psychology In The School, 13, 1 (January, 1976): 20-24.

The relationship between visual-motor perception as measured by Koppitz errors on the Bender Gestalt Test and classroom behavior as indicated by teacher ratings on the Devereaux Elementary School Behavior Rating Scale was investigated for

76 suburban first graders. Most of the subjects came from upper middle class homes and were within the bright/normal range of intelligence. Analysis of the regression of Koppitz errors on Devereaux ratings indicated that three types of classroom behavior tended to be associated with poor visual motor perception: 1) children with problems in this area seem to encounter difficulty understanding what is going on around them in the classroom, 2) these children appear to rush through their work without much concern for quality and 3) they did not seem to show overt disrespect or resistance toward their teacher, school, or schoolwork. See ERIC Abstract 0680456-4.

3763.   Wallbrown, J. D., Wallbrown, F. H., Engin, A. W., and Blaha, J. "Dimensions of Classroom Behavior for Kindergarten Children." Psychological Reports, 39, 3 Part II (December, 1976): 1163-1174.

The construct validity of the Devereux Elementary School Behavior Rating Scale was investigated with 408 children enrolled in fifteen kindergarten classes of a suburban school system. The nine teachers completed behavioral ratings of the children in their classes during a one week period. A principle-factor solution was obtained on inter-correlations among the forty-seven behaviors included in the Devereux Scale, and the factors thus obtained were rotated to varimax criterian. Results are generally positive in that nine of the eleven behavioral dimensions described were evident in the factor structure. There were, however, enough differences to suggest the possibility of modifying the score categories somewhat for use with suburban kindergarten children. See ERIC Abstract 0671758-4.

3764.   Wallin, K., Gutsch, K. U. & Koeppel, J. C. "The Impact of Two Behavioral Treatments on Highly Distractible Fifth and Sixth Grade Students." Southern Journal of Educational Research, 8, 5 (Winter, 1974): 182-191.

The effects of a classroom behavior management approach was investigated, and a classroom behavior management model reinforcement was studied on grade point averages and scores on classroom attention and movement. A controlled group of 24 subjects was used, and they received no treatment. Results showed that both approaches significantly modified the on-task behaviors of the subjects, although the modeling approach appeared to be more effective. See ERIC Abstract 0198952-5.

3765.   Walsh, K. & Cowles, M. "Social Consciousness and Discipline in the Urban Elementary School." Urban Review, 11, 1 (Spring, 1979): 25-35.

This article describes a discipline program for urban elementary school students. The program is based on several

theories of moral development and it emphasizes the importance of the social context of the school environment.   See
ERIC Abstract EJ 205729.

3766.   Walton, W. T. "The Use of a Relaxation Curriculum and
Bio-Feedback   Training   in   the   Classroom   to   Reduce
Inappropriate   Behaviors   of   Emotionally   Handicapped
Children."   Behavioral   Disorders,   5,   1   (November,   1979):
10-18.

Five emotionally handicapped fifth and sixth grade boys were
placed in a program of relaxation and bio-feedback training
over a 16 week period. Three times each week, the subjects
were trained in relaxation procedures, including isometric
exercises, autogenic training, and other mind-body relaxation techniques.   Bio-feedback therapy was conducted with
each subject once a week, using EMG procedures for muscle
relaxation.   A pre and post evaluation of each subject's
inappropriate classroom behavior and level of muscle relaxation were obtained.   Inappropriate behavior was reduced by
more than 50% in four subjects and muscle tension was also
significantly reduced. See ERIC Abstract 0381565-2.

3767.   Warner, S. P., Miller, F. D. and Cohen, M. W.   "Relative
Effectiveness of Teacher Attention and the Good Behavior
Game in Modifying Disruptive Classroom Behavior."   Journal
of Applied Behavior Analysis, 10, 4 (Winter, 1977):   737.

A study was conducted with two fourth grade teachers and two
fifth grade teachers and their 100 students to compare the
short terms effectiveness of the good behavior game and a
teacher attention procedure in reducing disruptive student
behavior.   Results   showed   that   the   good   behavior   game
reduced disruptive behavior significantly better than the
teacher attention procedure and that all teachers preferred
the game. See ERIC Abstract 0214561-1.

3768.   Warshaw,   M.   "Behavior   Modification   in   Secondary
Schools."   Educational   Technology,   15,   8   (August,   1975):
21-25.

The application of behavior modification principles is
discussed in relation to the cognitive and interpersonal
behaviors of secondary school students.   Suggestions are
made   for   determining   appropriate   reinforcers   through
activity interest ratings, interst inventories and questionnaires, and direct observation.   Examples from previous
research of the effective use of peer approval, wirtten
teacher comments, parent controlled contingencies, and self
contracting procedures are presented.   See ERIC Abstract
021461-1.

3769.   Wasserman, T. H. and Vogrin, D. J. "Relationship of Endorsement of Rationale Behavior, Age, Months in Teatment, and Intelligence to Overt Behavior of Emotionally Disturbed Children." Psychological Reports, 44, 3, Part 1 (June, 1979): 911-917.

The relationship between endorsement of the 11 irrational beliefs described by Ellis is investigated. It is discussed in terms of its relationship to overt behavior by 27 eight through thirteen year old emotionally disturbed and learning disabled children. Prior to involvement in the study, subjects received standardized training in rationale-emotive therapy. Analysis indicated that knowledge of the therapy was correlated with behaviorally measures of self reliance, control, and ability to take initiative in school situations. However, endorsement of the beliefs alone only predicted overt behavior when the subject's age was considered. Intelligence and month in treatment did not correlate with the behavioral demonstration of knowledge of the beliefs. See ERIC Abstract 1081564-5.

3770.   Wasson, A. S. "Stimulus-Seeking Perceived School Environment and School Misbehavior." Adolescence, 15, 59 (1980): 603-608.

It was hypothesized that there would be a) a positive relationship between stimulus seeking and school misbehavior, b) negative relationships between a positively perceived school environment and school misbehavior, and c) an interaction effect of stimulus seeking and perceived school environment on this behavior. Eighteen male and 41 female 11th graders from two classes completed the Sensation-Seeking Scale. Results supported all the hypothesized relationships. See ERIC Abstract 0415265-2.

3771.   Waters, B. J., Bill, M. D. and Lowell, E. L. "Precision Therapy: An Interpretation." Language, Speech and Hearing Services in the Schools, 8, 4 (October, 1977): 234-244.

An eclectic approach is described in relationship to case management that combines principles of programming, behavior modification, and traditional methods as applied to the school setting. This approach is seen as offering an alternative to commerical programs by allowing the clinician to individualize procedures while maintaining precise control of remedial events. Implementation of the treatment with 30 elementary school children having articulation, voice, fluency, and language disorders is described. See ERIC Abstract 0622960-3.

3772.   Wattenberg, W. W. "The Ecology of Classroom Behavior." Theory into Practice, 16, 4 (October, 1977): 256-261.

Alterations in the ecology of classroom behavior is discussed in terms of how it might increase the work involvement of students in learning activities. The results of

Kounin's research suggests ways of increasing work involvement by reducing the occurrence of behavior in inimical ot it. Kounin found that a significant ripple effect occurs during the first two or three weeks of the school year. Studies of this effect showed that a) unambiguous intervention had the greatest effect in reducing deviant behavior, b) follow-through behavior on the part of the teacher had the transatory effect of stopping deviance already in progress, and c) high power interventions decreased work involvement. Kounin subsequently identified four elements of teacher classroom style that were related to work involvement: a) with-itness, the ability of teachers to communicate behaviorally that they know what the children are doing, b) overlapping, the deftness with which the teacher deals with two or more matters concurrently, c) group alerting and accountability, the degree to which the teacher involves non-reciting children in a recitation task and holds them responsible for their task performances, and d) smoothness and momentum, the extent to which the teacher expedites activity. See ERIC Abstract 1289463-6.

3773.   Way, J. W.   "Verbal Interaction in Multi-Age Classrooms." Elementary School Journal, 79, 3 (Janaury, 1979): 178-186.

Verbal and interactions in multi-age classrooms were analyzed with three through 11 year old children. Classes containing two and three age levels were included. In classrooms with three age levels, older students initiated more interactions, but not in classrooms with two age levels. There was no age difference in the number of interactions initiated with the teacher. In classrooms with two age levels, cross age interactions were significant, but in classrooms with three age levels only the middle age group initiated interactions across age lines. There was no age difference found in the type of interactions initiated. See ERIC Abstract 1066363-5.

3774.   Webster, R. E.   "The Time-Out Procedure in a Public School Setting." Psychology in the Schools, 18 (January, 1976): 24-31.

This study uses time-out as the primary therapeutic intervention with a thirteen year old highly aggressive male in a public school setting. Specific behaviors were listed prior to beginning time-out and were explained to the child and teachers. Time-out was used over a ten week period with extinction of the specified behaviors occurring after the seventh week. During an eight week follow-up only three instances of the aggressive behaviors were observed. During the third and fourth week of time-out the child week began to show spontaneous interest in school work. It was concluded that time-out was sufficiently intensively adversive event of itself to alter some types of deviant behavior without direct application of positive reinforcers. It is most propitiously used when alternative response modes are made available for the child.

3775.   Weinrott, M. R., Garrett, B. and Todd, N. "The Influence of Observer Presence on Classroom Behavior." Behavior Therapy, 9, 5 (November, 1978): 900-911.

The appropriate classroom behavior of six socially aggressive children in kindergarten through grade three was monitored to assess their reactivity to non-participant observation. For 33 days, an observer was systematically placed in the room during a portion of two academic periods. Meanwhile, data for the entire period was gathered by observers stationed behind a one-way mirror. This procedure was carried out during all phases to evaluate the token program. Reactivity to the observation process was not evidenced in either period or in any phase of treatment. This was true for individual subjects and for the class as a whole. Results support the generalized ability to research findings based on naturalistic observation. See ERIC Abstract 0976362-4.

3776.   Weinrott, M. R. and Jones, R. R. "Differential Effects of Demand Characteristics on Teacher and Pupil Behavior." Journal of Educational Psychology, 69, 6 (December): 724-729.

Forty teachers of grade one through three classes were asked to manipulate the behavior of disrupted and withdrawn children in accordance with a socially desirable instructional set. Measures of disruptiveness and withdrawl were obtained using independent observers who recorded pupil and teacher behavior prior to, during, and following the manipulation. Results show that teachers were unable to decrease inappropriate behavior in disruptive children but were successful in raising the level of pro-social responding of withdrawn children. See ERIC Abstract 1032660-5.

3777.   Weinstein, C. S. "Modifying Student Behavior in an Open Classroom Through Changes in the Physical Design." American Educational Research Journal, 14, .3 (Summer, 1977): 249-262.

The spatial distribution of activity in a second and third grade open classroom was observed before and after a change in the physical design. It was hypothesized that minor changes in the physical setting could produce predictable, desirable changes in selected behaviors of 25 students. Behavioral goals included increased use of science and game areas, decreased use of math area, and decreased writing behavior in the reading area. The experimenter observed for two weeks using a time-sampling-by-child instrument. The activities and locations of the students were recorded on a floor plan of the room. Designed changes were then made with specific behavioral goals in mind, and a two week host change observation was begun. In most cases, the desired behavior changes were produced and the time-series analysis indicated that these changes were statistically significant. See ERIC Abstract 0827460-4.

3778.   Welsh, R. S. et al. "The Supreme Court Spanking Rule: An Issue in Debate." Paper presented at the annual convention of the American Psychological Association, Chicago, Illinois, April, 1976.

Few issues have polarized the educational community so completely as the 1975 and 1977 decisions by the United States Supreme Court to allow corporal punishment in the schools. The symposium reported here was organized and conducted following the 1975 decision, but prior to the 1977 one. Three papers in support and three papers against the ruling were read, after which the participants debated the matter. Finally, one pro and one con participant summed up the views for each side. The supporters of the ruling view corporal punishment as an effective deterent to misbehavior, insist that it is a necessary tool for keeping order in the classroom, and see it as an occasionally misused, but point to the fact that other useful tools of a civilized society are also subject to misuse. The nonsupporters of the ruling use corporal punishment as a type of legalized child abuse and are convinced that it compounds the teachers' problems by escalating anger in the child. They bolster their position by pointing out instances of abuse that have occurred in the past. Both groups agree that effective alternatives to physical discipline, coupled with teachers more adequately trained to handle disciplinary problems in the classroom, would largely remove the need for the continued future use of corporal punishment. See ERIC Abstract ED 151664.

3779.   West, J. et al. "A Study of Counseling and Counsulting in Appalachia." Elementary School Guidance and Counseling, 15, 1 (October, 1980): 5-13.

Students who underwent counseling displayed a positive difference in classroom behavior, relationships with teachers and peers, and self-understanding. Tutored children improved their academic behavior and teachers reported success with several strategies for behavior change. See ERIC Abstract. EJ 233764.

3780.   Wherry, J. H. "You Are Your Schools's Top P.R. Agent." Instructor, 87, 2 (September, 1977): 148-58.

The key to building good school public relations is good communication, that is, the quality of the personal contacts between teachers who are employees, and the parents of students, who are employers. Included are suggestions for helping teachers get their message across to parents and for evaluating their progress. See ERIC Abstract EJ 169102.

3781.   Whipple, W. S. "Changing Attitudes Through Behavior Modification." Paper presented at the annual meeting of the National Association of Secondary School Principals, New Orleans, Louisiana, January, 1977.

This article describes the philosophy and methods used by the staff at the Granite Alternative School in changing student attitudes through behavior modification. The students involved all have a failure syndrone or a low self-image, and are dropouts from traditional high schools. Among the techniques used are: 1) Reinforcing good behavior, 2) Caring for the student, 3) Modeling from teachers serving as good examples, 4) Token reinforcement, and 5) Creating a climate where success is obtainable by all students. See ERIC Abstract ED 146500.

3782.   White, B. G., Semb, G. & Semb, S.   "The Effects of Good-Behavior Contract on the Classroom Behaviors of Sixth Grade Students." Journal of Applied Behavior Analysis, 10, 2 (Summer, 1977): 312.

Results from the four participating sixth graders showed that a good behavior contract making use of existing facilities and privileges in a public school classroom can be effective. Subjects' on-task behavior and daily assignment completion increased, weekly grades were higher, and disruptive behavior decreased when the contract was in effect. See ERIC Abstract 1319359-6.

3783.   Whitmore, H. J. et al.   "Consultation and Counseling." Elementary School Guidance and Counseling, 9, 3 (March, 1975): 233-240.

This article describes step-by-step procedures used by a counselor in approaching a problem with a particular problem student. See ERIC Abstract EJ 114046.

3784.   Wilde, E. S. and Randolph, D.   "Effects Of Instructing Student Teachers In The Use Of Reinforcement Techniques For Classroom Behavior Management." Southern Journal Of Educational Research, 7, 3 (Summer, 1973): 100-113.

The classroom behaviors of fifteen student teachers who had received training in the techniques of behavioral control were compared with the behaviors of thirty who had not received this training. To measure the specific behavior changes designated as objectives for the study, trained observers recorded the frequencies of approval and disapproval responses, and frequencies of error of approval and error of disapproval responses for the two groups while teaching. Data from these observations were analyzed statistically to see if the difference that occurred were significant. The analyses support the belief that such training can increase the number of approval responses following appropriate classroom behaviors and lower the frequencies of disapproval responses. See ERIC Abstract 0621052-3.

3785.   Wilde, J. W. and Sommers, P. S.   "Disruption in High Schools: Could It Simply Be a Dysfunction of Classroom Structure?" High School Journal, 63, 5 (February, 1980): 191-194.

Author suggests that the way adults in a school behave is a major factor contributing to disruptive student behavior. They offer four suggestions for setting up a classroom that teaches appropriate behavior, and concludes that consistency is of ultimate importance. See ERIC Abstract EJ 226861.

3786.   Wilde, J. W. and Sommers, P. "Teaching Disruptive Adolescents: A Game Worth Winning." Phi Delta Kappan, 59, 5 (January, 1978): 342-3.

Four techniques are offered for preventing student behavior problems. See ERIC Abstract EJ 169849.

3787.   Wiley, R. L. "The Business of Education." Contemporary Education, 52, 1 (Fall, 1980): 47-49.

While many classroom problems can be solved by competent and able teachers, all discipline problems cannot be solved by teachers according to this author. It is possible to solve problems of discipline by involving the local community in making positive and needed changes. See ERIC Abstract EJ 237737.

3788.   Williams, R. L. and Anandam, K. "The Effect of Behavior Contracting on Grades." Journal of Educational Research, 66, 5 (January, 1973): 230-236.

Behavior contracting in two classes was used on urban disadvantaged seventh graders. The contract included both academic and social behaviors for which the subjects won or lost points. Subjects under contract received a grade each day on which their nine week grades were based. Grades of the subjects under contract increased significantly during the contract semester, while those of a similar control group declined slightly. See ERIC Abstract 0394450-2.

3789.   Williams, R. L., Long, J. E., and Yoakley, R. W. "The Utility of Behavior Contracts and Behavior Proclamation with Advantaged Senior High School Students." Journal of School Psychology, 10, 4 (December, 1972): 329-338.

The relative efficiency of behavioral contracts and behavioral proclamations in a parochial high school setting were empirically appraised. Subjects were a select group of academically oriented seniors studying problems in democracy. Results support the position that students attain higher rates of appropriate behavior when given the opportunity to assist in classroom mangement. Both behaviorally proclamations and contracts proved superior to the standard classroom procedures of the baselines. See ERIC Abstract 0394550-2.

3790.   Williamson, J. A. & Campbell, L. P. "The Student Teaching Experience Results In Greater Emphasis On Pupil Control." Southern Journal of Educational Research, 12, 1 (Winter, 1978)" 1-6.

Compared in the study with a pre and post student teaching scores of 131 female and 112 male student teachers in secondary education, utilizing a measure of pupil control ideology which defined a continuum from a humanistic to custodial ideology of pupil control, the Pupil Control Ideology Inventory. In addition, teachers who supervise subjects were administered the inventory at the beginning of each semester. Results showed that student teachers became significantly more custodial by the end of student teaching and that males were significantly more custodial than females both before and after student teaching. See ERIC Abstract 0940261-4.

3791.   Wilson, C. W. and Hopkins, B. L.   "The Effects of Contingent Music on the Intensity of Noise in Junior High Home Economics Classes: Journal of Applied Behavior Analysis, 6, 2 (Summer, 1973): 269-275.

The effects of quiet-contingent music on the general noise of two seventh and eighth grade home economics classes was studied. Seventy-two female students were used as subjects. Following a baseline procedure, popular radio music was used to reinforce maintenance of noise below an acceptable level of intensity. The teacher was free to engage in instructional activities because data collection and presentation of music were controlled by automatic apparatus. See ERIC Abstract 0181451-1.

3792.   Wilson, J. H.   "Iokyoks vs. The Shnoks."   Transactional Analysis Journal, 5, 3 (July, 1975): 247-249.

Personality factors were studied in the tendency of teachers to make disciplinary referrals. Thirty-three of forty-five junior high faculty members responded voluntarily to the sixteen personality factors. The eight with the lowest combined number of referrals were designated as the "I'm Okay--You're Okay" group, and the eight subjects with the highest combined numbers of referrals were designated as the "Somebody Here Is Not Okay" group. Analysis of test results showed significant differences between the two groups on five of the sixteen personality factors. The "I'm Okay" teachers could be characterized as inclusive and centripetally oriented, drawing students toward them; whereas, the "Somebody Here Is Not Okay" teachers could be characterized as exclusive and centrifugually oriented, throwing students from them. See ERIC Abstract 0877064-4.

3793.   Wilson, S. H. and Williams, R. L.   "The Effects of Group Contingencies on First Graders' Academic and Social Behaviors."   Journal of School Psychology, 11, 2 (Summer, 1973):

One hundred first graders were divided into smaller groups of nine to twelve students. Each group could earn free time by completing its work within a designated period and by minimizing disruptive activity. The group contingencies proved highly effective in increasing a percentage of work completed and reducing disruptive responses. After the study was completed, four teachers voluntarily organized the entire mornings activities around the group contingencies. A check of the same classroom the following year indicated that the teachers were continuing to make extensive use of group contingent free time. See ERIC Abstract 0793851-4.

3794.   Winett, R. A., Battersby, C. D. & Edwards, S. N. "The Effects of Architectural Change, Individualized Instruction, and Group Contingencies On The Academic Performance and Social Behavior of Sixth Graders." Journal of School Psychology, 13, 1 (Spring, 1975): 28-40.

Architectural changes, individualized instruction, and group contingencies placed on academic work were applied to the mathematics and language periods of an initially disruptive grade six classroom with twenty-seven children. Behavioral observations were made on ten of these children; work data was collected on all twenty-seven. Within classroom comparisons indicated that individualized instruction with group contingencies sharply increased the academic production of subjects from all ability levels, significantly improved social behavior, and changed the teacher's mode of instruction and interaction with the subjects. Individualized instruction alone had lesser effects, while the architectural changes produced no significant changes in the academic or social behavior of subjects or teachers. Results are discussed in terms of improvement of the intervention procedures, focus on academic programming, and a broadening of the base of behavior modification work. See ERIC Abstract 0629354-3.

3795.   Winger, J. "Peer Dynamics, 1978-79 Evaluation Report." Lincoln, Nebraska: Nebraska State Commission on Drugs, June, 1981.

This is an evaluation of the first year of a program designed to reduce the incidence of destructive risk-taking behavior among school-age youth. Background research indicates that peer group pressure is the single most important factor in dictating the presence of absence of juvenile delinquency behavior. The Peer Dynamics Process, involving fifty-six (56) schools in Nebraska, trains and supervises students who participated in a group interaction plan with others students to develop self-esteem and better communication skills, peer modeling takes place. The evaluation measures used were pre-post attitude tests, program evaluation by students and faculty, and an evaluation form which included such factors as vandalism, grades, dropouts, discipline and contacts with law enforcement agencies. Personal on-sight visits were made to each school to explain the evaluation measures. Results indicated an overall positive attitude change among peer group members due to participation in this program. See ERIC Abstract ED 197277.

3796.   Wiseman, F. "High School." Zipporah Films, 1969.

This is a documentary study of high school. It deals with the ideology and values of a large urban high school as seen through encounters between students, teachers and parents in guidance sessions, college counseling, discipline, faculty meetings, corridor patrol and classroom activities. Seventy-four minutes. 16mm film. See NICEM 0859893.

3797.   Witmer, J. N. "Is a Theory of Elementary Counseling Perse Passe for the Seventies? An Integrated Approach to Modifying Behavior: Individual and System Change." Paper presented at the American Personnel & Guidance Association Convention, Atlantic City, New Jersey, April, 1971.

Five models for the behavior change process at both the individual and the systemic level are proposed. The author sees them as comprising an integrated or eclectic approach, which he defines as using that which is most appropriate for achieving goals. The five models are: 1) The client-centered relationship model, 2) The behavioral model, which is based on learning theory, 3) The social psychological model, 4) The reality model, 5) The rational-cognitive model. The rational-cognitive model. The particular strengths and appropriateness of each model are discussed. The paper concludes by acknowledgement, that no one technique or model is adequate by itself. Whatever seems appropriate and workable from any one of the models should be used. See ERIC Abstract ED 048615.

3798.   Witty, E. P. "Training to Handle Learning and Behavioral Problems in the Regular Classroom." Journal of Teacher Education, 26, 2 (Summer, 1975): 135-138.

The Norfolk/Chesapeake Teacher Corps Project developed a special component which focused on helping teaching and interns become sensitive to the needs of exceptional children, and on helping them master competencies required to individualized instruction in the regular classroom for children without severe handicaps. See ERIC Abstract EJ 121717.

3799.   Wodarski, J. et al. "Reduction of Anti-Social Behavior in an Open Community Setting Through the Use of Behavior Modification in Groups." Child Care Quarterly, 5, 3 (Fall, 1976): 198-210.

The application of group level behavior modification techniques is examined with a group of ten fifth and sixth grade anti-social children. The author discusses the success of efforts to increase the incidence of pro-social behavior and decrease non-social and anti-social behavior. Described in the article is an assessment procedure for behavioral measurement. See ERIC Abstract EJ 154046.

3800.   Wodarski, J. S. et al. "The Reduction of Anti-Social Behavior in Ten, Eleven, and Twelve Year Old Boys Participation in a Recreation Center." Small Group Behavior, 7, 2 (May, 1976): 183-194.

This investigation represents an effort to evaluate the use of behavior modification techniques in a social setting. The attempt was made to decrease anti and non-social behaviors, while increasing pro-social behaviors in ten fifth and sixth graders. Data indicated that the techniques could be successful in an open environment. See ERIC Abstract EJ 146127.

3801.   Wodarski, J. S., Hamblin, R. L. & Buckholdt, D. R. "Individual Consequences Versus Different Shared Consequences Contingent on the Performance of Low Achieving Group Members." Journal of Applied Social Psychology, 3, 3 (July, 1973): 276-290.

In this study, the effects of four reinforcement conditions (individual consequence, group shared consequence, and two different portions of individual and group shared consequence) were measured on 1) peer tutoring, b. arithmetic performance, c. studying, d. non-studying, and 2) disruptive behavior employing sixty experimental and thirty-four comparison children from three fifth grade classes in the innercity school. The 100% shared consequence consistently produced the highest incidence of peer tutoring and the greatest incrament in the number of correct problems, both within and between periods. As the proportion of shared consequences decreased, the number of problems worked correctly decreased. Concurrently, the incidence in peer tutoring decreased as the proportion of shared consequences decreased. All consequences maintained high rates of study and behavior and low rates of non-studying and disruptive behaviors. Results suggest that shared consequences may be useful in creating cooperative work patterns and increasing arithmetic performance in classroom settings. See ERIC Abstract 0400352-2.

3802.   Wollam, S. A. "Try P.R.A.I.S.E." Momentum, 10, 4 (December, 1979): 34-38.

P.R.A.I.S.E. (Positive Reinforcement and Individualized Systematic Economics) is a multi-facted money system, which utilizes positive and negative reinforcement and, at the same time, incorporates peer pressure and reinforcement for behavior modification. The system motivates, relates closely to life situations, and can be applied to all areas of curriculum. See ERIC Abstract EJ 222914.

3803.   Workman, E. A. & Dickson, E. J. "The Use of Covert Positive Reinforcement in the Treatment of a Hyperactive Child: An Impurical Case Study." Journal of School Psychology, 17, 1 (Spring, 1979): 67-73.

This study evaluated the effects of covert positive reinforcement on a nine year old, third grade student who is causing classroom disturbances. There was an immediate improvement in three target behaviors following the implementation of the program by the school psychologist. See ERIC Abstract EJ 199259.

3804. Wright, W. E. & Jesness, C. F. "Delinquency in a Seventh Grade Cohort: Impact of School Climate on Problem Behavior." Rosenberg Foundation, San Francisco, California: California State Department of the Youth Authority, January, 1980.

The relationship between delinquency and school climate is defined as the aggregate-belief-value characteristics of people who make up the school. This relationship was investigated to determine if an aggregate measure of student attitudes about school, as measured by the quality of school life scale can be used as a measure of the characteristics of the school. Subjects were 2,184 students enrolled in eighth grade during the Spring of 1978. Tested were the effects of student background characteristic on the Q.S.L. Scores, and the independent contribution of school membership. Results indicated that as Q.S.L.: 1) Measured both school characteristics and student attitudes, 2) Is a fair measure of student affective responses to school, and 3) Effects both the obtrusive and unobtrusiveness behavior analysis skills. See ERIC Abstract ED 174936.

3805. Yates, J. B. "A New Alternative School: C.E.E.C." Clearing House, 52, 6 (February, 1979): 265-271.

The Community Experimental Education Center serves fifty (50) disadvantaged students, ages sixteen through twenty, unable to function well in traditional schools. Each student must complete thirty-three competencies in career, consumer, and life skills. This report discusses the report designed, funding and staffing, and lists the thirty-three (33) competencies. See ERIC Abstract EJ 199137.

3806. Yudof, M. G. "Student Discipline in Texas Schools." Journal of Law and Education, 3, 2 (April, 1974): 221-231.

Texas legislation is examined as well as court cases to determine the extent to which students should be afforded Constitutional guarantees. See ERIC Abstract EJ 099380.

3807. Zelie, K. et al. "Cognitive-Behavioral Intervention in School Discipline: A Preliminary Study." Personnel and Guidance Journal, 59, 2 (October, 1980): 80-83.

The results of this study support the effectiveness of the rational behavior therapy disciplinary intervention model. The specific problem behavior and the child's attention to classwork and homework was significantly improved. Disciplinary recidivism showed extraordinary differentiation between the groups. This improvement did not generalize to the students' overall behavior. See ERIC Abstract EJ 236045.

3808.   Zentall, S. S. "Behavioral Comparisons of Hyperactive and Normal Children in Natural Settings." Journal of Abnormal Psychology, 8, 1 (March, 1980): 93-109.

Matched pairs of 31 hyperactive and 31 normal active children were observed in 6 natural classroom settings. A number of specific behaviors were continuously recorded. Both groups of subjects showed differences in behavior as a function of settings, but only certain settings differentiated hyperactive from control subjects. Hyperactive subjects displayed significantly more noise-vocalization and more disruptive and off-task behavior in the most frequently observed classroom settings. Type of off-task behavior dependent on amount of classroom structure. Implications for identification and treatment of hyperactive children through the modification of the antecedent conditions of stimulation and structure are discussed. See PSYC Abstract 1124765-5.

3809.   Zentall, S. S. & Zentall, T. R. "Activity and Task Performance of Hyperactive Children as a Function of Environmental Stimulation." Journal of Consulting and Clinical Psychology, 44, 5 (October, 1976): 693-697.

Hyperactive children in a high stimulation environment were significantly less active and performed an academically related task no worse than when placed in a low stimulation environment. Under stimulation rather than over stimulation apparently precipitates hyperactive behavior. See ERIC Abstract EJ 146021.

3810.   Zigarmi, P. et al. "Implementing a New Approach to Discipline in a Junior High School: A Two-Year Study of Interventions in a Teacher Corps Project." Journal of Classroom Interaction, 14, 1 (Winter, 1978): 19-27.

This case study of a project designed to change a Junior High School's approach to discipline focuses on the change facilitators' interventions in implementing the innovation. Data assessing how teachers change are presented and discussed in relation to the intervention data. See ERIC Abstract EJ 197205.

3811.   Zimmerman, J. & Archbold, L. A. "On-Campus Suspension: What It Is and Why It Works." NASSP Bulletin, 63, 428 (September, 1979): 63-67.

A program where students are supervised and disciplined for improper actions operate successfully at Hemet High School in California. See ERIC Abstract EJ 206330.

3812.   Zimmerman, J. & Zimmerman, E. H. "Towards Humanizing Education: Classroom Behavior Management Re-visited." Psychological Record, 26, 3 (Summer, 1976): 387-397.

The author's experiences in conducting classroom management courses is described, and the critical comments and reactions of their practitioners and students which prompted changes in their teacher education concepts and approaches are discussed. The authors were often accused of being mechanistic, of being manipulators, and more interested in their own technology than in helping people, of presenting values as facts, of putting too heavy an emphasis on the use of precise language, of over-emphasizing concern with misconduct, and of paying too little attention to self-awareness, both the teacher's and the child's. Changes in the approach to teaching classroom management are described. Among their innovations was the acceptance of the use of the self-image concepts. Other major changes included emphasis on the teacher's self-awareness and communication skills. See ERIC Abstract 0900957-4.

4.

SCHOOL DISTRICT
PUBLICATIONS AND
NONPRINT MATERIALS

4001.   Acadia   Parish   School   Board.   "Student   Handbook."
         Crowley, Louisiana.

         Section five of the student handbook deals with the
         following discipline areas: school dress and grooming,
         leaving school grounds, policy on student attendance, drug
         policy, discipline of student and suspension from school,
         expulsions,   corporal   punishment,   punitive   measures,
         vandelism and/or theft, search and seizure policy for
         illegal items.

4002.   Akron Public Schools. Akron Public Schools code of
         student behavior. Akron, Ohio, September, 1981.

         Included in the code of student behavior are the following
         sections, student rights and responsibilities, administra-
         tive removal from school, rules and regulations for the
         behavior and discipline of students, procedures for suspen-
         sion and expulsion, attendance procedures, corporal punish-
         ment,   liability   of   parents   for   vandalism,   search   and
         seizure, and student interrogation.

4003.   Amphitheater Public Schools.   Goals and Self-Discipline.
         Tuscon, Arizona, 1981.

         A central goal of the educational system is to assist
         students in becoming self-disciplined.   Students need to be
         taught how to control themselves in order to function within
         reasonable limits of their environment.   Inner control is a
         significant element in discipline.   The home and the school
         must share in this responsibility for the development of
         this process.   The materials contained in this guidebook are
         the product of research and compellation by a committee of
         teachers in this school district.   There is no one answer on
         how to best tackle the problem of discipline.   The philos-
         ophy, procedures, codes and strategies are offered to help

the student, teacher and parent achieve the maximum benefit from the research. Included are the following sections: 1) introduction, 2) philosophy, 3) alternative approaches to discipline, 4) corporal punishment, 5) due process -- suspension and/or expulsion, 6) district policy on discipline record keeping, 7) appendix.

4004.   Andover, Massachusetts Public Schools. The Andover Peer Counseling Project. Andover, Massachusetts, Undated.

The peer group is bound to be a significant influence during childhood and adolescence. By providing extensive training for students who have motivated to help their peers, a core of well-informed, sensitive and capable teenagers are able to provide a variety of services for the entire Andover Public School system. The section of the brochure describes growth experience training. Services which are provided include the peer counseling drop-in center, elementary and junior high school divorce groups, big-brother/big-sister program, peer pressure groups, parents/teen educational programs, and the transition program.

4005.   Ann Arbor Public Schools. Discipline Policy K-12. Ann Arbor, Michigan, 1979.

The behavior of the student is the joint responsibility of the school, parent and pupil. To fulfill the school's responsibility, the Board Of Education, its administrators, and staff accepted as their duty to: 1) provide a school environment where learning can take place, 2) protect the rights and privileges of all members of the school community, 3) assure that the necessary corrective action is consistently applied, 4) assured disciplinary action is always coupled with counseling and positive guidance. Included are the following sections: Application and exceptions of deviation from policy, behavior offenses, restitution for vandalism, removal from class, student press, truancy, makeup responsibilities, conduct committee, grievance procedure, publication, distribution and orientation of policy, teachers' and administrators' role, hearings and procedure.

4006.   Arnold Missouri Public Schools. Student Handbook. Arnold, Missouri, Undated.

The policies and procedures contained in this handbook are the results of the concerted effort on the part of the faculty and administration. This information has been carefully prepared and presented so that it will be of great value in helping the student to adjust to school and to become an integral part of it. The ultimate purpose of education is to help each student to become an effective citizen in a democracy. To develop and accept the responsibilities and obligations of good citizenship would help students to participate successfully in the world of tomorrow. Included in this handbook are sections on the following disciplinary concerns: Leaving school grounds without authorization, in school suspension, truancy from school, drugs, student drivers, smoking, extortion, dress, student attitude and conduct in school, articles prohibited in school, and gambling.

4007.   Asheville Public Schools. Student Handbook. Asheville, North Carolina, 1981.

These statements of policy are written so that each student and teacher can be aware of the regulations governing behavior at school. The rules and regulations are enforced at all times for students who are representing these public schools whether on campus or on an organized field trip, as an athletic event, a dance or club activities. Students are expected to know and follow all rules and are held responsible for their actions. Included in this handbook is a section on school rules.

4008.   Atlanta, Georgia Public Schools. Guidelines For Student Behavior. Atlanta, Georgia, 1981.

The Fulton County School System operates on the philosophy that all students have the right to learn. To do so, each student must be in a school climate that is satisfying and productive, without disruptive behavior by any student infringing upon the rights of others. This publication presents guidelines to maintain an atmosphere in the schools that will give the students an opportunity to learn. Home and school, alike, must share the responsibility for acceptable conduct. Unacceptable behavior is divided into three categories in the Fulton County School System. This brochure describes the unacceptable behavior and student goals and objectives.

4009.   Baltimore City Public Schools. Student rights and responsibilities. Baltimore, Maryland, 1979.

All persons in a democratic society have both rights and responsibilities. The purpose of this brochure is to explain the rights and responsibilities of the students in the Baltimore City Public Schools. The students are to share this brochure with their parents so that parents and students will know the students' rights and responsibilities. Included are the following sections, right to education, freedom of expression, patriotic exercises, married students, student records, pregnant students, corporal punishment, student participation in making school rules, and locker searches. Student responsibility sections include non-discrimination, student behavior, drugs, and personal appearance.

4010.   Bartow County Alternative School. Bartow County Alternative School Handbook. Cartersville, Georgia, September, 1981.

Operating on the philosophy that every student needs to avail himself or herself of every available educational opportunity, the following purposes have been established for this school. They are: to offer an alternative educational environment to students who would normally have been suspended out of school while providing them the opportunity to continue their academic work with full credit and allowing them to be counted present at their home schools; to allow the home school the latitude to discipline students without penalizing them academically; to allow the home school to remove students temporarily who are so disruptive in their behavior as to impare the right of other students to receive an education; to provide suspended students time and opportunity to acquire the kinds of social attitudes, values, and skills which in turn will result in productive social behavior upon their return to their home schools; to allow the home schools to maintain a high average daily attendance; to staff an alternative school managed by professionals and paraprofessionals to provide educational activities and to counsel students; to serve as a deterrent at the home school to discourage those activities and behaviors which would normally result in the suspension of students. Included in the handbook are the following sections: objectives, educational design, behavioral expectations, coded discipline, assignments, attendance, dress code, parent conferences, personal hygiene, contraband, possession or use, and transportation.

4011.   Beaverton School District #48.   Elementary intervention program.   Beaverton, Oregon, 1981.

The following questions are answered in this publication: Which students benefit from intervention program? Where are these services currently available? What techniques are used in the intervention program? How long will a student remain in the intervention classroom? How are students reintegrated back into the regular program? How are students referred for intervention services? Included also is a section on seriously emotionally disturbed referral and placement process.

4012.   Beloit Public Schools.   "Policy Statement For Students And Parents -- Student Code Of Conduct And Alcohol And Drug Abuse." Beloit, Wisconsin, August, 1981.

The behavior and conduct of students attending the Beloit Public schools must reflect standards of good citizenship, high morality, self-discipline and responsibility for one's own action which should characterized all members of the democratic society. To this end, positive discipline is a necessary element, and provides all students with a healthy learning environment. Included are the following sections: Student code of conduct, sanctions, seclusion, alcohol and drug abuse.

4013.   Bergeth, R. "A Descriptive Picture of Minneapolis Public Schools' Title I Special Learning and Behavior Problem Students 1971-1972." Minneapolis, Minnesota: Department of Research and Evaluation, 1972.

A descriptive picture of the students in the Minneapolis Public Schools' Special Learning and Behavior Problem Title I EESEA Program is presented. Eighteen Title I teachers trained in special learning and behavior problems work in target area elementary schools. The teachers provide individual instruction for children with severe behavior problems which retard academic classes progress but do not necessitate placement in special education classes. The teachers work mainly on reading problems, but also work on math. The teachers also attempt to help a student who has some emotional or social problems. A total of 19 Title I schools with 325 children who could benefit by placement into program were studied. The third and fourth grades had the largest numbers of students in the program. The typical student was a white male who had been enrolled in the program for about ten months and who had a good chance of not living in a home where both parents resided. His parents had a strong possible of receiving ASDC Assistance, and there was a larger than average number of children in the family. He performed poorly on standardized achievement tests in reading and math. He does better on activities which are non-verbal in nature. See ERIC Abstract ED 084277.

4014.   Bethel Park School District. Discipline Handbooks. Bethel Park, Pennsylvania.

The Bethel Park School District publishes a manual for each of the six elementary, two middle and one senior high school. Each handbook contains information on staffing, regular school hours, health services, and discipline, the district corporal punishment policy, general safety regulations, student dress, and block parent program.

4015.   Binghamton City School District. Standards for students at the secondary level. Binghamton, New York, 1981.

This student handbook has been prepared by the teaching and administrative staffs of the city school district for the purpose of serving the student. It covers all areas of student life and answers most questions that students normally ask. Student rights are discussed. Included are sections on the following topics: educational philosophy, student attendance, field trips, textbooks, grading, written work, homework, pupil evaluation, discipline, disciplinary referral form, detention and study hall, student government, classroom materials and manners, use of school property and maintainance of public order and grievance procedure.

4016.   Binghamton City School District. Standards for the elementary schools. Binghamton, New York, July, 1977.

The handbook of standards for elementary schools include sections on the following: attendance, classroom management, complaints, conferences, cumulative records, discipline, curriculum, emergencies, evaluation, field trips, grade books, health, homework, promotion in retention, schedule, special services, standard building procedures, written work.

4017. Birmingham Public Schools. Student Rights, Responsibilities And Due Process Code. Birmingham, Michigan, June 26, 1979.

The Birmingham Public Schools recognizes the following: that the primary intent of society in establishing the public school is to provide an opportunity for learning; that the students have full rights of citizenship as delineated in the United States Constitution and its Amendments; that citizenship rights must not be abridged, obstructed or otherways altered except in accordance with due process of law; that education is one of these citizenship rights. In this code of conduct educators are concerned with the rights of the individual as a citizen of the United States. They see individuals carrying the same rights in all walks of life, and are concerned with the areas of education, specifically the school community. Included are the following sections: criminal acts, rules concerning conduct in school and school activities, student rights and responsibilities, types of corrective discipline, debarment, suspension, expulsion and due process.

4018. Bismarck Public Schools. "Discipline." Bismarck, North Dakota, February, 1977.

The establishment and maintenance of good learning environments in the various school of the city is the responsibility of many people. Once schools are established and students enrolled, the staff have the responsibility to develop within that school an environment conducive to learning. This needs to be an environment where teachers, students, parents, and administrators can interact in responsible ways, in a atmosphere of mutual respect and understanding. The staff and students within each school have certain obligations to one another. Included in this pamphlet are some of these obligations and outlines. Included are the following sections: 1) What is expected of students, 2) Rights of students, 3) Limits of students rights, 4) Steps in due process, 5) What is expected of teachers, 6) What is expected of administrators, 7) General recommendations, 8) School and community resources.

4019. Board Of Education, City Of Chicago. The Helping Handbook. Chicago, Illinois, 1980.

This handbook is intended primarily for teachers and it is hoped that it will act as a reference and informative guide for all people who interact with children who exhibit an

effective disorder and/or adaptive behavior which significantly interferes with their learning and/or social
function. The purpose of the written material is to enable
and assist the special education teacher implanting and
implementing a meaningful and successful individualized
program for the classroom. The format includes diagnositc
guides, methods and techniques for behavior management,
materials, and related services to implement a school
program. It was written and compiled by teachers who work
on a daily basis with students from all age levels who
display behavior disorders. They have drawn upon their own
knowledge and experiences in order to produce a practical
and useful guide. Included are the following chapers: 1)
Characteristics Of Children With Behavior Disorders, 2)
Behavior Management, 3) Individualization, 4) Observation
and Evaluation, 5) Use Of Supplementary Materials and
Supplies, 6) Field Trips and Extracurricular Activities, 7)
Inservice, 8) Parent Involvement, 9) Related Services.

4020.   Boston Public Schools. Code of Discipline. Boston,
Massachusetts, 1980.

It is the firm conviction of the Boston Public Schools that
equal educational opportunities and a safe and effective
educational environment are essential to good school discipline. The Boston Public Schools strives to develop and to
implement programs and approaches to learning and discipline
that will 1) ensure parental confidence in the ability of
the schools to provide climates that are safe and orderly,
2) assist administrators, teachers and other staff in their
quest for providing effective teaching and learning environments, and 3) provide students with the assurance that they
can learn in a non-disruptive atmosphere and can be treated
in a fair, consistent and nondiscriminatory manner. Included are the following sections: 1) equal educational
opportunities, 2) language and notices of conferences-
hearings, 3) informal conference procedures, 4) procedures
on establishing school-based rules on disciplinary problems,
5) alternative solutions to disciplinary problems, 6)
temporary removal from class, 7) grounds for suspension,
long-term suspension, transfer or expulsion, 8) emergency
suspension, 9) procedures for suspension, 10) long-term
suspension or transfer, 11) cumulative suspension, 12)
expulsion, 13) students with special needs, 14) discipline
in school work, 15) expunging records, 16) teacher appeal,
17) physical force, 18) promulgation and distribution, and
19) definitions.

4021.   Brunswick County Schools. Common Discipline Rules and
Regulations. South Fork, North Carolina, Undated.

Included in this brochure are the following sections:
in-school suspension center, automatic out-of-school suspension or expulsion, disciplinary regulations, administrative
policy for drug and alcohol, an overview of the project "The
New Model Me."

4022.   Buffalo Public Schools. <u>The Board, the student, and the</u> <u>parent responsibilities and roles.</u> Buffalo, New York, undated.

This brochure is divided into sections on students, board of education, and parents with their rights and responsibilities listed in numerical order.

4023.   Burlington Public Schools. <u>Burlington High Student</u> <u>Handbook.</u> Burlington, Massachusetts, 1981.

Included in this student handbook is a section on discipline, suspension, school policies and procedures. The main purpose of any disciplinary action is to correct and improve behavior so that the education process can proceed. There are circumstances in which the behavior of any individual transgresses the rights of other members of the school community. Therefore, there shall be consistent penalities imposed for all infractions of school rules. These penalities will become progressively severe for repeated infractions and parents are notified that all levels of suspension. No disciplinary action results in loss of makeup rights except as stated in the regulations governed by the policy.

4024.   Canton City School District. <u>Report Of The Task Force On</u> <u>Discipline.</u> Canton, Ohio, December 11, 1978.

Effective discipline is an important and necessary prerequisite for effective learning. The intent of rules and regulations is to establish guidelines which create a positive educational environment and which holds students accountable for their behavior and teaches them to live with the consequences of their decision. The Board of Education directs that the administration in consultation with the faculty, parents and students establish rules and regulations that will produce the best possible educational atmosphere and to teach students to be accountable for their actions. These rules have, as their educational objectives, the development of mature and responsible citizen and the maximum academic achievement possible. It is the responsibility of the administration and each staff member to see that rules are enforced fairly, firmly, consistently and impartially by all parties concerned. This report summarizes the Board of Education policies on student discipline.

4025.   Carman--Ainsworth Community Schools. <u>Citizenship</u> <u>Program.</u> Flint, Michigan, 1981.

In response to a district wide goal to raise student achievement and student expectations, the staff is implementing a program to provide and to evaluate citizenship responsibilities. The program was developed on these beliefs: 1) it is essential that a school clearly defines itself; to say what it believes in and stands for, 2) parents must consistently support the idea that students have responsibilities as well as rights and schools have an obligation to insist upon both, 3) there is nothing undemocratic in requiring students to do things which are demonstrated as being beneficial to them, 4) high performance takes place in a framework of high expectations. The program has four components, 1) a written list of rights and responsibilities, 2) a monthly citizenship report to report student progress in the areas of citizenship responsibilities and expectations. Parents receive this report the last school day of each month, 3) a recognition system for student who are identified as fulfulling their responsibilities, 4) a student code of conduct which defines various unacceptable behaviors and the consequences of such behavior.

4026.   Chandler Unified School District. Student Conduct Code, Grades Seven-Twelve. Chandler, Arizona, 1981.

This book descibes the Chandler Plan which is a cooperative effort between student, home and school. Included are the following sections: 1) Student rights, 2) Student responsibilities, 3) Conduct code violations and consequences, 4) Procedures for dealing with violations and right of appeal, 5) Citizenship, 6) A final word from parents.

4027.   Chapel Hill-Carlboro City School. Student Code of Behavior. Chapel Hill, North Carolina, undated.

These guidelines for student conduct reflect a mutual responsibility to maintain a safe and constructive atmosphere for learning. They are intended to define the limits of acceptable behavior and spell out the consequences for those who go beyond those limits. These guidelines are intended to be administered fairly, firmly and uniformly.

4028.   Chesterfield County Public Schools. School Discipline Policy. Chesterfield, Virginia, September 28, 1977.

Included are three major sections, the first on responsibilities, the second on enforcement and the third on due process. Students are responsible, with each principal, faculty and staff member, for maintaining the school environment in which educational programs can flourish in extracurricular programs can go forward for the pleasure and benefit of all participants.

4029.   Chicopee Public Schools. Discipline Code. Chicopee, Massachusetts, 1980.

Included are the following sections: Discrimination statement, philosophy of school committee and school administration towards students, towards administration, towards faculty, towards community, and towards peers; rules governing student conduct in the Chicopee Public Schools personal attendance, attendance, alcohol, drugs, transportation, grounds for suspension, exercise and due process, request for hearing by superintendent, expulsion, and exclusions.

4030.   City of Camden Board of Education. <u>Discipline Policy of</u> <u>the Camden Board of Education</u>. Camden, New Jersey, 1978.

The purpose of this policy is to assist students in developing a mode of behavior, self directed to as great an extent as possible, that will allow them to meet social expectations making them competitive with students from other environments for the challenges of constructive, productive social interaction. Included are the following sections: introduction, goals, expectations, policies, and glossary.

4031.   City School District of Elmira, New York. <u>Discipline</u> <u>Policy</u>. Elmira, New York, November 8, 1980.

The board of education and teachers association firmly believe that good schools are founded on good discipline. Each building principal must consult with the faculty to adopt such rules as are needed to insure that good discipline is maintained in each individual building. It is the responsibility of the building principal to be certain that all teachers understand and follow the rules and regulations established. Included in this brochure are procedures to assist in developing and maintaining good discipline. Sections include: 1) policy statements relative to teachers, 2) policy statements relative to students, 3) policy statements relative to parents, 4) disciplinary procedures, and 5) central office.

4032.   Clackamas County School District. <u>Student Code of</u> <u>Conduct Handbook</u>. Oregon City Public Schools, Oregon, 1981.

It is the responsibility of School District Number 62 to provide educational opportunities to equip students with basic skills, understandings, appreciations and attitudes necessary for living effectively in our society. It is the responsibility of the student, as a citizen of the community, to make his or her school a good place to live--a place where people can live and learn together. To help achieve this type of responsible citizenship, the Board of Education has developed a handbook to inform students of the policies and rules which govern conduct in school and to conform to the laws of the state of Oregon. Included are the following sections: 1) responsibility for student progress and behavior, 2) students rights and responsibilities, 3) community relationships, 4) attendance and enrollment, 5) student records, 6) student organization, 7) married students/expectant mothers, 8) bus regulations, 9) visitors to school, 10) motor vehicles, 11) campus regulations, 12) dress and grooming, 13) search and seizure, 14) acts and violation of school district rules, 15) school disciplinary procedures, 16) equal education opportunities, 17) equal education opportunity complaint procedure for students in the school district.

4033.   Clio Area Schools. Code of Conduct and Discipline Policy. Clio, Michigan, 1981.

It is important to note that every student has personal as well as legal responsibilities on issues pertaining to school related matters. This code of conduct delineates the rights of students and the responsibilities. It includes the following sections: (1) student rights and responsibilities (2) code for student conduct (3) guidelines for age of maturity legislation (4) legal basis for school discipline policy (5) law enforcement officers in the school.

4034.   Colonial School District. Code of Student Rights and Responsibilities. Plymouth Meeting, Pennsylvania, July, 1978.

The Code of Student Rights and Responsibilities is divided into three separate brochures one for the elementary, one for the junior high, and one for the senior high. Each brochure contains a philosophy of the disciplinary code, the goals of the disciplinary code, the purpose of the code, the rights and responsibilieies of students, kinds of discipline and procedures, and application of discipline, and definitions and procedures for exclusion from school.

4035.   Columbia Public Schools. "Pupil Control And Conduct Discipline." Columbia, Missouri, 1972.

The primary objectives of the school program of discipline are to: 1) To develop self-control, 2) Teach respect for proper authority, 3) Increase ability for assuming responsibility, 4) Develop the ability to excercise freedom wisely, 5) Develop positive attitudes in the area of human relations. Sections of this discipline code include: 1) Opening the school buidling, 2) Control of automobile use by pupils, 3) Control of smoking by pupils, 4) Control of drug use by students in school buildings, on school grounds, or at school sponsored activities.

4036.   Commonwealth Learning, Inc. "Morse Crisis Intervention Center -- Project Advance: Title III Project. Final Report." Washington, D.C., Department of Research and Evaluation, 1975.

The Morse Crisis Intervention Center is a program of survival for the youth of the District of Columbia Public Schools who have been removed from the public junior high school because of disruptive behavior. The center's ongoing activities were supplemented by Project Advance in the following specific areas during the 1974-75 school year: 1) psychotherapeutic services were provided to alleviate or minimize disturbing behavior, 2) individualized instruction was provided the students using a modified open classroom technique, and 3) enrichment activities were provided the students. The project director and staff developed 23 standards, which emphasized affective, behavioral, and educational objectives. These standards formed the basis for the program evaluation. Measures of program success included a staff survey, focusing on the attainment of the 23 standards, progress on the wide range achievement test, data from a classroom observation checklist, project director and counselor reports, and a survey by students. See ERIC Abstract ED 11757.

4037.   Community High School South District Ninety-Nine. Student Handbook. Downers Grove, Illinois, 1981.

Included in the student handbook is a section on Disciplinary Procedures. Outlined are acts of gross disobedience and the resulting disciplinary action. Also outlined are infractions involving misconduct and the resulting disciplinary action.

4038.   Cranston Public Schools. Disciplinary Procedures For Cranston Secondary Schools. Cranston, Rhode Island, January 17, 1977.

In an attempt to provide students and school authorities with a consistent set of reasonable rules and regulations to govern student behavior in a public school setting, rules were established by the Cranston School Committee. Through the establishment of these rules and dissemination to all families of secondary students, the rights, responsibilities and expectations of each student are protected and clearly defined.

4039.   Cranston Public Schools. Pupils' Conduct Code. Cranston, Rhode Island, November 2, 1977.

The Cranston School Committee is committed to provide each pupil with full opportunity to develop his or her potential in an orderly manner in which the rights and responsibility of each individual are considered. To provide this positive educational setting, the conduct, behavior, respect for authority and the use of school property are of utmost importance. To accomplish this goal, for the personal conduct of pupils, a set of reasonable rules and regulations have been developed for all elementary students. Included in this booklet are a list of those rules and regulations.

4040.   Criminal Justice and Behavior, 2, 4 (December, 1975, entire issue).

This special issue on schools and delinquency prevention is designed to bring together a number of diverse opinions and research findings on the prevention and control of school related delinquency, as well as on the role of the public school in generating and/or controlling delinquency among its youth population. Schools have been widely criticized for contributing to delinquency, for failing to adequately prepare youth for responsible adult roles, for labeling children negatively, for dealing with problem students by expulsion or for doing nothing at all about delinquency in youth crime. Included in this special issue are the following articles, 1) "Here, There, and Nowhere," 2) "Schools in the Community," 3) "Schools in the Delinquency Experience," 4) "Schools and Delinquency Prevention Strategies," 5) "Delinquency Programs in Schools," 6) "The School Relations Bureau," 7) "Preventing Drug Abuse," 8) "Self Report Measurement of Delinquent Orientation in Institutionalized Delinquent and High School Boards," 9) "Educational Intervention as a Preventive Measure," and 10) "Mutibility and Delinquency."

4041.   Culver City Unified School District. Discipline Policies. Culver City, California, Undated.

Included in the discipline policies are the following sections: suspension and expulsion of pupils, continuation education classes, exemption of pupils, exclusion of pupils, procedures for suspension, general rules: suspension, suspension of procedure, summary of suspension limitation/appeal process, pupil expulsion procedures, district office responsibilities, board responsibilities, annual review-reinstatement procedure, interdistrict permits, pupils with exceptional needs, exclusion procedures, annual review, involunteer transfer to continuation class.

4042.   Cumberland Public Schools. "Student Handbook -- Cumberland High School." Cumberland, Rhode Island, 1981.

Pages 26 to 41 of this handbook deal with student guidelines. Included are sections on class lateness policy, open campus, senior disciplinary code, arrival at school, passing to classes, smoking area, classroom conduct, study hall, general rules, media center procedure, detention, discipline. Within the discipline section are the following areas: Violations/disciplinary actions, attendance policies/in-school suspension, in-school suspension program, due process, general guidelines, suspension, temporary removal, short term suspension, long term suspension, hearing process, appeals process.

4043.   Dallas Independent School District. Student Rights And Responsibilities. Dallas, Texas, May 1, 1977.

Included in this handbook are sections on student rights and responsibilities: Involvement in decision making, student conduct, dress code, care of school property, hazing, smoking, alcohol and drug use, weapons, assaults on school personnel, disruption, married students, pregnant students, interegation and searches, student complaints, student discipline.

4044.   Davis Joint Unified School District. Discipline. Davis, California, August 24, 1977.

Discipline is a positive concept and is interpreted as application of order and control to the activities engaged in by people. Discipline and punishment should not be confused, although punishment may be necessary on occasion to achieve a good discipline. Punishment should never degrade or ridicule a person. The school has a prime educational responsibility for furthering among pupils a positive understanding and practice of discipline. There are three distinct basis of this responsibility. (1) the establishment of a school environment in which order and control are applied to the activities of the pupils and adults within the school (2) the development of under-standing on the part of the pupils of the need for disci-pline throughout the society in the ways in which this can be achieved (3) the development of the individual's ability for self-discipline and a provision of appropriate opportunity for the individual and group to be responsible for their own discipline. Included are the following sections (1) discipline (2) rights (3) responsibility (4) individual school code of behavior.

4045.   Dearborn Public Schools. Student Code Of Conduct -- Rights And Responsibility. Dearborn, Michigan, July, 1978.

A major objective of the code is the assurance of a school environment that is conducive to learning. To accomplish this objective the code provides for the fair, consistent and effective administration of student discipline. Further, the document acknowledges the right to appeal administrative decisions through procedures established in the code for instituting such appeals. Included are the following sections: 1) Philosophical and legal basis for a student code of conduct: rights and responsibilities, 2) Definition of terms, 3) Educational planning and placement committee, 4) Violations and maximum penalities, 5) Exclu-sion from school, 6) The appeal process, 7) Students' rights and responsibilities.

4046.   Decatur Public School District Sixty-One. Student Conduct. Decatur, Illinois, 1981.

Rules and regulations relating to the conduct of students during school hours and school sponsored activities have been formulated under the direction of the Superintendent of schools and approved by the Board of Education. Included are the following sections in the code of student conduct: 1) Philosophy, 2) General infractions, 3) Dress Code, 4) Procedures for handling misconduct on bus.

4047.   Denver Public School. Student Conduct And Discipline. Denver, Colorado, August 20, 1976.

The chief purpose of the schools is to educate those students in its charge. Behavior which tends to conflict with the educational program of the Denver Public Schools or which is inimical to the welfare of other students is subject to disciplinary action. Respect for constituted authority and obedience thereto is an essential lesson to qualify one for the duties of citizenship, and the classroom is an appropriate place to practice and teach that lesson. Student conduct and discipline policy and rules and their enforcement shall be consisted with applicable law. Students violating any of the policies and rules are subject to appropriate disciplinary action, including suspension, expulsion, and referral to the proper law enforcement authority. Included are the following sections: objectives, policy development, rule development in the school, enforcement, general policies on student conduct and discipline, specific policies on student conduct and discipline, policies on extra-curricular activities, policies relating to participants in the interscholastic athletic program.

4048.   Department of Public Instruction of Iowa. Search and Seizures in the Schools--A Model Policy and Rules. Des Moines, Iowa, November, 1976.

Included are the following sections: introduction, model statement of policy, model statement of rules, form 1, and selected source references.

4049.   Des Moines Independent Community District. Discipline Policy and Attendance Policy -- Des Moines Public Schools. Des Moines, Iowa, July, 1979.

The purpose of this discipline policy is to guide the conduct of pupils in a way which permits the orderly and efficient operation of the schook to define socially intolerable conducts so as to maintain a scholarly common discipline atmosphere to achieve maximum educational benefits for all pupils. The policy also defines the punishment for breaches of discipline and the due process procedures that are to be followed when correction is applied. Included are the following chapters, 10 Definition of School Discipline, 2) Definition of Breach of Discipline, 3) Sanctions for Breach of Discipline, 4) Restraint, 5) Areas in Which Disciplinary Control of Pupils is to be Exercised, 6) Non-Authorized Persons, 7) Actions for Physical Attack or Threats to School Personnel, 8) Procedure for Expulsion Cases, 9) Administrative Rules and Procedures Authorized.

4050.   Des Moines Public Schools. Discipline Policy and Attendance Policy. Des Moines, Iowa, Undated.

The purpose of the discipline policy is to guide the conduct of pupils in a way which permits the orderly and efficient operation of the school, to define socially intolerable conduct so as to maintain a scholarly, disciplined atmosphere to achieve maximum educational benefits for all pupils. The policy also defines the punishment for breaches of discipline and the due process procedures that are to be followed when correction is applied. Included are the following sections: (1) definition of school discipline (2)

definition of breach of discipline (3) sanctions for breach
of discipline (4) restraint (5) areas in which disciplinary
control of pupils is to be exercised (6) non-authorized
persons (7) actions for physical attack or threats to school
personnel (8) procedure for expulsion cases (9) administrative rules and procedures authorized.

4051.   Detroit Public Schools. Uniformed Code of Student
Conduct. Detroit, Michigan, 1976.

The purpose of this conduct code is to provide regulations
governing the behavior of students, to prevent actions or
activities interferring with the school program and/or
prohibited by law, and to provide for student rights and
responsibilities. Included are the following sections: 1)
student responsibilities, prohibited behavior, illegal
behavior, general prohibited behavior, disciplinary actions,
student rights, disciplinary procedures, records.

4052.   District 27. Handbook Guidance Procedures. Ozone Park,
New York, September, 1980.

The handbook contains up-to-date and revised materials which
serve as a guide and source of reference for all supervisors
and pupil personnel staff in the community school board.
Included are sections on procedures for suspension of
special education students, suspension profiles, medical
discharges, home instruction, truncated session, special day
schools, school transfers, child abuse and neglect, special
education, pupil behavior and discipline, community
services.

4053.   District 742 Community Schools. Welfare: Disci-
pline/Punishment-Secondary Students. St. Cloud, Minnesota,
March 22, 1979.

The Board of Education recognizes that the rights of all
students must be respected. Along with these rights, there
is a corresponding responsibility for students to follow
school rules and regulations. Students who fail to abide by
the established rules and regulations shall be handled as
outlined as policies suggest. Included are the following
sections: 1) general policies, 2) school regulations, 3)
disciplinary policies, 4) suspension procedures, 5) exclusion and expulsion procedures, 6) definitions.

4054.   Dothan City School. Out Alternative School--Dothan
Approach to School Suspension. Dothan, Alabama, Undated.

Included are the following sections in this description of
an alternative school: steps in the referral process,
alternative school-the first day, alternative school-the
last day, discipline referral, alternative school referral,
alternative school admission, alternative school rules,
counselor personal data sheet, anecdotal record, disclosure
record, counselor's daily log, and dismissal form.

4055.   Dufilho, L. P. et al. "Second Year Evaluation Report for
the Dothan City Schools for the Title Three Project,
'Comprehensive Services for Children'." Dothan City
Schools, Alabama, 1973.

This report summarizes the activities and results of the
second year of the Dothan City Schools Project, "Comprehensive Services for Children," funded under Elementary
Secondary Education Act Title Three. This project is
concerned with the provision of special services to meet the
needs of elementary school children suffering psycho-
emotional conflict problems. The mechanism for providing
such services is two-fold. One aspect is a special
inservice training program for elementary school teachers,
while the other involves the utilization of resource staff
members with specialized skills for the handling of such
problems. The principal outcomes of concern here are those
dealing with behavior and performance of the students.
During the second year of the project, a larger number of
teachers participated in the special inservice program than
in the first year. Of the fifty teachers in the program the
second year, five were in their second year of participation. Various types of data were collected on the students
of these fifty teachers. In addition, data were collected
on the students of nine teachers who were in the previous
year's program only, and on the students of 55 teachers who
did not participate in the special inservice program either
year. See ERIC Abstract ED 121906.

4056.   Duval County Public Schools. Code Of Student Conduct.
Jacksonville, Florida, 1981.

Instruction should occur in an environment that is conducive
to learning. Effective instruction requires good order and
discipline which may be described as the absence of distrac-
tions, frictions, and disturbances which interfere with the
effective functioning of the student, class and school. It
is also the presence of a friendly, yet businesslike atmosphere, in which students and school personnel work cooperatively toward mutually recognized and accepted goals. To
assist parents, administrators, and faculty in maintaining a
conducive atmosphere, the code of student conduct describes
roles of the home, student, school and school personnel;
describe student rights and responsibilities; identify
formal disciplinary action; standardize procedures for
administering formal discipline action; and identifying
classifications of violations and describe procedures for
disciplinary action.

4057.   East Hartford Public Schools. Guidelines For Enforcement
Of The Uniform Code Of Student Conduct. East Hartford,
Connecticut, October 22, 1980.

Sections of the brochure include: a) elementary school
guidelines for enforcement of uniform code of student
conduct and middle school guideline for enforcement of

uniform code of student conduct, and high school guidelines. Included also is the philosophy of discipline, student rights and responsibilities, and action plan, and an introduction to the code of conduct. Division of the code of conduct are explained.

4058.   Easton Area School District. Student Conduct Procedure for Elementary Schools. Easton, Pennsylvania, September, 1978.

This procedure presents the categories of student misbehaviors occuring in schools today as well as prescribed disciplinary responses. The basis tenant of this procedure is the belief that students grow in character as they come to understand more fully the consequences of their decisions and act in accordance with that understanding. Any action taken to correct behavior is intended to improve attitude, and subsequent behavior. The primary goal of this procedure is to promote the health, safety and educational welfare of students and staff. It is intended to facilitate educators' efforts to teach students to grow socially, emotionally, physically and academically. Included are the following sections: 1) introduction, 2) outline of misconduct/response structure, 3) addendum number 1: disciplinary alternatives, 4) addendum number 2: detention after school 5) addendum number 3: paddling, 6) addendum number 4: student suspension and expulsion, 7) student misconduct response charts.

4059.   Eastside Union High School District.   "District Policy Pertaining To Student Behavior." San Jose, California, 1980.

The following areas are included in the policies pertaining to student behavior: 1) Preface, 2) Objectives, 3) California State Law, 4) General conduct, 5) Attendance, 6) Habitual failure, 7) Health, safety, general welfare, 8) Tobacco, 9) Alcohol, drugs, stimulants or narcotics, 10) Insubordination, 11) Obsenities and vulgarities, 12) Fighting, 13) Dangerous or annoying instruments, 14) Memberships in organizations, 15) Thefts/damage to property, 16) Hazing, 17) Student-driven motor vehicles, 18) Suspensions, 19) Corporal Punishment, 20) Name calling, 21) Closed campus.

4060.   Eau Claire Area School District. "Student Code Of Rights And Responsibilities." Eau Claire, Wisconsin, 1979.

Included in this pamphlet are the following areas: Preamble, school responsibilites, definition of terms, anonymity, assemblage, assigned areas, attendance, truancy, bus riders safety and courtesy responsibility, gambling, general school conduct, grievance, illegal substances and non-prescribed drugs, tobacco, leaving the building or grounds without permission, profanity, behavior and weapons, loitering, personal dress, property, policy interviews, publications, solicitation of funds, student counsel, student vehicle.

4061.   Fillmore, E. H. "Goals and objectives for pupil personnel services." Student Booklet. Huntington Beach Union High School District, California. 87p, 1074.

The pupil personnel services unit goals and student objectives were produced by a counseling staff to comply with a state legislature mandate for accountability. Behavioral objectives have been set in five domains, including the educational, the social/personal, career development, the consultative, and job satisfaction. A brief implementation plan is outlined. See ERIC Abstract #ED 101075.

4062.   Findlay City School District. Student Discipline. Findlay, Ohio, October 10, 1977.

The school must maintain order because it is a prerequisite to learning. Even though the ultimate aim is self-discipline, the authority of teachers and principals is necessary as children are led to the point where they can practice self-discipline. It is wise to give freedom to children, but it is possible only when children have demonstrated that they can accept freedom by using it wisely. The essence of good discipline is to have a few simple rules of good behavior which are to be implicitly obeyed throughout the school and to permit no infraction of these rules. They should be devised to make sure that the safety and the welfare of all children are preserved. Included in this brochure are rules which must be observed when punishment is administered.

4063.   Forest Lake Independent School District 831. "Elementary School Student Code Of Conduct." Forest Lake, Minnesota.

Included in the elementary statement of policy is the written belief that learning can best take place in an orderly environment and that students can best learn individual and collective responsibility and gain maturity if they are provided opportunities in which to exercise responsibility within the school setting. Included are the following sections: 1) Statement of policy, 2) Elementary discipline procedures, 3) Corporal punishment.

4064.   Forest Lake Independent School District 831. "Secondary School Student Code Of Conduct." Forest Lake, Minnesota, 1981.

Included in this code of conduct are the following area: 1) Statement of policy, 2) Student bus application of the student code of conduct, 3) Rules governing eligibility for code-curricular activities, 4) Safety, 5) Unacceptable behavior, 6) Corrective measures, 7) Disciplinary action for some serious offenses, 8) The building students support team, 9) Corporal punishment.

4065.   Fort Zumwalt School District. <u>Guidelines for Discipline in Secondary Schools</u>. O'Fallon, Missouri, October 19, 1981.

These guidelines are intended to provide a guide for Saturday detention, Zumwalt Alternative Program, and Out-of-school suspension. The circumstances surrounding an incident and the student's previous disciplinary record should be taken into account in determining the appropriate punishment. The purpose of these guidelines is to further consistency from school-to-school and among administrators within a school. Deviations are appropriate when circumstances warrant. It is assumed that the classroom teacher will handle many of the more minor violations of rules which do not warrant referral to an administrator.

4066.   Fox, W. M. and Elder, N. "A study of practices and policies for discipline in drop-outs in ten selected schools." North Country, New York. 1980.

The report reviews the current literature on drop-outs and school discipline and discusses a survey of ten North Country high schools used to generate information to be used by schools when re-evaluating policies. Principals completed questionnaires in the ten schools. Recommendations wre made based on the literature review and survey results. They include: 1) early and systematic identification of potential drop-outs; 2) use of in-school suspensions as a disciplinary measure; 3) written guidelines for acceptable student behavior and the consequences if rules are broken; 4) involvement of students, parents, and faculty in the development of school disciplinary policies and 5) an emphasis on the positive aspects of student behavior. A check-list to aid early identification of potential drop-outs is included. See ERIC Abstract #ED 191974.

4067.   Freeport School District. <u>Discipline</u>. Freeport, Illinois, Undated.

Students, as citizens of the United States, are guaranteed certain individual rights and have corresponding individual responsibilities. Parents, teachers and administrators have a responsibility to protect the rights of students while maintaining an educational atmosphere conducive to the teaching and learning process. The concept of balancing the rights of the individual with the rights of society is as valid in the educational community as in the larger community. Certain special responsibilities required of a citizen who is a student in school are presented. Also presented are guidelines for the administration of discipline, level one behavior offenses, level two behavior offenses, level three behavior offenses, detention rules, suspension and expulsion.

4068.   Gary Community School Corporation. <u>Due Process and Pupil Discipline Manual</u>. Gary, Indiana, September, 1980.

Included are the following sections: 1) Introduction 2) Teacher 3) Principal 4) Hearing examiner 5) School attorney 6) Charges by student.

4069.   Gloucester Township Board Of Education. <u>Charles W. Lewis Middle School Student Guidebook</u>. Blackwood, New Jersey, 1981.

The Student Government Association compiled this handbook as a guide for the school year. School rules have been arranged in this handbook. A section entitled "Disciplinary Code" is included in this booklet. Included are general comments on the disciplinary code, a code of punishment for offenses, a list of infractions related to school attendance, class attendance and punctuality and infractions against good order, property and the necessary conditions for the health and safety of students and staff members, and infractions against the person.

4070.   Grand Blanc Community Schools. <u>Student Rights and Responsibilities Handbook</u>. Grand Blanc, Michigan, Undated.

In accordance with the laws of the state of Michigan the Board of Education has the authority to make reasonable rules and regulations relative to anything whatever necessary for the proper establishment, management in carrying on of the public school. This includes the establishment of regulations relative to the conduct of pupils while attending school or enroute to or from school. Because educational institutions must be orderly institutions, the freedom in each school may be reasonably restricted to protect the rights of all. 1) No idea or belief may be communicated in such a way as to cause a disruption of normal school activities. 2) The advocacy of immediate action, as opposed to the advocacy of ideas or beliefs, is not permitted when such action would disrupt normal school activities, violate any laws, or interfere with the rights of others. 3) No communication of a commercial, obscene or defamatory nature, nor any communication advocating racial or religious intolerances permitted. Included are the following sections: 1) Introduction to student rights and responsibilities. 2) Administrative policies and procedures- authority of the school board, limitation on freedom, freedom of speech, freedom of assembly, freedom to petition, right to publish, personal appearance, school records, search and seizure, attendance, instructional materials. 3) Student discipline--policy, philosophy, role responsibilities, discipline action short of suspension, suspension from school, expulsion, appeals procedure, makeup work, definitions of unacceptable behavior.

4071.   Grand Rapids Public Schools. <u>Student Handbook</u>. Grand Rapids, Minnesota, 1981.

Included in the student handbook is a section on rules and regulations, use of alcoholic drugs and tobacco, vandalism and theft, insubordination, insolence and fighting, suspension and expulsion, and student misconduct.

4072.   Greater Clark County Schools. Student Rights And Responsibilities -- A Guide For Parents And Students. Jefferson, Indiana, 1981.

In an effort to create a more democratic school society, the board of school trustees of the greater Clark County School Corporation has outlined some of the basic rights and responsibilities which allow the self-disciplined student to better govern himself within the total school environment. These policy statements made by the board of school trustees are summarized under three main headings: 1) Basic rights and responsibility of students, 2) Enforcement of rules and regulations, 3) Procedures for student due process hearings.

4073.   Greensboro Public School. Student Code of Conduct. May 20, 1980.

The Greensboro Public School Code enacted by the North Carolina General Assembly contains the following provisions: "To make and enforce such rules not in conflict with the General Law as it may deem it advisable for the Government in operation of the schools." It is the intention of the Board to enforce these rules fairly, firmly, without discrimination because of sex, race and with due respect for the Constitutional Rights of every student. The definitions used in the Code are described as well as eight rules for secondary students. These rules deal with (1) compliance with directions of principals, teachers and other school personnel (2) disruption of school (3) assault or physical injury to school employees or other persons (4) threatening, insulting, abusive or seriously discourteous words, signs or other acts (5) weapons and dangerous instruments (6) theft or damage to school or private property (7) narcotics, stimulants, alcholic beverages (8) cheating.

4074.   Gwinnett County Public Schools. Student Disciplinary Procedures. Lawrenceville, Georgia, January 8, 1980.

Included are the following sections: 1) student discipline, 2) procedures for student hearing, 3) student offenses and discipline procedures, 4) procedures for special education student for disciplinary action, and 5) appendixes.

4075.   Halifax County And South Boston City Schools. Discipline And Attendance Code. The Halifax County South Boston City School Board, Boston, Massachusetts, July 1, 1981.

Discipline problems are few in those schools where a positive learning environment exists. The responsibility for providing such a climate is with the administration and faculty of each school. When minor discipline problems do occur, teachers are encouraged to attempt to solve the problems themselves to a reasonable point. Realizing that the prime purpose of the school is to provide learning situations which allow each student the opportunity to maximize his potential, the philosophy of the Halifax County and South Boston City School Boards is that an atmosphere free of disruptive behavior contributes to the instructional program and provides for the rights of the students who are serious about learning. Included are the following sections: 1) School bus conduct, 2) Instructions for Halifax County and South Boston City School bus riders, 3) Teacher responsibility in administering code, 4) Principal responsibility in administering code, 5) Observance of due process, 6) Suspension, 7) Expulsion, 8) Definition, 9) Offenses and disposition, 10) Secondary and elementary cumulative disposition systems for disruptive behavior, 11) Attendance code, 12) Student and parent signature form.

4076.   The Hancock County Board Of Education. School Community Behavior. Weirton, West Virginia, February 19, 1973.

The board of education believes that the primary goal of the schools is to provide the opportunity for each individual to become educated to the fullest extent possible; the extent possible being the result of factors such as--ability, special learning disabilities, emotional stability, motiva- tion, health, aptitudes, available school funding, curricu- lum, available services, etc. The goal is to support school efforts which will maximize the opportunity for a individual to profit from his years of school attendance. The basic right of the individual to be a member of a school community, and, thereby, enjoy the opportunity to maximize his education in preparation for his adult role and pursuits, is contingent upon his respect for the rights of others to pursue the same opportunity and goals. Included are the following sections in this publication: services, truancy, behavior of pupils outside of school hours and off-school premises, law and probation officers, physical force, suspension of extracurricular activities and class organizational offices, pupil behavior at school activities, corporal punishment, suspension, expulsion, transportation, search and seizure, expression, equal education opportunity, assemblies and meetings, religion. Procedures for offenses referred to the administration are discussed.

4077.   Harford County Public Schools. Student disipline policies. Bel Air, Maryland, 1980.

The board of education has established policies to regulate, 1) student smoking, 2) student possession use, or distribu- tion of controlled dangerous substances and alcohol, 3) assault and/or battery, 4) malicious burning of property, 5) possession of dangerous weapons on school property. This leaflet is distributed to each student in the secondary schools to be certain they are familiar with the policies and understand the consequences of any violation of them.

4078.   Harlem School District. <u>Handbook On School Discipline</u>. Loves Park, Illinois, August 14, 1975.

Policies for the maintenance of discipline are included in this handbook. Discussed are first referral, second referral, and third referral. In the following disciplinary areas are discussed, 1) Truancy and tardiness, 2) Smoking on school grounds, 3) Personal appearance, 4) Loitering, 5) Possession of weapons of any type or fireworks, 6) Possession or consumption of alcohol or drugs, 7) Reckless driving on school property, 8). Inproper language and insubordination, 9) Stealing or destruction of property, 10) Fighting or assault, 11) Setting fire alarm, bomb threat or gross insubordination, 12) Study halls. Suspension and/or expulsion procedures are outlined. And a sample letter to parents and behavior contract are included.

4079.   Hartford Public Schools. "All Tuitive Secondary Centers, 1973-1974. Hartford Moves Ahead: An Evaluative Report." Hartford Public Schools, Connecticut, 1974.

The Alternate Secondary Center Program is the latest step in the series activities which have been taken to individualized prescriptive learning programs to meet the identified needs of alienated secondary school youngsters. As the external component to the chain of alternate secondary programs, Hartford's two centers focus on two operational concepts. Each center was staffed by one unit leader, five teachers, a secretary, and a paraprofessional. These instructional services were further supplemented by a half-time assignment of a social worker and a guidance counselor. With this staffing pattern, each center was set up to provide individualized instructional services to approximately 50 alienated youngsters enrolled in grades 7 through 12. The instructional focus was on basic skill mastery and particularly language arts for mediation, the development of a functional self concept which would enable each youngster to succeed in a mainstream environment, and both vocational and career exploration. Because regular school offerings had proven to be ineffective with the alienated youngster who produced symptoms of emotional and behavioral problems within his classroom, each center was held responsible for the identification construction, piloting, and validation of individualized learning materials which would work. See ERIC Abstract ED 097391.

4080.   Hartley, Wynona S. "Preventive Outcomes of Small Group Education With School Aged Children." An epidemiologic follow-up of the Kansas City School Behavior Project. National Institute of Mental Health, Bethesda, Maryland. 1977. 8p.

This project was an experiment intended to enhance the social-emotional development of individual pupils through treatment of mild behavioral disturbances and primary prevention programs, utilizing the teachers in their roles as group leaders. The teachers in the experimental group received training in the methods and techniques of small group interaction and were given support in the school year by staff in weekly meetings. An epidemiologic follow-up indicated more positive teacher ratings of work habits and fewer absences. Data from family files demonstrated prevention effects, whereas school data varied, showing limited positive effects and some negative effects. See ERIC Abstract ED 133668.

4081.   Haverford Township School District. Code of Student Behavior. Haverford, Pennsylvania. September, 1981.

One of the major goals of the school district is the development of the learning environment which will help provide students with the opportunity to receive the maximum benefits of the educational program. A major part of any successful school is the degree to which the students accept their responsibility to demonstrate the type of behavior that permits a healthy learning climate. Inappropriate behavior not only prevents a student from contributing to the educational process, it also affects other students' ability to learn. This code of student behavior was developed as a means of insuring that various types of inappropriate behavior are treated similarly in each district school. Included are four columns in this brochure: 1) Level of misconduct, 2) Examples, 3) Procedures, 4) Disciplinary options.

4082.   Hempfield School District. Student Handbook Of Hempfield High School. Landisville, Pennsylvania, 1981.

This handbook is a guide that offers specific suggestions and serves as a compilation of information about this high school's philosophy, policies, regulations, procedures and extracurricular opportunities. Included are sections on parent-teacher conferences, philosophy and objectives of the high school, the high school calendar, personnel, attendance policies, transportation, vocational-technical students, pupil personnel services, instructional materials center, student rights and responsibilities, exclusions from school, suspensions and expulsions, detention.

4083.   Higgins, Paul S. The Conflict Resolution Desegregation Aids Component of the Minneapolis Schools' 1973-74 Emergency School Aid Act Project: An Evaluation. May, 1976. 36p.

This component provided 20 para-professional desegregation aides for nine desegregating public schools. It also funded a coordinator of desegregation aids in a program of pre- and in-service training to help aids reduced various types of conflicts in school, and to act as liaisons between schools and the neighborhoods from which students were bused. The objectives were 1) prevention of major racial conflicts leading to school closing, 2) prevention of any increase of student-student conflict, as measured by suspension rates attributable to such conflicts, 3) prevention of any increase in student-teacher conflict and 4) among white students an increase in positive attitudes toward minority students. This report includes a brief description of aides and a discussion of their roles. See ERIC Abstract ED 117141.

4084.   Housden, Terry; and Fiedler, Patricia. "ElCamino's First Year as a Fundamental High School: A Descriptive Report." San Juan Unified School District, Carmichael, California. May, 1981. 61p.

Article describes the first year in this new fundamental high school. Students wanting to attend had to apply and agree to a new fundamental emphasis on school rules. As a result, the composition of the student body changed to one representing all ability levels. Other changes included 1) academic emphasis placed on basic skills and 2) school rules such as closed campus, dress code, and no smoking. Academic achievement during the first year was measured by minimum competency tests. Overall academic achievement remained high. Average test scores on the Test of Achievement and Proficiency were well above the national average. Attitudes were measured by surveys completed by parents, students, and staff. General observations where the course work was harder, students had more homework, students learned more, new rules were enforced but were unpopular with students and the school would hopefully improve more the second year. See ERIC Abstract ED 196940.

4085.   Howell Public Schools. "Student Attendance Policy, Student Grading System, Student Conduct Code For Grade Kindergarten Through Twelve." Howell, Michigan, 1982.

It is the desire of this Board of Education to provide the children of Howell with a safe learning environment, organized to meet the needs of each student and limited only by our creative ability and finances. The education of the children should be a joint effort of parents, students, and school personnel. Included are the following sections: 1) General school laws -- public education, 2) Student responsibilities -- good citizenship, 3) Student rights, 4) Code of conduct a) due process, b) violations, c) major violations, d) immediate recommendation for expulsion/police involvement, e) consequences of violations defined and explained, f) reasonable physical force/punishment, 5) Right of appeal, 6) Attendance policy, 7) Grading policy, 8) Citizenship.

4086.   Independent School District Of Boise City. "Attendance And Transportation Information." Boise, Idaho. 1977.

This booklet discusses attendance and discipline regulations in the Boise secondary schools. Included are the following sections: Introduction, attendance, discipline, corrective procedures, student management team, general guidelines, suspension and expulsion, suspension -- authoritive and procedural rules, and school transportation policies.

4087.   Iowa Department of Public Instruction. Absences--A Model Policy and Rules, Des Moines, Iowa, September, 1978.

Included are the following sections: 1) introduction, 2) model statement of policy, 3) model statement of rules, 4) Appendix A--1977 Code of Iowa, and Appendix B--Studies.

4088.   Iowa Department of Public Instruction. Model Policies and Rules for Assistance to Local Boards in Meeting Requirements of Procedural Due Process in Dealing With Student Suspension and Expulsion. Des Moines, Iowa, 1977.

Included are the following sections: 1) Introduction 2) Model policy and rules for suspension and expulsion procedures 3) Notice of hearing 4) Waver of hearing form 5) Findings of fact and resulted action form.

4089.   Iowa Department of Public Instruction. School Administrators and Law Enforcement Officials--A Model Policy and Rules. Des Moines, Iowa, May, 1977.

Included are the following sections: 1) Introduction 2) Model statement of policy 3) Model statement of rules.

4090.   Ithaca City School District. Handbook--student rights and responsibilities. Ithaca, New York, July 30, 1981.

The Ithaca City School District prepares students for life in American society. The Constitution of the United States grants each of the members of this society certain rights. In return for the granting of these rights, society requires all members to be respectful of the rights of others and to accept responsibility for the exercise of self discipline in the conduct of their lives. The board of education expects the members of the school community to be aware of their rights, the rights of others, and the responsibility which these rights place on its members for the conduct of their lives. To this end the board promotes procedures which insure the protection of these rights and the acceptance of these responsibilities by all. Included are the following sections: introduction, forward, student responsibilities, inforcement in penalties, student grievance procedure, and safety guidelines.

4091.   Jacobs, T. O. and others. "Princeton High School: A Needs Analysis." Consulting Report. Human Resources Research Organization, Alexandria, Virginia, 1971. 35p.

This report presents a description of the activities and findings of a research team providing consulting services to Princeton High School in the areas of classroom management, leadership and organizational development, and race relations. A predominantly middle class white school was merging with a predominantly black working class school. Problem areas were to be identified in the analysis. Areas of study included management, leadership, small group effectiveness, instructional methodology and contingency management technique applications, cross cultural and cross ethnic values, goals and aspirations. The findings consist mainly of what the teen found to be the existing perceptions among teachers, students, and administrators regarding their relative roles. See ERIC Abstract ED 128915.

4092.   Jefferson School District. Standards of Conduct. Daly City, California, July, 1981.

The purpose of this booklet is to assist students, parents, staff and other concerned individuals to understand the general behavior policies of the Jefferson School District. It is hoped that such understanding will assist the home, school and community to work cooperatively in coping with various problems that detract from conducive and effective learning atmosphere. The district and community believe that promoting positive standards of conduct will diminish discipline problems, and will contribute materially to the continuing excellence of the educational problem which the district's staff offers to the students and their parents. The school district believes that the purpose of any standard of conduct is to teach the individual what is expected behavior in and around the school. The district believes that it is a responsibility of the school to contribute to the students' understanding of their rights and the limits of those rights. Included are the following sections: 1) goals, 2) objectives, 3) standards of conduct, 4) parents, 5) principals, 6) teachers, 7) classified personnel. A second major section is on the rights of parents, teachers, principals, classified personnel and students. A third section deals with exceptions to school attendance. The concluding section discusses a problem entitled "Operation Stay/In School" which is a preventative program planned jointly by the school system, the city, and the police department. The purpose of the program is to locate and return students who are absent from school and do not have valid excuses.

4093.   Johnson, L. and Pearson, D. "Fundamental Schools in the Minneapolis School System: An Evaluation, 1978-1979." Minneapolis Public Schools, Minnesota Department of Research and Evaluation. 105p.

Three fundamental schools in Minneapolis, Minnesota, were evaluated using parent, student and teacher surveys, standardized test results and enrollment records. Parents reported their reasons for choosing this school with the most popular reason being its emphasis on reading, arithmetic, writing, discipline, self contained classrooms, citizenship, and character development. Parents were generally satisfied with the homework load, opportunity for involvement with teachers and their childrens progress and the communication about this project. All schools exceeded the gains expected by a national norm group, on standardized reading and mathematics tests. See ERIC Abstract ED 181057.

4094.   Joplin R-VII School District. Transitional Learning Center -- A Different Kind Of TLC. Joplin, Missouri, August, 1981.

The Transitional Learning Center is a means of dealing with student discipline and behavior problems that would normally result in suspension from school. Sending students home on suspension many times results in little improvement in attitude or behavior. In a certain sense, the student gets what he wants -- a vacation from school. This is not to say however, that suspension from school is not inappropriate penalty for certain violations. For some students, suspension is a meaningful penalty. This booklet outlines who will be served, basic principles, procedures for the TLC, transportation, classwork, absences, merit point system, exit interview, out-of-school suspension.

4095.   Kankakee School District Number 111. "Article Five Of Student Handbook." Kankakee, Illinois, 1975.

Included in this handbook are sections on moral attitude and sense of responsibility of students, administrative regulations for students, school attendance, procedure for handling school attendance problems, conduct at school activities, smoking, drugs, verbal or written threats, stealing, fighting, possession of or the use of dangerous weapons, the use of vulgar language or behavior, unauthorized person in buildings, harassment of school personnel or damage to personal property of school personnel, students having a grievance, inproper forms of protest, procedure for suspension, expulsion, procedures for expulsion.

4096.   Kankakee School District Number 111. "Code Of Conduct." Kankakee, Illinois, 1979.

Good discipline creates conditions favorable for efficient learning. Its ultimate purpose is the creation of mature, responsbile, and self-controlled individuals. Included are the following sections in this code of conduct: Smoking, possession or use of alcohol, use of drugs, verbal or written threats or acts of assualt and battery, stealing, robbery, verbal or written threats, fighting, possession or the use of dangerous weapons, the use of vulgar language or behavior.

4097.   Kent Public Schools. Policy on Discipline. Kent, Washington, June, 1980.

Included are the following sections: responsibilities and rights, conduct, control, procedures, due process. Including policy, procedures, administrative guidelines, a list of offenses, guidelines for elementary school sanctions, adult student policy, adult student procedures, adult student legal references, search and seizure, procedures, freedom of expression, student records, parental access to student records, law enforcement.

4098.   Knox County Schools. <u>Pupil Personnel Handbook</u>. Knoxville, Tennessee, August, 1981.

Any educational program includes three types of services -- instructional, administrative, and pupil personnel. Pupil personnel services are those that help each pupil to get the most out of his or her school experience. A program of pupil personnel services is more than a series of activities. It is also a point of view or a philosophy based upon a recognition of the needs of pupils, and understanding of the principles of human behavior, and a recognition of the unique features of the given school setting. A pupil personnel program has as its primary purpose to help the student and staff adjust to, and progress in the educational system. But in a much broader sense, the purpose of the program is also to help students adjust to the demands of their total environment and to help them, at the same time, achieve a degree of self-direction and self-realization. Included are the following sections: introduction, review of pupil personnel services, guidance, psychological services, social services, special education, procedures for obtaining pupil personnel services, general policies of concern to pupil personnel staff, suspension and expulsion, retention and acceleration of pupils, testing, student records, and community resources.

4099.   Lake Oswego Public Schools. <u>Policies Relating to Pupil Personnel--Discipline of Students in Appeals Procedure</u>. Lake Oswego, Oregon, June 6, 1977.

Included in this policy are the following areas, philosophy of discipline, objective of discipline, safeguards, physical discipline, physical restraint or force, guidelines for implementation of district policy are included.

4100.   Landcaster School District. <u>Discipline Procedures--A Working Copy</u>. Landcaster, California, July 31, 1981.

Included are the following sections: notification, record keeping, steps in the discipline process, grounds for suspension, and a summary of suspension limitations.

4101.   Laporte Community School Corporation. Student--Parent Guide. Laporte, Indiana, 1981.

The purpose of this publication is to inform parents, students and interested citizens of certain laws, regulations and policies that apply to students and parents of the Laporte Community School Corporation. Through the distribution of the Student--Parent Guide, the administration is attempting to give you information about the Federal Law on the Family Education Rights and Privacy Act and state laws on student due process, bus rules, etc.

4102.   Lenape High School. Discipline: It Doesn't Have to Mean Bad. Medford, New Jersey, undated.

This pamphlet includes the following sections, 1) Discipline: Instruction or Punishment?, 2) Is Your Child Misbehaving?, 3) Discipline Plus Love Equals Growing Togethter, 4) Discipline: It Doesn't Have to Mean Bad.

4103.   Lincoln Public Schools. Procedures for student exclusion, suspension, expulsion, and mandatory reassignment. Lincoln, Nebraska, August 10, 1976.

Included in this pamphlet are section: 1) emergency exclusion, 2) short term suspension, 3) long term suspension, 4) expulsion, 5) mandatory reassignment, 6) grounds for long term suspension or expulsion, 7) procedure for long term suspension, expulsion or mandatory reassignment, 8) hearing procedure.

4104.   Lincoln Public Schools. Rights and responsibilities of students--including provisions of Title IX legislation in the family rights and privacy act. Lincoln, Nebraska, August 10, 1976.

This brochure is intended to describe, in general terms some of the rights and responsibilities of students in the Lincoln Public Schools and to set forth appropriate regulations governing student conduct. In order to function properly, public school education must provide an equal learning opportunity for all students. In addition to the regular curriculum, principles and practices of good citizenship must be taught and demonstrated. The rules, rights, responsibilities and standards in this brochure apply to all school buildings or any school grounds during, immediately before or immediately after school hours. Included are the following sections: 1) establishment of policies, rules and regulations, 2) areas of prohibited student conduct, 3) student's responsibilities, 4) students' rights, 5) Title nine, 6) family rights and privacy act.

4105.   Lindgren, H. C.; and Patton, G.M. "Opinionnaire On Attitudes Toward Education." New Castle School District, Pennsylvania. 1975 4P.

As part of the instrumentation to assess the effectiveness Schools Without Failure Program in ten elementary schools in New Castle, Pennsylvania school district, the opinionnaire on Attitudes toward Education was used as a measure of teacher attitudes toward child-centered education, discipline, and the desirability of understanding pupil behavior. See ERIC Abstract ED 107687.

4106.   Louisiana Department of Education. Student rights and responsibilities--model handbook. Baton Rouge, Louisiana, November, 1976.

This guide addresses itself to the rights and responsibilities of the parties most intimately concerned with the education issue of discipline. Efforts have been made to eliminate statements which represent moral judgements and opinions and to confine this document to statements and positions which can be substantiated by recent court decisions or official action. The intent of this guide is to provide a source of information in suggested guidelines to local school districts in the development of their own policies, procedures, rules, and regulations on student rights and responsibilities. The major purpose of this guide is to present the legal rights and responsibilities of Louisiana Public School students under current state statute under United States law. Included are the following sections: student responsibilities, school attendance, appearance, freedom of expression, school newspaper/unofficial publications, patriotic ceremonies, school records, school organizations, physical punishment, suspension, expulsion, due process, conduct off school grounds, police on the school campus, alcohol, smoking, drugs, search and seizure, Title IX, special education in training.

4107.   Louisiana State Department of Education. Alternative Education Programs for Louisiana.

The purpose of this pamphlet is to present brief descriptions and other selected pertinent information on Act 689 Alternative Programs operating in Louisiana during the 1979-80 school term. Passed during the regular session of the 1978 Louisiana legislature, Act 689 authorizes the Louisiana State Department of Education to approve and fund a limited number of model pilot programs designed to reduce and/or eliminate crime and disruptive behaviors in the public schools of the state. The job of collecting and analyzing the date of use to write these descriptions was accomplished through onsight visits to the eleven programs currently in operation and a careful examination of project proposals by the state supervisor for student discipline at the department of education.

4108.   Loveless, Eugene J. "Impact Models For Guidance, School Year 1974-1975." New York City Board Of Education, Brooklyn, New York, Office of Educational Evaluation. 1975.

The purpose of the program evaluated in this report was to investigate the impact of increased guidance service on the educational performance of children. In the second year of the program, funded under the Elementary/Secondary Education Act, Title 3, all students in two elementary schools, one intermediate school, a junior high school and a cluster school consisting of three elementary schools and an intermediate school were included. The objectives of the program

were to enhance reading achievement and to reduce the number
of unruly disruptions in the classrooms, and to reduce the
number of disruptive incidences in the school at large. The
activities of the counselors included group and individual
counseling, special screening for learning problems,
tutorial systems and in-service. See ERIC Abstract ED
139894.

4109.   Lowell Public Schools. "Student Handbook -- Grades K-8."
Lowell, Massachusetts, 1979.

This handbook was issed in order that students and parents
become familiar with the general policies of the school. It
contains the information that should be known by all those
connected with the school. Good discipline originates in
the home. The parent is the first teacher of the child and
should develop in that child good behavior habits and proper
attitudes towards school. Included in the handbook are the
following sections: Student conduct, causes for suspension,
student conduct on school buses, out-of-classroom behavior,
attendance, tardiness, truancy, dismissals, guidance
services.

4110.   Lower Merion School District. "Code Of Student Conduct."
Ardmore, Pennsylvania, 1981.

Included in this code of student conduct are the following
area: Introduction, School environment, Responsiblities of
students, Misbehavior/Responses/Procedures, Group One,
Disciplinary options, Procedures, Group Two, Disciplinary
options, Procedures and Group Three, Disciplinary options
and procedures. Included also is a glossary with definitions used in the code.

4111.   Lyne, Evelyn. Paducah-Louisville Consortium Project
VIII: Focus On Dropouts, A New Design. Final Evaluation
Report, 1971-1972. Office of Education, Washington, D.C.
Paducah Public Schools, Kentucky.

Project VIII is an innovative behavioral science-oriented
educational program for potential dropouts. It is designed
to reduce the dropout rate in grades nine through twelve,
increase attendance in grades seven through twelve, decrease
discipline referrals and suspensions, increase reading and
math achievement in grades three through eleven, and improve
student self-concept. It is a consortium funded under a
Title VIII Elementary Secondary Education, which involves
the Paducah Public Schools, the Louisville Public Schools,
Indiana University and Murray State University. The project
consists of the instructional component (English, Mathematics, Social Studies and Reading) and the staff-
development component (parent involvement, counseling, and
health services). See ERIC Abstract ED 068614.

4112.   Maine Department of Educational and Cultural Services. <u>Early School Leaving--An Invitation to Disaster</u>. Augusta, Maine, undated.

A persistent recurring theme in several of the recent reports urging reform in secondary education is the call for changing compulsory school attendance laws so as to lower the school leaving age to fourteen. This paper discusses the reasons why lowering the school leaving age would not be good for the students for education in general and for the country.

4113.   Maine Department of Educational and Cultural Services. <u>State of Maine Laws Relating to Public Schools</u>. Augusta, Maine, 1981.

Included are all laws governing educational concerns in the state of Maine.

4114.   Maine State Department of Educational and Cultural Services. <u>Non-Traditional Programs</u>. Augusta, Maine, undated.

Included are the following sections: 1) background, 2) definitions, 3) overall purposes and intent, 4) historial roots, 5) current pratices, 6) possible senior high school options, 7) non-traditional options, 8) direction and recommendations.

4115.   Manchester Public Schools. <u>Code of Conduct</u>. Manchester, New Hampshire, August, 1979.

Included are the following sections: Section A, Student's Rights and Responsibilities (1) attendance (2) discipline and student conduct (3) motor vehicles (4) free public education (5) freedom of expression (6) press (7) dress and grooming (8) assembly and petition (9) privacy and student property. Section B, deals with rules of conduct and sanctions for violations and includes the following areas: A-Level 1--minor behavior, A- Level 2 major behavior, A-Level 3--asks director to get his persons or property whose consequences do not seriously endanger the health of safety of others inended or dismissed from school (3) who may suspend or dismiss a student from school. Also, included in this code of conduct are procedures for student suspension and dismissal.

4116.   Mapleton Public Schools. <u>Student Behavior Standards --Elementary</u>. Denver, Colorado, 1981.

A school is like a big family. If its members are going to be safe and happy, and things are going to get done, there must be rules. Rules must be fair and they must be the same for everyone. Rules do three things: they tell people what they can do, they tell people what they cannot do, and they make it possible for people to live and work together without too much trouble. Included are the following sections:

a word to students, a word to parents, student responsibilities, student rights, rules and what happens if they are broken, parent information, and signature of cooperation.

4117.   Mapleton Public Schools. Student Behavior Standard -- Secondary. Denver, Colorado, 1981.

The students in the school district like members of any community, have both rights and responsibilities. The obligation of the school district is to protect those rights and insist upon those responsibilities. To this end, student behavior standards have been developed. The purpose of these standards is to insure that all students understand their rights and responsibilities, the consequences of violating school rules and the procedures for dealing with violations. Included in this brochure are a prefix, a note to parents, student rights, student responsibilities, rule violations and consequences, due process/suspension-expulsion, and signature of cooperation.

4118.   McGee, J. C., et al. "A Three Year Study of Brown Middle School, 1974-1977. A Longitudinal Study of a Middle School in Hamilton County Tennessee." Middle Tennessee State University at Murfreesboro, 1977. 107p.

This report presents the findings of a three year study of the changes that occurred at Brown Middle School. It was converted from a junior high school to a middle school in 1974. A section is included on the improvement of discipline when switching to a middle school. See ERIC Abstract ED 147927.

4119.   McGreevy, P. & Gregory, R. "Management of Individual Behavior in the Classroom." Des Moines, Iowa: Iowa State Department of Public Instruction, 1972.

This short manual designed for teachers of the handicapped focused on management of individual behavior in the class- room and briefly explains principles of behavior change. Five basic steps in management are explained to specifica- tion of problem behavior, counting the occurence of the problem behavior, changing the problem behavior by formula- ting a plan, re-planning if necessary, and maintaining the appropriate behavior. Provision of appropriate conse- quences, reward or punishment, is then discussed. Reward and punishment are defined, and clarifying guidelines and comments are made concerning them. Common problems of implementation are then anticipated, followed by suggested solutions. A typical situation of classroom misbehavior is described in short, dramatic form to demonstrate the behavior principles. Mention is then made of a videotape presentation that illustrates the basic steps of the manage- ment process as the teacher would use them. See ERIC Abstract ED 065953.

4120.   Memphis City Public Schools. "Student Rights And Responsibilities." Memphis, Tennessee, 1981.

Student involvement in the educational process is a must. Schools exist for the purpose of creating a stimulating climate for all students. Active involvement of students in their education, including planning and evaluation, fosters a spirit of inquiry where students may freely express their own views and listen to and evaluate the opinions of others. To achieve this goal it is necessary to recognize and respect the worth of each individual. The statement in this document are made so that students may understand their rights as well as their responsibilities. Included are the following sections: The role of the Student Council, personal appearance, proms and dances, student communication, clubs, publications, elections, assemblies, freedom of expression, student property, code of behavior, drugs, drinking and smoking, appeals.

4121.   Michigan Department Of Education. A Recommended Guide To Students' Rights And Responsibilities In Michigan. Michigan Department Of Education, 1981.

Michigan education must recognize and protect the individual and legal rights of students as people and as citizens, regardless of race, religion or economic status. Together with these rights, students must accept responsibilities and discipline essential to our society. Implicit in this goal is the recognition of the corresponding rights of parents, teachers and other participants in the educational process. Included are the following sections: 1) Introduction, 2) Current law and practice, 3) Student behavior in terms of rights and responsibilites, 4) Suspension of students and procedural due process, 5) Summary.

4122.   Miller, S., et al. "An Integrated Curriculum for Chronic Disruptive Youth." Illinois State Office of Education at Springfield Division of Vocational and Technical Education. 1975. 641p.

This manual contains materials which provide educational coordinators with theoretical and operational operation on how to carry out an integrated curriculum designed to facilitate improved instructional and career programming for students in residential settings. The first chapter deals with chronically disruptive youth and outlines the behavioral needs of disruptive adolescent boys and girls, effective educational strategies, and programmatic directions. Chapter 2 assertains vocationally related behaviors, spells out types of diagnostic instruments that can be used with such youth and how such intruments are to be used. The third chapter discusses a meaningful career education plan and the fourth chapter discusses an integrated curriculum and its implications for chronic disruptive youth, discusses how integration of programmatic goals, the diagnostic process and the work stations neables the youth to establish and realize life-long goals. Chapter five presents information on job coaching and the second half of the manual consists of the integrated guide of courses, course outlines for eachers, counselors and coordinators and job coaches of chronic disruptive youth in various areas. See ERIC Abstract ED 147504.

4123.   Milwaukee Public Schools. Guidepost. Milwaukee, Wisconsin, August, 1979.

No organization or group of persons can function effectively without internal discipline. Guidelines the movement and activities of individual members of the group so that the individual in the group can achieve established objectives and serve community purposes. Included in this brochure are guidelines, policies, procedures, regulations, legal opinions, court decisions, state statutes, and federal regulations that are essential in management, welfare and safety of the students in the schools. Included are the following sections: 1) administrative procedures relating to pupil behavior, 2) school attendance, 3) drug and alcohol abuse, 4) physical assaults on school personnel, 5) building evacuation and student safety, 6) vandalism and loitering, 7) administrative guidelines for effecting emergency help and accident procedures in the schools, 8) index.

4124.   Minneapolis Public Schools. "Jefferson Junior High Pocket School and Positive Peer Culture: An Evaluation." Minneapolis, Minnesota: Department of Research and Evaluation, 1972.

This specialized curriculum in a Minneapolis junior high school was designed for students having considerable academic and behavioral problems. The curriculum emphasizes personalized help and team work with peers. The academic part of the program, the pocket school, emphasizes English, social studies and math. The second part of the program, the positive peer culture, involves group sessions in which a group leader and a few students meet to discuss students' personal problems and ways of solving them. Questionnaires and interviews are used to obtain information from adminis- trative staff, faculty and students for evaluation of the program. None of the 22 students in the peer group wanted to continue with the group for the coming year. About half wanted to continue with the pocket school. About 60% of the faculty felt that the pocket school should or could be continued if modifications were made. A similar percentage thought that the peer group could be continued with changes. It was apparent that the leaders and the faculty of the peer group did not share a common philosophy. Evaluators raised questions about the adequacy of training for teachers in the pocket school and for group leaders. Recommendations, if the program is to continue, include: a written statement of goals, formulations of a common philosophy, appointment of a director for the program, keeping the program entirely at one facility, and complete administrative support for the program. See ERIC Abstract ED 08311.

4125.   Montgomery County Public Schools. <u>Discipline Regulations</u>. Undated.

Included are the following regulations of the Montgomery Public Schools: 1) maintenance of classroom control and discipline, 2) suspension or expulsion of a pupil, 3) protection of employees, students and property.

4126.   Moore Public Schools. <u>Discipline Brochure</u>. Moore, Oklahoma, Undated.

The goal of the Moore Public Schools is to provide secondary students with a program of an in-school alternative education that would serve to modify deviant student behavior and prevent short term out-of-school suspension. Guidelines and objectives of such an in-school program are discussed.

4127.   Mount Diablo Unified School District. <u>Student Conduct and Discipline</u>. Concord, California, September, 1981.

This brochure is intended to familiarize readers with the rules regarding student conduct and discipline, truancy, detention, suspension and expulsion as defined by state law and is applied in the Mount Diablo Unified School District. Included are the following sections, 1) board of education statement, 2) definition of terms, 3) grounds for disciplinary action, 4) authority to invoke disciplinary action, 5) disciplinary action procedures, 6) rights and responsibilities.

4128.   Muskogee Public Schools <u>Student Handbook</u>. Muskogee, Oklahoma, 1981.

Included is a section on school logs of Oklahoma, and Muskogee secondary school code. The logs are presented in the following areas, 1) disruption of school, 2) damage or destruction of school property, 3) damage or destruction of private property, 4) assault on a school employee, 5) physical abuse of a student or other person not employed, 6) weapons and dangerous instruments, 7) narcotics, alcohol, and stimulant drugs, 8) repeated school violations.

4129.   Natrona County School District #1. <u>Student Disipline and Control</u>. Casper, Wyoming, June 26, 1978.

Included in the brochure on student disipline and control are sections on disiplinary action, principal responsibilities, teacher responsibilities, aides' responsibilities, general procedures and penalties for suspension and expulsion, the right of search, corporal punishment and physical restraint, interviewing of students, multiple misbehavior, smoking or tobacco products, closed campus, truancy, bus rules and regulations, citations, misconduct.

4130.   New Hanover County Schools. Policies, Rules and Procedures Relative to Student Conduct in the New Hanover County Schools. Wilmington, North Carolina, June 2, 1981.

To be successful, education must be a partnership involving the schools, the students, the parents and community. It is the objective and policy of the New Hanover County Board of Education to encourage and enforce the exercise of individual rights within the necessary framework of orderly, efficient and continuing school programs; yet, at the same time to recognize, preserve and protect the rights of all students in its educational system to an education therein. In order to deliniate and clarify the fundamental guidelines of student behavior in the New Hanover County Schools, and to establish procedures to be followed should serious disciplinary action by school authorities become necessary, rules and procedures have been adopted by the Board of Education and they are included in this publication. They are divided into the following rules (1) narcotics, alcoholic beverages and stimulant drugs (2) weapons and dangerous instruments (3) physical abuse to school personnel (4) verbal abuse of school personnel (5) extortion/intimidation (6) misdemeanors/felonies. These are all long-term suspensions behavior occurrences. Short-term suspensions involve (1) disrespect of school personnel (2) physical/verbal abuse of peers (3) theft/damage destruction of property (4) disruption (5) chronic offenders (6) trespassing (7) violation of school rules. Procedures relative to student discipline include exclusion, coverage, principal's investigation, limitation on principal's power to suspend or to request a hearing, short-term suspension, sending a suspended student home during the school day, informing parents in cases of short-term suspension, initiating long-term suspension or expulsion, notice, scheduling the hearing, group hearing, availability of the student's previous record, convener of the hearing board, hearing board members, appeal and automatic review.

4131.   New Haven Unified School District. Parent Handbook. Union City, California, 1981.

Included in the handbook are the following sections concerning discipline, attendance requirement, counseling services, closed campus/open campus, identification of property, philosophy of discipline, the Board of Education and pupil behavior, corporal punishment, suspension, expulsion, narcotics, tobacco, vandalism/misuse of school property, search of students and student lockers, exclusions, and state requirements.

4132.   New Jersey Department of Education. Alternative education programs--a guide from implementation. Trenton, New Jersey, July, 1981.

Current interest in alternative education programs stems from concerns about violence, vandalism and disruption in the schools. These and other behaviors, such truancy, absenteeism, substance abuse, the drop out rate and discipline problems, are only the obvious manifestations of larger, more generalized problems. Contributing factors are basic skills deficiencies, frustration, alienation, anxiety, poor or inappropriate motivations, and anger. These factors may stem from personal and family problems, a history of failure, negative self-concept, peer pressure, and a sometimes hostile, uncaring and punitive school environment that provides insufficient encouragement for the confused or angry student. Solutions designed to reduce violence, vandalism and disruptive behavior in schools without addressing the reasons underlying the behavior would be only partially effective. Alternative educational approaches that seek solutions to the fundamental educational problems associated with school disruption and failure must be used rather than curtailment of the symptoms. Included are the following sections, 1) introduction, 2) alternative education, a. definition, b. a national concern, c. New Jersey perspective, d. target population, e. funding, f. anticipated results, 3) guide to program planning, a. overview of the program completion alternative, b. alternative school option, 1) program elements, 2) recommended procedures for establishing an alternative school, 3) the individualized program plan, c. parental involvement, d. student participation for alternative education programs in New Jersey.

4133.   New Jersey State Department of Education. Handbook for developing a code of conduct for students. Trenton, New Jersey, February, 1981.

Disruption in the schools is a serious concern of New Jersey educators, students and the public. According to the Gallup poll the public perceives discipline as one of the most important problems facing public schools. The effect of individual incidents goes well beyond the individual acts; they affect the learning climate of the school, the moral of students and staff and the public's confidence in the schools. Included are the following sections: 1) statement by commissioner of education, 2) New Jersey State Board of Education resolution, 3) introduction, 4) considerations in developing codes, a. what to include, b. codes must provide certain assurances, c. code preparation and distribution, d. establishing minimum standards for rules, 5) grievance and appeals, 6) the role of school boards, 7) financial liability, 8) providing equal educational opportunity, 9) a final word.

4134.   New Mexico State Department Of Education. Rights And Responsibilities Of The Public Schools And Public School Students. Sante Fe, New Mexico, May 22, 1981.

Included in this publication are general provisions for public schools concerning authority, regulations superseded, jurisdiction over students, school authority over non-students, statement of policy, local school board authority, definitions. A second major sections deals with rules of conduct for New Mexico Public Schools and the third section deals with enforcing rules of conduct.

4135.   New Orleans Public Schools. Regulations For Suspension And Expulsions. New Orleans, Louisiana, 1975.

During the 1972-73 school session a task force composed of parents, students, community representatives, teachers and principals devoted many hours to studying the complex problems of school suspension and expulsion and revising previous board regulations. Explicit in this document is the philosophy that good discipline is essential to a good education. Suspension and expulsion are viewed as disciplinary measures to be invoked only as a last resort, when every lesser reasonable alternative has been sincerely attempted. Included are the following sections: 1) Discipline policy of the Orleans Parish School Board, 2) Overview of suspension and expulsion regulations, 3) Short term suspension procedures, 4) Long term suspension procedures, 5) Expulsion procedure, 6) Status and rehabilitation of suspended and expelled students.

4136.   Norfolk Public School. Rules, Rights, Regulations and Responsibilities. Norfolk, Virginia, September 2, 1980.

It is the policy of the Norfolk Public Schools to encourage student conduct that will promote good health, reasonable standards of behavior, effective citizenship and a favorable atmosphere for learning. Included are the following sections: Student expression, assembly, locker search, freedom from discrimination, flag salutes, school records, due process. Student responsibilities are presented as well as disciplinary rules. Rule (1) disruption of school (2) damage or destruction of school property (3) damage or destruction of private property (4) physical or verbal abuse or threatening (5) weapons and dangerous instruments (6) narcotics, alcoholic beverages, stimulant drugs and other intoxicants (7) smoking (8) Federal, State and local laws (9) misrepresentation (10) other school violations. An additional section is included on suspension and expulsion and miscellaneous procedural provisions.

4137.   Northborough-Southborough Regional School District. Student Handbook. Northborough, Massachusetts, 1981.

Included are the following sections dealing with behavior: Behavior at school sponsored activities, card playing, corridor traffic, disciplinary regulations, discrimination clause, drugs-alcohol offense procedures, general driving policy, guided services, guidelines for student rights and responsibilities, offenses calling for suspension, out-of-bounds areas, participation and activities after absence or during suspension, public display of affection, smoking regulation, student dress policy, student referrals to the office, student tardiness and students with special needs.

4138.   North Clackamas School District Number Twelve.   "Parent-Student Handbook." Milwaukie, Oregon, 1981.

This handbook was prepared to answer the questions of both parents and students at the beginning of the school year. It is the responsibility of each student to review and know the guidelines for conduct and discipline so that each can participate effectively as a member of the school community. Included is information on the following: The school community, student appeal procedure, discipline responsibility in the schools, discipline definitions and guidelines, bus regulations for students, search and seizure guidelines, law enforcement cooperation, activities resulting in disciplinary action, behavior acts, criminal acts.

4139.   North Carolina Department of Public Instruction. Discipline in Schools a Source Book. North Carolina, Undated.

Throughout the nation, and in practically all surveys, discipline is regarded as the schools' number problem -- superseding such concerns as finance, public apathy, intergration, bussing, teacher and militancy and lack of knowledge concerning the nature of change. Discipline problems never exist in a vacuum; they are intimately related to students and their perceptions, to teachers and their interpretations of goals, to administrators and their interpretation of responsibility and to the community with its sensitivity or lack of it for an atmosphere genuinely conducive to educational development. This source book approaches a problem of discipline forthrightly, and at the same time, the approach is altogether positive and always with overtones of encouragement. Included are the following sections: 1) The problem 2) Preventing discipline problems 3) Dealing with discipline problems 4) Barriers to constructive change 5) Legal aspects 6) Annotated appendices.

4140.   North Penn School District. Code of Student Discipline and Responsibilities. Lansdale, Pennsylvania, August, 1979.

This code of student discipline must (1) be preventative in nature (2) promote self-discipline (3) concern itself with the welfare of the individual as well as that of the school community as a whole (4) promote a close working relationship between parents and school staff (5) discriminate between minor and serious offenses as well as between first time and repeated offenses (6) provide disciplinary responses that are appropriate to the misbehavior (7) be administered by all in a way that is fair, firm, reasonable and consistent (8) encourage a high regard for every person's right to reasonable hearing procedures and due process when accused of misconduct (9) comply with the provisions of Federal, State and local law as well as with the guidelines and directives of the Pennsylvania Department of Education. Included are sections on responsibilities, regulations, and disciplinary structure.

4141.   Northside Independent School District. Disciplinary Procedures. San Antonio, Texas, 1981.

Included are the following sections: 1) student discipline procedures, 2) student discipline, 3) procedural examples, and 4) special provisions.

4142.   Northshore School District. "Special Education Department Opening Bulletin." Bothell, Washington, 1981-82.

This booklet includes the following sections: Goals, building multi-disciplinary team, confidentiality, parent participation in IEP meetings, questions and answer regarding IEP's, disciplining handicapped students, requests for interdisciplinary consultation, due process hearings.

4143.   North Syracuse Central School District. Discipline Policy. North Syracuse, New York, January 11, 1980.

The mission of this school district is to provide the programs, facilities, and climate for learning which will enable an individual to develop skills to a point where he or she strives for and is capable of achieving their potential. Included are the following sections 1) mission statement, 2) definition of discipline, 3) purposes of a discipline policy, 4) philosophy, 5) implementation, 6) regular school day, 7) outside regular school day.

4144.   Ohio Department Of Education. Governor's Study Committee On High School Dropouts And Unskilled Graduates. Columbus, Ohio, January 20, 1981.

The study committee had the following responsibilities: 1) access the reasons or the consequences of students dropping out of high school, and develop recommendations based upon its accessment of dropout prone students in order to reverse the accelerating frequency of student dropout in order that they may remain in school and receive adequate educational training; 2) examine the high school general education curriculum, and make recommendations to effect modifications, where necessary, so that students may receive adequate work related and skilled training for use after high school graduation. This publication describes the results and recommendations of this task force.

4145.   Ohio Department Of Education. Report: Governor's Task Force On School Discipline. Columbus, Ohio, October 5, 1981.

A task force was charged with three primary responsibilities: 1) to access the status and determine the cause of

student discipline problems and violence in Ohio schools; 2)
to develop recommendations, based on the task force's review
and analysis, for the implimentation of methods to identify,
correct, and remedy school discipline problems which could
be adopted as policy by local Boards of Education or the
State Board of Education; and 3) to develop recommendations,
based upon the above review, for legislative consideration
of statutory modifications, or for the repeal or enactment
of policies conducive to correcting discipline problems.
This publications describes the result and recommendations
of the task force.

4146.   Orange County Schools. Statement of Students' Rights and
Responsibilities. Hillsborough, North Carolina, July 1,
1978.

Statements of rights and responsibilities are designed to
protect all members of the school community so that they may
exercise their rights and carry out their responsibilities.
This code and any additional rules governing student discipline are distributed to students and parents at the beginning of each school year and are posted in conspicuous
places for each throughout the school year. Included are
the following sections, first amendment rights including
freedom of assembly, freedom of press, freedom of speech,
and right to petition personal rights such as right to an
education, right to freedom from discrimination, dress code
and personal appearance, right to a safe environment, right
to freedom from search and seizure, right to use of school
locker, the right to use of illegal drugs, right to use of
student vehicles, freedom from sales and solicitations,
right to health care, right to privilege of public school
transportation, right to make maintenance and privacy of
student records, procedures for a review by parents-students-
school personnel, procedures for releasing information to
other persons. Grievance rights that are discussed include
right to equitable resolutions of grievances and complaints,
concept of grievance procedure, grievance procedures.
Procedural rights which are discussed include right to due
process, concept of due process, minor disciplinary
problems, corporal punishment, major disciplinary problems,
legal basis for suspensions and expulsions, in-school suspension, procedures for short term suspension, long-term suspension or expulsion. Long-term expulsion hearing procedures.

4147.   Pattonville School District. Behavior Guide For Students
-- Pattonville School District. St. Louis County, Missouri,
1981.

Cooperative educational working relationships in the successful school district educational program involves review with
the acceptance, understanding and support primarily of
students, teachers, parents and administrators. To accomplish this understanding and support requires that all of
the participants accept the established philosophy of education within the educational goals written in Chapter I of

this policy book and comply with the provisions contained in subsequent chapters. Chapters include: 1) Guide, 2) Student Responsibility, 3) Student Rights, 4) Corrective and Remedial Disciplinary Processes, 5) Unacceptable Behavior, 6) State Regulations and Rules, 7) Procedures for Suspension, 8) Disciplinary Decisions, 9) Procedures for Appeal.

4148.   Pittsburgh Public Schools. School Discipline Code and Procedures. Pittsburgh, Pennyslvania, December, 1978.

Included are the following section of this brochure: 1) Major discipline areas, 2) Board of Education code prohibiting serious student misconduct, 3) Board of Education procedures for dealing with student misconduct, 4) Definition, 5) General information relating to school discipline, suspension and attendance, 6) Attendance standards and attendance related procedures.

4149.   Polk School District. Student Offenses And Discipline Procedures. Cedartown, Georgia, 1981.

The purpose of these discipline procedures is to ensure that all students are well aware of the actions which violate school rules and of the consequences of such behavior. Those who commit such violations take away from themselves and from others the educational opportunities which all students have a right to expect. The booklet is arranged with the offenses listed on the left side of the brochure and the dispositions listed on the right side of the page.

4150.   Port Huron School District. Student Code. Port Huron, Michigan, August 18, 1978.

The state code is as follows: 1) Each district promulgate a formal written code of student conduct, 2) Make it public and accessible to all students and parents, 3) Within the document, define as precisely as possible student rights and responsibilities, including unacceptable student behavior and penalities to be imposed when such behavior is exhibited. The district goal in this document is to review, update and revise the district student code for the purpose of providing a uniform and consistent district policy. Included are the following sections: Policy, Philosophy, Responsibilities, Students Rights and Responsibilities, Disciplinary Action Short of Expulsion, Expulsion, Appeals Procedure, Alternative Education, Definitions of Major Violations Within Designated Procedures.

4151.   Poway Unified School District. Student Discipline. Poway, California, June, 1979.

The Board of Education believes that the goal of discipline is the development of mature, self-disciplined individual who is a responsible, contributing member of a democratic society. The Board of Education holds all school personnel responsible for the control and proper conduct of students

while under the legal supervision of the school. Included
are student discipline and corporal punishment guidelines,
suspensions, expulsions, exclusions, exemptions, and
involuntary transfers.

4152.   Prince George's County Public Schools. Code Of Student
          Conduct. Upper Marlboro, Maryland, September 22, 1981.

This brochure answers the following questions: 1) What is
the code of student conduct and why do we need it? 2) What
does the code describe as a good school environment? 3)
What roles do the home, student, and school have in establishing this environment? 4) What types of conduct disrupt
a good learning environment? 5) What types of informal
disciplinary actions are emphasized in the code? 6) What
types of formal disciplinary actions are recognized in the
code? 7) What are the guidelines regarding drugs? 8) What
about school bus conduct? 9) What safeguards protect the
rights of students? 10) What about school work during
suspension? 11) Are there differences between elementary
and secondary schools? 12) When and where is the code of
student conduct enforced?

4153.   Prince George's County Public Schools. Pupil Services.
          Upper Marlboro, Maryland, 1981.

Included in this brochure are sections on the activity room
program, health services, guided services, student transfers, student records, pupil personnel services, the supervised discipline center program, psychological services, and
student concerns. The supervised discipline center program
presents an alternate consequence for students who violate
certain provisions of the code of student conduct.
Described is the program, the basis for assignment to supervised discipline centers and notification of parents and
guardians, and program administration and staffing.

4154.   Putnam City School District I-1. Student Discipline.
          Putnam City, Oklahoma, February 6, 1978.

Two leaflets prepared by the school district describe
student discipline and corporal punishment. Guides to good
discipline are recommended: 1) Good discipline is usually
positive rather than negative in nature. They consist of
keeping the student interested in and busy doing something
constructive rather than punishing them for doing things
that are anti-social. 2) Good discipline is always fair,
dignified, and in good temper. 3) Conferences with
teachers, principals, and parents should be effectively
employed to bring about acceptable classroom behavior.

4155.   Renton School District 403. Renton School District
          Policy Book. September 16, 1977.

Included is a list of actions which are prohibited on or
adjacent to school premises or at school sponsored

activities which constitute cause for discipline, suspension
or expulsion. The District reserves the right to refer to
the appropriate non-school agency any act or conduct of it's
pupils which may constitute crime under Federal, State,
County or local law. A section is included on disruptive
conduct and rules to enforce proper behavior.

4156.   Reynoldsburg City Schools. Student Conduct.
Reynoldsburg, Ohio, undated.

This is a general standard that is to be used as a guide by
all students. The following are some of the main areas of
conduct which may lead to disciplinary action. 1) a student
shall not behave in such a way that would cause physical
injury to another person, 2) a student shall not use violence, force or threat to cause disruption of school or the
educational program, 3) all students are to respect school
property and the property of others, 4) a student shall not
bring dangerous objects or weapons to school, 5) a student
shall not possess, handle, transmit or conceal or be under
the influency of tobacco, alcoholic beverages or drugs, 6) a
student shall not repeatedly fail to comply with directions
of teacher, principal or other authorized school personnel
during any period of time when a student is properly under
the authority of the school, and 7) students may not leave
school premises at any time during school hours without
permission from the office.

4157.   Rockdale County Public Schools. Sudent Offenses and
Discipline Procedures. Conyers, Georgia, 1981.

The purpose of the discipline procedures outlines in this
pamphlet are to insure that all students are well aware of
the actions which violate school rules and of the consequences of such behavior. The rules contained apply
primarily to middle and high school grades as outlined.
Parent involvement through conferences is the most desirable
avenue for correcting behavioral problems and is used whenever possible. Disciplinary actions subject to the discretion of the principal may include any or all of the
following: conferences, detention, work assignments, suspension of privileges, corporal punishment, suspension, referral to the student disciplinary committee for possible
recommendation for expulsion, and referral to the police.
Included in the pamphlet are a list of 22 rules and a list
of offenses and recommended maximum disposition.

4158.   Rock Island Public Schools. General Statements --
Discipline, Detention, Suspension and Expulsion. Rock
Island, Illinois, 1980.

The maintenance of good discipline is essential to the educational process and is the joint responsibility of the home
and school. The individual must adjust his behavior to the
standards of the school and not hinder in the education of
others. Each student has the responsibility to know and

abide by the regulations of the schools. Unacceptable behavior infringes on the rights of others to learn. Included are the following sections: 1) detention, 2) in-school suspension, 3) out-of-school suspension, 4) expulsion, 5) reasonable physical punishment.

4159.   Rollins, H. "Project Success Environment: An Approach to Community Educational Improvement." Atlanta: Georgia State Department of Education, 1975.

Between 1970 and 1973, Project Success Environment, funded under the Elementary Secondary Education Act Title III, developed an effective low cost classroom management program for use in grades one through eight of public schools. The program provides students with maximum opportunity to experience, on an individual basis, success in school. Teachers are trained to make their expectations clear, to emphasize, and reward appropriate social and academic behavior, to ignore most inappropriate behavior and to minimize student's opportunity for failure. At the end of the third year of funding, the program had been implemented in sixty-one classrooms of the Atlanta Public School System. Results consistently showed reduced disruptions, increased task involvement, and a positive, non-punitive classroom environment. See ERIC Abstract ED 124605.

4160.   Roseburg Public Schools. School Board Policy Handbook. Roseburg, Oregon, November 19, 1979.

Included in the policy handbook are the following areas: narcotics, dangerous drugs and alcholic beverages; physical discipline; discipline involving suspension, expulsion, and serious student misconduct, rights.

4161.   Roseburg School Board. Discipline In The Roseburg Public Schools. Roseburg, Oregon, November 13, 1972.

The Roseburg schools have traditionally emphasized good student discipline. However, in the interest of doing even better, the rules and responsibilities governing discipline and conduct are presented in this document so that all members of the school community -- students, parents, teachers and administrators, know what is required. By working together under clearly stated and consistently enforced regulations, the school system hopes to continue and improve Roseburg's tradition of firm and fair discipline.

4162.   Roswell Independence School District. Rights And Responsibilities Of The Schools And Students In the Roswell Independence School District. Roswell, New Mexico, 1981.

Included in this brochure are general provisions, rules of conduct for the Roswell Independence School System, specific policies concerning student behavior, enforcing rules of conduct.

4163.   Rowan County Schools. <u>Policies On Drugs And Discipline</u>
<u>For Elementary Students (Grades K Through Six</u>).

It is the policy of the Rowan County Board Of Education that
all students are entitled to an appropriate education conducted in an atmosphere free from all unnecessary disruptive
elements; to this end a policy on drugs and discipline is
adopted in order to ensure that such an atmosphere is
properly preserved. Included are several policy statements;
policy one deals with narcotics, drugs, and any controlled
substance.   Policy two deals with narcotics such as
marijuana, amphetamines and barbiturates.   Policy three
deals with alcoholic beverages and intoxicating liquors.
Policy four deals with weapons and dangerous instruments.
Policies are also presented in a separate brochure on grades
seven through twelve.

4164.   Saint Paul Public Schools. <u>Rights and Responsibilities</u>
<u>-- Student Behavior Handbook</u>.   St. Paul, Minnesota,
November, 1977.

This handbook has been prepared to define clearly the rights
and responsibilities of persons in the St. Paul Public
Schools.   The Board of Education believes that a self-
disciplined citizenry is essential for the maintenance of a
free society.   The Board of Education recognizes the causal
basis for behavior and expects all employees to be concerned
with students' behavior and when and where unacceptable
behavior occurs, to aid and assist students through positive
and supportive actions.   Included are the following
sections: school community responsibilities, student rights
and responsibilities, standards of conduct, and procedural
information.

4165.   Santa Barbara High School District. <u>School Discipline:</u>
<u>Suspension and Expulsion</u>.   Santa Barbara, California,
undated.

Included in this policy statement are the following
sections: 1) notification, 2) suspension, 3) involuntary
transfer, 4) expulsion, 5) professional assistance to
students and parents.

4166.   School District City of Pontiac. <u>Student Code of</u>
<u>Conduct</u>. Pontiac, Michigan, February, 1981.

Education is the mutual responsibility of the state of
Michigan, the Board of Education, staff, students, parents,
and the community.   In order to achieve excellence in education, the code of conduct is adopted to insure the safety
and welfare of all students, while providing an excellent
learning environment in due process for all. The philosophy
in regard to discipline, is to be corrective. Every effort
is made to keep a student in school so that he or she can
achieve a quality education. Students who violate the
student code are subject to corrective discipline. Every

effort is made to use the resources available to correct a student's behavior. Included are the following sections, 1) philosophy, 2) code of conduct, a) attendance, b) school bus behavior, c) personal appearance, d) police questioning, e) search and seizure, f) student lockers, g) marriage and pregnancy, h) right to petition, i) publication, j) loitering and trespassing, k) student record, 3) student violation, a) general misconduct, b) serious misconduct, c) illegal misconduct, 4) displinary action, a) suspension, b) expulsion, 5) hearing, a) informal procedures, b) formal procedures, 6) appeals, 7) pupil personnel services contact people.

4167.   School District City of St. Charles. Student Code of Conduct. St. Charles, Missouri, July 1, 1981.

The objective of this code is to establish rules with regard to the conduct of all secondary students in the school district of the City of St. Charles. These rules have been deemed appropriate and necessary for the maintenance of a wholesome school climate. This code of conduct should be reviewed by parents and students. These rules and standards apply to student conduct: (1) on school premises (2) on-school buses (3) involving school property (4) off-school premises which directly affect the school (5) school functions of any kind.

4168.   School District Of Riverview Gardens. Elementary Procedures And Implementation Of Disciplinary Rules And Regulations. St. Louis, Missouri, May 10, 1978.

Discipline is a state of mind that prompts a person to cooperate voluntarily with a group. The disciplinary program is interpreted to be a teaching device in a complimentary position to the rest of the instructional program. Freedom and self-direction are achieved only gradually as a child learns, through experience and guidance, to substitute self-imposed controls of behavior for adult imposed control. Special emphasis is placed upon methods and procedures used to transform discipline into self-discipline. Punishment for an offense committed may be only a temporary relief, discipline is approached through use of preventive measures. Correcting the cause of the antisocial behavior sets the stage for the proper type of behavior. Basic attitudes toward behavior are established and are accountable to the individual or the group. Treatment that is fair, just and consistent is mandatory.

4169.   School District of Superior. Students Rights and Responsibilities. Superior, Wisconsin, 1981.

Students in the Superior Public School system have certain rights guaranteed to them by the Constitution of the United States. Among these are the freedom of expression, freedom of speech, the right to petition, and the right to an education. Included in the Students Rights and Responsibilities brochure are specific areas in which students are insured rights by the Superior Board of Education. A list of students responsibilities is included as well as a statement of student conduct, student expulsion, student suspension, corporal punishment, secret societies, and student smoking/alcohol and drug abuse.

4170.   School District Number 2. Bronc Handbook. Billings, Montana.

The goal of Billings Senior High School is to ensure that each student attending has the opportunity to realize his or her potential--academically, socially, and personally. The total staff, both professional and support, are committed to helping students achieve that goal. The purpose of this handbook is to present information in the following areas: attendance, alcohol, drugs, tobacco, assemblies, the honor code, career center, dress, performance groups, special school services, extracurricular activities, parent advisory council, and the school calendar.

4171.   School District 66. Student Parent Handbook. Valleyview Junior High School, Omaha, Nebraska, 1979.

The administration, faculty and students who helped prepare this publication did so in order to answer many of the questions students have about the program of the school as well as its practices, procedures, and customs. This booklet is the most accurate source of information concerning school matters.

4172.   School District 66. Westbrook Registration Guide For Students And Parents. Omaha, Nebraska, 1980.

Included is all pertinent information needed concerning course selection at this Junior High School. Sections include seventh grade courses, eight grade courses, ninth grade courses, elective quarter courses, special courses and the elementary school.

4173.   Schwartz, L. "An Evaluation Of The Clinical And Guided Services, Non-Public Schools. Final Report" Brooklyn, New York: New York City Board Of Education.

The non-public schools' clinical and guidance service program was designed to provide clinical and guidance services to children attending designated non-public inner city schools in New York. The program was designed so that the clinical and guidance staff would engage in all the regular activities that they would normally perform in the public schools. Twenty elementary non-public schools were randomly selected for the study. Teachers referred large numbers of students for service. Students who presented behavior problems were most often referred. Of those students referred about three quarters received services. Students who received services demonstrated significant academic improvement. Teachers judged that referred students' classroom behavior had also improved.   See ERIC Abstract #ED 072132.

4174.   Scotch Plains -- Fanwood Public Schools.   "Regulations -- Student Attendance."   1981.

It is the policy of the Board of Education to establish regulations which actively encourage regular student attendance in school and in all classes in which each student is scheduled.   Recognizing that this is a shared responsibility, direct involvement of the student, parents, and staff is emphasized.   Included in the regulations are the following sections: absenteeism, absence verification, tardiness, exceptions to the policy and regulations, school sponsored activities, home instruction, appeals, appeals procedure, record keeping, appropriate notification, class cutting, contracts, attendance-truancy, guidelines for student attendance, conduct/behavior code, guidelines for possession or use of drugs, guidelines for vandalism, guidelines for possession of weapons, guidelines for disobedience or open defiance of authority.

4175.   Scottsdale School District.   Elementary Administrator's Handbook.   Phoenix, Arizona, February 3, 1976.

Included in this Handbook are recommendations in regard to a positive approach to school control, expectations, corporal punishment, clarification, suspension, expulsion, district discipline guidelines, and dress code.

4176.   Seattle Public Schools.   Discipline of Students Enrolled in Special Education.   Special Education Department, Seattle, Washington, 1981.

Included are the following sections: discipline of students enrolled in special education, building base planning for special education: discipline component, model for discipline the handicap student, 8-step hierarchy to disciplining the handicap student.   Principal workshop on discipline of the handicap student, positive alternatives to school suspension of handicap pupils.

4177.   Shaker Heights City School District.   The Policies and Procedures of Behavior and Discipline Governing Student Rights and Responsibilities.   Shaker Heights, Ohio, August 14, 1979.

The intent of this handbook is to assist students, parents teachers and school administrators in the maintenance of an environment which will enhance the achievement of positive behavior and discipline.   Included are the following sections: Shaker School policy, procedure, misconduct for which suspension/expulsion may be imposed, and student rights and responsibilities.

4178.   Sheboygan Area School District. "STRIBE"/Sheboygan Area Treatment For Reintergration Through Involvement In Vocation In Education--An Interagency Alternative Program For Disruptive Adolescents. Sheboygan, Wisconsin, 1981.

This publication discusses a community based treatment program for adolescents potentially facing removal from home and community because of serious emotional and behavior problems coupled with failure at school. The concept that the task force utilized involved in interdisciplinary treatment approach which is highly individualized, group oriented and success based. This project combines an alternative to the school with group and individual counseling along with off campus experiential learning. Staff is provided by participating agencies. There are fewer traditional distinctions between the professional discipline--teachers at times might counsel and counselors might assist in educational experiences. Included are the following sections: background and problem statements, basic premises, administrative model and committees, personnel, description of facility, referral information/intake process, education/treatment component, discharge (reintergration), follow-up services.

4179.   Sioux City Community Schools. Policies Governing Student Conduct. Sioux City, Iowa, 1981.

Sections of this policy include: 1) The Statement Of Policy Of The Maintenance Of Orderly Conduct, 2) The Attendance Policy, 3) Procedures And Dispositions, 4) Chronic Absenteeism, 5) Drugs And Alcohol, 6) Extortion, 7) Fighting, 8) Insubordination, 9) Physical Assault On A Student, 10) Physical Assault On A School Employee, 11) Smoking, 12) Threatening A School Employee, 13) Possession Of A Dangerous Weapon, 14) Corporal Punishment, 15) Procedure, 16) Transportation, 17) Fire Alarm Policy.

4180.   South Colonie Central Schools. Developing Positive Attitudes and Excellent Behavior. Albany, New York, 1981.

The mission of this project was to develop a K-12 Plan which addressed the need for establishing guidelines for the development of positive attitudes in students. The students and staff believe that the essence of discipline is to lead students from the need of external control and direction towards the development of self-discipline. The major premises are the following: (1) good discipline requires the cooperation of home, school and community (2) there is a strong relationship between excellent teaching of an academically challenging program and good discipline (3) all share in the responsibilities of providing discipline to all children (4) discipline should be humanistic in approach which does not encroach on the student's rightful respect and dignity (5) children who are given many and diverse ways to gain recognition for productive excellence are not so likely to engage in inappropriate or unexpectable behavior. Student discipline is discussed.

4181.   South Florida School Desegregation Consulting Center. "Discipline Practices in the Hillsborough County Public Schools." Washington, D.C.: Office of Education, 1977.

This study consists of an analysis of suspension patterns in the Hillsborough County Public Schools, Coral Gables, Florida. A description of in-house suspension programs is included with perceptions of secondary principals, teachers, and students about discipline in the schools. A review of the district's human relations program, an examination of student handbooks, and general recommendations and possible alternatives to current practices is included in the study. Among the conclusions and recommendations are the significant number of suspensions for minor offenses that are nondisruptive, that the suspension rate for black students is clearly disproportionate to their numbers in the school system, that in-house suspension programs are perceived as the clearest and quickest way to decrease discipline problems, that suspension should be used sparingly because of its disruption to the individual's education, and that regularly scheduled and planned communication sessions should be maintained and continued between minority group representatives and various levels of the school administration. See ERIC Abstract ED 145575.

4182.   Springfield Public Schools. Faculty Handbook--Rights and Responsibilities. Springfield, Illinois, 1981.

Student discipline is an issue that continues to be a vital concern to educators. The theme of the districts is "improved discipline through constructive change." This theme was adopted because of the acknowledged fact that teachers can successfully cope with the changes observed in society, in values and in behavior patterns in the young persons only if they, as professional educators, are able to make constructive change in their own behaviors and attitudes. In this approach to better discipline, there are two choices -- teachers can acquiesce to those changes that have resulted in increased misbehavior and disrespect for the rules and laws governing school or society, or they can develop and refine their skills and techniques in teaching in classroom management in order to foster desirable behavior and respect. Teachers must make constructive change to counter those changes in the last few decades which have resulted in the discipline problems faced in schools today. The following chapters are included in this manual: 1) philosophy of discipline, 2) a uniform code of conduct, 3) rights and responsibilities, 4) the roles--in discipline, 5) school discipline committees, 6) alternative programs, 7) appendix.

4183.   Springfield Public Schools. - <u>Parent Handbook -- Rights and Responsibilities</u>.

School discipline is an issue that continues to be a vital concern to all of us. Studies, surveys and opinion polls in the last decade verify the seriousness of school violence, crime and student misbehavior and lead credibility to the perceptions of educators and parents alike that discipline is one of the most serious problems facing schools today. This parent handbook was prepared as part of a discipline improvement plan. It is one of a series of handbooks designed to communicate information on student discipline to parents, students and faculty. Students have available handbooks suitable to their age group, and parents are encouraged to take time to review them with their children. This handbook has several objectives in mind -- to aid in establishment of a cooperative working relationship among all concerned by outlining the responsibilities and rights of each in relation to the school system; to specify the level of student misconduct and the disciplinary action associated with the various types of rules and fractions; to answer some of parents questions about discipline and school regulations in general. This handbook series is one part of a broad based program. Also included in the program to improve students discipline are a uniform code of conduct, alternative educational programs for students with behavior problems and a training program for teachers and administrators.

4184.   State College Area School. <u>Guidelines For Discipline</u>. State College, Pennsylvania, July, 1979.

This booklet provides a rationale for discipline in the schools, and contains a listing of the responsibilities of students, staff and parents in the promotion of appropriate behavior and discipline of students. Also included are specific guidelines that are used by school personnel in situations of student misbehavior. There are two major purposes for distribution of these procedures throughout the school district. First it is hoped that every student, parent and teacher in the district will read these guidelines and responsibilities of all groups involved in the educational process. Second it is emphasized that the attempt of district staff to utilize fair, consistent and definite procedures of discipline in the State College Area School is mandatory. Included are the following sections, 1) rationale, 2) responsibilities of students, 3) responsibilities of staff, 4) responsibilities of parents, 5) disciplinary guidelines for student misbehavior.

4185.   Sunnyvale School District. <u>Sunnyvale School District Student Discipline Policy</u>. Sunnyvale, California, 1981.

To promote a safe and secure environment it is necessary for all students to obey classroom and school rules. Students are expected to participate in class activities without

disrupting others. Consistent plans for positive consequences for appropriate student behavior and negative consequences for inappropriate student behavior help establish a
positive environment. Cooperation among parents, students
and school personnel is required to create a school where
teachers can teach and students can learn. Sections of this
brochure include: purpose, responsibilities, students
rights and due process, prohibitive behaviors, administrative action alternatives, and regulations.

4186.   Svoboda, C. T. & Koopman, E. J.   Reading and Human
Development and Learning.   Dubuque, Iowa: Kendall/Hunt
Publishing Company, 1976.

Authors believe that every human being has worth and
deserves respect. This is not merely an impressive
philosophical platitude; it is a responsibility each person
owes to the other. Because of the essential value of each
person, we owe to each other the regard and dignity we
accord to ourselves; not only ought we to love and treat our
neighbor as we treat ourselves, we should never let that
ideal be dimmed by prejudice or casual impressions. This
book contains the following chapters: 1) Physiological
Processes 2) Social Processes 3) Peer Group Processes 4)
Affectional Processes 5) Self-Developmental Processes 6)
Self-Adjustive Processes 7) Principles of Learning 8)
Contemporary Topics in Education. Chapter 7 deals with the
issue of discipline.

4187.   Swartz Creek Community Schools. Handbooks for Parents of
Elementary School Children. Swartz Creek, Michigan, August
10, 1981.

Included are the following sections concerning discipline:
promotion and retention, school discipline, due process,
safety, visitation, and special education.

4188.   Thompson, M. et al. "Project Success Environment: A
Behavior Modification Program for Innercity Teachers."
Atlanta, Georgia: Georgia State Department of Education,
1973.

The pilot study of Project Success Environment includes
eight experimental classes with appropriate comparison
classes. Following the initial effort, the program was
expanded to include twice the number of students within a
wider age range during the second year of operation in
1972-72. The Projects' purpose was to answer an actuarial
question: Can behavior modification solve the referring
social problem which has been analyzed into two sets of
behavior, those behaviors which are too high or too low in
rate? The central question in this study is whether or not
teachers can be trained to use the techniques made available
to behavioral analysis to provide large numbers of students
from economically disadvantaged backgrounds with some
modicum of individual success. The emphasis has been on the

training pre-service and in-service of teachers in the use of positive behavioral modification. A contingency management technique was implemented in a large number of inner-city classrooms for first to eight grade for an entire academic year. See ERIC Abstract ED 124604.

4189.   Thompson, M. et al. "Project Success Environment: A Positive Contingency Program for Elementary Teachers Management." Atlanta: Georgia State Department of Education, 1979.

The third year of this project, funded under Elementary Secondary Education Act Title III, had similar results to the second year. These results indicated that the success technique had provided inner city teachers with both an effective classroom management system, and an effective program for the ecceleration of the academic performance. To assess the effectiveness of training and the importance of experience as a success teacher, the in-class behavior of new teachers and of their students was compared to the behavior of the experienced teachers and their students throughout the school year. See ERIC Abstract ED 124606.

4190.   Thornton Township High School. Disciplinary Action Policy--Suspension and Expulsion. Harvey, Illinois, August 10, 1977.

Disobedience or misconduct, which may lead to suspension or expulsion of a student pursuant to the provision of the Illinois School Code, shall include any activity or behavior which might reasonably lead school authorities to forecast substantial disruption or material interference with school activities or which in fact include activities which take place in the school, on school property, on a school bus, or at a school-sponsored function. Violations of rules leading to suspension may also subject a student to being prohibited from participation and/or attending activities taking place after school. A list of activities for behaviors is presented and the disciplinary action resulting from these behaviors is then presented.

4191.   Topeka Unified School District No. 501. Board of Education Policies and Administrative Regulations. Topeka, Kansas, 1981.

This publication contains specific Board of Education policies and appropriate excerpts from regulations pertaining to school attendance, discipline and other matters which are necessary for students and parents to know. It is distributed to parents of elementary students at enrollment time and a copy is given to each middle and junior high school student at the opening of school. Included are major sections on students rights and responsibilities, discipline, special problems, general educational development testing programs, scheduling school activities, the instructional day.

4192.   Underwood, R. E. "Dropout Turnaround Through ESEA Title
          IV, Part C." Washington, D.C.: District of Columbia
          Department of Education, June, 1981.

          School dropouts not only limit the potential of their own
          lives but have a negative impact on society. This paper
          provides a brief description of efforts at federal, state,
          and local district levels in the area of dropout prevention.
          An overview is given of financial assistance that has been
          made available through the Elementary and Secondary Educa-
          tion Act of 1965 to assist educators working with school
          dropouts. Two different pilot projects were set up to
          develop innovative educational programs in target schools
          that would encourage potential dropouts to stay in school
          and increase their capacity to be productive citizens upon
          graduation from high school. The programs deal with a broad
          range of topics, including career exploration, improvement
          of overall attitude of potential dropouts, and involvement
          of parents of dropout prone students. Brief descriptions of
          dropout prevention projects funded in nine states are
          provided. Conclusions from this study data indicate that
          these programs were instrumental in reducing the number of
          school dropouts in the target schools by 52%. See ERIC
          Abstract ED 197274.

4193.   Union Township Public Schools. Student Behavior, Board
          Policy. Union, New Jersey, July, 1980.

          The intent of the Union Township Board of Education policy
          on student behavior is to assure the good order of the
          school. This intent will require students to conduct them-
          selves in keeping with their level of maturity, acting with
          due regard for the supervisory authority of the Board of
          Education employees. This is for the educational purpose
          underlying all school activities, for the widely shared use
          of school property, and for the rights and welfare of other
          students. The purpose of the policy is to ensure that
          physical and mental health, safety, and welfare of students
          in the schools will be protected in an orderly environment
          which is conducive to learning be maintained. Sections of
          this document include (1) purpose of policy (2) student
          responsibility (3) offenses against students (4) administra-
          tion of policy (5) policy dissemination. A digest of
          relevant laws is included along with the section on student
          rights and responsibilities, student complaints and griev-
          ances, hearing procedure, and suspension from attendance.

4194.   Vacaville School District. Discipline Handbook.
          Vacaville, California, September, 1981.

          For the maximum amount of learning to take place, all stu-
          dents must obey all classroom and school rules. The aim is
          to improve the learning environment through positive conse-
          quences for good behavior, and consistently apply conse-
          quences for inappropriate behavior. With the cooperation of
          parents, students and school personnel a school can be

maintained where teachers can teach and students can learn.
Elements of an effective discipline program include (1)
Care--for each child as a unique individual. (2) Con-
cern--for the rights of the individual and for the group.
(3) Commitment--to the belief that children are happier and
more productive academically when behavior is acceptable.
(4) Consistency--in the application and enforcement of rules
and consequences, and in recognizing efforts toward improvement. (5) Cooperation--between parents and school, working
together to solve problems which might arise. Unacceptable
student behavior deprives everyone of their right to learn,
and reduces the overall enthusiasm and effectiveness of
teachers. The key to an effective discipline program is the
spirit of cooperation between parents and school. Included
are the following sections: (1) Legal basis for school
discipline (2) Prevention--key to a positive school environment. (3) Consequences for misbehavior (4) Behavior
contract.

4195.   Vallejo City Unified School District. Standards for
Student Behavior. Vallejo, California, Undated.

This pamphlet describes the major behavior problem areas the
Vallejo City Unified School District will not tolerate.
Students who involve themselves in these problem areas will
receive corresponding disciplinary action, also listed in
the pamphlet. In all cases of disciplinary action, students
are protected by due process. Included are the following
sections: (1) problem areas, including tardiness, unexcused
absence and cutting, defiance of school personnel's
authority, disorderly conduct, including profanity and
obscene behavior, bus conduct, verbal abuse, forgery,
gambling, fact, smoking, destruction or defacement of
property, fighting, drugs/alcohol, weapons, extortion, and
explosive devices. A second major section discusses disciplinary action including informal talk, conference, parent
involvement, suspension from classes, suspension from
school, and expulsion. The third major area of this publication is the relationship between problem area and discipline
action. A chart indicates in general the types of disciplinary action applied to each problem area. In each
instance, a minimum and a maximum action is suggested, as
well as a suggested action for the first occurrence and for
repeated occurrences. A fourth section of the brochure
includes the student's rights and due process.

4196.   VanDyke Public Schools. Student Code Of Conduct.
Warren, Michigan, July, 1981.

The responsibility for the success of each student in school
is shared by many institutions in our society but the major
responsibility rests with the school, home and individual
student. Parents must assure regular attendance and appropriate behavior on the part of their student. Positive
encouragement is needed from the home in regard to the
pursuit of academic excellence and parents must stand in

support of the school. Included in this brochure are sections on: 1) Board of education authority and the rights and responsibilities of students, 2) Guidelines relative to student rights and responsibilities, 3) Suspension and expulsion of students, definitions of rules and procedural due process, 4) Student government, 5) Evaluation, 6) Graduation, 7) School rules.

4197.   Vidor Indepedent School District. "Vidor Junior High G/C -- Guidance Center." Vidor, Texas, 1978.

This pamphlet answers the following questions: 1) Who will be assigned to the guidance center?, 2) Who will assign students to the guidance center?, 3) How is the actual number of days determined? Guidelines are given for the following disciplinary actions: smoking, truancy, possession of knives or other dangerous weapons, fighting, gambling, forgery, obscene language, possession of fire works, hazing, cheating, theft, vandalism, verbal abuse.

4198.   Vigo County School Corporation Schools. Student--Parent Guide. Terre Haute, Indiana. August, 1981.

This guide places in one concise publication much of the information parents and students need to know about the county schools. Today's challenges to parents and the schools of their students remain significant. The children must be prepared to meet the responsibilities of productive citizenship in a democratic society. Beyond that each human being has personal, intellectual needs which must be fulfilled. Included in this brochure is a section on school behavior divided into the following areas: rights, responsibilities and regulations, student lockers, school admissions, establishment of policies, rules and regulations, areas of prohibited student conduct, other courses of action, suspension and right to hearing. Also included are sections on short-term suspension, corporal punishment and summary of policies on student records.

4199.   Walled Lake Consolidated Schools. Students Conduct Code For Secondary Schools. Walled Lake, Michigan, July, 1971.

The student conduct code for secondary schools recognizes: 1) that the primary intent of society in establishing the public schools is to provide an opportunity for learning, 2) that the students have full rights of citizenship as delineated in the United States Constitution and its Amendments, 3) that citizenship rights must not be abriged, obstructed, or in other way altered except in accordance with due process of law, 4) that education is one of these citizenship rights, 5) that students have responsibility to be accountable for their actions.

4200.   Wallingford Board of Education. Disciplinary Procedures. Wallingford, Connecticut, October 6, 1981.

A positive learning environment in the schools and a good state of discipline start with all involved students, parents and staff having knowledge and understanding of the basic standards of acceptable conduct and the procedures that are follwed at both high schools with regard to dealing with disciplinary problems. A list of fifteen basic standards are included in this brochure.

4201.   Wauwatosa School District. <u>Citizenship and Discipline</u>. Wauwatosa, Wisconsin, undated.

A major function of the public school is the development and preparation of youth for citizenship in the community. Most students are willing and anxious to be good citizens. There are a few who act without regard for their own welfare or the welfare of others. It is the responsibility of the schools to develop good attitudes of citizenship in each student, that is, the consideration of fellow students, respect for rules of the school, respect for rules and regulations of the community. The school must create and impose rules and regulations for protecting this oppor- tunity. It is the schools opportunity to see that these rules are fair to the individual student, as well as to the entire student body. Listed are the rules of the school.

4202.   Weber County School District. <u>Responsibilities and Rights</u>. Ogden, Utah, Undated.

Included are the following sections: the student goals and objectives, equal educational opportunities, student involve- ment, student conduct, personal behavior of students, dress, weapons and dangerous instruments, abuse of a student or other person not employed by the school, alcohol, controlled substances and tobacco, disruption of school, damage or destruction of public or private personal property, assault on school faculaty or staff, repeated school violation, cooperation with all law enforcement agencies, procedural definitions, four parts of the procedural process, written notification, procedural process of student discipline, search and seizure, and closed campus.

4203.   West Chester Area School District. <u>Discipline and Records Policies</u>. West Chester, Pennsylvania, Undated.

This brochure is divided into the following sections: 1) Some basic understanding, 2) Disciplinary action schedule for secondary schools, three disciplinary action schedules for elementary school. Some sections include offenses, administrative action, drug abuse, student detention, inter- rogation and searches by staff, corporal punishment, bus conduct, absenses and excuses, bomb threats, student smoking, other policies, and student records.

4204.   William S. Hart Union High School District. <u>Notice of Rights, Regulations and Responsibilities to Students, Parents and Guardians</u>. Newhall, California, 1981.

Included are the following sections, 1) legal requirements for notice, prevention and control of communicable diseases, medication during school day, exemption from physical examination, insurance, sex education, grades, transfer of pupil records, liability for loss or damage, special education, nutrition, student absence regulations, pupil records, alternative schools, non-discrimination, behavior regulations, suspension from school, expulsion, possession or use of tobacco, alcoholic beverage and drug abuse, exclusion or exemption, transer to/from continuation school participation in co-curricular activities.

4205.   Young, P. B. "Evaluation of the Academics Plus Program, 1979-1980: Technical Summary Report." Philadelphia, Pennsylvania: Office of Research and Evaluation. Philadelphia School District, 1980.

The Academics Plus Program, which stresses basic skills, discipline and dress codes, homework assignments, promotion requirements, and special parent conferences, served more than 10,000 students in 29 elementary and middle/junior high schools during the 1979-1980 school year. There is a single school model and a multi school model. A comprehensive survey of program principals, teachers and parents in the Spring of 1980, indicated that there was satisfactory implementation of all major program elements. In achievement on city-wide tests in 1980, the single school model showed improvement over 1979 performance in both total reading and total mathematics at every grade except one across one through seven. See ERIC Abstract ED 195565.

4206.   Youngstown Public Schools. Discipline Policies, Rules And Regulations Of Importance To Professional Staff. Youngstown, Ohio, 1981.

Included are sections on the following disciplinary concerns: 1) student attendance, 2) student conduct, 3) detention of pupils, 4) lack of parental responsibility, 5) corporal punishment, 6) suspension and expulsion of pupils, 7) suspensions, 8) expulsions, 9) emergency removal, 10) disruption of school, 11) damage or destruction or theft of school or private property, 12) assault on a school employee, 13) physical abuse of a student or other person not employed by the school, 14) weapons and dangerous instruments, 15) narcotics, alcoholic and stimulant drugs, 16) refusal to obey school rules, 17) use of tobacco on school property, 18) profanity, vulgarity and other obscenities, 19) truancy, class cutting and excessive tardiness, 20) gambling, 21) identification, 22) student conduct on school busses, 23) student dress code, 24) secret society, 25) hazing.

AUTHOR INDEX

The numbers below refer to entry numbers in the bibliography.

SUBJECT INDEX

The numbers below refer to entry numbers in the bibliography.

About the Compilers

ELIZABETH LUEDER KARNES is an Educational Consultant for Father Flanagan's Boys' Home. She has written *Philosophy, Policies & Programs of Early Adolescent Education: An Annotated Bibliography* (Greenwood, 1982).

DONALD D. BLACK is Director of Education for Father Flanagan's Boys' Home.

JOHN DOWNS is Administrative Assistant for Program Development for Father Flanagan's Boys' Home.